Axelrod & Cooper's
CONCISE
GUIDE
TO WRITING

FOURTH EDITION

Axelrod & Cooper's
CONCISE
GUIDE
TO WRITING

Rise B. Axelrod
UNIVERSITY OF CALIFORNIA, RIVERSIDE

Charles R. Cooper
UNIVERSITY OF CALIFORNIA, SAN DIEGO

BEDFORD/ST. MARTIN'S
Boston • New York

For Bedford/St. Martin's

Developmental Editor: Gregory S. Johnson
Senior Production Editor: Harold Chester
Senior Production Supervisor: Joe Ford
Art Direction and Cover Design: Lucy Krikorian
Text Design: Anna George
Cover Art: All images by Frank Stella (left to right): "Island, No. 10," "Hampton Roads," "Delaware Crossing," "Sabine Pass." All collection of the artist. (c) 2005 Frank Stella/Artists Rights Society (ARS), New York/Art Resource, NY.
Composition: Stratford Publishing Services, Inc.
Printing and Binding: R.R. Donnelley & Sons Company

President: Joan E. Feinberg
Editorial Director: Denise B. Wydra
Editor in Chief: Nancy Perry
Director of Marketing: Karen Melton Soeltz
Director of Editing, Design, and Production: Marcia Cohen
Managing Editor: Erica T. Appel

Library of Congress Control Number: 2005921117

Manufactured in the United States of America.

1   0   9   8

For information, write: Bedford/St. Martin's, 75 Arlington Street, Boston, MA 02116 (617-399-4000)

ISBN-10: 0-312-43439-1
ISBN-13: 978-0-312-43439-7

Acknowledgments

Acknowledgments and copyrights appear at the back of the book on page 466, which constitutes an extension of the copyright page.

To the Instructor

Axelrod & Cooper's Concise Guide to Writing, Fourth Edition, shows students how writing works and how written texts are shaped by the writing situations in which they arise. Through six essay assignment chapters, students experience four fundamentally different writing situations: reflecting on past events, presenting firsthand observations, explaining information, and arguing—taking a position, proposing a solution, or justifying an evaluation. Students see how the kinds of thinking and writing required by these situations are important for them as college students, workers, and citizens. We also show students that reading like a writer, planning essays systematically, getting and giving critical comments on drafts, revising thoughtfully, and thinking critically about their learning can improve their writing and confidence as writers. The *Concise Guide* challenges students, setting high standards for them with each essay they attempt, while also providing the scaffolding they need to achieve their goals.

An Overview of the Book

The *Concise Guide to Writing* has two sections, preceded by an introductory chapter. Chapter 1 explains how writing works and what it contributes to thinking and learning. The chapter also introduces students to the writing activities in Part One.

Part One, Writing Activities, presents six different essay assignments, all reflecting actual writing situations that students may encounter both in and out of college, genres of writing that they should learn to read critically and to write intelligently. The genres included are autobiography, profile, explanation, arguing a position, proposing a solution, and justifying an evaluation.

You may choose among these chapters and teach them in any order you wish, though they are sequenced here to move students from writing based on personal experience and firsthand observation to writing calling for the analysis and synthesis of ideas and information derived from a variety of sources.

Each chapter follows the same organizational plan.

- Six brief **scenarios** identify the genre covered in the chapter and suggest the range of occasions when such writing is done—in other courses, in the community, and in the workplace.

- A **collaborative activity** gets students working with the genre taught in that chapter.
- Three **readings,** including one student essay, are each accompanied by **critical apparatus** designed to help students explore connections to their culture and experience and to analyze writing strategies used in this genre.
- **Summaries** of the **purpose and audience** and the **basic features** of this genre help students make connections between what they have read and their own writing.
- A flexible **guide to writing,** tailored to the particular genre, gives the chapter's writing assignment and helps students find a topic and learn the kinds of questions they need to ask themselves to develop their ideas.
- A **critical reading guide** for peer review of drafts helps students work collaboratively and learn to read with a critical eye both their own and other's drafts.
- **Editing and proofreading guidelines** remind students to check for sentence-level problems.
- A **Reflecting on Your Writing** activity encourages students to explore what they have learned while writing the essay.

Part Two, Strategies for Writing and Research, looks at a variety of strategies that will help students at all stages of their writing and research. Writing strategies such as invention and cueing the reader are discussed in the assignment chapters and reinforced in Chapters 8 and 9. Chapter 10 focuses on a variety of critical reading strategies. Chapter 11 is devoted to such elements of argumentation as asserting a thesis, giving reasons and support, counterarguing, and understanding logical fallacies. In Chapter 12, students are introduced to the field research skills of observing, interviewing, and conducting surveys. The final two chapters of the book present comprehensive guidelines for doing research both in the library and on the Internet and for using and acknowledging sources.

Proven Features

The *Concise Guide to Writing* contains several special features that contribute to the book's effectiveness. Chief among these are the practical Guides to Writing, the integration of reading and writing, clear coverage of strategies for writing and critical reading, comprehensive chapters on research, and activities to promote group discussion and inquiry.

Practical Guides to Writing. We do not merely talk about writing; rather, we offer practical, flexible guides that escort students through the entire process for each genre covered, from invention through revision and self-evaluation. Thus, this book is more than just a rhetoric that students will refer to only occasionally. It is a guidebook that will help them write and develop as critical thinkers. Commonsensical and easy to follow, these writing guides teach students to assess a rhetorical situation, identify the kinds of information they will need, ask probing questions and find answers, organize their writing to achieve their purpose, and revise and edit their writing for clarity and effectiveness.

Systematic Integration of Reading and Writing.   Because we see a close relationship between the ability to read critically and the ability to write intelligently, the *Concise Guide* combines reading instruction with writing instruction. Each chapter in Part One introduces a specific genre for students to consider both as readers and as writers. Each reading is accompanied by carefully focused apparatus. First is a response activity, Connecting to Culture and Experience, that relates a central theme of the reading to the students' cultural knowledge and personal experience. Questions are designed to stimulate small-group discussion that helps students explore the essay's relevance to their lives as well as its broader social implications. The two sections following, Analyzing Writing Strategies and a brief Commentary, examine how each writer applies basic genre features and strategies to a particular rhetorical situation. Taken together, these analytical activities and commentaries prepare students to write an essay of their own in the genre. Finally, in Considering Topics for Your Own Essay, students are challenged to apply this new knowledge to their own writing by imagining what they could write about and how they might address their prospective readers.

Clear Coverage of Strategies for Writing and Critical Reading.   In Chapter 8, students learn how to use strategies for cueing readers, such as thesis statements, paragraphing, cohesive devices, topic sentences, transitions, and headings. In Chapter 9, they learn various mapping and writing strategies to discover and develop ideas. Chapter 10 catalogs important strategies for reading critically, including outlining, paraphrasing, summarizing, and evaluating the logic of an argument. These reading strategies, which students can use in their other courses as well, complement the attention given to critical reading in the writing assignment chapters.

Comprehensive Chapters on Research.   Chapters 12 through 14 present comprehensive strategies for field research, library and Internet research, and using, evaluating, and acknowledging sources that will help students address all aspects of writing research papers.

Activities to Promote Group Discussion and Inquiry.   The *Concise Guide* offers multiple opportunities for group work throughout Part One. At the start of each chapter is a collaborative activity that invites students to try out some of the thinking and planning they will be doing for the kind of writing covered in that chapter. The Connecting to Culture and Experience section that follows each reading is designed to provoke thoughtful responses about the social and political implications of the reading. The Guide to Writing contains another collaborative activity that gets students to discuss their work in progress with one another, along with a Critical Reading Guide, which keeps students focused on the genre's basic features as they read and comment on each other's drafts. All of these activities include questions and prompts that help students work together productively.

New to This Edition

Engaging New Readings.   In the fourth edition, we have replaced ten of the reading selections—half of the total—with new authors, including Barbara Ehrenreich, Stephen Holden, and Natalie Angier. Some new selections, including reviews of a movie and a computer game, show students ways that writers of a genre can make good use of visuals such as photographs and charts.

Web Activities in Every Guide to Writing.   Recognizing that many students turn to the World Wide Web when given a writing assignment, we have added to the Invention section in every Part One chapter a new activity that suggests ways students can use the Web selectively and productively. Topics range from searching for memorabilia for autobiographical writing to researching opposing views in argumentative essays.

Sentence Strategies for Each Genre.   To provide students with practical help to increase their rhetorical prowess, we have introduced in every Part One chapter new material explaining and illustrating certain sentence patterns writers typically use when composing in a particular genre. In the Drafting section of each Guide to Writing, a new subsection titled Sentence Strategies explains two sentence-level strategies that are rhetorically important for that genre—that is, likely to help students fulfill their purpose for their readers—and illustrates them with examples from the chapter's readings.

New Coverage of Editing and ESL Concerns.   The Editing and Proofreading section of each Guide to Writing now includes help with finding and correcting the most common editing and ESL concerns students are likely to encounter in a given genre. Hand-edited examples show students how to fix their errors, and cross-references to Exercise Central, an online database of more than 7,000 grammar exercises, provide students with opportunities for self-directed study.

Current, Concrete Advice on Technology throughout the Book.   Both the Guides to Writing and the rest of the text have been thoroughly revised to reflect the many ways students and instructors now rely on computers. New boxes provide concise information and advice about technological topics such as using grammar- and spellcheckers and software-based commenting, diagramming, and planning tools.

Up-to-Date Coverage of Electronic Research and Documentation.   Chapters 13 and 14 have been updated to reflect the latest aspects of electronic research—from the increasing intermeshing of online and library research to the most useful search tools and strategies—as well as the most recent MLA and APA documentation guidelines.

Ancillaries for the *Concise Guide*

Bedford/St. Martin's offers three ancillaries especially tailored for use with the *Concise Guide*.

- *Instructor's Resource Manual.* This useful manual contains information that will benefit novice and experienced instructors alike. The first section is devoted to teaching and evaluation practices, and the second section supplies suggested course plans, strategies for teaching major assignments, and detailed chapter plans. The appendix features a selected bibliography in composition studies.
- *Sticks and Stones and Other Student Essays,* **Fifth Edition.** This collection of essays was written by students across the nation using our Guides to Writing. For each chapter in the *Concise Guide,* there is a corresponding chapter in *Sticks and Stones.*
- **Companion Web site at bedfordstmartins.com/conciseguide.** This Web site provides quick access to our extensive new media resources for the *Concise Guide,* including both student aids—such as interactive grammar exercises—and support for instructors.

Contributing to the Next Edition of the *Concise Guide*

We are always looking for new student essays for the *Concise Guide, The St. Martin's Guide to Writing,* and *Sticks and Stones.* Please consider encouraging your students to send us contributions for publication consideration. Send contributions and completed agreement forms (located at the back of this student edition and in the *Instructor's Resource Manual*) to *Concise Guide,* Bedford/St. Martin's, 33 Irving Place, New York, NY, 10003. Instructors and students alike may also make submissions electronically at bedfordstmartins.com/conciseguide.

In addition, we would be delighted to receive comments and suggestions for improving the *Concise Guide.*

Acknowledgments

Our debt grows year by year to those teachers and students who have used *The St. Martin's Guide to Writing,* on which the *Concise Guide* is based, and who have so generously encouraged and advised us.

We would like to thank the reviewers who completed a detailed questionnaire and volunteered numerous suggestions for the *Concise Guide:* Vicky Byard, Northeastern Illinois University; Judy Casey, University of Puerto Rico–Mayagüez; Paul Cavalo, Asnuntuck Community-Technical College; Cynthia Crane, Raymond Walters College; Tricia Dahlquist, Bradley University; David Endicott, Tacoma Community College; Judith Garecht-Williams, Fashion Institute of Technology; Dorie Goldman-Rivera, Central Arizona College; Marlene Hess, Davenport University; Michael Knoll,

Bunker Hill Community College; Gary Leising, Northern Kentucky University; Ed Mortiz, Indiana University–Purdue University, Fort Wayne; Lee A. Newton, Bradley University; Douglas Okey, Illinois Central College; Ruth Oleson, Illinois Central College; Keith Otto, State University of New York at Buffalo; Catherine Schutz, University of Central Florida; Amy Shipley, Illinois Central College; Mary Wagner, Gannon University; Susan Youngs, Southern New Hampshire University.

We also wish to thank Lawrence Barkley of Mt. San Jacinto College–Menifee Valley for his contributions to the *Instructor's Resource Manual* and for coediting our collection of student essays, *Sticks and Stones*. We are especially grateful as well to the student authors who have so graciously allowed us to reprint their work in *Sticks and Stones and Other Student Essays* and in *Axelrod & Cooper's Concise Guide to Writing*.

We wish to thank many people at Bedford/St. Martin's, including editors John Elliott and Greg Johnson and senior project editor Harold Chester. Above all, we wish to express our appreciation to Nancy Perry, editor in chief, for helping us launch *The St. Martin's Guide* successfully so many years ago and continuing to stand by us; to Joan Feinberg and Denise Wydra for their adroit leadership of Bedford/St. Martin's; and to Karen Melton Soeltz, director of marketing, and Richard Cadman, marketing manager, and their extraordinarily talented and hardworking sales staff for their tireless efforts on behalf of our books.

Charles acknowledges the inspiration and advice of the other writing member of his family, his daughter Susanna, former member of the editorial board at the *Sacramento Bee* and now communications director for Preschool California, a nonprofit organization advocating statewide voluntary preschool programs.

Rise B. Axelrod
Charles R. Cooper

Contents

PART TWO   STRATEGIES FOR WRITING AND RESEARCH

Axelrod & Cooper's
CONCISE
GUIDE
TO WRITING

Introduction

"Why should learning to write well be important to me? What is the connection between writing and thinking? How will reading help me learn to write better? How can I learn to write more effectively and efficiently?" These are some of the questions you may be asking as you begin this writing course. Read on — for *Axelrod & Cooper's Concise Guide to Writing* offers some answers to these and other questions you may have.

■ WHY WRITING IS IMPORTANT

Writing has wide-ranging implications for the way we think and learn as well as for our chances of success, our personal development, and our relationships with other people.

Writing Influences the Ways We Think

First, the very act of writing encourages us to be creative as well as organized and logical in our thinking. When we write sentences, paragraphs, and whole essays, we generate ideas and connect these ideas in systematic ways. For example, by combining words into phrases and sentences with conjunctions such as *and, but,* and *because,* we can create complex new ideas. By grouping related ideas into paragraphs, we develop their similarities and differences and anchor our general ideas in specific facts and concrete examples.

By writing essays for different purposes and readers, we learn to develop our thinking in different ways. For example, writing about an important event in our lives develops our ability to select significant details and organize them into a meaningful narrative. Profiling people and places develops our observation and understanding of particular situations. Writing an explanation of a concept develops categorical thinking, as we connect new information to what we and our readers already know. Proposing solutions develops problem solving, arguing positions develops logical thinking, and justifying an evaluation develops judgment.

> Some of the things that happen to us in life seem to have no meaning, but when you write them down, you find the meanings for them. . . .
>
> – MAXINE HONG KINGSTON

1

Those who are learning to compose and arrange their sentences with accuracy and order are learning, at the same time, to think with accuracy and order.

–HUGH BLAIR

Writing Contributes to the Ways We Learn

Writing helps us learn by making us active, critical thinkers. When we take notes in class, for example, writing helps us identify and remember what is important. Writing in the margins as we read encourages us to question the reading's ideas and information in light of our experience and other reading. Writing in a journal frees us to explore our understanding of and response to what we are learning.

Writing essays of various kinds helps us to organize and present what we have learned and, in the process, to clarify and extend our own ideas. Writing an explanatory essay, for example, helps us better understand the concept or idea we are explaining. Researching a controversial issue helps us both learn from and question others' points of view.

The mere process of writing is one of the most powerful tools we have for clarifying our own thinking. I am never as clear about any matter as when I have just finished writing about it.

–JAMES VAN ALLEN

Writing keeps me from believing everything I read.

–GLORIA STEINEM

Writing Fosters Personal Development

In addition to influencing the ways we think and learn, writing can help us grow as individuals. We are led to reflect deeply on our personal experience, for example, when we write to understand the significance of a particular person in our life. Writing about a controversial issue can make us examine critically some of our most basic assumptions. Writing an evaluation requires that we think about what we value and how our values compare to those of others. Perhaps most important, becoming an author confers authority on us; it gives us confidence to assert our own ideas and feelings.

In a very real sense, the writer writes in order to teach himself, to understand himself, to satisfy himself. . . .

–ALFRED KAZIN

Writing has been for a long time my major tool for self-instruction and self-development.

–TONI CADE BAMBARA

Writing Connects Us to Others

It is easier now than ever before to connect with others via email and the Internet. We can use writing to keep in touch with friends and family, take part in academic discussions, and participate actively in democratic debate and decision making. By writing about our experiences, ideas, and observations, we reach out to readers, offering them our own point of view and inviting them to share theirs in return. Writing an argument on a controversial issue, for example, we not only assert our position on the issue but also give readers an opportunity to assert theirs. Moreover, when we respond constructively to each other's writing, we can clarify our differences, reexamine our reasoning, and ultimately influence each other's opinions. Similarly, writing a proposal requires us to work collaboratively with others to invent new, creative ways of solving complex problems.

> Writing is the act of saying *I*, of imposing oneself upon other people, of saying *listen to me, see it my way, change your mind*.
>
> —JOAN DIDION

> I think writing is really a process of communication. . . . It's the sense of being in contact with people who are part of a particular audience that really makes a difference to me in writing.
>
> —SHERLEY ANNE WILLIAMS

Writing Promotes Success in College and at Work

As students, you are probably most aware of the many ways writing can contribute to your success in school. Students who learn to write for different readers and purposes do well in courses throughout the curriculum. No doubt you have been able to use writing to demonstrate your knowledge as well as to add to it. Eventually, you will need to use writing to advance your career by writing persuasive application letters for jobs or graduate school admission. Many businesses and professions expect people to write effective email messages, formal letters, and reports that present clear explanations, convincing evaluations, or constructive proposals.

> The aim of school is to produce citizens who are able to communicate with each other, to defend points of view, and to criticize. . . .
>
> —ALBERT SHANKER

> People think it's sort of funny that I went to graduate school as a biologist and then became a writer. . . . What I learned [in science] is how to formulate or identify a new question that hasn't been asked before and then to set about solving it, to do original research to find the way to an answer. And that's what I do when I write a book.
>
> —BARBARA KINGSOLVER

■ **Exercise 1.1**

Think of an occasion when writing helped you accomplish something important. For example, you may recall a time when writing helped you better understand a difficult subject you were studying, when you used writing to influence someone else, when writing helped you achieve a goal, when you expressed your feelings or worked through a problem by writing, or when you used writing for some other worthwhile purpose.

Write a page or two describing what happened on this particular occasion. Describe how you came to write and what you wrote about. Then explain how you used writing on this occasion and what you wanted your writing to accomplish. For example, did you use it to help you learn something, express yourself, or connect to others?

■ HOW WRITING IS LEARNED

Writing is important. But can it be learned? This question is crucial because writing traditionally has been veiled in mystery. Some people believe that writers are born, not made. They assume that people who are good at writing do not have to spend a lot of time learning to write — that they just naturally know how to do so. Others may assume that if you have to spend time working on your writing — planning, rewriting, or editing — then you might as well give up and do something else. After all, "real" writers write perfectly the first time, every time, dashing off an essay with minimal effort. Their first draft is the last draft. They may need to spell-check their work, but nothing major needs to be clarified, developed, or corrected.

■ Exercise 1.2

List some of your ideas about writers and writing. Then write a few sentences speculating about where these ideas come from — from personal experience, teachers, textbooks, the media, or elsewhere.

Writers' testimonies, together with extensive research on how people write and learn to write, show that writing can — indeed must — be learned. Some writers may be more skilled than others. Some may find writing easier and more satisfying. But no one is born knowing how to write. Everyone must learn how to write.

However great a [person's] natural talent may be, the art of writing cannot be learned all at once.

– JEAN JACQUES ROUSSEAU

Learning to write well takes time and much effort, but it can be done.

– MARGARET MEAD

Axelrod & Cooper's Concise Guide to Writing, now in its fourth edition, has helped many students learn how to become effective, confident writers. Using the *Concise Guide,* you will read and write several different kinds of essays. From reading these essays, you will learn how other writers make their texts work for their particular readers. From writing the kinds of essays you are reading, you will learn to compose texts that work effectively for your readers. To take full advantage of what you are learning by reading and writing, the *Concise Guide* will also help you become self-reflective as a reader and writer. From thinking critically about your learning, you will be better able to remember and apply what you have learned, thereby earning a greater sense of confidence and control.

Reading

This section shows how reading texts that work well for their readers helps you learn to write texts for your own readers and how the *Concise Guide* supports your learning from reading.

How Written Texts Work.   How a text works depends on what purpose and what audience it is written for. A text's purpose and audience can be used to define the kind of writing it is, what we call its *genre*.

You may be familiar with genres as categories for literature (novel, poem, play) or film (science fiction, western, film noir, romance). College students read and write many different genres, such as lab reports in biology, ethnographies in anthropology, literary analyses or interpretations in English, or research reviews in education. Academic disciplines rely on certain genres that have become established ways of making meaning and communicating among students and specialists in the field. The same is true of writing in business (where genres include résumés and job-application letters, marketing reports, proposals, and personnel evaluations) and the professions (lawyers, for example, write briefs, appeals, closing arguments, and wills).

As these examples show, genres are shared by groups of people with common interests. Some genres are highly specialized and technical; to understand a biologist's lab report or a lawyer's brief, readers have to know the terminology and have to be able to judge the reliability of the lab report's research methods or the credibility of the brief's arguments. Many genres, however, are widely shared and therefore do not require specialized knowledge. For example, because of our shared experience, we can all read and understand most news reports, opinion essays, autobiographies, profiles, and advertisements we encounter in general audience publications such as newspapers, magazines, and Web sites.

Genres develop in different communities to serve particular purposes. Biologists use lab reports to inform readers interested in biology about the results of their research and to enable other researchers to duplicate their experiments. Lawyers use briefs to convince judges that certain points of law apply to their case. Reporters write about news events to inform readers. Columnists write opinion essays to persuade readers to adopt their views. Advertisers write ads to persuade readers to buy their clients' products.

A text's effectiveness—how well it achieves its purpose with its readers—depends on many factors, including how well it fulfills readers' expectations for the genre. Readers expect texts within a particular genre to have distinctive features, use specific strategies, and contain certain types of content. A remembered-event essay, for example, has several basic features: a well-told story about the event, a vivid presentation of the people involved in the event and of the place where it occurred, and an indication of the event's significance. Writers of such essays use strategies of narration and description to help readers imagine what happened and understand the event's significance. Readers expect the content of autobiographical writing to be about events they consider important, such as events that have had some lasting impact—changing, challenging, or complicating the writer's sense of self or connection with others.

Although individual texts within the same genre vary (no two proposals, even those arguing for the same solution, will be identical), they nonetheless follow a general pattern using distinctive basic features, strategies, and kinds of content to accomplish their purposes. This patterning allows for a certain amount of predictability, without which communication would be difficult, if not impossible. Language—whether spoken or written—is a system of social interaction. Everyone who speaks the same language learns to recognize certain patterns—how words should be ordered to make sentences comprehensible, how sentences can be related to one another to make coherent paragraphs, how examples can be used to explain new ideas, how arguments can be supported with quotations from authorities, and so forth. These language patterns, also called *conventions,* make communication possible.

To learn to write in genres for particular groups of readers, we need to pay attention to how texts work for their readers. We have to understand also that writing in a genre need not be mechanical or formulaic. Each genre's basic features, strategies, and kinds of content represent broad frameworks within which writers are free to be creative. Most writers, in fact, find that working within a framework allows them to be more creative, not less so. Some even blur the boundaries between genres and invent new genres for new media such as Web sites. And as groups change, developing new interests and new ways of adding to their knowledge, genre conventions also change.

> You would learn very little in this world if you were not allowed to imitate. And to repeat your imitations until some solid grounding... was achieved and the slight but wonderful difference—that made *you* and no one else—could assert itself.
>
> – MARY OLIVER

How the *Concise Guide* Helps You Write Texts That Work.   To learn the conventions of a particular genre, you need to read examples of that genre. At the same time, you should also practice writing in the genre.

> Read, read, read.... Just like a carpenter who works as an apprentice and studies the master. Read!
>
> – WILLIAM FAULKNER

Reading is crucial. As you read examples of a genre, you begin to recognize its predictable patterns as well as the possibilities for innovation. This knowledge is stored in your memory and used both when you read and when you write in that genre.

Experienced writers read and learn from positive examples as well as negative ones. Sometimes, they focus on a particular problem—how to write realistic-sounding dialogue or how to refute someone else's argument effectively, for example. They do not look for answers in a single example. Instead, they sample many texts to see how different writers work with a certain feature of the genre. This sampling is not slavish imitation but education. Like artists and craftspeople, writers have always learned from others. The *Concise Guide* presents a variety of examples in each genre accompanied by questions and commentary to help you see how writers use the conventional features and strategies of the genre to achieve their own purposes.

> I practiced writing in every possible way that I could. I wrote a pastiche of other people. Just as a pianist runs his scales for ten years before he gives his concert: because when he gives that concert, he can't be thinking of his fingering or of his hands, he has to be thinking of his interpretation. He's thinking of what he's trying to communicate.
>
> – KATHERINE ANNE PORTER

How the *Concise Guide* Helps You Design Texts That Work.   Writers have long recognized that no matter how well organized, well reasoned, or compelling a piece of writing may be, how it looks on the page influences to some extent how it works for readers. Today, writers have many more options for designing their documents than ever before. Recent advances in computer technology, digital photography and scanning, and integrated word processing and graphics programs make it relatively easy for writers to heighten the visual impact of the page. For example, they can change type fonts and add colors, charts, diagrams, and photographs to written documents. To construct multimedia Web pages or CD-ROMs, writers can add sound, moving images, and hyperlinks.

> Design is a funny word. Some people think design means how it looks. But of course, if you dig deeper, it's really how it works.
>
> – STEVE JOBS

These multiple possibilities, however, do not guarantee a more effective document. Writers need to learn to design effective texts by studying texts in their everyday lives that capture readers' attention and enhance understanding. As someone who has grown up watching television shows and videos, playing computer games, and looking at the photos, advertisements, cartoons, tables, and graphs in magazines, newspapers, and other sources, you are already a sophisticated visual consumer who has learned many of the conventions of document design for different genres and writing situations. This book will help you become aware of what you already know and help you make new discoveries about document design that you may be able to use in your own writing.

■ **Exercise 1.3**

> Make two lists—one of the genres you have *read* recently, such as explanations of how to do something, stories, news reports, opinion pieces, and movie reviews, and the other of the genres you have *written* recently, both for college courses and for other purposes. Then write a few sentences speculating about how your reading influences your writing and the design of your texts.

Writing

This section shows how your writing process can become a more productive process of *thinking and writing* and how the *Concise Guide* helps you develop a process to meet the demands of different writing situations.

How to MakeYour Writing Process Work. When you reflect on how you write, you probably think of the steps you take: First you read the writing assignment, next you decide which points to cover, then you begin writing the opening paragraph, and so forth. For familiar writing situations—when you know the subject well and feel confident writing in the genre for your particular readers—the process that works best may involve minimal planning and only one draft, followed by a little rewriting, spell-checking, and proofreading. But for most writing situations, you have to figure out what you can say about the subject and how to communicate effectively with your readers. In these situations, the writing process itself becomes a tool for discovery and not just a sequence of steps you take to produce a written text.

> I don't see writing as a communication of something already discovered, as "truths" already known. Rather, I see writing as a job of experiment. It's like any discovery job; you don't know what's going to happen until you try it.
>
> —WILLIAM STAFFORD

To make writing a true process of discovery, you need to recognize that the process of writing is a process of thinking—not simply a sequence of steps. Using writing as a process of discovery means that you do not think and then write but that the writing helps you think.

Few writers begin writing with a complete understanding of a subject. Most use writing as a way to learn about the subject, recording ideas and information they have collected, exploring connections and implications, letting the writing lead them to greater understanding. As they develop ideas and plan a draft, writers set goals for their writing: goals for the whole essay (to confront readers or inspire them, for example) and goals for particular passages (to make a sentence emphatic or include details in a paragraph).

> When I start a project, the first thing I do is write down, in longhand, everything I know about the subject, every thought I've ever had on it. This may be twelve or fourteen pages. Then I read it through, for quite a few days...then I try to find out what are the salient points that I must make. And then it begins to take shape.
>
> —MAYA ANGELOU

While writing, most writers pause occasionally to reread what they have written. They often reread with their readers in mind to see whether they can make their writing more effective. Rereading sometimes leads to further discovery—filling in a gap in the logic of an argument, for example—and frequently it leads to substantial rethinking and revising: cutting, reorganizing, rewriting.

> I think the writer ought to help the reader as much as he can without damaging what he wants to say; and I don't think it ever hurts the writer to sort of stand back now and then and look at his stuff as if he were reading it instead of writing it.
>
> —JAMES JONES

> The writer must survey his work critically, coolly, as though he were a stranger to it. At the end of each revision, a manuscript may look...worked over, torn apart, pinned together, added to, deleted from, words changed and words changed back.
>
> —ELEANOR ESTES

Rereading your own writing with a critical eye is necessary, but many writers also share their ideas and writing with others, actively seeking constructive critical comments from friends and colleagues. Playwrights, poets, and novelists often join writers' workshops to get help from other writers. F. Scott Fitzgerald depended on his editor, Maxwell Perkins. When Perkins criticized the way the title character was being introduced in an early version of the novel *The Great Gatsby,* Fitzgerald made significant changes in five chapters and completely rewrote two others.

Writers also sometimes write collaboratively. Engineers, business executives, and research scientists usually write proposals and reports in teams. Graduate students and professors in many fields do research together and cowrite conference papers and journal articles. This book is the product of extensive collaboration between the coauthors and numerous composition instructors, student writers, and editors over many years. Your instructor may ask you to try some of the *Concise Guide*'s collaborative activities with other students in your class.

> [Ezra Pound] was a marvelous critic because he didn't try to turn you into an imitation of himself. He tried to see what you were trying to do.
>
> —T. S. Eliot

> I like working collaboratively from time to time. I like fusing ideas into one vision. I like seeing that vision come to life with other people who know exactly what it took to get there.
>
> —Amy Tan

The continual shifting of attention—from setting goals to choosing words, from discovering new ideas to rereading to anticipate readers' likely objections, from adding supporting examples to reorganizing—characterizes the dynamic thinking that underlies the writing process. Although writing may seem to progress in a linear, step-by-step fashion—thinking about what to say and writing it down and then perhaps revising—discovery does not stop when drafting begins. It continues throughout drafting and revising. Most writers plan and revise their plans, draft and revise their drafts, write and read what they have written, and then write some more. This rereading and rethinking is what we mean when we describe the writing process as recursive rather than linear. Instead of progressing in a straight line from the first sentence to the last, from opening paragraph to conclusion, the experience of writing is more like taking a steep trail with frequent switchbacks; it appears that you are retracing old ground, but you are really rising to new levels.

Seasoned writers depend on this recursiveness to lead them to new ideas and to develop their insights. Many writers claim that it is only by writing that they can figure out what they think.

> How do I know what I think until I see what I say?
>
> —E. M. Forster

> As a writer I would find out most clearly what I thought, and what I only thought I thought, when I saw it written down.
>
> —Anna Quindlen

Even writers who plan extensively in their heads eventually have to work out their plans by writing them down. The advantage of writing down ideas is not only that writing makes a record you can review later but also that the process of writing itself can help you articulate and develop your ideas.

> You have to work problems out for yourself on paper. Put the stuff down and read it—to see if it works.
>
> —JOYCE CARY

Inexperienced writers or those writing in a new genre or on a difficult subject especially benefit from writing outlines of where they are and where they hope to go so that they can then focus on how to get there. But outlines should not be written in stone; they must be flexible if the writer is to benefit from the recursiveness of the writing process.

> Somebody starting to write should have a solid foundation to build on....When I first started to write I used to do two- or three-page outlines.
>
> —LILLIAN HELLMAN

> I began [*Invisible Man*] with a chart of the three-part division. It was a conceptual frame with most of the ideas and some of the incidents indicated.
>
> —RALPH ELLISON

> You are always going back and forth between the outline and the writing, bringing them closer together, or just throwing out the outline and making a new one.
>
> —ANNIE DILLARD

Sometimes the hardest part of writing is getting down to work. Writers may procrastinate, but they learn to deal with procrastination. Many writers make writing a habit by setting a time to write and trying to stick to their schedule. Most important, they know that the only way to make progress on a writing project is to keep at it. They work at their writing, knowing it takes time and perseverance.

> I have to write every day because, the way I work, the writing generates the writing.
>
> —E. L. DOCTOROW

> It's a matter of piling a little piece here and a little piece there, fitting them together, going on to the next part, then going back and gradually shaping the whole piece into something....You don't rely on inspiration—I don't anyway, and I don't think most writers do.
>
> —DAVE BARRY

Once immersed in figuring out what they want to say about the subject, contemplating what readers already think about it, and so forth, most writers find that they continue making discoveries even when away from their desks. Taking a walk or playing a game can be a productive part of the process rather than a means of procrastinating. Diverting a tired mind and body can help writers see connections or solve problems that had stymied them earlier.

> Often I write by not writing. I assign a task to my subconscious, then take a nap or go for a walk, do errands, and let my mind work on the problem.
>
> —DONALD MURRAY

Like most creative activities, writing is a form of problem solving. As they work on a draft, most writers continually discover and try to solve writing problems—how to bring a scene to life, how to handle objections, whether to begin with this point or that. The more writers know about their subjects, genres, and readers, the better they can anticipate and solve problems as they write.

Experienced writers develop a repertoire of strategies for solving problems they are likely to encounter. The *Concise Guide* will illustrate for you the strategies that will help you write well in several quite different genres.

How the *Concise Guide* Helps You Develop a Writing Process That Works.   As a student learning to write, you need to develop a writing process that is flexible and yet systematic. It should be a process that neither oversimplifies nor overwhelms, one that helps you learn about a subject and write a successful essay. The Guides to Writing in Part One of this book, which you will find on the pages bordered in blue, are designed to meet this need. These guides suggest what you need to think about for each different writing situation. The first few times you write in a new genre, you can rely on these guides. They provide a scaffolding to support your work until you become more familiar with each genre.

When engaging in any new and complex activity—driving, playing an instrument, skiing, or writing—we have to learn how to break down the activity into a series of manageable tasks. In learning to play tennis, for example, you can isolate lobbing from volleying or work on your backhand or serve. Similarly, in writing about an autobiographical event, you can work first on recalling what happened, imagining the scene, or reflecting on the event's significance. What is important is focusing on one aspect at a time. Dividing the process in this way enables you to tackle a complex writing project without oversimplifying it.

> You know when you think about writing a book, you think it is overwhelming. But, actually, you break it down into tiny little tasks any moron could do.
>
> —Annie Dillard

■ **Exercise 1.4**

Write a page or two describing the process you followed the last time you wrote something that took time and effort. Use the following questions to help you recall what you did, but feel free to write about any other aspects of your writing process that you remember.

- What initially led you to write? Who were you writing for, and what was the purpose of your writing?

- What kinds of thinking and planning did you do, if any, before you began writing the first draft?

- If you discussed your ideas and plans with someone, how did discussing them help you? If you had someone read your draft, how did getting a response help?

- If you rewrote, moved, added, or cut anything in your first draft, describe what you changed.

Thinking Critically

This section shows how thinking critically about your learning can help you make your writing more effective and how the *Concise Guide* helps you think critically about your reading, your writing process, and the genres you are using.

How to Think Critically about Your Learning.   Thinking critically means becoming self-aware or conscious of your own thinking and learning processes.

When writing, you will find that many of your decisions do not require conscious effort. You can rely on familiar strategies that usually produce effective writing for you in the genre. But there will nearly always be occasions as you write when you become aware of problems that require your full attention. Some problems may be fairly easy to remedy, such as an inappropriate word choice or a confusing sequence of events. Other problems may require considerable rethinking and writing—for example, if you discover that your readers' likely objections seriously undermine your argument.

After you have completed a final draft, reflecting on how you identified and tried to solve such problems can be a powerful aid to learning. Understanding the problem may enable you to anticipate similar problems in the future. It may also give you a firmer grip on the standards you need to apply when rereading your drafts. Most important, reflecting on a problem you solved should enhance your confidence as a writer, helping you realize that problems are not signs of bad writing but that problem-solving signifies good writing.

> That's what a writer is: someone who sees problems a little more clearly than others.
> – Eugene Ionesco

To think critically about your learning, it also helps to reflect on what you have learned from reading texts in the genre you are writing. Much of our language and genre-learning comes from modeling. As young children, for example, we learn from hearing our parents and peers tell stories and from watching stories portrayed on television and in film. We learn ways of beginning and ending, strategies for building suspense, techniques for making time sequences clear, how to use dialogue to develop character, and so on. As an adult, we can reinforce and increase our repertoire of storytelling patterns by analyzing how stories that we admire work and by consciously trying out in our own writing the strategies we have seen work in those stories.

> I went back to the good nature books that I had read. And I analyzed them. I wrote outlines of whole books—outlines of chapters—so that I could see their structure. And I copied down their transitional sentences or their main sentences or their closing sentences or their lead sentences. I especially paid attention to how these writers made transitions between paragraphs and scenes.
> – Annie Dillard

Finally, contemplating what you have learned about writing different genres can help you understand how genres are used to make possible certain kinds of social actions and ways of knowing while discouraging others. Concept explanations, for example, enable the efficient exchange of established knowledge, but they also discourage critical questioning about how certain kinds of knowledge, and not other kinds, get established as authoritative and by whom. Similarly, writing about remembered events enables self-presentation and perhaps even self-knowledge, but it discourages critical questioning about the social construction of identity and the idea of a single true or essential self.

> You leave out a lot, and emphasize this and not that. Your actual experience is a complete flux...[and yet] you want the readers to say, this is true...to believe [they are] getting the real Robert Lowell.
>
> – ROBERT LOWELL

How the *Concise Guide* Helps You Think Critically.   Thinking critically about your reading and writing experiences is not difficult. It simply requires that you shift focus from *what* you are reading and writing to *how* you are reading and writing.

The *Concise Guide* helps you talk and write about the hows of reading and writing different genres by providing a shared vocabulary of words and phrases that you can easily learn and others of which you already know. Words like *significance, narrating,* and *thesis,* for example, will help you identify the features and strategies of essays you are reading in different genres. Words and phrases like *invention, setting goals,* and *revising* will help you describe what you are doing as you write your own essays in these genres. Phrases like *established knowledge* and *essential self* will help you examine the social dimensions of genres you are reading and writing.

Each writing assignment chapter in Part One includes many opportunities for you to think critically about your understanding of the genre and to reflect on your writing process. A section entitled Reflecting on Your Writing concludes each chapter, giving you an opportunity to look back and reflect on how you used the writing process creatively.

■ **Exercise 1.5**

Read the following quotes to see how writers use similes ("Writing is like _____") and metaphors ("Writing is _____") to describe the processes and products of writing.

Writing is like exploring...as an explorer makes maps of the country he has explored, so a writer's works are maps of the country he has explored.

– LAWRENCE OSGOOD

Writing is manual labor of the mind: a job, like laying pipe.

– JOHN GREGORY DUNNE

Write two or three similes or metaphors of your own that express aspects of your experience as a writer. Then write a page or so explaining and expanding on the ideas and feelings expressed in your similes and metaphors.

■ USING THIS BOOK

Axelrod & Cooper's Concise Guide to Writing is divided into two major parts.

Part One presents writing assignments for six important genres: autobiographical events, profile, explanation, position paper, proposal, and evaluation. Each of these writing assignment chapters provides readings that demonstrate how written texts of that genre work and a Guide to Writing that will help you write an effective essay in the genre for your particular purpose and audience. Each chapter also includes a discussion of possible purposes and audiences for the genre and a summary of the genre's basic features and strategies. As we have mentioned, a section titled Reflecting on Your Writing concludes each of these chapters.

Part Two provides illustrations and practice using strategies for invention and critical reading, writing, and research. Also included are up-to-date guidelines for writing research papers, using a wide range of sources (library sources, the Internet, and your own field research).

■ Exercise 1.6

Preview each of the writing assignments in Part One (Chapters 2–7) of the *Concise Guide*. Begin by reading the opening paragraphs of the chapter, which introduce the genre, and skimming the examples of Writing in Your Other Courses, Writing in the Community, and Writing in the Workplace. Then turn to the Guide to Writing in the chapter (easily identified by the blue border around the pages), read the Writing Assignment, and skim the Invention activity immediately following the assignment to see examples of possible subjects for essays in the genre, including those listed under Identity and Community and Work and Career.

List at least two genres you would like to work on in this class. For each genre you list, write a few sentences explaining why you want to work on it.

The Part One Readings

Each Part One chapter includes readings, some written by professional writers and others by students who have used earlier editions of this book. All of the readings have been selected to reflect a wide range of topics and strategies. If you read these selections with a critical eye, you will see many different ways writers use a genre.

Each reading selection is accompanied by the following groups of questions, activities, and commentary to help you learn how essays in that genre work:

Connecting to Culture and Experience invites you to explore with other students an issue or question raised by the reading.

Analyzing Writing Strategies helps you examine closely the reading's basic features or writing strategies.

Commentary points out important features of the genre and strategies the writer uses in the essay.

Considering Topics for Your Own Essay suggests subjects related to the reading that you might write about in your own essay.

Most of the assignments in this book provide opportunities to explore your connections to the world. When you are choosing a topic to write about, you might consider suggestions listed under Identity and Community and under Work and Career in the Guides to Writing. These topics enable you to explore your personal connections to the various communities of which you are a part, visit and learn more about places in your community, debate issues important to your community, examine your ideas and attitudes about work, and consider issues related to your future career.

The Part One Guides to Writing

Each Part One assignment chapter provides detailed suggestions for thinking about your subject and purpose as well as your readers and their expectations. These Guides to Writing will help you develop a truly recursive process of discovery that will enable you to write an effective essay in the genre for your particular purpose and audience.

To make the process manageable, the Guide to Writing is divided into sections: The Writing Assignment, Invention and Research, Planning and Drafting, a Critical Reading Guide, Revising, and Editing and Proofreading. The "menu" preceding the Writing Assignment shows you at a glance the sections and the headings under each section. But to understand how the activities in the Guide to Writing will help you do the kinds of thinking you need to do, you must look closely at the types of activities included in each section.

The Writing Assignment.   Each Guide to Writing begins with an assignment that defines the general purpose and basic features of the genre you have been studying in the chapter. The assignment does not tell you what subject to write about or who your readers will be. You will have to make these decisions, guided by the invention activities in the next section.

Invention and Research.   Every Guide to Writing includes invention activities, and most also include suggestions for observational, library, or Internet research. The Invention and Research activities are designed to help you find a topic, discover what you already know about it, consider your purpose and audience, research the subject further to see what others have written about it, explore and develop your ideas, and compose a tentative thesis statement to guide your planning and drafting.

Remember that invention is not a part of the writing process you can skip. It is the basic, ongoing preoccupation of all writing. As writers, we cannot choose *whether* to invent; we can only decide *how*.

You can use the Invention activities before, during, and after you have written a first draft. However, the sequence of invention activities can be especially helpful before drafting because it focuses systematically on the basic genre features and writing strategies. The sequence reminds you of questions you need to think about as you collect, analyze, and synthesize ideas and information in light of your particular subject, purpose, and readers. A sequence of invention activities may take only two or three hours to complete. But it works best when spread over several days, giving yourself time to think. So if at all possible, begin the invention process far enough ahead of the deadline to let your thinking develop fully. Here is some general advice to keep in mind as you do the invention activities:

Use Writing to Explore Your Ideas. You can use writing to gather your thoughts and see where they lead. As you approach each invention activity, try to refrain from censoring yourself. Simply try writing for several minutes. Explore your ideas freely, letting one idea lead to another. Later, you can reread what you have written and select the most promising ideas to develop.

Focus on One Issue at a Time. Explore your topic systematically by dividing it into its component parts and exploring them one at a time. For example, instead of trying to think of your whole argument, focus on one reason and the support you would give for it, or focus on how you might refute one objection to your argument.

■ **Exercise 1.7**

Preview the Invention section of one of the Guides to Writing. First choose an assignment chapter that interests you (Chapters 2–7). Then find the Invention (or Invention and Research) section, and skim it from beginning to end. Notice the headings and subheadings, but also look closely at some of the activities to see what they ask you to do and think about.

Planning and Drafting.   To get you started writing the first draft of your essay, each Guide to Writing includes suggestions for planning. You set goals and try to implement them as you plan and write the draft. While drafting, you may make notes about new ideas or additional information you need to research, but you try to keep your focus on the ideas and information you have already discovered in order to work out their meanings.

The section is divided into four parts:

Seeing What You Have involves reviewing what you have discovered about your subject, purpose, and audience.

Setting Goals helps you think about your overall purpose as well as your goals for the various parts of your essay.

Outlining suggests some of the ways you might organize your essay.

Drafting launches you on the writing of your first draft.

As you begin your first draft, keep in mind the following practical points, many of which assist professional writers as they begin drafting:

Choose the Best Time and Place.   You can write a draft anytime and anyplace. As you probably already know, people write under the most surprising or arduous conditions. Drafting is likely to go smoothly, however, if you choose a time and place ideally suited for sustained and thoughtful work. Many professional writers have a place where they can concentrate for a few hours without repeated interruptions. Writers often find one place where they write best, and they return there whenever they have to write. Try to find such a place for yourself.

Make Revision Easy. If possible, compose your draft on a word processor. If you usually write with pen or pencil and paper, consider making the change to word processing for the ease of drafting and revising, as well as for the sake of long-term speed and efficiency. Even if you do not touch-type or if it seems strange at first, you may find, like most students, that you adjust relatively quickly to writing directly on the keyboard. If you do choose to compose on paper, leave plenty of space in the margins to make notes and revisions.

Do the Easy Parts First. Divide your task into manageable portions and do the easy parts first. Just aim to complete a small part of the essay — one section or paragraph — at a time. Try not to agonize over difficult parts, such as the first paragraph or the right word. Start with the part you understand best.

Lower Your Expectations — for the Time Being. Be satisfied with less than perfect writing in a first draft, and do not be overly critical of what you are getting down on paper at this stage. Remember, you are working on a draft that you will revise later. For now, try things out. Follow digressions. Let your ideas flow. Later you can go back and cross out a sentence, rework a section, or make other changes. Now and then, of course, you will want to reread what you have written, but do not reread obsessively. Return to drafting new material as soon as possible. Avoid editing or proofreading during this stage.

Take Short Breaks — and Reward Yourself. Drafting can be hard work, and you may need to take a break to refresh yourself. But be careful not to wander off for too long, or you may lose momentum. By setting small goals and rewarding yourself regularly, you will make it easier to complete the draft.

Critical Reading Guide. Each Guide to Writing includes a Critical Reading Guide that will help you get a good critical reading of your draft as well as help you read others' drafts. Once you have finished drafting your essay, you will want to make every effort to have someone else read the draft and comment on how to improve it. Experienced writers often seek out such advice from critical readers to help them see their drafts as others do.

Ask whether your critical reader would prefer an electronic version of your draft or a hard copy. Even a reader who is going to comment on the draft electronically may prefer to read a hard copy.

When you are asked to evaluate someone else's draft, you need to read it with a critical eye. You must be both positive and skeptical — positive in that you want to identify what is workable and promising in the draft, skeptical in that you need to question the writer's assumptions and decisions.

Here is some general advice on reading any draft critically:

Make a Written Record of Your Comments.   Although talking with the writer about your reading of the draft can be useful and even fun, you will be most helpful if you put your ideas into writing. When you write down your comments and suggestions—either within an electronic or hard copy of the draft or in a separate electronic or paper document—you leave a record that can be used later when the writer revises the material.

Read First for an Overall Impression.   On first reading, try not to be distracted by any errors in spelling, punctuation, or word choice. Look at the big issues: clear focus, compelling presentation, forcefulness of argument, novelty and quality of ideas. What seems particularly good? What problems do you see? Focus on the overall goal of the draft and how well it is met. Write just a few sentences expressing your initial reaction.

Read Again to Analyze the Draft.   For this second reading, focus on individual parts of the draft, bringing to bear what you know about the genre and the subject.

When you read the draft at this level, you must shift your attention from one aspect of the essay to another. Consider how well the opening paragraphs introduce the essay and prepare the reader for what follows. Pay attention to specific writing strategies, like narration or argument. Notice whether the parts seem logically sequenced. Look for detailing, examples, or other kinds of support.

As you analyze, you are evaluating as well as describing, but a critical reading involves more than criticism of the draft. A good critical reader helps a writer see how each part of an essay works and how all the parts work together. By describing what you see, you help the writer view the draft more objectively, a perspective that is necessary for thoughtful revising.

Offer Advice, but Do Not Rewrite.   As a critical reader, you may be tempted to rewrite the draft—to change a word here, correct an error there, add your ideas everywhere. Resist the impulse. Your role is to read carefully, to point out what you think is or is not working, to make suggestions and ask questions. Leave the revising to the writer.

In turn, the writer has a responsibility to listen to your comments but is under no obligation to do as you suggest. "Then why go to all the trouble?" you might ask. There are at least two good reasons. First, when you read someone else's draft critically, you learn more about writing—about the decisions writers make, about how a thoughtful reader reads, about the constraints of particular kinds of writing. Second, as a critical reader you embody for the writer the abstraction called "audience." By sharing your reactions with the writer, you complete the circuit of communication.

■ **Exercise 1.8**

Preview the Critical Reading Guide in the assignment chapter you chose for Exercise 1.7. Find the section and skim it. Then look closely at item 2 or 3 in the numbered list to get a sense of what you are being asked to think about when reading and responding to another writer's draft. If you have participated in draft workshops before, compare your previous experience as a reader to the experience you think you would have by following this Critical Reading Guide. Also compare the usefulness of the response you got in the past from readers of your draft to the kind of response you could expect from readers following this guide.

Revising.   Each Guide to Writing includes a Revising section to help you get an overview of your draft, chart a plan for revision, consider critical comments, and carry out the revisions. Productive invention and smooth drafting rarely result in the essay a writer has imagined. Experienced writers are not surprised or disappointed, however, because they expect revision to be necessary. They know that revising will bring them closer to the essay they really want to write. When writers read their drafts thoughtfully and critically—and perhaps reflect on the advice of critical readers—they are able to see many opportunities for improvement. They may notice sentence-level problems such as misspelled words or garbled syntax, but more important, they discover ways to delete, move, rephrase, and add material in order to develop their ideas and say what they want to say more clearly.

Here is some general advice on revising:

Reflect on Your Purpose and Audience.   Remind yourself of what you are trying to accomplish in this essay. If someone has read and responded to your draft, you may now have a better understanding of your readers' likely interests and concerns. You may also have refined your purpose. Keep your purpose and audience in mind as you reread the essay and revise in stages. Do not try to do everything at once.

Look at Major Problems First.   Identify any major problems preventing the draft from achieving its purpose. Major problems might include a lack of awareness of your audience, inadequate development of key parts, missing sections, or the need for further invention or research. Trying to solve these major problems will probably lead to some substantial rethinking and rewriting, so do not get diverted by sentence-level problems at this time.

Focus Next on Organization and Coherence.   Look at the introductory section of the essay to see how well it prepares readers for the parts that follow. It may help to make a paragraph-by-paragraph scratch outline to help you see at a glance what each paragraph does in the essay. If you have difficulty identifying the function of any paragraph, you may need to add an appropriate transition to clarify the paragraph's connection to the previous paragraphs or write a new topic sentence that better announces the subject of the paragraph. Or you may need to do some more extensive rewriting or reorganization.

Then Consider the Details.   As the saying goes, the devil is in the details. The details have to be selected for a specific purpose, such as to convey significance, support an argument, or provide a concrete example of an abstract idea. If any details seem unrelated to your larger purpose, you need to make the connections explicit. If your essay lacks details, you can review your invention notes or do some additional research to come up with the details you need.

Editing and Proofreading.   Once you have finished revising your essay, your next step is to edit and proofread it carefully. You want to make sure that every word, phrase, and sentence is clear and correct. Using language and punctuation correctly is an essential part of good writing. Errors will distract readers and lessen your credibility as a writer.

Be sure to save editing until the end—after you have planned and worked out a revision. Too much editing too early in the writing process can limit, or even block, invention and drafting.

Here are some other suggestions:

Proofread on Hard Copy.   If your essay exists only in electronic form, print out a copy and proofread that version. Electronic text is difficult and fatiguing to read, and you can easily miss errors that are obvious on the printed page.

Keep a List of Your Common Errors.   Note the grammatical and spelling errors you discover in your own writing. You will probably start to recognize error patterns to check for as you edit your work. Many word-processor grammar checkers allow you to customize, to some extent, what kinds of errors they call your attention to. If you find that you consistently make a particular error, cultivate the habit of using your word processor's Find function to locate instances of that error in the late stages of every piece of writing.

Begin Proofreading with the Last Word.   To focus your attention on word errors, it may help to read backward word for word, beginning with the last word of your essay. When you read backward, it is harder to pay attention to content and thus easier to recognize spelling and keying errors.

Exchange Drafts with Another Student.   Because it is usually easier to see errors in someone else's writing than in your own, consider trading essays with a classmate and proofreading one another's writing. If you do this, check whether your classmate would prefer an electronic version of your essay or a hard copy.

Reflecting on Your Writing.   Each chapter in Part One concludes with a set of activities to help you consider how you solved problems writing that particular kind of essay. If you are compiling a portfolio of your coursework that will be assessed at the end of the term, these activities may help you decide what to include in your portfolio as well as help you write a reflective essay on the work you select for the portfolio.

WRITING ACTIVITIES

Remembering
Events

When you write about remembered events in your life, you produce autobiography, a genre of writing that is very popular with both readers and writers. Autobiography is popular because reading as well as writing it leads people to reflect deeply on their own lives. When you reflect on the meaning of experience, you examine the forces within yourself and within society that have shaped you into the person you have become.

When you write about a remembered event, your purpose is to present yourself to readers by telling a story that discloses something significant about your life. Autobiographical writers do not just pour out their memories and feelings. Instead, they shape those memories into a compelling story that conveys the meaning and importance of an experience—what can be called its autobiographical significance.

Writing about your life for others to read is not the same as writing for yourself. As a writer, you must remember that autobiography is public, not private. While it requires self-presentation, it does not require you to make unwanted self-disclosures. You choose the event to write about and decide how you will portray yourself.

As you work through this chapter, you will learn to tell a story that entertains readers and lets them know something important about how you came to be the person you are now. You also will learn to describe people and places vividly so that readers can see what makes them memorable for you. As you learn to write well about a remembered event, you will be practicing two of the most basic writing strategies—narration and description. These strategies can play a role in almost every kind of writing. As you will see in Chapters 3–7, narration and description can contribute to explanatory reports and persuasive arguments, in addition to playing an essential role in the remembered-event assignment for this chapter.

You will encounter writing about a remembered event in many different contexts, as the following examples suggest.

Writing in Your Other Courses

- For an assignment in a psychology course, a student tests against her own experience an idea from the developmental psychologist Erik Erikson: "[Y]oung people ... are sometimes preoccupied with what they appear to be in the eyes of others as compared with what they feel they are." The student recounts a time when she cared tremendously about what the other members of her high school soccer team thought about her. Then she explains how her teammates' reactions influenced her feelings and sense of self.

- For a linguistics course, a student is asked to write about current research on men's and women's conversational styles. One researcher, Deborah Tannen, has reported that women and men have different expectations when they talk about problems. Women expect to spend a lot of time talking about the problem itself, especially about their feelings. Men, in contrast, typically want to cut short the analysis of the problem and the talk about feelings; they would rather discuss solutions to the problem. Applying Tannen's findings to her own experience, the student recounts a conversation about a family problem with her brother, who is one year older. She reconstructs as much of the conversation as she can remember and explains which parts constitute feelings talk and which indicate problem-solving talk. She concludes that her conversation with her brother well illustrates Tannen's findings.

Writing in the Community

- As part of a local history project in a small western ranching community, a college student volunteers to help an elderly rancher write about some of his early experiences. One experience seems especially dramatic and significant — a time in the winter of 1938 when a six-foot snowstorm isolated the rancher's family for nearly a month. The student tape-records the rancher talking about how he and his wife made preparations to survive and ensure the health of their infant sons and how he snowshoed eight miles to a logging train track, stopped the train, and gave the engineer a message to deliver to relatives in the nearest town explaining that they were going to be okay. On a second visit, the student and the rancher listen to the tape recording and afterward talk about further details that might make the event more complete and dramatic for readers. The rancher then writes a draft of the remembered event, and the student later helps him revise and edit the essay. The student copies an old snow-day photograph from the nearby town's newspaper files, and the rancher selects a photograph of his young family from a family photo album. The essay and photographs are published in a special supplement to the newspaper.

- To commemorate the retirement of the city's world-famous symphony orchestra conductor, a radio program director invites the conductor to talk about his early experiences with the orchestra. Aware of his tendency to ramble and digress in interviews, the conductor decides to write down a story about the first time he asked the orchestra members to play a never-before-performed modern composition noted for its lack of familiar tones, progressions, and rhythms. He describes how he tried to prepare the orchestra members for this experience and how they went about the hard, slow work of mastering the difficult music. The conductor expresses regret over posing this challenge so early in his experience of working with the orchestra members, but he proudly asserts that their great success with the music gave them the confidence to master any music they played together. For the radio program, he alternates reading this remembered event aloud with playing brief recorded excerpts from the orchestra's polished performance.

Writing in the Workplace

- As part of an orientation manual for new employees, the founder of a highly successful computer software company describes the day she spent with the Silicon Valley venture capitalists who lent her the money to start the company. She describes how other venture capitalists had turned her down and how desperately anxious she was for this group to fund her company. The meeting had barely begun when she spilled her coffee across the top of the gleaming conference table. She describes some of the questions and her answers and traces her rising and falling hopes during the discussion. She left dejected and resigned to giving up the dream of founding her own company. The next morning a member of the group who had not asked any questions at the meeting phoned her to praise her proposal and announce that his group would fund her company. He invited her to a celebratory lunch with the group at the best restaurant in town, where she was careful not to tip over her long-stemmed wine glass.

- The highway department offices of a large midwestern state have recently been the site of violence and threats of violence. One worker has killed another, and several managers have been threatened. To keynote a statewide meeting of highway department managers seeking solutions to this problem, a manager writes a speech that describes an incident when he was confronted in his office by an employee who was unhappy about an overtime assignment. The employee came into the manager's office without knocking and would not sit down. He talked loudly, waved his arms, and threatened to harm the manager and his family. He would not leave when asked to. The manager reflects on his fear and on his frustration about not knowing what to do when the employee finally left. The department's published procedures seemed not to apply to this case. He acknowledges his reluctance to report the incident to the state office because he did not want to appear to be ineffective and indecisive.

Practice Remembering an Event: A Collaborative Activity

The preceding scenarios suggest some occasions for writing about events in one's life. Think of an event in your life that you would feel comfortable describing to others in your class. The only requirements are that you remember the event well enough to tell the story and that the story lets your classmates learn something about you. Your instructor may schedule this collaborative activity as a face-to-face in-class discussion or ask you to conduct an online real-time discussion in a chat room. Whatever the medium, here are some guidelines to follow:

Part 1. Consider several events, and choose one you feel comfortable telling in this situation. Then, for two or three minutes, make notes about how you will tell your story.

Now, get together with two or three other students, and take turns telling your stories. Be brief: Each story should take only a few minutes.

Part 2. Take ten minutes to discuss what happened when you told about a remembered event:

- Tell each other how you chose your particular story. What did you think about when you were choosing an event? How did your purpose and audience — what you wanted your classmates to know and think about you — influence your choice?

- Review what each of you decided to include in your story. Did you plunge right into telling what happened, or did you first provide some background information? Did you decide to leave any of the action out of your story? If so, what did you leave out and why? Did you include a physical description of the scene? Did you describe any of the people, including yourself, or mention any specific dialogue? Did you tell your listeners how you felt at the time the event occurred, or did you say how you feel now looking back on it?

- What was the easiest part of telling a story about a remembered event in your life? What was the most difficult part?

READINGS

No two essays remembering an event are alike, and yet they share defining features. Together, the three readings in this chapter reveal a number of these features, so you will want to read as many of them as possible. If time permits, complete the activities in the Analyzing Writing Strategies section that follows each selection, and read the Commentary. Following the readings is a section called Basic Features: Remembering Events (p. 42), which offers a concise description of the features of writing about remembered events and provides examples from the three readings.

Annie Dillard *won the Pulitzer Prize for nonfiction writing with her first book,* Pilgrim at Tinker Creek *(1974). Since then, she has written nine books in a variety of genres, including the essay collections* Teaching a Stone to Talk *(1988) and* For the Time Being *(1999); a novel,* The Living *(1993); poetry,* Mornings like This *(1996); literary theory,* Living by Fiction *(1988); and an account of her work as a writer,* The Writing Life *(1990). Dillard also wrote an autobiography of her early years,* An American Childhood *(1987), from which the following reading comes.*

Dillard is a professor of English and writer in residence at Wesleyan College. In The Writing
Life, *she describes her writing as a process of discovery: "When you write, you lay out a line of
words. The line of words is a miner's pick, a woodcarver's gouge, a surgeon's probe. You wield
it, and it digs a path you follow. Soon you find yourself in new territory." Through this process,
she explains, the writing "changes from an expression of your notions to an epistemological
tool." In other words, the very act of writing helps her learn more about herself and others.*

*The reading that follows relates an event that occurred one winter morning when the
seven-year-old Dillard and a friend were chased relentlessly by an adult stranger at whom
they had been throwing snowballs. Dillard admits that she was terrified at the time, and yet she
asserts that she has "seldom been happier since." As you read, think about how this paradox
helps you grasp the autobiographical significance of this experience for Dillard.*

From *An American Childhood*

Annie Dillard

Some boys taught me to play football. This was fine sport. 1
You thought up a new strategy for every play and whis-
pered it to the others. You went out for a pass, fooling
everyone. Best, you got to throw yourself mightily at someone's running legs. Either you brought him down or you hit
the ground flat out on your chin, with your arms empty
before you. It was all or nothing. If you hesitated in fear, you would miss and get hurt: you
would take a hard fall while the kid got away, or you would get kicked in the face while the
kid got away. But if you flung yourself wholeheartedly at the back of his knees — if you
gathered and joined body and soul and pointed them diving fearlessly — then you likely
wouldn't get hurt, and you'd stop the ball. Your fate, and your team's score, depended on
your concentration and courage. Nothing girls did could compare with it.

Boys welcomed me at baseball, too, for I had, through enthusiastic practice, what 2
was weirdly known as a boy's arm. In winter, in the snow, there was neither baseball nor
football, so the boys and I threw snowballs at passing cars. I got in trouble throwing snowballs, and have seldom been happier since.

On one weekday morning after Christmas, six inches of new snow had just fallen. 3
We were standing up to our boot tops in snow on a front yard on trafficked Reynolds
Street, waiting for cars. The cars traveled Reynolds Street slowly and evenly; they were
targets all but wrapped in red ribbons, cream puffs. We couldn't miss.

I was seven; the boys were eight, nine, and ten. The oldest two Fahey boys were 4
there — Mikey and Peter — polite blond boys who lived near me on Lloyd Street, and who
already had four brothers and sisters. My parents approved Mikey and Peter Fahey.
Chickie McBride was there, a tough kid, and Billy Paul and Mackie Kean too, from across
Reynolds, where the boys grew up dark and furious, grew up skinny, knowing, and
skilled. We had all drifted from our houses that morning looking for action, and had found
it here on Reynolds Street.

It was cloudy but cold. The cars' tires laid behind them on the snowy street a complex 5
trail of beige chunks like crenellated castle walls. I had stepped on some earlier; they

squeaked. We could not have wished for more traffic. When a car came, we all popped it one. In the intervals between cars we reverted to the natural solitude of children.

I started making an iceball—a perfect iceball, from perfectly white snow, perfectly 6 spherical, and squeezed perfectly translucent so no snow remained all the way through. (The Fahey boys and I considered it unfair actually to throw an iceball at somebody, but it had been known to happen.)

I had just embarked on the iceball project when we heard tire chains come clanking 7 from afar. A black Buick was moving toward us down the street. We all spread out, banged together some regular snowballs, took aim, and, when the Buick drew nigh, fired.

A soft snowball hit the driver's windshield right before the driver's face. It made a 8 smashed star with a hump in the middle.

Often, of course, we hit our target, but this time, the only time in all of life, the 9 car pulled over and stopped. Its wide black door opened; a man got out of it, running. He didn't even close the car door.

He ran after us, and we ran away from him, up the snowy Reynolds sidewalk. At the 10 corner, I looked back; incredibly, he was still after us. He was in city clothes: a suit and tie, street shoes. Any normal adult would have quit, having sprung us into flight and made his point. This man was gaining on us. He was a thin man, all action. All of a sudden, we were running for our lives.

Wordless, we split up. We were on our turf; we could lose ourselves in the neighbor- 11 hood backyards, everyone for himself. I paused and considered. Everyone had vanished except Mikey Fahey, who was just rounding the corner of a yellow brick house. Poor Mikey, I trailed him. The driver of the Buick sensibly picked the two of us to follow. The man apparently had all day.

He chased Mikey and me around the yellow house and up a backyard path we knew 12 by heart: under a low tree, up a bank, through a hedge, down some snowy steps, and across the grocery store's delivery driveway. We smashed through a gap in another hedge, entered a scruffy backyard and ran around its back porch and tight between houses to Edgerton Avenue; we ran across Edgerton to an alley and up our own sliding woodpile to the Halls' front yard; he kept coming. We ran up Lloyd Street and wound through mazy backyards toward the steep hilltop at Willard and Lang.

He chased us silently, block after block. He chased us silently over picket fences, 13 through thorny hedges, between houses, around garbage cans, and across streets. Every time I glanced back, choking for breath, I expected he would have quit. He must have been as breathless as we were. His jacket strained over his body. It was an immense discovery, pounding into my hot head with every sliding, joyous step, that this ordinary adult evidently knew what I thought only children who trained at football knew: that you have to fling yourself at what you're doing, you have to point yourself, forget your- self, aim, dive.

Mikey and I had nowhere to go, in our own neighborhood or out of it, but away from 14 this man who was chasing us. He impelled us forward; we compelled him to follow our route. The air was cold; every breath tore my throat. We kept running, block after block; we kept improvising, backyard after backyard, running a frantic course and choosing it simultaneously, failing always to find small places or hard places to slow him down, and discovering always, exhilarated, dismayed, that only bare speed could save us—for he would never give up, this man—and we were losing speed.

He chased us through the backyard labyrinths of ten blocks before he caught us by our jackets. He caught us and we all stopped.   15

We three stood staggering, half blinded, coughing, in an obscure hilltop backyard: a man in his twenties, a boy, a girl. He had released our jackets, our pursuer, our captor, our hero: he knew we weren't going anywhere. We all played by the rules. Mikey and I unzipped our jackets. I pulled off my sopping mittens. Our tracks multiplied in the back-yard's new snow. We had been breaking new snow all morning. We didn't look at each other. I was cherishing my excitement. The man's lower pants legs were wet; his cuffs were full of snow, and there was a prow of snow beneath them on his shoes and socks. Some trees bordered the little flat backyard, some messy winter trees. There was no one around: a clearing in a grove, and we the only players.   16

It was a long time before he could speak. I had some difficulty at first recalling why we were there. My lips felt swollen; I couldn't see out of the sides of my eyes; I kept coughing.   17

"You stupid kids," he began perfunctorily.   18

We listened perfunctorily indeed, if we listened at all, for the chewing out was redun-   19
dant, a mere formality, and beside the point. The point was that he had chased us pas-sionately without giving up, and so he had caught us. Now he came down to earth. I wanted the glory to last forever.

But how could the glory have lasted forever? We could have run through every back-   20
yard in North America until we got to Panama. But when he trapped us at the lip of the Panama Canal, what precisely could he have done to prolong the drama of the chase and cap its glory? I brooded about this for the next few years. He could only have fried Mikey Fahey and me in boiling oil, say, or dismembered us piecemeal, or staked us to anthills. None of which I really wanted, and none of which any adult was likely to do, even in the spirit of fun. He could only chew us out there in the Panamanian jungle, after months or years of exalting pursuit. He could only begin, "You stupid kids," and continue in his ordi-nary Pittsburgh accent with his normal righteous anger and the usual common sense.

If in that snowy backyard the driver of the black Buick had cut off our heads, Mikey's   21
and mine, I would have died happy, for nothing has required so much of me since as being chased all over Pittsburgh in the middle of winter—running terrified, exhausted—by this sainted, skinny, furious redheaded man who wished to have a word with us. I don't know how he found his way back to his car.

Connecting to Culture and Experience: Childhood Play

"The point," Dillard tells us near the end, "was that he had chased us passionately without giving up" (paragraph 19). What seems to fascinate her is not that the man chased the kids to bawl them out, but that an adult could still do what she thought only children knew how to do: "you have to fling yourself at what you're doing, you have to point yourself, forget yourself, aim, dive" (paragraph 13). In fact, she explains at the beginning of the essay that in teaching her to play football, the neighborhood boys taught her something that few girls learned about: the joy of flinging yourself wholeheartedly, fearlessly, into play or, indeed, into anything you do in life.

With other students in your class, discuss what you have learned from childhood play about how to live your life. You might begin by telling one another about a particular kind of play you enjoyed as a child—something you did with others or alone such as team sports, computer games, playing a musical instrument, dancing, listening to music, or reading. Then, explore together what the kinds of play you enjoyed taught you about being yourself, facing challenges, getting along with others, or understanding your own body and mind or your attitude toward life.

Analyzing Writing Strategies

1. At the beginning of this chapter, we make several assertions about remembered-event essays. Consider which of these are true of Dillard's essay:

   - It tells an entertaining story.
   - It is vivid, letting readers see what makes the event as well as the people and places memorable for the writer.
   - It is purposeful, trying to give readers an understanding of why this particular event was significant in the writer's life.
   - It includes self-presentation but not unwanted self-disclosures.
   - It can lead readers to think in new ways about their own experiences or about how other people's lives differ from their own.

2. Visual description—naming objects and detailing their colors, shapes, sizes, textures, and other qualities—is an important writing strategy in remembered-event essays. To see how writers use naming and detailing to create vivid word pictures or images, let us look closely at Dillard's description of an iceball: "I started making an iceball—a perfect iceball, from perfectly white snow, perfectly spherical, and squeezed perfectly translucent so no snow remained all the way through" (paragraph 6). Notice that she names two things: *iceball* and *snow*. She adds to these names descriptive details—*white* (color), *spherical* (shape), and *translucent* (appearance)—that help readers imagine more precisely what an iceball looks like. She also repeats the words *perfect* and *perfectly* to emphasize the color, shape, and appearance of this particular iceball.

   To analyze Dillard's use of naming and detailing to present scenes and people, reread paragraphs 10–13, where she describes the man and the neighborhood through which he chases her and Mikey. As you read these paragraphs, underline the names of objects and people (nearly always nouns), and put brackets around all of the words and phrases that modify the nouns they name. Here are two examples from paragraph 10 to get you started: "[snowy] Reynolds sidewalk" and "[city] clothes."

Notice first how frequently naming and detailing occur in these paragraphs. Notice also how many different kinds of objects and people are named. Then consider these questions: Does naming sometimes occur without any accompanying detailing? How do you think the naming helps you as a reader visualize the scene and people? What do you think the detailing contributes?

Commentary: Organizing a Well-Told Story

An American Childhood is a well-told story. It provides a dramatic structure that arouses readers' curiosity, builds suspense, and concludes the action in a rather surprising way.

Writers of remembered-event essays usually begin at the beginning or even before the beginning. That is how Annie Dillard organizes *An American Childhood*—opening with two introductory paragraphs that give readers a context for the event and prepare them to appreciate its significance. Readers can see at a glance, by the space that separates the second paragraph from the rest of the essay, that the first two paragraphs are meant to stand apart as an introduction. They also are general, broad statements that do not refer to any particular incident.

In contrast, paragraph 3 begins by grounding readers in specifics. It is not any "weekday morning" but "one" in particular, one morning "after Christmas" and after a substantial snowfall. Dillard goes on to locate herself in a particular place "on a front yard on trafficked Reynolds Street," engaged in a particular set of actions with a particular group of individuals. She has not yet begun to tell what happened but is giving us the cast of characters (the "polite blond" Fahey boys, "tough" Chickie McBride) and setting the scene ("cloudy but cold"). The narrative, up to this point, has been moving slowly, like the cars making their way down Reynolds Street. But in paragraph 9, when the driver of the Buick "got out of it, running," Dillard's narrative itself suddenly springs into action, moving at breakneck speed for the next seven paragraphs until the man catches up with the kids in paragraph 15.

We can see this simple narrative organization in the following paragraph-by-paragraph scratch outline:

1. explains what she learned from playing football
2. identifies other sports she learned from boys in the neighborhood
3. sets the scene by describing the time and place of the event
4. describes the boys who were playing with her
5. describes what typically happened: a car would come down the street, they would throw snowballs, and then they would wait for another car
6. describes the iceball-making project she had begun while waiting
7. describes the Buick's approach and how they followed the routine
8. describes the impact of the snowball on the Buick's windshield
9. describes the man's surprising reaction: getting out of the car and running after them

10. narrates the chase and describes the man
11. explains how the kids split up and the man followed her and Mikey
12. narrates the chase and describes how the neighborhood looked as they ran through it
13. continues the narration, describing the way the man threw himself into the chase
14. continues the narration, commenting on her thoughts and feelings
15. narrates the ending or climax of the chase, when the man caught the kids
16. describes the runners trying to catch their breath
17. describes her own physical state
18. relates the man's words
19. explains her reactions to his words and actions
20. explains her later thoughts and feelings
21. explains her present perspective on this remembered event

From this simple scratch outline, we can see that Dillard's essay focuses on the chase. This focus on a single incident that occurred in a relatively short span of time is the hallmark of the remembered-event essay. A chase is by nature dramatic because it is suspenseful: Readers want to know whether the man will catch the kids and, if he does, what will happen. Dillard heightens the drama in a couple of ways. One strategy she uses is identification: She lets us into her point of view, helping us to see what she saw and feel what she felt. In addition, she uses surprise. In fact, Dillard surprises us from beginning to end. The first surprise is that the man gets out of the car. But the fact that he chases the kids and that he continues to chase them beyond the point that any reasonable person would do so ratchets up the suspense. We simply cannot know what such a man is capable of doing. Finally, the story reaches its climax when the man catches Mikey and Dillard. Even then, Dillard surprises readers by what the man says and doesn't say or do. All he says is, "You stupid kids" (paragraph 18). Moreover, Dillard tells us, he says it "perfunctorily," as if it is something he is supposed to say as an adult "in his ordinary Pittsburgh accent with his normal righteous anger and the usual common sense" (paragraph 20). Dillard's language here is ironic because it is obvious that she feels that the man's behavior was anything but *ordinary, normal,* or *usual*— which is, of course, precisely what Dillard wants us to appreciate.

Considering Topics for Your Own Essay

Dillard writes about throwing yourself body and soul into a sport, a chase, or whatever you are doing. Dillard explains that she learned "concentration and courage" (paragraph 1) from the boys who taught her to play football. What do you think you learned from playing or watching other kids play? Recall your own experiences at play as a child and as a young adult. List any sports events, school projects, musical performances, computer games, or other occasions that would enable you to reflect on your own ideas about play, commitment, or working with others or working alone to achieve a goal.

Tobias Wolff is probably best known for his short-story collections Back in the World *(1985),* In the Garden of the North American Martyrs *(1981), and* The Night in Question *(1996) and for his novel* The Barracks Thief *(1984), which won the PEN/Faulkner Award in 1985. Wolff has also written two autobiographies. The first,* A Boy's Life *(1989), won the* Los Angeles Times Book Award *for biography and was made into a movie (1993) in which Wolff was played by Leonardo DiCaprio. The second autobiography,* In Pharaoh's Army: Memories of the Lost War *(1994), about his experience serving as a Green Beret in the Vietnam War, was a finalist for a National Book Award and a* Los Angeles Times Award *for biography. In addition to his fiction and autobiography, Wolff has also edited several short-story collections, including* The Best American Short Stories. *Wolff has taught creative writing at Syracuse University and is currently the Ward W. and Priscilola B. Woods Professor at Stanford University, where he also has directed the creative writing program.*

In this selection from A Boy's Life, *Wolff tells the story of an experience he had when he was ten years old. He and his mother had just moved west from Florida to Salt Lake City, followed by Roy, his divorced mother's boyfriend. "Roy was handsome," Wolff writes, "in the conventional way that appeals to boys. He had a tattoo. He'd been to war and kept a silence about it that was full of heroic implication." As you read, notice how the young Wolff is motivated, at least in part, by a desire to be the kind of self-sufficient man he associates with soldiers and cowboys.*

On Being a Real Westerner

Tobias Wolff

Just after Easter Roy gave me the Winchester .22 rifle I'd learned to shoot with. It was a light, pump-action, beautifully balanced piece with a walnut stock black from all its oilings. Roy had carried it when he was a boy and it was still as good as new. Better than new. The action was silky from long use, and the wood of a quality no longer to be found. 1

The gift did not come as a surprise. Roy was stingy, and slow to take a hint, but I'd put him under siege. I had my heart set on that rifle. A weapon was the first condition of self-sufficiency, and of being a real Westerner, and of all acceptable employment—trapping, riding herd, soldiering, law enforcement, and outlawry. I needed that rifle, for itself and for the way it completed me when I held it. 2

My mother said I couldn't have it. Absolutely not. Roy took the rifle back but promised me he'd bring her around. He could not imagine anyone refusing him anything and treated the refusals he did encounter as perverse and insincere. Normally mute, he became at these times a relentless whiner. He would follow my mother from room to room, emitting one ceaseless note of complaint that was pitched perfectly to jelly her nerves and bring her to a state where she would agree to anything to make it stop. 3

After a few days of this my mother caved in. She said I could have the rifle if, and only if, I promised never to take it out or even touch it except when she and Roy were with me. Okay, I said. Sure. Naturally. But even then she wasn't satisfied. She plain didn't like the fact of me owning a rifle. Roy said he had owned several rifles by the time he was my age, but this did not reassure her. She didn't think I could be trusted with it. Roy said now was the time to find out. 4

For a week or so I kept my promises. But now that the weather had turned warm Roy   5
was usually off somewhere and eventually, in the dead hours after school when I found
myself alone in the apartment, I decided that there couldn't be any harm in taking the rifle
out to clean it. Only to clean it, nothing more. I was sure it would be enough just to break
it down, oil it, rub linseed into the stock, polish the octagonal barrel and then hold it up to
the light to confirm the perfection of the bore. But it wasn't enough. From cleaning the rifle
I went to marching around the apartment with it, and then to striking brave poses in front
of the mirror. Roy had saved one of his army uniforms and I sometimes dressed up in
this, together with martial-looking articles of hunting gear: fur trooper's hat, camouflage
coat, boots that reached nearly to my knees.

The camouflage coat made me feel like a sniper, and before long I began to act like   6
one. I set up a nest on the couch by the front window. I drew the shades to darken the
apartment, and took up my position. Nudging the shade aside with the rifle barrel, I followed people in my sights as they walked or drove along the street. At first I made shooting sounds — kyoo! kyoo! Then I started cocking the hammer and letting it snap down.

Roy stored his ammunition in a metal box he kept hidden in the closet. As with every-   7
thing else hidden in the apartment, I knew exactly where to find it. There was a layer of
loose .22 rounds on the bottom of the box under shells of bigger caliber, dropped there by
the handful the way men drop pennies on their dressers at night. I took some and put
them in a hiding place of my own. With these I started loading up the rifle. Hammer
cocked, a round in the chamber, finger resting lightly on the trigger, I drew a bead on
whoever walked by — women pushing strollers, children, garbage collectors laughing
and calling to each other, anyone — and as they passed under my window I sometimes
had to bite my lip to keep from laughing in the ecstasy of my power over them, and at
their absurd and innocent belief that they were safe.

But over time the innocence I laughed at began to irritate me. It was a peculiar kind   8
of irritation. I saw it years later in men I served with, and felt it myself, when unarmed Vietnamese civilians talked back to us while we were herding them around. Power can be
enjoyed only when it is recognized and feared. Fearlessness in those without power is
maddening to those who have it.

One afternoon I pulled the trigger. I had been aiming at two old people, a man and a   9
woman, who walked so slowly that by the time they turned the corner at the bottom of the
hill my little store of self-control was exhausted. I had to shoot. I looked up and down the
street. It was empty. Nothing moved but a pair of squirrels chasing each other back and
forth on the telephone wires. I followed one in my sight. Finally it stopped for a moment
and I fired. The squirrel dropped straight into the road. I pulled back into the shadows and
waited for something to happen, sure that someone must have heard the shot or seen
the squirrel fall. But the sound that was so loud to me probably seemed to our neighbors
no more than the bang of a cupboard slammed shut. After a while I sneaked a glance into
the street. The squirrel hadn't moved. It looked like a scarf someone had dropped.

When my mother got home from work I told her there was a dead squirrel in the   10
street. Like me, she was an animal lover. She took a cellophane bag off a loaf of bread

and we went outside and looked at the squirrel. "Poor little thing," she said. She stuck her hand in the wrapper and picked up the squirrel, then pulled the bag inside out away from her hand. We buried it behind our building under a cross made of popsicle sticks, and I blubbered the whole time.

I blubbered again in bed that night. At last I got out of bed and knelt down and did an imitation of somebody praying, and then I did an imitation of somebody receiving divine reassurance and inspiration. I stopped crying. I smiled to myself and forced a feeling of warmth into my chest. Then I climbed back in bed and looked up at the ceiling with a blissful expression until I went to sleep. 11

For several days I stayed away from the apartment at times when I knew I'd be alone there. 12

Though I avoided the apartment, I could not shake the idea that sooner or later I would get the rifle out again. All my images of myself as I wished to be were images of myself armed. Because I did not know who I was, any image of myself, no matter how grotesque, had power over me. This much I understand now. But the man can give no help to the boy, not in this matter nor in those that follow. The boy moves always out of reach. 13

Connecting to Culture and Experience: Role Playing

Wolff shows us that he took great delight in playing the role of a soldier—looking at himself in the mirror dressed in camouflage and "striking brave poses" (paragraph 5). The word *brave* suggests that the young Wolff wanted to see himself as possessing certain traits, like bravery, that we often associate with soldiers. Another part of the attraction of playing soldier, he admits, is the sense of power he experienced holding a rifle.

With other students in your class, discuss the roles you played as children. What personal and cultural factors influenced the roles that you and your classmates imagined for yourselves? You might begin by comparing your own childhood imaginings with Wolff's desire to play soldier. In addition to having firsthand experience with Roy, a soldier who impressed him with his masculine authority and power, Wolff grew up during World War II, when children were bombarded by media images of brave soldiers fighting heroic wars and lone cowboys bringing justice to the Wild West. What media images—from television, film, the Internet, and computer games—do you think influenced the kinds of role play that you engaged in as a child or young adult?

Analyzing Writing Strategies

1. Writers convey the significance of autobiographical events by telling how they felt at the time the event occurred and by telling how they feel now as they look back on the event. Skim paragraphs 7, 8, and 13, noting where Wolff expresses his

feelings and thoughts about the event. Try to distinguish between what he remembers thinking and feeling at the time and what he thinks and feels as he looks back on the event. What impression do you get of the young Wolff? What does the adult Wolff seem to think about his younger self?

2. Good stories show people in action—what we call specific narrative action—people moving or gesturing. Analyze paragraphs 7 and 9 by underlining the narrative actions and then putting brackets around the verb or verbal in each narrative action that specifically names the action. (A verbal is the -*ing* or *to* form of a verb: *laughing, to laugh*.) For example, here are the narrative actions (underlined) with their action verbs or verbals (in brackets) in paragraph 6:

   [set up] a nest, [drew] the shades, [took up] my position, [nudging] the shade aside, [followed] people, [walked] or [drove], [made] shooting sounds—kyoo! kyoo!, [started cocking] the hammer, [letting] it [snap] down.

   Now that you have completed your analysis of paragraphs 7 and 9, how do you think specific narrative action contributes to autobiographical stories?

3. Like other autobiographers, Wolff sometimes uses relatively short sentences. To understand why he might do so, compare the short and long sentences in the most dramatic and revealing action in the event. Begin by underlining every sentence of nine words or fewer (in paragraph 9). Then put brackets around the relatively long sentence at the end of paragraph 7 and the three relatively long sentences beginning "I had been aiming," "I pulled back," and "But the sound" in paragraph 9. Compare what the long and short sentences contribute to the action. How do their contents differ? What effect do the short sentences have on you as a reader? For more on the role of short sentences in remembered-event essays, turn to Sentence Strategies, pp. 54–55.

Commentary: Narrative Cueing in a Well-Told Story

This is a gripping story. The subject makes it inherently dramatic: Putting a rifle in a child's hands immediately alerts readers to the possibility that something dreadful could happen. Thus the potential for suspense is great. Contributing to the drama is Wolff's use of narrative strategies that move the action through time and help readers keep track of what happened.

If we look closely at Wolff's narration, we can see how two narrating strategies—verb tenses and temporal transitions—create the impression of time passing. These strategies serve as cueing devices because, like road signs, they enable readers to follow the action.

Verb Tenses.   Verb tenses signal when the action occurred—in the past, present, or future. Because remembered-event essays tell about past events, most of the verbs are in the past tense. Looking at the verbs in Wolff's essay, we can find several different kinds of past tense. In the first sentence of the essay, for example, Wolff shows an action that occurred at one point in the past (underlined) together with an action that was already completed (in brackets): "Just after Easter Roy gave me the Winchester .22 rifle [I'd learned to shoot with]." ("I'd learned" is a shortened form of "I had learned.") A second example shows an earlier action that was still going on (in brackets) when the more recent action occurred (underlined): "One afternoon I pulled the trigger. I [had been aiming] at two old people..." (paragraph 9).

Our final example is a little more complicated: "Roy took the rifle back but promised me [he'd bring] her around" (paragraph 3). This example presents three past actions. Whereas the first two actions (underlined) occurred at roughly the same time, the third (in brackets) predicts a future action that occurred after the first two actions were completed. (Here "he'd" is a short form of "he would.")

You probably do not know the technical names for these tenses, nor do you need to know them. However, you do need to know what the different verb tenses mean and how to use them. In your remembered-event essay, you will want to be sure that the verb tenses you use accurately indicate the time relations among various actions in your story.

Temporal Transitions.   In addition to using verb tense to show time, writers use transitions to move the narrative action forward in time and thereby keep readers oriented. Wolff uses many transitional words and phrases to locate an action at a particular point in time or to relate an action at one point in time to an action at another time. He uses four in the first paragraph alone: *just after, when, still,* and *no longer.* Time markers may appear at the beginning of a sentence or within a sentence. Notice how many paragraphs in Wolff's story include such a transition in the opening sentence: "Just after" (paragraph 1), "After a few days" (4), "For a week or so" (5), "before long" (6), "One afternoon" (9), "When" (10), "again" (11), and "For several days" (12). This extensive use of temporal transitions is not unusual in remembered-event essays. You will want to use them liberally in your own essay to orient readers and propel your narrative through time. (For more on temporal relationships, see Chapter 8, pp. 318–19.)

Considering Topics for Your Own Essay

In this selection, Wolff describes experiencing what he calls the "ecstasy of my power" to inflict harm on others (paragraph 7). Try to recall two or three incidents when you were in a position to exercise power over another person or when you were subject to someone else's power. You may have been in such relationships for long periods of time, but select only those relationships that can be well illustrated by one key incident that occurred within a day or two. Pick one such incident. Think about how you would present it, explaining what you did and how you felt.

Jean Brandt wrote this essay as a first-year college student. In it, she tells about a memorable event that occurred when she was thirteen. Reflecting on how she felt at the time, Brandt writes, "I was afraid, embarrassed, worried, mad." As you read, look for places where these tumultuous and contradictory remembered feelings are expressed.

Calling Home

Jean Brandt

As we all piled into the car, I knew it was going to be a 1 fabulous day. My grandmother was visiting for the holidays; and she and I, along with my older brother and sister, Louis and Susan, were setting off for a day of last-minute Christmas shopping. On the way to the mall, we sang Christmas carols, chattered, and laughed. With Christmas only two days away, we were caught up with holiday spirit. I felt light-headed and full of joy. I loved shopping—especially at Christmas.

The shopping center was swarming with frantic last-minute shoppers like ourselves. 2 We went first to the General Store, my favorite. It carried mostly knickknacks and other useless items which nobody needs but buys anyway. I was thirteen years old at the time, and things like buttons and calendars and posters would catch my fancy. This day was no different. The object of my desire was a 75-cent Snoopy button. Snoopy was the latest. If you owned anything with the Peanuts on it, you were "in." But since I was supposed to be shopping for gifts for other people and not myself, I couldn't decide what to do. I went in search of my sister for her opinion. I pushed my way through throngs of people to the back of the store where I found Susan. I asked her if she thought I should buy the button. She said it was cute and if I wanted it to go ahead and buy it.

When I got back to the Snoopy section, I took one look at the lines at the cashiers 3 and knew I didn't want to wait thirty minutes to buy an item worth less than one dollar. I walked back to the basket where I found the button and was about to drop it when suddenly, instead, I took a quick glance around, assured myself no one could see, and slipped the button into the pocket of my sweatshirt. I hesitated for a moment, but once the item was in my pocket, there was no turning back. I had never before stolen anything; but what was done was done. A few seconds later, my sister appeared and asked, "So, did you decide to buy the button?"

"No, I guess not." I hoped my voice didn't quaver. As we headed for the entrance, my 4 heart began to race. I just had to get out of that store. Only a few more yards to go and I'd be safe. As we crossed the threshold, I heaved a sigh of relief. I was home free. I thought about how sly I had been and I felt proud of my accomplishment.

An unexpected tap on my shoulder startled me. I whirled around to find a middle-aged 5 man, dressed in street clothes, flashing some type of badge and politely asking me to empty my pockets. Where did this man come from? How did he know? I was so sure that no one had seen me! On the verge of panicking, I told myself that all I had to do was give this man his button back, say I was sorry, and go on my way. After all, it was only a 75-cent item.

Next thing I knew, he was talking about calling the police and having me arrested 6 and thrown in jail, as if he had just nabbed a professional thief instead of a terrified kid. I couldn't believe what he was saying.

"Jean, what's going on?" 7

The sound of my sister's voice eased the pressure a bit. She always managed to get me out of trouble. She would come through this time too. 8

"Excuse me. Are you a relative of this young girl?" 9

"Yes, I'm her sister. What's the problem?" 10

"Well, I just caught her shoplifting and I'm afraid I'll have to call the police." 11

"What did she take?" 12

"This button." 13

"A button? You are having a thirteen-year-old arrested for stealing a button?" 14

"I'm sorry, but she broke the law." 15

The man led us through the store and into an office, where we waited for the police officers to arrive. Susan had found my grandmother and brother, who, still shocked, didn't say a word. The thought of going to jail terrified me, not because of jail itself, but because of the encounter with my parents afterward. Not more than ten minutes later, two officers arrived and placed me under arrest. They said that I was to be taken to the station alone. Then, they handcuffed me and led me out of the store. I felt alone and scared. I had counted on my sister being with me, but now I had to muster up the courage to face this ordeal all by myself. 16

As the officers led me through the mall, I sensed a hundred pairs of eyes staring at me. My face flushed and I broke out in a sweat. Now everyone knew I was a criminal. In their eyes I was a juvenile delinquent, and thank God the cops were getting me off the streets. The worst part was thinking my grandmother might be having the same thoughts. The humiliation at that moment was overwhelming. I felt like Hester Prynne being put on public display for everyone to ridicule. 17

That short walk through the mall seemed to take hours. But once we reached the squad car, time raced by. I was read my rights and questioned. We were at the police station within minutes. Everything happened so fast I didn't have a chance to feel remorse for my crime. Instead, I viewed what was happening to me as if it were a movie. Being searched, although embarrassing, somehow seemed to be exciting. All the movies and television programs I had seen were actually coming to life. This is what it was really like. But why were criminals always portrayed as frightened and regretful? I was having fun. I thought I had nothing to fear—until I was allowed my one phone call. I was trembling as I dialed home. I didn't know what I was going to say to my parents, especially my mother. 18

"Hi, Dad, this is Jean." 19

"We've been waiting for you to call." 20

"Did Susie tell you what happened?" 21

"Yeah, but we haven't told your mother. I think you should tell her what you did and where you are." 22

"You mean she doesn't even know where I am?" 23

"No, I want you to explain it to her." 24

There was a pause as he called my mother to the phone. For the first time that night, I was close to tears. I wished I had never stolen that stupid pin. I wanted to give the phone to one of the officers because I was too ashamed to tell my mother the truth, but I had no choice. 25

"Jean, where are you?" 26

"I'm, umm, in jail." 27

"Why? What for?"   28

"Shoplifting."   29

"Oh no, Jean. Why? Why did you do it?"   30

"I don't know. No reason. I just did it."   31

"I don't understand. What did you take? Why did you do it? You had plenty of money   32
with you."

"I know but I just did it. I can't explain why. Mom, I'm sorry."   33

"I'm afraid sorry isn't enough. I'm horribly disappointed in you."   34

Long after we got off the phone, while I sat in an empty jail cell, waiting for my par-   35
ents to pick me up, I could still distinctly hear the disappointment and hurt in my mother's
voice. I cried. The tears weren't for me but for her and the pain I had put her through. I felt
like a terrible human being. I would rather have stayed in jail than confront my mom right
then. I dreaded each passing minute that brought our encounter closer. When the officer
came to release me, I hesitated, actually not wanting to leave. We went to the front desk,
where I had to sign a form to retrieve my belongings. I saw my parents a few yards away
and my heart raced. A large knot formed in my stomach. I fought back the tears.

Not a word was spoken as we walked to the car. Slowly, I sank into the back seat   36
anticipating the scolding. Expecting harsh tones, I was relieved to hear almost the opposite from my father.

"I'm not going to punish you and I'll tell you why. Although I think what you did was   37
wrong, I think what the police did was more wrong. There's no excuse for locking a thirteen-year-old behind bars. That doesn't mean I condone what you did, but I think you've
been punished enough already."

As I looked from my father's eyes to my mother's, I knew this ordeal was over.   38
Although it would never be forgotten, the incident was not mentioned again.

Connecting to Culture and Experience: Shame and Social Disapproval

In paragraph 17, Brandt gives us a vivid portrait of how excruciating the feeling of shame can be: "I sensed a hundred pairs of eyes staring at me. My face flushed and I broke out in a sweat." Shame, as this description indicates, involves a desire for people's approval or a dread of their disapproval. (The words *shame* and *guilt* are often used interchangeably, but they have different connotations: Shame involves anxiety about social acceptance, whereas guilt is a more private, inward-looking emotion associated with morality.) We know that Brandt is feeling shame because of her emphasis on other people's opinions of her.

Identify one occasion when you felt ashamed. With other students, take turns briefly explaining what happened, who was ashamed of you, and why you felt shame. Then, keeping in mind that the social goal of shame is to constrain individuals' behavior, discuss what you think groups—families, friends, teams, employees—gain from creating fear of social disapproval among their members. Consider also what individuals might lose from undue pressure of social disapproval.

Analyzing Writing Strategies

1. Reread the essay, paying particular attention to Brandt's use of dialogue — reconstructed conversation from the time of the event. What do you learn about the author from what she says and how she says it? What do you learn about her relationship with her parents?

2. The story begins and ends in a car, with the two car rides framing the story. Framing, a narrative device, echoes something from the beginning in the ending. Review what happens in each car ride. The writer assumes that you might think of the beginning as you are reading the ending. What effect might this awareness have on your response to the ending car ride?

Commentary: A Vivid Presentation of Places and People

To present the people involved in the event and especially to dramatize her relationship with her parents, Brandt depends on dialogue. We can see from her use of dialogue the two ways that writers typically present remembered conversations: quoting and summarizing. Compare the two examples that follow. In the first example, Brandt quotes a brief exchange between herself and her sister as they were leaving the store (paragraphs 3 and 4):

> A few seconds later, my sister appeared and asked, "So, did you decide to buy the button?"
> "No, I guess not." I hoped my voice didn't quaver.

In this second example, Brandt summarizes what the store manager said to her as she left the store (paragraphs 5 and 6):

> An unexpected tap on my shoulder startled me. I whirled around to find a middle-aged man, dressed in street clothes, flashing some type of badge and politely asking me to empty my pockets. . . .
> Next thing I knew, he was talking about calling the police and having me arrested. . . .

As these examples indicate, writers usually summarize rather than quote when they need to give only the gist of what was said. Brandt apparently decides that the manager's actual words and way of speaking are not important for her purpose. However, presenting her response to her sister's question is important because it shows how she felt at the time. When you write a remembered-event essay, you too will have to decide in light of your overall purpose what to summarize and what to quote.

Considering Topics for Your Own Essay

Think of a few occasions when you did something uncharacteristic. Perhaps you acted on impulse or took a chance you would not ordinarily take. The events do not have to be reckless, dangerous, or illegal; they can be quite harmless or even pleasant. Pick one occasion you might like to write about. What would you want your readers to recognize about you on the basis of reading your story?

■ PURPOSE AND AUDIENCE

Writing autobiography, writers relive moments of pleasure and pain, and they also gain insight, learning who they are now by examining who they used to be and the forces that shaped them. Because autobiographers write to be read, though, they are as much concerned with self-presentation as with self-discovery. Writers present themselves to readers in the way they want to be perceived. The rest they keep hidden, though readers may read between the lines.

We read about others' experiences for much the same reason that we write about our own—to learn how to live our lives. Reading autobiography can validate our sense of ourselves, particularly when we see our own experience reflected in another's life. Reading about others' lives can also challenge our complacency and help us appreciate other points of view.

BASIC FEATURES: REMEMBERING EVENTS

A Well-Told Story

An essay about a remembered event should tell an interesting story. Whatever else the writer may attempt to do, he or she must shape the experience into a story that is entertaining and memorable. This is done primarily by building suspense, leading readers to wonder, for example, whether the driver of the Buick will catch Annie Dillard, Tobias Wolff will shoot the rifle, or Jean Brandt will get caught for shoplifting. The principal technique for propelling the narrative and heightening suspense is specific narrative action with its action verbs and verbals. Suspense increases, for instance, when Wolff gives a detailed close-up of his play with the rifle. In addition, writers use temporal transitions to cue readers and move the narrative through time, as when Tobias Wolff begins paragraphs with "Just after Easter," "For a week or so," and "One afternoon." Finally, writers often use dialogue to convey immediacy and drama, as Brandt does to dramatize her confrontation with her mother on the phone.

A Vivid Presentation of Places and People

Instead of giving a generalized impression, skillful writers attempt to re-create the place where the event occurred and let us hear what people said. Vivid language and specific details make the writing memorable. By moving in close, a writer can name specific objects at a place, such as when Brandt catalogs the store's knickknacks, calendars, and buttons. A writer may also provide details about some of the objects, as when Brandt describes the coveted "75-cent Snoopy button." Finally, writers use similes and metaphors to draw comparisons and thereby help readers understand the point. For example, when Brandt says she felt "like Hester Prynne being put on public display" (paragraph 17), readers familiar with *The Scarlet Letter* can imagine how embarrassed Brandt must have felt.

To present people who played an important role in a remembered event, autobiographers often provide some descriptive details and a snatch of dialogue. They may detail the person's appearance, as Annie Dillard does by describing the man who chased her "in city clothes: a suit and tie, street shoes" as "a thin man, all action" (paragraph 10). Dialogue can be an especially effective way of giving readers a vivid impression of someone. Wolff, for example, describes his mother by combining specific narrative actions with her empathetic words: "She took a cellophane bag off a loaf of bread and we went outside and looked at the squirrel. 'Poor little thing,' she said. She stuck her hand in the wrapper and picked up the squirrel, then pulled the bag inside out away from her hand" (paragraph 10).

An Indication of the Event's Significance

There are two ways a writer can communicate an event's autobiographical significance: by showing us that the event was important or by telling us directly what it meant. Most writers do both. Showing is necessary because the event must be dramatized for readers to appreciate its importance and understand the writer's feelings about it. Seeing the important scenes and people from the writer's point of view naturally leads readers to identify with the writer. We can well imagine what that "unexpected tap on [the] shoulder" (paragraph 5) must have felt like for Brandt and how Dillard felt when the man chased her and Mikey "silently over picket fences, through thorny hedges, between houses, around garbage cans, and across streets" (paragraph 13).

Telling also contributes to a reader's understanding, so most writers comment on the event's meaning and importance. Readers expect to understand the significance of the event, but they do not expect the essay to begin with the kind of thesis statement typical of argumentative writing. Instead, as the story moves along, writers tell us how they felt at the time or how they feel now as they look back on the experience. Often writers do both. Wolff, for example, tells us some of his remembered feelings when he recalls feeling "like a sniper" and delighting in the "ecstasy" of power. He also tells us what he thinks looking back on the experience: "Because I did not know who I was, any image of myself, no matter how grotesque, had power over me. This much I understand now" (paragraph 13). Telling is the main way that writers interpret the event for readers, but skillful writers are careful not to append these reflections artificially, like a moral tagged on to a fable.

GUIDE TO WRITING
Remembering Events

THE WRITING ASSIGNMENT

Write an essay about an event in your life that will be engaging for readers and that will, at the same time, help them understand the significance of the event. Tell your story dramatically and vividly.

THE WRITING ASSIGNMENT

INVENTION

Finding an Event to Write About

Describing the Place

Recalling Key People

Sketching the Story

Testing Your Choice

Exploring Memorabilia

Reflecting on the Event's Significance

Defining Your Purpose for Your Readers

Formulating a Tentative Thesis Statement

INVENTION

PLANNING & DRAFTING

Seeing What You Have

Setting Goals

Outlining

Drafting

PLANNING AND DRAFTING

CRITICAL READING GUIDE

First Impression

Storytelling

Vivid Description

Autobiographical Significance

Memorabilia

Organization

Final Thoughts

CRITICAL READING GUIDE

REVISING

A Well-Told Story

A Vivid Presentation of Places and People

Autobiographical Significance

Organization

REVISING

EDITING & PROOFREADING

Checking for Missing Commas after Introductory Elements

Checking for Fused Sentences

Checking Your Use of the Past Perfect

A Common ESL Problem

EDITING AND PROOFREADING

■ THE WRITING ASSIGNMENT

Write an essay about an event in your life that will be engaging for readers and that will, at the same time, help them understand the significance of the event. Tell your story dramatically and vividly.

■ INVENTION

The following invention activities will help you choose an appropriate event, recall specific details, sketch out the story, test your choice, and explore the event's autobiographical significance. Each activity is easy to do and takes only a few minutes. If you can spread out the activities over several days, it will be easier for you to recall details and to reflect deeply on the event's meaning in your life. Keep a written record of your invention work to use when you draft the essay and later when you revise it.

Finding an Event to Write About

To find the best possible event to write about, consider several possibilities rather than choosing the first event that comes to mind.

Listing Remembered Events. *Make a list of significant events from your past. Include only those events about which you can recall detail about what happened, where and when it happened, and the people involved.* Begin your list now, and add to it over the next few days. Include possibilities suggested by the Considering Topics for Your Own Essay activities following each reading in this chapter. Make your list as complete as you can. The following categories may give you some more ideas:

- An occasion when you realized you had a special skill, ambition, or problem
- A time when you became aware of injustice, selflessness, heroism, sexism, racism
- A difficult situation, such as when you had to make a tough choice, when someone you admired let you down (or you let someone else down), or when you struggled to learn or understand something hard
- An occasion when things did not turn out as expected, such as when you expected to be praised but were criticized or ignored or when you were convinced you would fail but succeeded
- An incident charged with strong emotion, such as love, fear, anger, embarrassment, guilt, frustration, hurt, pride, happiness, or joy
- An incident that you find yourself thinking about frequently or occasionally or one you know you will never forget

Listing Events Related to Identity and Community. Whenever you write about events in your life, you are likely to reveal important aspects of your sense of identity and your relationships with others. The suggestions that follow, however, will help you recall events that are particularly revealing of your efforts to know yourself and to discover your place in the communities to which you belong.

- An event that shaped you in a particular way or revealed an aspect of your personality you had not seen before, such as your independence, insecurity, ambitiousness, or jealousy
- An incident that made you reexamine one of your basic values or beliefs, such as when you were expected to do something that went against your better judgment or when your values conflicted with someone else's values
- An occasion when others' actions led you to consider seriously a new idea or point of view
- An incident that made you feel the need to identify yourself with a particular community, such as an ethnic group, a political or religious group, or a group of coworkers
- An event that made you realize that the role you were playing did not conform to what was expected of you as a student, as a male or female, as a parent or sibling, as a believer in a particular religious faith, or as a member of a particular community
- An incident in which a single encounter with another person changed the way you view yourself or changed your ideas about how you fit into a particular community

Listing Events Related to Work and Career. The following suggestions will help you think of events involving your work experiences as well as your career aspirations.

- An event that made you aware of your capacity for or interest in a particular kind of work or career or an event that convinced you that you were not cut out for a particular kind of work or career
- An incident of harassment or mistreatment at work
- An event that revealed to you other people's assumptions, attitudes, or prejudices about you as a worker, your fitness for a particular job, or your career goals
- An incident of conflict or serious misunderstanding with a customer, a fellow employee, a supervisor, or someone you supervised

Finding an Event to Write About: An Online Activity

Exploring Web sites where other people write about their own life experiences might inspire you by triggering memories of similar events in your own life and by suggesting a broad range of possibilities for the kinds of remembered events people find significant.

- If you do a search for remembered-event essays in Google (www.google.com) or Yahoo! Directory (http://dir.yahoo.com), you will find essays written by students in other composition classes throughout the country.
- Sites such as citystories.com and storypreservation.com where people post brief stories about their lives may suggest significant events in your own life.

Add to your list of possibilities any events suggested by your online research. But do not be disappointed if other people's stories do not help you think of events in your own life that you could write about.

Choosing an Event. *Look over your list of possibilities, and choose one event that you think will make an interesting story.* You should be eager to explore the significance of the event and comfortable about sharing the event with your instructors and classmates, who will be your first readers. You may find the choice easy to make, or you may have several equally promising possibilities from which to choose.

It may help you in choosing an event if you tentatively identify your ultimate readers, the people with whom you most want to share the story. They could include, for example, your personal friends, members of your family, people you work with, members of a group with which you identify or of an organization to which you belong, your classmates, an instructor, or even the public at large.

Make the best choice you can now. If this event does not work out, you can try a different one later.

Describing the Place

The following activities will help you decide which places are important to your story and what you remember about them. Take the time now to explore your memory and imagination. This exploration will yield descriptive language you can use in your essay.

Listing Key Places. *Make a list of all the places where the event occurred, skipping some space after each entry on your list.* Your event may have occurred in one or more places. For now, list all the places you remember without worrying about whether they should be included in your story.

Describing Key Places. *In the space after each entry on your list, make some notes describing each place.* As you remember each place, what do you see (excluding people for the moment)? What objects stand out? Are they large or small, green or brown, square or oblong? What sounds do you hear? Do you detect any smells? Does any taste come to mind? Do you recall anything soft or hard, smooth or rough?

Recalling Key People

These activities will help you remember the people who played a role in the event—what they looked like, did, and said.

Listing Key People.   *List the people who played more than a casual role in the event.* You may have only one person to list, or you may have several.

Describing Key People.   *Write a brief description of the people who played major roles in the event.* For each person, name and detail a few distinctive physical features or items of dress. Describe the person's way of talking or gesturing.

Re-Creating Conversations.   *Reconstruct any important conversations you had during the event.* Also try to recall any especially memorable comments, any unusual choice of words, or any telling remarks that you made or were made to you. You may not remember exactly what was said during an entire conversation, but try to re-create it so that readers will be able to imagine what was going on.

Sketching the Story

Write for a few minutes, telling what happened. You may find it easier to outline what happened rather than writing complete sentences and paragraphs. Any way you can put the main action into words is fine. Over the next few days, you may want to add to this rough sketch.

Testing Your Choice

Now you need to decide whether you recall enough detail to write a good story about this particular event. Reread your invention notes to see whether your initial memories seem promising. If you can recall clearly what happened and what the important scenes and people were like, then you have probably made a good choice. If at any point you lose confidence in your choice, return to your list, and choose another event.

Testing Your Choice: A Collaborative Activity

At this point, you will find it useful to get together with two or three other students to try out your story. Your instructor may ask you to do this collaborative activity in class or online using a chat room. Their reactions to your story will help you determine whether you have chosen an event you can present in an interesting way.

Storytellers: Take turns telling your story briefly. Try to make your story dramatic (by piquing your listeners' curiosity and building suspense) and vivid (by briefly describing the place and key people).

Listeners: Briefly tell each storyteller what you found most intriguing about the story. For example, were you eager to know how the story would turn out? Were you curious about any of the people? Were you able to identify with the story-teller? Could you imagine the place? Could you understand why the event is so memorable and significant for the storyteller?

Exploring Memorabilia

Memorabilia are visual images, sounds, and objects that can help you remember details and understand the significance of an event. Examples include photographs, newspaper or magazine clippings, recordings of popular music, souvenirs, medals or trophies, and even items not necessarily designated as mementoes (restaurant menus and movie, theater, or concert stubs and programs). *If you can obtain access to relevant memorabilia, take time to do so now. Add to your invention notes any details about the period, places, or people the memorabilia suggest.*

Consider including one or more pieces of memorabilia in your essay. You can simply append photographs or other items to your printed-out essay, or if you have the capability, you can scan them into your electronic document. If you include visual memorabilia in your essay, you should label and number them as Figure 1, Figure 2, and so on, and include captions identifying them.

Reflecting on the Event's Significance

You should now feel fairly confident that you can tell an interesting story about the event you have chosen. The following activities will help you to understand the meaning that the event holds in your life and to develop ways to convey this significance to your readers.

Recalling Your Remembered Feelings and Thoughts.   *Write for a few minutes about your feelings and thoughts during and immediately after the event.* The following questions may help stimulate your memory:

- What were my expectations before the event?
- What was my first reaction to the event as it was happening and right after it ended?
- How did I show my feelings? What did I say?
- What did I want the people involved to think of me? Why did I care what they thought of me?
- What did I think of myself at the time?
- How long did these initial feelings last?
- What were the immediate consequences of the event for me personally?

Pause now to reread what you have written. *Then write another sentence or two about the event's significance to you at the time it occurred.*

Exploring Your Present Perspective.   *Write for a few minutes about your current feelings and thoughts as you look back on the event.* These questions may help you get started:

- Looking back, how do I feel about this event? If I understand it differently now than I did then, what is the difference?
- What do my actions at the time of the event say about the kind of person I was then? How would I respond to the same event if it occurred today?
- Can looking at the event historically or culturally help explain what happened? For example, did I upset gender expectations? Did I feel torn between two cultures or ethnic identities? Did I feel out of place?
- Do I now see that there was a conflict underlying the event? For example, did I struggle with contradictory desires within myself? Did I feel pressured by others or by society in general? Were my desires and rights in conflict with someone else's? Was the event about power or responsibility?

Pause now to reflect on what you have written about your present perspective. *Then write another sentence or two, commenting on the event's significance as you look back on it.*

Defining Your Purpose for Your Readers

Write a few sentences, defining your purpose in writing about this particular event for your readers. Use these questions to focus your thoughts:

- Who are my readers? (Remember that in choosing an event, you considered several possible readers: your personal friends, members of your family, people you work with, members of a group with which you identify or of an organization to which you belong, your classmates, an instructor, even the public at large.)
- What do my readers know about me?
- What do my readers expect when they read autobiography?
- How do I expect my readers to understand or react to the event?
- How do I want my readers to feel about what happened? What is the dominant impression or mood I want my story to create?
- What specifically do I want my readers to think of me? What do I expect or fear they might think?

It is unlikely, but you may decide at this point that you feel uncomfortable disclosing this event. If so, choose another event to write about.

Formulating a Tentative Thesis Statement

Review what you wrote for Reflecting on the Event's Significance, and add another two or three sentences, not necessarily summarizing what you already have written but extending your insights into the significance of the event, what it meant to you at the time, and what it means now. These sentences must necessarily be speculative and tentative because you may not fully understand the event's significance in your life.

Keep in mind that readers do not expect you to begin your essay with the kind of explicit thesis statement typical of argumentative or explanatory writing. If you do decide to tell readers explicitly why the event was meaningful or significant, you will most likely do so as you tell the story, by commenting on or evaluating what happened, instead of announcing it at the beginning. Keep in mind that you are not obliged to tell readers the significance, but you should show it through the way you tell the story.

■ PLANNING AND DRAFTING

This section will help you review your invention writing and get started on your first draft.

Seeing What You Have

You have now done a lot of thinking and writing about the basic elements of a remembered-event essay: what happened, where it happened, who was involved, what was said, and how you felt. You have also begun to develop your understanding of why the event is so important to you. If you have done your invention writing on the computer, you may have sentences or whole paragraphs that can be copied and pasted into your draft. Reread what you have written so far to see what you have. Watch for specific narrative actions, vivid descriptive details, choice bits of dialogue. Note also any language that resonates with feeling or that seems especially insightful. Highlight any writing you think could be used in your draft.

Then ask yourself the following questions:

- Do I remember enough specific details about the event to describe it vividly?
- Do I understand how the event was significant to me?
- Does my invention material provide what I need to convey that significance to my readers?
- Does my present perspective on this event seem clear to me?
- Does the dominant impression I want to create in my essay seem relevant?

If you find little that seems promising, you are not likely to be able to write a good draft. Consider starting over with another event.

If, however, your invention writing offers some promising material, the following activities may help you develop more:

- To remember more of what actually happened, discuss the event with someone who was there or who remembers having heard about it at the time.
- To recall additional details about a person who played an important role in the event, look at any available photographs or letters, talk with the person, or talk with someone who remembers the person. If that is impossible, you might imagine having a conversation with the person today about the event: What would you say? How do you think the person would respond?
- To remember how you felt at the time of the event, try to recall what else was happening in your life during that period. What music, television shows, movies, sports, books, and magazines did you like? What concerns did you have at home, school, work, play?
- To develop your present perspective on the event, try viewing your experience as a historical event. If you were writing a news story or documentary about the event, what would you want people to know?
- To decide on the dominant impression you want your story to have on readers, imagine that you are making a film based on this event. What would your film look like? What mood or atmosphere would you try to create? Alternatively, imagine writing a song or poem about the event. Think of an appropriate image or refrain. What kind of song would you write—blues, hip-hop, country, ranchera, rock?

Setting Goals

Before starting to draft, set goals that will help you make decisions and solve problems as you draft and revise. Here are some questions that will help you set your goals:

Your Purpose and Readers

- What do I want my readers to think of me and my experience? Should I tell them how I felt and what I thought at the time of the event, as Dillard does? Should I tell them how my perspective has changed?
- If my readers are likely to have had a similar experience, how can I convey the uniqueness of my experience or its special importance in my life? Should I tell them more about my background or the particular context of the event? Should I give them a glimpse, as Dillard does, of its impact years later?
- If my readers are not likely to have had a similar experience, how can I help them understand what happened and appreciate its importance? Should I reveal the cultural influences acting on me, as Wolff does?

The Beginning

- What can I do in the opening sentences to arouse readers' curiosity? Should I begin with a surprising announcement, as Wolff does, or should I establish the setting and situation, as Dillard and Brandt do?
- How can I get my readers to identify with me? Should I tell them a few things about myself?
- Should I do something unusual, such as begin in the middle of the action or with a funny bit of dialogue?

The Story

- What should be the climax of my story—the point that readers anticipate with trepidation or eagerness?
- What specific narrative actions or dialogue would intensify the drama of the story?
- Should I follow strict chronological order? Or would flashback (referring to an event that occurred earlier) or flashforward (referring to an event that will occur later) make the narrative more interesting?
- How can I use vivid descriptive detail to dramatize the story?

The Ending

- If I conclude with some reflections on the meaning of the experience, how can I avoid tagging on a moral or being too sentimental?
- If I want readers to think well of me, should I conclude with a philosophical statement, as Wolff does? Should I end with a paradoxical statement, like Dillard? Should I be satirical? Should I be self-critical to avoid seeming smug?
- If I want to underscore the event's continuing significance in my life, can I show that the conflict was never fully resolved, as Brandt does? Could I contrast my remembered and current feelings and thoughts?
- Should I frame the essay by echoing something from the beginning to give readers at least a superficial sense of closure, as Brandt does by setting the last scene, like the first, in a car?

Outlining

The goals you have set should help you draft your essay, but first you might want to make a quick scratch outline to refocus on the basic story line. (For an example of a paragraph scratch outline, turn to the Commentary following Annie Dillard's essay on p. 31.) You could use the outlining function of your word processing program. In your outline, list the main actions in order, noting where you plan to describe the place, introduce particular people, present dialogue, and insert remembered or current feelings and thoughts. Use this outline to guide your drafting, but do not feel tied to it. As you draft, you may find a better way to sequence the action and integrate these features. Turn to Chapter 10 (p. 346) for more information on scratch outlining.

Drafting

General Advice.   Start drafting your essay, keeping in mind the goals you have set for yourself, especially the goal of telling the story dramatically. Turn off your grammar checker and spelling checker at this stage if you find them distracting. Don't be afraid to skip around in your story. Jump back and fill in a spontaneous idea, or leap ahead and write a later section first if you find that easier. Refer to your outline to help you sequence the action. If you get stuck while drafting, either make a note of what you need to fill in later or see if you can use something from your invention writing.

As you read over your first draft, you may see places where you can add new material to make the story dramatic. Or you may even decide that after this first draft you can finally see the story you want to write and set out to do so in a second draft.

Sentence Strategies.   As you draft a remembered-event essay, you will be trying to help readers feel the suspense of your story and recognize its significance. You will also need to orient readers to the time sequence of all the various actions in your narrative. In thinking about how to achieve these goals, you can often benefit by paying attention to how long your sentences are and where you place references to time.

Use short sentences to heighten the drama or suspense, point out autobiographical significance, and summarize action. Experienced writers of autobiography usually use both short and long sentences, as a glance at any reading in this chapter demonstrates. They write short sentences not to relieve the monotony or effort of writing long sentences but to achieve certain purposes they cannot achieve as easily with long sentences.

To dramatize actions or heighten suspense:

He caught us and we all stopped. (Annie Dillard, paragraph 15)

To emphasize the significance of the event to the writer:

I wanted the glory to last forever. (Annie Dillard, paragraph 19)
The humiliation at that moment was overwhelming. (Jean Brandt, paragraph 17)

To summarize actions:

One afternoon, I pulled the trigger. (Tobias Wolff, paragraph 9)

Short sentences are not the only way to achieve these purposes, but they do so notably well. Note, though, that most of these writers use short sentences infrequently. Because short sentences are infrequent, they attract the reader's attention: They seem to say, "Pay close attention here." But short sentences achieve this effect only in relation to long sentences, in context with them. (Some of the Sentence

Strategies presented in other chapters of this book illustrate ways that writers construct and purposefully deploy relatively long, complex sentences.) See how Dillard uses a series of longer sentences to build suspense that she brings to a peak with a short one:

> On one weekday morning after Christmas, six inches of new snow had just fallen. We were standing up to our boot tops in snow on a front yard on trafficked Reynolds Street, waiting for cars. The cars traveled Reynolds Street slowly and evenly; they were targets all but wrapped in red ribbons, cream puffs. We couldn't miss. (paragraph 3)

Place references to time toward the front of your sentences. Because your remembered-event essay is organized narratively—that is, it tells readers a story—you must regularly give them cues about when various actions occur. Without these time cues, readers may not know in which decade, year, or season the event occurred; whether it unfolded slowly or quickly; or in what sequence the various actions took place. When experienced writers of autobiography use these cues, they nearly always place them at the beginnings of sentences (or main clauses), as Annie Dillard does in this sentence from *An American Childhood:*

> *On one weekday morning after Christmas,* six inches of new snow had just fallen. (paragraph 3)

Placing these two important time cues—day of the week and time of the year—at the beginning of a sentence may not seem noteworthy, but in fact time cues can usually be placed nearly anywhere in a sentence. Consequently, Dillard might have written

> Six inches of new snow had just fallen *on one weekday morning after Christmas.*

Or she could have written

> *After Christmas,* six inches of new snow had just fallen *one weekday morning.*

Why might Dillard decide to locate these time cues at the beginning of the sentence, as she does with nearly all the time cues in her essay? Why not begin the sentence with the subject or main idea, in this case *six inches of snow?* The answer is that experienced writers of autobiography give highest priority to keeping readers oriented to time, specifically to the time of each action in the sequence of actions that make up a remembered event. To do so, they can rely on words, phrases, or clauses:

> Slowly, . . . (Jean Brandt, paragraph 36)
>
> For a week or so . . . (Tobias Wolff, paragraph 5)
>
> A few seconds later, . . . (Jean Brandt, paragraph 3)

In addition to using short sentences and locating explicit time cues at the beginning of sentences, you can strengthen your autobiographical writing with a kind of sentence that is important in observational writing—absolute phrases (p. 102).

CRITICAL READING GUIDE

Now is the time to get a good critical reading of your draft. Your instructor may schedule readings of drafts as part of your coursework—in class or online. If not, ask a classmate, friend, or family member to read your draft. You could also seek comments from a tutor at your campus writing center. The guidelines in this section can be used by anyone reviewing an essay about a remembered event. (If you are unable to have someone read your draft, turn ahead to the Revising section on p. 58, where you will find guidelines for reading your own draft critically.)

If you read another student's draft online, you may be able to use a word processing program to insert suggested improvements directly into the text of the draft or to write them out at the end of the draft. If you read a printout of the draft, you may write brief comments in the margins and lengthier suggestions on a separate page. When the writer sits down to revise, your thoughtful, extended suggestions written at the end of the draft or on separate pages will be especially helpful.

If You Are the Writer. To provide focused, helpful comments, your reader must know your essay's intended audience, your purpose, and a problem in the draft that you need help solving. Briefly write out this information at the top of your draft.

- *Readers:* Identify the intended readers of your essay.
- *Purpose:* What do you hope to achieve in writing this remembered-event essay? What features of your story do you hope will most interest readers? What do you want to disclose about yourself?
- *Problem:* Ask your reader to help you solve the single most important problem with your draft. Describe this problem briefly.

If You Are the Reader. Use the following guidelines to help you give critical comments to others on remembered-event essays.

1. *Read for a First Impression.* Read first to enjoy the story and to get a sense of its significance. Then, in just a few sentences, describe your first impression. If you have any insights about the meaning or importance of the event, share your thoughts. Next, consider the problem the writer identified, and respond briefly to that concern now. (If you find that the problem is covered by one of the other guidelines listed below, respond to it in more detail there if necessary.)

2. *Analyze the Effectiveness of the Storytelling.* Review the story, looking at the way the suspense builds and resolves itself. Point to any places where the

drama loses intensity—perhaps where the suspense slackens, where specific narrative action is sparse or action verbs are needed, where narrative transitions would help readers, or where dialogue could be added to dramatize people's interactions.

3. *Consider How Vividly the Places and People Are Described.* Point to any descriptive details, similes, or metaphors that are especially effective. Note any places or people that need more specific description. Also indicate any descriptive details that seem unnecessary. Identify any quoted dialogue that might be summarized instead or any dialogue that does not seem relevant.

4. *Assess Whether the Autobiographical Significance Is Clear.* Explain briefly what you think makes this event significant for the writer. Point out any places in the draft where the significance seems so overstated as to be sentimental or so understated as to be vague or unclear. If the event seems to lack significance, speculate about what you think the significance could be. Then point to one place in the draft where you think the significance could be made clearer by telling the story more fully or dramatically or by stating the significance.

5. *Assess the Use of Memorabilia.* If the writer makes use of memorabilia, evaluate how successfully each item is used. How is it relevant? Does it seem integrated into the narrative or merely appended? Is it placed in the most appropriate location? Does it make a meaningful contribution to the essay?

6. *Analyze the Effectiveness of the Organization.* Consider the overall plan, perhaps by making a scratch outline. Pay special attention to temporal transitions and verb tenses so that you can identify any places where the order of the action is unclear. Also indicate any places where you think the description or background information interrupts the action. If you can, suggest other locations for this material.

- *Look at the beginning.* If it does not arouse curiosity, point to language elsewhere in the essay that might serve as a better opening—for example, a bit of dialogue, a striking image, or a remembered feeling.

- *Look at the ending.* Indicate whether the conflict in the story is too neatly resolved at the end, whether the writer has tagged on a moral, or whether the essay abruptly stops without really coming to a conclusion. If there is a problem with the ending, try to suggest an alternative ending, such as framing the story with a reference to something from the beginning or projecting into the future.

7. *Give the Writer Your Final Thoughts.* What is the draft's strongest part? What part is most in need of further work?

■ REVISING

Now you have the opportunity to revise your essay. Your instructor or other students may have given you advice. You may have begun to realize that your draft requires not so much revising as rethinking. For example, you may recognize that the story you told is not the story you meant to tell. Or maybe you realize only now why the incident is important to you. Consequently, you may need to reshape your story radically or draft a new version of it, instead of working to improve the various parts of your first draft. Many students—and professional writers—find themselves in this situation. Often a writer produces a draft or two and gets advice on them from others and only then begins to see what might be achieved.

However, if instead you feel satisfied that your draft mostly achieves what you set out to do, you can focus on refining the various parts of it. Very likely you have thought of ways to improve your draft, and you may even have begun revising it. This section will help you get an overview of your draft and revise it accordingly.

Getting an Overview

Consider the draft as a whole, following these two steps:

1. *Reread.* If at all possible, put the draft aside for a day or two. When you do reread it, start by reconsidering your purpose. Then read the draft straight through, trying to see it as your intended readers will.
2. *Outline.* Make a quick scratch outline on paper, or use the headings and outline or summary functions of your word processor.

Planning for Revision. Resist the temptation to dive in and start changing your text until you have a comprehensive view of what needs to be done. Using your outline as a guide, move through the document, using the change-highlighting or commenting tools of your word processor to note comments received from others and problems you want to solve (or mark on a hard copy if you prefer).

Analyzing the Basic Features of Your Own Draft. Turn to the Critical Reading Guide on the preceding pages (pp. 56–57). Using this guide, reread the draft to identify problems you need to solve. Note the problems on your draft.

Studying Critical Comments. Review all of the comments you have received from other readers and add to your notes any that you intend to act on. For each comment, refer to the draft to see what might have led the reader to make that particular point. Try to be objective about any criticism. Ideally, these comments will help you to see your draft as others see it (rather than as you hoped it would be) and to identify specific problems.

Carrying Out Revisions

Having identified problems in your draft, you now need to figure out solutions and—most important—to carry them out. Basically, there are three ways to find solutions:

1. Review your invention and planning notes for material you can add to your draft.
2. Do additional invention writing to provide material you or your readers think is needed.
3. Look back at the readings in this chapter to see how other writers have solved similar problems.

The following suggestions, which are organized according to the basic features of remembered-event essays, will get you started solving some writing problems that are common in them.

A Well-Told Story

- **Is the climax difficult to identify?** Check to be sure your story has a climax. Perhaps it is the point when you get what you were striving for (Dillard), when you do what you were afraid you might do (Wolff), or when you get caught (Brandt). If you cannot find a climax in your story or reconstruct your story so that it has one, then you may have a major problem. If this is the case, you should discuss with your instructor the possibility of starting over with another event.

- **Does the suspense slacken instead of building to the climax?** Try showing people moving or gesturing, adding narrative transitions to propel the action, or substituting quoted dialogue for summarized dialogue. Remember that writers of autobiography often use short sentences to summarize action and heighten suspense, as when Dillard writes "We couldn't miss" and "He didn't even close the car door."

A Vivid Presentation of Places and People

- **Do any places or people need more specific description?** Try naming objects and adding sensory details to help readers imagine what the objects look, feel, smell, taste, or sound like. For people, describe a physical feature or mannerism that shows the role the person plays in your story.

- **Does any dialogue seem irrelevant or poorly written?** Eliminate any unnecessary dialogue, or summarize quoted dialogue that has no distinctive language or dramatic purpose. Liven up quoted dialogue with faster repartee to make it more dramatic. Instead of introducing each comment with the dialogue cue "he said," describe the speaker's attitude or personality with phrases like "she gasped" or "he joked."

- **Do any descriptions weaken the dominant impression?** Omit extraneous details or reconsider the impression you want to make. Add similes and metaphors that strengthen the dominant impression you want your story to have.

- *Do readers question any visuals you used?* Might you move a visual to a more appropriate place or replace an ineffective visual with a more appropriate one? Could you make clear the relevance of a visual by mentioning it in your text?

An Indication of the Event's Significance

- *Are readers getting a different image of you from the one you want to create?* Look closely at the language you use to express your feelings and thoughts. If you project an aspect of yourself you did not intend to, reconsider what the story reveals about you. Ask yourself again why the event stands out in your memory. What do you want readers to know about you from reading this essay?

- *Are your remembered or current feelings and thoughts about the event coming across clearly and eloquently?* If not, look in your invention writing for more expressive language. If your writing seems too sentimental, try to express your feelings more directly and simply, or let yourself show ambivalence or uncertainty.

- *Do readers appreciate the event's uniqueness or special importance in your life?* If not, consider giving them more insight into your background or cultural heritage. Also consider whether they need to know what has happened since the event took place to appreciate why it is so memorable for you.

The Organization

- *Is the overall plan ineffective or the story hard to follow?* Look carefully at the way the action unfolds. Fill in any gaps. Eliminate unnecessary digressions. Add or clarify temporal transitions. Fix confusing verb tenses. Remember that writers of autobiography tend to place references to time at the beginnings of sentences—"*When a car came,* we all popped it one"—to keep readers on track as the story unfolds.

- *Does description or other information disrupt the flow of the narrative?* Try integrating this material by adding smoother transitions. Or consider removing the disruptive parts or placing them elsewhere.

- *Is the beginning weak?* See whether there is a better way to start. Review the draft and your notes for an image, a bit of dialogue, or a remembered feeling that might catch readers' attention or spark their curiosity.

- *Does the ending work?* If not, think about a better way to end—with a memorable image, perhaps, or a provocative assertion. Consider whether you can frame the essay by referring back to something in the beginning.

Checking Sentence Strategies Electronically.   To check your draft for a sentence strategy especially useful in remembered-event essays, use your word processor's highlighting function to mark references to time. Then look at where each one appears in its sentence, and think about whether moving any of them closer to the beginning of the sentence would make it easier for readers to follow the sequence of actions in your narrative. For more on placement of time references, see p. 55.

■ EDITING AND PROOFREADING

Now is the time to check your revised draft for errors in grammar, punctuation, and mechanics and to consider matters of style. Our research has identified several errors that occur often in essays about remembered events: missing commas after introductory elements, fused sentences, and misused past-perfect verbs. The following guidelines will help you check your essay for these common errors. This book's Web site also provides interactive online exercises to help you learn to identify and correct each of these errors; to access the exercises for a particular error, go to the URL listed after each set of guidelines.

Checking for Missing Commas after Introductory Elements.   Introductory elements in a sentence can be words, phrases, or clauses. A comma tells readers that the introductory information is ending and the main part of the sentence is about to begin. If there is no danger of misreading, you can omit the comma after single words or short phrases or clauses, but you will never be wrong to include the comma. Remembered-event essays require introductory elements, especially those showing time passing. The following sentences, taken from drafts written by college students using this book, show several kinds of introductory sentence elements that should have a comma after them.

▶ **Through the nine-day run of the play‸ the acting just kept getting better and better.**

▶ **Knowing that the struggle was over‸ I felt through my jacket to find tea bags and cookies the robber had taken from the kitchen.**

▶ **As I stepped out of the car‸ I knew something was wrong.**

For practice, go to bedfordstmartins.com/conciseguide/comma.

Checking for Fused Sentences.   Fused sentences occur when two independent clauses are joined with no punctuation or connecting word between them. When you write about a remembered event, you try to re-create a scene. In so doing, you might write a fused sentence like this one:

▶ **Sleet glazed the windshield the wipers were frozen stuck.**

There are several ways to edit fused sentences:

• Make the clauses separate sentences.

    The
▶ **Sleet glazed the windshield‸the wipers were frozen stuck.**

• Join the two clauses with a comma and *and, but, or, nor, for, so,* or *yet.*

    ‸ and
▶ **Sleet glazed the windshield‸the wipers were frozen stuck.**

- Join the two clauses with a semicolon.

  ▶ Sleet glazed the windshield؛ the wipers were frozen stuck.

- Rewrite the sentence, subordinating one clause.

  As sleet   *became*
  ▶ ~~Sleet~~ glazed the windshield؛ the wipers ~~were~~ frozen stuck.
    ^   ^

For practice, go to bedfordstmartins.com/conciseguide/csplice.

Checking Your Use of the Past Perfect.   Verb tenses indicate the time an action takes place. As a writer, you will generally use the present tense for actions occurring at the time you are writing (we *see*), the past tense for actions completed in the past (we *saw*), and the future tense for actions that will occur in the future (we *will see*). When you write about a remembered event, you will often need to use various forms of the past tense: the past perfect to indicate an action that was completed at the time of another past action (she *had finished* her work when we saw her) and the past progressive to indicate a continuing action in the past (she *was finishing* her work). One common problem in writing about a remembered event is the failure to use the past perfect when it is needed. For example:

                                                              had
▶ I had three people in the car, something my father told me not to do on
                                                          ^
  several occasions.

In the following sentence, the meaning is not clear without the past perfect:

                      had run
▶ Coach Kernow told me I ~~ran~~ faster than ever before.
                        ^

For practice, go to bedfordstmartins.com/conciseguide/verbs.

A Common ESL Problem.   It is important to remember that the past perfect is formed with *had* followed by a past participle. Past participles usually end in *-ed, -d, -en, -n,* or *-t: worked, hoped, eaten, taken, bent.*

                                                      spoken
▶ Before Tania went to Moscow last year, she had not really ~~speak~~ Russian.
                                                          ^

For practice, go to bedfordstmartins.com/conciseguide/everb.

A Note on Grammar and Spelling Checkers.   These tools are good at catching certain types of errors, but currently there's no replacement for a good human proofreader. Grammar checkers in particular are extremely limited in what they can usually find, and often they only give you summary information that isn't helpful if you don't already understand the rule in question. They are also prone to give faulty advice for fixing problems and to flag correct items as wrong. Spelling checkers cause fewer problems but can't catch misspellings that are themselves words, such as *to* for *too.*

REFLECTING ON YOUR WRITING

Now that you have worked extensively in autobiography—reading it, talking about it, writing it—take some time for reflection. Reflecting on your writing process will help you gain a greater understanding of what you learned about solving the problems you encountered writing about an event.

Write a page or so telling your instructor about a problem you encountered in writing your essay and how you solved it. Before you begin, gather all of your writing—invention and planning notes, outlines, drafts, critical comments, revision plans, and final revision. Review these materials as you complete this writing task.

1. *Identify one problem you needed to solve as you wrote about a remembered event.* Do not be concerned with grammar and punctuation; concentrate on problems unique to writing a story about your experience. For example: Did you puzzle over how to present a particular place or person? Was it difficult to structure the narrative so it held readers' interest? Did you find it hard (or uncomfortable) to convey the event's autobiographical significance?

2. *Determine how you came to recognize the problem.* When did you first discover it? What called it to your attention? Did you notice it yourself, or did another reader point it out? Can you now see hints of it in your invention writing, your planning notes, or an earlier draft? If so, where specifically?

3. *Reflect on how you went about solving the problem.* Did you work on a particular passage, cut or add details, or reorganize the essay? Did you reread one of the essays in the chapter to see how another writer handled similar material? Did you look back at the invention guidelines? Did you discuss the problem with another student, a tutor, or your instructor? If so, how did talking about it help, and how useful was the advice you got?

4. *Write a brief explanation of the problem and your solution.* Be as specific as possible in reconstructing your efforts. Quote from your invention notes or early drafts, from readers' comments, from your revision plan, and from your final revision to show the various changes your writing underwent as you worked to solve the problem. Taking the time now to think about how you recognized and solved a real writing problem will help you become more aware of what works and does not work, making you a more confident writer.

3

Writing Profiles

Profiles tell about people, places, and activities. Some profile writers try to reveal the unapparent inner workings of places or activities we consider familiar. Other profile writers introduce us to the exotic places or people — peculiar hobbies, unusual places of business, bizarre personalities.

Whatever their subject, profile writers strive most of all to enable readers to imagine the person, place, or activity that is the focus of the profile. Writers succeed only by presenting many specific and vivid details: how the person dresses, gestures, and talks; what the place looks, sounds, and smells like; what the activity requires of those who participate in it. Not only must the details be vivid, but they also must help to convey a writer's perspective — some insight, idea, or interpretation — on the subject.

Because profiles share many features with essays about remembered events — such as description, narration, and dialogue — you may use many of the strategies learned in Chapter 2 when you write your profile. Yet profiles differ from writing that reflects on personal experience in that profiles present newly acquired knowledge gained from your observations. In acquiring this knowledge, you practice observing, interviewing, and notetaking. These field research activities are important in many areas of academic study, including anthropology, sociology, psychology, education, and business.

The scope of your profile may be large or small, depending on your assignment and your subject. You could attend a single event such as a parade, dress rehearsal for a play, or city council meeting and write your observations of the place, people, and activities. Or you might conduct an interview with a person who has an unusual occupation and write a profile based on your interview notes. If you have the time to do more extensive research, you might write a more complete profile based on several visits and interviews with various people.

Writing in Your Other Courses

- For an education course, a student who has been studying collaborative learning principles profiles a group of sixth-grade students working together on an Internet project. The student observes and takes extensive notes on the collaboration. To learn what the sixth graders think about working together, the student interviews them individually and as a group. She also talks with the classroom teacher about how students were prepared to do this kind of work and how their collaboration will be evaluated. She organizes the profile narratively, telling the story of one erratic but ultimately productive group meeting. She interweaves interpretive comments based on collaborative learning principles. From her descriptions and comments emerges a perspective that group work is unlikely to succeed unless the students together with the teacher frequently reflect on what they are learning and how they can work together more productively.

- For an anthropology assignment, a student plans to research and write an ethnography (somewhat like an in-depth profile) about the football program and team at a local high school. He interviews coaches, players, parents, a few teachers not directly involved in the football program, the school principal, and a sports reporter for the local newspaper. He attends several practices and games. His detailed description of the football program alternates observational details with his own perspective on what football means to this particular high school community, particularly the way it confers status on the players, their parents, and their friends.

Writing in the Community

- An art history student profiles a local artist recently commissioned to paint an outdoor mural for the city. The student visits the artist's studio and talks with him about the process of painting murals. The artist invites the student to spend the following day with a team of local art students and neighborhood volunteers working on the mural under his direction. This firsthand experience helps the student describe the process of mural painting almost from an insider's point of view. She organizes her profile around the main stages of this collaborative mural project, from conception to completion. As she describes each stage, she weaves in details about the artist, his helpers, and the site of their work, seeking to capture the civic spirit that pervades the mural project.

- For a small-town newspaper, a writer profiles a community activist who appears regularly at city council meetings to speak on various problems in his neighborhood. The writer interviews the activist as well as two of the council members. He also observes the activist speaking at one council meeting on the problem of trash being dumped in unauthorized areas. At this meeting, the activist describes an all-night vigil he made to capture on videotape a flagrant act of illegal dumping in an empty lot near his home. The writer uses the activist's appearance at this meeting as a narrative framework for the profile; he also integrates details of the activist's public life along with images from the videotape.

Writing in the Workplace

- To help a probation court judge make an informed decision about whether to jail a teenager convicted of a crime or return him to his family, a social worker prepares to write a report and make a recommendation to the court. She interviews the teenager and his parents and observes the interactions among the family members. Her report describes in detail what she saw and heard, concluding with a recommendation that the teenager be allowed to return to his parents' home.

- For a company newsletter, a public-relations officer profiles a day in the life of the new CEO. He follows the CEO from meeting to meeting—taking photographs, observing her interactions with others, and interviewing her between meetings about her management philosophy and her plans for handling the challenges facing the company. The CEO invites the writer to visit her at home and meet her family. He stays for dinner, helps clear the table, and then watches the CEO help her daughter with homework. He takes more photographs. The published profile is illustrated by two photographs, one showing the CEO engaged in an intense business conference and the other showing her helping her daughter with homework.

Practice Choosing a Profile Subject: A Collaborative Activity

The preceding scenarios suggest some occasions for writing profiles. Imagine that you have been assigned to write a profile of a person, a place, or an activity on your campus, in your community, or at your workplace. Think of subjects that you would like to know more about. Your instructor may schedule this collaborative activity as a classroom discussion or ask you to conduct an online discussion in a chatroom.

Part 1. List three to five subjects you are curious about. Choose subjects you can imagine yourself visiting and learning more about. If possible, name a specific subject—a particular musician, day-care center, or local brewery. Consider interesting *people* (for example, store owners, distinguished teachers, accomplished campus or community musicians or sports figures, newspaper columnists, public defenders, CEOs, radio talk show hosts), *places* (for example, a college health center or student newspaper office, day-care center, botanical garden, community police department, zoo, senior citizen center, farmer's market, artist's studio, museum or sculpture garden, historic building, public transportation center, or garage), and *businesses* or *activities* (for example, a comic-book store, wrecking company, motorcycle dealer, commercial fishing boat, local brewery or winery, homeless shelter, building contractor, dance studio, private tutoring service, or dog kennel).

Now get together with two or three other students, and take turns reading your lists of subjects to one another. The other group members will tell you which item on your list they personally find most interesting and why they chose that item and ask you any questions they have about it.

Part 2. After you have all read your lists and received responses, discuss these questions as a group:

- What surprised you most about group members' choices of interesting subjects from your list?

- If you were now choosing a subject from your list to write about, how would group members' comments and questions influence your choice?
- How might their comments and questions influence your approach to learning more about this subject?

READINGS

No two profiles are alike, and yet they share defining features. Together, the three readings in this chapter reveal a number of these features, so you will want to read as many of them as possible. If time permits, complete the activities in the Analyzing Writing Strategies section that follows each reading, and read the Commentary. Following the readings is a section called Basic Features: Profiles (p. 85), which offers a concise description of the features of profiles and provides examples from the three readings.

John T. Edge directs the Southern Foodways Symposium, which is part of the Center for the Study of Southern Culture at the University of Mississippi. He coordinates an annual conference on southern food. Food writer for the national magazine Oxford American, he has also written for Cooking Light, Food & Wine, and Gourmet. He has published several books, including A Gracious Plenty: Recipes and Recollections from the American South (1999); Southern Belly (2000), a portrait of southern food told through profiles of people and places; and, with photographer Robb Helfrick, Compass Guide Georgia (2001), a collection of new and archival photographs, literary excerpts, and practical travel information.

This reading (and the photograph shown on p. 68) first appeared in a 1999 issue of Oxford American and was reprinted in 2000 in Utne Reader. Edge profiles an unusual manufacturing business, Farm Fresh Food Supplier, in a small Mississippi town. He introduces readers to its pickled meat products, which include pickled pig lips. Like many other profile writers, Edge participates in his subject, in his case not by joining in the activities undertaken at Farm Fresh but by attempting to eat a pig lip at Jesse's Place, a nearby "juke" bar. You will see that the reading begins and ends with this personal experience.

As you read, enjoy Edge's struggle to eat a pig lip, but notice also how much you are learning about this bar snack food as Edge details his discomfort in trying to eat it. Be equally attentive to the information he offers about the history and manufacturing of pig lips at Farm Fresh.

I'm Not Leaving Until I Eat This Thing
John T. Edge

It's just past 4:00 on a Thursday afternoon in June at Jesse's Place, a country juke 17 miles south of the Mississippi line and three miles west of Amite, Louisiana. The air conditioner hacks and spits forth torrents of Arctic air, but the heat of summer can't be kept at bay. It seeps around the splintered doorjambs and settles in, transforming the

squat particleboard-plastered roadhouse into a sauna. Slowly, the dank barroom fills with grease-smeared mechanics from the truck stop up the road and farmers straight from the fields, the soles of their brogans thick with dirt clods. A few weary souls make their way over from the nearby sawmill. I sit alone at the bar, one empty bottle of Bud in front of me, a second in my hand. I drain the beer, order a third, and stare down at the pink juice spreading outward from a crumpled foil pouch and onto the bar.

I'm not leaving until I eat this thing, I tell myself.   2

Half a mile down the road, behind a fence coiled with razor wire, Lionel Dufour, pro-   3
prietor of Farm Fresh Food Supplier, is loading up the last truck of the day, wheeling case after case of pickled pork offal out of his cinder-block processing plant and into a semi-trailer bound for Hattiesburg, Mississippi.

His crew packed lips today. Yesterday, it was pickled sausage; the day before that,   4
pig feet. Tomorrow, it's pickled pig lips again. Lionel has been on the job since 2:45 in the morning, when he came in to light the boilers. Damon Landry, chief cook and mainte-nance man, came in at 4:30. By 7:30, the production line was at full tilt: six women in white smocks and blue bouffant caps, slicing ragged white fat from the lips, tossing the good parts in glass jars, the bad parts in barrels bound for the rendering plant. Across the aisle, filled jars clatter by on a conveyor belt as a worker tops them off with a Kool-Aid-red

slurry of hot sauce, vinegar, salt, and food coloring. Around the corner, the jars are capped, affixed with a label, and stored in pasteboard boxes to await shipping.

Unlike most offal—euphemistically called "variety meats"—lips belie their prove-nance. Brains, milky white and globular, look like brains. Feet, the ghosts of their cloven hoofs protruding, look like feet. Testicles look like, well, testicles. But lips are different. Loosed from the snout, trimmed of their fat, and dyed a preternatural pink, they look more like candy than like carrion. 5

At Farm Fresh, no swine root in an adjacent feedlot. No viscera-strewn killing floor lurks just out of sight, down a darkened hallway. These pigs died long ago at some Mid-western abattoir. By the time the lips arrive in Amite, they are, in essence, pig Popsicles, 50-pound blocks of offal and ice. 6

"Lips are all meat," Lionel told me earlier in the day. "No gristle, no bone, no nothing. They're bar food, hot and vinegary, great with a beer. Used to be the lips ended up in sausages, headcheese, those sorts of things. A lot of them still do." 7

Lionel, a 50-year-old father of three with quick, intelligent eyes set deep in a face the color of cordovan, is a veteran of nearly 40 years in the pickled pig lips business. "I started out with my daddy when I wasn't much more than 10," Lionel told me, his shy smile framed by a coarse black mustache flecked with whispers of gray. "The meatpack-ing business he owned had gone broke back when I was 6, and he was peddling out of the back of his car, selling dried shrimp, napkins, straws, tubes of plastic cups, pig feet, pig lips, whatever the bar owners needed. He sold to black bars, white bars, sweet shops, snowball stands, you name it. We made the rounds together after I got out of school, sometimes staying out till two or three in the morning. I remember bringing my toy cars to this one joint and racing them around the floor with the bar owner's son while my daddy and his father did business." 8

For years after the demise of that first meatpacking company, the Dufour family sold someone else's product. "We used to buy lips from Dennis Di Salvo's company down in Belle Chasse," recalled Lionel. "As far as I can tell, his mother was the one who came up with the idea to pickle and pack lips back in the '50s, back when she was working for a company called Three Little Pigs over in Houma. But pretty soon, we were selling so many lips that we had to almost beg Di Salvo's for product. That's when we started cooking up our own," he told me, gesturing toward the cast-iron kettle that hangs from the rafters by the front door of the plant. "My daddy started cooking lips in that very pot." 9

Lionel now cooks lips in 11 retrofitted milk tanks, dull stainless-steel cauldrons shaped like oversized cradles. But little else has changed. Though Lionel's father has passed away, Farm Fresh remains a family-focused company. His wife, Kathy, keeps the books. His daughter, Dana, a button-cute college student who has won numerous beauty titles, takes to the road in the summer, selling lips to convenience stores and whole-salers. Soon, after he graduates from business school, Lionel's younger son, Matt, will take over operations at the plant. And his older son, a veterinarian, lent his name to one of Farm Fresh's top sellers, Jason's Pickled Pig Lips. 10

"We do our best to corner the market on lips," Lionel told me, his voice tinged with 11
bravado. "Sometimes they're hard to get from the packing houses. You gotta kill a lot of
pigs to get enough lips to keep us going. I've got new customers calling every day; it's all
I can do to keep up with demand, but I bust my ass to keep up. I do what I can for my family—and for my customers.

"When my customers tell me something," he continued, "just like when my daddy told 12
me something, I listen. If my customers wanted me to dye the lips green, I'd ask, 'What
shade?' As it is, every few years we'll do some red and some blue for the Fourth of July.
This year we did jars full of Mardi Gras lips—half purple, half gold," Lionel recalled with a
chuckle. "I guess we'd had a few beers when we came up with that one."

Meanwhile, back at Jesse's Place, I finish my third Bud, order my fourth. *Now,* I tell 13
myself, my courage bolstered by booze, *I'm ready to eat a lip.*

They may have looked like candy in the plant, but in the barroom they're carrion once 14
again. I poke and prod the six-inch arc of pink flesh, peering up from my reverie just in
time to catch the barkeep's wife, Audrey, staring straight at me. She fixes me with a look
just this side of pity and asks, "You gonna eat that thing or make love to it?"

Her nephew, Jerry, sidles up to a bar stool on my left. "A lot of people like 'em with 15
chips," he says with a nod toward the pink juice pooling on the bar in front of me. I offer to
buy him a lip, and Audrey fishes one from a jar behind the counter, wraps it in tinfoil, and
places the whole affair on a paper towel in front of him.

I take stock of my own cowardice, and, following Jerry's lead, reach for a bag of 16
potato chips, tear open the top with my teeth, and toss the quivering hunk of hog flesh
into the shiny interior of the bag, slick with grease and dusted with salt. Vinegar vapors
tickle my nostrils. I stifle a gag that rolls from the back of my throat, swallow hard, and
pray that the urge to vomit passes.

With a smash of my hand, the potato chips are reduced to a pulp, and I feel the cold 17
lump of the lip beneath my fist. I clasp the bag shut and shake it hard in an effort to
ensure chip coverage in all the nooks and crannies of the lip. The technique that Jerry
uses—and I mimic—is not unlike that employed by home cooks mixing up a mess of
Shake 'n Bake chicken.

I pull from the bag a coral crescent of meat now crusted with blond bits of potato 18
chips. When I chomp down, the soft flesh dissolves between my teeth. It tastes like a flac-
cid cracklin', unmistakably porcine, and not altogether bad. The chips help, providing texture where there was none. Slowly, my brow unfurrows, my stomach ceases its fluttering.

Sensing my relief, Jerry leans over and peers into my bag. "Kind of look like Frosted 19
Flakes, don't they?" he says, by way of describing the chips rapidly turning to mush in the
pickling juice. I offer the bag to Jerry, order yet another beer, and turn to eye the pig feet
floating in a murky jar by the cash register, their blunt tips bobbing up through a pasty
white film.

Connecting to Culture and Experience: Gaining Firsthand Experience

Undoubtedly, Edge believed that he should visit a place where Farm Fresh Food Supplier's most popular product is consumed. He went further, however: He decided to experience the product firsthand by handling, smelling, and tasting it. Except for his own squeamishness, nothing prevented him from gaining the firsthand experience he sought. Aside from experiences in family and personal relationships, think about times when you have sought to gain firsthand experience and either succeeded or failed. Perhaps you yearned to sing but never took lessons, challenged yourself to go beyond watching basketball or soccer on television and won a spot on a school team, dreamed of an internship at a certain workplace but never could find the time to arrange it, imagined visiting a natural or historic site you had only read about and found a way to do so, or thought about joining others to protest a social injustice but never took action.

Identify one longed-for personal experience you missed out on and one you achieved, and think about why you failed in one case and succeeded in the other. At the time, how ready and able were you to gain access to the experience? What part did your personal decisiveness and effort play? Did you feel timid or bold about seeking what you wanted? Did you try to be accommodating, or did you have to be challenging or even disruptive? What roles did other people play? Who supported you, and who attempted to silence or exclude you? With whom did you have to negotiate? How did your gender or age affect the outcome? How important was money or other resources?

With two or three other students, discuss your attempts to gain longed-for personal experience. Begin by telling each other about one experience, explaining briefly what drew you to it, what happened, how you felt about the outcome, and why you think you succeeded or failed. Then, as a group, discuss what your stories reveal about what motivates and helps young Americans and what frustrates them as they try to gain longed-for experiences that may open new opportunities to them.

Analyzing Writing Strategies

1. The introduction to this chapter makes several generalizations about profile essays. Consider which of these assertions apply to Edge's essay:
   - It is based on the writer's newly acquired observations.
   - It takes readers behind the scenes of familiar places or introduces them to unusual places and people.
   - It is informative and entertaining.
   - It presents scenes and people vividly through description, action, and dialogue.
   - It suggests or asserts the writer's perspective on the subject—an idea about the subject or an insight into it.

2. Edge focuses on one of Farm Fresh's products, pickled pig lips. He probably assumes that most of his readers have never seen a pickled pig lip, much less eaten

one. Therefore, he describes this product carefully. To see how he does so, underline in paragraphs 4, 5, 7, 14, and 18 every detail of a pickled pig lip's appearance, size, texture or consistency, smell, and taste. If you have never seen a pickled pig lip, what more do you need to know to imagine what it looks like? Which details make a lip seem appealing to you? Which ones make it seem unappealing? Edge scatters the details across the profile, rather than collecting them in one place. For you as one reader, how did this scattering help or hinder your attempts to fully understand what a pig lip is like?

3. To present their subjects, profile writers occasionally make use of a sentence strategy that relies on a sentence structure known as an *absolute phrase*. To discover what absolute phrases contribute, underline these absolutes in Edge's profile: in paragraph 1, sentence 4, from "the soles" to the end of the sentence, and sentence 6, from "one empty bottle" to the end; in paragraph 8, sentence 2, from "his shy smile" to the end; and in paragraph 19, sentence 3, from "their blunt tips" to the end. Make notes in the margin about how the absolute phrase seems to be related to what comes before it in the sentence. Given that Edge's goal is to help readers imagine what he observes, what does each absolute contribute toward that goal? How are these four absolutes alike and different in what they add to their sentences? (To learn more about how absolute phrases contribute to profiles, see Sentence Strategies, p. 101.)

Commentary: A Topical Plan

A profile may be presented narratively, as a sequence of events observed by the writer during an encounter with the place, person, or activity; or it may be presented topically, as a series of topics of information gathered by the writer about the person, place, or activity. Though Edge frames (begins and ends) his profile with the narrative or story about attempting to eat a pig lip, he presents the basic information about Farm Fresh Food Supplier topically.

The following scratch outline of Edge's profile shows at a glance the topics he chose and how they are sequenced:

loading meat products on a truck (paragraph 3)

an overview of the production process, with a focus on that day's pig lips (4)

pig lips' peculiarity in not looking like where they come from on the pig (5)

the origin of Farm Fresh's materials — shipped frozen from the Midwest (6)

some characteristics of a pig lip (7)

Lionel's introduction to marketing food products and services (8)

Lionel's resurrection of the family meatpacking business (9)

family involvement in the business (10)

Lionel's marketing strategy (11)

Lionel's relations with customers (12)

Reviewing his interview and observation notes taken while he was at Farm Fresh, Edge apparently decided to organize them not as a narrative in the order in which he took them but as topics sequenced to be most informative for readers. He begins with the finished product, with Lionel loading the truck for shipment. Then he outlines the production process and mentions the various products. From there, he identifies the source of the products and briefly describes a pig lip, his main interest. Then he offers a history of Farm Fresh and concludes with Lionel's approach to his business. When you plan your profile essay, you will have to decide whether to organize your first draft topically or chronologically.

Considering Topics for Your Own Essay

Consider writing about a place that serves, produces, or sells something unusual, perhaps something that, like Edge, you could try yourself for the purpose of further informing and engaging your readers. If such places do not come to mind, you could browse the Yellow Pages of your local phone directory. There are many possibilities: producer or packager of a special ethnic or regional food or a local café that serves it, licensed acupuncture clinic, caterer, novelty and toy balloon store, microbrewery, chain saw dealer, boat builder, talent agency, manufacturer of ornamental iron, bead store, nail salon, pet fish and aquarium supplier, detailing shop, tattoo parlor, scrap metal recycler, fly fishing shop, handwriting analyst, dog or cat sitting service, photo restorer, burglar alarm installer, Christmas tree farm, wedding specialist, reweaving specialist, wig salon. You need not evaluate the quality of the work provided at a place as part of your observational essay. Instead, keep the focus on informing readers about the service or product the place offers. Relating a personal experience with the service or product is a good idea but not a requirement for a successful essay.

Trevor B. Hall runs a Boston nonprofit company, The Call Academy, that provides enrichment programs for low-income urban high school students. Program participants study literature, practice the documentary arts (writing, video and film, photography), and take part in adventure travel. DoubleTake, a magazine for the documentary arts, published Hall's "A Documentary Classroom," a profile of one teacher's efforts to bring documentary into the English classroom, in 2001. The following profile was published in DoubleTake in 2000. As you read, notice how Hall goes about presenting the Edison Café as an irreplaceable social asset to Skagit Valley, Washington.

The Edison Café
Trevor B. Hall

It is almost 6 A.M. in the town of Edison, Washington, and Julie Martin's headlights are cutting through fog and darkness. Julie is the cook and owner of the Edison Café. When she pulls up behind the small, crooked, fire-engine-red building, her first customer is waiting for her. Few words are passed as she opens the doors and begins to ready the kitchen. Soon the local farmers will begin to pour in.

They are tall, hearty men with weathered baseball caps or cowboy hats, earned dirt under every fingernail. Their entrance is always the same: the door creaks open; everyone looks at the new arrival, who swings around the lunch counter to the coffee machine.

"Mornin'," shouts Julie from the kitchen.   2

The new arrival quietly replies: "How-do?" The regulars each grab a mug, fill it, then   3
top off everyone else's cup. It's an unwritten rule that no one's coffee gets low or cold.

Outside it's still pitch black, and the only light in Edison comes from the café—the   4
fluorescent red EAT sign in the window and the dim yellow glow of the interior lights. Some mornings, there is playful banter; at times they all hold comfortable stares and listen quietly to the faux-antique, turquoise radio.

Edison is set in Washington State's Skagit Valley, some twenty-three thousand   5
square acres of the most plush, fertile farmland one can imagine. The valley has the look of a dark-green down comforter, creased by the water that travels down from the Cascade Mountains on its way to the Pacific Ocean. Dotting the horizon to the west are the rounded San Juan Islands. Directly to the east, the ten-thousand-foot volcanic Mount Baker stands watch (when, on occasion, the winter clouds split to allow its appearance). It is from this mountain that rainwater begins the journey down through the foothills and into the Samish River and its tributaries, creating a wetlands on this valley floor.

The valley gives life to a wide variety of birds: waterfowl (mostly ducks), eagles, blue   6
herons, huge flocks of sparrows, occasionally an exotic snowy egret or a mysterious Egyptian hawk. The valley is home to some of the best winter hawk-watching in the country. It is an active, lively place where nature and its doings are never far from the eye.

Most of Skagit Valley is farmland, and Edison is one of the only towns with remnants   7
of a main street (though Edison is no longer officially recognized by a postal zip code of its own). Established in 1869 and named after the inventor Thomas Alva Edison, the town enjoyed a heyday in the late 1880s, when it boasted three hotels, two churches, three grocery stores, a hardware store, a bank, a cheese factory, and four thirst-quenching establishments. For the most part, individually owned farms have since been pushed out

Mt. Baker's clouds over Edison, 2000

Early-rise breakfast, 2000

by larger industry, and the logging and fishing businesses have slowed to a near stand-still. The town has learned to be grateful for its two remaining bars and, of course, the Edison Café.

As the day progresses, the café will see three waves of customers: the early-morning farmers; the gamy, dice-wielding "shakers and rollers"; and the Edison Elementary School's rear-window gang.   8

The first crew is mostly men (and two of their wives, Rosie and Lucille) in their fifties   9
or sixties. They are people who have, in one way or another, worked the land of Skagit Valley: dairy farmers, potato farmers, fishermen, construction workers. The Edison Café is home for them—a combination dining room and kitchen.

One local asserts that while an estimated twenty-seven people have actually owned   10
the café since its beginnings in 1944, life in the café hasn't changed much over the years. Some of the owners have tried to fancy the place up a bit, but the changes were always met with either indifference or outright scorn by its customers. Julie understands: "It needs to be a place where people can come in with cow dung on their boots. You can't change that."

Julie is an attractive woman in her early forties, her blond hair usually pulled back for   11
cooking—a woman who knows what people around here like, to the point that almost no one actually places a food order. Customers sit down, chat with whoever is around, and eventually some food shows up—their meal, which is a day's selection of certain familiar possibilities: two pieces of bacon, a pancake, and a sausage; two eggs, a piece of bacon, and hash browns; an egg, two pancakes, and toast. The bill arrives on time. Everyone pays for the food (though some on mentally kept accounts), but if you're lucky, you can drink coffee for free.

"They roll me double or nothin' for the coffee," Julie declares. With five dice, in three   12
rolls, you must get a six, a five, a four, then the highest total of the remaining two dice wins. Those are the basic rules, but time has built many nuances into this game. Before people head out the door, they call to Julie, "Come roll me for this coffee." Julie emerges from the kitchen, dries her hands on her white apron, straightens her shoulders, peers at her competition, and grabs the dented leather dice cup. When Julie is on one of her winning streaks, she gets her fair share of suspicious looks, but it's part of the deal.

"Now, don't you bad mouth me for that one," she gently warns a loser as she makes   13
way back to the griddle.

By about 7:30 A.M., the first wave of customers is off to work, and the dice cup has   14
moved to the corner table, where the next wave will hit. It's not the last Julie will see of the morning crew, though; most will return periodically throughout the day (some of them four or five times). A little bit of light comes into the valley, and Julie can step out back for a moment's break.

Other than the arrival of her two waitresses—the sharp-tongued Roxy and the   15
charming woman known as Bear—or one of Julie's two high-school-aged daughters, the midmorning quiet lasts until about ten o'clock, when the shakers and rollers—a group of eight to ten local residents, mostly retired couples—show up, as they do every day, for The Game. The first half-hour or so is spent rolling for coffee, until someone rises to

Morning dice, 2000

the top as the day's winner. That person then rolls one-on-one against Julie, double or nothing, for the entire table's coffee. Talk of the weather, the nation, and town gossip rumble through the café. Then, promptly at 10:45, the usual breakfasts are delivered for everyone.

The meals are the standard fare—eggs, toast, hash browns, bacon—except in the   16 case of Peter Menth, who is in his late sixties and whose well-trimmed gray beard and black captain's hat give him the authority of a fishing-boat captain at sea. His meal commands an equally grand respect and even has its own name on the menu: the Peter Pan Hotcake. This is no ordinary hotcake, and is surely the mark of a man who "won't grow up." Simply put, it is huge—so big that Peter bought his own larger-than-life plate to accommodate it—but the hotcake still falls over the sides. Julie respectfully keeps the plate in back.

Yet the usual stack is nothing to ignore—especially when ordered as part of the   17
farmer's breakfast special: two eggs, two sausage links, two strips of bacon, hash
browns, and two pancakes, all for $7.25. Many adolescent appetites have made an
attempt at this one and come close—until the pancakes arrived, thudding on the counter
under their own weight.

In his book *Blue Highways,* William Least Heat-Moon offers that the measure of an   18
American café can be taken by the number of calendars on its wall; five calendars earns
his top rating. The Edison Café tops that by three, and I would add one twist to Least
Heat-Moon's measuring stick: if one of the calendars features pictures of tractors...
loosen your belt. This café offers such a calendar, and a meal for two, really, all for under
$10; a customer is hard pressed to spend more than $5, and further pressed not to leave
the Edison Café teetering, completely full. Nonetheless, at noon a gang of students from
the Edison Elementary School certainly tries their hand at this. (The café sits on the
school's property, always has, which is why the elementary-school students are allowed
to run over for lunch.) One local, Duane, recalls the café's presence in his life during his
days as a student in the late 1940s: "I remember being beat up in this café in 1947—by
my dad," he says with a smile—then explains: "I brought a white-face bull right in the front
door, did a one-eighty-degree turn with it, and headed out. They banned me for a month."
The school cafeteria food soon helped him mend his ways, and today's students are
quick to tell you that Julie's food is an "awesome" option.

The madness begins quietly enough as two of the students, Emma and Kyla, arrive   19
before the crowds. Through good grades, they have earned the right to "work the window"
and get a free lunch in exchange. Moments after their arrival, the rush is on. From the back
window of the café, it looks like a mob running in panic from a fire: backpacks bouncing off
of shoulders, sneakers squeaking across the wet pavement, eyes wide with anticipation.

"We keep them under control," Emma says. "They give us their order, we shout it out   20
to Julie, then we make sure everyone gets the right food. It's not too hard, and we get a
free lunch, which is great!" Julie loves her two helpers, referring to them as "my girls."

This last rush is usually over by twelve-thirty; then Julie can take a well-earned rest   21
on the bench out back. The sun is most likely to show its face about this time of the day,
and she leans against the café wall, her face aimed at the warmth. One of her waitresses
likely joins her, and the gossip begins. If it's her daughter, she often prods, "Didn't I fire
you this morning for being late?" Leaning on her mom's shoulder, the daughter shoots
back, "Mom, you fire me every morning."

So it has gone for years and years—a community tradition born of the need for food,   22
comfort, and ritual. Everyday service to others is willingly and eagerly offered as a café
owner's privilege—a service tendered with love, not because it promotes good corporate culture or because it will bolster profits, but because these are Julie's day husbands,
her shakers and rollers, her girls. The Edison Café is a town's reliable home away from
home, where personal politics and pettiness must be checked at the door. From the dark,
foggy mornings to the breaks of sunshine in the afternoon, Julie knows that day in and
day out, for better and for worse, in Edison, Washington, she "gets 'em fed."

Connecting to Culture and Experience: Community Social Life

You belong to several communities: your college, your neighborhood if you live off campus, perhaps a church or other spiritual community. You can see that communities are small-scale, local, and somewhat intimate, in that people at least recognize and greet each other and perhaps even talk casually. Besides these occasional brief, casual interactions, people in a community are likely to seek more substantial social interactions and look for places to find it, like the customers at the Edison Café.

Think about the communities you have belonged to or now belong to, and identify one place where you occasionally met or meet now to talk informally with others. These would be meetings, indoors or out, with two or more people you consider friends or perhaps only acquaintances. The meetings recur, at least for a few weeks. There is typically no agenda or purpose for the meeting, even though you might eat together, play cards, or watch a sports event on television. It may be scheduled, or it may occur spontaneously. There could be a different mix of people at each meeting.

With two or three other students, describe in turn this place, detailing where you meet, who typically shows up, how frequently and for how long you talk, and what you talk about. Then together explore the social meanings of these informal meetings. That is, what is your motive for meeting? What sustains your interest in meeting? What do you gain as individuals and as a group from these meetings? What do you think holds together groups like this, and what dissolves them?

Analyzing Writing Strategies

1. A profile writer attempts to convey a perspective on a subject — a point of view on it, an insight into it, an idea about it, an interpretation of it, or even a judgment about its worth. This perspective can be stated or implied, and all the details and information in the profile must be consistent with this perspective. Hall states his perspective quite directly in paragraph 22. In that paragraph, underline phrases that identify the role of the Edison Café in the community. Also underline relevant phrases in paragraphs 7, 9, and 15. From these various statements, write a sentence of your own that concisely expresses your understanding of Hall's perspective on his subject.

2. Photographs seem a natural partner to the written text of a profile. Hall includes three with his text. With film or digital camera, you can create visual images to combine with the text of your profile. Any images you choose to include should complement the information your text offers and be consistent with your perspective on the subject.

   Consider Hall's images in relation to his text, and make notes about what the images contribute to your understanding of the Edison Café. Try to think about the text without the images. What do the images add that you could not imagine or infer about the café from the text itself? How do the images support Hall's perspective on the café?

Commentary: A Role for the Writer

Depending on their subjects and personal inclinations, profile writers usually adopt one of two roles: participant observer or detached observer. In the participant-observer role, the writer reports his personal involvement and engagement in the subject. John T. Edge adopts this role in profiling Farm Fresh Food Supplier by narrating his personal experience with a real pig lip, oozing red-dyed vinegar and other unidentified juices, caked with soggy crushed potato chips, soft and yielding to the touch. He inserts himself in a vivid and humorous way into his profile. In contrast, Trevor B. Hall adopts the detached-observer role in profiling the Edison Café. He remains invisible, merely a reporter of what he observes. Although most readers would assume that Hall had eaten a meal at the café, he offers no clues that he did so. His chosen role as a writer may not correspond to his role as a researcher, however. Sitting quietly at the counter, sipping his coffee, not talking to anyone—only observing—he could have learned much of what he presents in the profile. He could have remained a cool observer of activities. Instead, it is evident that he interviewed owner Julie Martin, two or three of the adult customers, and two of the elementary school students. It seems very likely that he ate at least one, maybe two, meals, since he was at the café from before 6 A.M. to after 12:30 P.M. Even though Hall almost certainly initiated conversations, drank many cups of coffee, and ordered a meal or two, he nevertheless adopts a detached-observer role in writing the profile.

Considering Topics for Your Own Essay

Consider writing about places or activities that fulfill a major—or even essential—social function in your community, just as the Edison Café does for many people who live in Edison, Washington. You might visit a place where people, perhaps of different ages, gather occasionally and informally, like a senior citizens' center, local park, bowling alley, campaign headquarters, public library reading room, coffee house, café, or bar. Or you might profile an activity with a community purpose, such as a parade, Little League game, church youth group, college informal study group, benefit walk-athon or marathon, gallery opening, bake sale, or jazz festival.

Brian Cable wrote the following selection when he was a first-year college student. Cable's profile of a mortuary combines both seriousness and humor. He lets readers know his feelings as he presents information about the mortuary and the people working there. As you read, notice how Cable manages to inform you about the business of a mortuary while taking you on a guided tour of the premises. Notice also how he expresses his lack of seriousness about a serious place, a place of death and grief.

The Last Stop

Brian Cable

Let us endeavor so to live that when we come to die even the undertaker will be sorry.

—MARK TWAIN

Death is a subject largely ignored by the living. We don't discuss it much, not as children (when Grandpa dies, he is said to be "going away"), not as adults, not even as senior citizens. Throughout our lives, death remains intensely private. The death of a loved one can be very painful, partly because of the sense of loss but also because someone else's mortality reminds us all too vividly of our own. 1

Thus did I notice more than a few people avert their eyes as they walked past the dusty-pink building that houses the Goodbody Mortuaries. It looked a bit like a church— tall, with gothic arches and stained glass—and somewhat like an apartment complex— low, with many windows stamped out of red brick. 2

It wasn't at all what I had expected. I thought it would be more like Forest Lawn, serene with lush green lawns and meticulously groomed gardens, a place set apart from the hustle of day-to-day life. Here instead was an odd pink structure set in the middle of a business district. On top of the Goodbody Mortuaries sign was a large electric clock. "What the hell," I thought, "Mortuaries are concerned with time, too." 3

I was apprehensive as I climbed the stone steps to the entrance. I feared rejection or, worse, an invitation to come and stay. The door was massive, yet it swung open easily on well-oiled hinges. "Come in," said the sign. "We're always open." Inside was a cool and quiet reception room. Curtains were drawn against the outside glare, cutting the light down to a soft glow. 4

I found the funeral director in the main lobby, adjacent to the reception room. Like most people, I had preconceptions about what an undertaker looked like. Mr. Deaver fulfilled my expectations entirely. Tall and thin, he even had beady eyes and a bony face. A low, slanted forehead gave way to a beaked nose. His skin, scrubbed of all color, contrasted sharply with his jet black hair. He was wearing a starched white shirt, gray pants, and black shoes. Indeed, he looked like death on two legs. 5

He proved an amiable sort, however, and was easy to talk to. As funeral director, Mr. Deaver ("Call me Howard") was responsible for a wide range of services. Goodbody Mortuaries, upon notification of someone's death, will remove the remains from the hospital or home. They then prepare the body for viewing, whereupon features distorted by illness or accident are restored to their natural condition. The body is embalmed and then placed in a casket selected by the family of the deceased. Services are held in one of three chapels at the mortuary, and afterward the casket is placed in a "visitation room," where family and friends can pay their last respects. Goodbody also makes arrangements for the purchase of a burial site and transports the body there for burial. 6

All this information Howard related in a well-practiced, professional manner. It was obvious he was used to explaining the specifics of his profession. We sat alone in the lobby. His desk was bone clean, no pencils or paper, nothing—just a telephone. He did all his paperwork at home; as it turned out, he and his wife lived right upstairs. The phone rang. As he listened, he bit his lips and squeezed his Adam's apple somewhat nervously. 7

"I think we'll be able to get him in by Friday. No, no, the family wants him cremated." 8

His tone was that of a broker conferring on the Dow Jones. Directly behind him was a 9
sign announcing "Visa and Master Charge Welcome Here." It was tacked to the wall, right
next to a crucifix.

"Some people have the idea that we are bereavement specialists, that we can 10
handle the emotional problems which follow a death: Only a trained therapist can do that.
We provide services for the dead, not counseling for the living."

Physical comfort was the one thing they did provide for the living. The lobby was 11
modestly but comfortably furnished. There were several couches, in colors ranging from
earth brown to pastel blue, and a coffee table in front of each one. On one table lay some
magazines and a vase of flowers. Another supported an aquarium. Paintings of pastoral
scenes hung on every wall. The lobby looked more or less like that of an old hotel. Nothing seemed to match, but it had a homey, lived-in look.

"The last time the Goodbodys decorated was in '59, I believe. It still makes people 12
feel welcome."

And so "Goodbody" was not a name made up to attract customers but the owner's 13
family name. The Goodbody family started the business way back in 1915. Today, they do
over five hundred services a year.

"We're in *Ripley's Believe It or Not,* along with another funeral home whose owners' 14
names are Baggit and Sackit," Howard told me, without cracking a smile.

I followed him through an arched doorway into a chapel that smelled musty and old. 15
The only illumination came from sunlight filtered through a stained glass ceiling. Ahead of
us lay a casket. I could see that it contained a man dressed in a black suit. Wooden
benches ran on either side of an aisle that led to the body. I got no closer. From the red
roses across the dead man's chest, it was apparent that services had already been held.

"It was a large service," remarked Howard. "Look at that casket — a beautiful work of 16
craftsmanship."

I guess it was. Death may be the great leveler, but one's coffin quickly reestablishes 17
one's status.

We passed into a bright, fluorescent-lit "display room." Inside were thirty coffins, lids 18
open, patiently awaiting inspection. Like new cars on the showroom floor, they gleamed
with high-gloss finishes.

"We have models for every price range." 19

Indeed, there was a wide variety. They came in all colors and various materials. 20
Some were little more than cloth-covered cardboard boxes, others were made of wood,
and a few were made of steel, copper, or bronze. Prices started at $400 and averaged
about $1,800. Howard motioned toward the center of the room: "The top of the line."

This was a solid bronze casket, its seams electronically welded to resist corrosion. 21
Moisture-proof and air-tight, it could be hermetically sealed off from all outside elements.
Its handles were plated with 14-karat gold. The price: a cool $5,000.

A proper funeral remains a measure of respect for the deceased. But it is expensive. 22
In the United States the amount spent annually on funerals is about $2 billion. Among
ceremonial expenditures, funerals are second only to weddings. As a result, practices
are changing. Howard has been in this business for forty years. He remembers a time

when everyone was buried. Nowadays, with burials costing $2,000 a shot, people often opt instead for cremation—as Howard put it, "a cheap, quick, and easy means of disposal." In some areas of the country, the cremation rate is now over 60 percent. Observing this trend, one might wonder whether burials are becoming obsolete. Do burials serve an important role in society?

For Tim, Goodbody's licensed mortician, the answer is very definitely yes. Burials 23 will remain in common practice, according to the slender embalmer with the disarming smile, because they allow family and friends to view the deceased. Painful as it may be, such an experience brings home the finality of death. "Something deep within us demands a confrontation with death," Tim explained. "A last look assures us that the person we loved is, indeed, gone forever."

Apparently, we also need to be assured that the body will be laid to rest in comfort 24 and peace. The average casket, with its inner-spring mattress and pleated satin lining, is surprisingly roomy and luxurious. Perhaps such an air of comfort makes it easier for the family to give up their loved one. In addition, the burial site fixes the deceased in the survivors' memory, like a new address. Cremation provides none of these comforts.

Tim started out as a clerk in a funeral home but then studied to become a mortician. 25 "It was a profession I could live with," he told me with a sly grin. Mortuary science might be described as a cross between pre-med and cosmetology, with courses in anatomy and embalming as well as in restorative art.

Tim let me see the preparation, or embalming, room, a white-walled chamber about 26 the size of an operating room. Against the wall was a large sink with elbow taps and a draining board. In the center of the room stood a table with equipment for preparing the arterial embalming fluid, which consists primarily of formaldehyde, a preservative, and phenol, a disinfectant. This mixture sanitizes and also gives better color to the skin. Facial features can then be "set" to achieve a restful expression. Missing eyes, ears, and even noses can be replaced.

I asked Tim if his job ever depressed him. He bridled at the question: "No, it doesn't 27 depress me at all. I do what I can for people and take satisfaction in enabling relatives to see their loved ones as they were in life." He said that he felt people were becoming more aware of the public service his profession provides. Grade-school classes now visit funeral homes as often as they do police stations and museums. The mortician is no longer regarded as a minister of death.

Before leaving, I wanted to see a body up close. I thought I could be indifferent after 28 all I had seen and heard, but I wasn't sure. Cautiously, I reached out and touched the skin. It felt cold and firm, not unlike clay. As I walked out, I felt glad to have satisfied my curiosity about dead bodies, but all too happy to let someone else handle them.

Connecting to Culture and Experience: Death

"Death," Cable announces in his opening sentence, "is a subject largely ignored by the living. We don't discuss it much, not as children (when Grandpa dies, he is said to be 'going away'), not as adults, not even as senior citizens." Yet when a family member dies, every family is forced to mark death in some way.

With two or three other students, discuss how your families and friends prepare for and arrange a funeral or memorial service. Think of a funeral you have attended, or ask a family member to describe how your family traditionally marks the death of a loved one. Consider the following questions, for example: Is there a formal service? If so, where does it take place — in a house of worship, a funeral home, a private home, a cemetery, or somewhere else? Who typically attends? Do people dress formally or informally? Who speaks, and what kinds of things are said? What kind of music, if any, is played? Is the body cremated or buried? Is there usually a gathering after the formal service? If so, what is its purpose compared to the formal service?

Then, together, compare the different family traditions revealed in the services described by the members of your group. Try to answer these questions: What do you think the funeral or memorial service accomplishes for each family? What did it accomplish for you personally?

Analyzing Writing Strategies

1. How does the opening quotation from Mark Twain shape your expectations as a reader? Compare Cable's opening (the quotation and paragraphs 1 and 2) against the openings of the two other profile essays in this chapter. What can you conclude about the opening strategies of these profile writers? Given each writer's subject, materials, and purpose, which opening do you find most effective and why?

2. During his visit to the mortuary, Cable focuses on four rooms: the lobby (paragraph 11), the chapel where funeral services are conducted (15), the casket display room (18–21), and the embalming room (26). Reread Cable's descriptions of these four rooms, and then underline the details he uses to describe each room. What impression do you get of each room? What might Cable gain by contrasting them so sharply? How do these descriptions work together to convey Cable's perspective on the mortuary?

Commentary: Conveying a Perspective

By deciding to present himself as a participant in his profile, Cable can readily convey his perspective, his ideas and insights, by telling readers directly what he thinks and feels about the mortuary and the people who work there. He begins with some general ideas about death and the way that people tend to deal with death basically by ignoring it. Then, in paragraphs 3 and 4, he discusses his expectations and confesses his apprehensions about the initial visit.

Cable quotes Howard and Tim and summarizes their words, describing them and commenting on what the funeral director and mortician said. His descriptions and comments express his insights into these people and the kinds of work they do. For example, when Cable introduces Howard Deaver, the funeral director, in paragraphs 5–10, he begins by comparing Deaver to his preconceptions about what an undertaker looks like. Then he describes Deaver, no doubt emphasizing his stereotypical features:

> Tall and thin, he even had beady eyes and a bony face. A low, slanted forehead gave way to a beaked nose. His skin, scrubbed of all color, contrasted sharply with his jet black hair. He was wearing a starched white shirt, gray pants, and black shoes. Indeed, he looked like death on two legs. (5)

The description creates an image that reinforces the stereotype of an undertaker. But that is apparently not the perspective he wants to convey because Cable quickly replaces this stereotype with a different one when he describes Howard's tone on the telephone with a client as "that of a broker conferring on the Dow Jones" (paragraph 9). To make sure readers get the idea that mortuaries are a big business, Cable points out that on the wall directly behind Howard "was a sign announcing 'Visa and Master Charge Welcome Here.'" Skillfully combining direct comment and concise description (sometimes called telling and showing), Cable conveys a perspective on mortuaries as efficient, profit-seeking businesses that nevertheless understand that their services provide clients with what they want and need at a difficult time.

Considering Topics for Your Own Essay

Try to list at least two or three places or activities that you have strong preconceptions about, and add a few notes to each one describing the preconception. For example, you might think that fast-food places are popular because their customers have few other choices of places to eat, that counselors will put pressure on you to conform if you ask for help with a personal problem at the student counseling center, that car repair shops regularly perform unnecessary repairs and overcharge customers, or that college librarians are too busy to help students find sources for their essays. Choose one such place or activity, and think about how you would go about profiling it. How would you test your preconception? How might you use your preconception to heighten readers' interest in your profile?

■ PURPOSE AND AUDIENCE

A profile writer's primary purpose is to inform readers about the subject of the profile. Readers expect a profile to present information in an engaging way, however. Whether profiling people, places, or activities, the writer must engage as well as inform readers. Readers of profiles expect to be surprised by unusual subjects. If the subject is familiar, they expect it to be presented from an unusual perspective. When writing a profile, you will have an immediate advantage if your subject is a place, an activity, or a person that is likely to surprise and intrigue your readers. For example, the writer of "I'm Not Leaving Until I Eat This Thing" (pp. 67–70) has the triple advantage of being able to describe an unusual snack food, a little-known production process, and a colorful bar in which he can try out the unusual snack. Even when your subject is familiar, however, you can still engage your readers by presenting it in a way they have never before considered. For example, the writer of "The Last Stop" describes a mortuary owner as an ordinary, efficient businessman and not a "bereavement specialist."

A profile writer has one further concern: to be sensitive to readers' knowledge of a subject. Since readers must imagine the subject profiled and understand the new information offered about it, the writer must carefully assess what readers are likely to know already. For a profile of a pig-products processor, the decisions of a writer whose readers have likely never seen a pickled pig lip or foot will be quite different from those of a writer whose readers occasionally hang out in jukes and other bars where pickled pig products are always visible floating in a bottle of garish-colored vinegar. Given Edge's attention to detail, he is clearly writing for a general audience that has never before seen a pickled pig lip or foot, much less considered eating one.

BASIC FEATURES: PROFILES

Description of People and Places

Successful profile writers master the strategies of description. The profiles in this chapter, for example, evoke all the senses: *sight* ("the pink juice pooling on the bar in front of me," Edge, paragraph 15); *touch* ("slick with grease," Edge, 16; "the skin . . . felt cold and firm, not unlike clay," Cable, 28); *smell* ("Vinegar vapors tickle my nostrils," Edge, 16); *taste* ("hot and vinegary," Edge, 7); *hearing* ("[plates] thudding on the counter under their own weight," Hall, 17; "sneakers squeaking across the wet pavement," Hall, 19); and *physical sensation* ("a gag that rolls from the back of my throat," Edge, 16; "my stomach ceases its fluttering," Edge, 18). *Similes* (elementary school students "like a mob running in panic from a fire," Hall, 19) and *metaphors* ("the air conditioner hacks and spits forth torrents of Arctic air," Edge, 1) appear occasionally.

Profile writers often describe people in graphic detail ("his shy smile framed by a coarse black mustache," Edge, 8; "beady eyes and a bony face," Cable, 5). They show people moving and gesturing ("he bit his lips and squeezed his Adam's apple," Cable, 7; "I poke and prod the six-inch arc of pink flesh," Edge, 14). Writers rely on dialogue to reveal character ("Look at that casket — a beautiful work of craftsmanship," Cable, 16; "You gonna eat that thing or make love to it?," Edge, 14).

Information about the Subject

Profile writers give much thought to how and where to introduce information to their readers. After all, readers expect to be informed — to learn something surprising or useful. To meet this expectation, profile writers' basic strategy is to interweave information with descriptions of the subject (as Cable does profiling a mortuary) and with narratives of events (as Edge does when he struggles to eat a pig lip). Throughout their profiles, writers make good use of several strategies relied on by all writers of explanation: classification, example or illustration, comparison and contrast, definition, process narration, and cause and effect.

Edge classifies information about Farm Fresh when, in one part of his profile, he divides information about the business into four categories: rebirth of the family business, family involvement, marketing strategies, and customer relations. Hall gives several examples of the kinds of food served at the Edison Café. Cable defines the terms "mortuary science" and "embalming fluid." Edge narrates the process of preparing and bottling pig lips and, after receiving instruction, of eating one. Edge presents the causes of Farm Fresh's failure as a business and of its rebirth, and he discloses frankly the effects of his attempts to eat a pig lip.

A Topical or Narrative Plan

Profile writers rely on two basic plans for reporting their observations: *topical*, with the information grouped into topics; and *narrative*, with the information interwoven with elements of a story. The profiles by Hall and Cable are organized narratively. In each, the narrative is a story of a single visit to a place. For Hall, the visit is a long morning from 6:30 A.M. to 12:30 P.M. spent at the Edison Café; even the long chunk of information about Skagit Valley that Hall presumably acquired at a different time (paragraphs 5–7) is inserted into the morning narrative. For Cable, the visit is one of indeterminate length, probably two or three hours, to Goodbody Mortuaries. (Some profile writers present information gathered from several visits as though it was learned in a single visit.)

In the central segment of his profile of a southern pig-products producer, Edge organizes the information topically: He creates topics out of the many bits of information he gathers on the tour of Farm Fresh led by the owner, Lionel Dufour, and then sequences them in the profile in a way that he thinks will be most informative to readers. Yet Edge frames the information about Farm Fresh with a narrative of his attempts to eat one of its products, illustrating that a profile can be organized topically in some parts and narratively in others. Usually, however, one plan or the other predominates. Which plan you adopt will depend on your subject, the kinds of information you collect, and your assessment of what might be most engaging and informative for your readers.

A Role for the Writer

Profile writers must adopt a role or stance for themselves when they present their subjects. There are two basic options: detached observer and participant observer. Hall remains a detached and invisible observer throughout his profile. There is no evidence that he participates in any of the activities or conversations at the Edison Café. In the central part of his profile, where he presents what he learned on his visit to Farm Fresh Food Supplier, Edge, too, is a detached observer. We can easily infer that he asked questions and made comments, but he decides not to report any of them; instead, he focuses unwaveringly on the equipment, canning process, workers, and Dufour family members. By contrast, Cable adopts a participant-observer role. Even before he enters the mortuary, he inserts himself personally into the profile, reflecting on death, expressing his disappointment in the appearance of the place, admitting his apprehension about entering, revealing his sense of humor. Readers know where he is at all times as his tour of the building proceeds, and he seems as much a participant in the narrative of his visit as Deaver and Tim are. Before he leaves the mortuary, he touches a corpse, to satisfy his curiosity. Edge adopts a participant-observer role when he tries to eat a pig's lip in the juke.

A Perspective on the Subject

Profile writers do not simply present their observations of a subject; they also offer insights into the person, place, or activity being profiled. They may convey a perspective on their subjects by stating it explicitly, by implying it through the descriptive details and other information they include, or both. Cable shares his realization that Americans seem to capitalize on death as a way of coping with it. Hall comes to understand that the warm, civil social interactions he observes at the Edison Café are more than merely pleasurable for the patrons: They are essential to social cohesion in Skagit Valley. Edge's perspective on pig products is less explicit, but perhaps, as a specialist in southern cooking, he hopes to convey the impression that regional foods remain important to many of the people who live in a region. In small southern towns, bar patrons are not satisfied by peanuts, pretzels, and packaged cheese and crackers. They want a soft, pink, vinegary pig lip shaken in a bag of crushed potato chips.

GUIDE TO WRITING
Profiles

THE WRITING ASSIGNMENT

Write an essay about an intriguing person, place, or activity in your community. Observe your subject closely, and then present what you have learned in a way that both informs and engages readers.

THE WRITING ASSIGNMENT

INVENTION & RESEARCH

Finding a Subject to Write About

Exploring Your Preconceptions

Planning Your Project

Posing Some Preliminary Questions

Discovering a Perspective

Considering Your Own Role

Defining Your Purpose for Your Readers

Formulating a Tentative Thesis Statement

Considering Document Design

INVENTION AND RESEARCH

PLANNING & DRAFTING

Seeing What You Have

Setting Goals

Outlining

Drafting

PLANNING AND DRAFTING

CRITICAL READING GUIDE

First Impression

Organization

The Writer's Role

Description

Quality and Presentation of Information

The Writer's Perspective

Final Thoughts

CRITICAL READING GUIDE

REVISING

A Description of People and Places

Information about the Subject

A Topical or Narrative Plan

A Role for the Writer

A Perspective on the Subject

REVISING

EDITING & PROOFREADING

Checking the Punctuation of Quotations

A Common ESL Problem: Adjective Order

EDITING AND PROOFREADING

GUIDE TO WRITING

■ THE WRITING ASSIGNMENT

Write an essay about an intriguing person, place, or activity in your community. Observe your subject closely, and then present what you have learned in a way that both informs and engages readers.

■ INVENTION AND RESEARCH

Preparing to write a profile involves several activities, such as finding a subject, exploring your preconceptions about it, planning your project, and posing some preliminary questions. Each step takes no more than a few minutes, yet together these activities will enable you to anticipate problems likely to arise in a complex project like a profile, to arrange and schedule your interviews wisely, and to take notes and gather materials in a productive way. There is much to learn about observing, interviewing, and writing about what you have learned, and these activities will support your learning.

Finding a Subject to Write About

When you choose a subject, you consider various possibilities, select a promising one, and check that particular subject's accessibility.

Listing Subjects. *Make a list of subjects to consider for your profile.* Even if you already have a subject in mind, take a few minutes to consider some other possibilities. The more possibilities you consider, the more confident you can be about your choice. Do not overlook the subjects suggested by the Considering Topics for Your Own Essay activities following each reading in this chapter.

Before you list possible subjects, consider realistically the time you have available and the amount of observing and interviewing you will be able to accomplish. Whether you have a week to plan and write up one observational visit or interview or a month to develop a full profile will determine what kinds of subjects will be appropriate for you. Consult with your instructor if you need help defining the scope of your profile project.

Here we present some ideas you might use as starting points for a list of subjects. Try to extend your list to ten or twelve possibilities. Consider every subject you can think of, even unlikely ones. People like to read about the unusual.

People

- Anyone with an unusual or intriguing job or hobby—a private detective, beekeeper, classic-car owner, or dog trainer

- A prominent local personality—a parent of the year, labor organizer, politician, consumer advocate, television or radio personality, or community activist
- A campus personality—a coach, distinguished teacher, or ombudsman
- Someone recently recognized for outstanding service or achievement—a volunteer, mentor, or therapist

Places

- A weight-reduction clinic, martial arts studio, body-building gym, or health spa
- A small-claims court, juvenile court, or consumer fraud office
- A used-car lot, old movie house, used-book store, antique shop, historic site, auction hall, flower or gun show, or farmers' or flea market
- A hospital emergency room, hospice, birthing center, or psychiatric unit
- A local diner; the oldest, biggest, or quickest restaurant in town; or a coffeehouse
- A campus radio station, computer center, agricultural research facility, student center, faculty club, museum, newspaper office, or health center
- A book, newspaper, or Internet publisher; florist shop, nursery, or greenhouse; pawnshop; boatyard; or automobile restorer or wrecking yard
- A recycling center; fire station; airport control tower; theater, opera, or symphony office; refugee center; orphanage; or convent or monastery

Activities

- A citizens' volunteer program—a voter registration service, public television auction, meals-on-wheels project, tutoring program, or election campaign
- A sports event—a marathon, Frisbee tournament, chess match, or wrestling or boxing meet
- A hobby—folk dancing, roller blading, rock climbing, or poetry reading

Listing Subjects Related to Identity and Community.   Writing a profile about a person or a place in your community can help you learn more about particular individuals in your community and about institutions and activities fundamental to community life. By *community* we mean both geographic communities, such as towns and neighborhoods, and institutional and temporary communities, such as religious congregations, college students majoring in the same subject, volunteer organizations, and sports teams. The following suggestions will enable you to list several possible subjects.

People

- Someone who has made or is currently making an important contribution to a community

- Someone who is a prominent member of one of the communities you belong to and can help you define and understand that community
- Someone in a community who is generally tolerated but is not liked or respected, such as a homeless person, a gruff store owner, or an unorthodox church member, or someone who has been or is in danger of being shunned or exiled from a community
- Someone who has built a successful business, overcome a disability or setback, supported a worthy cause, served as a role model, or won respect from coworkers or neighbors

Places

- A facility that provides a needed service in a community, such as a legal advice bureau, child-care center, medical clinic, or shelter offering free meals
- A place where people of different ages, genders, ethnic groups, or some other attribute have formed a kind of ongoing community, such as a chess table in the park, political or social action headquarters, computer class, local coffeehouse, or barber or beauty shop
- A place where people come together because they are of the same age, gender, or ethnic group, such as a seniors-only housing complex, a boathouse for a men's crew team, a campus women's center, or an African American or Asian American student center
- An Internet site where people form a virtual community, such as a chat room, game parlor, or bulletin board

Activities

- A team practicing a sport or other activity (one you can observe as an outsider, not as a participant)
- A community improvement project, such as graffiti cleaning, tree planting, house repairing, church painting, or highway litter pickup
- A group of researchers working collaboratively on a project

Listing Subjects Related to Work and Career. The following categories will help you consider work- and career-related subjects. Writing a profile on one of these possibilities can help you learn more about your attitudes toward your own work and career goals by examining how others do their work and pursue their careers.

People

- A college senior or graduate student in a major you are considering
- Someone working in the career you are thinking of pursuing
- Someone who trains people to do the kind of work you would like to do

Places

- A place on campus where students work — the library, computer center, cafeteria, bookstore, office, or tutoring or learning center
- A place where you could learn more about the kind of career you would like to pursue — a law office, medical center, veterinary hospital, research institute, television station, newspaper, school, software manufacturer, or engineering firm
- A place where people do a kind of work you would like to know more about — a clothing factory, coal mine, dairy farm, racetrack, restaurant, bakery, commercial fishing boat, gardening nursery, nursing home, or delicatessen
- A place where people are trained for a certain kind of work or career — a police academy, cosmetology program, video repair course, or truck drivers' school

Activities

- The actual activities performed by someone doing a kind of work represented on television, such as that of a police detective, judge, attorney, newspaper reporter, taxi driver, novelist, or emergency room doctor
- The activities involved in preparing for a particular kind of work, such as a boxer preparing for a fight, an attorney preparing for a trial, a teacher or professor preparing a course, an actor rehearsing a role, or a musician practicing for a concert

Choosing a Subject. *Look over your list of possibilities, and choose a subject that you find you want to know more about and that your readers will find interesting.* Note, too, that most profile writers report the greatest satisfaction and the best results when they profile an unfamiliar person, place, or activity. If you choose a subject with which you are somewhat familiar, try to study it in an unfamiliar setting. For example, if you are a rock climber and decide to write a profile on rock climbing, do not rely exclusively on your own knowledge of and authority on the subject. Seek out other rock-climbing enthusiasts, even interview some critics of the sport to get another perspective, or visit a rock-climbing event or training class where you can observe without participating. By adopting an outsider's perspective on a familiar subject, you can make writing your profile a process of discovery for yourself as well as for your readers.

Stop now to focus your thoughts. *In a sentence or two, identify the subject you have chosen, and explain why you think it is a good choice for you and your readers.*

Checking on Accessibility. *Take steps to ensure that your subject will be accessible to you.* Having chosen a subject, you need to be certain you will be able to make observations and conduct interviews to learn more about it. Find out who might be able to give you information by making some preliminary phone calls. Explain that you need information for a school research project. You will be surprised how helpful people can be when they have the time. If you are unable to contact knowledgeable people or get access to the place you need to observe, you may not be able to write on this subject. Therefore, try to make these initial contacts early.

Exploring Your Preconceptions

Explore your initial thoughts and feelings about your subject in writing before you begin observing or interviewing. Write for a few minutes about your thoughts, using the following questions as a guide:

What I already know about this subject

- How can I define or describe it?
- What are its chief qualities or parts?
- Do I associate anyone or anything with it?
- What is its purpose or function?
- How does it compare with other, similar subjects?

My attitude toward this subject

- Why do I consider it intriguing?
- What about it most interests me?
- Do I like it? Respect it? Understand it?

My own and my readers' expectations

- How do my preconceptions of this subject compare with my readers'?
- What might be unique about my preconceptions?
- What attitudes about this subject do I share with my readers?
- How is this subject represented in the media?
- What values and ideas are associated with subjects of this kind?

Testing Your Choice: A Collaborative Activity

At this point, you will find it useful to get together with two or three other students and describe the subject you have chosen to profile. Your instructor may ask you to do this collaborative activity either in class or online, using a chat room for your real-time discussion. It will help you decide whether you have chosen a good subject to write about, one that will allow you to proceed confidently as you develop your profile.

Presenters: Take turns identifying your subjects. Explain your interest in the subject, and speculate about why you think it will interest your readers.

Listeners: Briefly tell each presenter what you already know about his or her subject, if anything, and what would make it interesting to readers.

Planning Your Project

Set up a tentative schedule for your observational and interview visits. Whatever the scope of your project—a single observation, an interview with one follow-up exchange, or multiple observations and interviews—you will want to get the most out of your time with your subject. Chapter 12 offers guidance in observing and interviewing and will give you an idea of how much time you will need to plan, carry out, and write up an observation or interview.

Take time now to consult Chapter 12. Figure out the amount of time you have to complete your essay, and then decide what visits you will need to make, whom you will need to interview, and what library or Internet research you might want to do, if any. Estimate the time necessary for each. You might use a chart like the following one:

Date	*Time Needed*	*Purpose*	*Preparation*
10/23	1 hour	Observe	Bring map, directions, paper
10/25	2 hours	Library research	Bring references, change or copycard for copy machine
10/26	45 minutes	Interview	Read brochure and prepare questions
10/30	3 hours	Observe and interview	Confirm appointment; bring questions and extra pen

You will probably have to modify your plan once you actually begin work, but it is a good idea to keep some sort of schedule in writing.

If you are developing a full profile, your first goal is to get your bearings. Some writers begin by observing; others start with an interview. Many read up on the subject before doing anything else to get a sense of its main elements. You may also want to read about other subjects similar to the one you have chosen. Save your notes.

Researching Your Profile Subject: An Online Activity

One way to get a quick initial overview of the information available on the subject of your profile is to search for the subject online. Use Google (www.google.com) or Yahoo! Directory (http://dir.yahoo.com) to discover possible sources of information about the subject:

- For example, if you are profiling a beekeeper, you could get some useful background information to guide you in planning your interview by entering "bee keeping."
- If you are profiling a person, enter the full name to discover whether he or she has a personal Web site. If you are profiling a business or institution, the chances are even better that it offers a site. Either kind of site would orient and inform you prior to your interview or first visit.

Bookmark or keep a record of promising sites. After your interview with or visit to the subject, download any materials, including visuals, you might consider including in your own essay. If you find little or no information about your subject online, do not lose confidence in your choice. All of the information you need to develop your profile can come from your observations and interviews when you visit your subject.

Posing Some Preliminary Questions

Write questions to prepare for your first visit. Before beginning your observations and interviews, try writing some questions for which you would like to find answers. These questions will orient you and allow you to focus your visits. As you work, you will find answers to many of these questions. Add to this list as new questions occur to you, and delete any that come to seem irrelevant.

Each subject invites its own special questions, and every writer has particular concerns. Consider, for example, how one student prepares interview questions for her profile of a local office of the Women's Health Initiative, a nationwide fifteen-year study of women's health established by the National Institutes of Health in 1991. After reading about the long-term health study in her local newspaper, the student calls the local WHI office to get further information. The administrator faxes her a fact sheet on the study and her office's special part in it. The student knows that she will need to mention the study in her profile of the local office and the people who work there. She also hopes to interview women who volunteer to participate in the research. Consequently, she devises the following questions to launch her research and prepare for her interview of the local director:

- Why has so little research been done until recently on women's health?
- How did the study come about, and what is the role of the National Institutes of Health?
- Why does the study focus only on women between the ages of fifty and eighty?
- Will women from all income levels be involved?
- Why will it take fifteen years to complete the study?
- When was this office established, and what role does it play in the national study?
- Does the office simply coordinate the study, or does it also provide health and medical advice to women participating in the study?
- Who works at the office, and what are their qualifications to work there?
- Will I be able to interview women who volunteer to participate in the research?
- Will I be permitted to take photographs at the office?
- Would it be appropriate to take photographs of the researchers and participants, if they give their consent?

Discovering a Perspective

After you have completed your observations and interviews, write for a few minutes, reflecting on what you now think is interesting and meaningful about the person, place, or activity you have chosen for your profile. Consider how you would answer these questions about your subject:

- What visual or other sensory impression is most memorable?
- What does this impression tell me about the person, place, or activity?
- What mood do I associate with my subject?
- What about my subject is most striking and likely to surprise or interest my readers?
- What is the most important thing I have learned about my subject? Why is it important?
- If I could find out the answer to one more question about my subject, what would that question be? Why is this question important?
- What about my subject says something larger about our culture and times?
- Which of my ideas, interpretations, or judgments do I most want to share with readers?

Considering Your Own Role

Decide tentatively whether you will adopt a detached-observer or participant-observer role to present your profile. As a detached observer, you would focus solely on the place and people, keeping yourself invisible to readers. As a participant-observer, you would insert yourself personally into the profile by reporting what you said or thought during interviews and commenting on the activities you observe.

Defining Your Purpose for Your Readers

Write a few sentences, defining your purpose in writing about this particular person, place, or activity for your readers. Use these questions to focus your thoughts:

- Who are my readers? Apart from my instructors and classmates, who would be interested in reading an essay about this particular subject? If I were to try to publish my essay, what magazine, newspaper, newsletter, or Web site might want a profile on this particular subject? Would people who work in a particular kind of business or who pursue certain kinds of hobbies or sports be interested in the essay?
- What do I want my readers to learn about the person, place, or activity from reading my essay?
- What insight can I offer my readers about the person, place, or activity?

Formulating a Tentative Thesis Statement

Review what you wrote for Discovering a Perspective (p. 96), and add another two or three sentences that will help you tell readers what you understand about the person, place, or activity on which you are focusing. Try to write sentences that extend your insights and interpretations and that do not simply summarize what you have already written.

Keep in mind that readers do not expect you to begin a profile essay with the kind of explicit thesis statement typical of argumentative essays. If you decide to tell readers your perspective on the person, place, or activity, you will most likely do so through interpretive or evaluative comments as you describe people and places, present dialogue, and narrate what you observed. You are not obliged to tell readers your perspective, but you should show it through the way you profile the subject.

Considering Document Design

Think about whether visual or audio elements—photographs, postcards, menus, or snippets from films, television programs, or songs—would strengthen your profile. These are not at all a requirement of an effective profile, but they sometimes are helpful. Consider also whether your readers might benefit from design features such as headings, bulleted or numbered lists, or other typographic elements that can make an essay easier to follow.

■ PLANNING AND DRAFTING

This section will help you review your invention writing and research notes and get started on your first draft.

Seeing What You Have

Read over your invention materials to see what you have. You probably have a great deal of material—notes from observational and interview visits or from library research, some idea of your preconceptions, a list of questions, and perhaps even some answers. You should also have a tentative perspective on the subject, some idea about it or insight into it. Your goals at this point are to digest all of the information you have gathered; to pick out the promising facts, details, anecdotes, and quotations; and to see how it all might come together to present your subject and your perspective on it to readers.

If you have done your invention writing on the computer, you may have sentences or whole paragraphs that can be copied and pasted into your draft. Whether your material is on screen or on paper, highlight key words, phrases, and sentences, and either make annotations in the margins or use your computer's annotating function.

As you sort through your material, try asking yourself the following questions to help clarify your focus and interpretation:

- How do my preconceptions of the subject contrast with my findings about it?
- Can I compare or contrast what different people say about my subject? Do I see any discrepancies between people's words and their behavior?
- How do my reactions compare with those of the people directly involved?
- How could I consider the place's appearance in light of the activity that occurs there?
- If I examine my subject as an anthropologist or archaeologist would, what evidence could explain its role in society at large?
- Could I use a visual or other graphic to complement the text?

Setting Goals

The following questions will help you establish goals for your first draft. Consider each question briefly now, and then return to them as necessary as you draft and revise.

Your Purpose and Readers

- Are my readers likely to be familiar with my subject? If not, what details do I need to provide to help them understand and visualize it?
- If my readers are familiar with my subject, how can I present it to them in a new and engaging way? What information do I have that is likely to be unfamiliar or entertaining to them?
- What design elements might make my writing more interesting or easier for readers to understand?

The Beginning

The opening is especially important in a profile. Because readers are unlikely to have any particular reason to read a profile, the writer must arouse their curiosity and interest. The best beginnings are surprising and specific; the worst are abstract. Here are some strategies you might consider:

- Should I open with a brief anecdote, as Edge does, or an intriguing epigraph, as Cable does? Or can I open with an emphatic statement?
- Should I simply begin at the beginning, as Hall does?
- Can I start with an amazing fact, anecdote, or question that would catch readers' attention?

Description of People and Places

- How might I give readers a strong visual image of people and places?
- Can I think of a simile or metaphor that would help me present an evocative image?

- Which bits of dialogue would convey information about my subject as well as a vivid impression of the speaker?
- What specific narrative actions can I include to show people moving and gesturing?

Information about the Subject

- How can I fully satisfy readers' needs for information about my subject?
- How can I manage the flow of information so that readers do not lose interest?
- What special terms will I need to define for my readers?
- Would comparisons or contrasts make the information clearer and more memorable?

A Narrative or Topical Plan

Profile writers use two basic methods of organizing information, arranging it narratively like a story or topically by grouping related materials.

If You Use a Narrative Plan

- How can I make the narrative interesting, perhaps even dramatic?
- What information should I present through dialogue, and what information should I interrupt the narrative to present?
- How much space should I devote to describing people and places and to telling what happened during a visit?
- If I have the option of including design elements, how might I use them effectively—to clarify the sequence of events, highlight a dramatic part of the narrative, or illustrate how the people and places in the profile changed over time?

If You Use a Topical Plan

- Which topics will best inform my readers and hold their interest?
- How can I sequence the topics to bring out significant comparisons or contrasts?
- What transitions will help readers make connections between topics?
- If I have the option of including design elements, are there ways I can use them effectively to reinforce the topical organization?

A Perspective on the Subject

- How can I convey a perspective on the subject that seems original or at least fresh?
- Should I state my perspective or leave readers to infer it from the details of my presentation?

The Ending

- Should I try to frame the essay by repeating an image or phrase from the beginning or by completing an action begun earlier in the profile?
- Would it be effective to end by stating or restating my perspective?
- Should I end with a telling image, anecdote, or bit of dialogue or with a provocative question or connection?

Outlining

If you plan to arrange your material narratively, plot the key events on a timeline. If you plan to arrange your material topically, you might use clustering or topic outlining to help you divide and group related information.

The following outline suggests one possible way to organize a narrative profile of a place:

Begin by describing the place from the outside.

Present background information.

Describe what you see as you enter.

Introduce the people and activities.

Tour the place, describing what you see as you move from one part to the next.

Fill in information, and comment about the place or the people.

Conclude with reflections on what you have learned about the place.

Here is a suggested outline for a topical profile about a person:

Begin with a vivid image of the person in action.

Use dialogue to present the first topic.

Narrate an anecdote or a procedure to illustrate the first topic.

Present the second topic.

Describe something related to it.

Evaluate or interpret what you have observed.

Present the third topic, etc.

Conclude with a bit of action or dialogue.

All of the material for these hypothetical essays would come from observations, interviews, and background reading. The plan you choose should reflect the possibilities in your material as well as your purpose and readers. At this point, your decisions must be tentative. As you begin drafting, you will almost certainly discover new ways of organizing your material. Once you have written a first draft, you and others may see better ways to organize the material for your particular audience.

Drafting

General Advice.   Start drafting your essay, keeping in mind the goals you set while you were planning. As you write, try to describe your subject in a way that conveys your perspective on it. Turn off your grammar checker and spelling checker at this stage if you find them distracting. Don't be afraid to skip around in your draft. Jump back and fill in a spontaneous idea, or leap ahead and write a later section first if you find that easier. If you get stuck while drafting, explore the problem by using some of the writing activities in the Invention and Research section of this chapter (pp. 89–97).

As you read over your first draft, you may see places where you can add new material to reveal more about the person, place, or activity. You may even decide that after this first draft, you can finally understand the complexity of your subject and set out to convey it more fully in a second draft.

Sentence Strategies.   As you draft a profile, you will need to present what people have said to you and others during your observations and interviews and to help your readers imagine the actions, people, and objects you have encountered. Two sentence strategies called *speaker tags* and *absolute phrases* are useful for these purposes.

Use general and specific speaker tags along with other words and phrases to present what people say. When you directly quote (rather than paraphrase or summarize) what someone has said, you will usually need to identify the speaker. The principal way to do so is to create what is called a *speaker tag.*

You may rely on a *general* or all-purpose speaker tag, using forms of *say* and *tell:*

"We keep them under control," Emma *says.* (Trevor B. Hall, paragraph 20)

"It was a large service," *remarked* Howard. (Brian Cable, paragraph 16)

Other speaker tags may be more *specific* or precise:

"We used to buy lips from Dennis Di Salvo's company down in Belle Chasse," *recalled* Lionel. (John T. Edge, paragraph 9)

"Mornin'," *shouts* Julie from the kitchen. (Trevor B. Hall, paragraph 2)

As you draft your profile, consider using specific speaker tags. They give readers more help with imagining speakers' attitudes and personal styles. In addition, to any speaker tag you may add a word or phrase to identify or describe the speaker or to reveal more precisely *how, where, when,* or *why* the speaker speaks:

"We're in *Ripley's Believe It or Not,* along with another funeral home whose owners' names are Baggit and Sackit," Howard told me, *without cracking a smile.* (Brian Cable, paragraph 14)

"We do our best to corner the market on lips," Lionel told me, *his voice tinged with bravado.* (John T. Edge, paragraph 11)

"Now, don't you bad mouth me for that one," *she gently warns* a loser as she makes way back to the griddle. (Trevor B. Hall, paragraph 13)

Even though all of these sentence resources are available to help you make speaker tags more precise and revealing, keep in mind that experienced writers rely on general speaker tags using forms of *say* and *tell* without any added material for most of their sentences with quotations. Also keep in mind that some dialogue can be introduced without speaker tags, if it is likely the reader can infer from the context who is speaking. Turn to Brian Cable's essay for examples in paragraphs 8 and 10. (For information on punctuating sentences with quotations, see Chapter 14, p. 434.)

Use absolute phrases to help readers better imagine actions and people or objects. In profiling a subject, an unusual but very effective kind of sentence enables you to show simultaneous parts of a complex action or to detail observations of a person or object. Such a sentence relies on a grammatical structure known as an *absolute phrase,* which adds meaning to a sentence but does not modify any particular word in the rest of the sentence. (You need not remember its name or the grammatical explanation for it to use the absolute phrase effectively in your writing.) Here is an example, with the absolute phrase in italics:

> Slowly, the dank barroom fills with grease-smeared mechanics from the truck stop up the road and farmers straight from the fields, *the soles of their brogans thick with dirt clods.* (John T. Edge, paragraph 1)

Edge could have presented his observations of the farmers' shoes in a separate sentence, but the sentence he actually wrote helps to make more concrete and vivid the general idea that the customers who frequent Jesse's Place are working people arriving "straight from" their labors. Absolute phrases nearly always are attached to the end of a main clause, adding various kinds of details to it to create a more complex, informative sentence. They are usually introduced by a noun or a possessive pronoun like *his* or *their.* Here are three further examples of absolute phrases from this chapter's readings:

> This was a solid bronze casket, *its seams electronically welded to resist corrosion.* (Brian Cable, paragraph 21)

> Inside were thirty coffins, *lids open,* patiently awaiting inspection. (Brian Cable, paragraph 18)

> I offer the bag to Jerry, order yet another beer, and turn to eye the pig feet floating in a murky jar by the cash register, *their blunt tips bobbing up through a pasty white film.* (John T. Edge, paragraph 19)

Absolute phrases are certainly not required for a successful profile—experienced writers use them only occasionally—yet they do offer writers an effective sentence option. Try them out in your own writing.

In addition to using specific speaker tags and absolute phrases, you can strengthen your profile with other kinds of sentences as well, and you may want to turn to the discussions of sentences that place references to time at the beginning (p. 55).

CRITICAL READING GUIDE

Now is the time to get a good critical reading of your draft. Writers usually find it helpful to have someone else read and comment on their drafts, and all writers know how much they learn about writing when they read other writers' drafts. Your instructor may schedule readings of drafts as part of your coursework—in class or online. If not, you can ask a classmate, friend, or family member to read your draft. You could also seek comments from a tutor at your campus writing center. The guidelines in this section can be used by *anyone* reviewing a profile. (If you are unable to have someone else read your draft, turn ahead to the Revising section on p. 105, where you will find guidelines for reading your own draft critically.)

If you read another student's draft online, you may be able to use a word processing program to insert suggested improvements directly into the text of the draft or to write them out at the end of the draft. If you read a printout of the draft, you may write brief comments in the margins and lengthier suggestions on a separate page. When the writer sits down to revise, your thoughtful, extended suggestions written at the end of the draft or on separate pages will be especially helpful.

If You Are the Writer. To provide comments that are focused and helpful, your reader must know your essay's intended audience, your purpose, and a problem in the draft that you need help solving. Briefly write out this information at the top of your draft.

- *Readers:* Identify the intended readers of your essay.
- *Purpose:* What do you hope your readers will see and learn about your subject?
- *Problem:* Ask your draft reader to help you solve the most important problem you see with your draft. Describe this problem briefly.

If You Are the Reader. The following guidelines can be useful for approaching a draft with a well-focused, questioning eye.

1. *Read for a First Impression.* Read first to get a general impression. Then briefly write about the profile's perspective on its subject or main insight into it, as you best understand it. Next, consider the problem the writer identified, and respond briefly to that concern now. (If you find that the problem is covered by one of the other guidelines listed below, respond to it in more detail there if necessary.)

2. *Analyze the Effectiveness of the Organization.* Consider the overall plan, perhaps by making a scratch outline. Keep in mind that the plan may be narrative or topical or a combination of the two. If the plan narrates a visit (or visits) to a place, point out places where the narrative slows unnecessarily or

shows gaps. Point out where time markers and transitions would help. Let the writer know whether the narrative arouses and holds your curiosity. Where does dialogue fall flat, and where does it convey immediacy and drama? If the plan is organized topically, note whether the writer presents too much or too little information for a topic and whether topics might be sequenced differently or connected more clearly. Finally, decide whether the writer might strengthen the profile by reordering any of the parts or the details.

- *Look again at the beginning* of the essay to see whether it captures your attention. If not, is there a quotation, a fact, or an anecdote elsewhere in the draft that might make a better opening?

- *Look again at the ending* to see whether it leaves you hanging, seems too abrupt, or oversimplifies the subject. If it does, suggest another way of ending, possibly by moving a part or a quotation from elsewhere in the essay.

- *Look again at any visuals.* Tell the writer how well the visuals—headings, lists, tables, photographs, drawings, video—are integrated into the profile. Advise the writer about any visuals that seem misplaced or unnecessary.

3. *Evaluate the Writer's Role.* Decide whether the writer has adopted the participant-observer or detached-observer role or a combination of the two roles to present the profile subject. The writer has likely chosen one role or the other, but if both roles are visibly present, evaluate whether the writer really needs both roles or whether the alternation between the two is too frequent or confusing in any way. If the writer remains throughout in a participant-observer role, look for places where the writer is perhaps too prominent, dominating rather than featuring the subject. Point out where the writer-participant is most appealing and informative and also, perhaps, most distracting and tiresome. If the writer remains throughout in the detached-observer role, notice whether the writer consistently directs you where and how to look at the subject, keeping you confidently moving through the profile.

4. *Analyze the Description of People and Places.* Begin by pointing out two or three places in the profile where the description of people, places, and activities or processes is most vivid for you, where your attention is held and you can readily imagine who or what is being described. Identify places where you would like more descriptive details. Also indicate where you need to see people in action—moving, talking, gesturing—to understand what is going on.

5. *Assess the Quality and Presentation of the Information about the Subject.* Show the writer where you learned something truly interesting, surprising, or useful. Point out where the information is too complex, coming at you

too quickly, or incomplete. Ask for definitions of words you do not understand or clarification of definitions that do not seem immediately clear. Ask for a fuller description of any activity or process you cannot readily understand. Assess the clarity and informativeness of all visuals and design features. If there are parts of the information about the subject that you think could be better presented or complemented by visuals, let the writer know. Show the writer where the interweaving of description and information seems out of balance — too much of one or the other for too long.

6. ***Question the Writer's Perspective on the Subject.*** Begin by trying to state briefly what you believe to be the writer's perspective on the subject — some idea or insight the writer wants to convey. (This perspective statement may differ from the one you wrote at the beginning of your critical reading of this draft.) Then look for and underline one or two places where the writer explicitly states or implies a perspective. If the perspective is stated, tell the writer whether you fully understand or would welcome some elaboration. If the perspective is only implied, let the writer know whether you are content with the implication or whether you would prefer to have the perspective explicitly stated. With the writer's perspective in mind, skim the draft one last time looking for unneeded or extraneous description and information.

7. ***Give the Writer Your Final Thoughts.*** What is the draft's strongest part? What part is most memorable? What part is weakest or most in need of further work?

■ REVISING

This section will help you get an overview of your draft and revise it accordingly.

Getting an Overview

Consider your draft as a whole, following these two steps:

1. ***Reread.*** If at all possible, put the draft aside for a day or two. When you do reread it, start by reconsidering your purpose. Then read the draft straight through, trying to see it as your intended readers will.

2. ***Outline.*** Make a quick scratch outline on paper, or use the headings and outline/summary functions of your word processor.

Planning for Revision.   Resist the temptation to dive in and start changing your text until after you have a comprehensive view of what needs to be done. Using your outline as a guide, move through the document, using the change-highlighting or commenting tools of your word processor to note comments received from others and problems you want to solve (or mark on a hard copy if you prefer).

Analyzing the Basic Features of Your Own Draft. Turn to the Critical Reading Guide on pp. 103–5. Using this guide, reread the draft to identify problems you need to solve. Note the problems on your draft.

Studying Critical Comments. Review all of the comments you have received from other readers. For each comment, look at the draft to determine what might have led the reader to make that particular point. Try to be objective about any criticism. Ideally, these comments will help you see your draft as others see it (rather than as you hoped it would be) and to identify specific problems. Add to your notes any problems readers have identified.

Carrying Out Revisions

Having identified problems in your draft, you now need to figure out solutions and carry them out. Basically, you have three options for finding solutions:

1. Review your observation or interview notes for other information and ideas.

2. Do additional observations or interviews to answer questions that you or other readers raised.

3. Look back at the readings in this chapter to see how other writers have solved similar problems.

The following suggestions, which are organized according to the basic features of profiles, will get you started solving some problems common to this kind of writing.

A Description of People and Places

- *Should people be described briefly?* Consider naming and detailing a few physical features of each person. Recall, for example, Hall's descriptive phrases: "the local farmers . . . tall, hearty men with weathered baseball caps or cowboy hats, earned dirt under every fingernail" (paragraph 1); "Julie is an attractive woman in her early forties, her blond hair usually pulled back for cooking" (paragraph 11). Add comparisons, as Cable does when he says Howard Deaver "looked like death on two legs" (paragraph 5). Also consider adding specific narrative action. Think of Deaver again, on the phone: "As he listened, he bit his lips and squeezed his Adam's apple" (paragraph 7).

- *Can you enliven the description of the place?* Add other senses to visual description. Recall, for example, these sensory descriptions from the readings: sound (plates thudding on a countertop), texture (the soft flesh of a pig lip, a cold and firm cadaver), smell (vinegar vapors), and taste (a pig lip that tastes porcine).

- *Do readers have difficulty seeing people in action or imagining what is involved in the activity?* Add specific narrative actions to show people moving, gesturing, or talking. For example, recall Edge's description of the production line: "six women in white smocks and blue bouffant caps, slicing ragged white fat from the lips, tossing the good parts in glass jars, the bad parts in barrels bound for the rendering plant" (paragraph 4).

Information about the Subject

- **Do readers feel bogged down by information?** Look for ways to reduce information or to break up long blocks of informational text with description of scenes or people, narration of events, lists, or other design elements. Consider presenting information through dialogue, as Edge does.

A Topical or Narrative Plan

- **Does your narratively arranged essay seem to drag or ramble?** Try adding drama through dialogue or specific narrative action. Try using comparison and contrast.
- **Does your topically arranged essay seem disorganized or out of balance?** Try rearranging topics to see if another order makes more sense. Add clearer, more explicit transitions or topic sentences. Move or condense information to restore balance.
- **Does the opening fail to engage readers' attention?** Consider alternatives. Think of questions you could open with, or look for an engaging image or dialogue later in the essay to move to the beginning. Go back to your observation or interview notes for other ideas. Recall how the writers in this chapter open their profile essays: Cable combines a quote by Mark Twain with comments about how people try to ignore death, Edge sits at a juke bar staring at a pig lip, Hall stands in the dark outside the Edison Café waiting for Julie to arrive.
- **Are transitions between stages in the narrative or between topics confusing or abrupt?** Add appropriate words or phrases, or revise sentences to make transitions clearer or smoother.
- **Does the ending seem weak?** Consider ending at an earlier point or moving something striking to the end. Review your invention and research notes to see if you overlooked something that would make for a strong ending. Consider ending your essay with a quotation, as several writers in this chapter do.
- **Are the design features effective?** Consider adding textual references to any visual elements in your essay or positioning visuals more effectively. Think of other possible design features you might incorporate to enhance your profile. Use images, as do Hall and Edge.

A Role for the Writer

- **Do readers want to see more of you in the profile?** Consider revealing yourself participating in some part of the activity. Add yourself to one of the conversations you participated in, re-creating dialogue for yourself.
- **Do readers find your participation so dominant that you seem to eclipse other participants?** Bring other people forward into more prominent view by adding material about them, reducing the material about yourself, or both.

A Perspective on the Subject

- *Are readers unsure what your perspective is?* Try stating it more directly. Be sure that the descriptive and narrative details reinforce the perspective you want to convey.

- *Are your readers' ideas about the person, place, or activity being profiled different from yours?* Consider whether you can incorporate any of their ideas into your essay or use them to develop your own ideas.

- *Do readers point to any details that seem especially meaningful?* Consider what these details suggest about your own perspective on the person, place, or activity.

Checking Sentence Strategies Electronically. To check your draft for a sentence strategy especially useful in profiles, use your word processor's highlighting function to mark sentences that include direct quotations. Then look at each sentence to see whether and, if so, how you have identified the speaker. Where you have not identified the speaker, think about whether you need to do so by adding a speaker tag. Also consider whether you could help your readers better imagine speakers' attitudes and personal styles by making any speaker tags more specific, either by using a verb other than *say* or *tell* or by adding a phrase that tells how, where, when, or why the speaker spoke. For more on using speaker tags, see pp. 101–2.

■ EDITING AND PROOFREADING

Now is the time to check your revised draft for errors in grammar, punctuation, and mechanics. Our research has identified several errors that occur often in profiles, including problems with the punctuation of quotations and the order of adjectives. The following guidelines will help you check your essay for these common errors. This book's Web site also provides interactive online exercises to help you learn to identify and correct each of these errors; to access the exercises for a particular error, go to the URL listed after each set of guidelines.

Checking the Punctuation of Quotations. Because most profiles are based in part on interviews, you probably have quoted one or more people in your essay. When you quote someone's exact words, you must enclose those words in quotation marks and observe strict conventions for punctuating quotations. Check your revised draft for your use of the following specific punctuation marks.

All quotations should have quotation marks at the beginning and the end.

▶ "What exactly is civil litigation?" I asked.

Commas and periods go *inside* quotation marks.

► "I'm here to see Anna Post," I replied nervously.

► Tony explained, "Fraternity boys just wouldn't feel comfortable at the Chez Moi Café®."

Question marks and exclamation points go *inside* closing quotation marks if they are part of the quotation, *outside* if they are not.

► After a pause, the patient asked, "Where do I sign?"

► Willie insisted, "You can *too* learn to play Super Mario!"

► When was the last time someone you just ticketed said to you, "Thank you, Officer, for doing a great job?"

Use commas with speaker tags (*he said, she asked,* etc.) that accompany direct quotations.

► "This sound system costs only four thousand dollars," Jorge said.

► I asked, "So where were these clothes from originally?"

For practice, go to bedfordstmartins.com/conciseguide/quote.

A Common ESL Problem: Adjective Order.   In trying to present the subject of your profile vividly and in detail, you probably have included many descriptive adjectives. When you include more than one adjective in front of a noun, you may have difficulty sequencing them. For example, do you write *a large old ceramic pot* or *an old large ceramic pot?* The following list shows the order in which adjectives are ordinarily arranged in front of a noun.

1. *Amount:* a/an, the, a few, six
2. *Evaluation:* good, beautiful, ugly, serious
3. *Size:* large, small, tremendous
4. *Shape, length:* round, long, short
5. *Age:* young, new, old
6. *Color:* red, black, green
7. *Origin:* Asian, Brazilian, German
8. *Material:* wood, cotton, gold
9. *Noun used as an adjective:* computer (as in *computer program*), cake (as in *cake pan*)
10. *The noun modified*

For practice, go to bedfordstmartins.com/conciseguide/order.

A Note on Grammar and Spelling Checkers. These tools are good at catching certain types of errors, but currently there's no replacement for a good human proofreader. Grammar checkers in particular are extremely limited in what they can usually find, and often they only give you summary information that isn't helpful if you don't already understand the rule in question. They are also prone to give faulty advice for fixing problems and to flag correct items as wrong. Spelling checkers cause fewer problems but can't catch misspellings that are themselves words, such as *to* for *too.*

REFLECTING ON YOUR WRITING

Now that you have spent several days discussing profiles and writing one of your own, take some time for reflection. Reflecting on your writing process will help you gain a greater understanding of what you learned about solving the problems you encountered in writing a profile.

   Write a one-page explanation, telling your instructor about a problem you encountered in writing your profile and how you solved it. Before you begin, gather all of your writing invention material, planning and interview notes, drafts, critical comments, revision notes and plans, and final revision. Review these materials as you complete this writing task.

1. ***Identify one writing problem you needed to solve as you worked on your profile.*** Do not be concerned with grammar or punctuation; concentrate instead on problems unique to developing a profile. For example: Did you puzzle over how to organize your diverse observations into a coherent essay? Was it difficult to convey your own perspective? Did you have any concerns about presenting your subject vividly or controlling the flow of information?

2. ***Determine how you came to recognize the problem.*** When did you first discover it? What called it to your attention? If someone else pointed out the problem to you, can you now see hints of it in your invention writings? If so, where specifically? When you first recognized the problem, how did you respond?

3. ***Reflect on how you went about solving the problem.*** Did you work on the wording of a passage, cut or add details about your subject, or move paragraphs or sentences around? Did you reread one of the essays in this chapter to see how another writer handled a similar problem, or did you look back at the invention suggestions? If you talked about the problem with another student, your instructor, or someone else, did talking about it help? How useful was the advice you received?

4. ***Write a brief explanation of the problem and your solution.*** Reconstruct your efforts as specifically as possible. Quote from your invention notes or draft essay, others' critical comments, your revision plan, or your revised essay to show the various changes your writing underwent as you tried to solve the problem. When you have finished, consider how explaining what you have learned about solving this writing problem can help you solve future writing problems.

Explaining a Concept

Explanatory writing serves primarily to inform readers. Successful explanatory writing presents information confidently and efficiently, usually with the purpose of educating the reader about a subject. College students, however, are required to write explanations not primarily to teach others but to demonstrate what they have learned. Whether the explanation is researched or written from memory, the writer must analyze and evaluate a variety of kinds of information and then organize and synthesize the information to make a coherent presentation. This type of writing—which includes much of what we find in newspapers, magazines, and research reports—may be based on firsthand observations and interviews (as in Chapter 3) as well as on library and Internet research. Although writers of explanation may be experts on a subject, more often they are people who study what experts have discovered to convey that knowledge to others, as in the essays in the chapter.

This chapter focuses on one important kind of explanatory writing—explanations of concepts. The chapter readings explain the concepts of romantic love, indirect aggression, and cannibalism. These concepts name processes and phenomena like those you are studying in your college courses or using at work. Every field of study has its concepts: Physics has entropy, mass, and fission; literature has irony, romanticism, and postmodernism; music has harmony; art has perspective; mathematics has probability; and so on. You can see from this brief list that concepts are central to the understanding of virtually every subject. Moreover, when you begin to study a new field, you are expected to learn a new set of concepts. That is why introductory courses and their textbooks teach a whole new vocabulary of technical terms and specialized jargon. When you read the opening chapter of this textbook, for example, you were introduced to many concepts important to the study of writing, such as genre, writing process, invention, and revision.

Learning to explain a concept is especially important to you as a college student. It will help you read explanatory writing, a staple of academic discourse; it will prepare you to write a common type of exam and paper assignment; it will acquaint you with the basic strategies common to all types of explanatory writing—definition, classification, comparison and contrast, cause and effect, and process narration; and it will sharpen your skill in researching and using sources, abilities essential for success in college, whatever your major.

You will encounter writing that explains concepts in many different contexts, as the following examples suggest:

Writing in Your Other Courses

- For a linguistics course, a student writes a term paper tracing children's gradual control of sentences—or syntax, as linguists say—from about eighteen months to five or six years of age. The student first explains how researchers go about studying children's syntax, using several well-known studies as examples. Then he presents the widely accepted classification of stages that children go through as they gain control of syntax. As he presents each stage, he gives examples of children's syntax in their monologues and conversations in different situations, examples chosen from many possibilities in the published research studies. Even though he writes for his instructor, who is an expert in child language development, he carefully defines key terms to show that he understands what he is writing about.

- For a history of religion course, a student writes a research paper on religious fundamentalism. To explain this concept, she relies primarily on a book by a noted religious scholar. She follows the scholar's classification of the ways that fundamentalist religious groups are similar and organizes her paper around these similarities, which include a sense of threat and an organized reaction to the threat, a reliance on authoritative texts, a resistance to ambiguity and ambivalence, an inclination to behave aggressively toward unbelievers, an allegiance to a grand past, and a belief in a bright future. She illustrates each of these features of fundamentalism with examples from the beliefs and histories of fundamentalist groups around the world. She concludes by pointing out that religious fundamentalism began to be a major political force in the late twentieth century.

Writing in the Community

- Community policing has just been adopted by the police department in a mid-sized city, and a writer in the department's public relations division has been assigned to write and produce a brochure explaining the new approach. The brochure will be mailed to all homes in the city. The writer designs a small, fold-out, six-panel, two-sided brochure that will feature both text and photographs. The text briefly explains the major features of community policing, including the involvement of neighborhood residents and businesses in police decisions about crime-control priorities, the long-term assignment of officers to particular neighborhoods, increased reliance on foot and bicycle patrols rather than on car patrols, and the establishment of neighborhood police mini-stations. Working with a photographer, the brochure writer arranges to have photographs taken that represent the different features of community policing explained in the text.

- As part of her firm's plan to encourage managers to volunteer in the community for a few hours each month, a manager at a marketing research firm has been tutoring fifth-grade students in math. Learning about the manager's expertise in surveys, the teacher encourages her to plan a presentation to the class about surveying, an important research method in the social sciences. The manager agrees to do so and begins her lesson by having students fill out a brief questionnaire on their television-watching habits. She explains that she is not collecting data for marketing purposes but rather introducing them to surveys. With the students helping, she tabulates the results on a computer, separating the results by sex, time of week (weekdays or weekends), and kinds of television shows. Using a PowerPoint program, she projects the data onto a large screen so that everyone can see how the tables represent the survey results. The manager first guides a brief discussion of the survey and the results, helping students understand its purpose, form, and graphic representation. Then she shows them on the screen examples of questions from other surveys and explains who does such surveys, what they hope to learn, and how they report and use the results. She explains that the state tests that the students take every year are a form of survey. Finally, she passes out a short-answer quiz so that she and each student can find out how much has been learned about surveys.

Writing in the Workplace

- Returning from a small invitational seminar on the national security implications of satellite photography, the CEO of a space-imaging company prepares a report to his employees on the international debate about symmetrical transparency, the concept of using satellite photography to make everything on the planet visible to everyone on the planet at one-meter resolution—enough detail to reveal individual cars in parking lots, small airplanes on runways, backyard swimming pools, and individual shrubs and trees planted in parks. Aware of the financial implications for his company of the outcome of the debate, the executive carefully organizes his information and prepares a written text to read aloud to his employees, a one-page handout that lists key issues in the debate, and a transparency to project on a large screen during his presentation. He begins by reminding employees that the company's cameras already provide high-resolution images to government and corporate purchasers. Addressing the question of whether symmetrical transparency and the multinational monitoring that it makes possible compromise national security—or promise greater worldwide security and peace—the CEO gives a brief overview of key issues in the debate. These issues include how closed societies (like that of North Korea) will be affected differently from more open ones, whether global terrorism will be reduced or become more prevalent or more effective, and whether the chance of a nuclear standoff will be lessened. He concludes by pointing out that the big question for the U.S. government to answer soon is whether to attempt to control space or insist that it be open to everyone.

- Legislation in a western state defines a new concept in tourism—agritourism. To explain the concept, a state senator invites farmers, vineyard owners, and ranchers in his part of the state to an informal meeting. To prepare for the meeting, he writes a four-page summary of the legislation and prepares a one-page list of the main points in his presentation for everyone to pick up and read before the meeting begins. Assuming that his listeners have all visited a bed and breakfast inn, the senator compares the rules in the new law with the rules governing B&Bs. He emphasizes that in agritourism, guests tour a farm or ranch and participate in supervised chores. Meals must be offered three times a day and prepared and served by people who have been certified through coursework at a community college. He also explains that the greatest beneficiaries of agritourism will be small and medium-sized farms and ranches, where income is relatively low and varies greatly from year to year.

Practice Explaining a Concept: A Collaborative Activity

The preceding scenarios suggest some occasions for writing about concepts. Think of concepts you are currently studying or have recently studied or concepts connected to a job, sport, or hobby you know a lot about. Here are some possibilities: hip-hop, squeeze play, critical thinking, ambition, hypertext, interval training, photosynthesis, civil rights, manifest destiny, postcolonialism. Your instructor may schedule this collaborative activity as a face-to-face in-class discussion or ask you to conduct an online real-time discussion in a chat room. Whatever the medium, here are some guidelines to follow:

Part 1. Choose one concept to explain to two or three other students. When you have chosen your concept, think about what others in the group are likely to know about it and how you can inform them about it in two or three minutes. Consider how you will define the concept and what other strategies you might use—description, comparison, and so on—to explain it in an interesting, memorable way.

Get together with two or three other students, and explain your concepts to one another. You might begin by indicating where you learned the concept and in what area of study or work or leisure it is usually used.

Part 2. When all group members have explained their concepts, discuss what you learned from the experience of explaining a concept. Begin by asking one another a question or two that elicits further information that you need to understand each concept more fully. Then consider these questions:

- How did you decide what to include in your explanation and what to leave out?
- What surprised you in the questions that readers asked about your presentation?
- If you were to repeat your explanation to a similar group of listeners, what would you add, subtract, or change?

READINGS

No two essays that explain concepts are much alike, and yet they share defining features. Together, the three readings in this chapter reveal a number of these features, so you will want to read as many of them as possible. If time permits, complete the activities in the Analyzing Writing Strategies section that follows each selection, and read the Commentary. Following the readings is a section called Basic Features: Explaining Concepts (p. 136), which offers a concise description of the features of concept explanations and provides examples from the three readings.

Anastasia Toufexis has been an associate editor of Time, *senior editor of* Discover, *and editor in chief of* Psychology Today. *She has written major reports, including some best-selling cover stories, on subjects as diverse as medicine, health and fitness, law, environment, education, science, and national and world news. Toufexis received a bachelor's degree from Smith College in 1967 and spent several years reporting for medical and pharmaceutical magazines. She has won a number of awards for her writing, including a Knight-Wallace Fellowship at the University of Michigan and an Ocean Science Journalism Fellowship at Woods Hole Oceanographic Institution. She has also lectured on science writing at Columbia University, the University of North Carolina, and the School of Visual Arts in New York.*

The following essay was originally published in 1993 in Time *magazine. As you read, notice how Toufexis brings together a variety of sources of information to present a neurochemical perspective on love.*

Love: The Right Chemistry

Anastasia Toufexis

Love is a romantic designation for a most ordinary biological — or, shall we say, chemical? — process. A lot of nonsense is talked and written about it.

— GRETA GARBO to Melvyn Douglas in *Ninotchka*

O.K., let's cut out all this nonsense about romantic love. Let's bring some scientific precision to the party. Let's put love under a microscope.

When rigorous people with Ph.D.s after their names do that, what they see is not some silly, senseless thing. No, their probe reveals that love rests firmly on the foundations of evolution, biology and chemistry. What seems on the surface to be irrational, intoxicated behavior is in fact part of nature's master strategy — a vital force that has helped humans survive, thrive and multiply through thousands of years. Says Michael Mills, a psychology professor at Loyola Marymount University in Los Angeles: "Love is our ancestors whispering in our ears."

It was on the plains of Africa about 4 million years ago, in the early days of the human species, that the notion of romantic love probably first began to blossom or at least that the first cascades of neurochemicals began flowing from the brain to the bloodstream to produce goofy grins and sweaty palms as men and women gazed deeply into each other's eyes. When mankind graduated from scuttling around on all fours to walking on two legs, this change made the whole person visible to fellow human beings for the first time. Sexual organs were in full display, as were other characteristics, from the color of eyes to the span of shoulders. As never before, each individual had a unique allure.

When the sparks flew, new ways of making love enabled sex to become a romantic encounter, not just a reproductive act. Although mounting mates from the rear was, and still is, the method favored among most animals, humans began to enjoy face-to-face couplings; both looks and personal attraction became a much greater part of the equation. 4

Romance served the evolutionary purpose of pulling males and females into long-term partnership, which was essential to child rearing. On open grasslands, one parent would have a hard—and dangerous—time handling a child while foraging for food. "If a woman was carrying the equivalent of a 20-lb. bowling ball in one arm and a pile of sticks in the other, it was ecologically critical to pair up with a mate to rear the young," explains anthropologist Helen Fisher, author of *Anatomy of Love.* 5

While Western culture holds fast to the idea that true love flames forever (the movie *Bram Stoker's Dracula* has the Count carrying the torch beyond the grave), nature apparently meant passions to sputter out in something like four years. Primitive pairs stayed together just "long enough to rear one child through infancy," says Fisher. Then each would find a new partner and start all over again. 6

What Fisher calls the "four-year itch" shows up unmistakably in today's divorce statistics. In most of the 62 cultures she has studied, divorce rates peak around the fourth 7

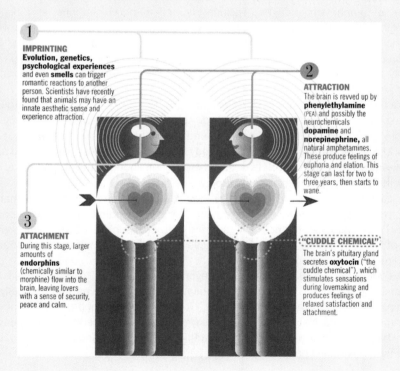

1 IMPRINTING
Evolution, genetics, psychological experiences and even **smells** can trigger romantic reactions to another person. Scientists have recently found that animals may have an innate aesthetic sense and experience attraction.

2 ATTRACTION
The brain is revved up by **phenylethylamine** (PEA) and possibly the neurochemicals **dopamine** and **norepinephrine,** all natural amphetamines. These produce feelings of euphoria and elation. This stage can last for two to three years, then starts to wane.

3 ATTACHMENT
During this stage, larger amounts of **endorphins** (chemically similar to morphine) flow into the brain, leaving lovers with a sense of security, peace and calm.

"CUDDLE CHEMICAL"
The brain's pituitary gland secretes **oxytocin** ("the cuddle chemical"), which stimulates sensations during lovemaking and produces feelings of relaxed satisfaction and attachment.

year of marriage. Additional youngsters help keep pairs together longer. If, say, a couple have another child three years after the first, as often occurs, then their union can be expected to last about four more years. That makes them ripe for the more familiar phenomenon portrayed in the Marilyn Monroe classic *The Seven-Year Itch*.

If, in nature's design, romantic love is not eternal, neither is it exclusive. Less than 8 5% of mammals form rigorously faithful pairs. From the earliest days, contends Fisher, the human pattern has been "monogamy with clandestine adultery." Occasional flings upped the chances that new combinations of genes would be passed on to the next generation. Men who sought new partners had more children. Contrary to common assumptions, women were just as likely to stray. "As long as prehistoric females were secretive about their extramarital affairs," argues Fisher, "they could garner extra resources, life insurance, better genes and more varied DNA for their biological futures. . . ."

Lovers often claim that they feel as if they are being swept away. They're not mis- 9 taken; they are literally flooded by chemicals, research suggests. A meeting of eyes, a touch of hands or a whiff of scent sets off a flood that starts in the brain and races along the nerves and through the blood. The results are familiar: flushed skin, sweaty palms, heavy breathing. If love looks suspiciously like stress, the reason is simple: the chemical pathways are identical.

Above all, there is the sheer euphoria of falling in love — a not-so-surprising reac- 10 tion, considering that many of the substances swamping the newly smitten are chemical cousins of amphetamines. They include dopamine, norepinephrine and especially phenylethylamine (PEA). Cole Porter knew what he was talking about when he wrote, "I get a kick out of you." "Love is a natural high," observes Anthony Walsh, author of *The Science of Love: Understanding Love and Its Effects on Mind and Body*. "PEA gives you that silly smile that you flash at strangers. When we meet someone who is attractive to us, the whistle blows at the PEA factory."

But phenylethylamine highs don't last forever, a fact that lends support to arguments 11 that passionate romantic love is short-lived. As with any amphetamine, the body builds up a tolerance to PEA; thus it takes more and more of the substance to produce love's special kick. After two to three years, the body simply can't crank up the needed amount of PEA. And chewing on chocolate doesn't help, despite popular belief. The candy is high in PEA, but it fails to boost the body's supply.

Fizzling chemicals spell the end of delirious passion; for many people that marks the 12 end of the liaison as well. It is particularly true for those whom Dr. Michael Liebowitz of the New York State Psychiatric Institute terms "attraction junkies." They crave the intoxication of falling in love so much that they move frantically from affair to affair just as soon as the first rush of infatuation fades.

Still, many romances clearly endure beyond the first years. What accounts for that? 13 Another set of chemicals, of course. The continued presence of a partner gradually steps up production in the brain of endorphins. Unlike the fizzy amphetamines, these are soothing substances. Natural pain-killers, they give lovers a sense of security, peace and calm. "That is one reason why it feels so horrible when we're abandoned or a lover dies," notes Fisher. "We don't have our daily hit of narcotics."

Researchers see a contrast between the heated infatuation induced by PEA, along   14
with other amphetamine-like chemicals, and the more intimate attachment fostered and
prolonged by endorphins. "Early love is when you love the way the other person makes
you feel," explains psychiatrist Mark Goulston of the University of California, Los Angeles.
"Mature love is when you love the person as he or she is." It is the difference between
passionate and compassionate love, observes Walsh, a psychobiologist at Boise State
University in Idaho. "It's Bon Jovi vs. Beethoven."

Oxytocin is another chemical that has recently been implicated in love. Produced by   15
the brain, it sensitizes nerves and stimulates muscle contraction. In women it helps uter-
ine contractions during childbirth as well as production of breast milk, and seems to
inspire mothers to nuzzle their infants. Scientists speculate that oxytocin might encourage similar cuddling between adult women and men. The versatile chemical may also
enhance orgasms. In one study of men, oxytocin increased to three to five times its normal level during climax, and it may soar even higher in women....

Chemicals may help explain (at least to scientists) the feelings of passion and com-   16
passion, but why do people tend to fall in love with one partner rather than a myriad of
others? Once again, it's partly a function of evolution and biology. "Men are looking for
maximal fertility in a mate," says Loyola Marymount's Mills. "That is in large part why
females in the prime childbearing ages of 17 to 28 are so desirable." Men can size up
youth and vitality in a glance, and studies indeed show that men fall in love quite rapidly.
Women tumble more slowly, to a large degree because their requirements are more complex; they need more time to check the guy out. "Age is not vital," notes Mills, "but the ability to provide security, father children, share resources and hold a high status in society
are all key factors."

Still, that does not explain why the way Mary walks and laughs makes Bill dizzy with   17
desire while Marcia's gait and giggle leave him cold. "Nature has wired us for one special
person," suggests Walsh, romantically. He rejects the idea that a woman or a man can be
in love with two people at the same time. Each person carries in his or her mind a unique
subliminal guide to the ideal partner, a "love map," to borrow a term coined by sexologist
John Money of Johns Hopkins University.

Drawn from the people and experiences of childhood, the map is a record of what-   18
ever we found enticing and exciting—or disturbing and disgusting. Small feet, curly hair.
The way our mothers patted our head or how our fathers told a joke. A fireman's uniform,
a doctor's stethoscope. All the information gathered while growing up is imprinted in the
brain's circuitry by adolescence. Partners never meet each and every requirement, but a
sufficient number of matches can light up the wires and signal, "It's love." Not every partner will be like the last one, since lovers may have different combinations of the characteristics favored by the map.

O.K., that's the scientific point of view. Satisfied? Probably not. To most people—   19
with or without Ph.D.s—love will always be more than the sum of its natural parts. It's a
commingling of body and soul, reality and imagination, poetry and phenylethylamine. In
our deepest hearts, most of us harbor the hope that love will never fully yield up its
secrets, that it will always elude our grasp.

Connecting to Culture and Experience: Love Maps

The chemistry of love is easily summarized: Amphetamines fuel romance; endorphins and oxytocin sustain lasting relationships. As Toufexis makes clear, however, these chemical reactions do not explain why specific people are initially attracted to each other. Toufexis observes that an initial attraction occurs because each of us carries a "unique subliminal guide" or "love map" (paragraph 17) that leads us unerringly to a partner. Moreover, she explains that men look for maximal fertility, whereas women look for security, resources, status, and a willingness to father children.

Discuss these explanations for attraction between the sexes. Consider where your love map comes from and how much it may be influenced by your family, your ethnicity, or images in the media or advertising. Consider whether it is possible for an individual's love map to change over time — from adolescence to adulthood, for example.

Analyzing Writing Strategies

1. At the beginning of this chapter, we made several generalizations about essays explaining concepts. Consider which of these assertions are true of Toufexis's essay:
   - It seeks to inform readers about a specific subject.
   - It presents information confidently and efficiently.
   - It relies almost exclusively on established information.

2. To explain a concept, you have to classify the information; that is, group or divide it into meaningful categories. Otherwise, you struggle to write about a jumble of information, and your readers quickly give up trying to make sense of it. For example, a writer setting out to explain testing in American colleges to a college student in Thailand would first try to classify the subject by dividing it into categories like the following: short-answer, essay, multiple-choice, lab demonstration, artistic performance.

   To understand more about how Toufexis classifies her information, make a scratch outline of paragraphs 9–15, where she presents the centrally important information on specific chemicals. How is the information divided and sequenced in these paragraphs? What cues does Toufexis provide to help you follow the sequence? What do you find most and least successful about the division?

Commentary: A Focused Concept and Careful Use of Sources

Unless they are writing entire books, writers explaining concepts must focus their attention on particular aspects of concepts. For instance, Toufexis focuses in her relatively brief magazine article on the chemistry of love between adult human heterosexual mates. She excludes homosexual love, parents' love for their children, dogs' love for their masters, views on love by various religions, the history of romance as revealed in literature, courtship rituals through time, and dozens of other possible subjects related to love. Toufexis holds to her chemical focus throughout the essay, except for a brief but relevant digression about "love maps" toward the end. When they finish the essay, readers have learned nothing new about love in general, but they are well informed about the neurochemistry of love. By keeping to this narrow focus, Toufexis is able to present information that is likely to be new to most readers and therefore is more likely to hold readers' attention.

Besides maintaining a focus on a specific aspect of a concept, concept explanations rely on authoritative, expert sources, on established material gleaned from reputable publications or interviews. Toufexis uses both these kinds of sources. She apparently arranged telephone or in-person interviews with six different professors specializing in diverse academic disciplines: psychology, anthropology, psychiatry, and sexology. (She does not immediately identify the discipline of one professor — Walsh, in paragraph 10 — but from the title of his book, we might guess that he is a biochemist, and in paragraph 14 we are not surprised to learn that he is a psychobiologist.) We assume that Toufexis read at least parts of the two books she names in paragraphs 5 and 10, and perhaps she also read other sources, which may have led her to some of the professors she interviewed.

What is most notable about Toufexis's use of sources is that she does not indicate precisely where she obtained all the information she includes. For example, she does not cite the source of the anthropological information in paragraphs 3–5, although a reader might guess that she summarized it from *Anatomy of Love*, cited at the end of paragraph 5. We cannot be certain whether the quote at the end of paragraph 5 comes from the book or from an interview with its author. As long as she gives general indications of where her information comes from, Toufexis can safely assume that her readers will not fault her for failing to provide exact bibliographical information. These liberties in citing sources are expected by experienced readers of magazines and newspapers, including the leading ones that educated readers count on to keep them up to date on developments in various fields. Readers would be surprised to find footnotes or works cited lists in popular publications.

In most college writing, however, sources must be cited. Moreover, college writers — whether students or professors — are expected to follow certain styles for citing and acknowledging their sources, such as MLA style in English and APA style in psychology. Academic writers cite sources because credit must be given to the authors of any work that contributes to a new piece of work. To learn more about avoiding plagiarism and documenting sources using MLA or APA styles, turn to Chapter 14.

Observing a third important requirement of essays that explain concepts, Toufexis provides several different kinds of cues to keep readers on track. In addition to paragraph-opening transitions, Toufexis carefully forecasts the topics and direction of her essay in her second paragraph: "their probe reveals that love rests firmly on the foundations of evolution, biology and chemistry." This forecast helps readers anticipate the types of scientific information Toufexis has selected for her special focus on love and the sequence that she will use to introduce them.

Considering Topics for Your Own Essay

Like Toufexis, you could write an essay about love or romance, but you could choose a different focus: on its history (how and when did it develop as an idea in the West?), its cultural characteristics (how is love regarded currently among different American ethnic groups or world cultures?), its excesses or extremes, its expression between parent and child, or the phases of falling in and out of love. Also consider writing about other concepts involving personal relationships, such as jealousy, codependency, idealization, stereotyping, or homophobia.

Natalie Angier studied English, physics, and astronomy in college and "dreamed of starting a popular magazine about science for intelligent lay readers who wanted to know more about what's going on across the great divide of C. P. Snow's two cultures"—the sciences and the humanities. At the age of twenty-two, she realized her dream when she joined the founding staff of Discover *magazine. Since then, she has worked as a science writer for newspapers (winning a Pulitzer Prize for her* New York Times *writing on biology and medicine), magazines (such as* Time, *the* Atlantic Monthly, *and* Reader's Digest), *and television (Fox and the Canadian Broadcasting Corporation). In addition to the Pulitzer, Angier has won other distinguished honors for science writing, including the Lewis Thomas Award and recognition from the American Association for the Advancement of Science (AAAS). She also has taught science writing at New York University's Graduate Program in Science and Environmental Reporting and edited* The Best American Science and Nature Writing 2002. *Angier has written four books, including* Natural Obsessions: Striving to Unlock the Deepest Secrets of the Cancer Cell *(1988);* The Beauty of the Beastly: New Views on the Nature of Life *(1995); and* Woman: An Intimate Geography *(1999), a National Book Award finalist, from which the following selection explaining the concept of indirect aggression is excerpted.*

Like Toufexis writing for Time *magazine, Angier is writing for a popular audience, the "intelligent lay readers" she dreamed of writing for when she was still a college student. As an experienced popularizer or translator of scientific research, Angier knows that she needs to present information authoritatively and show readers that she has done her research so that they will have confidence in the credibility of the information she is presenting. As you read, consider how well she succeeds in convincing you to accept her authority.*

Indirect Aggression
Natalie Angier

This study has been done many times. If you take a group of babies or young toddlers and dress them in nondescript, non-sex-specific clothes—yellow is always a good color!—and make sure that their haircuts don't give them away, and if you put them in a room with a lot of adults watching, the adults will not be able to sex the children accurately. The adults will try, based on the behaviors of each child, but they will be right no more often than they would be if they flipped a coin. This has been shown again and again, but still we don't believe it. We think we can tell a boy or a girl by the child's behavior, specifically by its level of aggressiveness. If you show a person a videotape of a crying baby and tell her the baby is a boy, the observer will describe the baby as looking angry; if you tell the person the baby is a girl, she will say the child is scared or miserable.

I am at a party with my daughter, who is sixteen months old. A boy who is almost eighteen months comes into the room and takes a toy away from my daughter. I say something humorous to her about how she's got to watch out for those older kids, they'll always try to push you around. And the boy's mother says, "It's also because he's a boy." That's what happens at this age, she says. The boys become very boyish. A little while later, a girl who is almost eighteen months old takes my daughter's cup of milk away from her. The mother of the other girl doesn't say, "It's because she's a girl, she's becoming girlish." Of course she doesn't say that; it would make no sense, would it? An older girl taking a cup away from a younger girl has nothing to do with the girlness of either party. But taking the toy away is viewed as inherent to the older boy's boyness.   2

I felt very aggressive about the whole thing; alas, not being a toddler, I couldn't go and kick anybody in the kneecap. Which is the sort of thing that toddlers do, whatever their sex. They kick, they hit, they scream, they throw objects around, they act like pills past their expiration date. And we adults put up with it, and we subscribe to the myth of the helpless, innocent child, and it's a good thing we do and that children are cute, because otherwise we might well see the truth: that our children are born with astonishing powers, and with brains that seem by default to counsel aggression.   3

"Young children are like animals," says Kaj Björkqvist, of Turku Akademi University in Finland. "Before they have language, they have their bodies. And through their bodies they can be aggressive, and so that is what they do, that is how they are. They are physically aggressive—boys, girls, all of them." Björkqvist studies female aggression. He has done cross-cultural comparisons of children in Europe, North America, the Middle East, and Asia. Everywhere he has found that young children are physically aggressive, and that before the age of three, there are no significant differences between girl aggression and boy aggression.   4

We grow into our sex-specific aggressions. We own the code of aggression from birth, and we perfect its idiom through experience and experimentation. . . . When the mind comes into its own and the child starts speaking fluently, purposefully, adults become less tolerant of physical aggression. Today, in most cultures, acceptance of physical aggression declines as the child gets older; by the time a person reaches puberty, the tendency to use physical force to wrest a desired object or behavior from another is considered frankly pathological. This is true for both sexes, but particularly for girls. Physical aggression is discouraged in girls in manifold and aggressive ways. Not only are they instructed against offensive fighting; they are rarely instructed in defensive fighting. Girls don't learn how to throw a punch. Humor is another form of aggression, and until recently humor has been used to squelch the very notion of a warrior female. Just the thought of a girl-fight, and people snicker and rub their hands with glee. Cat fight! Scratching, screeching, pulling hair, and falling on butt with skirt hiked in the air! Happily, the smirky parody of girl-fights has gotten a bit paunchy and dated of late, and instead we've been treated to images of GI Janes and bodiced Xenas wielding swords and Klingon women   5 with brickbat fists, though whether the mass media's revisionist fighting female has been driven by attitudinal change or by the need to jolt a bored and distracted audience is unclear.

Whatever the media moment may be, girls still do not often engage in physical fights. The older children get, the less physically aggressive they become — though not always, and not everywhere — but the dropoff rate for the use of physical aggression in girls is much sharper than it is for boys. At least in the developed West, by the time girls and boys are in third grade, boys are about three times as likely as girls to kick or strike at somebody who makes them mad. What then do girls do with that aggressiveness, which in the bliss of preverbalism could speak through hands and feet? It does not go away. It finds a new voice. It finds words. Girls learn to talk hornet talk. Mastering curse words and barbed insults is an essential task of childhood. Girls also learn to use their faces as weapons. Expressions like sticking out your tongue or rolling your eyes or curling your lip all seem funny to adults, but studies show that they aren't funny to children, and that they can be effective in conveying anger and dislike or in ostracizing an undesirable. Aggression researchers initially thought that girls had the edge over boys in verbal aggression and that they were more likely than boys to belittle their peers with words and facial flexions, but a series of Finnish studies of eight- and eleven-year-olds suggested otherwise. The researchers sought to determine how children responded when they were angry. They asked the children to describe themselves and their reactions to being roused to rage; they asked teachers and parents to describe how the children reacted in conflict; and they asked children to talk about each other, to rate each other's rileability and behaviors in a squall. The scientists found that boys and girls were equally likely to use verbal aggression against their cohorts, to call them nasty names to their faces, to yell, to mock, to try to make the despised ones look stupid. And so boys kick and fight more than girls do, and the sexes argue and chide in equal amounts. We might then conclude that boys are more aggressive, for they shout with their mouths and on occasion with their bodies, while the girls keep their fists to themselves.   6

There are other ways in which rage emerges among girls, though, ways that are roughly girl-specific. A girl who is angry often responds by stalking off, turning away, snubbing the offender, pretending she doesn't exist. She withdraws, visibly so, aggressively so. You can almost hear the thwapping of her sulk. Among eleven-year-olds, girls are three times more likely than boys to express their anger in the form of a flamboyant snub. In addition, girls at this age, more than boys, engage in a style of aggression called indirect aggression.   7

I'll admit up front that I dislike this form of aggression, and that to mention it is to reinforce clichés about female treachery and female conniving. Yet it is an aggression that we gals know, because we grew up as girls and we saw it and struggled against it and hated it and did it ourselves. Indirect aggression is anonymous aggression. It is backbiting, gossiping, spreading vicious rumors. It is seeking to rally others against the despised but then denying the plot when confronted. The use of indirect aggression increases over time, not just because girls don't generally use their fists to make their point, but because the effectiveness of indirect aggression is tied to the fluency of a person's social intelli-   8 gence; the more sophisticated the person, the cleverer her use of the dorsal blade. In this sense, then, a girl's supposed head start over boys in verbal fluency may give her an edge in applying an indirect form of aggression. But the advantage, such as it is, doesn't last, for males catch up, and by the time we reach adulthood we have all become political animals, and men and women are, according to a number of studies, equally likely to express their aggression covertly. Despite rumors to the contrary, systematic eavesdroppings have revealed that men and women gossip an equal amount about their friends, families, colleagues, and celebrities. Adults of both sexes go to great lengths to express their antipathy toward one another indirectly, in ways that mask their hostile intent while still getting the jab done. For example, a person might repeatedly interrupt an opponent during an office meeting, or criticize the antagonist's work, rather than attacking his or her character—even though the source of the aggressor's ire has nothing to do with the quality of the opponent's performance.

Indirect aggression is not pretty, nor is it much admired. To the contrary it is universally condemned. When children and adults are asked to describe their feelings about the various methods of expressing anger, backstabbing behavior ranks at the bottom, below a good swift kick to the crotch. Yet there it is, with us, among us, not exclusively female by any means, but a recognizable hazard of girlhood. Part of the blame lies with the myth of the good-girl, for the more girls are counseled against direct forms of aggression and the more geniality of temperament is prized, the greater is the likelihood that the tart girls will resort to hidden machinations to get what they want. In cultures where girls are allowed to be girls, to speak up and out, they are in fact more verbally, directly aggressive and less indirectly aggressive than in cultures where girls and women are expected to be demure. In Poland, for example, a good smart mouth is considered a female asset, and girls there rag each other and pull no punches and report feeling relatively little threat of intragroup skullduggery. Among female Zapotec Indians in Mexico, who are exceedingly subordinate to men, indirect aggression prevails. Among the Vanatinai of Papua New Guinea, one of the most egalitarian and least stratified societies known to anthropologists, women speak and move as freely as they please, and they sometimes use their fists and feet to demonstrate their wrath, and there is no evidence of a feminine edge in covert operations.

Another reason that girls may resort to indirect aggression is that they feel such extraordinary aggression toward their friends—lashing, tumbling, ever-replenishing aggression. Girl friendships are fierce and dangerous. The expression "I'll be your best friend" is not exclusively a girl phrase, but girls use it a lot. They know how powerful the words are, how significant the offer is. Girls who become good friends feel a compulsion to define the friendship, to stamp it and name it, and they are inclined to rank a close friend as a best friend, with the result that they often have many best friends. They think about their friends on a daily basis and try to figure out where a particular friend fits that day in their cosmology of friendships. Is the girl her best friend today, or a provisional best friend, pending the resolution of a minor technicality, a small bit of friction encountered the day before? The girl may want to view a particular girl as her best friend, but she worries how her previous best friend will take it—as a betrayal or as a potential benefit, a bringing in of a new source of strength to the pair. Girls fall in love with each other and feel an intimacy for each other that is hard for them to describe or understand.

When girls are in groups, they form coalitions of best friends, two against two, or two in edgy harmony with two. A girl in a group of girls who doesn't feel that she has a specific ally feels at risk, threatened, frightened. If a girl who is already incorporated into the group decides to take on a newcomer, to sponsor her, the resident girl takes on a weighty responsibility, for the newcomer will view her as (for the moment) her best friend, her only friend, the guardian of her oxygen mask. 11

When girls have a falling-out, they fall like Alice down the tunnel, convinced that it will never end, that they will never be friends again. The Finnish studies of aggression among girls found that girls hold grudges against each other much longer than boys do. "Girls tend to form dyadic relationships, with very deep psychological expectations from their best friends," Björkqvist said. "Because their expectations are high, they feel deeply betrayed when the friendship falls apart. They become as antagonistic afterwards as they had been bonded before." If a girl feels betrayed by a friend, she will try to think of ways to get revenge in kind, to truly hurt her friend, as she has been hurt. Fighting physically is an unsatisfactory form of punishing the terrible traitor. It is over too quickly. To express anger might work if the betrayer accepts the anger and responds to it with respect. But if she doesn't acknowledge her friend's anger or sense of betrayal, if she refuses to apologize or admit to any wrongdoing, or if she goes further, walking away or mocking or snubbing her friend, at that point a girl may aim to hurt with the most piercing and persistent tools for the job, the psychological tools of indirect, vengeful aggression, with the object of destroying the girl's position, her peace of mind, her right to be. Indirect aggression is akin to a voodoo hex, an anonymous but obsessive act in which the antagonist's soul, more than her body, must be got at, must be penetrated, must be nullified. 12

Connecting to Culture and Experience: Gender and Aggression

Angier makes the point that although both boys and girls use both direct and indirect aggression, adolescent boys are more likely to use direct aggression and girls of the same age are more likely to use indirect aggression. Try to recall one experience from your adolescent and teenage years of each kind of aggression — indirect and direct — when you were either the aggressor or the victim of aggression.

With two or three other students, discuss your experience with these two kinds of aggression. For each of the experiences you recall, tell what happened, who was involved, and what was said and done. Then discuss whether your experience supports the research Angier cites showing that adolescent boys use direct aggression more often than girls, and girls use indirect aggression more often than boys. Also discuss your attitudes toward these two kinds of aggression. Note that Angier states that she personally dislikes indirect aggression and that it is "universally condemned" (paragraph 9). Which kind of aggression, if any, do you think is more acceptable, and by whom? If you think that one kind of aggression tends to be preferred or relied on more than the other, how would you explain the preference?

Analyzing Writing Strategies

1. Reread paragraphs 1–3 to see how Angier begins this concept explanation. Focus first on paragraph 1. What is the point of this paragraph? Having already read the rest of the selection, how do you think this first paragraph prepares readers for the explanation that follows? What does it lead readers to expect will follow?

    Now focus on paragraphs 2 and 3. What is the point of these paragraphs? How do they prepare readers for the explanation that follows?

    Finally, speculate on why Angier chose to begin her essay with these two different openings. How effective for you is this way of beginning? If you were to choose, which opening would you keep, and why? If you think they work together well, comment on why you think so.

2. In paragraphs 9–12, Angier presents two causes for girls' apparent preference for indirect over direct aggression. Reread these paragraphs to identify the two causes and to notice that Angier is not arguing for her own speculations about why girls prefer indirect aggression. Instead, she has decided that for readers to understand the concept of indirect aggression, they need to know what researchers have determined to be the causes for girls' reliance on indirect aggression. Therefore, she devotes several paragraphs to reporting the causes established by field and experimental research studies. Review these paragraphs, and highlight the passages where she is referring to sources she has read in the library and possibly on the Internet.

    Notice also that Angier explains one cause rather quickly but spends several paragraphs elaborating her explanation of the other cause. How well do you think she explains each of these causes? Why do you think she decided to go into more detail about one cause and not the other?

3. To explain indirect aggression, Angier makes effective use of a sentence strategy that relies on a grammatical structure known as an *appositive*. Underline these appositives: in paragraph 10, sentence 1, from *lashing* to the end; paragraph 10, sentence 8, from *bringing in* to the end; paragraph 11, sentence 1, from *two against two* to the end; paragraph 12, the second from last sentence, from *psychological* through *aggression;* paragraph 12, the last sentence, from *an anonymous* to the end. Now compare each appositive to what comes before in its sentence. Make notes in the margin about how the appositive and what comes before seem to be related to each other. What does each appositive contribute? How are the five of them alike and different in what they add to the sentence? (For more on sentence strategies important to writers explaining concepts, turn to Sentence Strategies, p. 150.)

Commentary: Using Comparison/Contrast to Explain Concepts

As a writer experienced in explaining new concepts, Angier knows that perhaps the best way to explain something unfamiliar is to relate it to something familiar. Comparing and contrasting seeks to make clear how the unfamiliar is like or unlike the familiar. In this selection, Angier sets up three kinds of comparisons: between indirect aggression and other kinds of aggression, between girls and boys, and between different age groups.

Let us look first at the comparison of indirect aggression to other types of aggression. Although her readers are unlikely to know what indirect aggression is, Angier can assume they will know other types of aggression with which she can compare it. In the opening paragraphs, she discusses the most common type of aggression—physical aggression. She lists many examples of physical aggression, including kicking, hitting, and throwing objects. In paragraph 6, she brings up a second type of aggression: "hornet talk" or verbal aggression. This kind of aggression is exemplified by cursing, belittling, insulting, yelling, and mocking. In paragraph 7, Angier introduces a third type of aggression, which she identifies at the end of the paragraph as "indirect aggression" and contrasts with the other kinds of aggression. In contrast to the confrontation and body contact associated with physical aggression, she tells us that indirect aggression involves withdrawing or turning away. In contrast to calling people "nasty names to their faces" (paragraph 6), which is typical of verbal aggression, indirect aggression includes backstabbing behaviors such as gossiping, spreading rumors, and plotting (paragraph 8). These contrasts help readers understand that indirect aggression has both physical and verbal elements but differs from physical and verbal aggression chiefly by being indirect or by masking its "hostile intent," as Angier explains in paragraph 8.

In addition to comparing indirect aggression to other types of aggression, Angier also compares boys and girls in terms of which type of aggression they use. At the same time, she compares aggressive behaviors at different ages. In paragraphs 1–3, she shows that people assume there is a difference between girls and boys as toddlers. In paragraph 4, however, she summarizes the research finding that "before the age of three, there are no significant differences between girl aggression and boy aggression." In paragraph 5, she makes explicit the idea that "sex-specific aggressions" change through time. This point is developed in subsequent paragraphs where she contrasts girls' and boys' preferences at different ages. She explains that as children grow older, girls become less physically aggressive and more verbally aggressive and boys become both more physically and more verbally aggressive. In paragraph 8, she explains that although girls develop indirect aggression earlier, by the time they are adults both sexes are equally adept at this covert form of aggression.

Comparison and contrast are important explanatory writing strategies that you may want to consider using in your own concept explanation.

Considering Topics for Your Own Essay

Angier mentions several concepts associated with behavior that you might consider explaining, such as hostility, aggression, obsession, grudge, coalition, friendship, intimacy, betrayal, and rileability. She also refers to kinds of communication such as gossip and rumor. Other kinds of communication you could write about include body language, metaphor, instant messaging, sign language, and semiotics.

Linh Kieu Ngo wrote this essay as a first-year college student. In it, he defines a concept that is of importance in anthropology and of wide general interest—cannibalism, the eating of human flesh by other humans. Most Americans know about survival cannibalism—eating human flesh to avoid starvation—but Ngo also explains the historical importance of dietary and ritual cannibalism in his essay. As you read, notice how he relies on examples to illustrate the types.

Cannibalism: It Still Exists

Linh Kieu Ngo

Fifty-five Vietnamese refugees fled to Malaysia on a small fishing boat to escape communist rule in their country following the Vietnam War. During their escape attempt, the captain was shot by the coast guard. The boat and its passengers managed to outrun the coast guard to the open sea, but they had lost the only person who knew the way to Malaysia, the captain. 1

The men onboard tried to navigate the boat, but after a week fuel ran out, and they drifted farther out to sea. Their supply of food and water was gone; people were starving, and some of the elderly were near death. The men managed to produce a small amount of drinking water by boiling salt water, using dispensable wood from the boat to create a small fire near the stern. They also tried to fish but had little success. 2

A month went by, and the old and weak died. At first, the crew threw the dead overboard, but later, out of desperation, they turned to human flesh as a source of food. Some people vomited as they attempted to eat it, while others refused to resort to cannibalism and see the bodies of their loved ones sacrificed for food. Those who did not eat died of starvation, and their bodies in turn became food for others. Human flesh was cut out, washed in salt water, and hung to dry for preservation. The liquids inside the cranium were drunk to quench thirst. The livers, kidneys, hearts, stomachs, and intestines were boiled and eaten. 3

Five months passed before a whaling vessel discovered the drifting boat, looking like a graveyard of bones. There was only one survivor. 4

Cannibalism, the act of human beings eating human flesh (Sagan 2), has a long history and continues to hold interest and create controversy. Many books and research reports offer examples of cannibalism, but a few scholars have questioned whether it actually was ever practiced anywhere, except in cases of ensuring survival in times of famine or isolation (Askenasy 43–54). Recently, some scholars have tried to understand why people in the West have been so eager to attribute cannibalism to non-Westerners (Barker, Hulme, and Iversen). Cannibalism has long been a part of American popular culture. For example, Mark Twain's "Cannibalism in the Cars" tells a humorous story about cannibalism by well-to-do travelers on a train stranded in a snowstorm, and cannibalism is still a popular subject for jokes ("Cannibal Jokes"). 5

If we assume there is some reality to the reports about cannibalism, how can we   6
best understand this concept? Cannibalism can be broken down into two main categories: exocannibalism, the eating of outsiders or foreigners, and endocannibalism, the
eating of members of one's own social group (Shipman 70). Within these categories are
several functional types of cannibalism, three of the most common being survival cannibalism, dietary cannibalism, and religious and ritual cannibalism.

Survival cannibalism occurs when people trapped without food have to decide   7
"whether to starve or to eat fellow humans" (Shipman 70). In the case of the Vietnamese
refugees, the crew and passengers on the boat ate human flesh to stay alive. They did
not kill people to get human flesh for nourishment but instead waited until the people had
died. Even after human carcasses were sacrificed as food, the boat people ate only
enough to survive. Another case of survival cannibalism occured in 1945, when General
Douglas MacArthur's forces cut supply lines to Japanese troops stationed in the Pacific
Islands. In one incident, Japanese troops were reported to have sacrificed the Arapesh
people of northeastern New Guinea for food in order to avoid death by starvation (Tuzin
63). The most famous example of survival cannibalism in American history comes from
the diaries, letters, and interviews of survivors of the California-bound Donner Party, who
in the winter of 1846 were snowbound in the Sierra Nevada Mountains for five months.
Thirty-five of eighty-seven adults and children died, and some of them were eaten (Hart
116–117; Johnson).

Unlike survival cannibalism, in which human flesh is eaten as a last resort after   8
a person has died, in dietary cannibalism humans are purchased or trapped for food and
then eaten as a part of a culture's traditions. In addition, survival cannibalism often involves people eating other people of the same origins, whereas dietary cannibalism usually involves people eating foreigners.

In the Miyanmin society of the west Sepik interior of Papua, New Guinea, villagers   9
do not value human life over that of pigs or marsupials because human flesh is part
of their normal diet (Poole 7). The Miyanmin people observe no differences in "gender,
kinship, ritual status, and bodily substance"; they eat anyone, even their own dead. In
this respect, then, they practice both endocannibalism and exocannibalism; and to
ensure a constant supply of human flesh for food, they raid neighboring tribes and drag
their victims back to their village to be eaten (Poole 11). Perhaps, in the history of this
society, there was at one time a shortage of wild game to be hunted for food, and
because people were more plentiful than fish, deer, rabbits, pigs, or cows, survival cannibalism was adopted as a last resort. Then, as their culture developed, the Miyanmin may
have retained the practice of dietary cannibalism, which has endured as a part of their
culture.

Similar to the Miyanmin, the people of the Leopard and Alligator societies in South   10
America eat human flesh as part of their cultural tradition. Practicing dietary exocannibalism, the Leopard people hunt in groups, with one member wearing the skin of a leopard
to conceal the face. They ambush their victims in the forest and carry their victims back to
their village to be eaten. The Alligator people also hunt in groups, but they hide them-

selves under a canoelike submarine that resembles an alligator, then swim close to a fisherman's or trader's canoe to overturn it and catch their victims (MacCormack 54).

Religious or ritual cannibalism is different from survival and dietary cannibalism in that it has a ceremonial purpose rather than one of nourishment. Sometimes only a single victim is sacrificed in a ritual, while at other times many are sacrificed. For example, the Bangala tribe of the Congo River in central Africa honors a deceased chief or leader by purchasing, sacrificing, and feasting on slaves (Sagan 53). The number of slaves sacrificed is determined by how highly the tribe members revered the deceased leader.

Ritual cannibalism among South American Indians often serves as revenge for the dead. Like the Bangalas, some South American tribes kill their victims to be served as part of funeral rituals, with human sacrifices denoting that the deceased was held in high honor. Also like the Bangalas, these tribes use outsiders as victims. Unlike the Bangalas, however, the Indians sacrifice only one victim instead of many in a single ritual. For example, when a warrior of a tribe is killed in battle, the family of the warrior forces a victim to take the identity of the warrior. The family adorns the victim with the deceased warrior's belongings and may even force him to marry the deceased warrior's wives. But once the family believes the victim has assumed the spiritual identity of the deceased warrior, the family kills him. The children in the tribe soak their hands in the victim's blood to symbolize their revenge of the warrior's death. Elderly women from the tribe drink the victim's blood and then cut up his body for roasting and eating (Sagan 53–54). The people of the tribe believe that by sacrificing a victim, they have avenged the death of the warrior and the soul of the deceased can rest in peace.

In the villages of certain African tribes, only a small part of a dead body is used in ritual cannibalism. In these tribes, where the childbearing capacity of women is highly valued, women are obligated to eat small, raw fragments of genital parts during fertility rites. Elders of the tribe supervise this ritual to ensure that the women will be fertile. In the Bimin-Kuskusmin tribe, for instance, a widow eats a small, raw fragment of flesh from the penis of her deceased husband in order to enhance her future fertility and reproductive capacity. Similarly, a widower may eat a raw fragment of flesh from his deceased wife's vagina along with a piece of her bone marrow; by eating her flesh, he hopes to strengthen the fertility of his daughters borne by his dead wife, and by eating her bone marrow, he honors her reproductive capacity. Also, when an elder woman of the village who has shown great reproductive capacity dies, her uterus and the interior parts of her vagina are eaten by other women who hope to benefit from her reproductive power (Poole 16–17).

Members of developed societies in general practice none of these forms of cannibalism, with the occasional exception of survival cannibalism when the only alternative is starvation. It is possible, however, that our distant-past ancestors were cannibals who through the eons turned away from the practice. We are, after all, descended from the same ancestors as the Miyanmin, the Alligator, and the Leopard people, and survival cannibalism shows that people are capable of eating human flesh when they have no other choice.

Works Cited

Askenasy, Hans. *Cannibalism: From Sacrifice to Survival.* Amherst, NY: Prometheus, 1994.

Barker, Francis, Peter Hulme, and Margaret Iversen, eds. *Cannibalism and the New World.* Cambridge: Cambridge UP, 1998.

Brown, Paula, and Donald Tuzin, eds. *The Ethnography of Cannibalism.* Washington: Society of Psychological Anthropology, 1983.

"Cannibal Jokes." *The Loonie Bin of Jokes.* 22 Sept. 1999 <http://www.looniebin.mb.ca/cannibal.html>

Hart, James D. *A Companion to California.* Berkeley: U of California P, 1987.

Johnson, Kristin. "New Light on the Donner Party." 28 Sept. 1999 <http://www.metrogourmet.com/crossroads.KJhome.htm>.

MacCormack, Carol. "Human Leopard and Crocodile." Brown and Tuzin 54–55.

Poole, Fitz John Porter. "Cannibals, Tricksters, and Witches." Brown and Tuzin 11, 16–17.

Sagan, Eli. *Cannibalism.* New York: Harper, 1976.

Shipman, Pat. "The Myths and Perturbing Realities of Cannibalism." *Discover* Mar. 1987: 70+.

Tuzin, Donald. "Cannibalism and Arapesh Cosmology." Brown and Tuzin 61–63.

Twain, Mark. "Cannibalism in the Cars." *The Complete Short Stories of Mark Twain.* Ed. Charles Neider. New York: Doubleday, 1957. 9–16.

Connecting to Culture and Experience: Taboos

The author of a respected book on the Donner Party has this to say about the fact that some members of the party ate other members after they had died:

> Surely the necessity, starvation itself, had forced them to all they did, and surely no just man would ever have pointed at them in scorn, or assumed his own superiority.... Even the seemingly ghoulish actions invoked in the story may be rationally explained. To open the bodies first for the heart and liver, and to saw apart the skulls for the brain were not acts of perversion. We must remember that these people had been living for months upon the hides and lean meat of half-starved work oxen; their diet was lacking not only in mere quantity, but also in all sorts of necessary vitamin and mineral constituents, even in common salt. Almost uncontrollable cravings must have assailed them, cravings which represented a real deficiency in diet to be supplied in some degree at least by the organs mentioned.
>
> – GEORGE R. STEWART, *Ordeal by Hunger*

With two or three other students, discuss this author's argument and his unwillingness to pass judgment on the Donner Party's cannibalism. Individually, are you inclined to agree or disagree with the author? Give reasons for your views. Keep in mind that no one, perhaps with one exception toward the very end of the Donner Party's isolation, was murdered to be eaten. Therefore, the issue is not murder but the eating of human flesh and body parts by other humans to remain alive. Humans do eat many other animals' flesh and body parts for nourishment. Where do you think the taboo against cannibalism comes from in our society? What are your views on whether the taboo should be observed in all circumstances? What do you think about extending the taboo to the consumption of animal flesh?

Analyzing Writing Strategies

1. At the end of paragraph 6, Ngo names three types of cannibalism, which he defines in the subsequent paragraphs. Find where these types are defined in paragraphs 7, 8, and 12, and underline the definitions. Some definitions are given in a single phrase, and others are made up of several phrases, not always contiguous. Exclude the examples from your underlining. Then look over the definitions you have underlined with the following questions in mind: What makes these definitions easy or hard for you to understand? In what ways does the example that begins the essay (paragraphs 1–4) prepare you to understand the definitions? How do the examples that follow the definitions help you understand each concise definition?

2. As he explains the different types of cannibalism, Ngo makes good use of examples in paragraphs 7–13. Choose one of the longer examples in paragraph 9, 12, or 13, and analyze how it is put together and how effective it is. What kinds of information does it offer? What sources does the writer rely on? What seems most memorable or surprising to you in the example? How does it help you understand the type of cannibalism being illustrated? In general, how effective does it seem to you in explaining the concept?

Commentary: A Logical Plan

Writers face special challenges in planning essays that explain concepts. First they gather a lot of information about a concept. Then they find a focus for the explanation. With the focus in mind, they research the concept further, looking for information to help them develop the focus. At this point, they have to find a way to arrange the information into logically related topics. This process is known formally as *classifying*. Sometimes, as in Ngo's research, one of the sources provides the classification, but sometimes the writer has to create it. This borrowing or creation allows writers to plan their essays to identify the topics in the order in which they will present them.

Ngo's explanation of cannibalism illustrates the importance of a logical plan. The following topical scratch outline of the essay will help you see Ngo's classification and plan:

- Narration of a specific recent incident of cannibalism (paragraphs 1–4)
- Context for the concept (5)
- Definition of cannibalism and introduction of its two main categories and three types (6)

- Definition of survival cannibalism, with two brief examples (7)
- Definition of dietary cannibalism (8)
- Two extended examples of dietary cannibalism (9–10)
- Definition of ritual cannibalism, with one brief example (11)
- Two extended examples of ritual cannibalism (12–13)
- Conclusion (14)

Ngo presents the classification in paragraph 6. It has two levels. On the first level, the information is divided into exocannibalism and endocannibalism. On the second level, each of the first two divisions is divided into three parts: survival, dietary, and ritual cannibalism. That is, either outsiders or members of one's own group can be eaten in each type of cannibalism. Ngo relies on the three types of cannibalism to create a plan for his essay. First he explains survival cannibalism, then dietary cannibalism, and finally, ritual cannibalism. This plan may be considered logical in at least two ways: It moves from most to least familiar and from least to most complex. Perhaps Ngo assumes that his readers will know about the Donner Party, an unfortunate group of 1846 immigrants to California who were trapped high in the Sierra Nevada Mountains by early, heavy snowstorms and ended up practicing survival endocannibalism. Therefore, Ngo explains this type of cannibalism first and then moves on to the less familiar types, whose complex practice takes different forms around the world. Ngo devotes two or three times more space to explaining dietary and ritual cannibalism than he does to explaining survival cannibalism, and he presents detailed examples of these forms.

Ngo does more than adopt a classification and use it to plan his essay. He helps readers anticipate and follow the plan by forecasting it and then providing cues to the steps in the plan. At the end of paragraph 6, Ngo forecasts the types of cannibalism he will focus on: survival cannibalism, dietary cannibalism, and religious and ritual cannibalism. This forecast introduces the names or terms that Ngo will use consistently throughout the explanation and presents the types of cannibalism in the order that Ngo will discuss them. Readers are thereby prepared for the step-by-step plan of the explanation.

Ngo lets readers know when he is leaving one type of cannibalism and addressing the next type by constructing visible transitions at the beginnings of paragraphs. Here are the three key transition sentences:

Survival cannibalism occurs when people trapped without food have to decide "whether to starve or to eat fellow humans. . . ." (paragraph 7)

Unlike survival cannibalism, in which human flesh is eaten as a last resort after a person has died, in dietary cannibalism humans are purchased or trapped for food and then eaten as a part of a culture's traditions. (8)

Religious or ritual cannibalism is different from survival and dietary cannibalism in that it has a ceremonial purpose rather than one of nourishment. (11)

You can feature these types of cues—forecasts and transitions—in your essay explaining a concept. Whereas forecasting is optional, transitions are essential; without them, your readers will struggle to follow your explanation and may throw up their hands in confusion and irritation. For more information on forecasting and transitions, see Chapter 8.

Considering Topics for Your Own Essay

Consider writing about some other well-established religious or cultural taboo such as murder, incest, or pedophilia. Or you might consider writing about a concept that tells something about current or historical social values, practices, or attitudes. To look at changing attitudes toward immigration, for example, think about concepts like assimilation, multiculturalism, the melting pot, and race. To look at changing attitudes toward dating, consider concepts like courtship, calling, and flirting.

■ PURPOSE AND AUDIENCE

Though it often seeks to engage readers' interests, explanatory writing gives prominence to facts about a subject. It aims to engage readers' intellects rather than their imaginations, to instruct rather than entertain or argue.

Setting out to teach readers about a concept is no small undertaking. To succeed, you must know the concept so well that you can explain it simply, without jargon or other confusing language. You must be authoritative without showing off or talking down. You must also estimate what your readers already know about the concept to decide which information will be truly new to them. You want to define unfamiliar words and pace the information carefully so that your readers are neither bored nor overwhelmed.

This assignment requires a willingness to cast yourself in the role of expert, which may not come naturally to you at this stage in your development as a writer. Students are most often asked to explain things in writing to readers who know more than they do — their instructors. When you plan and draft this essay, however, you will be aiming at readers who know less — maybe much less — than you do about the concept you will explain. Like Toufexis and Angier, you could write for a general audience of adults who regularly read a newspaper and subscribe to a few magazines. Even though some of them may be highly educated, you can readily and confidently assume the role of expert after a couple of hours of research into your concept. Your purpose may be to deepen your readers' understanding of a concept they may already be familiar with. If you choose to write for upper elementary or secondary school students, you could introduce them to an unfamiliar concept, or if you write for your classmates, you could demonstrate to them that a concept in an academic discipline that they find forbidding can actually be made both understandable and interesting. Even if you are told to consider your instructor your sole reader, you can assume that your instructor is eager to be informed about nearly any concept you choose.

You have spent many years in school reading explanations of concepts: Your textbooks in every subject have been full of concept explanations. Now, instead of receiving these explanations, you will be delivering one. To succeed, you will have to accept your role of expert. Your readers will expect you to be authoritative and well informed; they will also expect that you have limited the focus of your explanation but that you have not excluded anything essential to their understanding.

BASIC FEATURES: EXPLAINING CONCEPTS

A Focused Concept

The primary purpose for explaining a concept is to inform readers, but writers of explanatory essays do not hope to communicate everything that is known about a concept. Instead, they make choices about what to include, what to emphasize, and what to omit. Most writers focus on one aspect of the concept. Anastasia Toufexis focuses on the neurochemistry of love, Natalie Angier focuses on girls' preference for indirect aggression, and Linh Kieu Ngo focuses on three specific types of cannibalism.

An Appeal to Readers' Interests

Most people read explanations of concepts for work or study. Consequently, they expect the writing to be simply informative and not necessarily entertaining. Yet readers appreciate explanations that both identify the concept's importance and engage them with lively writing and vivid detail. The essays in this chapter show some of the ways in which writers may appeal to readers. For example, Toufexis uses humor and everyday language to attract readers' attention. She opens her essay with this direct address to readers: "O.K., let's cut out all this nonsense about romantic love." Calling romantic love "nonsense" arrests readers' attention as they thumb through the magazine in which the essay originally appeared. An opening strategy like this can do much to interest readers in the concept.

A Logical Plan

Since concept explanations present information that is new to readers and can therefore be hard to understand, writers need to develop a plan that presents new material step by step in a logical order. The most effective explanations are carefully organized and give readers all the obvious cues they need, such as forecasting statements, topic sentences, transitions, and summaries. In addition, the writer may try to frame the essay for readers by relating the ending to the beginning. We have seen these features repeatedly in the readings in this chapter. For example, Toufexis frames her essay with references to Ph.D.'s, forecasts the three sciences from which she has gleaned her information about the neurochemistry of love, and begins nearly all of her paragraphs with a transition sentence.

Good writers never forget that their readers need clear signals. Because writers already know the information and are aware of how their essays are organized, they can find it difficult to see the essay the way someone reading it for the first time would. That is precisely how it should be seen, however, to be sure that the essay includes all the necessary cues.

Clear Definitions

Essays explaining concepts depend on clear definitions. To relate information clearly, a writer must be sensitive to readers' knowledge; any key terms that are likely to be unfamiliar or misunderstood must be explicitly defined, as Toufexis defines *attraction junkies* (paragraph 12) and *endorphins* (paragraph 13) and as Ngo defines the *categories* of cannibalism (paragraph 6) and *types* of cannibalism (at the beginnings of paragraphs where he illustrates them). In a sense, all the readings in this chapter are extended definitions of concepts, and all the authors offer relatively concise, clear definitions of their concepts at some point in their essays.

Appropriate Writing Strategies

Many writing strategies are useful for presenting information. The strategies that a writer uses are determined by the way he or she focuses the essay and the kind of information available. The following strategies are particularly useful in explaining concepts:

Classification. One way of presenting information is to divide it into groups and discuss the groups one by one. For example, Toufexis divides the chemicals she discusses into those associated with falling in love and those associated with lasting relationships. Ngo divides cannibalism into three types.

Process Narration. Process narration typically explains how something is done. Many concepts involve processes that unfold over time, such as the geologic scale, or over both time and space, such as bird migration. Process narration involves some of the basic storytelling strategies covered in Chapter 2: narrative time signals, actors and action, and connectives showing temporal relationships. For example, Ngo briefly narrates one process of ritual cannibalism (paragraph 12).

Comparison and Contrast. The comparison/contrast strategy is especially useful for explaining concepts because it helps readers understand something new by showing how it is similar to or different from things they already know. Every essayist in this chapter makes use of comparison and contrast. For example, Angier compares indirect aggression with physical and verbal aggression, girls with boys, and different age groups with one another. Ngo compares the three types of cannibalism as well as different cultures.

Cause and Effect. Another useful strategy for explaining a concept is to report its causes or effects. Toufexis explains the evolutionary benefits of romantic love, and Angier reports the causes established by research to explain why adolescent girls rely on indirect aggression. Note that writers of explanatory essays ordinarily either report established causes or effects or report others' speculated causes or effects as if they were established facts. They usually do not themselves speculate about possible causes or effects.

Careful Use of Sources

To explain concepts, writers usually draw on information from many different sources. Although they often draw on their own experiences and observations, they almost always do additional research into what others have to say about their subject. Referring to expert sources always lends authority to an explanation.

How writers treat sources depends on the writing situation. Certain formal situations, such as college assignments or scholarly papers, have rules for citing and documenting sources. Students and scholars are expected to cite their sources formally because readers judge their work in part by what the writers have read and how they have used their reading. Ngo's essay illustrates this academic form of citing sources. For more informal writing—magazine articles, for example—readers do not expect or want page references or publication information, but they do expect sources to be identified. This identification often appears within the text of the article, as illustrated in the selection by Toufexis, which was originally published in a magazine. Other nonacademic writing—popular books, for example—may be based on research, but those authors may choose not to impose on readers the formal documentation style of academic writing. Angier, for example, mentions in her preface that she interviewed hundreds of experts. She also includes a list of sources at the end of the book and identifies most of them in the text—such as Björkqvist in paragraphs 4 and 12—so that her readers can find their names in the alphabetical list at the end.

GUIDE TO WRITING
Explaining Concepts

THE WRITING ASSIGNMENT

Write an essay about a concept that interests you and that you want to study further. When you have a good understanding of the concept, explain it to your readers, considering carefully what they already know about it and how your essay might add to what they know.

THE WRITING ASSIGNMENT

INVENTION AND RESEARCH

PLANNING AND DRAFTING

PLANNING & DRAFTING

Seeing What You Have

Setting Goals

Outlining

Drafting

CRITICAL READING GUIDE

REVISING

Revising

A Focused Concept

An Appeal to Readers' Interests

A Logical Plan

Clear Definitions

Appropriate Writing Strategies

Careful Use of Sources

EDITING AND PROOFREADING

INVENTION & RESEARCH

Finding a Concept to Write About

Surveying Information about the Concept

Focusing the Concept

Testing Your Choice

Researching Your Topic Focus

Considering Explanatory Strategies

Considering Document Design

Defining Your Purpose for Your Readers

Formulating a Tentative Thesis Statement

CRITICAL READING GUIDE

First Impression

Clear Focus and Explanation of Concept

Appropriate Content

Organization

Clarity of Definitions

Use of Sources

Effectiveness of Visuals

Final Thoughts

EDITING & PROOFREADING

Checking the Punctuation of Adjective Clauses

Checking for Commas around Interrupting Phrases

GUIDE TO WRITING

■ THE WRITING ASSIGNMENT

Write an essay about a concept that interests you and that you want to study further. When you have a good understanding of the concept, explain it to your readers, considering carefully what they already know about it and how your essay might add to what they know.

■ INVENTION AND RESEARCH

The following guidelines will help you find a concept, understand it fully, select a focus that is appropriate for your readers, test your choice, and devise strategies for presenting your discoveries in a way that will be truly informative for your particular readers. Each activity is easy to do and takes only a few minutes. If you can spread out the activities over several days, you will have adequate time to understand the concept and decide how to present it. Keep a written record of your invention work to use when you draft the essay and later when you revise it. If you write on the computer, you may be able to copy and paste into your draft material from your invention and research notes.

Finding a Concept to Write About

Even if you already have a concept in mind, completing the following activities will help you to be certain of your choice.

Listing Concepts. *Make a list of concepts you could write about.* The longer your list, the more likely you are to find just the right concept for you. And should your first choice not work out, you will have a ready list of alternatives. Include concepts you already know something about as well as some you know only slightly and would like to research further. Also include concepts suggested by the Considering Topics for Your Own Essay activities following each reading in this chapter.

Your courses provide many concepts you will want to consider. Here are some typical concepts from a number of academic and other subjects. Your class notes or textbooks will suggest many others.

- *Literature:* irony, metaphysical conceit, semiotics, hero, dystopian novel, humanism, picaresque, the absurd, canon, representation, figurative language, modernism, identity politics, queering
- *Philosophy:* existentialism, nihilism, logical positivism, determinism, metaphysics, ethics, natural law, Zeno's paradox, epistemology, ideology
- *Business management:* autonomous work group, quality circle, cybernetic control system, management by objectives, zero-based budgeting, liquidity gap

140

- *Psychology:* metacognition, Hawthorne effect, assimilation/accommodation, social cognition, moratorium, intelligence, divergent/convergent thinking, operant conditioning, short-term memory, the Stroop effect, sleep paralysis
- *Government:* majority rule, minority rights, federalism, popular consent, exclusionary rule, political party, political machine, interest group, hegemony
- *Biology:* photosynthesis, mitosis, karyotype analysis, morphogenesis, ecosystem, electron transport, plasmolysis, phagocytosis, homozygosity, diffusion
- *Art:* cubism, Dadaism, surrealism, expressionism
- *Math:* polynomials, boundedness, null space, permutations and combinations, factoring, Rolle's theorem, continuity, derivative, indefinite integral
- *Physical sciences:* matter, mass, weight, energy, gravity, atomic theory, law of definite proportions, osmotic pressure, first law of thermodynamics, entropy
- *Public health:* alcoholism, seasonal affective disorder, contraception, lead poisoning, prenatal care, toxicology
- *Environmental studies:* acid rain, recycling, ozone depletion, toxic waste, endangered species
- *Sports:* squeeze play, hit and run (baseball); power play (hockey); nickel defense, wishbone offense (football); serve and volley offense (tennis); setup (volleyball); pick and roll, inside game (basketball)
- *Personal finance:* mortgage, budget, insurance, deduction, revolving credit, interest rates, dividend, bankruptcy
- *Law:* tort, contract, garnishment, double indemnity, reasonable doubt, class-action suits, product liability, lemon law
- *Sociology:* norm, deviance, role conflict, ethnocentrism, class, social stratification, conflict theory, action theory, acculturation, Whorf-Sapir hypothesis, machismo

Listing Concepts Related to Identity and Community.   Many concepts are important in understanding identity and community. As you consider the following concepts, try to think of others in this category: self-esteem, character, personality, autonomy, individuation, narcissism, multiculturalism, ethnicity, race, racism, social contract, communitarianism, community policing, social Darwinism, identity politics, special-interest groups, diaspora, colonialism, public space, the other, agency, difference, yuppie, generation X.

Listing Concepts Related to Work and Career.   Concepts like the following enable you to gain a deeper understanding of your work experiences and career aspirations: free enterprise, minimum wage, affirmative action, stock option, sweatshop, glass ceiling, downsizing, collective bargaining, service sector, market, entrepreneur, bourgeoisie, underclass, working class, middle class, division of labor, monopoly, automation, robotics, management style, deregulation, multinational corporation.

Choosing a Concept.   *Look over your list of possibilities, and select one concept to explore.* Pick a concept that interests you, one you feel eager to learn more about. Consider also whether it might interest others. You may know very little about the concept now, but the guidelines that follow will help you research it and understand it fully.

Surveying Information about the Concept

Your research efforts for a concept essay must be divided into two stages. First, you want to achieve quickly a far-reaching survey or overview of information about the concept you have chosen. Your goal in this first stage is to learn as much as you can from diverse sources so that you may decide whether you want to write about this topic and whether you can identify an aspect of it to focus on.

In the second stage, when you know what your focus will be, you begin in-depth research for information that will educate you about this focus. When Natalie Angier arrived at this stage, she would have been learning as much as possible about indirect aggression between girls, not aggression in general. When Linh Kieu Ngo arrived at this stage, he would have been digging for information on ways to classify the different types of cannibalism.

The activities that follow will guide you through this two-stage research process.

Discovering What You Already Know.   *Before doing any research on your concept or even looking at any handy references, take a few minutes to write about what you already know about the concept.* Also say why you have chosen the concept and why you find it interesting and worth knowing about. Write quickly, without planning or organizing. Write phrases or lists as well as sentences. You could even add drawings or quick sketches or write down questions about the concept, questions that express your curiosity or uncertainty. If you find that you know very little about the concept, you still might want to write about it — out of personal motivation, which is not a bad reason to commit yourself to the study of an unfamiliar concept.

Sorting Through Your Personal Resources.   *Check any materials you already have at hand that explain your concept.* If you are considering a concept from one of your academic courses, you will find explanatory material in your textbook or perhaps your lecture notes.

To acquire a comprehensive, up-to-date understanding of your concept, however, you will need to know how experts other than your textbook writer and instructor define and illustrate it. To find this information, you might locate relevant articles or books in the library, search for resources or make inquiries on the Internet, or consult experts on campus or in the community.

Going Online.   *Keep a list of Web sites you find that invite more than a quick glance, sites that hold your attention and inform you about your concept. Bookmark each site, or record its name and URL. You might make a few brief notes about key contents or features of sites from which you learn the most. Also keep a list of possible focuses you discover.*

Keep your goal for this stage in mind: to educate yourself quickly about the concept and look for a possible focus for your essay. It is too early to begin downloading a lot of material.

Going to the Library.   *Keep a list of the most promising materials you discover in the library. Continue your other list of possible focuses, trying to come up with at least two or three possibilities.* Besides taking a quick look at relevant encyclopedias and disciplinary guides, look for your concept name in the subject headings of the *Library of Congress Subject Headings* and also in the library catalog, using the keyword search option. The library can give you access to special online resources; ask a librarian for advice. Remember that moving through your search quickly will give you a good overview of information about your concept. Consult Chapter 13, "Strategies for Library and Internet Research," for help with using the library productively.

Researching Concepts: An Online Activity	One way to get a quick initial overview of the information available on a concept is to search for the concept online. You can do this in several ways:

- Enter the name of your concept in a search tool such as Google (www.google .com) or Yahoo! Directory (http://dir.yahoo.com) to discover possible sources of information about the concept.
- Check an online encyclopedia in the field to which the concept belongs. Here are a few specialized encyclopedias that may be helpful:
  - *Encyclopedia of Psychology* www.psychology.org/
  - *The Internet Encyclopedia of Philosophy* www.utm.edu/research/iep/
  - *Webopedia* www.webopedia.com

  Bookmark or keep a record of promising sites. When you proceed to a narrower search for information about your topic focus, you could then download any materials, including visuals, that you might consider including in your own essay.

Focusing the Concept

Once you have an overview of your concept, you must choose a focus for your essay. More is known about most concepts than you can include in an essay, and concepts can be approached from many perspectives (for example, history, definition, significance), so you must limit your explanation. Doing this will help you avoid the common problem of trying to explain too much. Because the focus must reflect both your special interest in the concept and your readers' likely knowledge and interest, you will want to explore both.

Exploring Your Own Interests. *Make a list of two or three aspects of the concept that could become a focus for your essay, and evaluate what you know about each focus. Leave some space after each item in the list.* Under each possible focus in your list, make notes about why it interests you and why it seems just the right size (not so small that it is trivial and not so large that it is overwhelming). Indicate whether you know enough to begin writing about that aspect of the concept, what additional questions you would need to answer, and what is important or interesting to you about that particular aspect.

Analyzing Your Readers. *Take a few minutes to analyze in writing your readers.* To decide what aspect of the concept to focus on, you also need to think about who your prospective readers are likely to be and to speculate about their knowledge of and interest in the concept. Even if you are writing only for your instructor, you should give some thought to what he or she knows and thinks about the concept.

The following questions are designed to help you with your analysis:

- Who are my readers, and what are they likely to know about this concept?
- What, if anything, might they know about the field of study to which this concept applies?
- What could I point out that would be useful for them to know about this concept, perhaps something that could relate to their life or work?
- What connections could I make between this concept and others that my readers are likely to be familiar with?

Choosing a Focus. *With your interests and those of your readers in mind, choose an aspect of your concept on which to focus, and write a sentence justifying its appropriateness.*

Testing Your Choice

Pause now to test whether you have chosen a workable concept and focused it appropriately. As painful as it may be to consider, starting fresh with a new concept is better than continuing with an unworkable one. The following questions can help you test your choice:

- Do I understand my concept well enough to explain it?
- Have I discovered a focus for writing about this concept?
- Do I think I can find enough information for an essay with such a focus?
- Do I see possibilities for engaging my readers' interest in this aspect of my concept?

If you cannot answer yes to all four questions, consider choosing another focus or selecting another concept to write about.

<table>
<tr><td>

Testing Your Choice: A Collaborative Activity

</td><td>

Get together with two or three other students to find out what your readers are likely to know about your subject and what might interest them about it. Your instructor may ask you to complete this activity in class or online in a chat room.

</td></tr>
</table>

Presenters: Take turns briefly explaining your concept, describing your intended readers, and identifying the aspect of the concept that you will focus on.

Listeners: Briefly tell the presenter whether the focus sounds appropriate and interesting for the intended readers. Share what you think readers are likely to know about the concept and what information might be especially interesting and memorable for them.

Researching Your Topic Focus

Now begins stage two of your research process. With a likely focus in mind, you are ready to mine both the Internet and the library for valuable nuggets of information. Your research becomes selective and deliberate, and you will now want to keep careful records of all sources you believe will contribute in any way to your essay. If possible, make photocopies of print sources, and print out sources you download from CD-ROMs or the Internet. If you must rely on notes, be sure to copy any quotations exactly and enclose them in quotation marks so that later you can quote sources accurately.

Since you do not know which sources you will ultimately use, keep a careful record of the author, title, publication information, page numbers, and other required information for each source you gather. Check with your instructor about whether you should follow the Modern Language Association (MLA) or American Psychological Association (APA) style of acknowledging sources. In this chapter, the Ngo essay follows the MLA style.

Going Online.   *Return to online searching, with your focus in mind. Download and print out essential material if possible, or take careful notes. Record all of the details you will need to acknowledge sources in your essay, should you decide to use them.*

Going to the Library.   *Return to the library to search for materials relevant to your focus. Photocopy, print out, or take notes on promising print and electronic materials. Keep careful records so that you can acknowledge your sources.*

Considering Explanatory Strategies

Before you move on to plan and draft your essay, consider some possible ways of presenting the concept. Try to answer each of the following questions in a sentence or two.

Questions that you can answer readily may identify strategies that can help you explain your concept.

- What term is used to name the concept, and what does it mean? (definition)
- How is this concept like or unlike related concepts? (comparison and contrast)
- How can an explanation of this concept be divided into parts? (classification)
- How does this concept happen, or how does one go about doing it? (process narration)
- What are this concept's known causes or effects? (cause and effect)

Considering Document Design

Think about whether visual elements—tables, graphs, drawings, photographs—would make your explanation clearer. These are not a requirement of an essay explaining a concept, but they could be helpful. Consider also whether your readers might benefit from design features such as headings, bulleted or numbered lists, or other elements that would present information efficiently or make your explanation easier to follow. You could construct your own graphic elements, download materials from the Internet, copy images from television or other sources, or scan into your document visuals from books and magazines. Remember that you should cite the source of any visual you do not create yourself, and you should also request permission from the source of the visual if your paper is going to be posted on the Web.

Defining Your Purpose for Your Readers

Write a few sentences that define your purpose in writing about this particular concept for your readers. Remember that you have already identified and analyzed your readers and that you have begun to research and develop your explanation with these readers in mind. Given these readers, try now to define your purpose in explaining the concept to them. Use these questions to focus your thoughts:

- Are my readers familiar with the concept? If not, how can I overcome their resistance or puzzlement? Or, if so, will my chosen focus allow my readers to see the familiar concept in a new light?
- If I suspect that my readers have misconceptions about the concept, how can I correct the misconceptions without offending readers?
- Do I want to arouse readers' interest in information that may seem at first to be less than engaging?
- Do I want readers to see that the information I have to report is relevant to their lives, families, communities, work, or studies?

Formulating a Tentative Thesis Statement

Write one or more sentences that could serve as a thesis statement. State your concept and focus. You might also want to forecast the topics you will use to explain the concept.

Anastasia Toufexis begins her essay with this thesis statement:

> O.K., let's cut out all this nonsense about romantic love. Let's bring some scientific precision to the party. Let's put love under a microscope.
>
> When rigorous people with Ph.D.s after their names do that, what they see is not some silly, senseless thing. No, their probe reveals that love rests firmly on the foundations of evolution, biology and chemistry.

Toufexis's concept is love, and her focus is the scientific explanation of love — specifically the evolution, biology, and chemistry of love. In announcing her focus, she forecasts the order in which she will present information from the three most relevant academic disciplines — anthropology (which includes the study of human evolution), biology, and chemistry. These discipline names become her topics.

In his essay on cannibalism, Linh Kieu Ngo offers his thesis statement in paragraph 6:

> Cannibalism can be broken down into two main categories: exocannibalism, the eating of outsiders or foreigners, and endocannibalism, the eating of members of one's own social group (Shipman 70). Within these categories are several functional types of cannibalism, three of the most common being survival cannibalism, dietary cannibalism, and religious and ritual cannibalism.

Ngo's concept is cannibalism, and his focus is on three common types of cannibalism. He carefully forecasts how he will divide the information to create topics and the order in which he will explain each of the topics, the common types of cannibalism.

As you draft your own tentative thesis statement, take care to make the language clear and unambiguous. Although you may want to revise your thesis statement as you draft your essay, trying to state it now will give your planning and drafting more focus and direction. Keep in mind that the thesis in an explanatory essay merely announces the subject; it never asserts a position that requires an argument to defend it.

■ PLANNING AND DRAFTING

The following guidelines will help you get the most out of your invention notes, determine specific goals for your essay, and write a first draft.

Seeing What You Have

Reread everything you have written so far. This is a critically important time for reflection and evaluation. Before beginning the actual draft, you must decide whether your subject is worthwhile and whether you have sufficient information for a successful essay.

It may help, as you read, to annotate your invention writings. Look for details that will help you explain the concept in a way that your readers can grasp. Highlight key words, phrases, or sentences; make marginal notes or electronic annotations of any material you think could be useful. If you have done your invention writing on the computer, you may have sentences or whole paragraphs that can be copied and pasted into your draft.

Be realistic. If at this point your notes do not look promising, you may want to choose a different focus for your concept or select a different concept to write about. If your notes seem thin but promising, do further research to find more information before continuing.

Setting Goals

Successful writers are always looking beyond the next sentence to larger goals. Indeed, the next sentence is easier to write if you keep larger goals in mind. The following questions can help you set these goals. Consider each one now, and then return to them as necessary while you write.

Your Purpose and Readers

- How can I build on my readers' knowledge?
- What new information can I present to them?
- How can I organize my essay so that my readers can follow it easily?
- What tone would be most appropriate? Would an informal tone like Toufexis's or a formal one like Ngo's be more appropriate to my purpose?

The Beginning

- How shall I begin? Should I open with a provocative quotation, as Toufexis does? With an incident illustrating the concept, as Angier and Ngo do? With an explanation of why readers need to understand the concept? With a question?
- How can I best forecast the plan that my explanation will follow? Should I offer a detailed forecast, as Toufexis and Ngo do?

Writing Strategies

- What terms do I need to define? Can I rely on brief sentence definitions, or will I need to write extended definitions? Should I give a history of the concept term?
- Are there ways to classify the information?
- What examples can I use to make the explanation more concrete?
- Would any comparisons or contrasts help readers understand the information?
- Do I need to explain any processes or known causes or effects?

The Ending

- Should I frame the essay by relating the ending to the beginning, as Toufexis does?
- Should I end by suggesting what is special about the concept, as Angier does?
- Should I end with a speculation about the past, as Ngo does?
- Should I end by suggesting how my readers can apply the concept to their own lives?

Outlining

The goals that you have set should help you draft your essay, but first you might want to make a quick scratch outline to refocus on the basic story line. You could use the outlining function of your word processing program. In your outline, list the main topics into which you have divided the information about your concept. Use this outline to guide your drafting, but do not feel tied to it. As you draft, you may find a better way to sequence the action and integrate these features.

An essay explaining a concept is made up of four basic parts:

- An attempt to engage readers' interest
- The thesis statement, announcing the concept, its focus, and its topics
- An orientation to the concept, which may include a description or definition of the concept
- Information about the concept

Here is a possible outline for an essay explaining a concept:

An attempt to gain readers' interest in the concept

Thesis statement

Definition of the concept

Topic 1 with illustration

Topic 2 with illustration

(etc.)

Conclusion

An attempt to gain readers' interest could take as little space as two or three sentences or as much as four or five paragraphs. The thesis statement and definition are usually quite brief—sometimes only a few sentences. A topic illustration may occupy one or several paragraphs, and there can be few or many topics, depending on how the information has been divided up. A conclusion might summarize the information presented, give advice about how to use or apply the information, or speculate about the future of the concept.

Consider any outlining that you do before you begin drafting to be tentative. As you draft, be ready to revise your outline, shift parts around, or drop or add parts. If you use the outlining function of your word processing program, changing your outline will be simple, and you may be able to write the essay simply by expanding the outline.

Drafting

General Advice. Start drafting your essay, keeping in mind the goals you set while you were planning. Remember also the needs and expectations of your readers; organize, define, and explain with them in mind. Work to increase readers' understanding of your concept. Turn off your grammar checker and spelling checker at this stage if you find them distracting. Do not be afraid to skip around in your document. Jump back and fill in a spontaneous idea, or leap ahead and write a later section first if you find that easier. If you get stuck while drafting, try using some of the writing activities in the Invention and Research section of this chapter. You may want to review the general drafting advice on pp. 16–17.

Sentence Strategies. As you draft an essay explaining a concept, you must introduce library and Internet research sources and their authors within your sentences. You must also devise sentences that allow you to subordinate some information to other information and to introduce many examples or illustrations for readers to understand the concept. Precise verbs and a versatile sentence modifier called an *appositive* can help you achieve these goals.

Use informative, precise verbs to introduce sources and authors. Experienced writers of all kinds of explanatory and informational writing take great care in choosing verbs to introduce sources and authors, as these examples illustrate (the verbs are in italics):

> Lovers…are literally flooded by chemicals, research *suggests*. (Anastasia Toufexis, paragraph 9)

> The scientists *found* that boys and girls were equally likely to use verbal aggression against their cohorts.…(Natalie Angier, paragraph 6)

> In one incident, Japanese troops *were reported* to have sacrificed the Arapesh people of northeastern New Guinea for food in order to avoid death by starvation. (Linh Kieu Ngo, paragraph 7)

When you explain a concept to readers unfamiliar with it, you usually are presenting information that is well established and currently considered reliable by experts on your topic. Because you are not making an argument either for or against your sources or authors, you need to introduce them to readers using somewhat neutral language — like the italicized verbs *suggests, found,* and *were reported* in the preceding examples. Yet there are important distinctions in meaning among these three verbs. *Found* connotes that Natalie Angier is merely reporting a research discovery or an earlier discovery newly confirmed. *Suggests* may indicate that Anastasia Toufexis is referring to broad implications of research rather than to findings. Paraphrasing a source with *were reported,* Linh Kieu Ngo makes clear to readers that the writer relied on secondhand information.

As you refer to sources in your concept explanation, you will be able to choose carefully among a wide variety of precise verbs. Every writer in this chapter uses a great variety of verbs for this purpose — sometimes for the sake of variety, no doubt, but usually in an effort to help readers better understand how the writer is using a source. As you draft your essay, you may find this partial list of verbs from the readings helpful in selecting precisely the right verbs to introduce your sources:

reveals	contends	questions
explains	brings into focus	tells

observes	pulls together	reports
notes	documents	finds
shows	warns	according to [name of
speculates	mounts	author or source]
rejects	tries to understand	

Use appositives to identify people, define terms, and give examples and specifics. An appositive can be defined as a group of words, usually based on a noun or pronoun, that identifies or gives more information about another noun or pronoun just preceding it. Appositives come in many forms, as shown in these examples (the appositives are in italics):

Says Michael Mills, *a psychology professor at Loyola Marymount University in Los Angeles:* "Love is our ancestors whispering in our ears." (Anastasia Toufexis, paragraph 2)

Cannibalism, *the act of human beings eating human flesh* (Sagan 2), has a long history and continues to hold interest and create controversy. (Linh Kieu Ngo, paragraph 5)

In this chapter's three readings, appositives appear frequently. Writers explaining concepts rely to such an extent on appositives because they serve so many purposes. Among the most common are the following:

- Identifying a thing or person, often to establish a source's authority

  "Love is a natural high," observes Anthony Walsh, *author of* The Science of Love: Understanding Love and Its Effects on Mind and Body. (Anastasia Toufexis, paragraph 10)

- Giving examples or more specific information

  Girls who become good friends feel a compulsion to define the friendship, *to stamp it and name it*....(Natalie Angier, paragraph 10)

- Introducing a new term

  Each person carries in his or her mind a unique subliminal guide to the ideal partner, *a "love map."*...(Anastasia Toufexis, paragraph 17)

Appositives accomplish these and other purposes very efficiently by enabling the writer to put related bits of information next to each other in the same sentence, thereby merging two potential sentences into one or shrinking a potential clause to a phrase. For example, Ngo, instead of making use of the appositive, could have written either of the following:

Cannibalism can be defined as the act of human beings eating human flesh. It has a long history and continues to hold interest and create controversy.

Cannibalism, which can be defined as the act of human beings eating human flesh, has a long history and continues to hold interest and create controversy.

Both of these versions are readable and clear. By using an appositive, however, Ngo saves four or five words, subordinates the definition of cannibalism to his main idea about history and controversy, and yet locates the definition exactly where readers need to see it.

In addition to using precise verbs to introduce sources and examples and to relying on appositives, you can strengthen your concept explanation with other kinds of sentences as well, and you may want to turn to the information about sentences that express comparison and contrast (pp. 293–94) and sentences that use conjunctions and phrases to indicate the logical relationships between clauses and sentences (pp. 198–99). If you frequently quote from sources, you may want to review the examples of integrating quoted material into your sentences (pp. 432–36).

CRITICAL READING GUIDE

Now is the time to get a good critical reading of your draft. Your instructor may arrange such a reading as part of your coursework—in class or online. If not, you can ask a classmate, friend, or family member to read your draft using this guide. If your campus has a writing center, you might ask a tutor there to read and comment on your draft. (If you are unable to have someone else review your draft, turn ahead to the Revising section on p. 154, where you will find guidelines for reading your own draft critically.)

If you read another student's draft online, you may be able to use a word processing program to insert suggested improvements directly into the text of the draft or to write them out at the end of the draft. If you read a printout of the draft, you may write brief comments in the margins and lengthier suggestions on a separate page. When the writer sits down to revise, your thoughtful, extended suggestions written at the end of the draft or on separate pages will be especially helpful.

If You Are the Writer. To provide focused, helpful comments, your reader must know your essay's intended audience, your purpose, and a problem in the draft that you need help solving. Briefly write out this information at the top of your draft.

- *Readers:* To whom are you directing your concept explanation? What do you assume they know about the concept? How do you plan to engage and hold their interest?
- *Purpose:* What do you hope to achieve with your readers?
- *Problem:* Ask your reader to help you solve the most important problem you see in the draft. Describe this problem briefly.

If You Are the Reader. Use the following guidelines to help you give constructive, helpful comments to others on essays explaining concepts.

1. *Read for a First Impression.* Read first to get a sense of the concept. Then briefly write out your impressions. What in the draft do you think will especially interest the intended readers? Where might they have difficulty in following the explanation? Next, consider the problem the writer identified, and respond briefly to that concern now. (If you find that the problem is covered by one of the other guidelines listed below, respond to it in more detail there if necessary.)

2. *Assess Whether the Concept Is Clearly Explained and Focused.* Restate, in one sentence, what you understand the concept to mean. Indicate any confusion or uncertainty you have about its meaning. Given the concept, does the focus seem appropriate, too broad, or too narrow for the intended readers? Can you think of a more interesting aspect of the concept on which to focus the explanation?

3. *Consider Whether the Content Is Appropriate for the Intended Readers.* Does it tell them all that they are likely to want to know about the concept? Can you suggest additional information that should be included? What unanswered questions might readers have about the concept? Point out any information that seems either superfluous or too predictable.

4. *Evaluate the Organization.* Look at the way the essay is organized by making a scratch outline. Does the information seem to be logically divided? If not, suggest a better way to divide it. Also consider the order or sequence of information. Can you suggest a better way of sequencing it?

   - *Look at the beginning.* Does it pull readers into the essay and make them want to continue? Does it adequately forecast the direction of the essay? If possible, suggest a better way to begin.

   - *Look for obvious transitions in the draft.* Tell the writer how they are helpful or unhelpful. Try to improve one or two of them. Look for additional places where transitions would be helpful.

   - *Look at the ending.* Explain what makes it particularly effective or less effective than it might be, in your opinion. If you can, suggest a better way to end.

5. *Assess the Clarity of Definitions.* Point out any definitions that may be unclear or confusing to the intended readers. Identify any other terms that may need to be defined.

6. *Evaluate the Use of Sources.* If the writer has used sources, review the list of sources cited. Given the purpose, readers, and focus of the essay, does the list seem balanced, and are the selections appropriate? Try to suggest concerns or questions about sources that readers knowledgeable about the concept might raise. Then consider the use of sources within the text of the essay. Are there places where summary or paraphrase would be preferable to quoted material or vice versa? Note any places where the writer has

placed quotations awkwardly into the text, and recommend ways to smooth them out.

7. ***Evaluate the Effectiveness of Visuals.*** If charts, graphs, tables, or other visuals are included, let the writer know whether they help you understand the concept. Suggest ideas you have for changing, adding, moving, or deleting visuals.

8. ***Give the Writer Your Final Thoughts.*** Which part needs the most work? What do you think the intended readers will find most informative or memorable? What do you like best about the draft essay?

■ REVISING

Now you are ready to revise your essay. Your instructor or other students may have given you advice on improving your draft. Nevertheless, you may have begun to realize that your draft requires not so much revision as rethinking. For example, you may recognize that the focus you chose is too broad to be explained adequately in a few pages, that you need to make the information more engaging or interesting for your intended readers, or that you need substantially more information to present the concept adequately. Consequently, instead of working to improve parts of the draft, you may need to write a new draft that radically reenvisions your explanation. It is not unusual for students—and professional writers—to find themselves in this situation. Seek your instructor's advice if you must plan a radical revision.

On the other hand, you may feel quite satisfied that your draft achieves most, if not all, of your goals. In that case, you can focus on refining specific parts of your draft. Very likely you have thought of ways to improve your draft, and you may even have begun improving it. This section will help you get an overview of your draft and revise it accordingly.

Getting an Overview

Consider your draft as a whole. It may help to do so in two steps:

1. ***Reread.*** If at all possible, put the draft aside for a day or two before rereading it. When you return to it, start by reconsidering your readers and purpose. Then read the draft straight through, trying to see it as your intended readers will.

2. ***Outline.*** Make a scratch outline to get an overview of the essay's development. Consider using the headings and outline/summary functions of your word processor.

Planning for Revision.   Resist the temptation to dive in and start changing your text until after you have a clear view of the big picture. Using your outline as a guide, move through the document, using the highlighting or commenting tools of your word processor to note comments received from others and problems you want to solve (or mark on a hard copy if you prefer).

Analyzing the Basic Features of Your Own Draft.   Using the Critical Reading Guide on the preceding pages, reread the draft to identify problems you need to solve. Note the problems on your draft.

Studying Critical Comments.   Review all of the comments you have received from other readers, and add to your notes any that you intend to act on. Try not to react defensively. For each comment, look at the draft to determine what might have led the reader to make the comment. By letting you see how others respond to your draft, these comments provide valuable information about how you might improve it.

Carrying Out Revisions

Having identified problems in your draft, you now need to come up with solutions and—most important—to carry them out. Basically, there are three ways to find solutions:

1. Review your invention and planning notes and your sources for information and ideas to add to the draft.
2. Do further invention or research to answer questions your readers raised.
3. Look back at the readings in this chapter to see how other writers have solved similar problems.

The following suggestions, which are organized according to the basic features of explanatory essays, will get you started solving some writing problems common to them.

A Focused Concept

- *Is the focus too broad?* Consider limiting it further so that you can explain one part of the concept in more depth. If readers were uninterested in the aspect you focused on, consider focusing on some other aspect.

- *Is the focus too narrow?* You may have isolated too minor an aspect. Go back to your invention and research notes, and look for larger or more significant aspects.

An Appeal to Readers' Interests

- *Do you fail to connect to readers' interests and engage their attention throughout the essay?* Help readers see the significance of the information to them personally. Eliminate superfluous or too-predictable content. Open with an unusual piece of information that catches readers' interest.

- *Do you think readers will have unanswered questions?* Review your invention writing and sources for further information to answer them.

A Logical Plan

- **Does the beginning successfully orient readers to your purpose and plan?** Try making your focus obvious immediately. Forecast the plan of your essay.

- **Is the explanation difficult to follow?** Look for a way to reorder the parts so that the essay is easier to follow. Try constructing an alternative outline. Add transitions or summaries to help keep readers on track. Or consider ways you might classify and divide the information to make it easier to understand or provide a more interesting perspective on the topic.

- **Is the ending inconclusive?** Consider moving important information there. Try summarizing highlights of the essay or framing it by referring to something in the beginning. Or you might speculate about the future of the concept or assert its usefulness.

Clear Definitions

- **Do readers need a clearer or fuller definition of the concept?** Add a concise definition early in your essay, or consider adding a brief summary that defines the concept later in the essay (in the middle or at the end). Remove any information that may blur readers' understanding of the concept.

- **Are other key terms inadequately defined?** Supply clear definitions, searching your sources or checking a dictionary if necessary.

Appropriate Writing Strategies

- **Does the content seem thin or the definition of the concept blurred?** Consider whether any other writing strategies would improve the presentation.
  - Try comparing or contrasting the concept with a related one that is more familiar to readers.
  - Add some information about its known causes or effects.
  - See whether adding examples enlivens or clarifies your explanation. Remember that appositive phrases are a good way to introduce brief examples.
  - Tell more about how the concept works or what people do with it.
  - Add design features or visuals such as charts, headings, drawings, or photographs.

Careful Use of Sources

- **Do readers find your sources inadequate?** Return to the library or the Internet to find additional ones. Consider dropping weak or less reliable sources. Make sure that your sources provide coverage in a comprehensive, balanced way.

- **Do you rely too much on quoting, summarizing, or paraphrasing?** Change some of your quotations to summaries or paraphrases, or vice versa.

- **Does quoted material need to be more smoothly integrated into your own text?** Revise to make it so. Remember to use precise verbs to introduce sources and authors.

- *Are there discrepancies between your in-text citations and the entries in your list of sources?* Compare each citation and entry against the examples given in Chapter 14 for the documentation style you are using. Be sure that all of the citations and entries follow the style exactly. Check to see that your list of sources has an entry for each source that you cite in the text.

Checking Sentence Strategies Electronically. To check your draft for a sentence strategy especially useful in explaining concepts, use your word processor's highlighting function to mark places where you refer to sources and their authors. Then look at the verbs that you use to introduce each source or author, and think about whether changing any of them to a more precise, informative verb would help your readers understand better how you are using the source. For more on using informative, precise verbs to introduce sources, see p. 150.

■ EDITING AND PROOFREADING

Now is the time to check your revised draft carefully for errors in usage, punctuation, and mechanics and to consider matters of style. Our research on students' writing has identified several errors that are especially common in writing that explains concepts. The following guidelines will help you check and edit your essay for these errors. This book's Web site also provides interactive online exercises to help you learn to identify and correct each of these errors; to access the exercises for a particular error, go to the URLs listed after each set of guidelines.

Checking the Punctuation of Adjective Clauses. Adjective clauses include both a subject and a verb. They give information about a noun or a pronoun. They often begin with *who, which,* or *that.* Here is an example from a student essay explaining the concept of schizophrenia, a type of mental illness:

> **It is common for schizophrenics to have delusions** *that they are being persecuted.*

Because adjective clauses add information about the nouns they follow—defining, illustrating, or explaining—they can be useful in writing that explains a concept. Adjective clauses may or may not need to be set off with a comma or commas. To decide, first you have to determine whether the clause is essential to the meaning of the sentence. Clauses that are essential to the meaning of a sentence should not be set off with a comma; clauses that are not essential to the meaning must be set off with a comma. Here are two examples from the student essay about schizophrenia:

ESSENTIAL   **It is common for schizophrenics to have delusions** *that they are being persecuted.*

The adjective clause defines and limits the word *delusions*. If the clause were removed, the basic meaning of the sentence would change, saying that schizophrenics commonly have delusions of all sorts.

NONESSENTIAL   Related to delusions are hallucinations, *which are very common in schizophrenics.*

The adjective clause gives information that is not essential to understanding the main clause (*Related to delusions are hallucinations*). Taking away the adjective clause (*which are very common in schizophrenics*) in no way changes the basic meaning of the main clause.

To decide whether an adjective clause is essential or nonessential, mentally delete the clause. If taking out the clause changes the basic meaning of the sentence or makes it unclear, the clause is probably essential and should not be set off with commas. If the meaning of the main part of the sentence or the main clause does not change enormously, the clause is probably nonessential and should be set off with commas.

▶ Postpartum neurosis, which can last for two weeks or longer, can adversely affect a mother's ability to care for her infant.

▶ The early stage starts with memory loss, which usually causes the patient to forget recent life events.

▶ Seasonal affective disorders are mood disturbances, that occur with a change of season.

▶ The coaches, who do the recruiting should be disciplined.

Adjective clauses following proper nouns always require commas.

▶ Nanotechnologists defer to K. Eric Drexler, who speculates imaginatively about the uses of nonmachines.

For practice, go to bedfordstmartins.com/conciseguide/comma and bedfordstmartins.com/conciseguide/uncomma.

Checking for Commas around Interrupting Phrases.   When writers are explaining a concept, they need to supply a great deal of information. They add much of this information in phrases that interrupt the flow of a sentence. Words that interrupt are usually set off with commas. Be especially careful with interrupting phrases that fall in the middle of a sentence. Such phrases must be set off with two commas, one at the beginning and one at the end:

▶ People on the West Coast, especially in Los Angeles, have always been receptive to new ideas.

▶ Alzheimer's disease, named after the German neuropathologist Alois Alzheimer, is a chronic degenerative illness.

▶ These examples, though simple, present equations in terms of tangible objects.

For practice, go to bedfordstmartins.com/conciseguide/comma and bedfordstmartins.com/conciseguide/uncomma.

A Note on Grammar and Spelling Checkers. These tools are good at catching certain types of errors, but currently there's no replacement for a good human proofreader. Grammar checkers in particular are extremely limited in what they can usually find, and often they only give you summary information that isn't helpful if you don't already understand the rule in question. They are also prone to give faulty advice for fixing problems and to flag correct items as wrong. Spelling checkers cause fewer problems but can't catch misspellings that are themselves words, such as *to* for *too*.

REFLECTING ON YOUR WRITING

Now that you have read and discussed several essays that explain concepts and written one of your own, take some time for reflection. Reflecting on your writing process will help you gain a greater understanding of what you learned about solving the problems you encountered in explaining a concept.

Write a one-page explanation, telling your instructor about a problem you encountered in writing your essay and how you solved it. Before you begin, gather all of your writing—invention and planning notes, drafts, critical comments, revision notes and plans, and final revision. Review these materials, and refer to them as you complete this writing task.

1. *Identify one writing problem you had to solve as you worked to explain the concept in your essay.* Do not be concerned with grammar and punctuation; concentrate instead on problems unique to developing a concept explanation. For example: Did you puzzle over how to focus your explanation? Did you worry about how to appeal to your readers' interests or how to identify and define the

terms that your readers would need explained? Did you have trouble integrating sources smoothly?

2. ***Determine how you came to recognize the problem.*** When did you first discover it? What called it to your attention? If you did not become aware of the problem until someone else pointed it out, can you now see hints of it in your invention writings? If so, where specifically? How did you respond when you first recognized the problem?

3. ***Reflect on how you went about solving the problem.*** Did you work on the wording of a particular passage, cut or add information, move paragraphs or sentences around, add transitions or forecasting statements, experiment with different writing strategies? Did you reread one of the essays in this chapter to see how another writer handled the problem, or did you look back at the invention suggestions? If you talked about the writing problem with another student, a tutor, or your instructor, did talking about it help? How useful was the advice you received?

4. ***Write a brief explanation of how you identified the problem and how you solved it.*** Be as specific as possible in reconstructing your efforts. Quote from your invention notes and draft essay, others' critical comments, your revision plan, or your revised essay to show the various changes your writing underwent as you tried to solve the problem. If you are still uncertain about your solution, say so. Thinking in detail about how you identified a particular problem, how you went about solving it, and what you learned from this experience can help you solve future writing problems more easily.

5

Arguing a Position

You may associate arguing with quarreling or with the in-your-face debating we hear so often on radio and television talk shows. These ways of arguing may let us vent strong feelings, but they seldom lead us to consider seriously other points of view or to look critically at our own thinking.

This chapter presents a more deliberative way of arguing that we call *reasoned argument* because it depends on giving reasons rather than raising voices. It demands that positions be supported rather than merely asserted. It also commands respect for the right of others to disagree with you as you may disagree with them. Reasoned argument requires more thought than quarreling but no less passion or commitment, as you will see when you read the essays in this chapter arguing about controversial issues.

Controversial issues are, by definition, issues about which people may have strong feelings. The issue may involve a practice that has been accepted for some time, like fraternity hazing, or it may concern a newly proposed or recently instituted policy, like the Peacekeepers school program. People may agree about goals but disagree about the best way to achieve them, as in the perennial debate over how to guarantee adequate health care for all citizens. Or they may disagree about fundamental values and beliefs, as in the debate over euthanasia or abortion.

As you can see from these examples, controversial issues have no obvious right answer, no truth that everyone accepts, no single authority on which everyone relies. Writers cannot offer absolute proof in debates about controversial issues because such issues are matters of opinion and judgment. Simply gathering information — finding the facts or learning from experts — will not settle disputes like these, although the more that is known about an issue, the more informed the positions will be.

Although it is not possible to prove that a position on a controversial issue is right or wrong, it is possible through reasoned argument to convince others to accept or reject a particular position. To be convincing, not only must an argument present convincing reasons and plausible support for its position, but it also should anticipate readers' likely objections and opposing arguments, conceding those that are reasonable and refuting those that are not. Vigorous debate that sets forth arguments and counterarguments on all sides of an issue can advance everyone's thinking.

Learning to make reasoned arguments on controversial issues and to think critically about our own as well as others' arguments is not a luxury; it is a necessity if our

161

increasingly diverse society is to survive and flourish. As citizens in a democracy, we have a special duty to inform ourselves about pressing issues and to participate constructively in the public debate. Honing our thinking and arguing skills also has practical advantages in school, where we often are judged by our ability to write convincingly, and in the workplace, where we often need to recommend or defend controversial policy decisions.

You will encounter writing that argues a position in many different contexts, as the following examples suggest.

Writing in Your Other Courses

- For a sociology class, a student writes an essay on surrogate mothering. She finds several newspaper and magazine articles and checks the Internet for surrogate mothering Web sites. In her essay, she acknowledges that using *in vitro* fertilization and a surrogate may be the only way some couples can have their own biological children. Although she respects this desire, she argues that from a sociological perspective surrogate mothering does more harm than good. She gives two reasons: that the practice has serious emotional consequences for the surrogates and their families and that it exploits poor women by creating a class of professional breeders. She supports her argument with anecdotes from surrogates and their families as well as with quotations from sociologists and psychologists who have studied surrogate mothering.

- For a business course, a student writes an essay arguing that the glass ceiling that prevents women from advancing up the corporate ladder still exists at the highest executive levels. She acknowledges that in the nearly twenty years after the phrase "glass ceiling" was coined by a writer at the *Wall Street Journal* in 1986, the percentage of corporate officers who are women has grown. Nevertheless, she argues, the statistics are misleading. Because it is good business to claim gender equity, many companies define to their own advantage the positions counted as corporate officers. The student cites statistics from the Catalyst research group indicating that only 7 percent of the corporate officers in line positions—those responsible for the bottom line and therefore most likely to be promoted to chief executive positions—are women.

Writing in the Community

- For the campus newspaper, a student writes an editorial condemning the practice of fraternity hazing. He acknowledges that most hazing is harmless but argues that hazing can get out of hand and even be lethal. He refers specifically to two incidents reported in the national news in which one student died of alcohol poisoning after being forced to drink too much liquor and another student had a heart attack after being made to run too many laps around the school's track. To show that the potential for a similar tragedy exists on his campus, the writer recounts several anecdotes told to him by students there about their experiences pledging for fraternities. He concludes with a plea to the fraternities on campus to radically change—or at least, curtail—their hazing practices before someone is seriously hurt or killed.

- In a letter to the school board, parents protest a new Peacekeepers program that is being implemented at the local middle school. The writers acknowledge that the aim of the program—to teach students to avoid conflict—is worthwhile. But they argue that the program's methods unduly restrict students' freedoms. Moreover, they claim that the program teaches children to become passive and submissive rather than thinking adults who are willing and able to fight for what is right. To support their argument, they list some of the rules that have been instituted at the middle school: Students must wear uniforms to school, must keep their hands clasped behind their backs when walking down the halls, may not raise their voices in anger or use obscenities, and cannot play aggressive games like dodge ball or contact sports like basketball and football.

Writing in the Workplace

- For a business magazine, a corporate executive writes an essay arguing that protecting the environment is not only good citizenship, but also good business. She supports her position with examples of two companies that became successful by developing innovative methods of reducing hazardous wastes. She also reminds readers of the decisive actions taken in the late 1980s by established corporations to help solve the problem of ozone depletion, such as DuPont's decision to discontinue production of chlorofluorocarbons (CFCs) and McDonald's elimination of styrofoam cartons. Finally, she points out that *Fortune* magazine agrees with her position, noting that the eight deciding factors in its annual ranking of America's Most Admired Corporations include community and environmental responsibility alongside financial soundness.

- In a memo to the director of personnel, a loan company manager argues that written communication skills should be a more important factor in hiring. He acknowledges that math skills are necessary but tries to convince the director that mistakes in writing are too costly to ignore. To support his argument, he cites examples of bad writing in letters and memos that cost the company money and time. For additional examples and suggestions on solving the problem, he refers the personnel director to an ongoing discussion about writing on a listserv to which the manager subscribes.

Practice Arguing a Position: A Collaborative Activity

The preceding scenarios suggest some occasions for arguing a position. Your instructor may schedule this collaborative activity as a face-to-face in-class discussion or ask you to conduct an online real-time discussion in a chat room. Whatever the medium, here are some guidelines to follow:

To construct an effective argument, you must assert a position and offer support for it. This activity gives you a chance to practice constructing an argument with other students.

Part 1. Get together with two to three other students, and choose an issue. You do not have to be an expert on the issue, but you should be familiar with some of the arguments people typically make about it. If you do not have an issue in mind, the following list might help you think of possibilities.

- Should all students be required to wear uniforms in school?
- Should college athletes be paid a portion of the money the school gains from sports events?
- Should community service be a requirement for graduation from high school or college?

In your group, spend two to three minutes quickly exchanging your opinions, and then agree together to argue for the same position on the issue, whether you personally agree with the position or not. Also decide who you would want to read your argument and what you expect these readers to think about the issue. Choose someone in the group to write down the results of your discussion like this:

Issue: Should grades in college be abolished?

Position: Grades should be abolished.

Readers: Teachers who think grades measure learning accurately and efficiently.

Take another ten to fifteen minutes to construct an argument for your position, giving several reasons and noting the kinds of support you would need. Also try to anticipate one or two objections you would expect from readers who disagree with your position. Write down what you discover under the following headings: Reasons, Support Needed, and Likely Objections. Following is an example of this work for the position that grades should be abolished.

Reasons

1. Tests are not always the best way to judge students' knowledge because some students do poorly on tests even though they know the material.
2. Tests often evaluate only what is easily measurable, such as whether students remember facts, rather than whether students can use facts to support their ideas.

Support Needed

1. Research on testing anxiety
2. Anecdotes from students' experience with testing anxiety
3. Teachers' comments on why they rely on tests and how they feel about alternatives to testing (such as group projects)

Likely Objections

1. Tests are efficient for teachers and for students, especially in comparison with research papers.
2. Tests are evaluated strictly on what students have learned about the subject, not on how well they write or how well a group collaborates.

Part 2. Discuss for about five minutes what you did as a group to construct an argument:

Reasons: What did you learn about giving reasons? If you thought of more reasons than you needed, how did you choose? If you had difficulty thinking of reasons, what could you do?

Support: What did you learn about supporting an argument? How many different kinds of support (such as quotations, examples, or anecdotes) did you consider? Which reasons seemed the easiest to support? Which the hardest?

Objections: What did you learn about anticipating objections to your argument? How did you come up with these objections? Given your designated readers, was it easy or hard to think of their likely objections? How could you learn more about your readers' likely objections?

READINGS

No two essays taking a position are alike, and yet they share defining features. Together, the three readings in this chapter reveal a number of these features, so you will want to read as many of them as possible. If time permits, complete the activities in the Analyzing Writing Strategies section that follows each selection, and read the Commentary. Following the readings is a section called Basic Features: Arguing Positions (p. 182), which offers a concise description of the features of writing that takes a position and provides examples from the three readings.

Richard Estrada *was the associate editor of the* Dallas Morning News *editorial page and a syndicated columnist whose essays appeared regularly in the* Washington Post, *the* Los Angeles Times, *and other major newspapers. He was best known as a thoughtful, independent-minded commentator on immigration and social issues. Before joining the* Dallas Morning News *in 1988, Estrada worked as a congressional staff member and as a researcher at the Center for Immigration Studies in Washington, D.C. In the 1990s, he was appointed to the U.S.*

Commission on Immigration Reform. Following his death at the age of forty-nine in 1999, the Richard Estrada Fellowship in Immigration Studies was established in his honor.

Estrada wrote this essay during the 1995 baseball World Series in which the Atlanta Braves played the Cleveland Indians. The series drew the public's attention to the practice of dressing team mascots like Native Americans on the warpath and encouraging fans to rally their team with gestures like the "tomahawk chop" and pep yells like the "Indian chant." The controversy over these practices revitalized a longstanding debate over naming sports teams with words associated with Native Americans. Several high schools and at least one university, Stanford, have changed the names of their sports teams because of this ongoing controversy. A coworker remarked that in his newspaper columns, Estrada "firmly opposed separating the American people into competing ethnic and linguistic groups." As you read this essay, think about his purpose in writing this position essay and how it seeks to bring different groups together.

Sticks and Stones and Sports Team Names

Richard Estrada

When I was a kid living in Baltimore in the late 1950s, there was only one professional sports team worth following. Anyone who ever saw the movie *Diner* knows which one it was. Back when we liked Ike, the Colts were the gods of the gridiron and Memorial Stadium was their Mount Olympus.   1

Ah, yes: The Colts. The Lions. Da Bears. Back when defensive tackle Big Daddy Lipscomb was letting running backs know exactly what time it was, a young fan could easily forget that in a game where men were men, the teams they played on were not invariably named after animals. Among others, the Packers, the Steelers and the distant 49ers were cases in point. But in the roll call of pro teams, one name in particular always discomfited me: the Washington Redskins. Still, however willing I may have been to go along with the name as a kid, as an adult I have concluded that using an ethnic group essentially as a sports mascot is wrong.   2

The Redskins and the Kansas City Chiefs, along with baseball teams like the Atlanta Braves and the Cleveland Indians, should find other names that avoid highlighting ethnicity.   3

By no means were such names originally meant to disparage Native Americans. The noble symbols of the Redskins or college football's Florida State Seminoles or the Illinois Illini are meant to be strong and proud. Yet, ultimately, the practice of using a people as mascots is dehumanizing. It sets them apart from the rest of society. It promotes the politics of racial aggrievement at a moment when our storehouse is running over with it.   4

The World Series between the Cleveland Indians and the Atlanta Braves re-ignited the debate. In the chill night air of October, tomahawk chops and war chants suddenly became far more familiar to millions of fans, along with the ridiculous and offensive cartoon logo of Cleveland's "Chief Wahoo."   5

The defenders of team names that use variations on the Indian theme argue that tradition should not be sacrificed at the altar of political correctness. In truth, the nation's No. 1 P.C. [politically correct] school, Stanford University, helped matters some when it   6 changed its team nickname from "the Indians" to "the Cardinals." To be sure, Stanford did the right thing, but the school's status as P.C. without peer tainted the decision for those who still need to do the right thing.

Another argument is that ethnic group leaders are too inclined to cry wolf in alleging racial insensitivity. Often, this is the case. But no one should overlook genuine cases of political insensitivity in an attempt to avoid accusations of hypersensitivity and political correctness. 7

The real world is different from the world of sports entertainment. I recently heard a father who happened to be a Native American complain on the radio that his child was being pressured into participating in celebrations of Braves baseball. At his kid's school, certain days are set aside on which all children are told to dress in Indian garb and celebrate with tomahawk chops and the like. 8

That father should be forgiven for not wanting his family to serve as somebody's mascot. The desire to avoid ridicule is legitimate and understandable. Nobody likes to be trivialized or deprived of their dignity. This has nothing to do with political correctness and the provocations of militant leaders. 9

Against this backdrop, the decision by newspapers in Minneapolis, Seattle and Portland to ban references to Native American nicknames is more reasonable than some might think. 10

What makes naming teams after ethnic groups, particularly minorities, reprehensible is that politically impotent groups continue to be targeted, while politically powerful ones who bite back are left alone. How long does anyone think the name "Washington Blackskins" would last? Or how about "the New York Jews"? 11

With no fewer than 10 Latino ballplayers on the Cleveland Indians' roster, the team could change its name to "the Banditos." The trouble is, they would be missing the point: Latinos would correctly object to that stereotype, just as they rightly protested against Frito-Lay's use of the "Frito Bandito" character years ago. 12

It seems to me that what Native Americans are saying is that what would be intolerable for Jews, blacks, Latinos and others is no less offensive to them. Theirs is a request not only for dignified treatment, but for fair treatment as well. For America to ignore the complaints of a numerically small segment of the population because it is small is neither dignified nor fair. 13

Connecting to Culture and Experience: Name-Calling

As children, we may say, "Sticks and stones will break my bones, but words will never hurt me." Most children, however, recognize the power of words, especially words that make them feel different or inferior.

Make a list of derogatory words that are used to refer to groups with which you identify. Try to think of words associated with your ethnicity, religion, gender, interests, geographic region, or any other factor. (Are you perhaps a redneck Okie good ole boy religious fanatic?) Which of the words on your list, if any, do you consider insulting? Why? Would you consider someone who called you these names insensitive?

With two or three other students, discuss your name-calling lists, giving examples from your list. Tell when, where, and by whom you or others in your group have been called these names. Speculate about motives of the name callers, and describe your reactions.

Analyzing Writing Strategies

1. At the beginning of this chapter, we discuss several features of essays that argue a position. Consider which of these is true of Estrada's essay:

   - It presents a controversial issue.
   - It asserts a clear position on the issue.
   - It argues for the position by presenting plausible reasons and support.
   - It anticipates readers' objections and arguments, either conceding or refuting them.

2. Reread paragraphs 11–13, where Estrada offers hypothetical examples of team names for ethnic groups, such as the "Washington Blackskins" and "the New York Jews." How do these examples support Estrada's argument? Given his readers, how convincing do you think they are likely to be? How effective are they for you, as one reader?

Commentary: Presenting the Issue and Plausible Reasons

Although the title of his essay implies its subject, Estrada does not identify the issue explicitly until the end of the second paragraph. He begins the essay by remembering his childhood experience as a football fan and explaining that, even as a child, he was made uncomfortable by the practice of naming sports teams for Native Americans. In paragraphs 2–4, he lists team names (Washington Redskins, Kansas City Chiefs, Atlanta Braves, Cleveland Indians, Florida State Seminoles, Illinois Illini) to remind readers how common the practice is. Then, in paragraph 8, he relates an anecdote about a father who not only feels uncomfortable but also feels personally ridiculed as a Native American when his son's school celebrates Braves' victories with Indian costumes and tomahawk chops. Estrada uses this anecdote to demonstrate that the issue is important and worth taking seriously.

Estrada presents the issue in this way to appeal to the readers of his column in the politically conservative *Dallas Morning News*. He apparently assumes that unless he can convince his readers that the issue of sports teams' names is significant, many readers would dismiss it as unimportant or as advancing a liberal agenda. Therefore, Estrada tries to make his readers empathize with what he calls a real-world issue, one that actually hurts kids (paragraph 8). When you present the issue in your own essay, you also may need to help readers understand why it is important and for whom. In the next reading, for example, you will notice that the primary purpose of Barbara Ehrenreich's essay is to make readers appreciate the seriousness of the issue she is addressing.

Presenting the issue is just a beginning. To convince readers, Estrada has to give the reasons that he believes naming sports teams for ethnic groups is detrimental. He gives two: because it treats people like team mascots and it singles out a politically weak group. Moreover, to be convincing, the reasons have to seem plausible to readers. The position (naming sports teams for Native Americans is wrong) has to follow logically from the reason: If readers accept the reason, then they also should accept the position. In other words, if readers are convinced by the support Estrada provides to show the effects of treating people like mascots, then they will be inclined to agree with Estrada that the practice is wrong. Similarly, if readers are convinced also that naming sports teams for Native Americans unfairly singles out a politically weak group, then they would be even more likely to agree with Estrada's conclusion.

Considering Topics for Your Own Essay

List some issues that involve what you believe to be unfair treatment of a marginalized minority group. For example, should a law be passed to make English the official language in this country, requiring that ballots and drivers' tests be printed only in English? Should elementary schools continue bilingual education to help non-English-speaking students learn subjects like math, science, and history while they are learning to read and write fluently in English? What is affirmative action, and should it be used in college admissions for underrepresented groups?

Barbara Ehrenreich published her first article in a science journal when she was a graduate student in biology. After earning her Ph.D., she chose a career as a writer instead of as a research scientist, but Ehrenreich believes that her science background has helped her to look at things both analytically and systematically, seeing the "ways things fit together." A prolific author, she has published essays in such journals as Time, *the* Atlantic Monthly, *the* New York Times Magazine, *the* Nation, *and* Harper's, *for which she is also a contributing editor. Ehrenreich has researched and written more than a dozen books, including* The American Health Empire: Power, Profits, and Politics *(1970);* Fear of Falling: The Inner Life of the Middle Class *(1989), which was nominated for a National Book Critics' Award; and* Blood Rites: Origins and History of the Passions of War *(1997). For the critically acclaimed* Nickel and Dimed: On (Not) Getting By in America *(2001), from which this reading comes, Ehrenreich went "undercover" as a waitress, a maid, a nursing home aide, and a Wal-Mart sales associate. A chapter from* Nickel and Dimed *published in* Harper's *won the Sydney Hillman Award for Journalism, and Ehrenreich has also received a National Magazine Award for Excellence in Reporting, a Ford Foundation Award for Humanistic Perspectives on Contemporary Society, a Guggenheim Fellowship, and a John D. and Catherine T. MacArthur Foundation grant.*

At the time Ehrenreich began her research in 1998, most Americans were enjoying unprecedented economic prosperity stimulated by the dot-com bubble that burst by the time her book was published in 2001. Controversial welfare reform that required single mothers to find jobs was considered a success because more than half of former welfare recipients were employed and the unemployment rate in general was at an all-time low. Nevertheless, reports like that of the Economic Policy Institute, which Ehrenreich refers to in the first paragraph of this reading, indicated that the working poor were struggling just to keep their heads above water. Of course, economic conditions change, and when you read this essay, the situation for the working poor may be better or worse than it was when Ehrenreich completed her research. As you read the essay, think about your own economic situation and that of your family and friends.

Nickel and Dimed

Barbara Ehrenreich

Many people earn far less than they need to live on. How much is that? The Economic Policy Institute recently reviewed dozens of studies of what constitutes a "living wage" and came up with an average figure of $30,000 a year for a family of one adult and two children, which amounts to a wage of $14 an hour. This is not the very minimum such a family could live on; the budget includes health insurance, a telephone, and child care at a licensed center, for example, which are well beyond the reach of millions. But it does not include restaurant meals, video rentals, Internet access, wine and liquor, cigarettes and lottery tickets, or even very much meat. The shocking thing is that the majority of American workers, about 60 percent, earn less than $14 an hour. Many of them get by by teaming up with another wage earner, a spouse or grown child. Some draw on government help in the form of food stamps, housing vouchers, the earned income tax credit, or—for those coming off welfare in relatively generous states—subsidized child care. But others—single mothers, for example—have nothing but their own wages to live on, no matter how many mouths there are to feed. 1

Employers will look at that $30,000 figure, which is over twice what they currently pay entry-level workers, and see nothing but bankruptcy ahead. Indeed, it is probably impossible for the private sector to provide everyone with an adequate standard of living through wages, or even wages plus benefits, alone: too much of what we need, such as reliable child care, is just too expensive, even for middle-class families. Most civilized nations compensate for the inadequacy of wages by providing relatively generous public services such as health insurance, free or subsidized child care, subsidized housing, and effective public transportation. But the United States, for all its wealth, leaves its citizens to fend for themselves—facing market-based rents, for example, on their wages alone. For millions of Americans, that $10—or even $8 or $6—hourly wage is all there is. 2

It is common, among the nonpoor, to think of poverty as a sustainable condition—austere, perhaps, but they get by somehow, don't they? They are "always with us." What is harder for the nonpoor to see is poverty as active distress: The lunch that consists of Doritos or hot dog rolls, leading to faintness before the end of the shift. The "home" that is also a car or a van. The illness or injury that must be "worked through," with gritted teeth, because there's no sick pay or health insurance and the loss of one day's pay will mean no groceries for the next. These experiences are not part of a sustainable lifestyle, even a lifestyle of chronic deprivation and relentless low-level punishment. They are, by almost any standard of subsistence, emergency situations. And that is how we should see the poverty of so many millions of low-wage Americans—as a state of emergency.... 3

Some odd optical property of our highly polarized and unequal society makes the poor almost invisible to their economic superiors. The poor can see the affluent easily enough—on television, for example, or on the covers of magazines. But the affluent rarely see the poor or, if they do catch sight of them in some public space, rarely know what they're seeing, since—thanks to consignment stores and, yes, Wal-Mart—the poor are usually able to disguise themselves as members of the more comfortable classes. Forty years ago the hot journalistic topic was the "discovery of the poor" in their inner-city and Appalachian "pockets of poverty." Today you are more likely to find commentary on their "disappearance," either as a supposed demographic reality or as a shortcoming of the middle-class imagination.

In a 2000 article on the "disappearing poor," journalist James Fallows reports that, from the vantage point of the Internet's nouveaux riches, it is "hard to understand people for whom a million dollars would be a fortune . . . not to mention those for whom $246 is a full week's earnings."[1] Among the reasons he and others have cited for the blindness of the affluent is the fact that they are less and less likely to share spaces and services with the poor. As public schools and other public services deteriorate, those who can afford to do so send their children to private schools and spend their off-hours in private spaces— health clubs, for example, instead of the local park. They don't ride on public buses and subways. They withdraw from mixed neighborhoods into distant suburbs, gated communities, or guarded apartment towers; they shop in stores that, in line with the prevailing "market segmentation," are designed to appeal to the affluent alone. Even the affluent young are increasingly unlikely to spend their summers learning how the "other half" lives, as lifeguards, waitresses, or housekeepers at resort hotels. The *New York Times* reports that they now prefer career-relevant activities like summer school or interning in an appropriate professional setting to the "sweaty, low-paid and mind-numbing slots that have long been their lot."[2]

Then, too, the particular political moment favors what almost looks like a "conspiracy of silence" on the subject of poverty and the poor. . . . Welfare reform itself is a factor weighing against any close investigation of the conditions of the poor. Both parties heartily endorsed it, and to acknowledge that low-wage work doesn't lift people out of poverty would be to admit that it may have been, in human terms, a catastrophic mistake. In fact, very little is known about the fate of former welfare recipients because the 1996 welfare reform legislation blithely failed to include any provision for monitoring their post-welfare economic condition. Media accounts persistently bright-side the situation, highlighting the occasional success stories and downplaying the acknowledged increase in hunger.[3] And sometimes there seems to be almost deliberate deception. In June 2000, the press rushed to hail a study supposedly showing that Minnesota's welfare-to-work program had sharply reduced poverty and was, as *Time* magazine put it, a "winner."[4] Overlooked in these reports was the fact that the program in question was a pilot project that offered far more generous child care and other subsidies than Minnesota's actual welfare reform program. Perhaps the error can be forgiven—the pilot project, which ended in 1997, had the same name, Minnesota Family Investment Program, as Minnesota's much larger, ongoing welfare reform program.[5]

You would have to read a great many newspapers very carefully, cover to cover, to   7
see the signs of distress. You would find, for example, that in 1999 Massachusetts food
pantries reported a 72 percent increase in the demand for their services over the previous year, that Texas food banks were "scrounging" for food, despite donations at or above
1998 levels, as were those in Atlanta.[6] You might learn that in San Diego the Catholic
Church could no longer, as of January 2000, accept homeless families at its shelter, which
happens to be the city's largest, because it was already operating at twice its normal
capacity.[7] You would come across news of a study showing that the percentage of Wis-
consin food-stamp families in "extreme poverty"—defined as less than 50 percent of the
federal poverty line—has tripled in the last decade to more than 30 percent.[8] You might
discover that, nationwide, America's food banks are experiencing "a torrent of need which
[they] cannot meet" and that,[9] according to a survey conducted by the U.S. Conference of
Mayors, 67 percent of the adults requesting emergency food aid are people with jobs.[10]

One reason nobody bothers to pull all these stories together and announce a wide-   8
spread state of emergency may be that Americans of the newspaper-reading professional middle class are used to thinking of poverty as a consequence of unemployment.
During the heyday of downsizing, in the Reagan years, it very often was, and it still is for
many inner-city residents who have no way of getting to the proliferating entry-level jobs
on urban peripheries. When unemployment causes poverty, we know how to state the
problem—typically, "the economy isn't growing fast enough"—and we know what the
traditional liberal solution is—"full employment." But when we have full or nearly full
employment, when jobs are available to any job seeker who can get to them, then the
problem goes deeper and begins to cut into that web of expectations that make up the
"social contract." According to a recent poll conducted by Jobs for the Future, a Boston-
based employment research firm, 94 percent of Americans agree that "people who work
fulltime should be able to earn enough to keep their families out of poverty."[11] I grew up
hearing over and over, to the point of tedium, that "hard work" was the secret of success:
"Work hard and you'll get ahead" or "It's hard work that got us where we are." No one ever
said that you could work hard—harder even than you ever thought possible—and still
find yourself sinking ever deeper into poverty and debt.

When poor single mothers had the option of remaining out of the labor force on wel-   9
fare, the middle and upper middle class tended to view them with a certain impatience, if
not disgust. The welfare poor were excoriated for their laziness, their persistence in
reproducing in unfavorable circumstances, their presumed addictions, and above all for
their "dependency." Here they were, content to live off "government handouts" instead of
seeking "self-sufficiency," like everyone else, through a job. They needed to get their act
together, learn how to wind an alarm clock, get out there and get to work. But now that
government has largely withdrawn its "handouts," now that the overwhelming majority of
the poor are out there toiling in Wal-Mart or Wendy's—well, what are we to think of
them? Disapproval and condescension no longer apply, so what outlook makes sense?

Guilt, you may be thinking warily. Isn't that what we're supposed to feel? But guilt   10
doesn't go anywhere near far enough; the appropriate emotion is shame—shame at our
own dependency, in this case, on the underpaid labor of others. When someone works

for less pay than she can live on—when, for example, she goes hungry so that you can eat more cheaply and conveniently—then she has made a great sacrifice for you, she has made you a gift of some part of her abilities, her health, and her life. The "working poor," as they are approvingly termed, are in fact the major philanthropists of our society. They neglect their own children so that the children of others will be cared for; they live in substandard housing so that other homes will be shiny and perfect; they endure privation so that inflation will be low and stock prices high. To be a member of the working poor is to be an anonymous donor, a nameless benefactor, to everyone else. As Gail, one of my restaurant coworkers put it, "you give and you give."

Someday, of course—and I will make no predictions as to exactly when—they are   11
bound to tire of getting so little in return and to demand to be paid what they're worth. There'll be a lot of anger when that day comes, and strikes and disruption. But the sky will not fall, and we will all be better off for it in the end.

Notes

1. "The Invisible Poor," *New York Times Magazine,* March 19, 2000.
2. "Summer Work Is out of Favor with the Young," *New York Times,* June 18, 2000.
3. The *National Journal* reports that the "good news" is that almost six million people have left the welfare rolls since 1996, while the "rest of the story" includes the problem that "these people sometimes don't have enough to eat" ("Welfare Reform, Act 2," June 24, 2000: 1,978–93).
4. "Minnesota's Welfare Reform Proves a Winner," *Time,* June 12, 2000.
5. Center for Law and Social Policy, "Update," Washington, D.C., June 2000.
6. "Study: More Go Hungry since Welfare Reform," *Boston Herald,* January 21, 2000; "Charity Can't Feed All while Welfare Reforms Implemented," *Houston Chronicle,* January 10, 2000; "Hunger Grows as Food Banks Try to Keep Pace," *Atlanta Journal and Constitution,* November 26, 1999.
7. "Rise in Homeless Families Strains San Diego Aid," *Los Angeles Times,* January 24, 2000.
8. "Hunger Problems Said to Be Getting Worse," *Milwaukee Journal Sentinel,* December 15, 1999.
9. Deborah Leff, the president and CEO of the hunger-relief organization America's Second Harvest, quoted in the *National Journal,* "Welfare Reform, Act 2."
10. "Hunger Persists in U.S. despite the Good Times," *Detroit News,* June 15, 2000.
11. "A National Survey of American Attitudes toward Low-Wage Workers and Welfare Reform," Jobs for the Future, Boston, May 24, 2000.

Connecting to Culture and Experience: The American Dream

In paragraph 8, Barbara Ehrenreich writes about "that web of expectations that make up the 'social contract.'" She explains the essential feature of this social contract in these terms: "'hard work' was the secret of success: 'Work hard and you'll get ahead.'" What she is referring to here is the ideology of the American dream, a set of beliefs and values held by people in the United States and around the world. The American dream assumes that if you work hard enough, you—or at least your children—will be better off financially.

Make a list of the values and beliefs that you associate with the American dream. Then get together with two or three other students, and compare your lists. What do your lists say about the value and rewards of hard work?

Analyzing Writing Strategies

1. In arguing a position on a controversial issue, writers usually state their position in a thesis statement. At the end of paragraph 3, Ehrenreich asserts her thesis: "And that is how we should see the poverty of so many millions of low-wage Americans—as a state of emergency." For a position to be effective, it must be arguable. That is, it should not be a simple statement of fact that can be proven true or false. Nor should a thesis be a matter of faith. Instead, it should be an opinion about which others disagree. It also should be clear and unambiguous as well as appropriately qualified. Use these criteria—that the position be arguable, clear, and appropriately qualified—to decide how effectively Ehrenreich states her position.

2. Ehrenreich sprinkles her argument with statistics. For example, in the opening paragraph, she specifies $14 an hour as the "living wage" that a family of one adult and two children needs. In the same paragraph, she also writes that 60 percent of American workers earn less than this hourly wage. Statistics like these can carry a lot of weight if readers are confident that they come from a reliable source that collects data objectively and professionally. Writers usually cite their sources so that readers can decide for themselves whether the statistics can be believed. For example, if you did a Google search on the Economic Policy Institute, you would find the institute's Web site and learn about EPI's purpose; its corporate, academic, or other affiliations; and its membership. This information could help you judge with some confidence the source's credibility and whether you can count on its statistics.

   Underline the statistics Ehrenreich presents in paragraphs 7 and 8, and put brackets around the sources. Then check Ehrenreich's notes to see what information she gives about each source that could help you determine its credibility.

   (Notice that Ehrenreich does not follow either of the formal styles of documentation, MLA and APA, that are explained in this book; instead she uses a modified form of the *Chicago Manual of Style* system that is often used in books for a general audience. Instead of giving parenthetical citations in the text that are keyed to a list of works cited, she provides notes and does not include a list of works cited. She also does not systematically include page references. When you write a research paper for any of your classes, be sure to ask your instructor what style you should use. For more information on citing sources, see Chapter 14.)

Commentary: Supporting Examples

In the book from which this selection comes, Ehrenreich has the luxury of space to present extended examples to show how particular individuals struggle every day to make ends meet. In this selection from the book's conclusion, however, she needs to make her point quickly with a few brief examples.

Notice how she gives examples in paragraph 3. She provides a list of three examples, and the list is framed by introductory and concluding sentences:

> It is common, among the nonpoor, to think of poverty as a sustainable condition—austere, perhaps, but they get by somehow, don't they? They are "always with us." What is harder for the nonpoor to see is poverty as active distress: The lunch that consists of Doritos or hot dog rolls, leading to faintness before the end of the shift. The "home" that is also a car or a van. The illness or injury that must be "worked through," with gritted teeth, because there's no sick pay or health insurance and the loss of one day's pay will mean no groceries for the next. These experiences are not part of a sustainable lifestyle, even a lifestyle of chronic deprivation and relentless low-level punishment. They are, by almost any standard of subsistence, emergency situations.

This set of examples provides vivid images of the "active distress" Ehrenreich is trying to help her readers to see. Each example refers to a fundamental human need: food, shelter, and health. By emphasizing needs such as these, she reinforces a point she makes at the beginning of her essay: The working poor lack basic necessities, not luxuries. Examples like these help readers to understand what Ehrenreich means by "active distress," and they can also help to convince readers that the problem she is trying to call attention to is serious indeed.

As a writer, you will want to notice not only that Ehrenreich uses examples to support her argument but also that she uses punctuation and sentence structure to present the examples in a way that emphasizes her point:

> What is harder for the nonpoor to see is poverty as active distress: The lunch that.... The "home" that.... The illness or injury that....

Notice that she introduces the list with a colon, a punctuation mark that often precedes a series of examples. Notice also that Ehrenreich uses the same sentence structure for each example: beginning with *the* and a noun (*lunch, home, illness*) followed by a clause beginning with *that*. By consistently beginning each clause with a noun— *lunch, home,* and *illness*—Ehrenreich focuses readers' attention on the basic necessities that many of the working poor lack, thereby repeatedly stressing the point she is making in the paragraph. You might also note that the examples are not full sentences in themselves but are grammatical because they complete the first part of the sentence ("What is harder...is").

When you are writing your own argument, you may want to provide examples for your readers to help them appreciate your point. Following Ehrenreich, try to arrange your sentences in a way that will draw your readers' attention to what you think is most important for them to notice.

Considering Topics for Your Own Essay

You might want to write an essay arguing your own position on the issue that Ehren-reich addresses. If you agree with her that the working poor need help, you might want to argue that the minimum wage should be raised. (The federal minimum wage is currently $5.15 an hour, although some states have higher rates. The minimum wage for employees who earn tips is $2.13 an hour.) Or you might want to argue that citizens should be provided a better social safety net that guarantees quality health care, food stamps, housing subsidies, child care, or other support services. Consider any other social issues you might want to write about. Identify an issue on which you have a position, and think about how you would gather information to construct an argument for your position.

Jessica Statsky wrote the following essay about children's competitive sports for her college composition course. Before reading, recall your own experiences as an elementary student playing competitive sports, either in or out of school. If you were not actively involved yourself, did you know anyone who was? Looking back, do you think that winning was unduly empha-sized? What value was placed on having a good time? On learning to get along with others? On developing athletic skills and confidence?

Children Need to Play, Not Compete

Jessica Statsky

Over the past three decades, organized sports for chil-dren have increased dramatically in the United States. And though many adults regard Little League Baseball and Peewee Football as a basic part of childhood, the games are not always joyous ones. When overzealous parents and coaches impose adult standards on children's sports, the result can be activ-ities that are neither satisfying nor beneficial to children. 1

I am concerned about all organized sports activities for children between the ages of six and twelve. The damage I see results from noncontact as well as contact sports, from sports organized locally as well as those organized nationally. Highly organized competi-tive sports such as Peewee Football and Little League Baseball are too often played to adult standards, which are developmentally inappropriate for children and can be both physically and psychologically harmful. Furthermore, because they eliminate many chil-dren from organized sports before they are ready to compete, they are actually counter-productive for developing either future players or fans. Finally, because they emphasize competition and winning, they unfortunately provide occasions for some parents and coaches to place their own fantasies and needs ahead of children's welfare. 2

One readily understandable danger of overly competitive sports is that they entice children into physical actions that are bad for growing bodies. Although the official Little League Web site acknowledges that children do risk injury playing baseball, they insist that severe injuries are infrequent, "far less than the risk of riding a skateboard, a bicycle, or even the school bus" ("What about My Child?"). Nevertheless, Leonard Koppett in 3

Sports Illusion, Sports Reality claims that a twelve-year-old trying to throw a curve ball, for example, may put abnormal strain on developing arm and shoulder muscles, sometimes resulting in lifelong injuries (294). Contact sports like football can be even more hazardous. Thomas Tutko, a psychology professor at San Jose State University and coauthor of the book *Winning Is Everything and Other American Myths,* writes:

> I am strongly opposed to young kids playing tackle football. It is not the right stage of development for them to be taught to crash into other kids. Kids under the age of fourteen are not by nature physical. Their main concern is self-preservation. They don't want to meet head on and slam into each other. But tackle football absolutely requires that they try to hit each other as hard as they can. And it is too traumatic for young kids. (qtd. in Tosches A1)

As Tutko indicates, even when children are not injured, fear of being hurt detracts   4
from their enjoyment of the sport. The Little League Web site ranks fear of injury as the seventh of seven reasons children quit ("What about My Child?"). One mother of an eight-year-old Peewee Football player explained, "The kids get so scared. They get hit once and they don't want anything to do with football anymore. They'll sit on the bench and pretend their leg hurts . . ." (qtd. in Tosches). Some children are driven to even more desperate measures. For example, in one Peewee Football game, a reporter watched the following scene as a player took himself out of the game:

> "Coach, my tummy hurts. I can't play," he said. The coach told the player to get back onto the field. "There's nothing wrong with your stomach," he said. When the coach turned his head the seven-year-old stuck a finger down his throat and made himself vomit. When the coach turned back, the boy pointed to the ground and told him, "Yes there is, coach. See?" (Tosches A33)

Besides physical hazards and anxieties, competitive sports pose psychological dan-   5
gers for children. Martin Rablovsky, a former sports editor for the *New York Times,* says that in all his years of watching young children play organized sports, he has noticed very few of them smiling. "I've seen children enjoying a spontaneous pre-practice scrimmage become somber and serious when the coach's whistle blows," Rablovsky says. "The spirit of play suddenly disappears, and sport becomes joblike" (qtd. in Coakley 94). The primary goal of a professional athlete — winning — is not appropriate for children. Their goals should be having fun, learning, and being with friends. Although winning does add to the fun, too many adults lose sight of what matters and make winning the most important goal. Several studies have shown that when children are asked whether they would rather be warming the bench on a winning team or playing regularly on a losing team, about 90 percent choose the latter (Smith, Smith, and Smoll 11).

Winning and losing may be an inevitable part of adult life, but they should not be part   6
of childhood. Too much competition too early in life can affect a child's development. Children are easily influenced, and when they sense that their competence and worth are based on their ability to live up to their parents' and coaches' high expectations — and on their ability to win — they can become discouraged and depressed. Little League advises

parents to "keep winning in perspective" ("Your Role"), noting that the most common reasons children give for quitting, aside from change in interest, are lack of playing time, failure and fear of failure, disapproval by significant others, and psychological stress ("What about My Child?"). According to Dr. Glyn C. Roberts, a professor of kinesiology at the Institute of Child Behavior and Development at the University of Illinois, 80 to 90 percent of children who play competitive sports at a young age drop out by sixteen (Kutner).

This statistic illustrates another reason I oppose competitive sports for children: because they are so highly selective, very few children get to participate. Far too soon, a few children are singled out for their athletic promise, while many others, who may be on the verge of developing the necessary strength and ability, are screened out and discouraged from trying out again. Like adults, children fear failure, and so even those with good physical skills may stay away because they lack self-confidence. Consequently, teams lose many promising players who with some encouragement and experience might have become stars. The problem is that many parent-sponsored, out-of-school programs give more importance to having a winning team than to developing children's physical skills and self-esteem.   7

Indeed, it is no secret that too often scorekeeping, league standings, and the drive to win bring out the worst in adults who are more absorbed in living out their own fantasies than in enhancing the quality of the experience for children (Smith, Smith, and Smoll 9). Recent newspaper articles on children's sports contain plenty of horror stories. *Los Angeles Times* reporter Rich Tosches, for example, tells the story of a brawl among seventy-five parents following a Peewee Football game (A33). As a result of the brawl, which began when a parent from one team confronted a player from the other team, the teams are now thinking of hiring security guards for future games. Another example is provided by an *L.A. Times* editorial about a Little League manager who intimidated the opposing team by setting fire to one of their team's jerseys on the pitching mound before the game began. As the editorial writer commented, the manager showed his young team that "intimidation could substitute for playing well" ("The Bad News").   8

Although not all parents or coaches behave so inappropriately, the seriousness of the problem is illustrated by the fact that Adelphi University in Garden City, New York, offers a sports psychology workshop for Little League coaches, designed to balance their "animal instincts" with "educational theory" in hopes of reducing the "screaming and hollering," in the words of Harold Weisman, manager of sixteen Little Leagues in New York City (Schmitt). In a three-and-one-half-hour Sunday morning workshop, coaches learn how to make practices more fun, treat injuries, deal with irate parents, and be "more sensitive to their young players' fears, emotional frailties, and need for recognition." Little League is to be credited with recognizing the need for such workshops.   9

Some parents would no doubt argue that children cannot start too soon preparing to live in a competitive free-market economy. After all, secondary schools and colleges require students to compete for grades, and college admission is extremely competitive. And it is perfectly obvious how important competitive skills are in finding a job. Yet the ability to cooperate is also important for success in life. Before children are psychologi-   10

cally ready for competition, maybe we should emphasize cooperation and individual performance in team sports rather than winning.

Many people are ready for such an emphasis. In 1988, one New York Little League   11
official who had attended the Adelphi workshop tried to ban scoring from six- to eight-
year-olds' games—but parents wouldn't support him (Schmitt). An innovative children's
sports program in New York City, City Sports for Kids, emphasizes fitness, self-esteem,
and sportsmanship. In this program's basketball games, every member on a team plays
at least two of six eight-minute periods. The basket is seven feet from the floor, rather
than ten feet, and a player can score a point just by hitting the rim (Bloch). I believe this
kind of local program should replace overly competitive programs like Peewee Football
and Little League Baseball. As one coach explains, significant improvements can result
from a few simple rule changes, such as including every player in the batting order and
giving every player, regardless of age or ability, the opportunity to play at least four
innings a game (Frank).

Authorities have clearly documented the excesses and dangers of many competitive   12
sports programs for children. It would seem that few children benefit from these programs
and that those who do would benefit even more from programs emphasizing fitness,
cooperation, sportsmanship, and individual performance. Thirteen- and fourteen-year-
olds may be eager for competition, but few younger children are. These younger children
deserve sports programs designed specifically for their needs and abilities.

Works Cited

Bloch, Gordon B. "Thrill of Victory Is Secondary to Fun." *New York Times* 2 Apr. 1990, late
    ed.: C12.
"The Bad News Pyromaniacs?" Editorial. *Los Angeles Times* 16 June 1990: B6.
Coakley, Jay J. *Sport in Society: Issues and Controversies.* St. Louis: Mosby, 1982.
Frank, L. "Contributions from Parents and Coaches." Online posting. 8 July 1997. CYB
    Message Board. 14 May 1999 <http://members.aol.com/JohnHoelter/b-parent
    .html>.
Koppett, Leonard. *Sports Illusion, Sports Reality.* Boston: Houghton, 1981.
Kutner, Lawrence. "Athletics, through a Child's Eyes." *New York Times* 23 Mar. 1989, late
    ed.: C8.
Schmitt, Eric. "Psychologists Take Seat on Little League Bench." *New York Times* 14 Mar.
    1988, late ed.: B2.
Smith, Nathan, Ronald Smith, and Frank Smoll. *Kidsports: A Survival Guide for Parents.*
    Reading: Addison, 1983.
Tosches, Rich. "Peewee Football: Is It Time to Blow the Whistle?" *Los Angeles Times*
    3 Dec. 1988: A1+.
"What about My Child?" *Little League Online.* 1999. Little League Baseball, Inc. 30 June
    1999 <http://www.littleleague.org/about/parents/yourchild.htm>.
"Your Role as a Little League Parent." *Little League Online.* 1999. Little League Baseball,
    Inc. 30 June 1999 <http://www.littleleague.org/about/parents/yourrole.htm>.

Connecting to Culture and Experience: Competition versus Cooperation

Statsky makes the point that competition is highly valued in our culture and that cooperation tends to be downplayed. With two or three other students, discuss some of the ways in which schools encourage competition, especially through courses, instruction, and testing; tutoring and counseling; and sports or other activities. Consider also how cooperation is encouraged. Think about whether, in your own experience, the schools you attended encouraged one more than the other.

If you believe that your schools preferred either competition or cooperation, reflect on why they might have done so. Who in society might benefit most from such a preference — men or women, the poor or the middle class or upper class, your school's administrators or teachers or students? Who loses most?

Analyzing Writing Strategies

1. Anecdotes can provide convincing support if they are clearly relevant to the point they support, believable, and vivid enough to enable readers to imagine what happened. In paragraph 4, Statsky presents one fully developed anecdote that includes dialogue and a detailed narrative. In paragraph 8, she offers two brief anecdotes that summarize rather than detail the events: One is about a brawl among parents, and the other about a team manager who set fire to a jersey of the opposing team. Locate and reread these anecdotes to find out what each one contributes to Statsky's argument and to judge how convincing they are likely to be for her readers. (For more on using anecdotes and authorities, see Chapter 11.)

2. To support her argument, Statsky repeatedly quotes authorities, experts who agree with her position. Skim the essay, underlining each authority she cites. Note where she quotes whole sentences or individual words and phrases. Then pick one source you think adds something important to her argument, and briefly explain what it adds. (For more on quoting and summarizing, see Chapter 14.)

3. Several times in her argument, Statsky adopts a strategy that is favored by writers taking positions on issues and that you can identify. To analyze two examples of the strategy, underline the second and third sentences of paragraph 1 and the first sentence of paragraph 9. What do these two examples have in common? Begin by thinking about the relation of the opening "though" and "although" clauses to what follows in the sentences. For more on sentence strategies important to writers taking positions, turn to Sentence Strategies, p. 196.

Commentary: A Clear Position

Writers arguing a position must state their position clearly, but they also try not to overstate it. By avoiding absolute, unconditional language and carefully qualifying her position, Statsky makes clear her concerns without making enthusiasts of competitive sports overly defensive. Throughout the essay, she qualifies with words like *not always*, *can, maybe,* and *it would seem*—words that potentially have a major effect on readers, making Statsky's position seem reasonable without making her seem indecisive. Similarly, Statsky qualifies her position by focusing on a particular age group. To ensure that readers know the particular kind of sports she is talking about, she gives two familiar examples: Peewee Football and Little League Baseball.

Statsky's unambiguous word choice and appropriate qualification satisfy two of the three requirements for an effective thesis. The third requirement, that the position be arguable, is indicated clearly in paragraph 2, where Statsky forecasts the three reasons for opposing organized competitive sports for young children that she develops later in the essay:

1. Such sports are "both physically and psychologically harmful" (developed in paragraphs 3–6)

2. They are "counterproductive for developing either future players or fans" (developed in paragraph 7)

3. They allow adults "to place their own fantasies and needs ahead of children's welfare" (developed in paragraphs 8–9)

Inexperienced writers are sometimes reluctant to state a thesis and forecast their reasons as clearly and directly as Statsky does. They fear that being direct will oversimplify or give away their whole argument. But we can see from Statsky's essay that the effectiveness of her argument is enhanced, not diminished, by her directness. Nor does directness prevent her from advancing a complex and thoughtful argument on an issue that is certain to arouse strong feelings in many readers.

Considering Topics for Your Own Essay

Make a list of issues related to childhood and adolescence. For example, should elementary and secondary schools be on a year-round schedule? Should children have the right to divorce their parents? Should adolescents who commit serious crimes be tried as adults? Then choose an issue that you think you could write about. What position would you take?

■ PURPOSE AND AUDIENCE

Purpose and audience are closely linked when you write an essay arguing a position. In defining your purpose, you also need to anticipate your readers. Most writers compose essays arguing for a position because they care deeply about the issue. As they develop an argument with their readers in mind, however, writers usually feel challenged to think critically about their own as well as their readers' feelings and thoughts about the issue.

Writers with strong convictions seek to influence their readers. Assuming that logical argument will prevail over prejudice, they try to change readers' minds by presenting compelling reasons and support based on shared values and principles. Nevertheless, they also recognize that in cases where disagreement is profound, it is highly unlikely that a single essay will be able to change readers' minds, no matter how well written it is. When they are addressing an audience that is completely opposed to their position, most writers are satisfied if they can simply win their readers' respect for a different point of view. Often, however, all that they can do is to sharpen the differences.

BASIC FEATURES: ARGUING POSITIONS

A Focused Presentation of the Issue

Writers use a variety of strategies to present the issue and prepare readers for their argument. For current, hotly debated issues, the title may be enough to identify the issue. Estrada's allusion to the familiar children's chant in his title "Sticks and Stones and Sports Team Names" is enough to identify the issue for many readers. Statsky gives a brief history of the debate about competitive sports for children. Many writers provide concrete examples early on to make sure that readers can understand the issue. Statsky mentions Peewee Football and Little League Baseball as examples of the kind of organized sports she opposes. Ehrenreich opens her essay by detailing what would constitute a "living wage," noting how few American workers earn that amount.

How writers present the issue depends on what they assume readers already know and what they want readers to think about the issue. Therefore, they try to define the issue in a way that promotes their position. Estrada defines the issue of naming sports teams after Native Americans in terms of how it affects individuals, especially children, rather than in terms of liberal or conservative politics. Similarly, Ehrenreich presents the issue of a living wage in terms of its practical impact on society.

A Clear Position

Very often writers declare their position in a thesis statement early in the essay. This strategy has the advantage of letting readers know right away where the writer stands. Statsky places her thesis in the opening paragraph, whereas Estrada puts his in the second paragraph. Moreover, all of the writers in this chapter restate the thesis at places in the argument where readers could lose sight of the central point. And they reiterate the thesis at the end.

In composing a thesis statement, writers try to make their position unambiguous, appropriately qualified, and clearly arguable. For example, to avoid ambiguity, Estrada uses common words like *wrong*. But because readers may differ on what they consider to be wrong, Estrada demonstrates exactly what he thinks is wrong about naming teams for ethnic groups. To show readers he shares their legitimate concerns about hypersensitivity, Estrada qualifies his thesis to apply only to genuine cases of political insensitivity. Finally, to show that his position is not based solely on personal feelings, Estrada appeals to readers' common sense of right and wrong.

Plausible Reasons and Convincing Support

To argue for a position, writers must give reasons. Even in relatively brief essays, writers sometimes give more than one reason and state their reasons explicitly. Estrada, for instance, gives two reasons for his position that naming sports teams for ethnic groups is detrimental: It treats people like team mascots, and it singles out politically weak groups. Statsky gives three reasons for her opposition to competitive sports for children: They are harmful to the children, discourage most from participating, and encourage adults to behave badly.

Writers know they cannot simply assert their reasons. They must support them with examples, statistics, authorities, or anecdotes. We have seen all of these kinds of support used in this chapter. For instance, Statsky uses all of them in her essay—giving examples of common sports injuries that children incur, citing statistics indicating the high percentage of children who drop out of competitive sports, quoting authorities on the physical and psychological hazards of competitive sports for young children, and relating an anecdote of a child vomiting to show the enormous psychological pressure competitive sports put on some children. Ehrenreich depends primarily on examples and statistics to support her position that the working poor are living in a perpetual state of emergency that must be acknowledged and remedied.

An Anticipation of Opposing Positions and Objections

Writers also try to anticipate other widely held positions on the issue as well as objections and questions readers might raise to an argument. The writers in this chapter counterargue by either accommodating or refuting opposing positions and objections. Estrada does both, implying that he shares his readers' objection to political correctness but arguing that naming sports teams after ethnic groups is a genuine case of political insensitivity and not an instance of hypersensitivity.

Anticipating readers' positions and objections can enhance the writer's credibility and strengthen the argument. When readers holding an opposing position recognize that the writer takes their position seriously, they are more likely to listen to what the writer has to say. It can also reassure readers that they share certain important values and attitudes with the writer, building a bridge of common concerns among people who have been separated by difference and antagonism.

GUIDE TO WRITING
Arguing Positions

THE WRITING ASSIGNMENT

THE WRITING ASSIGNMENT

Write an essay on a controversial issue. Learn more about the issue, and take a position on it. Present the issue to readers, and develop an argument for the purpose of confirming, challenging, or changing your readers' views on the issue.

INVENTION & RESEARCH

Finding an Issue to Write About

Exploring the Issue

Analyzing Potential Readers

Testing Your Choice

Developing Your Argument

Anticipating Readers' Objections and Questions

Anticipating Opposing Positions

Considering Document Design

Defining Your Purpose for Your Readers

Formulating a Tentative Thesis Statement

INVENTION AND RESEARCH

PLANNING & DRAFTING

Seeing What You Have

Doing Further Research

Setting Goals

Outlining

Drafting

PLANNING AND DRAFTING

CRITICAL READING GUIDE

First Impression

Presentation of the Issue

Clear Statement of the Position

Reasons and Support

Treatment of Opposing Positions, Likely Objections

Effectiveness of Organization

Final Thoughts

CRITICAL READING GUIDE

REVISING

A Focused Presentation of the Issue

A Clear Position

Plausible Reasons and Convincing Support

An Anticipation of Opposing Positions and Objections

The Organization

REVISING

EDITING & PROOFREADING

Checking for Commas before Coordinating Conjunctions

Checking the Punctuation of Conjunctive Adverbs

A Common ESL Problem: Subtle Differences in Meaning

EDITING AND PROOFREADING

GUIDE TO WRITING

■ THE WRITING ASSIGNMENT

Write an essay on a controversial issue. Learn more about the issue, and take a position on it. Present the issue to readers, and develop an argument for the purpose of confirming, challenging, or changing your readers' views on the issue.

■ INVENTION AND RESEARCH

The following activities will help you find an issue, explore what you know about it, and do any necessary research to develop an argument and counterargument. Each activity is easy to do and in most cases takes only a few minutes. Spreading the activities over several days will help you think critically about your own as well as other people's positions on the issue. Keep a written record of your invention and research to use when you draft and revise your essay.

Finding an Issue to Write About

To find the best possible issue for your essay, list as many possibilities as you can. The following activities will help you make a good choice.

Listing Issues. *Make a list of issues you might consider writing about.* Begin your list now, and add to it over the next few days. Include issues on which you already have a position and ones you do not know much about but would like to explore further. Do not overlook the issues suggested by the Considering Topics for Your Own Essay activities following each reading in this chapter.

Put the issues you list in the form of questions, like the following examples:

- Should local school boards be allowed to ban books (like *The Adventures of Huckleberry Finn* and *Of Mice and Men*) from school libraries?
- Should teenagers be required to get their parents' permission to obtain birth-control information and contraceptives?
- Should public libraries and schools be allowed to block access to selected Internet sites?
- Should undercover police officers be permitted to pose as high school students to identify sellers and users of drugs?
- Should training in music performance or art (drawing, painting, sculpting) be required of all high school students?
- Should college admission be based solely on academic achievement in high school?
- Should colleges be required to provide child-care facilities for children of students taking classes?

- Should students attending public colleges be required to pay higher tuition fees if they have been full-time students but do not graduate within four years?
- Should elected state or national representatives vote primarily on the basis of their individual conscience, their constituents' interests, or the general welfare?
- Should scientists attempt to clone human beings as they have done with animals?
- Should more money be directed into research to cure [any disease you want to name]?

Listing Issues Related to Identity and Community.   As the following suggestions indicate, many controversial issues will enable you to explore your understanding of identity and community. List issues that interest you.

- Should student athletes be required to maintain a certain grade point average to participate in college sports?
- Should parents be held responsible legally and financially for crimes committed by their children under age eighteen?
- Should students choose a college or courses that would confirm or challenge their beliefs and values?
- Should high schools or colleges require students to perform community service as a condition for graduation?
- Should children of immigrants who do not speak English be taught in their native language while they are learning English?
- Should all materials related to voting, driving, and income-tax reporting be written only in English or in other languages read by members of the community?
- Should the racial, ethnic, or gender makeup of a police force parallel the makeup of the community it serves?

Listing Issues Related to Work and Career.   Many current controversial issues will allow you to explore work and career topics. Identify issues that you would consider writing about.

- Should businesses remain loyal to their communities, or should they move to wherever labor costs, taxes, or other conditions are more favorable?
- When they choose careers, should people look primarily for jobs that are well paid or for jobs that are personally fulfilling, morally acceptable, or socially responsible?
- Should the state or federal government provide job training or temporary employment to people who are unemployed but willing to work?
- Should the primary purpose of a college education be job training?
- Should drug testing be mandatory for people in high-risk jobs such as bus drivers, heavy-equipment operators, and airplane pilots?

Choosing an Interesting Issue. *Select an issue from your list that you think would be interesting to explore further.* You may already have an opinion on the issue, or you may have chosen it because you want to learn more about it.

Your choice may be influenced by whether you have time for research or whether your instructor requires you to do research. Issues that have been written about extensively make excellent topics for extended research projects. In contrast, you may feel confident writing about a local community or campus issue without doing much, if any, research.

Exploring the Issue

To explore the issue, you need to define it, determine whether you need to do research, and decide tentatively on your position.

Defining the Issue. *To begin thinking about the issue, write for a few minutes explaining how you currently understand it.* If you have strong feelings about the issue, briefly explain why, but do not try to present your argument at this time. Focus on clarifying the issue by considering questions like these:

- Who has taken a position on this issue, and what positions have they taken?
- How does the issue affect different groups of people? What is at stake for them?
- What is the issue's history? How long has it been an issue? Has it changed over time? What makes it important now?
- How broad is the issue? What other issues are related to it?

Doing Research. *If you do not know very much about the issue or the different views people have taken on it, do some research before continuing.* You can gather information by talking to others and by reading what others have written. Choosing one or two key terms of your issue, look for them in the subject headings of the *Library of Congress Subject Headings* and also in the library catalog, using the keyword search option. The library can also give you access to special online resources; check the library's Web site or ask a librarian for advice. Keep a list of the most promising materials you discover.

If you do not have time for research and lack confidence in your knowledge of the issue, you should switch to another issue about which you are better informed. Return to your list of possible issues, and start over.

Exploring Your Opinion. *Write for a few minutes exploring your current thinking on the issue.* What is your current position? Why do you hold this position? What other positions on the issue do you know about? As you develop your argument and learn more about the issue, you may change your mind. Your aim now is merely to record your thinking as of this moment.

Analyzing Potential Readers

Write several sentences describing the readers to whom you will be addressing your argument. Begin by briefly identifying your readers; then use the following questions to help you describe them.

- What position or positions will my readers take on this issue? How entrenched are these positions likely to be?
- What do my readers know about the issue? In what contexts are they likely to have encountered it? In what ways might the issue affect them personally or professionally?
- How far apart on the issue are my readers and I likely to be? What fundamental differences in worldview or experience might keep us from agreeing? Which of my readers' values might most influence their view of the issue?
- Why would I want to present my argument to these particular readers? What could I realistically hope to achieve — convincing them to adopt my point of view, getting them to reconsider their own position, confirming or challenging some of their underlying beliefs and values?

Testing Your Choice

Decide whether you should proceed with this particular issue. Review your invention notes to see whether you understand the issue well enough to continue working with it and whether you can feel confident that you will be able to construct a convincing argument for your prospective readers. To make these decisions, ask yourself the following questions:

- Have I begun to understand the issue and my own position well enough to begin constructing a well-reasoned, well-supported argument?
- Do I have a good enough sense of how my readers view this issue to begin formulating an argument that is appropriate for them?
- Do I now know enough about the issue, or can I learn what I need to know in the time I have remaining?

If you cannot answer these questions affirmatively at this point in the process, it might be wise to consider a different issue. Giving up on a topic after you have worked on it is bound to be frustrating, but if you have little interest in the issue and do not have any idea how you could address your readers, starting over may be the wisest course of action. The following collaborative activity may help you decide whether to go on with this issue or to begin looking for an alternative.

Testing Your Choice: A Collaborative Activity	At this point in your invention work, you will find it helpful to get together with two or three other students to discuss the issue you have tentatively chosen.

Arguers: In turn, each of you identify the issue you are planning to write about. Explain briefly why you care about it personally and why you think your intended readers might see it as important. Then tell the most important reason that you have taken your position on the issue.

Listeners: Tell the arguer what you know about the issue and what you think makes it worth arguing about. Then try to suggest one thing the arguer could say to make the favored reason most convincing to the intended readers.

Developing Your Argument

To construct a convincing argument, you need to list reasons for your position, choose the most plausible ones, and support them.

Listing Reasons.   *Write down every reason you can think of for why you have taken your position.* You can discover reasons for your position by trying to come up with "because" statements—for example, "I believe that my college should provide day care for the young children of full-time students *because these students are most likely to drop out if they cannot count on reliable day care.*" Given that few convincing arguments rely on only one reason, try to come up with at least two or three.

Choosing the Most Plausible Reasons.   *Write several sentences on each reason to determine which reasons seem most plausible—that is, most likely to be convincing to your particular readers. Then identify your most plausible reasons.* If you decide that none of your reasons seems very plausible, you might need to reconsider your position, do some more research, or choose another issue.

Anticipating Readers' Objections and Questions

To construct a convincing argument, you also need to anticipate and decide how you will counterargue readers' objections and questions.

Listing Your Most Plausible Reasons.   *Review the choices you made at the end of the preceding activity, and list your two or three most plausible reasons.*

Listing Objections and Questions.   *Under each reason, list one or more objections to or questions about it that readers could raise.* You may know how readers will respond to some of your reasons. For others, you may need to be inventive. Imagining yourself as a critical reader, look for places where your argument is vulnerable to criticism. For example, think of an assumption that you are making that others might not accept or a value others might not share. Imagine how people in different situations—different neighborhoods, occupations, age groups, living arrangements—might react to your argument.

Accommodating a Legitimate Objection or Question. *Choose one objection or question that makes sense to you, and write for a few minutes on how you could accommodate it into your argument.* You may be able simply to acknowledge an objection or answer a question and explain why you think it does not negatively affect your argument. If the criticism is more serious, try not to let it shake your confidence. Instead, consider how you can accommodate it, perhaps by conceding the point and qualifying your position or changing the way you argue for it.

If the criticism seems so damaging that you cannot accommodate it into your argument, however, you may need to rethink your position or even consider writing on a different issue. If you arrive at such an impasse, discuss the problem with your instructor; do not abandon your issue unless it is absolutely necessary.

Refuting an Illegitimate Objection or Question. *Choose one objection or question that seems to challenge or weaken your argument, and write for a few minutes on how you could refute it.* Do not choose to refute only the weakest objection (to make what is sometimes called a *straw-man argument*) while ignoring the strongest one. Consider whether you can show that an objection is based on a misunderstanding or that it does not really damage your argument.

Anticipating Opposing Positions

Now that you have planned your argument and counterargument, you need to consider how you can respond to the arguments for other positions on the issue.

Considering Other Positions. *Identify one or more widely held positions other than your own that people take on the issue.* If you can, identify the individuals or groups who support the positions you list.

Researching Opposing Positions: An Online Activity   To learn more about opposing positions, search for your issue online. To do so, enter a key term—a word or brief phrase—of your issue into a search tool such as Google (www.google.com) or Yahoo! Directory (http://dir.yahoo.com). If possible, identify at least two positions different from your own. No matter how well argued, they need not weaken your confidence in your position. Your purpose is to understand opposing positions so well that you can represent one or more of them accurately and counterargue them effectively.

Bookmark or keep a record of promising sites. Download any materials that may help you represent and counterargue opposing positions.

Listing Reasons for the Opposing Position. *Choose the opposing position you think is likely to be most attractive to your particular readers, and list the reasons people give for it.* Given what you now know, try to represent the argument accurately and fairly. Later, you may need to do some research to find out more about this opposing position.

Accommodating a Plausible Reason. *Choose one reason that makes sense to you, and write for a few minutes on how you could accommodate it into your argument.* Consider whether you can accommodate the point and put it aside as not really damaging to your central argument. You may also have to consider qualifying your position or changing the way you argue for it.

Refuting an Implausible Reason. *Choose one reason that you do not accept, and write for a few minutes on how you will plan your refutation.* Do not choose to refute a position no one really takes seriously. Also be careful not to misrepresent other people's positions or to criticize people personally (sometimes called an *ad hominem attack*). Do try to get at the heart of your disagreement.

You may want to argue that the values on which the opposing argument is based are not widely shared or are just plain wrong. Or perhaps you can point out that the reasoning is flawed (for instance, showing that an example applies only to certain people in certain situations). Or maybe you can show that the argument lacks convincing support (for instance, that the opposition's statistics can be interpreted differently or that quoted authorities do not qualify as experts). If you do not have all the information you need, make a note of what you need and where you might find it. Later, you can do more research to develop this part of your argument.

Considering Document Design

Think about whether including visual or audio elements—cartoons, photographs, tables, graphs, or snippets from films, television programs, or songs—would strengthen your argument. These are not a requirement of an effective essay arguing a position, but they could be helpful. Consider also whether your readers might benefit from design features such as headings, bulleted or numbered lists, or other elements that would make your essay easier to follow. You could construct your own graphic elements, download materials from the Internet, tape images and sounds from television or other sources, or scan into your document visuals from books and magazines. If you do use visual or audio materials you did not create yourself, be sure to acknowledge your sources in your essay (and request permission from the sources if the essay will be posted on the Web).

Defining Your Purpose for Your Readers

Write a few sentences, defining your purpose in writing about your position on this issue for your particular readers. Remember that you already have analyzed your potential readers and developed your argument with these readers in mind. Given these readers, try now to define your purpose by considering the following possibilities and any others that might apply to your writing situation:

- If my readers are likely to be sympathetic to my point of view, what do I hope to achieve — give them reasons to commit to my position, arm them with ammunition to make their own arguments, or win their respect and admiration?

- If my readers are likely to be hostile to my point of view, what do I hope to accomplish — get them to concede that other points of view must be taken seriously, make them defend their reasons, show them how knowledgeable and committed I am to my position, or show them how well I can argue?

- If my readers are likely to take an opposing position but are not staunchly committed to it, what should I try to do — make them think critically about the reasons and the kinds of support they have for their position, give them reasons to change their minds, show them how my position serves their interests better, appeal to their values and sense of responsibility, or disabuse them of their preconceptions and prejudices against my position?

Formulating a Tentative Thesis Statement

Write several sentences that could serve as a thesis statement. Assert your position carefully. You might also forecast your reasons, listing them in the order in which you will take them up in your argument. In other words, draft a thesis statement that tells your readers simply and directly what you want them to think about the issue and why. (For more on thesis and forecasting statements, see Chapter 8, pp. 307–9.)

Estrada states his thesis at the end of the second paragraph: "Still, however willing I may have been to go along with the name as a kid, as an adult I have concluded that using an ethnic group essentially as a sports mascot is wrong." Perhaps the most explicit and fully developed thesis statement in this chapter's readings is Jessica Statsky's. She asserts her thesis at the end of the first paragraph and then qualifies it and forecasts her reasons in the second paragraph:

> When overzealous parents and coaches impose adult standards on children's sports, the result can be activities that are neither satisfying nor beneficial to children.
>
> I am concerned about all organized sports activities for children between the ages of six and twelve. The damage I see results from noncontact as well as contact sports, from sports organized locally as well as those organized nationally. Highly organized competitive sports such as Peewee Football and Little League Baseball are too often played to adult standards, which are developmentally inappropriate for children and can be both physically and psychologically harmful. Furthermore, because they eliminate many children from organized sports before they are ready to compete, they are actually counterproductive for developing either future players or fans. Finally, because they emphasize competition and winning, they unfortunately provide occasions for some parents and coaches to place their own fantasies and needs ahead of children's welfare.

As you formulate your own tentative thesis statement, pay attention to the language you use. It should be clear and unambiguous, emphatic but appropriately qualified, as well as arguable and based on plausible reasons. Although you will most probably refine this thesis statement as you work on your essay, trying now to articulate it will help give your planning and drafting direction and impetus. (For more on asserting a thesis, see Chapter 11, pp. 362–65.)

■ PLANNING AND DRAFTING

You should now review what you have learned about the issue, do further research if necessary, and plan your first draft by setting goals and making an outline.

Seeing What You Have

Pause now to reflect on your invention and research notes. Reread everything carefully to decide whether you have enough plausible reasons and convincing support to offer readers and whether you understand the debate well enough to anticipate and respond to your readers' likely objections. It may help, as you read, to annotate your invention writings. If you have done your invention writing on the computer, you may have sentences or whole paragraphs that can be copied and pasted into your draft. Reread what you have written so far to identify the potentially useful material. Look for details that will help you clarify the issue for readers, present a strong argument for your position, and counterargue possible objections and alternative positions. Highlight key words, phrases, or sentences; make marginal notes or electronic annotations.

If your invention notes are skimpy, you may not have given enough thought to the issue or know enough at this time to write a convincing argument about it. You can do further research at this stage or begin drafting and later do research to fill in the blanks.

If you fear that you are in over your head, consult your instructor to determine whether you should make a radical change. For example, your instructor might suggest that you tackle a smaller, more doable aspect of the issue, perhaps one with which you have firsthand experience. It is also possible that your instructor will advise you to give up on this topic for the time being and to try writing on a different issue.

Doing Further Research

If you think you lack crucial information that you will need to plan and draft your essay, this is a good time to do some further research. Consider possible sources, including people you could interview as well as library materials and Internet sites. Then do your research, making sure to note down all the information you will need to cite your sources.

Setting Goals

Before you begin writing your draft, consider some specific goals for your essay. The draft will be easier to write and more focused if you have some clear goals in mind. The following questions will help you set them. You may find it useful to return to them while you are drafting, for they are designed to help you look at specific features and strategies of an essay arguing a position on a controversial issue.

Your Purpose and Readers

- Who are my readers, and what can I realistically hope to accomplish by addressing them?
- Should I write primarily to change readers' minds, to get them to consider my arguments seriously, to confirm their opinions, to urge them to do something about the issue, or to accomplish some other purpose?
- How can I present myself so that my readers will consider me informed, knowledgeable, and fair?

The Beginning

- What opening would capture readers' attention?
- Should I begin as if I were telling a story, with phrases like "When I was" (Estrada) or "Over the past three decades" (Statsky)?
- Should I open with a rhetorical question, an arresting quotation, or a surprising statistic? Ehrenreich combines all three in her opening sentences.
- Should I open by summarizing an opposing argument that I will refute?
- Should I make clear at the outset exactly what my concerns are and how I see the issue, as Statsky does?

Presentation of the Issue

- Should I place the issue in a historical context or in a personal context, as Estrada does?
- Should I use examples—real or hypothetical—to make the issue concrete for readers, as Estrada does?
- Should I try to demonstrate that the issue is important by citing statistics, quoting authorities, or describing its negative effects, as Statsky and Ehrenreich do?

Your Argument and Counterargument

- How can I present my reasons so that readers will see them as plausible, leading logically to my position?
- If I have more than one reason, how should I sequence them?
- Should I forecast my reasons or counterarguments early in the essay, as Statsky does?

- Which objections should I anticipate? Can I concede any objections without undermining my argument, as Estrada does?
- Which opposing positions should I anticipate? Can I counterargue by showing that the statistics offered by others are not relevant? Can I support my position with anecdotes, as Estrada does?

The Ending

- How can I conclude my argument effectively? Should I reiterate my thesis?
- Should I try to unite readers with different allegiances by reminding them of values we share, as Estrada and Ehrenreich do?
- Could I conclude by looking to the future or by urging readers to take action or make changes, as Statsky does?

Outlining

An essay arguing a position on a controversial issue contains as many as four basic parts:

1. Presentation of the issue
2. A clear position
3. Reasons and support
4. Anticipation of opposing positions and objections

These parts can be organized in various ways. If you expect some of your readers to oppose your argument, you might try to redefine the issue so that these readers can see the possibility that they may share some common values with you after all. To reinforce your connection to readers, you could go on to concede the wisdom of an aspect of their position before presenting the reasons and support for your position. You would conclude by reiterating the shared values on which you hope to build agreement. In this case, an outline might look like this:

Presentation of the issue

Accommodation of some aspect of an opposing position

Thesis statement

First reason with support

Second reason with support (etc.)

Conclusion

If you have decided to write primarily for readers who agree rather than disagree with you, then you might choose to organize your argument as a refutation of opposing arguments to strengthen your readers' convictions. Begin by presenting the issue, stating your position, and reminding readers of your most plausible reasons. Then take up each opposing argument, and try to refute it. You might conclude by calling your supporters to arms. Here is an outline showing what this kind of essay might look like:

Presentation of the issue

Thesis statement

Your most plausible reasons

First opposing argument with refutation

Second opposing argument with refutation

Conclusion

There are, of course, many other possible ways to organize an essay arguing for a position on a controversial issue, but these outlines should help you start planning your own essay. (For more on outlining, see Chapter 9, pp. 326–29.)

Consider tentative any outlining you do before you begin drafting. Never be a slave to an outline. As you draft, you will usually see ways to improve on your original plan. Be ready to revise your outline, shift parts around, or drop or add parts as you draft. If you use the outlining function of your word processing program, changing your outline will be simple, and you may be able to write the essay simply by expanding the outline.

Drafting

General Advice.   Start drafting your essay, keeping in mind the goals you set while you were planning. Remember also the needs and expectations of your readers; organize, define, and explain with them in mind. Turn off your grammar checker and spelling checker at this stage if you find them distracting. Don't be afraid to skip around in your draft; jump back and fill in a spontaneous idea, or leap ahead and write a later section first if you find that easier. If, as you draft, you find that you need more information, just make a note of what you have to find out and go on to the next point. When you are done drafting, you can search for the information you need. If you get stuck while drafting, explore the problem by using some of the writing activities in the Invention and Research section of this chapter. You may want to review the general drafting advice in Chapter 1.

As you draft, keep in mind that the basis for disagreement about controversial issues often depends on values as much as on credible support. Try to think critically about the values underlying your own as well as others' views so that your argument can take these values into account. Consider the tone of your argument and how you want to come across to readers.

Sentence Strategies.   As you draft, you will need to move back and forth smoothly between direct arguments for your position and counterarguments for your readers' likely objections, questions, and preferred positions on the issue. One useful strategy for making this move is to concede the value of a likely criticism and then to attempt to refute it immediately, either in the same sentence or in the next one. You will also need to use conjunctions and similar phrases to indicate explicitly and precisely the logical relationships between your sentences.

Counterargue by conceding and then immediately refuting. How do you introduce brief concession followed by refutation into your argument? The following sentences from Jessica Statsky's essay illustrate several ways to do so (the concessions are in italics, the refutations in bold):

> The primary goal of professional athletes — winning — is not appropriate for children. Their goals should be having fun, learning, and being with friends. *Although winning does add to the fun,* **too many adults lose sight of what matters and make winning the most important goal.** (paragraph 5)

> *And it is perfectly obvious how important competitive skills are in finding a job.* **Yet the ability to cooperate is also important for success in life.** (10)

In both these examples from different stages in her argument, Statsky concedes the importance or value of some of her readers' likely objections, but then firmly refutes them. (Because these illustrations are woven into an extended argument, you may be better able to appreciate them if you look at them in context by turning to the paragraphs where they appear.) The following example comes from another reading in the chapter:

> *Guilt, you may be thinking warily. Isn't that what we're supposed to feel?* **But guilt doesn't go anywhere near far enough; the appropriate emotion is shame.**.... (Barbara Ehrenreich, paragraph 10)

This important counterargument strategy sometimes begins not with concession but with acknowledgment; that is, the writer simply accurately restates part of an opponent's argument without conceding the wisdom of it. Here is an example:

> *Another argument is that ethnic group leaders are too inclined to cry wolf in alleging racial insensitivity. Often, this is the case.* **But no one should overlook genuine cases of political insensitivity in an attempt to avoid accusations of hypersensitivity and political correctness.** (Richard Estrada, paragraph 7)

The concession-refutation move, sometimes called the "yes-but" strategy, is important in most arguments; in fact, it usually recurs, as it does in all the readings in this chapter. Following is an outline of some of the other language this chapter's authors rely on to introduce their concession-refutation moves:

Introducing the concession	*Introducing the refutation that follows*
I understand that	What I think is
I can't prove	But I think
I am grateful	But surely
It is true that	But my point is
Another argument	But

And it is not difficult to imagine other concession-refutation pairings:

It has been argued that	Nevertheless,
We are told that	My own belief is

Proponents argue that	This argument, however,
This argument seems plausible	But experience and evidence show
One common complaint is	In recent years, however,
I'm not saying. . . . Nor am I saying	But I am saying
Activists insist	Still, in spite of their good intentions
A reader might ask	But the real issue

Use conjunctions and phrases like them to indicate explicitly and precisely the logical relationships between clauses and sentences. In all writing, conjunctions serve to indicate the specific ways that clauses and sentences relate in meaning to each other, but reasoned arguments are especially dependent on these logical links. There are three main types of conjunctions: coordinating conjunctions like *and, but,* or *so;* subordinating conjunctions like *while, because,* and *although;* and, of special importance in arguments taking a position, conjunctive adverbs like *furthermore, consequently, however, nevertheless,* and *therefore.* Here is an example from a reading in this chapter, with the conjunctive adverb in italics:

> Highly organized competitive sports such as Peewee Football and Little League Baseball are too often played to adult standards, which are developmentally inappropriate for children and can be both physically and psychologically harmful. *Furthermore,* because they eliminate many children from organized sports before they are ready to compete, they are actually counterproductive for developing either future players or fans. (Jessica Statsky, paragraph 2)

Statsky chooses the conjunctive adverb *furthermore* because in the previous sentence she has given one reason that she opposes highly competitive organized sports for children and she wants readers to understand that she is about to give another one. In this situation, she might also have chosen *moreover, in addition,* or *at the same time.*

Now look at this example:

> Like adults, children fear failure, *and so* even those with good physical skills may stay away because they lack self-confidence. *Consequently,* teams lose many promising players who with some encouragement and experience might have become stars. (Jessica Statsky, paragraph 7)

Here Statsky uses *and so* to link the two main clauses in the first sentence and the conjunctive adverb *consequently* to link the second sentence to the first. In both cases, she is arguing that what comes after the conjunction is an unfortunate effect or consequence of what comes before it: Fear of failure causes staying away, which in turn causes the loss of promising players. Instead of *consequently,* she might have chosen *therefore, as a result,* or *in effect* to make this logical relationship explicit.

Notice that conjunctive adverbs seem somewhat formal. This level of formality would be appropriate in most arguments taking positions on public issues. Should you be writing for a familiar audience of peers or a publication aimed at a popular audience, however, you might want to adopt less formal conjunctions or phrases for indicating logical relationships between your clauses and sentences. For example, you could use *but* instead of *however, and* or *in addition* instead of *moreover, still* for *nev-*

ertheless, or *so* instead of *consequently.* In this chapter's readings, Barbara Ehrenreich consistently uses informal conjunctions, and Jessica Statsky mostly uses formal ones.

You might find the following list helpful when you are searching for precisely the right conjunctive adverb or phrase for the logical relationship you want to signal. If you are unsure about which one to choose, look up the most likely one in a dictionary or, better, a dictionary of synonyms. Keep in mind that these useful expressions serve only to *signal* a logical relationship; they cannot *create* such a relationship, which is determined by the content of the clauses or sentences they join. Your readers will not necessarily see the similarities between two things, for example, just because you have joined them with *similarly.*

> To expand or add: *moreover, further, furthermore, in addition, at the same time, in the same way, by the same token, that is, likewise*
>
> To reformulate or replace: *in other words, better, rather, again, alternatively, on the other hand*
>
> To exemplify: *for example, as an example, thus, for instance*
>
> To qualify: *however, nevertheless, on the other hand, at the same time*
>
> To dismiss: *in any case, in either case, whichever way it is, anyhow, at any rate, however it is*
>
> To show cause or effect: *therefore, consequently, as a result, in effect, for this reason, otherwise, in that case, accordingly, hence, thus*
>
> To show comparison: *in comparison, by comparison, in the same way, similarly, likewise*
>
> To show contrast: *instead, on the contrary, rather, by contrast, in opposition, on the other hand*
>
> To show emphasis: *indeed, again*

In addition to making the concession-refutation move and using conjunctions to signal logical relationships, you can strengthen your reasoned arguments with other kinds of sentence strategies as well, and you may want to turn to the discussions of sentences that feature appositives to identify or establish the authority of a source (pp. 151–52).

CRITICAL READING GUIDE

Now is the time to get a good critical reading of your draft. Your instructor may arrange such a reading as part of your coursework; if not, you can ask a classmate, friend, or family member to read it over. If your campus has a writing center, you might ask a tutor there to read and comment on your draft using this guide to critical reading. (If you are unable to have someone else review your draft, turn ahead to the Revising section on p. 202, where you will find guidelines for reading your own draft critically.)

If you read another student's draft online, you may be able to use a word processing program to insert suggested improvements directly into the text of the draft or to write them out at the end of the draft. If you read a printout of the draft, you may write brief comments in the margins and lengthier suggestions on a separate page. When the writer sits down to revise, your thoughtful, extended suggestions written at the end of the draft or on separate pages will be especially helpful.

If You Are the Writer. To provide focused, helpful comments, your critical reader must know your essay's intended audience, your purpose, and a problem in the draft that you need help solving. Briefly write out this information at the top of your draft.

- *Readers:* To whom are you directing your argument? What do you assume they think about this issue? Do you expect them to be receptive, skeptical, resistant, antagonistic?

- *Purpose:* What effect do you realistically expect your argument to have on these particular readers?

- *Problem:* Ask your reader to help you solve the most important problem you see in your draft. Describe this problem briefly.

If You Are the Reader. Use the following guidelines to help you give constructive, critical comments to others on their position papers.

1. *Read for a First Impression.* Tell the writer what you think the intended readers would find most and least convincing. If you personally think the argument is seriously flawed, share your thoughts. Then try to help the writer improve the argument for the designated readers. Next, consider the problem the writer identified, and respond briefly to that concern now. (If you find that the problem is covered by one of the other guidelines listed below, respond to it in more detail there if necessary.)

2. *Analyze the Way the Issue Is Presented.* Look at the way the issue is presented, and indicate whether you think that most readers would understand the issue differently. If you think that readers will need more information to grasp the issue and appreciate its importance, ask questions to help the writer fill in whatever is missing.

3. *Assess Whether the Position Is Stated Clearly.* Write a sentence or two summarizing the writer's position as you understand it from reading the draft.

Then identify the sentence or sentences in the draft where the thesis is stated explicitly. (It may be restated in several places.) If you cannot find an explicit statement of the thesis, let the writer know. Given the writer's purpose and audience, consider whether the thesis statement is too strident or too timid and whether it needs to be more qualified, more sharply focused, or more confidently asserted. If you think that the thesis, as presented, is not really arguable — for example, if it asserts a fact no one questions or a matter of personal belief — let the writer know.

4. *Evaluate the Reasons and Support.* Identify the reasons given for the writer's position. Have any important reasons been left out or any weak ones overemphasized? Indicate any contradictions or gaps in the argument. Point to any reasons that do not seem plausible to you, and briefly explain why. Then note any places where support is lacking or unconvincing. Help the writer think of additional support or suggest sources where more or better support might be found.

5. *Assess How Well Opposing Positions and Likely Objections Have Been Handled.* Identify places where opposing arguments or objections are mentioned, and point to any where the refutation could be strengthened or where shared assumptions or values offer the potential for accommodation. Also consider whether the writer has ignored any important opposing arguments or objections.

6. *Consider Whether the Organization Is Effective.* Get an overview of the essay's organization, perhaps by making a scratch outline. Point to any parts that might be more effective earlier or later in the essay. Point out any places where more explicit cueing — transitions, summaries, or topic sentences — would clarify the relationship between parts of the essay.

   - *Reread the beginning.* Will readers find it engaging? If not, see whether you can recommend something from later in the essay that might work better as an opening.

   - *Study the ending.* Does the essay conclude decisively and memorably? If not, suggest an alternative. Could something be moved to the end?

   - *Assess the design features and visuals.* Comment on the contribution of any headings, tables, or other design features and illustrations. Help the writer think of additional design features and illustrations that could make a contribution to the essay.

7. *Give the Writer Your Final Thoughts.* What is this draft's strongest part? What part is most in need of further work?

■ REVISING

Now you are ready to revise your essay. Your instructor or other students may have given you advice on improving your draft. Nevertheless, you may have begun to realize that your draft requires not so much revising as rethinking. For example, you may recognize that your reasons do not lead readers to accept your position, that you cannot adequately support your reasons, or that you have been unable to refute damaging objections to your argument. Consequently, instead of working to improve parts of the draft, you may need to write a new draft that radically reenvisions your argument. It is not unusual for students—and professional writers—to find themselves in this situation. Learning to make radical revisions is a valuable lesson for all writers.

On the other hand, you may feel quite satisfied that your draft achieves most, if not all, of your goals. In that case, you can focus on refining specific parts of your draft. Very likely you have thought of ways of improving your draft, and you may even have begun improving it. This section will help you get an overview of your draft and revise it accordingly.

Getting an Overview

Consider your draft as a whole, following these two steps:

1. *Reread.* If at all possible, put the draft aside for a day or two before rereading it. When you return to it, start by reconsidering your purpose. Then read the draft straight through, trying to see it as your intended readers will.

2. *Outline.* Make a scratch outline, indicating the basic features as they appear in the draft. Consider using the headings and outline/summary functions of your word processor.

Planning for Revision. Resist the temptation to dive in and start changing your text until after you have a clear view of the big picture. Using your outline as a guide, move through the document, using the highlighting or commenting tools of your word processor to note comments received from others and problems you want to solve (or mark on a hard copy if you prefer).

Analyzing the Basic Features of Your Own Draft. Using the questions presented in the Critical Reading Guide on pp. 199–201, reread your draft to identify specific problems you need to solve. Note the problems on your draft.

Studying Critical Comments. Review all of the comments you have received from other readers, and add to your notes any suggestions you intend to act on. For each comment, look at the draft to see what might have led the reader to make that particular point. Try to be receptive to any criticism. By letting you see how other readers respond to your draft, these comments provide valuable information about how you might improve it.

Carrying Out Revisions

Having identified problems in your draft, you now need to come up with solutions and — most important — to carry them out. Basically, you have three ways of finding solutions:

1. Review your invention and planning notes for information and ideas to add to your draft.
2. Do additional invention and research to provide material you or your readers think is needed.
3. Look back at the readings in this chapter to see how other writers have solved similar problems.

The following suggestions, which are organized according to the basic features of position papers, will help you get started solving some problems common to them.

A Focused Presentation of the Issue

- *Do readers have difficulty summarizing the issue, or do they see it differently from the way you do?* Try to anticipate possible misunderstandings or other ways of seeing the issue.

- *Do readers need more information?* Consider adding examples, quoting authorities, or simply explaining the issue further.

- *Does the issue strike readers as unimportant?* State explicitly why you think it is important and why you think your readers should think so, too. Try to provide an anecdote, facts, or a quote from an authority that would demonstrate its importance.

A Clear Position

- *Do readers have difficulty summarizing your position or finding your thesis statement?* You may need to announce your thesis statement more explicitly or rewrite it to prevent misunderstanding.

- *Do any words seem unclear or ambiguous?* Use other words, explain what you mean, or add an example to make your position more concrete.

- *Do you appear to be taking a position that is not really arguable?* Consider whether your position is arguable. If you believe in your position as a matter of faith and cannot provide reasons and support, then your position probably is not arguable. Consult your instructor about changing your position or topic.

- *Could you qualify your thesis to account for exceptions or strong objections to your argument?* Add language that specifies when, where, under what conditions, or for whom your position applies.

Plausible Reasons and Convincing Support

- *Do readers have difficulty identifying your reasons?* Announce each reason explicitly, possibly with topic sentences. Consider adding a forecast early in the essay so readers know what reasons to expect.

- *Have you left out any reasons?* Consider whether adding particular reasons would strengthen your argument. To fit in new reasons, you may have to reorganize your whole argument.

- *Do any of your reasons seem implausible or contradictory?* Either delete such reasons, or show how they relate logically to your position or to your other reasons.

- *Does your support seem unconvincing or scanty?* Where necessary, explain why you think the support should lead readers to accept your position. Review your invention notes, or do some more research to gather additional examples, statistics, anecdotes, or quotations from authorities.

An Anticipation of Opposing Positions and Objections

- *Do readers have difficulty finding your responses to opposing arguments or objections?* Add transitions that call readers' attention to each response.

- *Do you ignore any important objections or arguments?* Consider adding to your response. Determine whether you should replace a response to a relatively weak objection with a new response to a more important one.

- *Are there any concessions you could make?* Consider whether you should acknowledge the legitimacy of readers' concerns or accommodate particular objections. Show on what points you share readers' values, even though you may disagree on other points. Remember that all of the authors in this chapter concede and then attempt to refute, relying on useful sentence openers like *I understand that, What I think is,* and *It is true that . . . , but my point is. . . .*

- *Do any of your attempts at refutation seem unconvincing?* Try to strengthen them. Avoid attacking your opponents. Instead, provide solid support—respected authorities, accepted facts, and statistics from reputable sources—to convince readers that your argument is credible.

The Organization

- *Do readers have trouble following your argument?* Consider adding a brief forecast of your main reasons at the beginning of your essay and adding explicit topic sentences and transitions to announce each reason as it is developed. As all the authors do in this chapter, consider signaling explicitly the logical relations between steps and sentences in your argument. Remember that they use both informal signals like *yet* and *still* and formal signals like *moreover, consequently,* and *therefore.*

- *Does the beginning seem vague and uninteresting?* Consider adding a striking anecdote or surprising quotation to open the essay, or find something in the essay you could move to the beginning.

- *Does the ending seem indecisive or abrupt?* Search your invention notes for a strong quotation, or add language that will reach out to readers. Try moving your strongest point to the ending.

- *Can you add illustrations or any other design features to make the essay more interesting to read and to strengthen your argument?* Consider incorporating a visual you came across in your research or one you can create on your own.

Checking Sentence Strategies Electronically. To check your draft for a sentence strategy especially useful in essays arguing a position, use your word processor's highlighting function to mark places where you are either making concessions or trying to refute opposing arguments or objections that readers might have to your argument. Then look at each place, and think about whether you could strengthen your argument at that point by combining concession and refutation, either by moving or adding a concession just before a refutation or by moving or adding a refutation immediately following a concession. For more on the concession-refutation strategy, see pp. 196–98.

■ EDITING AND PROOFREADING

Now is the time to edit your revised draft for errors in grammar, punctuation, and mechanics and to consider matters of style. Our research has revealed several errors that are especially likely to occur in student essays arguing a position. The following guidelines will help you check and edit your draft for these common errors. This book's Web site also provides interactive online exercises to help you learn to identify and correct some of these errors; to access the exercises for a particular error, go to the URLs listed after each set of guidelines.

Checking for Commas before Coordinating Conjunctions. An independent clause is a group of words that can stand alone as a complete sentence. Writers often join two or more such clauses with coordinating conjunctions *(and, but, for, or, nor, so, yet)* to link related ideas in one sentence. Look at one example from Jessica Statsky's essay:

> Winning and losing may be an inevitable part of adult life, but they should not be part of childhood. (paragraph 6)

In this sentence, Statsky links two ideas: (1) that winning and losing may be part of adult life and (2) that they should not be part of childhood. In essays that argue a position, writers often join ideas in this way as they set forth the reasons and support for their positions.

When you join independent clauses, use a comma before the coordinating conjunction so that readers can easily see where one idea stops and the next one starts:

▶ The new immigration laws will bring in more skilled people⌃ but their presence will take jobs away from other Americans.

▶ Sexually transmitted diseases are widespread⌃ and many students are sexually active.

Do not use a comma when the coordinating conjunction joins phrases that are not independent clauses:

▶ Newspaper reporters have visited pharmacies⁄ and observed pharmacists selling steroids illegally.

▶ We need people with special talents⁄ and diverse skills to make the United States a stronger nation.

For practice, go to bedfordstmartins.com/conciseguide/comma and bedfordstmartins .com/conciseguide/uncomma.

Checking the Punctuation of Conjunctive Adverbs. When writers take a position, the reasoning they need to employ seems to invite the use of conjunctive adverbs (*consequently, furthermore, however, moreover, therefore, thus*) to connect sentences and clauses. Conjunctive adverbs that open a sentence should be followed by a comma:

▶ Consequently⌃ many local governments have banned smoking.

▶ Therefore⌃ talented nurses will leave the profession because of poor working conditions and low salaries.

If a conjunctive adverb joins two independent clauses, it must be preceded by a semi-colon and followed by a comma:

▶ The recent vote on increasing student fees produced a disappointing turnout⌃ moreover⌃ the presence of campaign literature on ballot tables violated voting procedures.

▶ Children watching television recognize violence but not its intention⌃ thus⌃ they become desensitized to violence.

Conjunctive adverbs that fall in the middle of an independent clause are set off with commas:

▶ Due to trade restrictions⌃ however⌃ sales of Japanese cars did not surpass sales of domestic cars.

For practice, go to bedfordstmartins.com/conciseguide/comma, bedfordstmartins .com/conciseguide/uncomma, and bedfordstmartins.com/conciseguide/semi.

A Common ESL Problem: Subtle Differences in Meaning.   Because the distinctions in meaning among some common conjunctive adverbs are subtle, nonnative speakers often have difficulty using them accurately. For example, the difference between *however* and *nevertheless* is small; each is used to introduce statements that contrast with what precedes it. But *nevertheless* emphasizes the contrast, whereas *however* softens it. Check usage of such terms in an English dictionary rather than a bilingual one. *The American Heritage Dictionary of the English Language* has special usage notes to help distinguish frequently confused words.

A Note on Grammar and Spelling Checkers.   These tools are good at catching certain types of errors, but currently there's no replacement for a good human proofreader. Grammar checkers in particular are extremely limited in what they can usually find, and often they only give you summary information that isn't helpful if you don't already understand the rule in question. They are also prone to give faulty advice for fixing problems and to flag correct items as wrong. Spelling checkers cause fewer problems but can't catch misspellings that are themselves words, such as *to* for *too.*

REFLECTING ON YOUR WRITING

Now that you have read and discussed several essays that argue a position on a controversial issue and written one of your own, take some time for reflection. Reflecting on your writing process will help you gain a greater understanding of what you learned about solving the problems you encountered in writing an argument.

   Write a one-page explanation telling your instructor about a problem you encountered in writing your essay and how you solved it. Before you begin, gather all of your invention and planning notes, drafts, critical comments, revision plan, and final revision. Review these materials as you complete this writing task.

1. *Identify one writing problem you needed to solve as you worked on the essay.* Do not be concerned with grammar and punctuation; concentrate instead on problems unique to developing an essay arguing for a position. For example: Did you puzzle over how to convince your readers that the issue is important? Did you have trouble asserting your position forcefully while acknowledging other points

of view? Was it difficult to refute an important objection you knew readers would raise?

2. ***Determine how you came to recognize the problem.*** When did you first discover it? What called it to your attention? If you did not become aware of the problem until someone pointed it out to you, can you now see hints of it in your invention writings? If so, where specifically?

3. ***Reflect on how you went about solving the problem.*** Did you work on the wording of a passage, cut or add reasons or refutations, conduct further research, or move paragraphs or sentences around? Did you reread one of the essays in this chapter to see how another writer handled a similar problem, or did you look back at your invention writing? If you talked about the problem with another student, a tutor, or your instructor, did talking about it help? How useful was the advice you received?

4. ***Write a brief explanation of how you identified the problem and tried to solve it.*** Be as specific as possible in reconstructing your efforts. Quote from your invention notes and draft essay, others' critical comments, your revision plan, or your revised essay to show the various changes your writing—and thinking—underwent as you tried to solve the problem. If you are still uncertain about your solution, say so. Taking time to explain how you identified a particular problem, how you went about solving it, and what you learned from this experience can help you solve future writing problems more easily.

Proposing a Solution

Proposals are vital to a democracy. They inform citizens about problems affecting their well-being and suggest actions that could be taken to remedy these problems. People write proposals every day in business, government, education, and the professions. Proposals are a basic ingredient of the world's work.

As a special form of argument, proposals have much in common with position papers, described in Chapter 5. Both analyze a subject about which there is disagreement and take a definite stand on it. Both make an argument, giving reasons and support and acknowledging readers' likely objections or questions. Proposals, however, go further: They urge readers to take specific action. They argue for a proposed solution to a problem, and they succeed or fail by the strength of that argument.

Problem-solving is basic to most disciplines and professions. For example, scientists use the scientific method, a systematic form of problem-solving; political scientists and sociologists propose solutions to troubling political and social problems; engineers employ problem-solving techniques in building bridges, automobiles, and computers; teachers make decisions about how to help students with learning problems; counselors devote themselves to helping clients solve personal problems; business owners and managers daily solve problems large and small.

Problem-solving depends on a questioning attitude—wondering about alternative approaches to bringing about change, puzzling over how a goal might be achieved, questioning why a process unfolds in a particular way, posing challenges to the status quo. In addition, it demands imagination and creativity. To solve a problem, you need to see it anew, to look at it from new angles and in new contexts.

Because a proposal tries to convince readers that its way of defining and solving the problem makes sense, proposal writers must be sensitive to readers' needs and expectations. Readers need to know details of the solution and to be convinced that it will solve the problem and can be implemented. If readers initially favor a different solution, knowing why the writer rejects it will help them decide whether to support or reject the writer's proposed solution. Readers may be wary of costs, demands on their time, and grand schemes.

As you plan and draft a proposal, you will have to determine whether your readers are aware of the problem and whether they recognize its seriousness, and you will have to consider their views on alternative possible solutions. Knowing what your readers know—their knowledge of the problem and willingness to make changes, their assumptions and biases, the kinds of arguments likely to appeal to them—is a central part of proposal writing.

The writing of proposals occurs in many different contexts, as the following examples suggest.

Writing in Your Other Courses

- For an economics class, a student writes an essay proposing a solution to the problem of inadequate housing for Mexican workers in the nearly three thousand maquiladora factories clustered along the Mexican side of the border with the United States. She briefly describes the binational arrangement that has produced over a million low-paying jobs for Mexican workers and increased profits for American manufacturers who own the assembly plants—along with job losses for thousands of American workers. She sketches the history of maquiladoras since the 1970s and then surveys some of the problems they have spawned. Focusing on inadequate housing, she argues that it, of all the problems, should be addressed first and is most amenable to modest, short-term solutions. The student argues that maquiladora owners must share with Mexican city and state governments the costs of planning and installing water delivery systems and minimal house plumbing installations, and provide low-interest loans to workers who want to buy indoor plumbing fixtures. Recognizing that this is only a first-stage solution to a major problem requiring long-term efforts, the student calls for an international competition to design entire maquiladora workers' communities, along with plans for adequate low-cost houses with plumbing and electricity.

- For an education class, a student researches the history of educational television production and programming for two- to thirteen-year-old children, beginning with the 1969 production of Children's Television Workshop's *Sesame Street*. He also researches children's television in Australia, Great Britain, and Japan and learns that these countries provide much more support for children's television programming than the United States does. For an assignment to write an essay proposing a solution, he proposes a plan to develop government support for children's programming. He presents the problem by comparing other countries' support for children's television to U.S. support. Influenced by a book by the founder of Children's Television Workshop, the student argues that television is the most efficient and effective way to teach preschool-age children basic math and English skills. Arguing to support his proposal, the student concedes that attractive new programs continue to appear—for example, *Bill Nye, the Science Guy*—but argues that these are sporadic and cannot provide the amount or diversity of programming that is needed.

Writing in the Community

- A California high school junior enters an essay contest, "There Ought to Be a Law," sponsored by her state legislator. The goal of the contest is to encourage high school students to propose solutions to community problems. The student wins the contest with a proposal for a state law requiring school districts to replace textbooks every ten years. She presents the problem by describing her own battered, marked-up, dated textbooks, particularly a chemistry text published before she was born. To gain a better understanding of the problems caused by outdated textbooks, she talks with several other students and with teachers. Recognizing that she lacks the expertise to outline a legislative solution, she speculates about the probable obstacles, chief among them the costs of implementing her solution. The legislator drafts a law based on the student's proposal, invites the student to attend the opening of the next legislative session, and introduces the law at that session.

- A social services administrator in a large northeastern city becomes increasingly concerned about the rise in numbers of adolescents in jail for minor and major crimes. From his observations and the research studies he reads, he becomes convinced that a partial solution to the problem would be to intervene at the first sign of delinquent behavior in eight- to twelve-year-olds. In developing a proposal to circulate among influential people in the local police department, juvenile justice system, school system, and business and religious communities, the administrator begins by describing the long-term consequences of jailing young criminals. Trying to make the problem seem significant and worth solving, he focuses mainly on the costs and the high rate of return to criminal activity after release from jail. He then lists and discusses at length the major components of his early intervention program. These components include assigning mentors to young people who are beginning to fail in school, placing social workers in troubled families to help out daily before and after school, hiring neighborhood residents to work full-time on the streets to counter the influence of gangs, and encouraging businesses to hire high school students as paid interns. The administrator acknowledges that early intervention to head off serious criminal activity will require the cooperation of many city agencies. He offers to take the lead in bringing about this cooperation and in launching the program.

Writing in the Workplace

- Frustrated by what they see as the failure of schools to prepare students for the workplace, managers of a pharmaceuticals corporation in the Midwest decide to develop a proposal to move vocational and technical training out of ill-equipped high school vocational programs and onto the plant's floor. Seven division managers meet weekly for four months to develop a proposal for schools in the region. They are joined by one of the firm's experienced technical writers, who takes notes of discussions, writes progress reports, and eventually drafts the proposal. They define the problem as schools being unable to offer the cutting-edge teaching, modern equipment, motivation, or accountability of on-the-job training. They eventually propose a vocational track that would begin in grade 10, with all of the job training taking place in businesses and industries. Each year students would spend more time on the job, and by grade 12 they would work thirty-two hours a week and spend ten hours a week in school, mainly in courses in English (reading and writing) and advanced math. As the managers detail their solution, develop a timetable for implementing it, and speculate about how current school budgets could be reworked to support the program, they seek advice on early drafts of their proposal from business leaders, school board members, school administrators, representatives of teachers' unions, newspaper editorial boards, and key members of the state legislature. The final draft incorporates suggestions from these advisers and attempts to refute known arguments against the proposal.

- A woman in her sixties who has been hauling asphalt and gravel in a double-bottom dump truck for sixteen years writes a proposal for trucking company owners and managers, who face a continual shortage of well-qualified drivers for heavy diesel tractor-and-trailer trucks, suggesting that the companies focus on recruiting more women. As she plans her proposal, she talks to the owner of the company she drives for and to the few women drivers she knows. She begins the proposal by describing her work briefly and explaining how she got a lucky break when her brother taught her how to drive his truck. She then points out the problem: that few women ever get the chance to learn this skill. She proposes her solution to this problem: an in-house training program in which women recruits would be trained by company drivers on the job and after hours. Drivers would be paid for their after-hours training contributions, and the students would be paid a small stipend after agreeing to drive for the company for a certain number of months at a reduced salary. She argues that her proposal would succeed only if trucking companies sponsor a well-designed recruitment program relying on advertisements published on Web sites and in magazines read by working women, and she lists titles of several such publications. She attempts to refute the alternative solution of relying on already established truck-driving schools by arguing that many women cannot afford the tuition. Her proposal is first published in her company's internal newsletter and later, in slightly revised form, in a leading magazine read by trucking company owners and managers.

**Practice
Proposing
a Solution
to a Problem:
A Collaborative
Activity**

The preceding scenarios suggest some occasions for writing proposals to solve problems. To get a sense of the complexities and possibilities involved in proposing solutions, think through a specific problem, and try to come up with a feasible proposal. Your instructor may schedule this collaborative activity as a face-to-face in-class discussion or ask you to conduct an online real-time discussion in a chat room. Whatever the medium, here are some guidelines to follow:

Part 1. Form a group with two or three other students, and select one person to take notes during your discussion.

- First, identify two or three problems within your college or community, and select one that you all recognize and agree needs to be solved.

- Next, consider possible solutions to this problem, and identify one solution that you can all support. You need not all be equally enthusiastic for this solution.

- Finally, determine which individual or group has the authority to take action on your proposed solution and how you would go about convincing this audience that the problem is serious and must be solved and that your proposed solution is feasible and should be supported. Make notes also about questions this audience might have about your proposal and what objections the audience might raise.

Part 2. As a group, discuss your efforts at proposing a solution to a problem. What surprised or pleased you most about this activity? What difficulties did you encounter in coming up with arguments that the problem must be solved and that your proposed solution would solve it? How did the objections you thought of influence your confidence in your proposed solution?

READINGS

The three readings in this chapter illustrate a number of the features of essays that propose solutions to problems and many of the strategies that writers rely on to realize the features. No two proposals are alike, and yet they share defining features. Together, the three essays cover many of the possibilities of proposals, so you will want to read as many of them as possible. If time permits, complete the activities in the Analyzing Writing Strategies section that follows each selection, and read the Commentary. Following the readings is a section called Basic Features: Proposing Solutions (p. 233), which offers a concise description of the features of proposals and provides examples from the three readings.

Mark Hertsgaard is a journalist and a regular contributor to National Public Radio. His essays have appeared in numerous newspapers and magazines such as the New York Times, the New Yorker, the Atlantic Monthly, Outside, Harper's, and Rolling Stone. He also teaches non-fiction writing at Johns Hopkins University and has written five books, including Nuclear, Inc.: The Men and Money behind Nuclear Energy (1983), A Day in the Life: The Music and Artistry of the Beatles (1995), and The Eagle's Shadow: Why America Fascinates and Infuriates the World (2002). This proposal was originally published in Time magazine's special Earth Day edition in 2000, and it reflects the extensive research he did for his 1999 book Earth Odyssey: Around the World in Search of Our Environmental Future.

Hertsgaard probably titled his proposal "A Global Green Deal" to remind readers of President Franklin D. Roosevelt's New Deal, which helped the United States recover from the Great Depression of the 1930s. Hertsgaard proposes that government encourage businesses to develop and use new, more efficient and environmentally friendly technologies. You will see that toward the end of his essay, Hertsgaard admits that his proposal is "no silver bullet" but argues that it will take us in the right direction and "buy us time to make the more deep-seated changes" that are needed (paragraph 16). As you read, notice how sensitive he is to readers who fear the problem is too daunting. Pay attention to the ways he tries to bolster readers' confidence that the problem can be solved while at the same time trying to be realistic about what his proposed solution can accomplish.

A Global Green Deal

Mark Hertsgaard

The bad news is that we have to change our ways—and fast. Here's the good news: it could be a hugely profitable enterprise. 1

So what do we do? Everyone knows the planet is in bad shape, but most people are resigned to passivity. Changing course, they reason, would require economic sacrifice and provoke stiff resistance from corporations and consumers alike, so why bother? It's easier to ignore the gathering storm clouds and hope the problem magically takes care of itself. 2

Such fatalism is not only dangerous but mistaken. For much of the 1990s I traveled the world to write a book about our environmental predicament. I returned home sobered by the extent of the damage we are causing and by the speed at which it is occurring. But there is nothing inevitable about our self-destructive behavior. Not only could we dramatically reduce our burden on the air, water and other natural systems, we could make money doing so. If we're smart, we could make restoring the environment the biggest economic enterprise of our time, a huge source of jobs, profits and poverty alleviation. 3

What we need is a Global Green Deal: a program to renovate our civilization environmentally from top to bottom in rich and poor countries alike. Making use of both market incentives and government leadership, a twenty-first-century Global Green Deal would do for environmental technologies what government and industry have recently done so well for computer and Internet technologies: launch their commercial takeoff. 4

Getting it done will take work, and before we begin we need to understand three facts about the reality facing us. First, we have no time to lose. While we've made progress in certain areas—air pollution is down in the U.S.—big environmental problems like climate change, water scarcity and species extinction are getting worse, and faster than ever. Thus we have to change our ways profoundly—and very soon. 5

Second, poverty is central to the problem. Four billion of the planet's 6 billion people face deprivation inconceivable to the wealthiest 1 billion. To paraphrase Thomas Jefferson, nothing is more certainly written in the book of fate than that the bottom two-thirds of humanity will strive to improve their lot. As they demand adequate heat and food, not to mention cars and CD players, humanity's environmental footprint will grow. Our challenge is to accommodate this mass ascent from poverty without wrecking the natural systems that make life possible. 6

Third, some good news: we have in hand most of the technologies needed to chart a   7
new course. We know how to use oil, wood, water and other resources much more efficiently than we do now. Increased efficiency—doing more with less—will enable us to
use fewer resources and produce less pollution per capita, buying us the time to bring
solar power, hydrogen fuel cells and other futuristic technologies on line.

Efficiency may not sound like a rallying cry for environmental revolution, but it packs   8
a financial punch. As Joseph J. Romm reports in his book *Cool Companies,* Xerox, Com-
paq and 3M are among many firms that have recognized they can cut their greenhouse-
gas emissions in half—and enjoy 50 percent and higher returns on investment through
improved efficiency, better lighting and insulation and smarter motors and building
design. The rest of us (small businesses, homeowners, city governments, schools) can
reap the same benefits.

Super-refrigerators use 87% less electricity than older, standard models while cost-   9
ing the same (assuming mass production) and performing better, as Paul Hawken and
Amory and L. Hunter Lovins explain in their book *Natural Capitalism.* In Amsterdam the
headquarters of ING Bank, one of Holland's largest banks, uses one-fifth as much energy
per square meter as a nearby bank, even though the buildings cost the same to construct. The ING center boasts efficient windows and insulation and a design that enables
solar energy to provide much of the building's needs, even in cloudy Northern Europe.

Examples like these lead even such mainstream voices as AT&T and Japan's energy   10
planning agency, NEDO, to predict that environmental restoration could be a source of
virtually limitless profit. The idea is to retrofit our farms, factories, shops, houses, offices
and everything inside them. The economic activity generated would be enormous. Better
yet, it would be labor intensive; investments in energy efficiency yield two to 10 times
more jobs than investments in fossil fuel and nuclear power. In a world where 1 billion
people lack gainful employment, creating jobs is essential to fighting the poverty that
retards environmental progress.

But this transition will not happen by itself—too many entrenched interests stand in   11
the way. Automakers often talk green but make only token efforts to develop green cars
because gas-guzzling sport-utility vehicles are hugely profitable. But every year the U.S.
government buys 56,000 new vehicles for official use from Detroit. Under the Global
Green Deal, Washington would tell Detroit that from now on the cars have to be hybrid-
electric or hydrogen-fuel-cell cars. Detroit might scream and holler, but if Washington
stood firm, carmakers soon would be climbing the learning curve and offering the com-
petitively priced green cars that consumers say they want.

We know such government pump-priming works; it's why so many of us have com-   12
puters today. America's computer companies began learning to produce today's affordable systems during the 1960s while benefiting from subsidies and guaranteed markets
under contracts with the Pentagon and the space program. And the cyberboom has
fueled the biggest economic expansion in history.

The Global Green Deal must not be solely an American project, however. China and   13
India, with their gigantic populations and ambitious development plans, could by themselves doom everyone else to severe global warming. Already, China is the world's

second largest producer of greenhouse gases (after the U.S.). But China would use 50% less coal if it simply installed today's energy-efficient technologies. Under the Global Green Deal, Europe, America and Japan would help China buy these technologies, not only because that would reduce global warming but also because it would create jobs and profits for workers and companies back home.

Governments would not have to spend more money, only shift existing subsidies   14 away from environmentally dead-end technologies like coal and nuclear power. If even half the $500 billion to $900 billion in environmentally destructive subsidies now offered by the world's governments were redirected, the Global Green Deal would be off to a roaring start. Governments need to establish "rules of the road" so that market prices reflect the real social costs of clearcut forests and other environmental abominations. Again, such a shift could be revenue neutral. Higher taxes on, say, coal burning would be offset by cuts in payroll and profits taxes, thus encouraging jobs and investment while discouraging pollution. A portion of the revenues should be set aside to assure a just transition for workers and companies now engaged in inherently anti-environmental activities like coal mining.

All this sounds easy enough on paper, but in the real world it is not so simple. Bene-   15 ficiaries of the current system—be they U.S. corporate-welfare recipients, redundant German coal miners, or cutthroat Asian logging interests—will resist. Which is why progress is unlikely absent a broader agenda of change, including real democracy: assuring the human rights of environmental activists and neutralizing the power of Big Money through campaign-finance reform.

The Global Green Deal is no silver bullet. It can, however, buy us time to make the   16 more deep-seated changes—in our often excessive appetites, in our curious belief that humans are the center of the universe, in our sheer numbers—that will be necessary to repair our relationship with our environment.

None of this will happen without an aroused citizenry. But a Global Green Deal is in   17 the common interest, and it is a slogan easily grasped by the media and the public. More-over, it should appeal across political, class and national boundaries, for it would stimu-late both jobs and business throughout the world in the name of a universal value: leaving our children a livable planet. The history of environmentalism is largely the story of ordi-nary people pushing for change while governments, corporations and other established interests reluctantly follow behind. It's time to repeat that history on behalf of a Global Green Deal.

Connecting to Culture and Experience:
Acting to Create a More Livable Planet

Hertsgaard acknowledges in this proposal that his solution is "no silver bullet," but he hopes it will "buy us time to make the more deep-seated changes" that are needed (paragraph 16).

With two or three other students, discuss other actions that can be taken to buy us time and possibly also help to repair the environment. Begin by telling each other about conservation efforts you have made. For example, you may buy recycled paper, or your family may compost food remains. What other actions could you take? Then discuss whether helping the environment is a high priority for you. If you were buying a car, for instance, would getting an energy-efficient car be a high priority? If you have a choice between driving a car or taking public transportation to school or work, would you take public transportation to reduce energy costs and air pollution?

Analyzing Writing Strategies

1. At the beginning of this chapter, we make several generalizations about essays that propose solutions to problems. Consider which of these assertions are true of Hertsgaard's proposal:

   - It defines the problem and helps readers realize the seriousness of the problem.
   - It describes the proposed solution.
   - It attempts to convince readers that the solution will help solve the problem and can be implemented.
   - It anticipates readers' likely questions and objections.
   - It evaluates alternative solutions that readers may initially favor.

2. The most important part of a proposal is the solution. To be effective, the proposal has to describe the solution in a way that convinces readers that it can be implemented. Hertsgaard first presents his solution in paragraph 4, where he describes in broad terms the "Global Green Deal" he is proposing. But he does not describe how his solution to renovate the environment can be implemented until paragraphs 11–14. Reread these paragraphs to see how convincing he is in arguing that his solution can and should be implemented. Highlight in paragraphs 11 and 13–14 what would need to be done to implement the solution. Also look closely at paragraph 12 to see what it adds to his argument.

Commentary: Defining the Problem

Every proposal begins with a problem. Writers usually spend some time defining the problem—establishing that the problem exists and is serious enough to warrant action. What writers say about the problem and how much space they devote to it depend on what they assume their readers already know and think about it. In this proposal, Hertsgaard assumes the readers of *Time* magazine's special Earth Day edition know that "the planet is in bad shape," as he puts it in paragraph 2.

He identifies the problem more specifically at various points in the essay: "big environmental problems like climate change, water scarcity and species extinction" (5), "pollution" (7), and "global warming" (13). In paragraphs 5–9, Hertsgaard elaborates further by presenting "three facts about the reality" of the problem (5). The first two facts make the problem seem overwhelming, but the third is a ray of hope. He notes that we have made progress but that time is running out as developing countries become wealthier and place increasing pressures on the environment. The third fact, however, provides the "good news" that is an essential ingredient of his proposed solution: We already have the technological efficiency to make a difference.

Hertsgaard knows that many of his readers feel defeated by the enormity of the problem and that his proposal will fall on deaf ears if his readers do not believe that the steps he is proposing will do any good. Therefore, he tries to allay his readers' fears, in particular their feeling of "fatalism" (3). To reassure readers, he tries to be optimistic yet realistic. He tempers his own enthusiasm with language like this: "If we're smart, we could" (3) and "The Global Green Deal is no silver bullet. It can, however, buy us time to make the more deep-seated changes" (16). Ultimately, Hertsgaard tries to represent the problem as a "challenge" (6), something that "will take work" (5) but that can be done.

As you plan your proposal, you also will need to consider your readers' feelings as well as their knowledge. Remember that defining the problem is part of your argument. It should be designed to convince readers that you know what you are talking about and can be trusted. Hertsgaard builds his credibility with readers in part by referring to his extensive research (3, 8–9) but also by showing readers he understands the complexity of the problem.

Considering Topics for Your Own Essay

Hertsgaard's admittedly limited proposal might suggest to you other proposals to solve environmental problems. For example, you might consider writing a proposal for increasing the use of carpools on campus, reducing energy consumption in dormitories, or instituting a campus recycling program. You might interview people in your community about the feasibility of subsidizing alternative energy sources, such as solar-heating panels that could be installed in public buildings and parks. You might also research promising newer technologies for a proposal addressed to your college administration or local government.

Katherine S. Newman is the Malcolm Wiener Professor of Urban Studies at Harvard University; chair of the joint doctoral program in sociology, government, and social policy at Harvard's Kennedy School of Government; and dean of social science at the Radcliffe Institute for Advanced Studies. She has written many books, including Declining Fortunes: The Withering of the American Dream *(1993),* No Shame in My Game: The Working Poor in the Inner City *(1999), and* A Different Shade of Gray: Mid-Life and Beyond in the Inner City *(2003). Her essays have appeared in popular newspapers and magazines such as the* New York Times *and* Newsweek *as well as in numerous scholarly journals such as the* American Anthropologist, *the* International Journal of Sociology and Social Policy, *and the* Brookings Review, *a journal concerned with public policy, in which "Dead-End Jobs: A Way Out" was originally published.*

This proposal resulted from Newman's research for No Shame in My Game, *a book that was awarded the Sidney Hillman Book Prize and the Robert F. Kennedy Book Award. As you read her proposal, notice her analysis of why the social networks that inner-city fast-food workers belong to fail to lead them to better jobs, and evaluate whether you think the proposed solution—an employer consortium (a group of cooperating employers)—"might re-create the job ladders that have disappeared," as Newman explained in an interview.*

Dead-End Jobs: A Way Out

Katherine S. Newman

Millions of Americans work full-time, year-round in jobs that still leave them stranded in poverty. Though they pound the pavement looking for better jobs, they consistently come up empty-handed. Many of these workers are in our nation's inner cities. 1

I know, because I have spent two years finding out what working life is like for 200 employees—about half African-American, half Latino—at fast-food restaurants in Harlem. Many work only part-time, though they would happily take longer hours if they could get them. Those who do work full-time earn about $8,840 (before taxes)—well below the poverty threshold for a family of four. 2

These fast-food workers make persistent efforts to get better jobs, particularly in retail and higher-paid service-sector occupations. They take civil service examinations and apply for jobs with the electric company or the phone company. Sometimes their efforts bear fruit. More often they don't. 3

A few workers make their way into the lower managerial ranks of the fast-food industry, where wages are marginally better. An even smaller number graduate into higher management, a path made possible by the internal promotion patterns long practiced by these firms. As in any industry, however, senior management opportunities are limited. Hence most workers, even those with track records as reliable employees, are locked inside a low-wage environment. Contrary to those who preach the benefits of work and persistence, the human capital these workers build up—experience in food production, inventory management, cash register operation, customer relations, minor machinery repair, and cleaning—does not pay off. These workers are often unable to move upward out of poverty. And their experience is not unusual. Hundreds of thousands of low-wage workers in American cities run into the same brick wall. Why? And what can we do about it? 4

Stagnation in the Inner City

Harlem, like many inner-city communities, has lost the manufacturing job base that once sustained its neighborhoods. Service industries that cater to neighborhood consumers, coupled with now dwindling government jobs, largely make up the local economy. With official jobless rates hovering around 18 percent (14 people apply for every minimum-wage fast-food job in Harlem), employers can select from the very top of the preference "queue." Once hired, even experienced workers have virtually nowhere to go. 5

One reason for their lack of mobility is that many employers in the primary labor market outside Harlem consider "hamburger flipper" jobs worthless. At most, employers credit the fast-food industry with training people to turn up for work on time and to fill out 6 job applications. The real skills these workers have developed go unrecognized. However inaccurate the unflattering stereotypes, they help keep experienced workers from "graduating" out of low-wage work to more remunerative employment. . . .

As Harry Holzer, an economist at Michigan State University, has shown, "central-city" employers insist on specific work experience, references, and particular kinds of formal training in addition to literacy and numeracy skills, even for jobs that do not require a college degree. Demands of this kind, more stringent in the big-city labor markets than in the surrounding suburbs, clearly limit the upward mobility of the working poor in urban areas. If the only kind of job available does not provide the "right" work experience or formal training, many better jobs will be foreclosed.

Racial stereotypes also weaken mobility prospects. Employers view ghetto blacks, especially men, as a bad risk or a troublesome element in the workplace. They prefer immigrants or nonblack minorities, of which there are many in the Harlem labor force, who appear to them more deferential and willing to work harder for low wages. As Joleen Kirshenman and Kathryn Neckerman found in their study of Chicago workplaces, stereotypes abound among employers who have become wary of the "underclass." Primary employers exercise these preferences by discriminating against black applicants, particularly those who live in housing projects, on the grounds of perceived group characteristics. The "losers" are not given an opportunity to prove themselves. . . .

Social Networks

Social networks are crucial in finding work. Friends and acquaintances are far more useful sources of information than are want ads. The literature on the urban underclass suggests that inner-city neighborhoods are bereft of these critical links to the work world. My work, however, suggests a different picture: the working poor in Harlem have access to two types of occupational social networks, but neither provides upward mobility. The first is a homogeneous *lateral* network of age mates and acquaintances, employed and unemployed. It provides contacts that allow workers to move sideways in the labor market—from Kentucky Fried Chicken to Burger King or McDonald's—but not to move to jobs of higher quality. Lateral networks are useful, particularly for poor people who have to move frequently, for they help ensure a certain amount of portability in the low-wage labor market. But they do not lift workers out of poverty; they merely facilitate "churning" laterally in the low-wage world.

Young workers in Harlem also participate in more heterogeneous *vertical* networks with their older family members who long ago moved to suburban communities or better urban neighborhoods to become homeowners on the strength of jobs that were more widely available 20 and 30 years ago. Successful grandparents, great-aunts and uncles, and distant cousins, relatives now in their 50s and 60s, often have (or have retired from) jobs in the post office, the public sector, the transportation system, public utilities, the military, hospitals, and factories that pay union wages. But these industries are now shedding workers, not hiring them. As a result, older generations are typically unable to help job-hunting young relatives.

7

8

9

10

Although little is known about the social and business networks of minority business   11
owners and managers in the inner city, it seems that Harlem's business community, particularly its small business sector, is also walled off from the wider economy of midtown.
Fast-food owners know the other people in their franchise system. They do business with
banks and security firms inside the inner city. But they appear less likely to interact with
firms outside the ghetto.

For that reason, a good recommendation from a McDonald's owner may represent a   12
calling card that extends no farther than the general reputation of the firm and a prospective employer's perception—poor, as I have noted—of the skills that such work represents. It can move someone from an entry-level job in one restaurant to the same kind of
job in another, but not into a good job elsewhere in the city.

Lacking personal or business-based ties that facilitate upward mobility, workers in   13
Harlem's fast-food market find themselves on the outside looking in when it comes to the
world of "good jobs." They search diligently for them, they complete many job applications, but it is the rare individual who finds a job that pays a family wage. Those who do
are either workers who have been selected for internal promotion or men and women
who have had the luxury of devoting their earnings solely to improving their own educational or craft credentials. Since most low-wage service workers are under pressure to
support their families or contribute to the support of their parents' households, this kind of
human capital investment is often difficult. As a result, the best most can do is to churn
from one low-wage job to another.

The Employer Consortium

Some of the social ills that keep Harlem's fast-food workers at the bottom of a short job   14
ladder—a poor urban job base, increasing downward mobility, discrimination, structural
problems in the inner-city business sector—are too complex to solve quickly enough to
help most of the workers I've followed. But the problem of poor social networks may be
amenable to solution if formal organizations linking primary and secondary labor market
employers can be developed. An "employer consortium" could help to move hard-working
inner-city employees into richer job markets by providing the job information and pre-
cious referrals that "come naturally" to middle-class Americans.

How would an employer consortium function? It would include both inner-city   15
employers of the working poor and downtown businesses or nonprofit institutions with
higher-paid employees. Employers in the inner city would periodically select employees
they consider reliable, punctual, hard-working, and motivated. Workers who have successfully completed at least one year of work would be placed in a pool of workers eligible for hiring by a set of linked employers who have better jobs to offer. Entry-level
employers would, in essence, put their own good name behind successful workers as
they pass them on to their consortium partners in the primary sector.

Primary-sector employers, for their part, would agree to hire from the pool and meet   16
periodically with their partners in the low-wage industries to review applications and follow up on the performance of those hired through the consortium. Employers "up the line"

would provide training or educational opportunities to enhance the employee's skills. These training investments would make it more likely that hirees would continue to move up the new job ladders.

As they move up, the new hirees would clear the way for others to follow. First, their performance would reinforce the reputation of the employers who recommended them. Second, their achievements on the job might begin to lessen the stigma or fear their new employers may feel toward the inner-city workforce. On both counts, other consortium-based workers from the inner city would be more likely to get the same opportunities, following in a form of managed chain migration out of the inner-city labor market. Meanwhile, the attractiveness of fast-food jobs, now no better reputed among inner-city residents than among the rest of society, would grow as they became, at least potentially, a gateway to something better.   17

Advantages for Employers

Fast-food employers in Harlem run businesses in highly competitive markets. Constant pressure on prices and profit discourage them from paying wages high enough to keep a steady workforce. In fact, most such employers regard the jobs they fill as temporary placements: they *expect* successful employees to leave. And despite the simple production processes used within the fast-food industry to minimize the damage of turnover, sudden departures of knowledgeable workers still disrupt business and cause considerable frustration and exhaustion.   18

An employer consortium gives these employers—who *can't* raise wages if they hope to stay in business—a way to compete for workers who will stay with them longer than usual. In lieu of higher pay, employers can offer access to the consortium hiring pool and the prospect of a more skilled and ultimately better-paying job upon graduation from this real world "boot camp." . . .   19

Consortiums would also appeal to the civic spirit of minority business owners, who often choose to locate in places like Harlem rather than in less risky neighborhoods because they want to provide job opportunities for their own community. The big franchise operations mandate some attention to civic responsibility as well. Some fast-food firms have licensing requirements for franchisees that require demonstrated community involvement.   20

At a time when much of the public is voicing opposition to heavy-handed government efforts to prevent employment discrimination, employer consortiums have the advantage of encouraging minority hiring based on private-sector relationships. Institutional employers in particular—for example, universities and hospitals, often among the larger employers in East Coast cities—should find the consortiums especially valuable. These employers typically retain a strong commitment to workforce diversity but are often put off by the reputation of secondary-sector workers as unskilled, unmotivated, and less worthy of consideration.   21

The practical advantages for primary-sector managers are clear. Hirees have been vetted and tested. Skills have been assessed and certified in the most real world of settings. A valuable base of experience and skills stands ready for further training and   22 advancement. The consortium assures that the employers making and receiving recommendations would come to know one another, thus reinforcing the value of recommendations — a cost-effective strategy for primary-sector managers who must make significant training investments in their workers.

Minimal Government Involvement

Despite the evident advantages for both primary and secondary labor market employers, it may be necessary for governments to provide modest incentives to encourage wide participation. Secondary-sector business owners in the inner city, for example, might be deterred from participating by the prospect of losing some of their best employees at the end of a year. Guaranteeing these employers a lump sum or a tax break for every worker they promote into management internally or successfully place with a consortium participant could help break down such reluctance.   23

Primary-sector employers, who would have to provide support for training and possibly for schooling of their consortium employees, may also require some kind of tax break to subsidize their efforts at skill enhancement. Demonstration projects could experiment with various sorts of financial incentives for both sets of employers by providing grants to underwrite the costs of training new workers.   24

Local governments could also help publicize the efforts of participating employers. Most big-city mayors, for example, would be happy to shower credit on business people looking to boost the prospects of the deserving (read working) poor.   25

Government involvement, however, would be minimal. Employer consortiums could probably be assembled out of the existing economic development offices of U.S. cities, or with the help of the Chamber of Commerce and other local institutions that encourage private-sector activity. Industry- or sector-specific consortiums could probably be put together with the aid of local industry councils.   26

Moreover, some of the negative effects of prior experiments with wage subsidies for the "hard to employ" — efforts that foundered on the stigma assigned to these workers and the paperwork irritants to employers — would be reversed here. Consortium employees would be singled out for doing well, for being the cream of the crop. And the private-sector domination of employer consortiums would augur against extensive paperwork burdens.   27

Building Bridges

The inner-city fast-food workers that I have been following in Harlem have proven themselves in difficult jobs. They have shown that they are reliable, they clearly relish their economic independence, and they are willing to work hard. Still, work offers them no escape from poverty. Trapped in a minimum-wage job market, they lack bridges to the kind of work that can enable them to support their families and begin to move out of poverty. For reasons I have discussed, those bridges have not evolved naturally in our inner cities. But where they are lacking, they must be created and fostered. And we can begin with employer consortiums, to the benefit of everyone, workers and employers alike.   28

Connecting to Culture and Experience: The Value of Routine, Repetitive Work

Newman explains that one reason fast-food workers cannot find better jobs is that employers believe such workers learn only routine, repetitive skills that do not prepare them for other types of jobs.

With several students, discuss this possible limitation of fast-food jobs and other kinds of routine jobs. You may hold such a job now, or you may have held one in the past. Maybe you parked cars, delivered pizzas, ran a cash register, wiped down cars in a car wash, bagged and carried groceries or other merchandise, wrapped holiday packages, or did cleanup work. Tell each other about the routine jobs you have held. Then consider Newman's criticism of these jobs: that they only teach workers how to show up on time and follow rudimentary directions. Is this a fair criticism, do you think? Have critics overlooked certain important kinds of learning on these jobs? If so, what might these kinds of learning be? Or if you agree that these jobs are as limiting as the critics contend, what other kinds of low-paying work might teach more important skills?

Analyzing Writing Strategies

1. Reread paragraphs 1–8, where Newman defines the problem she believes needs to be solved. In a sentence or two, state what you understand the problem to be.

   At the end of paragraph 4, Newman asks why this problem continues. Underline the main reasons she gives in paragraphs 6–8. For her purpose and readers, how well does she define the problem? What questions might readers have about her presentation of the problem? Finally, how well does her proposed solution (employer consortiums) address the reasons the problem continues?

2. Readers are often aware of previous attempts to solve a problem, or they might think of solutions they believe are better than the one the writer is proposing. Writers who hope to win readers' support must evaluate alternative solutions that readers are likely to be aware of. To evaluate an alternative solution, writers usually either concede that it has some merit or refute it as meritless and not worth further consideration.

   Newman evaluates an alternative solution in paragraphs 9–13. How would you summarize this alternative to Newman's proposed solution of an employer consortium? What are the main reasons Newman gives for not taking this alternative solution seriously and encouraging readers to do the same? How well do you think she refutes this alternative to her proposed solution?

Commentary: Describing the Proposed Solution and Anticipating Objections

The heart of an essay proposing a solution to a problem is the proposed solution and the direct argument supporting the solution. Readers need to know exactly what is being proposed and how it can be implemented before they can decide whether it is feasible — cost-effective and likely to help solve the problem. Newman describes her proposed solution relatively fully. In paragraphs 14–17, she provides many details about the employer consortium. She begins paragraph 14 acknowledging the scope and complexity of the problem and admitting that the solution she is proposing focuses on only one aspect of the problem, "poor social networks." She ends the paragraph by explaining the goal of her proposed solution: to find better jobs for hard-working, ambitious fast-food workers. An "employer consortium," as she envisions it, would provide information about jobs and referrals to specific available jobs — the two main resources that inner-city fast-food employees lack.

Newman then describes in detail how easy it would be to implement or put into effect her solution (15–17). In explaining how an employer consortium would function, she outlines the responsibilities of the two key players in the consortium she envisions: the inner-city fast-food employers and the downtown employers with the better-paying jobs. Notice that she does not hesitate to specify criteria for eligible inner-city employees: They must be "reliable, punctual, hard-working, and motivated," and they must "have successfully completed at least one year of work" (15). To make it clear that inner-city employers will not be doing all the work, she describes how downtown employers would meet with fast-food employers, review workers' job applications, and pay attention to workers once they are on the job. The downtown employers would also be required to offer on-the-job training to prepare the new workers for better jobs (16).

She also points out some of the advantages of her solution for everyone involved. She argues that it offers inner-city employers a competitive edge without requiring them to raise wages (19). For other business owners and institutions, she argues that not only does her plan provide them with new employees who are well-trained, conscientious workers, but it also increases diversity in the workplace without government interference.

In addition to the direct argument for the solution, proposal writers usually try to anticipate readers' likely objections. To respond to the concern of inner-city employers that they would be continually giving up their best workers, Newman suggests that employers' reputations would be enhanced and the image of fast-food work would improve as the jobs came to be seen as a step to better jobs (17). She also argues that fast-food workers would presumably be more committed to doing a good job if the quality of their work could lead to a better job downtown — and their employers would benefit as a result. In addition, she acknowledges both that the loss of experienced workers would be a financial disadvantage to inner-city employers and that the costs of training employees would be an added burden to consortium employers. To accommodate these concerns, she adds to her proposal government subsidies to compensate employers (23–24).

When you plan your essay, you will need to develop an argument with your readers in mind, trying to convince them that your proposed solution makes sense and can be put into effect.

Considering Topics for Your Own Essay

Think of barriers or obstacles you have met or expect to meet in realizing your goals and dreams. You might want to think specifically about obstacles to preparing for and entering the career of your choice, but you need not limit yourself to career goals. Perhaps you are not able to get into an internship program that would give you some experience with the kind of work you hope to do. Perhaps your high school did not offer the courses you needed to prepare for the college major you want to pursue. Perhaps at some crucial point in your life you received inadequate medical care or counseling. Identify an obstacle you faced and think of it as a general problem to be solved; that is, assume that other people have confronted the same obstacle. How would you define the problem? How might you propose to solve it? To be more than a personal complaint about bad luck or mistreatment, your proposal would need to appeal to readers who have experienced a similar obstacle or who would be able to remove the obstacle or give sound advice on getting around it.

Patrick O'Malley wrote the following proposal while he was a first-year college student. He proposes that college professors give students frequent brief examinations in addition to the usual midterm and final exams. After discussing with his instructor his unusual rhetorical situation—a student advising professors—he decided to revise the essay into the form of an open letter to professors at his college, a letter that might appear in the campus newspaper.

O'Malley's essay may strike you as unusually authoritative. This tone of authority is due in large part to what O'Malley learned about the possibilities and problems of frequent exams as he interviewed two professors (his writing instructor and the writing program director) and talked with several students. As you read his essay, notice particularly how he anticipates professors' likely objections to his proposal and evaluates their preferred solutions to the problem he identifies.

More Testing, More Learning
Patrick O'Malley

It's late at night. The final's tomorrow. You got a C on the midterm, so this one will make or break you. Will it be like the midterm? Did you study enough? Did you study the right things? It's too late to drop the course. So what happens if you fail? No time to worry about that now—you've got a ton of notes to go over. 1

Although this last-minute anxiety about midterm and final exams is only too familiar to most college students, many professors may not realize how such major, infrequent, high-stakes exams work against the best interests of students both psychologically and intellectually. They cause unnecessary amounts of stress, placing too much importance on one or two days in the students' entire term, judging ability on a single or dual performance. They don't encourage frequent study, and they fail to inspire students' best performance. If professors gave additional brief exams at frequent intervals, students would 2 be spurred to study more regularly, learn more, worry less, and perform better on midterms, finals, and other papers and projects.

Ideally, a professor would give an in-class test or quiz after each unit, chapter, or focus of study, depending on the type of class and course material. A physics class might require a test on concepts after every chapter covered, while a history class could necessitate quizzes covering certain time periods or major events. These exams should be given weekly or at least twice monthly. Whenever possible, they should consist of two or three essay questions rather than many multiple-choice or short-answer questions. To preserve class time for lecture and discussion, exams should take no more than 15 or 20 minutes.

The main reason professors should give frequent exams is that when they do and when they provide feedback to students on how well they are doing, students learn more in the course and perform better on major exams, projects, and papers. It makes sense that in a challenging course containing a great deal of material, students will learn more of it and put it to better use if they have to apply or "practice" it frequently on exams, which also helps them find out how much they are learning and what they need to go over again. A recent Harvard study notes students' "strong preference for frequent evaluation in a course." Harvard students feel they learn least in courses that have "only a midterm and a final exam, with no other personal evaluation." They believe they learn most in courses with "many opportunities to see how they are doing" (Light, 1990, p. 32). In a review of a number of studies of student learning, Frederiksen (1984) reports that students who take weekly quizzes achieve higher scores on final exams than students who take only a midterm exam and that testing increases retention of material tested.

Another, closely related argument in favor of multiple exams is that they encourage students to improve their study habits. Greater frequency in test taking means greater frequency in studying for tests. Students prone to cramming will be required—or at least strongly motivated—to open their textbooks and notebooks more often, making them less likely to resort to long, kamikaze nights of studying for major exams. Since there is so much to be learned in the typical course, it makes sense that frequent, careful study and review are highly beneficial. But students need motivation to study regularly, and nothing works like an exam. If students had frequent exams in all their courses, they would have to schedule study time each week and gradually would develop a habit of frequent study. It might be argued that students are adults who have to learn how to manage their own lives, but learning history or physics is more complicated than learning to drive a car or balance a checkbook. Students need coaching and practice in learning. The right way to learn new material needs to become a habit, and I believe that frequent exams are key to developing good habits of study and learning. The Harvard study concludes that "tying regular evaluation to good course organization enables students to plan their work more than a few days in advance. If quizzes and homework are scheduled on specific days, students plan their work to capitalize on them" (Light, 1990, p. 33).

By encouraging regular study habits, frequent exams would also decrease anxiety by reducing the procrastination that produces anxiety. Students would benefit psychologically if they were not subjected to the emotional ups and downs caused by major exams, when after being virtually worry-free for weeks they are suddenly ready to check into the psychiatric ward. Researchers at the University of Vermont found a strong relationship among procrastination, anxiety, and achievement. Students who regularly put off studying for exams had continuing high anxiety and lower grades than students who procrastinated less. The researchers found that even "low" procrastinators did not study regularly and recommended that professors give frequent assignments and exams to reduce procrastination and increase achievement (Rothblum, Solomon, & Murakami, 1986, pp. 393–394).

Research supports my proposed solution to the problems I have described. Common sense as well as my experience and that of many of my friends support it. Why, then, do so few professors give frequent brief exams? Some believe that such exams take up too much of the limited class time available to cover the material in the course. Most courses meet 150 minutes a week—three times a week for 50 minutes each time. A 20-minute weekly exam might take 30 minutes to administer, and that is one-fifth of each week's class time. From the student's perspective, however, this time is well spent. Better learning and greater confidence about the course seem a good trade-off for another 30 minutes of lecture. Moreover, time lost to lecturing or discussion could easily be made up in students' learning on their own through careful regular study for the weekly exams. If weekly exams still seem too time-consuming to some professors, their frequency could be reduced to every other week or their length to 5 or 10 minutes. In courses where multiple-choice exams are appropriate, several questions could be designed to take only a few minutes to answer. 7

Another objection professors have to frequent exams is that they take too much time to read and grade. In a 20-minute essay exam, a well-prepared student can easily write two pages. A relatively small class of 30 students might then produce 60 pages, no small amount of material to read each week. A large class of 100 or more students would produce an insurmountable pile of material. There are a number of responses to this objection. Again, professors could give exams every other week or make them very short. Instead of reading them closely they could skim them quickly to see whether students understand an idea or can apply it to an unfamiliar problem; and instead of numerical or letter grades they could give a plus, check, or minus. Exams could be collected and responded to only every third or fourth week. Professors who have readers or teaching assistants could rely on them to grade or check exams. And the Scantron machine is always available for instant grading of multiple-choice exams. Finally, frequent exams could be given *in place of* a midterm exam or out-of-class essay assignment. 8

Since frequent exams seem to some professors to create too many problems, however, it is reasonable to consider alternative ways to achieve the same goals. One alternative solution is to implement a program that would improve study skills. While such a program might teach students how to study for exams, it cannot prevent procrastination or reduce "large test anxiety" by a substantial amount. One research team studying anxiety and test performance found that study skills training was not effective in reducing anxiety or improving performance (Dendato & Diener, 1986, p. 134). This team, which also reviewed other research that reached the same conclusion, did find that a combina- 9 tion of "cognitive/relaxation therapy" and study skills training was effective. This possible solution seems complicated, however, not to mention time-consuming and expensive. It seems much easier and more effective to change the cause of the bad habit rather than treat the habit itself. That is, it would make more sense to solve the problem at its root: the method of learning and evaluation.

Still another solution might be to provide frequent study questions for students to 10 answer. These would no doubt be helpful in focusing students' time studying, but students would probably not actually write out the answers unless they were required to. To get students to complete the questions in a timely way, professors would have to collect and check the answers. In that case, however, they might as well devote the time to grading an exam. Even if it asks the same questions, a scheduled exam is preferable to a set of study questions because it takes far less time to write in class, compared to the time students would devote to responding to questions at home. In-class exams also ensure that each student produces his or her own work.

Another possible solution would be to help students prepare for midterm and final 11 exams by providing sets of questions from which the exam questions will be selected or announcing possible exam topics at the beginning of the course. This solution would have the advantage of reducing students' anxiety about learning every fact in the textbook, and it would clarify the course goals, but it would not motivate students to study carefully each new unit, concept, or text chapter in the course. I see this as a way of complementing frequent exams, not as substituting for them.

From the evidence and from my talks with professors and students, I see frequent, 12 brief in-class exams as the only way to improve students' study habits and learning, reduce their anxiety and procrastination, and increase their satisfaction with college. These exams are not a panacea, but only more parking spaces and a winning football team would do as much to improve college life. Professors can't do much about parking or football, but they can give more frequent exams. Campus administrators should get behind this effort, and professors should get together to consider giving exams more frequently. It would make a difference.

References

Dendato, K. M., & Diener, D. (1986). Effectiveness of cognitive/relaxation therapy and study-skills training in reducing self-reported anxiety and improving the academic performance of test-anxious students. *Journal of Counseling Psychology, 33,* 131–135.

Frederiksen, N. (1984). The real test bias: Influences of testing on teaching and learning. *American Psychologist, 39,* 193–202.

Light, R. J. (1990). *Explorations with students and faculty about teaching, learning, and student life.* Cambridge, MA: Harvard University Graduate School of Education and Kennedy School of Government.

Rothblum, E. D., Solomon, L., & Murakami, J. (1986). Affective, cognitive, and behavioral differences between high and low procrastinators. *Journal of Counseling Psychology, 33,* 387–394.

Connecting to Culture and Experience: Experience with Frequent Exams

O'Malley advocates frequent brief exams as a solution to the problems of midterm- and final-exam anxiety, poor study habits, and disappointing exam performance. With two or three other students, discuss O'Malley's proposal in light of your own experience. To what extent do your courses without frequent exams produce the problems he identifies? Which of your high school or college courses included frequent exams? Describe these courses and the kinds of exams they offered. When you were taking these courses, what effect did the frequent exams have on your study habits, anxiety level, and mastery of the coursework?

Analyzing Writing Strategies

1. O'Malley devotes almost a third of his essay to anticipating readers' likely objections to his proposal. This section of the essay begins in the middle of paragraph 5 (with the sentence "It might be argued...") and then resumes in paragraphs 7 and 8. Begin by underlining the three objections, one each in paragraphs 5, 7, and 8. Then make notes about how O'Malley counterargues these objections. Finally, evaluate how successful each counterargument seems to be for its intended readers—college professors. What seems most and least convincing in each counterargument? (For more on counterarguing, see Chapter 11.)

2. Readers of proposals are nearly always aware of solutions different from the one the writer is proposing. Readers may know of alternatives to the writer's solution—a solution someone has already proposed or one that has been tried with mixed results. Or—as readers have a tendency to do—they may think of an alternative solution after learning about the writer's preferred one. Consequently, effective proposals try to evaluate one or more likely alternative solutions. O'Malley evaluates alternative solutions in paragraphs 9–10, a different one in each paragraph. Reread these counterarguments and notice two things: the strategies and resources that O'Malley relies on and the extent to which he either concedes that some good ideas can be found in each alternative or refutes alternatives as unworkable. How do you think his intended readers will react to these paragraphs? What might they find most and least convincing?

Commentary: Supporting the Proposed Solution

O'Malley's essay demonstrates the importance of taking readers seriously. Not only does he interview both those who would carry out his proposal (professors) and those who would benefit from it (students), but he also features in his essay what he has learned from these interviews. Paragraphs 7–11 directly acknowledge professors' objections, their questions, and the alternative solutions they would probably prefer. These counterarguments, which may be essential to convincing readers to support a proposal, are only part of the overall argument, which centers on the writer's direct support of the proposed solution. Most of O'Malley's direct argument can be found in paragraphs 4–6, in which O'Malley presents three reasons that professors should give frequent exams: Students will (1) learn more and perform better on major exams, projects, and essays; (2) acquire better study habits; and (3) experience decreased anxiety and improved performance. He supports each reason with a combination of assertions based on his own experience and references to reputable research studies carried out at three universities. He quotes and paraphrases these studies. (For more on quoting and paraphrasing, see Chapter 14.)

Argument and counterargument can be woven together in many different ways in an essay proposing a solution to a problem. Because O'Malley succeeds at balancing argument and counterargument, the organization of his proposal is worth noting. The following is a scratch outline of his essay:

> opening: a scenario to introduce the problem (paragraph 1)
>
> presentation of the problem and introduction of the solution (2)
>
> details of the solution (3)
>
> reason 1: improved learning and performance (4)
>
> reason 2: improved study habits (5)
>
> refutation of objection 1: students as adults (5)
>
> reason 3: less procrastination and anxiety (6)
>
> accommodation of objection 2: limited class time (7)
>
> accommodation of objection 3: too much work (8)
>
> refutation of alternative solution 1: study-skills training (9)
>
> refutation of alternative solution 2: study questions (10)
>
> accommodation of alternative solution 3: sample exam questions (11)
>
> closing: reiteration of the proposed solution and advice on implementing it (12)

Except for a brief refutation in paragraph 5, O'Malley first presents the direct argument for frequent exams (paragraphs 4–6) and then counterargues (paragraphs 7–11). The outline reveals that counterargument takes up most of the space, not an unusual balance in proposals to solve problems. O'Malley might have counterargued first or counterargued as he presented his direct argument, as he does briefly in paragraph 5. The approach you take depends on what your readers know about the problem and their experience with other proposed solutions to it.

Considering Topics for Your Own Essay

Much of what happens in high school and college is predictable and conventional. Examples of conventional practices that have changed very little over the years are exams, group instruction, graduation ceremonies, required courses, and lowered admission requirements for athletes. Think of additional examples of established practices in high school or college; then select one that you believe needs to be improved or refined in some way. What changes would you propose? What individual or group might be convinced to take action on your proposal for improvement? What questions or objections should you anticipate? How could you discover whether others have previously proposed improvements in the practice you are concerned with? Whom might you interview to learn more about the practice and the likelihood of changing it?

■ PURPOSE AND AUDIENCE

Most proposals are calls to action. Because of this clear purpose, a writer must anticipate readers' needs and concerns more when writing a proposal than in any other kind of writing. The writer attempts not only to convince readers but also to inspire them, to persuade them to support or implement the proposed solution. What your particular readers know about the problem and what they are capable of doing to solve it determine how you address them.

Readers of proposals are often unaware of the problem. In this case, your task is clear: to present them with evidence that will convince them of its existence. This evidence may include statistics, testimony from witnesses or experts, and examples, including the personal experiences of people involved with the problem. You can also speculate about the cause of the problem and describe its ill effects.

Sometimes readers recognize the existence of a problem but fail to take it seriously. When readers are indifferent, you may need to connect the problem closely to their own concerns. For instance, you might show how much they have in common with the people directly affected by it or how it affects them indirectly. However you appeal to readers, you must do more than alert them to the problem; you must also make them care about it. You want to touch readers emotionally as well as intellectually.

At other times, readers concerned about the problem may assume that someone else is taking care of it and that they need not become personally involved. In this situation, you might want to demonstrate that the people they thought were taking care of the problem have failed. Another assumption readers might make is that a solution they supported in the past has already solved the problem. You might point out that the original solution has proved unworkable or that new solutions have become available through changed circumstances or improved technology. Your aim is to rekindle these readers' interest in the problem.

Perhaps the most satisfying proposals are addressed to parties who can take immediate action to remedy the problem. You may have the opportunity to write such a proposal if you choose a problem faced by a group to which you belong. Not only do you have a firsthand understanding of the problem, but you also have a good idea of the kinds of solutions that other members of the group will support. (You might informally survey some of them before you submit your proposal to test your definition of the problem and your proposed solution.) When you address readers who are in a position to take action, you want to assure them that it is wise to do so. You must demonstrate that the solution is feasible — that it can be implemented and that it will work.

BASIC FEATURES: PROPOSING SOLUTIONS

A Well-Defined Problem

A proposal is written to offer a solution to a problem. Before presenting the solution, the writer must be sure that readers know and understand what the problem is. Patrick O'Malley, for example, devotes the first three paragraphs of his essay to defining the problem of infrequent course exams. It is wise to define the problem explicitly, as all the writers in this chapter do.

Stating the problem is not enough, however; the writer also must establish the problem as serious enough to need solving. Sometimes a writer can assume that readers will recognize the problem and its seriousness. For example, Hertsgaard assumes his readers understand the seriousness of the problem; his challenge is to help them overcome their feeling of fatalism so that they will pay attention to the solution he is proposing. At other times, readers may not be aware of the problem and will need to be convinced that it deserves their attention. Katherine S. Newman, for instance, does not assume that her readers will understand how difficult it is for inner-city fast-food workers to find better jobs.

In addition to defining the problem and establishing its seriousness for readers, a proposal writer may have to analyze the problem, exploring its causes, consequences, and history and past efforts at dealing with it.

A Clearly Described Solution

Once the problem is defined and its existence established, the writer must describe the solution so that readers can readily imagine what it would be like. Because O'Malley assumes that his readers know what brief exams are like, he runs little risk in not describing them. He does, however, identify their approximate lengths and possible forms—brief essay, short answer, or multiple choice. In contrast, because Newman cannot assume her readers will know what she means by an employer consortium, she describes it at length, focusing on who would be involved and the roles they would play.

A Convincing Argument in Support of the Proposed Solution

The main purpose of a proposal is to convince readers that the writer's solution will help to solve the problem. To this end, O'Malley gives three reasons why he thinks more brief exams will solve the problem and supports each reason with published research studies as well as his own experience.

Writers must also argue that the proposed solution is feasible—that it can actually be implemented and that it will work. The easier it is to implement, the more likely it is to win readers' support. Therefore, writers sometimes set out the steps required to put the proposed solution into practice, an especially important strategy when the solution might seem difficult, time-consuming, or expensive to enact. All the writers in this chapter offer specific suggestions for implementing their proposals, though none outlines all the steps required. For example, O'Malley offers professors several specific ways to give their students frequent, brief exams; Hertsgaard explains how government pump priming would work; and Newman offers many details about how an employer consortium would function.

An Anticipation of Readers' Objections and Questions

The writer arguing for a proposal must anticipate objections or reservations that readers may have about the proposed solution. Probably the greatest concern Hertsgaard anticipates is his readers' sense that the problem is too overwhelming to be solved. He accommodates or concedes the scope and seriousness of the problem but refutes his readers' hopelessness, arguing that we have already made progress in some areas and we possess the technology to make additional progress.

An Evaluation of Alternative Solutions

Proposal writers sometimes try to convince readers that the proposed solution is preferable to other possible solutions. They may compare the proposed solution to other solutions readers may know about or ones they may think of themselves. O'Malley, for example, evaluates three alternative solutions — study-skills training, study questions, and sample exam questions as alternatives to frequent exams — and demonstrates what is wrong with each one. He rejects study-skills training because it is overly complicated, time-consuming, and expensive. He rejects study questions because, compared with exams, they would not save either students or professors any time or ensure that students each do their own individual work. He rejects sample exam questions by arguing that they solve only part of the problem.

GUIDE TO WRITING
Proposing Solutions

THE WRITING ASSIGNMENT

Write an essay proposing a solution to a problem. Choose a problem faced by a community or group to which you belong, and address your proposal to one or more members of the group or to outsiders who might help solve the problem.

THE WRITING ASSIGNMENT

INVENTION AND RESEARCH

INVENTION & RESEARCH

Finding a Problem to Write About

Analyzing and Defining the Problem

Identifying Your Readers

Finding a Tentative Solution

Defending Your Solution

Testing Your Choice

Offering Reasons for Your Proposal

Considering Alternative Solutions

Doing Research

Considering Document Design

Defining Your Purpose for Your Readers

Formulating a Tentative Thesis Statement

PLANNING & DRAFTING

Seeing What You Have

Setting Goals

Outlining

Drafting

PLANNING AND DRAFTING

CRITICAL READING GUIDE

CRITICAL READING GUIDE

First Impression

Definition of the Problem

Description of the Solution

Convincing Argument in Support of Proposed Solution

Anticipation of Readers' Objections, Questions

Evaluation of Alternative Solutions

Effectiveness of Organization

Final Thoughts

REVISING

A Well-Defined Problem

A Clearly Described Solution

A Convincing Argument in Support of the Proposed Solution

An Anticipation of Readers' Objections and Questions

An Evaluation of Alternative Solutions

The Organization

REVISING

EDITING AND PROOFREADING

EDITING & PROOFREADING

Checking for Ambiguous Use of *This* and *That*

Checking for Sentences That Lack an Agent

GUIDE TO WRITING

■ THE WRITING ASSIGNMENT

Write an essay proposing a solution to a problem. Choose a problem faced by a community or group to which you belong, and address your proposal to one or more members of the group or to outsiders who might help solve the problem.

■ INVENTION AND RESEARCH

The following activities will help you prepare to write a proposal. You will choose a problem you can write about, analyze and define the problem, identify your prospective readers, decide on and defend your proposed solution, test your choice, offer reasons and support for adopting your proposal, and consider readers' objections and alternative solutions, among other things. These activities are easy to complete. Doing them over several days will give your ideas time to ripen and grow. Be sure to keep a written record of your invention and research to use later when you draft and revise.

Finding a Problem to Write About

You may have already thought about a problem you could write about. Or you may have been drawn to one of the problems suggested by the Considering Topics for Your Own Essay activities following the readings in this chapter. Even so, you will want to consider several problems that need solving before making your final choice. The following activity will help you get started.

Listing Problems.   *Make a list of problems you could write about.* Make a double-column chart like the following one. Divide a piece of paper or your computer screen into two columns. In the left-hand column, list communities, groups, or organizations to which you belong. Include as many communities as possible: college, neighborhood, hometown, and cultural or ethnic groups. Also include groups you participate in: sports, musical, work, religious, political, support, hobby, and so on. In the right-hand column, list any problems that exist within each group. Here is how such a chart might begin:

Community	*Problem*
My college	Poor advising or orientation
	Shortage of practice rooms in music building
	No financial aid for part-time students
	Lack of facilities for disabled students
	Lack of enough sections of required courses

Class scheduling that does not accommodate working
students or students with children

My neighborhood   Need for traffic light at dangerous intersection
Unsupervised children getting into trouble
Megastores driving away small businesses
Lack of safe places for children to play

Listing Problems Related to Identity and Community.   Writing a proposal can
give you special insight into issues of identity and community by helping you understand how members of a community negotiate their individual needs and concerns.
You may already have made a chart of communities to which you belong and problems in those communities. The following categories may help you think of additional
problems in those or other communities that you could add to your list:

- Disagreement over conforming to community standards
- Conflicting economic, cultural, or political interests within the community
- Problems with equity or fairness between men and women, rich and poor, differ-
ent ethnic groups
- Lack of respect or trust among the members of the community
- Struggles for leadership of the community

Listing Problems Related to Work and Career.   Proposals are frequently written
on the job and about the work people do. Based on your work experience, make a
double-column chart like the following one. List the places you have worked in the
left column and the problems you encountered on the job in the right column.

Workplace	*Problem*
Restaurant	Inadequate training
	Conflicts with supervisor
	Unfair shift assignments
Department store	Inadequate inventory
	Computer glitches
	Overcomplicated procedures
Office	Unfair workloads
	Changing requirements
	Inflexible work schedules
	Lack of information about procedures
	Difficulty in scheduling vacations
	Outdated technology

Choosing a Problem.   *Choose one problem from your list that seems especially important to you, that concerns others in the group or community, and that seems solvable. (You*

need not know the exact solution now.) The problem should also be one that you can explore in detail and are willing to discuss in writing.

Proposing to solve a problem in a group or community to which you belong gives you an inestimably important advantage: You can write as an expert, an insider. You know about the history of the problem, have felt the urgency to solve it, and perhaps have already thought of possible solutions. Equally important, you will know precisely to whom to address the proposal, and you can interview others in the group to get their views of the problem and to understand how they might resist your solution. From such a position of knowledge and authority comes confident, convincing writing.

Should you want to propose a solution for a social problem of national scope, concentrate on one with which you have direct experience and for which you can suggest a detailed plan of action. Even better, focus on unique local aspects of the problem. For example, if you would like to propose a solution to the lack of affordable child care for children of college students or working parents, you have a great advantage if you are a parent who has experienced the frustration of finding professional, affordable child care. Moreover, even though such a problem is national in scope, it may be solvable only campus by campus, business by business, or neighborhood by neighborhood.

Analyzing and Defining the Problem

Before you can begin to consider the best possible solution, you must analyze the problem carefully and then try to define it. Keep in mind that you will have to demonstrate to readers that the problem exists, that it is serious, and that you have a more than casual understanding of its causes and consequences. If you find that you cannot do so, you will want to select some other problem to write about.

Analyzing. *Start by writing a few sentences in response to these questions:*

- Does the problem really exist? How can I tell?
- What caused this problem? Can I identify any immediate causes? Any deeper causes? Is the problem caused by a flaw in the system, a lack of resources, individual misconduct or incompetence? How can I tell?
- What is the history of the problem?
- What are the bad effects of the problem? How does it harm members of the community or group? What goals of the group are endangered by the existence of this problem? Does it raise any moral or ethical questions?
- Who in the community or group is affected by the problem? Be as specific as possible: Who is seriously affected? Minimally affected? Unaffected? Does anyone benefit from its existence?
- What similar problems exist in this same community or group? How can I distinguish my problem from these?

Defining. *Write a definition of the problem, being as specific as possible.* Identify who or what seems responsible for it, and give one recent, telling example.

Identifying Your Readers

In a few sentences, describe your readers, stating your reason for directing your proposal to them. Then take a few minutes to write about these readers. Whom do you need to address—everyone in the community or group, a committee, an individual, an outsider? You want to address your proposal to the person or group who can help implement it. The following questions will help you develop a profile of your readers:

- How informed are my readers likely to be about the problem? Have they shown any awareness of it?
- Why would this problem be important to my readers? Why would they care about solving it?
- Have my readers supported any other proposals to solve this problem? If so, what do those proposals have in common with mine?
- Do my readers ally themselves with any group, and would that alliance cause them to favor or reject my proposal? Do we share any values or attitudes that could bring us together to solve the problem?
- How have my readers responded to other problems? Do their past reactions suggest anything about how they might respond to my proposal?

Finding a Tentative Solution

Solving problems takes time. Apparent solutions often turn out to be impossible. After all, a solution has to be both workable and acceptable to the community or group involved. Consequently, you should strive to come up with several possible solutions whose advantages and disadvantages you can weigh. You may notice that the most imaginative solutions sometimes occur to you only after you have struggled with a number of other possibilities.

Look back at the way you defined the problem and described your readers. Then with these factors in mind, list as many possible solutions to the problem as you can think of. You might come up with only two or three possible solutions; but at this stage, the more the better. To come up with different solutions, use the following problem-solving questions:

- What solutions to this problem have already been tried?
- What solutions have been proposed for related problems? Might they solve this problem as well?
- Is a solution required that would disband or change the community or group in some way?
- What solution might eliminate some of the causes of the problem?
- What solution would eliminate any of the bad effects of the problem?
- Is the problem too big to be solved all at once? Can I divide it into several related problems? What solutions might solve one or more of these problems?
- If a series of solutions is required, which should come first? Second?

- What solution would ultimately solve the problem?
- What might be a daring solution, arousing the most resistance but perhaps holding out the most promise?
- What would be the most conservative solution, acceptable to nearly everyone in the community or group?

Give yourself enough time to let your ideas percolate as you continue to add to your list of possible solutions and to consider the advantages and disadvantages of each one in light of your prospective readers. If possible, discuss your solutions with those members of the community or group who can help you consider the advantages and disadvantages of each one.

Choosing the Most Promising Solution.   *In a sentence or two, state what you consider the best possible way of solving the problem.*

Determining Specific Steps.   *Write down the major stages or steps necessary to carry out your solution.* This list of steps will provide an early test of whether your solution can, in fact, be implemented.

Defending Your Solution

Proposals have to be feasible—that is, they must be both reasonable and practical. Imagine that one of your readers strongly opposes your proposed solution and confronts you with the following statements. *Write a few sentences refuting each one.*

- It would not really solve the problem.
- I am comfortable with things as they are.
- We cannot afford it.
- It would take too long.
- People would not do it.
- Too few people would benefit.
- I do not even see how to get started on your solution.
- We already tried that, with unsatisfactory results.
- You support this proposal merely because it would benefit you personally.

Answering these questions should help you prepare responses to possible objections. If you feel that you need a better idea of how others are likely to feel about your proposal, talk with a few people who are directly involved with or affected by the problem. The more you know about your readers' concerns, the better you will be able to anticipate their reservations and preferred alternative solutions.

Testing Your Choice

Now examine the problem and your proposed solution to see whether you can write a strong proposal. Start by asking yourself the following questions:

- Is this a significant problem? Do other people in the community or group really care about it, or can they be persuaded to care?
- Will my solution really solve the problem? Can it be implemented?
- Can I answer objections from enough people in the community or group to win support for my solution?

As you plan and draft your proposal, you will probably want to consider these questions again. If at any point you decide that you cannot answer them with a confident yes, you may want to consider proposing a different, more feasible solution to the problem; if none exists, you may need to choose a different problem to write about.

Testing Your Choice: A Collaborative Activity

At this point, you will find it useful to get together with two or three other students and present your plans to one another. This collaborative activity will help you determine whether you can write this proposal in a way that will interest and convince others.

Presenters: Take turns briefly defining the problem you hope to solve, identifying your intended readers, and describing your proposed solution.

Listeners: Tell the presenter whether the proposed solution seems appropriate and feasible for the situation and intended readers. Suggest objections and reservations you believe readers may have.

Offering Reasons for Your Proposal

To make a convincing case for your proposed solution, you must offer your readers good reasons for adopting your proposal.

Listing Reasons.   *Write down every plausible reason you could give that might persuade readers to accept your proposal.* These reasons should answer your readers' key question: Why is this the best possible solution?

Choosing the Strongest Reasons.   *Put an asterisk next to the strongest reasons—the reasons most likely to be convincing to your intended readers.* If you do not consider at least two or three of your reasons strong, you will probably have difficulty developing a strong proposal and should reconsider your topic.

Evaluating Your Strongest Reasons.   *Now look at your strongest reasons and explain briefly why you think each one will be effective with your particular readers, the members of the group or community you are addressing.*

Considering Alternative Solutions

List alternative solutions that members of the group or community might offer when they learn about your solution, and consider the advantages and disadvantages of each one relative to your solution. Even if members are likely to consider your proposal reasonable, they will probably want to compare your proposed solution with other possible solutions. You might find it helpful to chart the information as follows:

Possible Solutions	Advantages	Disadvantages
My solution		
Alternative solution 1		
Alternative solution 2		
Etc.		

Researching Alternative Solutions: an Online Activity

Searching the Web can be a productive way of learning about solutions other people have proposed or tried out. If possible, use your online research to identify at least two alternative solutions. Your purpose is to gain information about these solutions that will help you evaluate them fairly. Here are some specific suggestions for finding information about solutions:

- Enter keywords—words or brief phrases related to the problem or a solution—into a search tool such as Google (www.google.com) or Yahoo! Directory (http://dir.yahoo.com). For example, if you are concerned that many children in your neighborhood have no adult supervision after school, you could try keywords associated with the problem such as *latchkey kids,* or keywords associated with possible solutions such as *after-school programs.*

- If you think solutions to your problem may have been proposed by a government agency, you could try adding the word *government* to your keywords or searching on FirstGov.gov, the U.S. government's official Web portal. For example, you might explore the problem of latchkey children by following links at the Web site of the U.S. Department of Health & Human Services (www.hhs.gov). If you want to see whether the problem has been addressed in your state or local government, you can go to the Library of Congress Internet Resource Page on State and Local Governments (www.loc.gov/global/state/) and follow the links.

Add to your chart of the advantages and disadvantages of alternative solutions any information you find from your online research. Bookmark or keep a record of promising sites. You may want to download or copy information you could use in your essay, including visuals; if so, remember to record documentation information.

Doing Research

So far you have relied largely on your own knowledge and experience for ideas about solving the problem. You may now feel that you need to do some research to learn more about the causes of the problem and to find more technical information about implementing the solution. For guidelines on library and Internet research, see Chapter 13.

If you are proposing a solution to a problem about which others have written, you will want to find out how they have defined the problem and what solutions they have proposed. You may need to acknowledge these solutions in your essay, either accommodating or refuting them. Now is a good time — before you start drafting — to get any additional information you need. If you are proposing a solution to a local problem, you will want to conduct informal interviews with several people who are aware of or affected by the problem. Find out whether they know anything about its history and current ill effects. Try out your solution on them. Discover whether they have other solutions in mind. (For more on interviewing, see Chapter 12.)

Considering Document Design

Think about whether your readers might benefit from design features, such as headings, numbered lists, or other elements that would make your presentation of the problem easier to follow and your solution more convincing. Earlier in this chapter's readings, for instance, Katherine S. Newman uses headings to introduce the major sections of her proposal. Consider also whether visuals — drawings, photographs, tables, or graphs — would strengthen your argument. These are not required for essays proposing a solution, but they could be helpful. You may come across promising visuals in your research and either download them from the Internet or make photocopies from library materials. When you reproduce visuals, make sure to acknowledge their sources. If you are going to post your essay on the Web, you also need to ask the source for permission.

Defining Your Purpose for Your Readers

Write a few sentences defining your purpose in proposing a solution to a problem of concern to the particular readers you have in mind. Remember that you have already identified your readers in the group or community you are addressing and developed your proposal with these readers in mind. Given these readers, try now to define your purpose by considering the following questions:

- Do I seek incremental, moderate, or radical change? Am I being realistic about what my readers are prepared to do? How can I overcome their natural aversion to change of any kind?

- How can I ensure that my readers will not remain indifferent to the problem?

- Who can I count on for support, and what can I do to consolidate that support? Who will oppose my solution? Shall I write them off or seek common ground with them?

- What exactly do I want my readers to do? To take my proposed solution as a starting point for further discussion about the problem? To take action immediately to implement my solution? To commit themselves to take certain preliminary steps, like seeking funding or testing the feasibility of the solution? To take some other action?

Formulating a Tentative Thesis Statement

Write one or more sentences that could serve as your tentative thesis statement. In most essays proposing solutions to problems, the thesis statement is a concise assertion or announcement of the solution. Think about how emphatic you should make the thesis and whether you should include in it a forecast of your reasons. (For more on thesis and forecasting statements, see Chapter 8, pp. 307–9.)

Review the readings in this chapter to see how other writers construct their thesis statements. For example, recall that Patrick O'Malley states his thesis early in his essay: "If professors gave additional brief exams at frequent intervals, students would be spurred to study more regularly, learn more, worry less, and perform better on midterms, finals, and other papers and projects" (paragraph 2). O'Malley's thesis announces his solution—brief, frequent exams—to the problems created for students in courses limited to anxiety-producing, high-stakes midterms and finals. The thesis lists the reasons students will benefit from the solution in the order in which the benefits appear in the essay. A forecast is not a requirement of a thesis statement, but it does enable readers to predict the stages of the argument, thereby increasing their understanding.

As you draft your own thesis statement, pay attention to the language you use. It should be clear and unambiguous, emphatic but appropriately qualified. Although you will probably refine your thesis statement as you draft and revise your essay, trying now to articulate it will help give your planning and drafting direction and impetus. (For more on asserting a thesis, see Chapter 11, pp. 362–65.)

■ PLANNING AND DRAFTING

This section will help you review your invention writing and research notes, determine specific goals for your essay, prepare a rough outline, and get started on your first draft.

Seeing What You Have

You have now produced a lot of writing for this assignment about a problem and why it needs attention, about alternative solutions, and about the solution you want to propose and why it is preferable to the other proposed solutions. If you have done your invention writing on the computer, you may have sentences or whole paragraphs that can be copied and pasted into your draft. Reread what you have written so far to identify the potentially useful material. Look for details that will help you present a convincing argument for your solution and a strong counterargument in response to readers' likely objections to your solution and their preference for alternative solutions. Highlight key words, phrases, or sentences; make marginal notes or electronic annotations.

If at this point you doubt the significance of the problem or question the success of your proposed solution, you might want to consider a new topic. If you are unsure about these basic points, you cannot expect to produce a convincing draft.

However, if your invention material seems thin but promising, you may be able to strengthen it with additional invention writing. Ask yourself the following questions:

- Can I make a stronger case for the seriousness of the problem?
- Can I think of additional reasons for readers to support my solution?
- Are there any other ways of refuting alternative solutions to or troubling questions about my proposed solution?

Setting Goals

Before beginning to draft, think seriously about the overall goals of your proposal. Not only will the draft be easier to write once you have clear goals, but it will almost surely be more convincing as well.

Here are some questions that will help you set goals now. You may find it useful to return to them while drafting, for they are designed to help you focus on exactly what you want to accomplish with this proposal.

Your Purpose and Readers

- What do my readers already know about this problem?
- Are they likely to welcome my solution or resist it?
- How can I anticipate any specific reservations or objections they may have?
- How can I gain readers' enthusiastic support? How can I get them to want to implement the solution?
- How can I present myself so that I seem both reasonable and authoritative?

The Beginning

- How can I immediately engage my readers' interest? Should I open with a dramatic scenario, as O'Malley does? With statistics that highlight the seriousness of the problem, as Newman does? With a recitation of facts or events? Or with a rhetorical question, anecdote, or quotation?
- What information should I give first? Next? Last?

Defining the Problem

- How much do I need to tell about the problem's causes or history?
- How can I show the seriousness of the problem? Should I stress negative consequences, as O'Malley does? Should I cite statistics, as Newman does?

- Is it an urgent problem? Should I emphasize its urgency, as Hertsgaard does?
- How much space should I devote to defining the problem? Only a little space (like O'Malley) or much space (like Hertsgaard and Newman)?

Describing the Proposed Solution

- How can I describe my solution so that it will look like the best way to proceed? Should I show how to implement it, as Hertsgaard and Newman do? Or should I focus on my reasons to support it, as O'Malley does?
- How can I make the solution seem easy to implement? Or should I acknowledge that the solution may be difficult to implement and argue that it will be worth the effort?

Anticipating Readers' Objections

- Should I acknowledge every possible objection to my proposed solution? How might I choose among these objections?
- Has anyone already raised these objections? Should I name the person?
- Should I accommodate certain objections and refute others, as O'Malley does?
- How can I support my refutation? Should I cite an authority my readers are likely to respect?
- How can I refute my readers' objections without seeming to attack anyone? Can I accommodate as well as refute objections, as Hertsgaard and O'Malley do?

Evaluating Alternative Solutions

- How many alternative solutions do I need to mention? Which ones should I discuss at length? Should I indicate where each one comes from?
- How can I support my refutation of the alternative solutions? Can I argue that they are too expensive and time-consuming, as O'Malley does, or that they will not really solve the problem, as Newman does?
- How can I reject these other solutions without seeming to criticize their proponents? Newman and O'Malley, for example, succeed at rejecting other solutions respectfully.

The Ending

- How should I conclude? Should I end by restating the problem or by summarizing my solution and its advantages, as O'Malley and Newman do? Should I end with an inspiring call to action, as Hertsgaard and Newman do?
- Is there something special about the problem that I should remind readers of at the end?
- Should I end with a scenario suggesting the consequences of a failure to solve the problem?
- Might a shift to humor or satire provide an effective way to end?

Outlining

After setting goals for your proposal, you are ready to make a working outline—a scratch outline or a more formal outline using the outlining function of your word processing program. The basic outline for a proposal is quite simple:

> The problem
>
> The solution
>
> The reasons for accepting the solution

This simple plan is nearly always complicated by other factors, however. In outlining your material, you must take into consideration many other details, such as whether readers already recognize the problem, how much agreement exists on the need to solve the problem, how many alternative solutions are available, how much attention must be given to these other solutions, and how many objections should be expected.

Here is a possible outline for a proposal where readers may not understand the problem fully and other solutions have been proposed:

> Presentation of the problem
>
> > Its existence
> >
> > Its seriousness
> >
> > Its causes
>
> Consequences of failing to solve the problem
>
> Description of the proposed solution
>
> List of steps for implementing the solution
>
> Reasons and support for the solution
>
> > Acknowledgment of objections
> >
> > Accommodation or refutation of objections
>
> Consideration of alternative solutions and their disadvantages
>
> Restatement of the proposed solution and its advantages

(See p. 231 for another sample outline.)

Your outline will of course reflect your own writing situation. As you develop it, think about what your readers know and feel about your own writing goals. Once you have a working outline, you should not hesitate to change it as necessary while drafting and revising. For instance, you might find it more effective to hold back on presenting your own solution until you have dismissed other possible solutions. Or you might find a better way to order the reasons for adopting your proposal. The purpose of an outline is to identify the basic features of your proposal and to help you organize them effectively, not to lock you into a particular structure. If you use the outlining function of your word processing program, changing your outline will be simple and you may be able to write the essay simply by expanding the outline.

Most of the information you will need to develop each feature of a proposal can be found in your invention writing and research notes. How much space you devote to each feature is determined by the topic, not the outline. Do not assume that each entry on your outline must be given one paragraph. For example, each reason for supporting the solution may require a paragraph, but you might instead present the reasons, objections, and refutations all in one paragraph. (For more on outlining, see Chapter 9, pp. 326–29.)

Consider tentative any outlining you do before you begin drafting. Never be a slave to an outline. As you draft, you will usually see ways to improve on your original plan. Be ready to revise your outline, shift parts around, or drop or add parts as you draft.

Drafting

General Advice.   Start drafting your proposal, keeping in mind the goals you set while you were planning and the needs and expectations of your readers; organize, define, and argue with them in mind. Also keep in mind the two main goals of proposals: (1) to establish that a problem exists and is serious enough to require a solution and (2) to demonstrate that your proposed solution is both feasible and the best possible alternative. Use your outline to guide you as you write, but do not hesitate to stray from it whenever you find that drafting takes you in an unexpected direction.

Turn off your grammar checker and spelling checker at this stage if you find them distracting. Don't be afraid to skip around in your document. Jump back and fill in a spontaneous idea, or leap ahead and write a later section first if you find that easier. If you get stuck while drafting, explore the problem by using some of the writing activities in the Invention and Research section of this chapter (p. 236). You may want to review the general drafting advice in Chapter 1 (p. 16).

Sentence Strategies.   As you draft an essay proposing a solution to a problem, you will want to connect with your readers. You will also want readers to become concerned with the seriousness of the problem and thoughtful about the challenge of solving it. Sentences that take the form of rhetorical questions and sentences that feature either assertive or tentative language can help you achieve these goals.

Use rhetorical questions to engage your readers, orient them to reading a proposal, and forecast the plan of your proposal. A rhetorical question is conventionally defined as a sentence posing a question to which the writer expects no answer from the reader. (Of course, not being face to face with the writer, a reader could not possibly answer.) In proposals, however, rhetorical questions do important rhetorical work—that is, they assist a writer in realizing a particular purpose and they influence readers in certain ways. Here are two examples from Katherine S. Newman's proposal:

> Why? And what can we do about it? (paragraph 4)

> How would an employer consortium function? (15)

These questions help readers understand that they will be reading a proposal: Newman implies through the questions that she will be explaining why inner-city workers are trapped in low-wage jobs and outlining a proposal to solve the problem. In addition, she engages readers by sharing with them the questions behind her research project and voicing one of the specific questions they are likely to have about her proposed solution. Consequently, readers have confidence that she will answer the questions she has posed so boldly.

Here are further examples from the other readings in this chapter:

So what do we do? (Mark Hertsgaard, paragraph 2)

Why, then, do so few professors give frequent brief exams? (Patrick O'Malley, paragraph 7)

All of the authors in this chapter use at least one carefully placed rhetorical question. Nevertheless, rhetorical questions are not a requirement for a successful proposal; and when they are used, they appear only occasionally.

Present the problem assertively, and argue the solution tentatively. To stress the seriousness of the problem and the urgency of solving it, use assertive language freely. In contrast, to convince readers to join you in taking action to solve the problem, use tentative language. These language contrasts—assertiveness versus tentativeness—play out quite predictably in this chapter's readings, as in the following example from Katherine S. Newman's proposal:

- Asserting the seriousness of the problem and the urgency of solving it

  Millions of Americans work full-time, year-round in jobs that leave them *stranded in poverty*. (Newman, paragraph 1)

This sentence features language that is blunt, unqualified, and attention-getting. Newman uses a familiar image of being stranded—isolated, alone, beyond reach of help—to dramatize the plight of low-paid full-time workers. Such language seems chosen to expose the failure of the status quo—of business as usual, of the way things have always been done—and to make clear that the problem is serious and urgently requires a solution. It expresses exasperation, even anger. It expresses a moral judgment: Something is wrong, and it is best to admit it.

- Arguing tentatively for the solution to the problem

  Second, their achievements on the job *might begin to lessen* the stigma or fear their new employers *may feel* toward the inner-city workforce. (Newman, paragraph 17)

This sentence features language that is cautious, provisional, and diffident: *might, begin to, may.* It acknowledges that every proposal is untried, its outcome unknowable. At the same time, it does not give the impression that Newman lacks confidence in her proposal. It simply recognizes that every proposal will inevitably be greeted with skepticism and that proposers must strategically overcome readers' resistance by showing themselves to be tentative, if not cautious, about advocating change, even though they may fervently wish for change.

In addition to using rhetorical questions and sentences that feature assertive or tentative language, you can strengthen your proposal with other kinds of sentences as well; and you may want to turn to the discussions of sentences that introduce concession and refutation (pp. 197–98) and that signal explicitly their logical relationship to a previous sentence (pp. 198–99).

CRITICAL READING GUIDE

Now is the time to get a good critical reading of your draft. Writers usually find it helpful to have someone else read and comment on their drafts, and all writers know how much they learn when they read other writers' drafts. Your instructor may arrange such a reading as part of your coursework—in class or online. If not, you can ask a classmate, friend, or family member to read your draft. You could also seek comments from a tutor at your campus writing center. (If you are unable to have someone else read your draft, turn ahead to the Revising section at p. 252, where you will find guidelines for reading your own draft critically.)

If you read another student's draft online, you may be able to use a word processing program to insert suggested improvements directly into the text of the draft or to write them out at the end of the draft. If you read a printout of the draft, you may write brief comments in the margins and lengthier suggestions on a separate page. When the writer sits down to revise, your thoughtful, extended suggestions written at the end of the draft or on separate pages will be especially helpful.

If You Are the Writer. To provide focused, helpful comments, your reader must know your essay's intended audience, your purpose, and a problem in the draft that you need help solving. Briefly write out this information at the top of your draft.

- *Readers:* Identify the intended readers of your essay. How much do they know about the problem? How will they react to your proposed solution?

- *Purpose:* What do you want your readers to do or think as a result of reading your proposal?

- *Problem:* Ask your reader to help you solve the single most important problem you see with your draft. Describe this problem briefly.

If You Are the Reader. Reading a draft critically means reading it more than once—first to get a general impression and then to analyze its basic features. Use the following guidelines to help you give critical comments to others on essays that propose solutions to problems.

1. *Read for a First Impression.* Read first to get a basic understanding of the problem and the proposed solution to it. After reading the draft, briefly write out your impressions. How convincing do you think the proposal will be for its particular readers? What do you notice about the way the problem is presented and the way the solution is argued for? Next, consider the problem the writer identified, and respond briefly to that concern now. (If you find that the problem is covered by one of the other guidelines listed below, respond to it in more detail there if necessary.)

2. *Evaluate How Well the Problem Is Defined.* Decide whether the problem is stated clearly. Does the writer give enough information about its causes and consequences? What more might be done to establish its seriousness? Is there more that readers might need or wish to know about it?

3. *Consider Whether the Solution Is Described Adequately.* Does the presentation of the solution seem immediately clear and readable? How could the presentation be strengthened? Has the writer laid out steps for implementation? If not, might readers expect or require them? Does the solution seem practical? If not, why?

4. *Assess Whether a Convincing Argument Is Advanced in Support of the Proposed Solution.* Look at the reasons offered for advocating this solution. Are they sufficient? Which are likely to be most and least convincing to the intended readers? What kind of support does the writer provide for each reason? How believable do you think readers will find it? Has the writer argued forcefully for the proposal without offending readers?

5. *Evaluate How Well the Writer Anticipates Readers' Objections and Questions.* Which accommodations and refutations seem most convincing? Which seem least convincing? Are there other objections or reservations that the writer should acknowledge?

6. *Assess the Writer's Evaluation of Alternative Solutions.* Are alternative solutions discussed and either accommodated or refuted? Which are the most convincing reasons given against other solutions? Which are least convincing, and why? Has the writer sought out common ground with readers who may advocate alternative solutions? Are such solutions accommodated or rejected without a personal attack on those who propose them? Try to think of other solutions that readers may prefer.

7. *Consider the Effectiveness of the Organization.* Evaluate the overall plan of the proposal, perhaps by outlining it briefly. Would any parts be more effectively placed earlier or later in the essay?

   - *Look at the beginning.* Is it engaging? If not, how might it be revised to capture readers' attention? Does it adequately forecast the main ideas and the plan of the proposal? Suggest other ways the writer might begin.

   - *Look closely at the way the writer orders the argument* for the solution — the presentation of the reasons and the accommodation or refutation of objections and alternative solutions. How might the sequence be revised to strengthen the argument? Point out any gaps in the argument.

   - *Look at the ending.* Does it frame the proposal by echoing or referring to something at the beginning? If not, how might it do so? Does the ending convey a sense of urgency? Suggest a stronger way to conclude.

- *Look at any design elements and visuals* the writer has incorporated. Assess how well they are incorporated into the essay. Point to any items that do not strengthen either the presentation of the problem or the argument in support of the solution.

8. *Give the Writer Your Final Thoughts.* What is the draft's strongest part? What part is most in need of further work?

■ REVISING

Now you have the opportunity to revise your essay. Your instructor or other students may have given you advice on how to improve your draft. Or you may have begun to realize that your draft requires not so much revising as rethinking. For example, you may recognize that you are no longer convinced that the problem is serious, that you feel it is serious but cannot be solved now or anytime soon, that you cannot decide to whom to address the proposal, that you cannot come up with a set of convincing reasons that readers should support your solution, or that you have been unable to accommodate or refute readers' objections and questions or to evaluate alternative solutions. Consequently, instead of working to improve the various parts of your first draft, you may need to write a new draft that reshapes your argument. Many students—and professional writers—find themselves in this situation. Often a writer produces a draft or two and gets advice on them from others and only then begins to see what might be achieved.

If you feel satisfied that your draft mostly achieves what you set out to do, you can focus on refining the various parts of it. This section will help you get an overview of your draft and revise it accordingly.

Getting an Overview

Consider your draft as a whole, following these two steps:

1. *Reread.* If at all possible, put the draft aside for a day or two before rereading it. When you do go back to it, start by reconsidering your audience and purpose. Then read the draft straight through, trying to see it as your intended readers will.

2. *Outline.* Make a scratch outline, indicating the basic features as they appear in the draft. Consider using the headings and outline or summary functions of your word processor.

Planning for Revision.   Resist the temptation to dive in and start changing your text until after you have a clear view of the big picture. Using your outline as a guide, move through the document, using the change-highlighting or commenting tools of

your word processor to note comments received from others and problems you want
to solve (or mark a hard copy if you prefer).

Analyzing the Basic Features of Your Own Draft.   Turn to the Critical Reading
Guide that begins on p. 250. Using this guide, reread the draft to identify problems
you need to solve. Note the problems on your draft.

Studying Critical Comments.   Review all of the comments you have received from
other readers. For each comment, look at the draft to determine what might have led
the reader to make that particular point. Try to be receptive to constructive criticism.
Ideally, these comments will help you see your draft as others see it. Add to your notes
any problems readers have identified.

Carrying Out Revisions

Having identified problems in your draft, you now need to find solutions and—most
important—to carry them out. You have three ways of finding solutions:

1. Review your invention and planning notes for additional information and ideas.
2. Do further invention writing or research to provide material you or your readers
   think is needed.
3. Look back at the readings in this chapter to see how other writers have solved
   similar problems.

   The following suggestions, which are organized according to the basic features of
essays that propose solutions, will get you started solving some common writing
problems. For now, focus on solving the problems identified in your notes. Avoid tin-
kering with grammar and punctuation; those tasks will come later, when you edit and
proofread.

A Well-Defined Problem

- **Is the definition of the problem unclear?** Consider sketching out its history,
  including past attempts to deal with it, discussing its causes and consequences
  more fully, dramatizing its seriousness more vividly, or comparing it to other
  problems that readers may be familiar with. Remember that all the authors of the
  readings in this chapter use assertive language to stress the seriousness of the
  problem.

A Clearly Described Solution

- **Is the description of the solution inadequate?** Try outlining the steps or phases
  involved in its implementation. Help readers see how easy the first step will be, or
  acknowledge the difficulty of the first step.

A Convincing Argument in Support of the Proposed Solution

- *Does the argument seem weak?* Try to think of more reasons for readers to support your proposal.
- *Is the argument hard to follow?* Try to put your reasons in a more convincing order — leading up to the strongest one rather than putting it first, perhaps.

An Anticipation of Readers' Objections and Questions

- *Does your refutation of any objection or question seem unconvincing?* Consider accommodating it by modifying your proposal.
- *Have you left out any likely objections to the solution?* Acknowledge those objections and either accommodate or refute them. Remember that all the authors of the readings in this chapter use tentative language in arguing to support their solutions.

An Evaluation of Alternative Solutions

- *Have you neglected to mention alternative solutions that some readers are likely to prefer?* Do so now. Consider whether you want to accommodate or refute these alternatives. For each one, try to acknowledge its good points, but argue that it is not as effective a solution as your own. You may in fact want to strengthen your own solution by incorporating into it some of the good points from alternatives.

The Organization

- *Is the beginning weak?* Think of a better way to start. Would an anecdote or an example of the problem engage readers more effectively?
- *Is the ending flat?* Consider framing your proposal by mentioning something from the beginning of your essay or ending with a call for action that expresses the urgency of implementing your solution.
- *Would design elements make the problem or proposed solution easier to understand?* Consider adding headings or visuals.

Checking Sentence Strategies Electronically.   To check your draft for a sentence strategy especially useful in proposals, use your word processor's highlighting function to mark specific language where you present the problem and where you propose the solution. Then think about whether you could strengthen your proposal either by making the language about the problem more assertive, so that the problem seems more serious or urgent, or by making the language about the solution more tentative and cautious, so that readers are less likely to resist it. For more on assertive and tentative language in proposals, see p. 249.

■ EDITING AND PROOFREADING

Now is the time to check your revised draft for errors in grammar, punctuation, and mechanics as well as to consider matters of style. Our research has identified several errors that are especially common in essays that propose solutions. The following guidelines will help you check and edit your essay for these common errors.

Checking for Ambiguous Use of *This* and *That*.   Using *this* and *that* vaguely to refer to other words or ideas can confuse readers. Because you must frequently refer to the problem and the solution in a proposal, you will often use pronouns to avoid the monotony or wordiness of repeatedly referring to them by name. Check your draft carefully for ambiguous use of *this* and *that*. Often the easiest way to edit such usage is to add a specific noun after *this* or *that*, as Patrick O'Malley does in the following example from his essay in this chapter:

> Another possible solution would be to help students prepare for midterm and final exams by providing sets of questions from which the exam questions will be selected or announcing possible exam topics at the beginning of the course. *This solution* would have the advantage of reducing students' anxiety about learning every fact in the textbook. . . .

O'Malley avoids an ambiguous *this* in the second sentence by repeating the noun *solution*. (He might just as well have used *preparation* or *action* or *approach*.)

The following sentences from proposals have been edited to avoid ambiguity:

▶ Students would not resist a reasonable fee increase of about $40 a year.
    increase
This would pay for the needed dormitory remodeling.
  ^

▶ Compared to other large California cities, San Diego has the weakest
                              neglect
programs for conserving water. This and our decreasing access to Colorado
                                   ^
River water give us reason to worry.

                                                        one
▶ Compared to other proposed solutions to this problem, that is clearly the
                                                           ^
most feasible.

Checking for Sentences That Lack an Agent.   A writer proposing a solution to a problem usually needs to indicate who exactly should take action to solve it. Such actors are called "agents." An agent is a person who is in a position to take action. Look at this sentence from O'Malley's proposal:

> To get students to complete the questions in a timely way, professors would have to collect and check the answers.

In this sentence, *professors* are the agents. They have the authority to assign and collect study questions, and they would need to take this action in order for this solution to be successfully implemented. Had O'Malley instead written "the answers would have to be collected and checked," the sentence would lack an agent. Naming an agent makes his argument convincing, demonstrating to readers that O'Malley has thought through one of the key parts of any proposal: who is going to take action.

The following sentences from student-written proposals illustrate how you can edit agentless sentences:

> *Your staff should plan a survey*
> ▶ ~~A survey could be planned~~ to find out more about students' problems in
>   ^
>   scheduling the courses they need.

> *The registrar should extend*
> ▶ ~~Extending~~ the deadline to mid-quarter ~~would make sense.~~
>   ^

Sometimes it is appropriate to write agentless sentences, however. Study the following examples from O'Malley's essay:

> These exams should be given weekly, or at least twice monthly.

> Exams could be collected and responded to only every third or fourth week.

> Still another solution might be to provide frequent study questions for students to answer.

Even though these sentences do not name explicit agents, they are all fine because it is clear from the larger context who will perform the action. In each case, it is obvious that the action will be carried out by a professor.

A Note on Grammar and Spelling Checkers.   These tools are good at catching certain types of errors, but currently there's no replacement for a good human proofreader. Grammar checkers in particular are extremely limited in what they can usually find, and often they only give you summary information that isn't helpful if you don't already understand the rule in question. They are also prone to give faulty advice for fixing problems and to flag correct items as wrong. Spelling checkers cause fewer problems but can't catch misspellings that are themselves words, such as *to* for *too*.

REFLECTING ON YOUR WRITING

Now that you have worked extensively with essays that propose solutions to problems—reading them, talking about them, writing one of your own—take some time for reflection. Reflecting on your writing process will help you gain a greater understanding of what you learned about solving the problems you encountered in writing a proposal.

Write a page or two telling your instructor about a problem you encountered in writing an essay that proposes a solution and how you solved it. Before you begin, gather all of your writing—invention and planning notes, drafts, critical comments, revision notes and plans, and final revision. Review these materials as you complete this writing task.

1. ***Identify one writing problem you had to solve as you worked on your proposal essay.*** Do not be concerned with grammar and punctuation; concentrate instead on problems unique to developing a proposal. For example: Did you puzzle over how to convince readers that your proposed solution would actually solve the problem you identified? Did you find it difficult to support the reasons you gave for recommending the solution? Did you have trouble coming up with alternative solutions that your readers might favor?

2. ***Determine how you came to recognize the writing problem.*** When did you first discover it? What called it to your attention? If someone else pointed out the problem to you, can you now see hints of it in your invention writings? If so, where specifically? When you first recognized the problem, how did you respond?

3. ***Reflect on how you went about solving the problem.*** Did you reword a passage, cut or add details about the problem or solution, or move paragraphs or sentences around? Did you reread one of the essays in this chapter to see how another writer handled a similar problem, or did you look back at the invention suggestions? If you discussed the writing problem with another student, a tutor, or your instructor, did talking about it help? How useful was the advice you received?

4. ***Write a page or so explaining the problem and your solution.*** Be as specific as possible in reconstructing your efforts. Quote from your invention notes, your draft essay, others' critical comments, your revision plan, and your revised essay to show the various changes your writing underwent as you tried to solve the problem. If you are still uncertain about your solution, say so. The point is not to prove that you have solved the problem perfectly but rather to show what you have learned about solving problems when writing proposals. Taking time to explain how you identified a particular problem, how you went about trying to solve it, and what you learned from this experience can help you solve future writing problems more easily.

7

Justifying an Evaluation

Evaluation involves making judgments. Many times each day, we make judgments about subjects as diverse as the weather, food, music, computer programs, sports events, politicians, and films. In everyday conversation, we often express judgments casually ("I like it" or "I don't like it"), only occasionally giving our reasons (for example, "I hate cafeteria food because it is bland and overcooked") or supporting them with specific examples ("Take last night's spaghetti. That must have been a tomato sauce because it was red, but it didn't have the tang of tomatoes. And the noodles were so overdone that they were mushy").

When we write an evaluation, however, we know most readers expect that instead of merely asserting a judgment, we will provide reasons and support for the judgment. We know that unless we argue convincingly, readers who disagree will simply dismiss our judgments as personal preferences.

Evaluators can argue convincingly in several ways. One way is by making the reasons for your judgment explicit and by providing specific examples to support your reasons. You can also demonstrate knowledge of the particular subject being evaluated and the general category to which the subject belongs. For example, in an evaluation of *The Matrix Revolutions*, you would want to reassure readers that you are judging this particular film against other action and science-fiction films, including the first two films in the *Matrix* trilogy, *The Matrix* and *The Matrix Reloaded*. Given the film's genre, readers will expect you to base your judgment on qualities such as special effects, action sequences, and ideas or themes. Showing readers you understand how your particular subject relates to other subjects in the same general category demonstrates that your judgment is based on standards that readers recognize as appropriate for judging that kind of subject. For example, most people would agree that taste and consistency are appropriate standards for judging spaghetti served in the school cafeteria, but they would reject the high noise level and uncomfortable seating in a cafeteria as appropriate reasons for evaluating cafeteria food (although these reasons would be appropriate for judging the cafeteria itself).

As you can see, writing evaluations contributes to your intellectual growth by teaching you to develop reasoned, well-supported arguments for your judgments. Evaluations also require you to look critically at the standards underlying your own judgments as well as those of other people. You will encounter evaluative writing in many different contexts, as the following examples suggest.

Writing in Your Other Courses

- For a film-study course, a student evaluates two films (*Emma* and *Clueless*) based on the Jane Austen novel *Emma*. The student reads the novel, watches both films on videotape, and takes extensive notes. He also does an Internet search for reviews of the films. In his evaluation, the student argues that *Emma,* a period piece that faithfully follows the novel, is less successful than *Clueless,* a loose adaptation set in contemporary Beverly Hills, in capturing the spirit and romance of the novel. He supports his judgment with examples from the films and the novel as well as a few quotations from the movie reviews.

- For a political science course, a student writes a research paper evaluating the two major presidential candidates' performances during the first of their scheduled televised debates. Before watching the debate, she researches newspaper and magazine reports on two previous presidential debates to see what standards others have used to evaluate televised debates. Then she watches the debate and records it so that she can review it later. As she views the debate, she makes notes evaluating each candidate's performance. Afterward, she copies the transcript of the debate from the newspaper and collects published, televised, and online reviews of the debate. She uses this material both to support her own judgment and to respond to opposing judgments. Her final multimedia research paper includes downloaded Internet materials and videotaped excerpts from the debate.

Writing in the Community

- For the travel section of a local newspaper, a motorcycle enthusiast writes an article called "Hog Heaven" evaluating a tour of the Harley-Davidson factory and museum in York, Pennsylvania. He argues that Harley fans will enjoy the two dozen antique bikes on display and that people interested in business will be fascinated by the Harley plant because it includes both a classic assembly line (in which each worker performs an isolated operation on the motorcycles as they move along a conveyor belt) and a Japanese-inspired assembly team (in which three workers assemble an entire motorcycle from beginning to end, following whatever procedure they think works best). He concludes by emphasizing that the free tour offers something for everyone.

- For a campus publication, a college student writes an evaluation of a history course. She explains that the course includes three one-hour lectures per week by the professor plus a one-hour-per-week discussion led by a teaching assistant (TA). She states her judgment that although the lectures are boring, hard to follow, and seemingly unrelated to the assigned reading, the TA-led discussions are stimulating and help students grasp important information in each week's lectures and readings. To support her judgment, she describes a typical lecture and contrasts it to a typical discussion. She praises the TA for his innovative "term game," in which two teams of students compete to identify important concepts brought up in the week's lectures and reading, and for reviewing essay drafts via email. She concludes by recommending the course even though she wishes the TA could conduct the lectures as well as the discussions.

Writing in the Workplace

- In a written review of the work of a probationary employee, a supervisor judges the employee's performance as being adequate overall but still needing improvement in two key areas: completing projects on time and communicating effectively with others. To support his judgment, the supervisor explains that in one instance the employee's lateness derailed a team of workers and tells how the employee's lack of tact and clarity in communicating with coworkers created serious misunderstandings during the six-month probation period.

- For a conference on innovations in education, an elementary school teacher evaluates *Schoolhouse Rock,* an animated educational television series developed in the 1970s and recently reissued in several new formats: books, CD-ROM learning games, and music CDs. She praises the series as an entertaining and inventive way of presenting information, giving two reasons why it is an effective teaching tool: Witty lyrics and catchy tunes make the information memorable, and cartoonlike visuals make the lessons painless. She supports each reason by showing and discussing videotaped examples of popular *Schoolhouse Rock* segments, such as "Conjunction Junction," "We the People," and "Three Is a Magic Number." She ends by expressing her hope that teachers and developers of multimedia educational software will learn from the example of *Schoolhouse Rock.*

Practice Evaluating a Subject: A Collaborative Activity

The preceding scenarios suggest some occasions for evaluating a subject. You can discover how much you already know about evaluating by completing the following collaborative activity. Your instructor may schedule it for an in-class discussion or ask you to conduct an online discussion in a chat room.

Part 1. Get together with two or three other students to choose a reading from an earlier chapter that you have all already read. Review the reading, and decide whether you think the reading was helpful or unhelpful to you in learning to write well in the genre of the reading. Everyone in the group does not have to share the same judgment.

- First, take turns telling the group whether the reading was helpful in learning to write in the genre and giving two reasons for that judgment. Do not try to convince the others that your judgment is right or your reasons are sound; simply state your judgment and reasons.

- Next, after each person gives a judgment and reasons, discuss briefly as a group whether the reasons seem appropriate for judging a reading in a writing course. Again, you do not have to agree about whether the reading was helpful or unhelpful; all you have to do is discover whether you can agree on the kinds of reasons that make sense when evaluating a reading in the context of a writing course.

Part 2. As a group, spend a few minutes discussing what happened when you tried to agree on appropriate reasons for evaluating the reading:

- Begin by focusing on the reasons your group found easiest to agree on. Discuss why your group found these reasons so easy to agree on.
- Then focus on the reasons your group found hardest to agree on. Discuss why your group found these particular reasons so hard to agree on.

What can you conclude about community standards for judging readings in a writing course?

READINGS

No two essays justifying an evaluation are alike, and yet they share defining features. Together, the three readings in this chapter reveal a number of these features, so you will want to read as many of the essays as possible. If time permits, complete the activities in the Analyzing Writing Strategies section that follows each selection, and read the Commentary. Following the readings is a section called Basic Features: Evaluations (p. 280), which offers a concise description of the features of evaluative essays and provides examples from the three readings.

Stephen Holden *is a film reviewer for the* New York Times *and member of the New York Film Critics Circle. He began his writing career as a freelance rock critic, and his music reviews have appeared in* Rolling Stone, *the* Village Voice, *and other major publications. He briefly was a record producer for RCA Records and later wrote a novel about the record industry entitled* Triple Platinum *(1979). Holden still occasionally writes evaluations of musical performances and recordings, but since 2000 he has been one of the* Times's *primary film reviewers. He also wrote the introduction to a book based on a series of* Times *articles about the cultural significance of the television series* The Sopranos.

Like The Sopranos, *the film* Road to Perdition *is about the psychological and moral angst of mobsters and their families. In his review, "A Hell for Fathers and Sons," Holden mentions* The Sopranos *and argues that* Road to Perdition *is "a period gangster film that achieves the grandeur of a classic Hollywood western." Evaluations, as you will see, often make comparisons of this kind. As you read, notice how Holden develops the comparison, and think about why he uses the writing strategy of comparing and contrasting. What does it add to his evaluation?*

A Hell for Fathers and Sons

Stephen Holden

Early in *Road to Perdition,* a period gangster film that achieves the grandeur of a classic Hollywood western, John Rooney (Paul Newman), the crusty old Irish mob boss in a town somewhere outside Chicago, growls a lament that echoes through the movie like a subterranean rumble: "Sons are put on the earth to trouble their fathers." 1

Rooney is decrying the trigger-happy behavior of his corrupt, hot-headed son, Connor (Daniel Craig), who in a fit of paranoid rage impulsively murdered one of Rooney's loyal lieutenants. The ear into which Rooney pours his frustration belongs to Michael Sullivan (Tom Hanks), his personal hit man, who witnessed the killing. An orphan whom Rooney brought up as a surrogate son and who has married and fathered two boys, Sullivan is in some ways more beloved to Rooney than his own flesh and blood. He is certainly more trustworthy. 2

But as the film shows, Rooney's bitter observation about fathers and sons also works in reverse: fathers are eternal mysteries put on the earth to trouble their sons as well as teach them. The story is narrated by the older of Sullivan's two boys, 12-year-old Michael Jr. (Tyler Hoechlin), who in a prologue establishes the movie's tone and setting (most of the events take place over six weeks in the winter of 1931) and invites us to decide, once his tale has been told, whether his father was "a decent man" or "no good at all." 3

Road to Perdition, which opens today nationwide, is the second feature film directed by Sam Mendes, the British theatrical maestro who landed at the top of Hollywood's A-list with his cinematic debut, *American Beauty.* The new movie reteams him with Conrad L. Hall, the brilliant cinematographer responsible for that film's surreal classicist shimmer. With *Road to Perdition* they have created a truly majestic visual tone poem, one that is so much more stylized than its forerunners that it inspires a continuing and deeply satisfying awareness of the best movies as monumental "picture shows." 4

Because Sullivan is played by Mr. Hanks, an actor who invariably exudes conscientiousness and decency, his son's question lends the fable a profound moral ambiguity. *Road to Perdition* ponders some of the same questions as *The Sopranos,* a comparably great work of popular art, whose protagonist is also a gangster and a devoted family man. But far from a self-pitying boor lumbering around a suburban basement in his undershirt, Mr. Hanks's antihero is a stern, taciturn killer who projects a tortured nobility. Acutely aware of his sins, Sullivan is determined that his son, who takes after him temperamentally, not follow in his murderous footsteps. Yet when driven to the brink, Sullivan gives his son a gun with instructions to use it, if necessary, and enlists him to drive his getaway car. 5

In surveying the world through Michael Jr.'s eyes, the movie captures, like no film I've seen, the fear-tinged awe with which young boys regard their fathers and the degree to 6

E1
B1 NE
FRIDAY, JULY 12, 2002

Weekend

MOVIES
PERFORMING ARTS

The New York Times

FILM REVIEW

A Hell for Fathers and Sons

An epic of
murderous
family
values.

Tom Hanks as Michael Sullivan, a Chicago hit man, ordering Michael Jr. (Tyler Hoechlin) to wait for him while he attends to business in "Road to Perdition," directed by Sam Mendes. The film opens today nationwide.

which that awe continues to reverberate into adult life. Viewed through his son's eyes, Sullivan, whose face is half-shadowed much of the time by the brim of his fedora, is a largely silent deity, the benign but fearsome source of all knowledge and wisdom. An unsmiling Mr. Hanks does a powerful job of conveying the conflicting emotions roiling beneath Sullivan's grimly purposeful exterior as he tries to save his son and himself from mob execution. It's all done with facial muscles.

Yet Sullivan is also beholden to his own surrogate father, who has nurtured and pro-   7
tected him since childhood. Mr. Newman's Rooney, with his ferocious hawklike glare, sepulchral rasp and thunderous temper, has the ultimate power to bestow praise and shame, to bless and to curse. The role, for which the 77-year-old actor adopts a softened Irish brogue, is one of Mr. Newman's most farsighted, anguished performances.

What triggers the movie's tragic chain of events is Michael Jr.'s worshipful curiosity   8
about his father. Desperate to see what his dad actually does for a living, he hides in the back of the car that Sullivan drives to the fatal meeting at which Connor goes haywire.

After the boy is caught spying, Connor, who hates and envies Sullivan, decides without consulting Rooney that the boy can't be trusted to keep silent and must die. He steals into Sullivan's house and shoots his wife, Annie (Jennifer Jason Leigh), and his other son, Peter (Liam Aiken), mistaking Peter for Michael Jr., who returns on his bicycle as the murders are taking place.

Arriving home, Sullivan finds his surviving son sitting alone in the dark, and as the 9 camera waits downstairs, Sullivan climbs to the second floor and discovers the bodies. As his world shatters, all we hear is a far-off strangled cry of grief and horror. Minutes later he is frantically packing Michael Jr. into a car, and the two become fugitives, making one deadly stop before heading toward Chicago where Sullivan hopes to work for Frank Nitti (Stanley Tucci), Al Capone's right-hand man. For the rest of the movie, Sullivan plots his revenge on Connor, who remains secreted in a Chicago hotel room, protected by Rooney. Sullivan's plan involves a Robin Hood-style scheme of robbing banks but stealing only mob money.

The film, adapted from a comic-book novel by Max Allan Collins with illustrations by 10 Richard Piers Rayner, portrays the conflicts as a sort of contemporary Bible story with associations to Abraham and Isaac, and Cain and Abel. The very word *perdition,* a fancy term for hell, is meant to weigh heavily, and it does.

True to the austere moral code of classic westerns, the film believes in heaven and hell 11 and in the possibility of redemption. In that spirit its characters retain the somewhat remote, mythic aura of figures in a western, and the movie's stately tone and vision of gunmen striding to their fates through an empty Depression-era landscape seems intentionally to recall *High Noon, Shane* and *Unforgiven.* When the characters speak in David Self's screenplay, their pronouncements often have the gravity of epigraphs carved into stone.

A scary wild card slithering and hissing like a coiled snake through the second half of 12 the film is Maguire (Jude Law), a ghoulish hit man and photojournalist with a fanatical devotion to taking pictures of dead bodies. When he opens fire, his cold saucer-eyed leer and bottled-up volatility explode into frenzied seizures that suggest a demonically dancing puppet. And just when you have almost forgotten the character, he reappears like an avenging fury.

The look of the film maintains a scrupulous balance between the pop illustration of a 13 graphic novel (Michael Jr. himself is shown reading one, *The Lone Ranger*) and Depression-era paintings, especially the bare, desolate canvases of Edward Hopper. The camera moves with serene, stealthy deliberation (nothing is rushed or jagged), while the lighting sustains a wintry atmosphere of funereal gloom. Mr. Hall embraces shadow as hungrily as Gordon Willis in the *Godfather* movies, but where the ruddy palette of *The Godfather* suggested a hidden, sensual, blood-spattered twilight, *Road to Perdition* comes in shades of gray fading to black.

Those shades are matched by Thomas Newman's symphonic score, which infuses 14 a sweeping Coplandesque evocation of the American flatlands with Irish folk motifs. In the flashiest of many visually indelible moments, a cluster of gangsters silhouetted in a heavy rain are systematically mowed down on a Chicago street in a volley of machine-gun flashes that seem to erupt out of nowhere from an unseen assassin. But no shots or voices are heard. The eerie silence is filled by the solemn swell of Mr. Newman's score. It is one of many scenes of violence in which the camera maintains a discreet aesthetic distance from the carnage.

Although *Road to Perdition* is not without gore, it chooses its bloodier moments with 15 exquisite care. The aftermath of another cold-blooded murder is seen only for an instant in the swing of a mirrored bathroom door. Another is shown as a reflection on a window overlooking an idyllic beach on which a boy frisks with a dog. Here the overlapping images evoke more than any words the characters' tragic apprehension of having to choose between two simultaneous, colliding worlds. One is a heaven on earth, the other hell.

Connecting to Culture and Experience: Parables and Fables

In evaluating *Road to Perdition*, Holden seems to think that the moral dilemma the film presents makes it interesting. He characterizes the comic-book novel from which the film is derived as "a sort of contemporary Bible story" (paragraph 10). Bible stories like those of Abraham and Isaac or Cain and Abel, to which Holden refers, are often parables or fables, simple stories that illustrate a moral or religious lesson — for example, "Thou shalt not kill." Holden calls *Road to Perdition* a fable with "a profound moral ambiguity" (paragraph 5).

With two or three other students, try to think of other films or television programs you have seen that also resemble parables or fables. If you can think of several examples, see whether you agree on what lessons they teach. If, on the other hand, you cannot think of any other examples, consider why contemporary media rarely presents moral lessons. Then discuss whether morality should be taken into account when evaluating films in general or only those films that, like *Road to Perdition*, try to make a point about morality.

Analyzing Writing Strategies

1. At the beginning of this chapter, we make several generalizations about evaluative essays. Consider which of these statements is true of Holden's essay:

   - It asserts an overall judgment.
   - It makes explicit the reasons for the judgment.
   - It provides specific support for the judgment.
   - It tries to demonstrate knowledge of the particular subject as well as the general category to which the subject belongs.

2. One reason Holden thinks highly of *Road to Perdition* is what he calls its "look" (paragraph 13), which is created by camera movements, lighting, sound, and silence. Reread paragraphs 13–14 to see how Holden uses comparisons to support his enthusiasm for the look of the film.

   Underline the comparisons. To what does Holden compare *Road to Perdition*? If any of these comparisons are familiar to you and you have seen *Road to*

Perdition, explain how well they help you understand what Holden is saying about the look of the film. Also notice that for many of these comparisons, Holden adds descriptive language. In talking about lighting, for example, he compares the use of shadow and color in *Road to Perdition* to that in the *Godfather* films (13). Explain how adding a little description helps readers, both those who are familiar with the comparison and those who are not.

3. Holden makes good use of another kind of comparison: the simile. There are three of them in paragraph 12, two beginning with *like* and one with *suggest*. Underline these similes. (Holden also uses metaphors: *wild card, ghoulish, saucer-eyed, explode.*) Explain how the similes help you imagine (or remember, if you have seen the film) the character Maguire. To write comparisons and similes, you have to rely on certain kinds of sentences. For more information on the sentences of comparison and contrast, turn to p. 293.

Commentary: Presenting the Subject and the Overall Judgment

Film reviews, like other evaluations, usually begin by presenting the subject and stating the writer's overall judgment. Stephen Holden identifies the movie by name in the first sentence, and in the first four paragraphs he categorizes it ("a period gangster film" [paragraph 1]), and tells where and when it takes place ("a town somewhere outside Chicago" [1], "six weeks in the winter of 1931" [3]), what the story is about, who the actors are and what characters they play, and who the director is.

Because they can usually assume their readers are trying to decide whether to see the film, reviewers have to think carefully about how much plot detail to include and why. At least in the opening paragraphs, Holden chooses to give information that is shown in the trailer used to advertise the film. Later, in paragraphs 8 and 9, he gives additional information but does not reveal the ending. In contrast, your instructor may want you to assume your readers have seen the film.

In addition to presenting the subject, writers of evaluation usually state their overall judgment early in the essay. In the first sentence, for example, Holden indicates his judgment is positive when he describes *Road to Perdition* as achieving "the grandeur of a classic Hollywood western." At the end of paragraph 4, after he has described the film and the people responsible for it, he reiterates this judgment in a clear, definitive thesis statement: "With *Road to Perdition* they have created a truly majestic visual tone poem, one that is so much more stylized than its forerunners that it inspires a continuing and deeply satisfying awareness of the best movies as monumental 'picture shows'" (4). This thesis statement has the three qualities expected of a good thesis: It is clear, arguable, and appropriately qualified. The key words *majestic* and *monumental* in this thesis sentence (like the words *grandeur* and *classic* in the first sentence) clearly express praise. The thesis is also obviously arguable since some viewers would very likely disagree with Holden's judgment. (For more information on thesis statements, see Chapter 11, pp. 362–65.

Because his is a rave review, Holden does not point out weaknesses of any kind. He does not qualify or limit his thesis. Most film reviews as well as other kinds of evaluations, however, combine praise and criticism. Rarely do critics find nothing to criticize. Even in highly positive evaluations, writers often acknowledge minor shortcomings to show readers that their evaluation is fair and balanced. Similarly, in negative reviews, the writer usually finds something to praise. As you read the next selection, you will see how a writer can express a positive overall judgment but still point out shortcomings.

Considering Topics for Your Own Essay

List several movies that you would enjoy reviewing, and choose one from your list that you recall especially well. Of course, if you were actually to write about this movie, you would need to see it at least twice to develop your reasons and find supporting examples. For this activity, however, you do not have to view your film again. Just be sure you have a strong overall judgment about it. Then consider how you would argue for your judgment. Specifically, what reasons do you think you would give your readers? Why do you assume that your readers would accept these reasons as appropriate for evaluating this particular film?

Jonah Jackson evaluates computer games for TechTV. He also writes reviews for Computer Gaming World *and Gamers.com. This evaluation of a game called The Elder Scrolls III: Morrowind was initially published on the TechTV Web site and also aired on the TechTV show* Extended Play. *It was originally posted December 30, 2002, and modified on April 23, 2003, for a "best picks" program. Jackson gives the game five stars, TechTV's highest rating. According to TechTV, "Five-star games are a rarity. This is a landmark title that every gamer should consider owning. Even gamers who aren't fans of the genre will enjoy playing this game. It may have some slight flaws, but the ambition of the title and what the developer was able to successfully pull off more than make up for any shortcomings. If games are indeed art, these are masterpieces." As you read Jackson's review, notice that he points out the game's weaknesses as well as its strengths. Consider whether balancing the good with the bad in a review like this makes his argument more convincing or less so.*

The Elder Scrolls III: Morrowind

Jonah Jackson

Morrowind, the third title in Bethesda Softworks' Elder Scrolls series, has hit the shelves. In this week's episode of *Extended Play* we sink our teeth into one of the largest and most richly detailed fantasy worlds ever to wear a set of polygons.[1] There are literally hundreds of hours of gameplay. A second CD that contains a construction set promises countless more hours of gameplay as gamers all over the world work hard on [your favorite mod here].[2] It's a good time to be a gamer.

---

[1] Polygons are used to create virtual three-dimensional space in video games.
[2] *Mod* is a modification of a computer game's technical features.

Outstanding Graphics

Morrowind would be worth the price of admission for the graphics alone. Building on past games, the island of Vvardenfell was meticulously created with dozens of climates and landscapes. Unique architectural detail differentiates cities and towns across the various regions. The sense of scope and grandeur is well maintained from the open canals of Vivec to the modest

Ashlander yurt villages. Seeing the ruined ornate spires of an ancient city appear out of the mist as you walk through the countryside is something to behold.

Fog enshrouds the mountaintops, the water glistens and reflects landscape features, lightning, rain, and dust storms howl through the land, and night skies shine with stars. The Bethesda team has created a world that pulls you in with wide eyes from the moment you step off the slave boat onto the port of Seyda Neen.

Though the game is best played in the first person, there is a third-person camera position that's worth it if for nothing more than checking out the new duds you pick up in town. The few graphical quirks, such as shadows that get cast through walls and robe sleeves that obscure your ranged weapon targeting, are easy to forgive once you see your character reach up and shield his eyes while turning into the teeth of a windstorm.

Free to Explore

Morrowind begins with your arrival in Vvardenfell on an Imperial slave ship. After a short and clever character-generation segment disguised as a new-arrival check-in, you're off and running. Though you're given an initial task related to the game's main story, from the very beginning you're given the freedom to explore and adventure at your own pace.

2

3

4

5

Unlike many games that promise you the freedom to play however you want, Morrowind goes a long way toward meeting that promise. There are hundreds of side quests and locations to explore all over the map. You'll visit many of them and have a satisfying experience by simply following the main story. Alternatively, you can head into the countryside and make your way along a story line on your own. The sheer volume of quests and plot lines ensures that independent exploration will not hamper you when you want to return to the more traditional style of RPG[3] play. Plus it's downright fun to head into the nearest ancestral tomb to pick up a few goodies while walking down a nice country road.

6

Still, the best way to experience Morrowind is to attach yourself to a guild or two and start role-playing the quests you receive. While the ubiquitous fed-ex and find-my-lost-armor quests are well represented, many of your tasks will have more than one solution, depending on your skills, and you'll often find that the overlapping or conflicting interests of the guilds make the plot lines more interesting. The main story follows an engaging plot line as well and includes a huge back story that's interesting on its own. The island of Vvardenfell is a somewhat troubled section of the Empire. The native Dunmers or Dark Elves are at odds among themselves and with the Imperial presence. As the story unfolds you find that you play a larger and more important role in the future of Vvardenfell.

7

Quests and plots are revealed most often through interaction with the hundreds of characters found throughout Vvardenfell. Conversation is based on keywords and the interface[4] keeps track of questions and responses in a separate journal. Many of the generic townspeople do begin to look and sound alike after a while and the canned responses to certain questions do get old or even nonsensical. More than once townspeople seemed completely oblivious to world-changing events that had just taken place.

8

Customization

Every part of the game's design is implemented with an eye toward flexibility and customization to the player's desires. There are 10 races and 21 predefined classes, and you can create custom classes by choosing preferences from 27 skills among three specialization categories: Combat, Magic, and Stealth.

9

---

[3] *RPG* stands for *role-playing game.*
[4] *Interface* is the part of a program that presents information and allows user input.

Skills are improved through training or successful use of the skill. Level advance- 10
ment is based on improving a combination of any skills a total of 10 times. Level advancement brings additional Health and the opportunity to assign additional points to your base
attributes.

Any character class can improve any skill, although advancement is easier in the 11
skills related to your class. The game has no time limit, though, so you can work to create a mighty sorcerer who's also the most skilled swordsman and deft pickpocket in the
land.

With a few exceptions, all skills are useful and the game is well balanced. Playing a 12
skilled orator and acrobat with limited combat skills is just as rewarding as hacking
through the hordes with a barbarian warrior. Bethesda has done an excellent job writing a
story that can be played through with many different character types.

Control

Navigation is similar to many FPS[5] titles and will be familiar to players of the first two 13
Elder Scrolls games. The seamless combat interface is also easy to use, although the
various types of weapon swing (slash, jab, and so on) are awkwardly related to your
movement direction. A group of windowed menus is available with a simple click of the
right mouse button. This pauses the game and lets you access inventory, map, magic
items, and your character's detailed status. Basics such as health, mana, and spell
effects, plus a minimap, are always available on screen. Some of the interface design
is less than optimal. Your inventory, which you can sort by type, can become unwieldy
as you collect a lot of potions or scrolls. It's especially difficult to manage all the potion-
making ingredients if your character has the Alchemy skill.

The many quests you'll receive along the way are recorded in a chronological journal 14
that's autoindexed as you go. This journal manages to record everything of importance,
but it's missing the ability to sort or group items by quest. Nor does it separate completed
quests and ongoing quests. Although the sheer volume of information is a bit much in
later stages, the index feature does prevent the journal from becoming unusable.

Sound

Bethesda gave the music and sound effects the same care it gave the visuals. The 15
grand scope of the story is served well by the basic theme music. Given 50-plus hours of
game time, it was important to produce something that was unobtrusive enough to hear a
few hundred times while still providing atmosphere. The combat music is a little flat, but it
does provide important auditory clues about nearby enemies. The ambiance of the game
is also helped by the carefully crafted sound of footsteps, creaking doors, howling wind,
moaning spirits, unsheathing swords, rippling water, and dozens of other effects that
really pull the game together.

---

[5] *FPS* refers to *first-person shooter* games, a multiplayer genre of computer games.

Summary

Morrowind is a flawed jewel, but flawed only because its scope is so grand. Beautiful   16
graphics, compelling stories, a huge map to explore, engaging quests, and a simple
interface all add up to a premier game. Its bugs and design quirks are more than com-
pensated for by a core game that's just fantastic. It may have just missed the center of
the bull's eye, but Bethesda gets five stars for hitting a target that no one else even dares
aim for.

Connecting to Culture and Experience: Freedom of Play in Computer Games

According to Jonah Jackson, an important attraction of role-playing computer games
is the freedom they give players to explore and play in any way they choose. In addition, computer game enthusiasts can also join online "mod communities" to modify
their favorite games.

With two or three other students, discuss your experiences with role-playing
computer games. Take turns describing what kinds of games you enjoy playing and
what you like about playing these particular games. For example, how much do you
value the freedom to play as you choose and the opportunity to be creative? Consider
also how you feel about the game's rules. Do the rules restrict your enjoyment or contribute in some way to it? Does it matter to you—and do you think it should matter
to Jackson—that what he calls freedom is really scripted?

Analyzing Writing Strategies

1. Writers of evaluations give readers a lot of information about the subject in the
   course of the essay. But they usually present the subject in the opening paragraph
   by identifying it in certain ways. Reread paragraph 1 to see how Jackson presents
   the subject he is evaluating. Underline the information he gives readers, and speculate about why you think he begins with this information.

2. Jackson indicates his overall judgment in the opening and then reasserts it as a
   thesis statement in the concluding paragraph. Reread paragraph 16 to see whether
   the thesis statement meets the three standards for a good thesis: that it be clear
   and unambiguous, arguable, and appropriately qualified.

Commentary: Giving Appropriate Reasons

The argument is probably the most important part of an evaluative essay. Writers
argue by giving reasons and support for their overall judgment. In addition to this
direct argument, writers also usually counterargue, anticipating and responding to
readers' objections and alternative judgments. Here we focus on the way writers give
reasons for their judgment.

Reasons in evaluative arguments are often statements praising or criticizing particular qualities of the subject. Jackson uses headings to focus attention on qualities such as graphics, customization, and control. Headings make his argument easy for readers to follow. They are especially useful for text posted online, as was the case with Jackson's original review, because reading long stretches of text onscreen can be difficult. Here is a scratch outline of Jackson's essay, including the headings:

Introduces the subject and states the judgment (paragraph 1)

Develops and supports the first reason: "Outstanding Graphics" (2–4)

Develops and supports the second reason: "Free to Explore" (5–8)

Develops and supports the third reason: "Customization" (9–12)

Develops and supports the fourth reason: "Control" (13–14)

Develops and supports the fifth reason: "Sound" (15)

Concludes and reiterates judgment (16)

Under each heading, Jackson presents his reason in topic sentences like these:

Outstanding Graphics: Morrowind would be worth the price of admission for the graphics alone. Building on past games, the island of Vvardenfell was meticulously created with dozens of climates and landscapes. (paragraph 2)

Free to Explore: Though you're given an initial task related to the game's main story, from the very beginning you're given the freedom to explore and adventure at your own pace. (5)

Customization: Every part of the game's design is implemented with an eye toward flexibility and customization to the player's desires. (9)

He does not simply assert his reasons, he supports them with particular examples. Look at the way he specifies in paragraphs 2–4 what makes the graphics good. In his topic sentence, he claims that the graphics are praiseworthy because the island was "meticulously created with dozens of climates and landscapes" (2). He supports this assertion with numerous examples. In paragraph 2, he points out how each city and town—from "the ruined ornate spires of an ancient city" to "the open canals of Vivec" and "the modest Ashlander yurt villages"—is given its own look with "[u]nique architectural detail." In paragraph 3, he illustrates the different climates—fog, lightning, rain, dust storms, night skies—that the player encounters. In addition to praising the good graphics, Jackson points out the bad ones, what he calls a "few graphical quirks" (4). He gives examples of these "quirks": "shadows that get cast through walls and robe sleeves that obscure your ranged weapon targeting" (4). Supporting reasons with this kind of detail helps to convince readers that the writer is making an informed as well as a balanced evaluation. As you plan your argument, make sure that you support your reasons with specific examples.

Writers also sometimes need to argue that their reasons are appropriate because they are based on the kinds of standards that people knowledgeable about the subject normally use. Jackson, however, does not have to make this kind of argument because he can assume that his original TechTV audience of experienced computer game players agree that his reasons for evaluating a game are appropriate because they are based on important aesthetic and technical features of role-playing games. The order in which Jackson presents his reasons suggests that for this particular kind of game, graphics are the most important standard for judgment. Presumably, if something serious was wrong with the control interface, his review would have been much more negative, and he might have made control the first reason. Notice that he devotes eleven paragraphs to the first three reasons and only three paragraphs to the last two reasons. The Guide to Writing in this chapter (beginning on p. 282) will help you decide which reasons to present, how to support them, whether you need to argue for their appropriateness, and how to organize your essay.

Considering Topics for Your Own Essay

Like Jonah Jackson, you might have a favorite computer game. Or you might do a lot of digital photography and be able to evaluate digital cameras or a software program like Photoshop. Alternatively, you might be interested in evaluating a particular Web site you use regularly. Choose one particular game, software program, or Web site, and list its obvious strengths and weaknesses.

Christine Romano wrote the following essay when she was a first-year college student. In it she evaluates an argument essay written by another student, Jessica Statsky's "Children Need to Play, Not Compete," which appears in Chapter 5 of this book (pp. 176-79). Romano focuses not on the writing strategies or basic features of an essay arguing a position but rather on its logic—on whether the argument is likely to convince its intended readers. She evaluates the logic of the argument according to the standards presented in Chapter 10. You might want to review these standards on pp. 356–59 before you read Romano's evaluation. Also, if you have not already read Statsky's essay, you might want to do so now, thinking about what seems most and least convincing to you about her argument that competitive sports can be harmful to young children.

"Children Need to Play, Not Compete," by Jessica Statsky: An Evaluation

Christine Romano

Parents of young children have a lot to worry about and to hope for. In "Children Need to Play, Not Compete," Jessica Statsky appeals to their worries and hopes in order to convince them that organized competitive sports may harm their children physically and psychologically. Statsky states her thesis clearly and fully forecasts the reasons she will offer to justify her position: Besides causing physical and psychological harm, competitive sports discourage young people from becoming players and fans when they are older and inevitably put parents' needs and fantasies ahead of children's welfare. Statsky also carefully defines her key terms. By *sports,* for example, she means to include both contact and noncontact sports that emphasize competition. The sports may be organized locally at schools or summer sports camps or nationally, as in the examples of Peewee Football and Little League Baseball. She is concerned only with children six to twelve years of age.

In this essay, I will evaluate the logic of Statsky's argument, considering whether the support for her thesis is appropriate, believable, consistent, and complete. While her logic *is* appropriate, believable, and consistent, her argument also has weaknesses. I will focus on two: Her argument seems incomplete because she neglects to anticipate parents' predictable questions and objections and because she fails to support certain parts of it fully.

Statsky provides appropriate support for her thesis. Throughout her essay, she relies for support on different kinds of information (she cites eleven separate sources, including books, newspapers, and Web sites). Her quotations, examples, and statistics all support the reasons she believes competitive sports are bad for children. For example, in paragraph 3, Statsky offers the reason that "overly competitive sports" may damage children's growing bodies and that contact sports, in particular, may be especially hazardous. She supports this reason by paraphrasing Koppett that muscle strain or even lifelong injury may result when a twelve-year-old throws curve balls. She then quotes Tutko on the dangers of tackle football. The opinions of both experts are obviously appropriate. They are relevant to her reason, and we can easily imagine that they would worry many parents.

Not only is Statsky's support appropriate, but it is also believable. Statsky quotes or summarizes authorities to support her argument in paragraphs 3–6, 8, 9, and 11. The question is whether readers would find these authorities credible. Since Statsky relies almost entirely on authorities to support her argument, readers must believe these authorities for her argument to succeed. I have not read Statsky's sources, but I think there are good reasons to consider them authoritative. First of all, the newspaper authors she quotes write for two of America's most respected newspapers, the *New York Times* and the *Los Angeles Times*. These newspapers are read across the country by political leaders and financial experts and by people interested in the arts and popular culture. Both have sports reporters who not only report on sports events but also take a critical look at sports issues. In addition, both newspapers have reporters who specialize in children's health and education. Second, Statsky gives background information about the authorities she quotes, which is intended to increase the person's believability in the eyes of parents of young children. In paragraph 3, she tells readers that Thomas Tutko is "a psychology professor at San Jose State University and coauthor of the book *Winning Is Everything and Other American Myths*." In paragraph 5, she announces that Martin Rablovsky is "a former sports editor for the *New York Times*," and she notes that he has watched children play organized sports for many years. Third, she quotes from two Web sites—the official Little League site and an AOL message board. Parents are likely to accept the authority of the Little League site and be interested in what other parents and coaches (most of whom are also parents) have to say.

In addition to quoting authorities, Statsky relies on examples and anecdotes to support the reasons for her position. If examples and anecdotes are to be believable, they must seem representative to readers, not bizarre or highly unusual or completely unpredictable. Readers can imagine a similar event happening elsewhere. For anecdotes to be believable, they should, in addition, be specific and true to life. All of Statsky's examples and anecdotes fulfill these requirements, and her readers would find them believable. For example, early in her argument, in paragraph 4, Statsky reasons that fear of being hurt greatly reduces children's enjoyment of contact sports. The anecdote comes from Tosches's investigative report on Peewee Football as does the quotation by the mother of an eight-year-old player who says that the children become frightened and pretend to be injured in order to stay out of the game. In the anecdote, a seven-year-old makes himself vomit to avoid playing. Because these echo the familiar "I feel bad" or "I'm sick" excuse children give when they do not want to go somewhere (especially school) or do something, most parents would find them believable. They could easily imagine their own children pretending to be hurt or ill if they were fearful or depressed. The anecdote is also specific. Tosches reports what the boy said and did and what the coach said and did.

Other examples provide support for all the major reasons Statsky gives for her position: 6

- That competitive sports pose psychological dangers—children becoming serious and unplayful when the game starts (paragraph 5)
- That adults' desire to win puts children at risk—parents fighting each other at a Peewee Football game and a coach setting fire to an opposing team's jersey (paragraph 8)
- That organized sports should emphasize cooperation and individual performance instead of winning—a coach banning scoring but finding that parents would not support him and a New York City basketball league in which all children play an equal amount of time and scoring is easier (paragraph 11)

All of these examples are appropriate to the reason they support. They are also believable. Together, they help Statsky achieve her purpose of convincing parents that organized, competitive sports may be bad for their children and that there are alternatives.

If readers are to find an argument logical and convincing, it must be consistent and 7
complete. While there are no inconsistencies or contradictions in Statsky's argument, it is seriously incomplete because it neglects to support fully one of its reasons, it fails to anticipate many predictable questions parents would have, and it pays too little attention to noncontact competitive team sports. The most obvious example of thin support comes in paragraph 11, where Statsky asserts that many parents are ready for children's team sports that emphasize cooperation and individual performance. Yet the example of a Little League official who failed to win parents' approval to ban scores raises serious questions about just how many parents are ready to embrace noncompetitive sports teams. The other support, a brief description of City Sports for Kids in New York City, is very convincing but will only be logically compelling to those parents who are already inclined to agree with Statsky's position. Parents inclined to disagree with Statsky would need additional evidence. Most parents know that big cities receive special federal funding for evening, weekend, and summer recreation. Brief descriptions of six or eight noncompetitive teams in a variety of sports in cities, rural areas, suburban neighborhoods—some

funded publicly, some funded privately—would be more likely to convince skeptics. Statsky is guilty here of failing to accept the burden of proof, a logical fallacy.

Statsky's argument is also incomplete in that it fails to anticipate certain objections and questions that some parents, especially those she most wants to convince, are almost sure to raise. In the first sentences of paragraphs 6, 9, and 10, Statsky does show that she is thinking about her readers' questions. She does not go nearly far enough, however, to have a chance of influencing two types of readers: those who themselves are or were fans of and participants in competitive sports and those who want their six- to twelve-year-old children involved in mainstream sports programs despite the risks, especially the national programs that have a certain prestige. Such parents might feel that competitive team sports for young children create a sense of community with a shared purpose, build character through self-sacrifice and commitment to the group, teach children to face their fears early and learn how to deal with them through the support of coaches and team members, and introduce children to the principles of social cooperation and collaboration. Some parents are likely to believe and to know from personal experience that coaches who burn opposing team's jerseys on the pitching mound before the game starts are the exception, not the rule. Some young children idolize teachers and coaches, and team practice and games are the brightest moments in their lives. Statsky seems not to have considered these reasonable possibilities, and as a result her argument lacks a compelling logic it might have had. By acknowledging that she was aware of many of these objections—and perhaps even accommodating more of them in her own argument, as she does in paragraph 10, while refuting other objections—she would have strengthened her argument. 8

Finally, Statsky's argument is incomplete because she overlooks examples of non-contact team sports. Track, swimming, and tennis are good examples that some readers would certainly think of. Some elementary schools compete in track meets. Public and private clubs and recreational programs organize competitive swimming and tennis competitions. In these sports, individual performance is the focus. No one gets trampled. Children exert themselves only as much as they are able to. Yet individual performances are scored, and a team score is derived. Because Statsky fails to mention any of these obvious possibilities, her argument is weakened. 9

The logic of Statsky's argument, then, has both strengths and weaknesses. The support she offers is appropriate, believable, and consistent. The major weakness is incompleteness—she fails to anticipate more fully the likely objections of a wide range of readers. Her logic would prevent parents who enjoy and advocate competitive sports from taking her argument seriously. Such parents and their children have probably had positive experiences with team sports, and these experiences would lead them to believe that the gains are worth whatever risks may be involved. Many probably think that the risks Statsky points out can be avoided by careful monitoring. For those parents inclined to agree with her, Statsky's logic is likely to seem sound and complete. An argument that successfully confirms readers' beliefs is certainly valid, and Statsky succeeds admirably at this kind of argument. Because she does not offer compelling counterarguments to the legitimate objections of those inclined not to agree with her, however, her success is limited. 10

Connecting to Culture and Experience: Competitive Team Sports and Social Cooperation

Romano reasons in paragraph 8 that some parents "feel that competitive team sports for young children create a sense of community with a shared purpose, build character through self-sacrifice and commitment to the group, teach children to face their fears early and learn how to deal with them through the support of coaches and team members, and introduce children to the principles of social cooperation and collaboration."

With two or three other students, discuss this view of the role that sports plays in developing a child's sense of social cooperation by giving children insights into how people cooperate in communities like neighborhoods, schools, workplaces, or even nations. Begin by telling one another about your own, your siblings', or your children's experiences with team sports between the ages of six and twelve. Explain how participating in sports at this young age did or did not teach social cooperation. If you think team sports failed to teach cooperation or had some other effect, explain the effect it did have.

Analyzing Writing Strategies

1. In paragraph 2, Romano presents her overall judgment. Underline the thesis statement, and evaluate it in terms of how well it meets the three standards for a good thesis: that it be clear and unambiguous, arguable, and appropriately qualified.

2. In addition to presenting her judgment in her thesis statement, Romano forecasts her reasons in paragraph 2. Reread Romano's essay, noting in the margin where she addresses each of these reasons. Then explain what you learn from the way Romano presents her reasons. Are they clear and easy to follow? Do you think her intended readers — her instructor and parents of young children (the same audience Statsky is trying to convince) — are likely to consider her reasons plausible? In other words, are these reasons appropriate for evaluating an essay that argues a position, based on standards her readers are likely to share? If you see a potential problem with any of the reasons she uses, explain the problem you see.

3. In paragraph 8, Romano observes that Statsky fails to anticipate certain objections and questions that her readers are almost sure to raise. Romano herself has analyzed her readers and tried to anticipate their likely objections and questions as well as the judgments they may be inclined to make of the subject.

Commentary: Presenting Convincing Support

Because she is evaluating a written text, Romano uses textual evidence to support her argument. To provide textual evidence, writers can quote, paraphrase, or summarize passages from the text. (For more on using textual evidence as support, see Chapter 11, p. 371.) Romano quotes selectively, usually brief phrases. In paragraph 4, for example, Romano supports her argument about the believability of Statsky's sources with a quote showing how Statsky presents authorities:

In paragraph 3, she tells readers that Thomas Tutko is "a psychology professor at San Jose State University and coauthor of the book *Winning Is Everything and Other American Myths.*" In paragraph 5, she announces that Martin Rablovsky is "a former sports editor for the *New York Times.*"

In addition to quoting, Romano paraphrases and summarizes passages from Statsky's essay. A summary — a distillation of the main ideas — tends to be briefer than a paraphrase. Paraphrasing, in contrast, tries to capture the rich detail of the original. A good example of paraphrasing appears in the opening paragraph, where Romano represents Statsky's argument. Compare Romano's paraphrase to the original passage from Statsky's essay:

Statsky's Original Version

Highly organized competitive sports such as Peewee Football and Little League Baseball are too often played to adult standards, which are developmentally inappropriate for children and can be both physically and psychologically harmful. Furthermore, because they eliminate many children from organized sports before they are ready to compete, they are actually counterproductive for developing either future players or fans. (paragraph 2)

Romano's Paraphrase

Besides causing physical and psychological harm, competitive sports discourage young people from becoming players and fans when they are older and inevitably put parents' needs and fantasies ahead of children's welfare. (paragraph 1)

Notice that in the paraphrase, Romano mostly uses her own words, with a few significant exceptions for key terms like *physical* and *psychological, players* and *fans.*

Romano summarizes primarily to present parts of Statsky's argument, as in the following excerpt:

Romano's Summary

[I]n paragraph 3, Statsky offers the reason that "overly competitive sports" may damage children's growing bodies and that contact sports, in particular, may be especially hazardous. She supports this reason by paraphrasing Koppett that muscle strain or even lifelong injury may result when a twelve-year-old throws curve balls. She then quotes Tutko on the dangers of tackle football. (paragraph 3)

If you compare this summary with Romano's paraphrase, you will notice another important distinction between summarizing and paraphrasing. When summarizing, writers usually describe what the author is doing in the passage. In the summarized passage, for instance, Romano uses Statsky's name and the pronoun *she* to relate the different strategic moves Statsky makes in the paragraph being summarized. When paraphrasing, however, writers typically leave out references to the author and his or her moves. Like Romano does in the preceding sample paraphrase, they simply restate what the author has written.

Especially when you write an evaluation of a written document, these are the strategies you need to employ for presenting textual evidence from the document itself. For additional examples of paraphrasing and summarizing, see Chapter 14, pp. 436–38. For guidance on integrating quotations into your writing, see Chapter 14, pp. 432–34.

Considering Topics for Your Own Essay

List several written texts you would consider evaluating. For example, you might include in your list an essay from one of the chapters in this book. If you choose an argument from Chapters 5–7, you could evaluate its logic, its use of emotional appeals, or its credibility. You might prefer to evaluate a children's book that you read when you were young or that you now read to your own children, a magazine for people interested in a particular topic like computers or cars, a scholarly article you read for a research paper, or a short story. You need not limit yourself to texts written on paper; also consider texts available online. Choose one possibility from your list, and come up with two or three reasons why it is a good or bad text.

■ PURPOSE AND AUDIENCE

When you evaluate something, you seek to influence readers' judgments and possibly their actions. Your primary aim is to convince readers that your judgment is well informed and reasonable and therefore that they can feel confident in making decisions based on it. Readers do not simply accept reviewers' judgments, however, especially on important subjects. More likely they read reviews to learn more about a subject so that they can make an informed decision themselves. Consequently, most readers care less about the forcefulness with which you assert your judgment than about the reasons and support you give for it.

Effective writers develop an argument designed for their particular readers. Given what you can expect your readers to know about your subject and the standards they would apply when evaluating this kind of subject, you decide which reasons to use as well as how much and what kind of support to give.

You may want to acknowledge directly your readers' knowledge of the subject, perhaps revealing that you understand how they might judge it differently. You might even let readers know that you have anticipated their objections to your argument. In responding to objections or different judgments, you could agree to disagree on certain points but try to convince readers that on other points you do share the same or at least similar standards.

BASIC FEATURES: EVALUATIONS

A Well-Presented Subject

The subject must be clearly identified if readers are to know what is being evaluated. Most writers name it explicitly. When the subject is a film, an essay, a video game, or a Web site, naming it is easy. When it is something more general, naming may require more imagination or just an arbitrary choice.

Evaluations should provide only enough information to give readers a context for the judgment. However, certain kinds of evaluations—such as reviews of films, computer games, television programs, and books—usually require more information than others because reviewers have to assume that readers will be unfamiliar with the subject and are reading in part to learn more about it. Holden tells readers the names of the actors and director of *Road to Perdition,* the place and time in which the film's story unfolds, and a general outline of what happens to the main characters. For a recently released film, the writer must decide how much of the plot to reveal—trying not to spoil the suspense while explaining how well or poorly the suspense is managed. For a classic film or in certain classroom situations, reviewers need not worry about giving anything away.

A Clear Overall Judgment

Evaluation essays are built around an overall judgment—an assertion that the subject is good or bad or that it is better or worse than something else of the same kind. This judgment is the thesis of the essay. The thesis statement may appear in the first sentence or elsewhere in the essay. Romano puts hers in the second paragraph. Holden asserts his thesis in the fourth paragraph. Writers also may restate the thesis at the end of the essay, summarizing their main points, as Jackson does. Wherever the thesis appears, it must satisfy three requirements: that it be clear and unambiguous, arguable, and appropriately qualified.

Although readers expect a definitive judgment, they also appreciate a balanced one. All of the writers in this chapter, except Holden, acknowledge both good and bad qualities of the subject they are evaluating. Romano praises the strengths and criticizes the weaknesses of Statsky's logic. Jackson gives the computer game his show's highest five-star rating, but he points out its shortcomings.

Appropriate Reasons and Convincing Support

Writers assert the reasons for their judgment, often explain their reasons in some detail, and provide support for their reasons.

For an argument to be convincing, readers have to accept the reasons as appropriate for evaluating the subject. Jackson, for example, assumes that his audience of computer game players will agree that his reasons are appropriate because they are based on standards that knowledgeable gamers apply when evaluating a game.

Evaluators not only give reasons but must also support their reasons. They may use various kinds of support. Romano, for example, relies primarily on textual evidence to support her reasons, presenting it in quotations, paraphrases, and summaries. In evaluating a video game, Jackson supports his argument with examples and descriptions.

Many writers also use comparisons to support an evaluative argument. For example, Holden refers to other films (such as *High Noon, Unforgiven,* and the *Godfather* movies), graphic novels *(The Lone Ranger),* Depression-era paintings (by artists like Edward Hopper), and music (by composers like Aaron Copland). Comparisons like these both support the argument and help to convince readers that the writer is an expert who knows the kinds of standards that knowledgeable people normally apply when evaluating this kind of film. Similarly, Jackson compares the video game he is reviewing to other role-playing games.

An Anticipation of Readers' Objections and Alternative Judgments

Sometimes reviewers try to anticipate and respond to readers' possible objections and alternative judgments, but counterarguing is not as crucial for evaluation as is arguing directly for a judgment by giving reasons and support. When they do counterargue, reviewers may simply acknowledge that others perhaps disagree, may accommodate into their argument points others have made, or may try to refute objections and alternative judgments. Romano, in her evaluation of Statsky's essay, accommodates various criticisms she thinks Statsky's readers would have. Thus, her evaluation turns out to be mixed — praising the strengths but also acknowledging the weaknesses of the argument she is evaluating. Evaluation essays often counterargue in just this way.

GUIDE TO WRITING
Justifying an Evaluation

THE WRITING ASSIGNMENT

Write an essay evaluating a particular subject. Examine your subject closely, and make a judgment about it. Give reasons for your judgment, reasons based on widely recognized standards for evaluating a subject like yours. Support your reasons with examples and other details from your subject.

THE WRITING ASSIGNMENT

INVENTION & RESEARCH

Finding a Subject to Write About

Exploring Your Subject and Possible Readers

Testing Your Choice

Testing Your Choice: A Collaborative Activity

Becoming an Expert on Your Subject

Developing Your Evaluation

Considering Document Design

Defining Your Purpose for Your Readers

Formulating a Tentative Thesis Statement

INVENTION AND RESEARCH

PLANNING & DRAFTING

Seeing What You Have

Setting Goals

Outlining

Drafting

PLANNING AND DRAFTING

CRITICAL READING GUIDE

First Impression

Presentation of the Subject

Clear Judgment

Reasons and Support

Treatment of Readers' Objections, Questions, Alternative Judgments

Effectiveness of the Organization

Final Thoughts

CRITICAL READING GUIDE

REVISING

A Well-Presented Subject

A Clear Overall Judgment

Appropriate Reasons and Convincing Support

An Anticipation of Readers' Objections and Alternative Judgments

The Organization

REVISING

EDITING AND PROOFREADING

EDITING & PROOFREADING

Checking Comparisons

Combining Sentences

■ THE WRITING ASSIGNMENT

Write an essay evaluating a particular subject. Examine your subject closely, and make a judgment about it. Give reasons for your judgment, reasons based on widely recognized standards for evaluating a subject like yours. Support your reasons with examples and other details from your subject.

■ INVENTION AND RESEARCH

The following activities will help you choose and explore a subject, consider your judgment, and develop your argument. These activities are easy to complete. Doing them over several days will give your ideas time to ripen and grow. Keep a written record of your invention and research to use later when you draft and revise.

Finding a Subject to Write About

You may already have a subject in mind and some ideas on how you will evaluate it. Even so, it is wise to take a few minutes to consider some other possible subjects. That way you can feel confident not only about having made the best possible choice but also about having one or two alternative subjects in case your first choice does not work. The following activities will help you make a good choice.

Listing Subjects.   *Make a list of subjects you might be interested in evaluating.* Make your list as complete as you can, including, for example, the subjects suggested by the Considering Topics for Your Own Essay activity following each reading in this chapter. The following categories may give you some ideas.

- *Culture:* Television program, magazine or newspaper, computer game, band, songwriter, recording, film, actor, performance, dance club, coffeehouse, artist, museum exhibit, individual work of art
- *Written work:* Poem, short story, novel, Web site, magazine article, newspaper column, letter to the editor, textbook, autobiography, essay from this book
- *Education:* School, program, teacher, major department, library, academic or psychological counseling service, writing center, campus publication, sports team
- *Government:* Government department or official, proposed or existing law, agency or program, candidate for public office
- *Leisure:* Amusement park, museum, restaurant, resort, sports team, sports equipment, national or state park

Listing Subjects Related to Identity and Community. The following are ideas for an evaluative essay on issues of identity and community.

- Evaluate how well one of the following meets the needs of residents of your town or city: a community center, public library, health clinic, college, athletic team, festival, neighborhood watch or block parent program, meals-on-wheels program, theater or symphony, school or school program.

- Evaluate how well one of the following serves the members of your religious community: a religious school, youth or senior group, religious leader, particular sermon, bingo, revival meeting, choir, building and grounds.

- Evaluate how well one of the following aspects of local government serves the needs of the community: mayor, city council, police, courts, social services, park system, zoning commission.

Listing Subjects Related to Work and Career. Following are some suggestions for an evaluative essay on issues involving work and career.

- Evaluate a job you have had or currently have, or evaluate someone else you have observed closely, such as a coworker or supervisor.

- Evaluate a local job-training program, either one in which you have participated or one where you can observe and interview trainees.

Choosing a Subject. *Review your list, and choose the one subject that seems most promising.* Your subject should be one that you can evaluate with some authority, either one that you already know quite well or one that you can study closely over the next week or two.

Exploring Your Subject and Possible Readers

To explore the subject, you need to review what you now know about it, become more familiar with it, make a tentative judgment about it, and think seriously about who your readers may be before you proceed to study your subject in depth. You then will be in a good position to decide whether to stick with this subject for your essay or choose a different subject, making this initial brief period of invention work a very good investment of your time.

Reviewing What You Now Know about the Subject. *Write for a few minutes about what you already know about your subject right at this moment.* Focus your thinking by considering questions like these:

- Why am I interested in this subject?
- What do I like and dislike about this subject?

- What do I usually look for in evaluating a subject of this kind? What do other people look for?
- How can I arrange to become very familiar with my subject over the next week or two?

Familiarizing Yourself with the Subject. *Take notes about what you observe and learn as you get acquainted with your subject, notes that include the kinds of details that make your subject interesting and special.* Whatever your subject, you must now take the time to experience it. If you are evaluating a one-time performance, it must be scheduled within the next few days, and you must be exceedingly attentive to the one performance and take careful notes. If you plan to evaluate a film, it would be best if you could rent the video so that you can reexamine parts you need to refer to. If you are evaluating an agency, a service, or a program, observe and talk to people and make notes about what you see and hear.

Making a Tentative Judgment. *Review what you have written as you have been getting to know your subject; then write a few sentences stating your best current overall judgment of the subject.* Your judgment may be only tentative at this stage, or you may feel quite confident in it. Your judgment may also be mixed: You may have a high regard for certain aspects of the subject and, at the same time, a rather low assessment of other aspects. As you consider your overall judgment, keep in mind that readers of evaluative essays expect writers not only to balance their evaluation of a subject (by pointing out things they like as well as things they dislike) but also to state a definitive judgment, not a vague, wishy-washy, or undecided judgment.

Identifying and Understanding Potential Readers. *Write several sentences about possible readers, with the following questions in mind:*

- For what particular kinds of readers do I want to write this evaluation?
- What are my readers likely to know about my subject? Will I be introducing the subject to them (as in a film or book review)? Or will they already be familiar with it, and if so, how expert on the subject are they likely to be?
- How are my readers likely to judge my subject? What about it might they like, and what might they dislike?
- What reasons might they give for their judgment?
- On what standards is their overall judgment likely to be based? Do I share these standards or at least recognize their appropriateness?

Testing Your Choice

Pause now to decide whether you have chosen a subject about which you can make a convincing evaluative argument. Reread your invention notes to see whether you know enough about your subject or can get the information you need to write a convincing evaluation for the readers you have identified. Also consider whether you feel confident in your judgment.

As you develop your argument, you should become even more confident. If, however, you begin to doubt your choice, consider beginning again with a different subject selected from your list of possibilities. Before changing your subject, however, discuss your ideas with another student or your instructor to see whether they make sense to someone else.

Testing Your Choice: A Collaborative Activity

At this point in your invention work, you will find it helpful to get together with two or three other students to discuss your subjects and test ways of evaluating them.

Presenters: Each of you in turn briefly describe your subject without revealing your overall judgment.

Evaluators: Explain to each presenter how you would evaluate a subject of this kind. For example, would you judge a science-fiction film by the story, acting, ideas, special effects, or some other aspect of the film? Would you judge a lecture course by how interesting or entertaining the lectures are, how hard the tests are, how well the lectures are organized, or how well it succeeds in some other aspect of the class? In other words, tell the presenter what standards you would apply to his or her particular subject. (Presenters: Take notes about what you hear.)

Becoming an Expert on Your Subject

Now that you are confident about your choice of subject and have in mind some standards for judging it, you can confidently move ahead to become an expert on your subject. Over the next few days, you can immerse yourself in it to prepare to evaluate it confidently.

Immersing Yourself in Your Subject. *Take careful notes at every stage of gradually becoming thoroughly familiar with your subject.* If you are writing about a film, for example, you will need to view the film at least twice by attending screenings or renting a video or DVD. If you are evaluating the effectiveness of a public official, you will need to read recent public statements by the official and perhaps observe the official in action. If you decide to evaluate a local sports team, you will need to study the team, attend a game and if possible a practice, and review films of recent games. Consult with other students and your instructor about efficient strategies for becoming an expert on your subject. Your goal is to gather the details, facts, examples, or stories you will need to write an informative, convincing evaluation.

If you think you will need to do more research than time permits or you cannot view, visit, or research your subject to discover the details needed to support an evaluation of it, then you may need to consider choosing a different, more accessible subject.

Learning More about Standards for Judging Your Subject. *Make a list of prominent, widely recognized standards for judging your subject.* If you do not know the standards usually used to evaluate your subject, you could do some research. For example, if you are reviewing a film, you could read a few recent film reviews online or in the library, noting the standards that reviewers typically use and the reasons that they assert for liking or disliking a film. If you are evaluating a soccer team or one winning (or losing) game, you could read a book on coaching soccer or talk to an experienced soccer coach to learn about what makes an excellent soccer team or winning game. If you are evaluating a civic, governmental, or religious program, look for information online or in the library about what makes a good program of its type. If you are evaluating an essay in this book, you will find standards in the Purpose and Audience section and in the Basic Features section of the chapter where the essay appears. If you are evaluating an argument essay from Chapters 5–7, you will find additional standards in Evaluating the Logic of an Argument, Recognizing Emotional Manipulation, and Judging the Writer's Credibility, Chapter 10, pp. 356–61.

Developing Your Evaluation

Now you are ready to discover how you might proceed to make a plausible, even convincing, argument to justify your judgment. Each of the following activities requires only a few minutes of your time spread out over a day or two, and they are all essential to your success in organizing and drafting your evaluation.

Listing Reasons. *Write down every reason you can think of to convince readers of your overall judgment.* Try stating your reasons like this: "My judgment is X because..." or "A reason I like (or dislike) X is that...." Then look over your list to consider which reasons you regard as most important and likely to be most convincing to your readers. Highlight these reasons.

Finding Support. *Make notes about how to support your most promising reasons.* From your invention notes made earlier, select a few details, facts, comparisons, contrasts, or examples about your subject that might help you support each reason.

Anticipating Readers' Alternative Judgments, Questions, and Objections. *List a few questions your particular readers would likely want to ask you or objections they might have to your argument. Write for a few minutes responding to at least two of these questions or objections.* Now that you can begin to see how your argument might shape up, assume that some of your particular readers would judge your subject differently from the way you do. Remember that your responses—your counterargument—could simply acknowledge the disagreements, accommodate readers' views by conceding certain points, or refute readers' arguments as uninformed or mistaken.

Researching Alternative Judgments: An Online Activity
One way to learn more about judgments of your subject that differ from your own judgment is to search for reviews or evaluations of your subject online. You may even decide to incorporate quotations from or references to alternative judgments as part of your counterargument, although you need not do so in order to write a successful evaluation. Enter the name of your subject, such as a movie title, restaurant name, compact disc title, title of a proposed law, or the name of a candidate for public office, in a search engine such as Google (www.google.com) or Yahoo! Directory (http://dir.yahoo.com). (Sometimes you can narrow the search usefully by including the keyword *review* as well.) Of course, not all subjects are conveniently searchable online, and some subjects—a local concert, a college sports event, a campus student service, a neighborhood program—will likely not have been reviewed by anyone but you.

Bookmark or keep a record of promising sites. Download any materials you might wish to cite in your evaluation, making sure you have all the information necessary to document the source.

Considering Document Design

Think about whether visual or audio elements—cartoons, photographs, tables, graphs, or snippets from films, television programs, or songs—would strengthen your argument. These are not at all a requirement of an effective evaluation essay, but they could be helpful. Consider also whether your readers might benefit by such design features as headings, bulleted or numbered lists, or other elements that would make your essay easier to follow. You could construct your own graphic elements, download materials from the Internet, tape images and sounds from television or other sources, or scan visuals into your document from books and magazines. If you do use visual or audio elements you did not create yourself, remember to document the sources in your essay (and request permission from the sources if the essay will be posted on the Web).

Defining Your Purpose for Your Readers

Write a few sentences defining your purpose in writing this evaluation for your readers. Remember that you already have analyzed your potential readers and developed your argument with these readers in mind. Given these readers, try now to define your purpose by considering the following possibilities and any others that might apply to your writing situation:

- If my readers are likely to agree with my overall judgment, should I try to strengthen their resolve by giving them well-supported reasons, helping them refute others' judgments, or suggesting how they might respond to questions and objections?

- If my readers and I share certain standards for evaluating a subject of this kind but we disagree on our overall judgment of this particular subject, can I build a convincing argument based on these shared standards or at least get readers to acknowledge the legitimacy of my judgment?

- If my readers use different standards of judgment, what should I try to do—urge them to think critically about their own judgment, to consider seriously other standards for judging the subject, or to see certain aspects of the subject they might have overlooked?

Formulating a Tentative Thesis Statement

Write several sentences that could serve as your thesis statement. Think about how you should state your overall judgment—how emphatic you should make it, whether you should qualify it, and whether you should include in the thesis a forecast of your reasons and support. Remember that a strong thesis statement should be clear, arguable, and appropriately qualified. (For more on thesis and forecasting statements, see Chapter 8, pp. 307–9.)

Review the readings in this chapter to see how other writers construct thesis statements. For example, recall that Holden boldly asserts an overall judgment he knows will not be expected by his readers. His thesis statement is simple and direct: "With *Road to Perdition* they have created a truly majestic visual tone poem, one that is so much more stylized than its forerunners that it inspires a continuing and deeply satisfying awareness of the best movies as monumental 'picture shows'" (paragraph 4).

Romano uses the thesis statement to forecast her reasons as well as to express her overall judgment. She begins by indicating the standards she thinks are appropriate for evaluating her subject. Her thesis statement shows that she bases her reasons on these standards. In addition, it lets readers know in advance what she likes about the subject she is evaluating as well as what she does not like: "While [Statsky's] logic *is* appropriate, believable, and consistent, her argument also has weaknesses" (paragraph 2). Romano makes her thesis statement seem thoughtful and balanced. There is no ambivalence or confusion, however, about Romano's judgment. She is clear and emphatic, not vague or wishy-washy.

As you draft your own tentative thesis statement, think carefully about the language you use. It should be clear and unambiguous, emphatic but appropriately qualified. Although you will most probably refine your thesis statement as you draft and revise your essay, trying now to articulate it will help give direction and impetus to your planning and drafting. (For more on asserting a thesis, see Chapter 11, pp. 362–65.)

■ PLANNING AND DRAFTING

This section will help you review what you have learned about evaluating your subject, determine specific goals for your essay, make a tentative outline, and get started on your first draft.

Seeing What You Have

Pause now to reread your invention and research notes. Watch for language that describes the subject vividly, states your judgment clearly, presents your reasons and support convincingly, and counterargues objections to your argument or readers' alternative judgments. Highlight key words, phrases, and sentences; make marginal notes or electronic annotations. If you have done your invention writing on the computer, you may have sentences or whole paragraphs that can be copied and pasted into your draft.

If your invention notes seem skimpy, you may need to do further research at this stage, or you could begin drafting now and later do research to fill in the blanks.

If your confidence in your judgment has been shaken or if you are concerned that you will not be able to write an argument to support your judgment, consult your instructor to determine whether you should try evaluating a different subject.

Setting Goals

Before you begin drafting, set some specific goals to guide the decisions you will make as you draft and revise your essay. The draft will be easier to write and more focused if you start with clear goals in mind. The following questions will help you set goals. You may find it useful to return to them while you are drafting, for they are designed to help you focus on specific features and strategies of evaluative essays.

Your Purpose and Readers

- What do I want my readers to think about the subject after reading my essay? Do I want to show them how the subject that I am evaluating fails, how it succeeds (as Holden does), or how it includes both strengths and weaknesses (as Jackson and Romano do)?

- Should I assume that my readers are likely to have read other evaluations of the subject (perhaps like Holden and Jackson) or to have developed their own evaluation of it (like Romano)? Or should I assume that I am introducing readers to the subject?

- How should I present myself to my readers—as knowledgeable, balanced, or impassioned or in some other way?

The Beginning

- What opening would capture readers' attention? Should I open by stating my overall judgment, as Holden and Jackson do? Or should I begin by giving readers a context for my evaluation, as Romano does?

- Should I try to make clear to readers at the outset the standards I will apply, as Romano does? Should I begin by comparing my subject with a subject more familiar to readers, as Jackson and Holden do?

The Presentation of the Subject

- How should I identify the subject? If it doesn't have a specific name, should I name it after something readers will recognize? Should I place it in a recognized category or genre, as Holden does when he refers to period gangster and classic western films or as Romano does by announcing the title of an essay she evaluates?

- What about the subject should I describe? Can I use visuals to illustrate, as Holden and Jackson do?

- If the subject has a story, how much of it should I tell? Should I simply set the scene and identify the characters, or should I give details of the plot, as Holden does?

Your Evaluative Argument

- How should I state my thesis? Should I forecast my reasons early in the essay, as Romano does? Should I place my thesis at the beginning or wait until after I have provided a context?

- How can I convince readers to consider my overall judgment seriously even if they disagree with it? Should I build my argument on shared standards or defend my standards (like Romano)? Should I try to present a balanced judgment by praising some things and criticizing others, as all the writers in this chapter but Holden do?

- How can I present my reasons? Should I explain the standards on which I base my reasons, as Romano does, or can I assume that my readers will share my standards, as Jackson does?

- If I have more than one reason, how should I order them? Should I begin with the ones I think are most important for judging a subject of this kind, as Jackson does? Or should I begin with the strongest and likely most convincing reason?

- How can I support my reasons? Can I find examples from the text to quote, paraphrase, or summarize, as Holden and Romano do? Can I call on authorities and cite statistics? Can I give examples, as Jackson and Romano do?

- What objections or alternative judgments should I anticipate? How should I respond—by merely acknowledging them, by conceding legitimate objections and qualifying my judgment, or by trying to refute objections I consider illegitimate or weak?

The Ending

- How should I conclude? Should I try to frame the essay by echoing something from the opening or from another part of the essay?

- Should I conclude by restating my overall judgment, as Romano and Jackson do?

- Should I end by making a recommendation?

Outlining

An evaluative essay contains as many as four basic parts:

1. A presentation of the subject
2. A judgment of the subject
3. A presentation of reasons and support
4. A consideration of readers' objections and alternative judgments

These parts can be organized in various ways. If, for example, you expect readers to disagree with your judgment, you could show them what you think they have overlooked or misjudged about the subject. You could begin by presenting the subject; then you could assert your thesis, present your reasons and support, and anticipate and refute readers' likely objections.

> Presentation of the subject
>
> Thesis statement (judgment)
>
> First reason and support
>
> Anticipation and refutation of objection
>
> Second reason and support
>
> Anticipation and accommodation of objection
>
> Conclusion

If you expect some of your readers to disagree with your negative judgment even though they base their judgment on the same standard on which you base yours, you could try to show them that the subject really does not satisfy the standard. You could begin by reinforcing the standard you share and then demonstrate how the subject fails to meet it.

> Establish shared standard
>
> Acknowledge alternative judgment
>
> State thesis (judgment) that subject fails to meet shared standard
>
> First reason and support showing how subject falls short of standard
>
> Second reason and support (etc.)
>
> Conclusion

There are, of course, many other possible ways to organize an evaluative essay, but these outlines should help you start planning your own essay. (For more on outlining, see Chapter 9, pp. 326–29.)

Consider tentative any outlining you do before you begin drafting. Never be a slave to an outline. As you draft, you will usually see ways to improve your original plan. Be ready to revise your outline, shift parts around, or drop or add parts as you draft. If you use the outlining function of your word processing program, changing your outline will be simple, and you may be able to write the essay simply by expanding the outline.

Drafting

General Advice.   Start drafting your essay, keeping in mind the goals you set while you were planning. Remember also the needs and expectations of your readers; organize, define, and explain with them in mind. Turn off your grammar checker and spelling checker at this stage if you find them distracting. Don't be afraid to skip around in your draft; jump back and fill in a spontaneous idea, or leap ahead and write a later section first if you find that easier. If you discover that you need more information, just make a note of what you have to find out, and go to the next point. When you are done drafting, you can search for the information you need. If you get stuck while drafting, explore the problem by using some of the writing activities in the Invention and Research section of this chapter (pp. 283–89).

You may want to review the general drafting advice on pp. 16–17. In addition, keep in mind that in writing an evaluative argument, you must accept the burden of proof by offering reasons and support for your judgment. Remember, too, that the basis for judgment often depends on standards as much as reasons and support. Try to think critically about the standards on which you base your judgment as well as the standards that others apply to subjects of the kind you are evaluating.

Sentence Strategies.   As you draft an essay evaluating a subject, you may want to compare or contrast your subject with similar subjects to establish your authority with readers to evaluate a subject like yours. In addition, you are likely to want to balance the evaluation of your subject — by criticizing one or more aspects of the subject if you generally praise it or by praising one or more aspects of it if you generally criticize it. To do so, you will need to use sentences that clearly and efficiently express comparisons or contrasts, specifically ones that contrast criticism with praise and vice versa.

Use sentences comparing or contrasting your subject with similar subjects to help convince readers that you are knowledgeable about the kind of subject you are evaluating. These sentences often make use of key comparative terms like *more, less, most, least, as, than, like, unlike, similar,* or *dissimilar,* as readings in this chapter well illustrate:

> The role, for which the 77-year-old actor adopts a softened Irish brogue, is one of Mr. Newman's *most* farsighted, anguished performances. (Stephen Holden, paragraph 7)

In this sentence Holden compares Newman's performance in *Road to Perdition* to his performances in earlier movies, asserting that it is as good and perhaps even superior.

> The film . . . portrays the conflicts *as* a sort of contemporary Bible story with associations to Abraham and Isaac, and Cain and Abel. (Stephen Holden, paragraph 10)

In this sentence Holden compares the conflicts among the characters in the movie to the conflicts between father and son and between brother and brother in two memorable Bible stories: Abraham was willing to kill his son Isaac when commanded by God to do so (but was not required to actually kill the boy), and Cain killed his brother Abel out of jealous anger because God favored Abel's gift over Cain's. (Comparisons introduced by *like* or *as* are called *similes*.)

> *Unlike* many games that promise you the freedom to play however you want, Morrowind goes a long way toward meeting that promise. (Jonah Jackson, paragraph 6)

In this sentence Jackson contrasts one feature of Morrowind with the corresponding feature of other computer games. Some comparisons or contrasts do not rely on an explicitly comparative term:

> *True to the austere moral code of classic westerns,* the film believes in heaven and hell and in the possibility of redemption. (Stephen Holden, paragraph 11)

Increase your authority with readers by using certain kinds of sentences to balance criticism and praise. The sentence strategies are similar for introducing criticism followed by praise and introducing praise followed by criticism, strategies we refer to in this chapter as *counterargument.* In general, these strategies rely on words expressing contrast, like *but, although, however, while,* and so on to set up the shift between the two responses.

- Praise followed by criticism:

> This journal manages to record everything of importance, *but* it's missing the ability to sort or group items by quest. (Jonah Jackson, paragraph 14)

> ...Statsky does show that she is thinking about her readers' questions. She does not go nearly far enough, *however,* to have a chance of influencing two types of readers.... (Christine Romano, paragraph 8)

> The seamless combat interface is also easy to use, *although* the various types of weapon swing (slash, jab, and so on) are awkwardly related to your movement direction. (Jonah Jackson, paragraph 13)

- Criticism followed by praise:

> The combat music is a little flat, *but* it does provide important auditory clues about nearby enemies. (Jonah Jackson, paragraph 15)

> Its bugs and design quirks are *more than compensated for* by a core game that's just fantastic. (Jonah Jackson, paragraph 16)

Notice that the last example does not use an explicitly comparative term to set up the contrast.

In addition to using sentences that make comparisons or contrasts with other subjects and sentences that balance criticism and praise, you can strengthen your evaluation with other kinds of sentences as well. You may want to turn to the information about using appositives (pp. 151–52), writing sentences introducing concession and refutation (pp. 197-98), and expressing logical relationships between sentences (pp. 198–99).

CRITICAL READING GUIDE

Now is the time to get a good critical reading of your draft. Writers usually find it helpful to have someone else read and comment on their drafts, and all writers know how much they learn about writing when they read other writers' drafts. Your instructor may arrange such a reading as part of your coursework—in class or online. If not, you can ask a classmate, friend, or family member to read your draft. You could also seek comments from a tutor at your campus writing center. (If you are unable to have someone else read your draft, turn ahead to the Revising section on p. 297, where you will find guidelines for reading your own draft critically.)

If you read another student's draft online, you may be able to use a word processing program to insert suggested improvements directly into the text of the draft or to write them out at the end of the draft. If you read a printout of the draft, you may write brief comments in the margins and lengthier suggestions on a separate page. When the writer sits down to revise, your thoughtful, extended suggestions written at the end of the draft or on separate pages will be especially helpful.

If You Are the Writer. To provide focused, helpful comments, your reader must know your essay's intended audience, your purpose, and a problem in the draft that you need help solving. Briefly write out this information at the top of your draft.

- *Readers:* Identify the intended readers of your essay. What do you assume that they think about your subject? Do you expect them to be receptive, skeptical, resistant, or antagonistic?

- *Purpose:* What effect do you realistically expect your argument to have on these particular readers?

- *Problem:* Ask your reader to help you solve the most important problem you see in your draft. Describe this problem briefly.

If You Are the Reader. Use the following guidelines to help you give constructive, critical comments to others on evaluation essays:

1. *Read for a First Impression.* Tell the writer what you think the intended readers would find most and least convincing. If you personally think the evaluation is seriously flawed, share your thoughts. Then try to help the writer improve the argument for the designated readers. Next, consider the problem the writer identified, and respond briefly to that concern now. (If you find that the problem is covered by one of the other guidelines listed below, respond to it in more detail there if necessary.)

2. *Analyze How Well the Subject Is Presented.* Locate where in the draft the subject is presented, and ask questions that will help the writer strengthen

the presentation. If you are surprised by the way the writer has presented the subject, briefly explain how you usually think of this particular subject or subjects of this kind. Also indicate whether any of the information about the subject seems unnecessary. Finally, and most important, let the writer know whether any of the information about the subject seems to you possibly inaccurate or only partly true.

3. *Assess Whether the Judgment Is Stated Clearly.* Write a sentence or two summarizing the writer's judgment as you understand it from reading the draft. Then identify the sentence or sentences in the draft where the judgment is stated explicitly. (It may be restated in several places.) If you cannot find an explicit statement of the judgment, let the writer know. Given the writer's purpose and audience, consider whether the judgment is arguable, clear, and appropriately qualified. If it seems indecisive or too extreme, suggest how the writer might make it clearer or might qualify it by referring at least occasionally to the strengths of a criticized subject or the weaknesses of a praised subject.

4. *Evaluate the Reasons and Support.* Identify the reasons, and look closely at them and the support that the writer gives for them. If anything seems problematic, briefly explain what bothers you. For example, the reason may not seem appropriate for judging this kind of subject, you may not fully understand the reason or how it applies to this particular subject, the connection between a particular reason and its support may not be clear or convincing to you, the support may be too weak, or there may not be enough support to sustain the argument. Be as specific and constructive as you can, pointing out what does not work and also suggesting what the writer might do to solve the problem. For example, if the reason seems inappropriate, explain why you think so, and indicate what kinds of reasons you expect the intended readers to recognize as acceptable for judging this kind of subject. If the support is weak, suggest how it could be strengthened.

5. *Assess How Well Readers' Objections, Questions, and Alternative Judgments Have Been Handled.* Mark where the writer acknowledges, accommodates, or tries to refute readers' objections, questions, or alternative judgments. Point to any places where the counterargument seems superficial or dismissive, and suggest how it could be strengthened. Help the writer anticipate any important objections or questions that have been overlooked, providing advice on how to respond to them. Keep in mind that the writer may choose to acknowledge, accommodate, or refute opposing arguments.

6. *Consider the Effectiveness of the Organization.* Get an overview of the essay's organization, and point out any places where more explicit cueing—transitions, summaries, or topic sentences—would clarify the relationship between parts of the essay.

- *Look at the beginning.* Do you think readers will find it engaging? If not, propose an alternative or suggest moving something from later in the essay that might work as a better opening.
- *Look at the ending.* Does the essay conclude decisively and memorably? If not, suggest an alternative. Could something be moved to the end?
- *Look at the design features.* Comment on the contribution of figures, headings, tables, and other design features. Indicate whether any visual or audio elements that have been included fail to support the evaluation effectively, and offer suggestions for improvement. Help the writer think of additional visual or audio elements that could make a contribution to the essay.

7. *Give the Writer Your Final Thoughts.* What is this draft's strongest part? What part is most in need of further work?

■ REVISING

Now you are ready to revise your essay. Your instructor or other students may have given you advice on improving your draft. Nevertheless, you may have begun to realize that your draft requires more rethinking than revising. For example, you may recognize that your reasons do not lead readers to accept your evaluation, that you cannot adequately support your reasons, or that you are unable to refute damaging objections to your argument. Consequently, instead of working to improve parts of the draft, you may need to write a new draft that radically reenvisions your argument. It is not unusual for students—and professional writers—to find themselves in this situation. Learning to make radical revisions is a valuable lesson for any writer.

If you feel satisfied that your draft achieves most, if not all, of your goals, you can focus on refining specific parts of it. Very likely you have thought of ways of improving your draft, and you may even have begun revising it. This section will help you get an overview of your draft and revise it accordingly.

Getting an Overview

Consider your draft as a whole, following these two steps:

1. *Reread.* If at all possible, put the draft aside for a day or two before rereading it. When you return to it, start by reconsidering your purpose. Then read the draft straight through, trying to see it as your intended readers will.
2. *Outline.* Make a scratch outline, indicating the basic features as they appear in the draft. Consider using the headings and outline/summary functions of your word processor.

Planning for Revision. Resist the temptation to dive in and start changing your text until after you have a solid grasp of the big picture. Using your outline as a guide, move through the document, using the change-highlighting or commenting tools of your word processor to note useful comments received from others and problems you want to solve (or mark on a hard copy if you prefer).

Analyzing the Basic Features of Your Own Draft. Using the Critical Reading Guide that begins on p. 295, identify problems that you now see in your draft.

Studying Critical Comments. Review all of the comments you have received from other readers, and add to your revision plan any that you intend to act on. For each comment, look at the draft to determine what might have led the reader to make that particular point. Try to be objective about any criticism. Ideally, these comments will help you see your draft as others see it, providing valuable information about how you can improve it.

Carrying Out Revisions

Having identified problems in your draft, you now need to come up with solutions and—most important—to carry them out. Basically, you have three ways of finding solutions:

1. Review your invention and planning notes for information and ideas to add to your draft.
2. Do additional invention and research to provide additional material that you or your readers think is needed.
3. Look back at the readings in this chapter to see how other writers have solved similar problems.

The following suggestions, which are organized according to the basic features of evaluation essays, will help you solve some common problems in this genre.

A Well-Presented Subject

- **Is the subject unclear or hard to identify?** Try to give it a name or to identify the general category to which it belongs. If you need more information about the subject, review your invention writing to see if you have left out any details you could now add. You may also need to revisit your subject or do further invention writing to answer questions that your classmates and instructor have raised or your intended readers might have.

- **Is the subject presented in too much detail?** Cut extraneous and repetitive details. If your subject is a film or book, consider whether you are giving away too much of the plot or whether your readers will expect you to give a lot of detail.

- **Is any of the information inaccurate or only partly true?** Reconsider the accuracy and completeness of the information you present. If any of the information will be surprising to readers, consider how you might reassure them that the information is accurate.

A Clear Overall Judgment

- *Is your overall judgment hard to find?* Announce your thesis more explicitly. If your judgment is mixed—pointing out what you like and do not like about the subject—let readers know this from the beginning. Use sentences that balance praise and criticism, as most of the authors of this chapter's readings do.
- *Does your overall judgment seem indecisive or too extreme?* If your readers do not know what your overall judgment is or if they think you are either too positive or too negative, you may need to clarify your thesis statement or qualify it more carefully.

Appropriate Reasons and Convincing Support

- *Do any of the reasons seem inappropriate to readers?* Explain why you think the reason is appropriate, or show that your argument employs a standard commonly used for evaluating subjects of this kind.
- *Is any of the support thin or unconvincing?* To find additional support, review your invention writing, or reexamine the subject. Look closely again at your subject for more details that would support your reasons. As do all the authors of readings in this chapter, consider comparing or contrasting aspects of your subject with those of other subjects like yours.
- *Are any of your reasons and support unclear?* To clarify them, you may need to explain your reasoning in more detail or use examples and comparisons to make your ideas understandable. You may need to do some additional exploratory writing or research to figure out how to explain your reasoning. Consider also whether any of the reasons should be combined, separated, or cut.

An Anticipation of Reader's Objections and Alternative Judgments

- *Do readers fail to recognize your counterargument?* Make your responses to readers' likely questions or objections or alternative judgments more explicit.
- *Are any important objections or questions overlooked?* Revisit your subject or invention notes to think more deeply about why and where readers might resist your argument. Try to imagine how a reader who strongly disagrees with your judgment (praising a movie or college program or restaurant, for example) might respond to your evaluation.

The Organization

- *Does the essay seem disorganized or confusing?* You may need to add a forecasting statement, transitions, summaries, or topic sentences. You may also need to do some major restructuring, such as moving your presentation of the subject or reordering your reasons.

- *Is the beginning weak?* Review your notes to find an interesting quotation, comparison, image, or example to use in your first paragraph.

- *Is the ending weak?* See if you can restate your judgment, summarize your reasoning, or frame the essay by echoing a point made earlier.

- *Can you add any visuals or design features to make the essay more interesting to read and to strengthen your argument?* Consider taking features from your subject or creating visual or audio elements of your own.

Checking Sentence Strategies Electronically. To check your draft for a sentence strategy especially useful in evaluation essays, use your word processor's highlighting function to mark sentences where you praise or criticize various aspects of the subject. Then think about whether you could make your evaluation more authoritative and convincing to readers by making any of the sentences more balanced, either by praising something in an aspect that you have generally criticized or by criticizing something in an aspect that you have generally praised. For more on sentences that balance criticism and praise, see p. 294.

■ EDITING AND PROOFREADING

Now is the time to check your revised draft for errors in grammar, punctuation, and mechanics and to consider matters of style. Our research has identified several errors that are especially likely to occur in evaluative writing. The following guidelines will help you proofread and edit your revised draft for these common errors.

Checking Comparisons. Whenever you evaluate something, you are likely to engage in comparison. You might want to show that a new recording is inferior to an earlier one, that one film is stronger than another, that this café is better than that one. Make a point of checking to see that all comparisons in your writing are complete, logical, and clear.

Editing to Make Comparisons Complete

▶ *Jazz* is as good $\overset{as}{\wedge}$, if not better than, Morrison's other novels.

▶ I liked the Lispector story because it's so different $\overset{\text{from anything else I've ever read.}}{\wedge}$

Editing to Make Comparisons Logical

▶ Will Smith's Muhammad Ali is more serious than any $\overset{other}{\wedge}$ role he's played.

▶ Ohio State's offense played much better than ~~Michigan~~. *Michigan's did.*

Check also to see that you say *different from* instead of *different than*.

▶ Carrying herself with a confident and brisk stride, Katherine Parker seems

different ~~than~~ the other women in the office. *from*

▶ Films like *Pulp Fiction* that glorify violence for its own sake are different

~~than~~ films like *Apocalypse Now* that use violence to make a moral point. *from*

Combining Sentences.   When you evaluate something, you generally present your subject in some detail—defining it, describing it, placing it in some context. Inexperienced writers often give such details almost one by one, in separate sentences. Combining closely related sentences can make your writing more readable, helping readers to see how ideas relate.

▶ In paragraph 5, the details provide a different impression/, ~~It is~~ a comic or

perhaps even pathetic impression/, ~~This impression comes from~~ the boy's *based on*

attempts to dress up like a real westerner.

From three separate sentences, this writer combines details about the "different impression" into one sentence, using two common strategies for sentence combining:

- Changing a sentence into an appositive phrase (a noun phrase that renames the noun or pronoun that immediately precedes it: "a comic or perhaps even pathetic impression")
- Changing a sentence into a verbal phrase (phrases with verbals that function as adjectives, adverbs, or nouns: "based on the boy's attempts to dress up like a real westerner")

Using Appositive Phrases to Combine Sentences

▶ "Something Pacific" was created by Nam June Paik/, ~~He is~~ a Korean artist who is considered a founder of video art.

▶ One of Dylan's songs ridiculed the John Birch Society. ~~This song was called~~ *"Talkin' John Birch Paranoid Blues"*
~~"Talkin' John Birch Paranoid Blues."~~

Using Verbal Phrases to Combine Sentences

▶ Spider-Man's lifesaving webbing sprung from his wristbands/. ~~They carried~~ *carrying*
Mary Jane Watson and him out of peril.

▶ The coffee bar flanks the bookshelves/. ~~It entices~~ *enticing* readers to relax with a
book.

A Note on Grammar and Spelling Checkers.   These tools are good at catching certain types of errors, but currently there's no replacement for a good human proofreader. Grammar checkers in particular are extremely limited in what they can usually find, and often they only give you summary information that isn't helpful if you don't already understand the rule in question. They are also prone to give faulty advice for fixing problems and to flag correct items as wrong. Spelling checkers cause fewer problems but can't catch misspellings that are themselves words, such as *to* for *too*.

REFLECTING ON YOUR WRITING

Now that you have read and discussed several evaluation essays and written one of your own, take some time for reflection. Reflecting on your writing process will help you gain a greater understanding of what you learned about solving the problems you encountered in writing an evaluation.

Write a one-page explanation, telling your instructor about a problem you encountered in writing your essay and how you solved it. Before you begin, gather all of your writing—invention and planning notes, drafts, critical comments, revision plan, and final revisions. Review these materials as you complete this writing task.

1. *Identify one writing problem you needed to solve as you worked on the essay.* Do not be concerned with grammar and punctuation problems; concentrate instead on problems unique to developing an evaluation essay. For example: Did you puzzle over how to present your subject? Did you have trouble acknowledging what you liked as well as what you disliked? Was it difficult to refute an important objection or answer a question you knew readers would raise?

2. *Determine how you came to recognize the problem.* When did you first discover it? What called it to your attention? If you did not become aware of the problem

until someone else pointed it out to you, can you now see hints of it in your invention writings? If so, where specifically? When you first recognized the problem, how did you respond?

3. ***Reflect on how you went about solving the problem.*** Did you work on the wording of a passage, cut or add reasons or refutations, conduct further research, or move paragraphs or sentences around? Did you reread one of the essays in this chapter to see how another writer handled a similar problem, or did you look back at your invention writing? If you talked about the problem with another student, a tutor, or your instructor, did talking about it help? How useful was the advice you received?

4. ***Write a brief explanation of the problem and your solution.*** Be as specific as possible in reconstructing your efforts. Quote from your invention notes or draft essay, others' critical comments, your revision plan, or your revised essay to show the various changes that your writing — and thinking — underwent as you tried to solve the problem. If you are still uncertain about your solution, say so. Taking time to explain how you identified a particular problem, how you went about trying to solve it, and what you learned from this experience can help you solve future writing problems more easily.

STRATEGIES
FOR WRITING
AND RESEARCH

Strategies for Cueing Readers

Readers need guidance. To guide readers through a piece of writing, a writer can provide five basic kinds of cues or signals:

1. *Thesis and forecasting statements,* to orient readers to ideas and organization
2. *Paragraphing,* to group related ideas and details
3. *Cohesive devices,* to connect ideas to one another and bring about coherence and clarity
4. *Connectives,* to signal relationships or shifts in meaning
5. *Headings and subheadings,* to group related paragraphs and help readers locate specific information quickly

This chapter illustrates how each of these cueing strategies works.

■ ORIENTING STATEMENTS

To help readers find their way, especially in difficult and lengthy texts, you can provide two kinds of *orienting statements:* a thesis statement, which declares the main point, and a forecasting statement, which previews subordinate points, showing the order in which they will be discussed in the essay.

Thesis Statements

To help readers understand what is being said about a subject, writers often provide a thesis statement early in the essay. The *thesis statement* operates as a cue by letting readers know which is the most important general idea among the writer's many ideas and observations. Here are three thesis statements from essays in Part One:

> O.K., let's cut out all this nonsense about romantic love. Let's bring some scientific precision to the party. Let's put love under a microscope.
>
> When rigorous people with Ph.D.s after their names do that, what they see is not some silly, senseless thing. No, their probe reveals that love rests firmly on the foundations of evolution, biology and chemistry.
>
> —ANASTASIA TOUFEXIS, Chapter 4

It seems to me that what Native Americans are saying is that what would be intolerable for Jews, blacks, Latinos and others is no less offensive to them. Theirs is a request not only for dignified treatment, but for fair treatment as well. For America to ignore the complaints of a numerically small segment of the population because it is small is neither dignified nor fair.

— RICHARD ESTRADA, Chapter 5

. . . I could not shake the idea that sooner or later I would get the rifle out again. All my images of myself as I wished to be were images of myself armed. Because I did not know who I was, any image of myself, no matter how grotesque, had power over me. This much I understand now. But the man can give no help to the boy, not in this matter nor in those that follow. The boy moves always out of reach.

— TOBIAS WOLFF, Chapter 2

Most thesis statements, like Toufexis's, can be expressed in a single sentence; others may require two or more sentences, like Estrada's and Wolff's. Wolff's thesis explicitly states the point of a remembered event, but many autobiographical essays imply the thesis rather than state it directly.

Readers naturally look for something that will tell them the point of an essay, a focus for the many diverse details and ideas they encounter as they read. The lack of an explicit thesis statement can make this task more difficult. Therefore, careful writers keep readers' needs and expectations in mind when deciding how to state the thesis as clearly and directly as possible.

Another important decision is where to place the thesis statement. Most readers expect to find some information early on that will give them a context for reading the essay, particularly if they are reading about a new and difficult subject. Therefore, a thesis statement, like that of Toufexis, placed at the beginning of an essay enables readers to anticipate the content of the essay and helps them to understand the relationships among its various ideas and details.

Occasionally, however, particularly in fairly short, informal essays and in some autobiographical and argumentative essays, a writer may save a direct statement of the thesis until the conclusion, which is where Estrada and Wolff put theirs. Ending with the thesis brings together the various strands of information or supporting details introduced over the course of the essay and makes clear the essay's main idea.

■ Exercise 8.1

In the essay by Jessica Statsky in Chapter 5, underline the thesis statement, the last sentence in paragraph 1. Notice the key terms in this thesis, the words that seem to be essential to presenting Statsky's ideas: "overzealous parents and coaches," "impose adult standards," "children's sports," "activities . . . neither satisfying nor beneficial." Then skim the essay, stopping to read the sentence at the beginning of each paragraph. Also read the last paragraph.

Consider whether the idea in every paragraph's first sentence is anticipated by the thesis key terms. Consider also the connection between the ideas in the last paragraph and the thesis key terms. What can you conclude about how a thesis might assert the point of an essay, anticipate the ideas that follow, and help readers relate the ideas to each other?

Forecasting Statements

Some thesis statements include a *forecast,* which overviews the way a thesis will be developed. For example, note the role of the forecasting statement in this opening paragraph from an essay by William Langer on the bubonic plague:

> In the three years from 1348 through 1350 the pandemic of plague known as the Black Death, or, as the Germans called it, the Great Dying, killed at least a fourth of the population of Europe. It was undoubtedly the worst disaster that has ever befallen mankind. Today we can have no real conception of the terror under which people lived in the shadow of the plague. For more than two centuries plague has not been a serious threat to mankind in the large, although it is still a grisly presence in parts of the Far East and Africa. Scholars continue to study the Great Dying, however, as a historical example of human behavior under the stress of universal catastrophe. <u>In these days when the threat of plague has been replaced by the threat of mass human extermination by even more rapid means, there has been a sharp renewal of interest in the history of the fourteenth-century calamity. With new perspective, students are investigating its manifold effects: demographic, economic, psychological, moral and religious.</u>
>
> —WILLIAM LANGER, "The Black Death"

This introductory paragraph informs us that Langer's article is about the effects of the Black Death. His thesis (underlined) states that there is renewed interest in studying the social effects of the bubonic plague and that these new studies focus on five particular categories of effects. As a reader would expect, Langer then goes on to divide his essay into explanations of the research into these five effects, addressing them in the order in which they appear in the forecasting statement.

■ **Exercise 8.2**

Turn to Christine Romano's essay in Chapter 7, and underline the forecasting statement in paragraph 2. (After the first sentence, which states Romano's thesis, the remaining sentences offer a forecast of Romano's main points and the order in which she will address them.) Then skim the essay, pausing to read the first sentence in each paragraph. Notice whether Romano takes up every point she mentions in the forecasting statement and whether she sticks to the order she promises readers. What can you conclude about how a forecasting statement assists readers?

■ PARAGRAPHING

Paragraph cues as obvious as indentation keep readers on track. You can also arrange material in a paragraph to help readers see what is important or significant. For example, you can begin with a topic sentence, help readers see the relationship between the previous paragraph and the present one with an explicit transition, and place the most important information toward the end. This section illustrates these cues and others. (For additional visual cues for readers, see Headings and Subheadings on pp. 320–22.)

Paragraph Cues

One *paragraph cue*—the indentation that signals the beginning of a new paragraph—is a relatively modern printing convention. Old manuscripts show that paragraph divisions were not always marked. To make reading easier, scribes and printers began to use the symbol ¶ to mark paragraph breaks, and later, indenting became common practice. Even that relatively modern custom, however, has been abandoned by most business writers, who now distinguish one paragraph from another by leaving a line of space above and below each paragraph. Writing on the Internet is also usually paragraphed in this way.

Paragraphing helps readers by signaling when a sequence of related ideas begins and ends. Paragraphing also helps readers judge what is most important in what they are reading. Writers typically emphasize important information by placing it at the two points where readers are most attentive—the beginning and the end of a paragraph. Many writers put information to orient readers at the beginning of a paragraph and save the most important information for last.

You can give special emphasis to information by placing it in its own paragraph.

■ **Exercise 8.3**

Turn to Patrick O'Malley's essay in Chapter 6, and read paragraphs 4–6 with the following questions in mind: Does all the material in each paragraph seem to be related? Do you feel a sense of closure at the end of each paragraph? Does the last sentence offer the most important or significant or weighty information in the paragraph?

Topic Sentence Strategies

A *topic sentence* lets readers know the focus of a paragraph in simple and direct terms. It is a cueing strategy for the paragraph, much as a thesis or forecasting statement is for the whole essay. Because paragraphing usually signals a shift in focus, readers expect some kind of reorientation in the opening sentence. They need to know whether the new paragraph will introduce another aspect of the topic or develop one already introduced.

Announcing the Topic.   Some topic sentences simply announce the topic. Here are some examples taken from Barry Lopez's book *Arctic Dreams:*

A polar bear walks in a way all its own.

What is so consistently striking about the way Eskimos used parts of an animal is the breadth of their understanding about what would work.

The Mediterranean view of the Arctic, down to the time of the Elizabethan mariners, was shaped by two somewhat contradictory thoughts.

These topic sentences do more than merely identify the topic; they also indicate how the topic will be developed in subsequent sentences—by describing how bears walk, giving examples of animal parts Eskimos used and explaining what they understood about how each part could be useful, or contrasting two preconceptions about the Arctic.

The following paragraph shows how one of Lopez's topic sentences (underlined) is developed:

> <u>What is so consistently striking about the way Eskimos used parts of an animal is the breadth of their understanding about what would work.</u> Knowing that muskox horn is more flexible than caribou antler, they preferred it for making the side prongs of a fish spear. For a waterproof bag in which to carry sinews for clothing repair, they chose salmon skin. They selected the strong, translucent intestine of a bearded seal to make a window for a snowhouse—it would fold up for easy traveling and it would not frost over in cold weather. To make small snares for sea ducks, they needed a springy material that would not rot in salt water—baleen fibers. The down feather of a common eider, tethered at the end of a stick in the snow at an angle, would reveal the exhalation of a quietly surfacing seal. Polar bear bone was used anywhere a stout, sharp point was required, because it is the hardest bone.
>
> – BARRY LOPEZ, *Arctic Dreams*

■ **Exercise 8.4**

Turn to Jessica Statsky's essay in Chapter 5. Underline the topic sentence in paragraphs 3–8. Consider how these sentences help you anticipate the paragraph's topic and development.

Making a Transition.   Not all topic sentences simply point to what will follow. Some also refer to earlier sentences. Such sentences work both as topic sentences, stating the main point of the paragraph, and as transitions, linking that paragraph to the previous one. Here are a few topic sentences from "Quilts and Women's Culture," by Elaine Hedges, that use specific transitions (underlined) to tie the sentence to a previous statement:

> Within its broad traditionalism and anonymity, <u>however</u>, variations and distinctions developed.

> Regionally, <u>too</u>, distinctions were introduced into quilt making through the interesting process of renaming.

> <u>With equal inventiveness</u> women renamed traditional patterns to accommodate to the local landscape.

> <u>Finally</u>, out of such regional and other variations come individual, signed achievements.

> Quilts, <u>then</u>, were an outlet for creative energy, a source and emblem of sisterhood and solidarity, and a graphic response to historical and political change.

Sometimes the first sentence of a paragraph serves as a transition, and a subsequent sentence states the topic. The underlined sentences in the following example illustrate this strategy:

> . . . What a convenience, what a relief it will be, they say, never to worry about how to dress for a job interview, a romantic tryst, or a funeral!

Convenient, perhaps, but not exactly a relief. Such a utopia would give most of us the same kind of chill we feel when a stadium full of Communist-bloc athletes in identical sports outfits, shouting slogans in unison, appears on TV. Most people do not want to be told what to wear any more than they want to be told what to say. In Belfast recently four hundred Irish Republican prisoners "refused to wear any clothes at all, draping themselves day and night in blankets," rather than put on prison uniforms. Even the offer of civilian-style dress did not satisfy them; they insisted on wearing their own clothes brought from home, or nothing. Fashion is free speech, and one of the privileges, if not always one of the pleasures, of a free world.

— ALISON LURIE, *The Language of Clothes*

Occasionally, whole paragraphs serve as transitions, linking one sequence of paragraphs with those that follow. This transition paragraph summarizes what went before (evidence of contrast) and sets up what will follow (evidence of similarity):

Yet it was not all contrast, after all. Different as they were — in background, in personality, in underlying aspiration — these two great soldiers had much in common. Under everything else, they were marvelous fighters. Furthermore, their fighting qualities were really very much alike.

— BRUCE CATTON, "Grant and Lee: A Study in Contrasts"

■ **Exercise 8.5**

Turn to Anastasia Toufexis's essay in Chapter 4, and read paragraphs 6–18. As you read, underline the part of the first sentence in paragraphs 7, 11, and 18 that refers to the previous paragraph, creating a transition from the one paragraph to the next. Notice the different ways Toufexis creates these transitions. Consider whether they are all equally effective.

Positioning the Topic Sentence.   Although topic sentences may occur anywhere in a paragraph, stating the topic in the first sentence has the advantage of giving readers a sense of how the paragraph is likely to be developed. The beginning of the paragraph is therefore the most common position for a topic sentence.

A topic sentence that does not open a paragraph is most likely to appear at the end. When a topic sentence concludes a paragraph, it usually summarizes or generalizes preceding information. In the following example, the topic is not stated explicitly until the last sentence.

Even black Americans sometimes need to be reminded about the deceptiveness of television. Blacks retain their fascination with black characters on TV: Many of us buy *Jet* magazine primarily to read its weekly television feature, which lists every black character (major or minor) to be seen on the screen that week. Yet our fixation with the presence of black characters on TV has blinded us to an important fact that *Cosby,* which began in 1984, and its offshoots over the years demonstrate convincingly: There is very little connection between the social status of black Americans and the fabricated images of black people that Americans consume each day. The representation of blacks on TV is a very poor index to our social advancement or political progress.

— HENRY LOUIS GATES JR., "TV's Black World Turns — but Stays Unreal"

When a topic sentence is used in a narrative, it often appears as the last sentence as a way to evaluate or reflect on events:

> A cold sun was sliding down a gray fall sky. Some older boys had been playing tackle football in the field we took charge of every weekend. In a few years, they'd be called to Southeast Asia, some of them. Their locations would be tracked with push-pins in red, white, and blue on maps on nearly every kitchen wall. But that after-noon, they were quick as young deer. They leapt and dodged, dove from each other and collided in midair. Bulletlike passes flew to connect them. Or the ball spiraled in a high arc across the frosty sky one to another. In short, they were mindlessly agile in a way that captured as audience every little kid within running distance of the yellow goalposts.
>
> – MARY KARR, *Cherry*

It is possible for a single topic sentence to introduce two or more paragraphs. Subsequent paragraphs in such a sequence have no separate topic sentences of their own. Here is a two-paragraph sequence in which the topic sentence opens the first paragraph:

> Anthropologists Daniel Maltz and Ruth Borker point out that boys and girls socialize differently. Little girls tend to play in small groups or, even more common, in pairs. Their social life usually centers around a best friend, and friendships are made, maintained, and broken by talk—especially "secrets." If a little girl tells her friend's secret to another little girl, she may find herself with a new best friend. The secrets themselves may or may not be important, but the fact of telling them is all-important. It's hard for newcomers to get into these tight groups, but anyone who is admitted is treated as an equal. Girls like to play cooperatively; if they can't cooperate, the group breaks up.
>
> Little boys tend to play in larger groups, often outdoors, and they spend more time doing things than talking. It's easy for boys to get into the group, but not every-one is accepted as an equal. Once in the group, boys must jockey for their status in it. One of the most important ways they do this is through talk: verbal display such as telling stories and jokes, challenging and sidetracking the verbal displays of other boys, and withstanding other boys' challenges in order to maintain their own story—and status. Their talk is often competitive talk about who is best at what.
>
> – DEBORAH TANNEN, *That's Not What I Meant!*

■ Exercise 8.6

Consider the variety and effectiveness of the topic sentences in your most recent essay. Begin by underlining the topic sentence in each paragraph after the first one. The topic sentence may not be the first sentence in a paragraph, though often it will be.

Then double-underline the part of the topic sentence that provides an explicit transition from one paragraph to the next. You may find a transition that is separate from the topic sentence. You may not always find a topic sentence.

Reflect on your topic sentences, and evaluate how well they serve to orient your readers to the sequence of topics or ideas in your essay.

■ COHESIVE DEVICES

Cohesive devices guide readers, helping them follow your train of thought by connecting key words and phrases throughout a passage. Among such devices are pronoun reference, word repetition, synonyms, repetition of sentence structure, and collocation.

Pronoun Reference

One common cohesive device is *pronoun reference.* As noun substitutes, pronouns refer to nouns that either precede or follow them and thus serve to connect phrases or sentences. The nouns that come before the pronouns are called *antecedents.* In the following paragraph, the pronouns (*it* or *its*) form a chain of connection with their antecedent, *George Washington Bridge.*

> In New York from dawn to dusk to dawn, day after day, you can hear the steady rumble of tires against the concrete span of the George Washington Bridge. The bridge is never completely still. It trembles with traffic. It moves in the wind. Its great veins of steel swell when hot and contract when cold; its span often is ten feet closer to the Hudson River in summer than in winter.
>
> – GAY TALESE, "New York"

This example has only one pronoun-antecedent chain, and the antecedent comes first, so all the pronouns refer back to it. When there are multiple pronoun-antecedent chains with references forward as well as back, writers have to make sure that readers will not mistake one pronoun's antecedent for another's.

Word Repetition

To avoid confusion, writers often use *word repetition.* The device of repeating words and phrases is especially helpful if a pronoun might confuse readers:

> Some odd optical property of our highly polarized and unequal society makes the poor almost invisible to their economic superiors. The poor can see the affluent easily enough—on television, for example, or on the covers of magazines. But the affluent rarely see the poor or, if they do catch sight of them in some public space, rarely know what they're seeing, since—thanks to consignment stores and, yes, Wal-Mart—the poor are usually able to disguise themselves as members of the more comfortable classes.
>
> – BARBARA EHRENREICH, *Nickel and Dimed*

In the next example, several overlapping chains of word repetition prevent confusion and help the reader follow the ideas:

> Natural selection is the central concept of Darwinian theory—the fittest survive and spread their favored traits through populations. Natural selection is defined by Spencer's phrase "survival of the fittest," but what does this famous bit of jargon really mean? Who are the fittest? And how is "fitness" defined? We often read that fitness involves no more than "differential reproductive success"—the production of more

surviving offspring than other competing members of the population. Whoa! cries Bethell, as many others have before him. This formulation defines fitness in terms of survival only. The crucial phrase of natural selection means no more than "the survival of those who survive"—a vacuous tautology. (A tautology is a phrase—like "my father is a man"—containing no information in the predicate ["a man"] not inherent in the subject ["my father"]. Tautologies are fine as definitions, but not as testable scientific statements—there can be nothing to test in a statement true by definition.)

— STEPHEN JAY GOULD, *Ever Since Darwin*

Notice that Gould uses repetition to keep readers focused on the key concepts of "natural selection," "survival of the fittest," and "tautology." These key terms may vary in form—*fittest* becomes *fitness,* and *survival* changes to *surviving* and *survive*—but they serve as links in the chain of meaning.

Synonyms

In addition to word repetition, you can use *synonyms,* words with identical or very similar meanings, to connect important ideas. In the following example, the author develops a careful chain of synonyms and word repetitions:

Over time, small bits of knowledge about a region accumulate among local residents in the form of stories. These are remembered in the community; even what is unusual does not become lost and therefore irrelevant. These narratives comprise for a native an intricate, long-term view of a particular landscape.... Outside the region this complex but easily shared "reality" is hard to get across without reducing it to generalities, to misleading or imprecise abstraction.

— BARRY LOPEZ, *Arctic Dreams*

Note the variety of synonym sequences:

"particular landscape," "region"

"local residents," "community," "native"

"stories," "narratives"

"accumulate," "remembered," "does not become lost," "comprise"

"intricate, long-term view," "complex ... reality," "without reducing it to generalities"

The result is a coherent paragraph that constantly reinforces the author's point.

Sentence Structure Repetition

Writers occasionally use *sentence structure repetition* to emphasize the connections among their ideas, as in this example:

But the life forms are as much part of the structure of the Earth as any inanimate portion is. It is all an inseparable part of a whole. If any animal is isolated totally from other forms of life, then death by starvation will surely follow. If isolated from water, death by dehydration will follow even faster. If isolated from air, whether free or dis-solved in water, death by asphyxiation will follow still faster. If isolated from the Sun, animals will survive for a time, but plants would die, and if all plants died, all animals would starve.

– ISAAC ASIMOV, "The Case against Man"

From the third sentence to the last, Asimov repeats the same sentence structure—"If this...then that"—to show that the sentences or clauses are logically related; every one expresses a consequence of isolation.

Collocation

Collocation—the positioning of words together in expected ways around a particular topic—occurs quite naturally to writers and usually forms recognizable networks of meaning for readers. For example, in a paragraph on a high school graduation, a reader might expect to encounter such words as *valedictorian, diploma, commence-ment, honors, cap and gown,* and *senior class.* The paragraph that follows uses five col-location chains:

housewife, cooking, neighbor, home

clocks, calculated cooking times, progression, precise

obstinacy, vagaries, problem

sun, clear days, cloudy ones, sundial, cast its light, angle, seasons, sun, weather

cooking, fire, matches, hot coals, smoldering, ashes, go out, bed-warming pan

The seventeenth-century housewife not only had to make do without thermometers, she also had to make do without clocks, which were scarce and dear throughout the six-teen hundreds. She calculated cooking times by the progression of the sun; her cooking must have been more precise on clear days than on cloudy ones. Marks were sometimes painted on the floor, providing her with a rough sundial, but she still had to make allowance for the obstinacy of the sun in refusing to cast its light at the same angle as the seasons changed; but she was used to allowing for the vagaries of sun and weather. She also had a problem starting her fire in the morning; there were no matches. If she had allowed the hot coals smoldering under the ashes to go out, she had to borrow some from a neighbor, carrying them home with care, perhaps in a bed-warming pan.

– WAVERLY ROOT AND RICHARD DE ROUCHEMENT, *Eating in America*

■ Exercise 8.7

Now that you know more about pronoun reference, word repetition, synonyms, sen-tence structure repetition, and collocation, turn to Trevor B. Hall's essay in Chap-ter 3, and identify the cohesive devices you find in paragraphs 1–6. Underline each cohesive device you can find; there will be many devices. You might also want to con-nect with lines the various pronoun, related-word, and synonym chains you find. You could also try listing the separate collocation chains. Consider how these cohesive devices help you read and make sense of the passage.

■ **Exercise 8.8**

Choose one of your recent essays, and select any three contiguous paragraphs. Identify the cohesive devices you find in these three paragraphs. Underline every cohesive device you can find; there will be many devices. Try to connect with lines the various pronoun, related-word, and synonym chains you find. Also try listing the separate collocation chains.

You will be surprised and pleased at how extensively you rely on cohesive ties. Indeed, you could not produce readable text without cohesive ties. Consider these questions relevant to your development as a writer: Are all of your pronoun references clear? Are you straining for synonyms when repeated words would do? Do you ever repeat sentence structures to emphasize connections? Do you trust yourself to put collocation to work?

■ CONNECTIVES

A *connective* serves as a bridge to connect one paragraph, sentence, clause, or word with another. It also identifies the kind of connection by indicating to readers how the item preceding the connective relates to the one that follows it. Connectives help readers anticipate how the next paragraph or sentence will affect the meaning of what they have just read. There are three basic groups of connectives, based on the relationships they indicate: logical, temporal, and spatial.

Logical Relationships

Connectives help readers follow the *logical relationships* within an argument. How such connectives work is illustrated in this tightly and passionately reasoned paragraph by James Baldwin:

> The black man insists, by whatever means he finds at his disposal, that the white man cease to regard him as an exotic rarity and recognize him as a human being. This is a very charged and difficult moment, for there is a great deal of will power involved in the white man's naïveté. Most people are not naturally malicious, and the white man prefers to keep the black man at a certain human remove because it is easier for him thus to preserve his simplicity and to avoid being called to account for crimes committed by his forefathers, or his neighbors. He is inescapably aware, nevertheless, that he is in a better position in the world than black men are, nor can he quite put to death the suspicion that he is hated by black men therefore. He does not wish to be hated, neither does he wish to change places, and at this point in his uneasiness he can scarcely avoid having recourse to those legends which white men have created about black men, the most unusual effect of which is that the white man finds himself enmeshed, so to speak, in his own language which describes hell, as well as the attributes which lead one to hell, as being black as night.
>
> – JAMES BALDWIN, "Stranger in the Village"

Connectives Showing Logical Relationships

- *To introduce another item in a series:* first, second; in the second place; for one thing . . . , for another; next; then; furthermore; moreover; in addition; finally; last; also; similarly; besides; and; as well as

- *To introduce an illustration or other specification:* in particular; specifically; for instance; for example; that is; namely

- *To introduce a result or a cause:* consequently; as a result; hence; accordingly; thus; so; therefore; then; because; since; for

- *To introduce a restatement:* that is; in other words; in simpler terms; to put it differently

- *To introduce a conclusion or summary:* in conclusion; finally; all in all; evidently; clearly; actually; to sum up; altogether; of course

- *To introduce an opposing point:* but; however; yet; nevertheless; on the contrary; on the other hand; in contrast; still; neither; nor

- *To introduce a concession to an opposing view:* certainly; naturally; of course; it is true; to be sure; granted

- *To resume the original line of reasoning after a concession:* nonetheless; all the same; even though; still; nevertheless

Temporal Relationships

In addition to showing logical connections, connectives may indicate *temporal relationships*—a sequence or progression in time—as this example illustrates:

> That night, we drank tea and then vodka with lemon peel steeped in it. The four of us talked in Russian and English about mutual friends and American railroads and the Rolling Stones. Seryozha loves the Stones, and his face grew wistful as we spoke about their recent album, *Some Girls.* He played a tape of "Let It Bleed" over and over, until we could translate some difficult phrases for him; after that, he came out with the phrases at intervals during the evening, in a pretty decent imitation of Jagger's Cockney snarl. He was an adroit and oddly formal host, inconspicuously filling our teacups and politely urging us to eat bread and cheese and chocolate. While he talked to us, he teased Anya, calling her "Piglet," and she shook back her bangs and glowered at him. It was clear that theirs was a fiery relationship. After a while, we talked about ourselves. Anya told us about painting and printmaking and about how hard it was to buy supplies in Moscow. There had been something angry in her dark face since the beginning of the evening; I thought at first that it meant she didn't like Americans; but now I realized that it was a constant, barely suppressed rage at her own situation.
>
> —ANDREA LEE, *Russian Journal*

Connectives Showing Temporal Relationships

- *To indicate frequency:* frequently; hourly; often; occasionally; now and then; day after day; every so often; again and again

- *To indicate duration:* during; briefly; for a long time; minute by minute; while
- *To indicate a particular time:* now; then; at that time; in those days; last Sunday; next Christmas; in 2003; at the beginning of August; at six o'clock; first thing in the morning; two months ago; when
- *To indicate the beginning:* at first; in the beginning; since; before then
- *To indicate the middle:* in the meantime; meanwhile; as it was happening; at that moment; at the same time; simultaneously; next; then
- *To indicate the end and beyond:* eventually; finally; at last; in the end; subsequently; later; afterward

Spatial Relationships

Spatial relationships connectives orient readers to the objects in a scene, as illustrated in these paragraphs:

> On Georgia 155, I crossed Troublesome Creek, then went through groves of pecan trees aligned one with the next like fenceposts. The pastures grew a green almost blue, and syrupy water the color of a dusty sunset filled the ponds. Around the farmhouses, from wires strung high above the ground, swayed gourds hollowed out for purple martins.
>
> The land rose again on the other side of the Chattahoochee River, and Highway 34 went to the ridgetops where long views over the hills opened in all directions. Here was the tail of the Appalachian backbone, its gradual descent to the Gulf. Near the Alabama stateline stood a couple of LAST CHANCE! bars. . . .
>
> —WILLIAM LEAST HEAT MOON, *Blue Highways*

Connectives Showing Spatial Relationships

- *To indicate closeness:* close to; near; next to; alongside; adjacent to; facing
- *To indicate distance:* in the distance; far; beyond; away; there
- *To indicate direction:* up/down; sideways; along; across; to the right/left; in front of/behind; above/below; inside/outside; toward/away from

■ Exercise 8.9

Turn to Patrick O'Malley's essay in Chapter 6. Relying on the lists of connectives just given, underline the *logical* and *temporal* connectives in paragraphs 5–10. Notice the different connectives O'Malley uses and how they work to make the relationships among his ideas clear.

■ Exercise 8.10

Select a recent essay of your own. Choose at least three paragraphs, and, relying on the lists of connectives given in the text, underline the logical, temporal, and spatial connectives. Depending on the kind of writing you were doing, you may find few, if any, connectives in one category or another. For example, an essay speculating about causes may not include any spatial connectives; writing about a remembered event might not contain connectives showing logical relationships.

Consider how your connectives relate the ideas from sentence to sentence. Comparing your connectives to those in the lists, do you find that you are making full use of the repertoire of connectives? Do you find gaps between any of your sentences that a well-chosen connective would close?

■ HEADINGS AND SUBHEADINGS

Headings and subheadings—brief phrases set off from the text in various ways—can provide visible cues to readers about the content and organization of a text. Headings can be distinguished from text in numerous ways, including the selective use of capital letters, bold or italic type, or different sizes of type. To be most helpful to readers, headings should be phrased similarly and follow a predictable system.

Heading Systems and Levels

In this chapter, the headings in the section Paragraphing, beginning on p. 309, provide a good example of a system of headings that can readily be outlined:

PARAGRAPHING

Paragraph Cues

Topic Sentence Strategies

    Announcing the Topic.

    Making a Transition.

    Positioning the Topic Sentence.

Notice that in this example the heading system has three levels. The first-level heading sits on its own line, and all the letters are capitalized; this heading stands out most visibly among the others. (It is one of five such capitalized headings in this chapter.) The second-level heading also sits on its own line, but only the first letter in each word (except for articles and prepositions) is capitalized, and the others are lowercased. Like the heading in the first level, this second-level heading is aligned with the left margin. The first of these second-level headings has no subheadings beneath it, while the second has three. These third-level headings run into the paragraph they introduce, as you can see if you pause now to turn to pp. 310–12.

All of these headings are set apart from the surrounding text by the special use of capital letters or spacing or both. At each level, they follow a parallel grammatical structure: nouns at the first level, which you can confirm by skimming the chapter in order to look at the other four first-level heads; nouns at the second level ("cues" and "strategies"); and "-ing" nouns at the third level.

Headings and Genres

Headings may not be necessary in the short essays you will be writing for this composition course. Short essays offer readers thesis statements, forecasting statements, well-positioned topic sentences, and transition sentences so that they have all the cues they may need. Headings are rare in some genres, like essays about remembered events (Chapter 2) and essays profiling people and places (Chapter 3). Headings appear more frequently in genres such as concept explanations, position papers, public policy proposals, and evaluations (Chapters 4–7).

Frequency and Placement of Headings

Before dividing their essays into sections with headings and subheadings, writers need to make sure their discussion is detailed enough to support at least one heading at each level. The frequency and placement of headings depend entirely on the content and how it is divided and organized. Keep in mind that headings do not reduce the need for other cues to keep readers on track.

"The Elder Scrolls III: Morrowind" by Jonah Jackson in Chapter 7 uses six headings to cue readers, which define his criteria for evaluating a video game:

Outstanding Graphics

Free to Explore

Customization

Control

Sound

Summary

If you read or skim this essay, you will find that the text following the first heading discusses the quality of the game's graphics. The second heading begins a section that discusses users' ability to either follow the game's main storyline or to set out on their own, non-preprogrammed role-playing adventure. The third heading introduces a section on the game's customizability. The fourth heading introduces a section in which the writer discusses how users control their gameplay. The fifth heading introduces a discussion of the game's music and sound effects. Finally, the sixth heading leads into a discussion of the game's overall strengths and weaknesses, summing up the writer's evaluation.

■ **Exercise 8.11**

Turn to Katherine S. Newman's essay in Chapter 6, and survey that essay's system of headings. If you have not read the essay, read or skim it now. Also read Basic Features: Proposing Solutions at the end of the Chapter 6 Readings section (pp. 233–34) to familiarize yourself with the genre — proposing a solution. Consider how Newman's headings help readers anticipate what is coming and how the argument is organized. Analyze whether the headings substitute for or complement a strong system of other cues for keeping readers on track. Decide whether the headings guide readers through the particular stages of the genre. Finally, try to answer these questions: Do any of the headings suggest subheadings? Might fewer or more headings be helpful to readers? Are the headings grammatically parallel?

■ **Exercise 8.12**

Select one of your essays that might benefit from headings. Develop a system of headings, and insert them where appropriate. Be prepared to justify your headings in light of the discussion about headings in this section.

Strategies for All-Purpose Invention

Writers are like scientists: They ask questions, systematically inquiring about how things work, what they are, where they occur, and how more information can be learned about them. Writers are also like artists in that they use what they know and learn to create something new and imaginative.

The invention and inquiry strategies—also known as *heuristics*—described in this chapter are not mysterious or magical. They are available to all writers, and one or more of them may appeal to your common sense and experience. These techniques represent ways creative writers, engineers, scientists, composers—in fact, all of us—solve problems.

Once you have mastered these strategies, you can use them to tackle many of the writing situations you will encounter in college, on the job, and in the community. The best way to learn them is to use them as you write an actual essay. Chapters 2–7 show you when these strategies can be most helpful and how to make the most efficient use of them. The Guides to Writing in those chapters offer easy-to-use adaptations of these general strategies, adaptations designed to satisfy the special requirements of each kind of writing. You will learn how and when to use these strategies and see how to combine them to achieve your goals.

The strategies for invention and inquiry in this chapter are grouped into two categories:

Mapping: A brief visual representation of your thinking or planning

Writing: The composition of phrases or sentences to discover information and ideas and to make connections among them

These invention and inquiry strategies can be powerful tools for thinking about your topic and planning your writing. They will help you explore and research a topic fully before you begin drafting and then help you creatively solve problems as you draft and revise your draft. In this chapter, strategies are arranged alphabetically within each of the two categories.

■ MAPPING

Mapping strategies involve making a visual record of invention and inquiry. Many writers find that mapping helps them think about a topic. In making maps, they usually use key words and phrases to record material they want to remember, questions they need to answer, and new sources of information they want to check. The maps show the ideas, details, and facts they are examining. They also show possible ways to connect and focus materials. Maps might be informal graphic displays with words and phrases circled and connected by lines to show relationships, or they might be formal sentence outlines. Mapping can be especially useful for working in collaborative writing situations, for preparing oral presentations, and for creating visual aids for written or oral reports. Mapping strategies include clustering, listing, and outlining.

Software-Based Diagramming Tools.   Software vendors have created a variety of electronic tools to help people working in business and technical fields better visualize complex projects. The features of these software packages allow you to enter, store, and rearrange information in a variety of visual formats such as flowcharts, webs, and outlines. For some types of complex writing assignments, these graphical depictions can make it easier for you (or your instructor) to see how to proceed on the project, where more information is needed, or other pitfalls that might not otherwise be apparent. If you are comfortable with any of these packages or if you are primarily a visual thinker, you may find the use of a diagramming tool helpful in the invention as well as later stages of your project.

Clustering

Clustering is a strategy for revealing possible relationships among facts and ideas. Unlike listing (the next mapping strategy), clustering requires a brief period of initial preparation when you divide your topic into parts or main ideas. Clustering works as follows:

1. In a word or phrase, write your topic in the center of a piece of paper. Circle it.
2. Also in words or phrases, write down the main parts or ideas of your topic. Circle these, and connect them with lines to the topic in the center.
3. Next, think of facts, details, examples, or ideas related in any way to these main parts. Cluster these around the main parts.

Clustering can be useful for any kind of writing. You can use it in the early stages of planning an essay to find subtopics and organize information. You may try out and

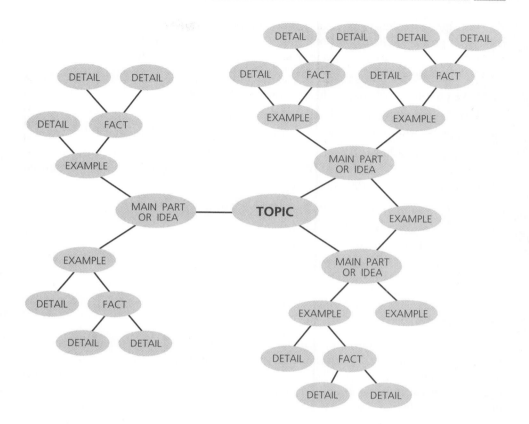

discard several clusters before finding one that is promising. Many writers use clustering to plan brief sections of an essay as they are drafting or revising. (See above for a model of clustering.)

Listing

Listing is a familiar activity. We make shopping lists and lists of errands to do or people to call. Listing can also be a great help in planning an essay. It enables you to recall what you already know about a topic and suggests what else you may need to find out. It is an easy way to get started with your invention writing, instead of just worrying about what you will write. A list rides along on its own momentum, the first item leading naturally to the next.

A basic activity for all writers, listing is especially useful to those who have little time for planning—for example, reporters facing deadlines and college students taking essay exams. Listing lets you order your ideas quickly. It can also serve as a first step in discovering possible writing topics.

Listing is a solitary form of brainstorming, a popular technique of problem-solving in groups. When you work with a group to generate ideas for a collaborative writing project, you are engaged in true brainstorming. Here is how listing works best for invention work:

1. Give your list a title that indicates your main idea or topic.

2. Write as fast as you can, relying on short phrases.

3. Include anything that seems at all useful. Try not to be judgmental at this point.

4. After you have finished or even as you write, reflect on the list, and organize it in the following way. This step is very important, for it may lead you to further discoveries about your topic.

   Put an asterisk next to the most promising items.

   Number key items in order of importance.

   Put items in related groups.

   Cross out items that do not seem promising.

   Add new items.

Outlining

Like listing and clustering, *outlining* is both a means of inventing what you want to say in an essay and a way of organizing your ideas and information. As you outline, you nearly always see new possibilities in your subject, discovering new ways of dividing or grouping information and seeing where you need additional information to develop your ideas. Because outlining lets you see at a glance where your essay's strengths and weaknesses lie, outlining can also help you read and revise your essay with a critical eye.

There are two main forms of outlining: informal scratch outlining and formal topic or sentence outlining. (Keep in mind that clustering is also a type of informal outlining.)

A *scratch outline* is considered an informal outline because it is little more than a list of the essay's main points. You have no doubt made scratch outlines many times—to plan essays or essay exams, to revise your own writing, and to analyze a difficult reading passage. Here are sample scratch outlines for two different kinds of essays. The first outlines Annie Dillard's essay in Chapter 2, and the second shows one way to organize a position paper (Chapter 5):

Scratch Outline: Essay about a Remembered Event

1. Explains what she learned from playing football

2. Identifies other sports she learned from boys in the neighborhood

3. Sets the scene by describing the time and place of the event

4. Describes the boys who were playing with her

5. Describes what typically happened: a car would come down the street, they would throw snowballs, and then they would wait for another car
6. Describes the iceball-making project she had begun while waiting
7. Describes the Buick's approach and how they followed the routine
8. Describes the impact of the snowball on the Buick's windshield
9. Describes the man's surprising reaction: getting out of the car and running after them
10. Narrates the chase and describes the man
11. Explains how the kids split up and the man followed her and Mikey
12. Narrates the chase and describes how the neighborhood looked as they ran through it
13. Continues the narration, describing the way the man threw himself into the chase
14. Continues the narration, commenting on her thoughts and feelings
15. Narrates the ending or climax of the chase, when the man caught the kids
16. Describes the runners trying to catch their breath
17. Describes her own physical state
18. Relates the man's words
19. Explains her reactions to his words and actions
20. Explains her later thoughts and feelings
21. Explains her present perspective on this remembered event

Scratch Outline: Essay Arguing a Position

Presentation of the issue

Concession of some aspect of an opposing position

Thesis statement

First reason with support

Second reason with support (etc.)

Conclusion

Remember that the items in a scratch outline do not necessarily coincide with paragraphs. Sometimes two or more items may be developed in the same paragraph or one item may be covered in two or more paragraphs.

Chunking, a type of scratch outline commonly used by professional writers in business and industry and especially well suited to writing in the electronic age, consists of a set of headings describing the major points to be covered in the final document. What makes chunking distinctive is that the blocks of text—or "chunks"—under each heading are intended to be roughly the same length and scope. These headings can be discussed and passed around among several writers and editors before writing begins, and different chunks may be written by different authors, simply by typing notes or text on a word processor into the space under each heading. The list of headings is subject to change during the writing, and new headings may be added or old ones subdivided or discarded as part of the drafting and editing process.

The advantage of chunking in your own individual writing is that it breaks the large task of drafting into smaller tasks in a simple, evenly balanced way; once the headings are determined, the writing becomes just a matter of filling in the specifics that go in each chunk. Organization tends to improve as you get a sense of the weight of different parts of the document while filling in the blanks. Places where the essay needs more information or there is a problem with pacing tend to stand out because of the chunking structure, and the headings can either be taken out of the finished essay or left in as devices to help guide readers. If they are left in, they should be edited into parallel grammatical form like the items in a formal topic or sentence outline, as discussed below.

Topic and *sentence outlines* are considered more formal than scratch outlines because they follow a conventional format of numbered and lettered headings and subheadings:

    I. (Main topic)
       A. (Subtopic of I)
       B.
          1. (Subtopic of I.B)
          2.
             a. (Subtopic of I.B.2)
             b.
                (1) (Subtopic of I.B.2.b)
                (2)
       C.
          1. (Subtopic of I.C)
          2.

The difference between a topic and sentence outline is obvious: topic outlines simply name the topics and subtopics, whereas sentence outlines use complete or abbreviated sentences. To illustrate, here are two partial formal outlines of an essay arguing a position, Jessica Statsky's "Children Need to Play, Not Compete," from Chapter 5.

Formal Topic Outline

    I. Organized sports harmful to children
       A. Harmful physically
          1. Curve ball (Koppett)
          2. Tackle football (Tutko)
       B. Harmful psychologically
          1. Fear of being hurt
             a. Little League Web site
             b. Mother
             c. Reporter

2. Competition
  a. Rablovsky
  b. Studies

Formal Sentence Outline

I. Highly organized competitive sports such as Peewee Football and Little League Baseball can be physically and psychologically harmful to children, as well as counterproductive for developing future players.
  A. Physically harmful because sports entice children into physical actions that are bad for growing bodies.
    1. Koppett claims throwing a curve ball may put abnormal strain on developing arm and shoulder muscles.
    2. Tutko argues that tackle football is too traumatic for young kids.
  B. Psychologically harmful to children for a number of reasons.
    1. Fear of being hurt detracts from their enjoyment of the sport.
      a. Little League Web site ranks fear of injury seventh among the seven top reasons children quit.
      b. One mother says, "kids get so scared. . . . They'll sit on the bench and pretend their leg hurts."
      c. A reporter tells about a child who made himself vomit to get out of playing Peewee Football.
    2. Too much competition poses psychological dangers for children.
      a. Rablovsky reports: "The spirit of play suddenly disappears, and sport becomes joblike."
      b. Studies show that children prefer playing on a losing team to "warming the bench on a winning team."

In contrast to an informal outline in which anything goes, a formal outline must follow many conventions. The roman numerals and capital letters are followed by periods. In topic and sentence outlines, the first word of each item is capitalized, but items in topic outlines do not end with a period as items in sentence outlines do. Every level of a formal outline except the top level (identified by the roman numeral *I*) must include at least two items. Items at the same level of indentation in a topic outline should be grammatically parallel—all beginning with the same part of speech. For example, *I.A.* and *I.B.* are parallel when they both begin with an adverb (*Physically harmful* and *Psychologically harmful*) or with a noun (*Harmful physically* and *Harmful psychologically*); they would not be parallel if one began with an adverb *(Physically harmful)* and the other with a noun *(Harmful psychologically)*.

■ WRITING

Writing is itself a powerful tool for thinking. As you write, you can recall details, remember facts, develop your ideas, find connections in new information you have collected, examine assumptions, and critically question what you know.

Unlike most mapping strategies, *writing strategies* of invention invite you to produce complete sentences. Sentences provide considerable generative power. Because they are complete statements, they take you further than listing or clustering. They enable you to explore ideas and define relationships, bring ideas together or show how they differ, and identify causes and effects. Sentences can also help you develop a logical chain of thought.

Some of these invention and inquiry strategies are systematic, while others are more flexible. Even though they call for complete sentences that are related to one another, they do not require preparation or revision. You can use them to develop oral as well as written presentations.

These writing strategies include cubing, dialoguing, dramatizing, keeping a journal, looping, questioning, and quick drafting.

Cubing

Cubing is useful for quickly exploring a writing topic, probing it from six different perspectives. It is known as *cubing* because a cube has six sides. These are the six perspectives in cubing:

Describing: What does your subject look like? What size is it? What is its color? Its shape? Its texture? Name its parts.

Comparing: What is your subject similar to? Different from?

Associating: What does your subject make you think of? What connections does it have to anything else in your experience?

Analyzing: What are the origins of your subject? What are its parts or features? How are its parts related?

Applying: What can you do with your subject? What uses does it have?

Arguing: What arguments can you make for your subject? Against it?

Here are some guidelines to help you use cubing productively.

1. Select a topic, subject, or part of a subject. This can be a person, a scene, an event, an object, a problem, an idea, or an issue. Hold it in focus.

2. Limit your writing to three to five minutes for each perspective. The whole activity should take no more than half an hour.

3. Keep going until you have written about your subject from all six perspectives. Remember that cubing offers the special advantage of enabling you to generate multiple perspectives quickly.

4. As you write from each perspective, begin with what you know about your subject. However, do not limit yourself to your present knowledge. Indicate what else you would like to know about your subject, and suggest where you might find that information.

5. Reread what you have written. Look for bright spots, surprises. Recall the part that was easiest for you to write. Recall the part where you felt a special momen-

tum and pleasure in the writing. Look for an angle or an unexpected insight. These special parts may suggest a focus or topic within a larger subject, or they may provide specific details to include in a draft.

Dialoguing

A dialogue is a conversation between two or more people. You can use *dialoguing* to search for topics, find a focus, explore ideas, or consider opposing viewpoints. When you write a dialogue as an invention strategy, you need to make up all parts of the conversation (unless, of course, you are writing collaboratively—on a network, for example). To construct a dialogue by yourself, imagine two particular people talking, hold a conversation yourself with some imagined person, or simply talk out loud to yourself. To construct a dialogue independently or collaboratively, follow these steps:

1. Write a conversation between two speakers. Label the participants *Speaker A* and *Speaker B,* or make up names for them.
2. If you get stuck, you might have one of the speakers ask the other a question.
3. Write brief responses to keep the conversation moving fast. Do not spend much time planning or rehearsing responses. Write what first occurs to you, just as in a real conversation, where people take quick turns to prevent any awkward silences.

Dialogues can be especially useful with personal experience and persuasive essays because they help you remember conversations and anticipate objections.

Dramatizing

Dramatizing is an invention activity developed by the philosopher Kenneth Burke as a way of thinking about how people interact and as a way of analyzing stories and films.

Thinking about human behavior in dramatic terms can be very productive for writers. Drama has action, actors, setting, motives, and methods. Since stars and acting go together, you can use a five-pointed star to remember these five points of dramatizing: Each point on the star provides a different perspective on human behavior. We can think of each point independently and in combination. Let us begin by looking at each point to see how it helps us to analyze people and their interactions.

Action.   An action is anything that happens, has happened, will happen, or could happen. Action includes events that are physical (running a marathon), mental (thinking about a book you have read), and emotional (falling in love). This category also refers to the results of activity (an essay).

Actor.   The actor is involved in the action—either responsible for it or simply affected by it. (The actor does not have to be a person. It can be a force, something that causes an action. For example, if the action is a rise in the price of gasoline, the actor could be increased demand or short supply.) Dramatizing may also include a number of coactors working together or at odds.

Setting.   The setting is the situation or background of the action. We usually think of setting as the place and time of an event, but it may also be the historical background of an event or the childhood of a person.

Motive.   The motive is the purpose or reason for an action—the actor's intention. Actions may have multiple, even conflicting, motives.

Method.   The method explains how an action occurs, including the techniques an actor uses. It refers to whatever makes things happen.

Each of these points suggests a simple invention question:

Action: What?

Actor: Who?

Setting: When and where?

Motive: Why?

Method: How?

This list looks like the questions reporters typically ask. But dramatizing goes further: It enables us to ask a much fuller set of invention questions that we generate by considering relations between and among these five elements. We can think about actors' motives, the effect of the setting on the actors, the relations between actors, and so on.

You can use this invention strategy to learn more about yourself or about other significant people in your life. You can use it, as well, to explore, analyze, or evaluate characters in stories or movies. Moreover, dramatizing is especially useful in analyzing the readers you want to inform or convince.

To use dramatizing, imagine the person you want to understand better in a particular situation. Holding this image in mind, write answers to any questions in the following list that apply. You may draw a blank on some questions, have little to say to some, and find a lot to say to others. Be exploratory and playful with the questions. Write responses quickly, relying on words and phrases, even drawings.

- What is the actor doing?
- How did the actor come to be involved in this situation?
- Why does the actor do what he or she does?
- What else might the actor do?
- What is the actor trying to accomplish?
- How do other actors influence — help or hinder — the main actor?
- What do the actor's actions reveal about him or her?
- What does the actor's language reveal about him or her?
- How does the event's setting influence the actor's actions?
- How does the time of the event influence what the actor does?
- Where does this actor come from?
- How is this actor different now from what he or she used to be?
- What might this actor become?
- How is this actor like or unlike the other actors?

Keeping a Journal

Professional writers often use *journals* to keep notes, and so might you. Starting a writer's journal is easy. Buy a special notebook, or open a new file on your computer, and start writing. Here are some possibilities:

- Keep a list of new words and concepts you learn in your courses. You could also write about the progress and direction of your learning in particular courses — the experience of being in the course, your feelings about what is happening and what you are learning.

- Respond to your reading, both assigned and personal. As you read, write about your personal associations, reflections, reactions, and evaluations. Summarize or copy memorable or especially important passages, and comment on them. (Copying and commenting have been practiced by students and writers for centuries in special journals called *commonplace books.*)

- Write to prepare for particular class meetings. Write about the main ideas you have learned from assigned readings and about the relationship of these new ideas to other ideas in the course. After class, write to summarize what you have learned. List questions you have about the ideas or information discussed in class. Journal writing of this kind involves reflecting, evaluating, interpreting, synthesizing, summarizing, and questioning.

- Record observations and overheard conversations.

- Write for ten or fifteen minutes every day about whatever is on your mind. Focus these meditations on your new experiences as you try to understand, interpret, and reflect on them.

- Write sketches of people who catch your attention.
- Organize your time. Write about your goals and priorities, or list specific things to accomplish and what you plan to do.
- Keep a log over several days or weeks about a particular event unfolding in the news—a sensational trial, an environmental disaster, a political campaign, a campus controversy, the fortunes of a sports team.

You can use a journal in many ways. All of the writing in your journal has value for learning. You may also be able to use parts of your journal for writing in your other courses.

Looping

Looping is especially useful for the first stages of exploring a topic. As its name suggests, *looping* involves writing quickly to explore some aspect of a topic and then looping back to your original starting point or to a new starting point to explore another aspect. Beginning with almost any starting point, looping enables you to find a center of interest and eventually a thesis for your essay. The steps are simple:

1. Write down your area of interest. You may know only that you have to write about another person or a movie or a cultural trend that has caught your attention. Or you may want to search for a topic in a broad historical period or for one related to a major political event. Although you may wander from this topic as you write, you will want to keep coming back to it. Your purpose is to find a focus for writing.

2. Write nonstop for ten minutes. Start with the first thing that comes to mind. Write rapidly, without looking back to reread or to correct anything. *Do not stop writing. Keep your pencil moving.* Continuous writing is the key to looping. If you get stuck for a moment, rewrite the last sentence. Trust the act of writing to lead you to new insights. Follow diversions and digressions, but keep returning to your topic.

3. After ten minutes, pause to reread what you have written. Decide what is most important—a single insight, a pattern of ideas, an emerging theme, a visual detail, anything at all that stands out. Some writers call this a "center of gravity" or a "hot spot." To complete the first loop, restate this center in a single sentence.

4. Beginning with this sentence, write nonstop for another ten minutes.

5. Summarize in one sentence again to complete the second loop.

6. Keep looping until one of your summary sentences produces a focus or thesis. You may need only two or three loops; you may need more.

Questioning

Asking *questions* about a subject is a way to learn about it and decide what to write. When you first encounter a subject, however, your questions may be scattered. Also, you are not likely to think right away of all the important questions you ought to ask. The advantage of having a basic list of questions for invention, like the ones for cubing and for dramatizing discussed earlier in this chapter, is that it provides a systematic approach to exploring a subject.

The questions that follow come from classical rhetoric (what the Greek philosopher Aristotle called *topics*) and a modern approach to invention called *tagmemics*. Based on the work of linguist Kenneth Pike, tagmemics provides questions about different ways we make sense of the world, the ways we sort and classify experience in order to understand it.

Here are the steps in using questions for invention:

1. In a sentence or two, identify your subject. A subject could be any event, person, problem, project, idea, or issue — in other words, anything you might write about.

2. Start by writing a response to the first question in the following list, and move right through the list. Try to answer each question at least briefly with a word or a phrase. Some questions may invite several sentences or even a page or more of writing. You may draw a blank on a few questions. Skip them. Later, when you have more experience with questions for invention, you can start anywhere in the list.

3. Write your responses quickly, without much planning. Follow digressions or associations. Do not screen anything out. Be playful.

What Is Your Subject?

- What is your subject's name? What other names does it have? What names did it have in the past?
- What aspects of the subject do these different names emphasize?
- Imagine a still photograph or a moving picture of your subject. What would it look like?
- What would you put into a time capsule to stand for your subject?
- What are its causes and results?
- How would it look from different vantage points or perspectives?
- What particular experiences have you had with the subject? What have you learned?

What Parts or Features Does Your Subject Have, and How Are They Related?

- Name the parts or features of your subject.
- Describe each one, using the questions in the preceding subject list.
- How is each part or feature related to the others?

How Is Your Subject Similar to and Different from Other Subjects?

- What is your subject similar to? In what ways are these subjects alike?
- What is your subject different from? In what ways are the subjects different?

- What seems to you most unlike your subject? In what ways are the two things unlike each other? Now, just for fun, note how they are alike.

How Much Can Your Subject Change and Still Remain the Same?

- How has your subject changed from what it once was?
- How is it changing now—moment to moment, day to day, year to year?
- How does each change alter your way of thinking about your subject?
- What are some different forms your subject takes?
- What does it become when it is no longer itself?

Where Does Your Subject Fit in the World?

- When and where did your subject originate?
- What would happen if at some future time your subject ceased to exist?
- When and where do you usually experience the subject?
- What is this subject a part of, and what are the other parts?
- What do other people think of your subject?

Quick Drafting

Sometimes you know what you want to say or have little time for invention. In these situations, *quick drafting* may be a good strategy. There are no special rules for quick drafting, but you should rely on it only if you know your subject well, have had experience with the kind of writing you are doing, and will have a chance to revise your draft. Quick drafting can help you discover what you already know about the subject and what you need to find out. It can also help you develop and organize your thoughts.

Strategies for Reading Critically

To become a thoughtful, effective writer, you must also become a critical reader. This chapter presents strategies to help you *read with a critical eye*. Reading critically means not just comprehending passively and remembering what you read but also scrutinizing actively and making thoughtful judgments about your reading. When you read a text critically, you need to alternate between understanding and questioning—on the one hand, striving to understand the text on its own terms; on the other hand, taking care to question its ideas and authority. You will benefit greatly from reading what others have written—and reading your own writing—in this way.

The strategies here complement and supplement reading strategies presented in Part One, Chapters 2–7. Critical reading is central to your success with the writing assignments in those chapters. The Connecting to Culture and Experience activity following each reading in Part One helps you think about the selection in light of your own experience and awareness of social issues, while the Analyzing Writing Strategies questions help you understand how the text works and evaluate how well it achieves its purpose with its readers. The Critical Reading Guide in each Part One chapter helps you read other students' drafts as well as your own to find out what is working and what needs improvement.

Reading is, after all, inextricably linked to writing, and the reading strategies in this chapter can help you enrich your thinking as a reader and participate in conversations as a writer. These strategies include the following:

- *Annotating:* Recording your reactions to, interpretations of, and questions about a text as you read it
- *Taking inventory:* Listing and grouping your annotations and other notes to find meaningful patterns
- *Outlining:* Listing the text's main ideas to reveal how it is organized
- *Paraphrasing:* Restating what you have read to clarify or refer to it
- *Summarizing:* Distilling the main ideas or gist of a text
- *Synthesizing:* Integrating into your own writing ideas and information gleaned from different sources
- *Contextualizing:* Placing a text in its historical and cultural contexts

- *Exploring the significance of figurative language:* Examining how metaphors, similes, and symbols are used in a text to convey meaning and evoke feelings
- *Looking for patterns of opposition:* Analyzing the values and assumptions embodied in the language of a text
- *Reflecting on challenges to your beliefs and values:* Critically examining the bases of your personal responses to a text
- *Evaluating the logic of an argument:* Determining whether a thesis is well reasoned and adequately supported
- *Recognizing emotional manipulation:* Identifying texts that unfairly and inappropriately use emotional appeals based on false or exaggerated claims
- *Judging the writer's credibility:* Considering whether writers represent different points of view fairly and know what they are writing about

These critical reading strategies can help you connect information from different sources and relate it to what you already know; distinguish fact from opinion; uncover and question assumptions; and subject other people's ideas as well as your own to reasoned argument. You can readily learn these strategies and apply them not only to a critical reading of the selections in Part One but also to your other college reading. Although mastering the strategies will not make critical reading easy, it can make your reading much more satisfying and productive and thus help you handle even difficult material with confidence. Critical reading strategies will, in addition, often be useful in your reading outside of school — for instance, these strategies can help you understand, evaluate, and comment on what political figures, advertisers, and other writers are saying.

■ ANNOTATING

Annotations are the marks — underlines, highlights, and comments — you make directly on the page as you read. *Annotating* can be used to record immediate reactions and questions, outline and summarize main points, and evaluate and relate the reading to other ideas and points of view. Especially useful for studying and preparing to write, annotating is also an essential element of many other critical reading strategies. Your annotations can take many forms, such as the following:

Writing comments, questions, or definitions in the margins

Underlining or circling words, phrases, or sentences

Connecting ideas with lines or arrows

Numbering related points

Bracketing sections of the text

Noting anything that strikes you as interesting, important, or questionable

Annotating Onscreen. Although this discussion of annotating assumes you are reading printed pages, you can also annotate many kinds of text on the computer screen by using your word processor's highlighting and commenting functions. Even if these functions are not available, you may be able to type annotations into the text using a different color or font. If electronic annotation is impossible, print out the text, and annotate by hand.

Most readers annotate in layers, adding further annotations on second and third readings. Annotations can be light or heavy, depending on the reader's purpose and the difficulty of the material. Your purpose for reading also determines how you use your annotations.

The following selection, excerpted from Martin Luther King Jr.'s "Letter from Birmingham Jail," is annotated to illustrate some of the ways you can annotate as you read. Add your own annotations, if you like.

Martin Luther King Jr. (1929–1968) first came to national notice in 1955, when he led a successful boycott against the policy of restricting African American passengers to rear seats on city buses in Montgomery, Alabama, where he was minister of a Baptist church. He subsequently formed a national organization, the Southern Christian Leadership Conference, that brought people of all races from all over the country to the South to fight nonviolently for racial integration. In 1963, King led demonstrations in Birmingham, Alabama, that were met with violence; a bomb was detonated in a black church, killing four young girls. King was arrested for his role in organizing the protests, and while in prison, he wrote the famous "Letter from Birmingham Jail" to answer the criticism of local clergy and to justify to the nation his strategy of civil disobedience, which he called "nonviolent direct action."

King begins his letter by discussing his disappointment with the lack of support he has received from white moderates, such as the group of clergy who published criticism in the local newspaper. As you read the following excerpt from his letter, try to infer from King's written response what the clergy's specific criticisms might have been. Also, notice the tone King uses to answer his critics. Would you characterize the writing as apologetic, conciliatory, accusatory, or in some other way?

An Annotated Sample from "Letter from Birmingham Jail"

Martin Luther King Jr.

I must confess that over the past few years I have been gravely disappointed with the white moderate. I have almost reached the regrettable conclusion that the Negro's [great stumbling block in his stride toward freedom] is not the White Citizen's Counciler or the Ku Klux Klanner, but the white moderate, who is more devoted to "order" than to justice; who prefers a negative peace

1

¶1. White moderates block progress

order vs. justice

which is the absence of tension to a positive peace which is the presence of justice; who constantly says: "I agree with you in the goal you seek, but I cannot agree with your methods of direct action"; who paternalistically believes he can set the timetable for another man's freedom; who lives by a mythical concept of time and who constantly advises the Negro to wait for a "more convenient season." Shallow understanding from people of good will is more frustrating than absolute misunderstanding from people of ill will. Lukewarm acceptance is much more bewildering than outright rejection.

negative vs. positive

ends vs. means treating others like children

2   I had hoped that the white moderate would understand that law and order exist for the purpose of establishing justice and that when they fail in this purpose they become the dangerously structured dams that block the flow of social progress. I had hoped that the white moderate would understand that the present tension in the South is a necessary phase of the transition from an obnoxious negative peace, in which the Negro passively accepted his unjust plight, to a substantive and positive peace, in which all men will respect the dignity and worth of human personality. Actually, we who engage in nonviolent direct action are not the creators of tension. We merely bring to the surface the hidden tension that is already alive. We bring it out in the open, where it can be seen and dealt with. Like a boil that can never be cured so long as it is covered up but must be opened with all its ugliness to the natural medicines of air and light, injustice must be exposed, with all the tension its exposure creates, to the light of human conscience and the air of national opinion before it can be cured.

¶2. Tension necessary for progress.

Tension already exists anyway.

True?

Simile: hidden tension is "like a boil"

3   In your statement you assert that our actions, even though peaceful, must be condemned because they precipitate violence. But is this a logical assertion? Isn't this like condemning a robbed man because his possession of money precipitated the evil act of robbery? Isn't this like condemning Socrates because his unswerving commitment to truth and his philosophical inquiries precipitated the act by the misguided populace in which they made him drink hemlock? Isn't this like condemning Jesus because his unique God-consciousness and never-ceasing devotion to God's will precipitated the evil act of crucifixion? We must come to see that, as the federal courts have consistently affirmed, it is wrong to urge an individual to cease his efforts to gain his basic constitutional rights because the question may precipitate violence. Society must protect the robbed and punish the robber.

¶3. Questions clergymen's logic: condemning his actions = condemning victims, Socrates, Jesus.

Yes!

4   I had also hoped that the white moderate would reject the myth concerning time in relation to the struggle for freedom. I have just received a letter from a white brother in Texas. He writes:

"All Christians know that the colored people will receive equal rights eventually, but it is possible that you are in too great a religious hurry. It has taken Christianity almost two thousand years to accomplish what it has. The teachings of Christ take time to come to earth." Such an attitude stems from a tragic misconception of time, from the strangely irrational notion that there is something in the very flow of time that will inevitably cure all ills. Actually, time itself is neutral; it can be used either destructively or constructively. More and more I feel that the people of ill will have used time much more effectively than have the people of good will. We will have to repent in this generation not merely for the [hateful words and actions of the bad people] but for the [appalling silence of the good people.] Human progress never rolls in on [wheels of inevitability;] it comes through the tireless efforts of men willing to be co-workers with God, and without this hard work, time itself becomes an ally of the forces of social (stagnation.) We must use time creatively, in the knowledge that the time is always ripe to do right. Now is the time to make real the promise of democracy and transform our pending [national elegy] into a creative [psalm of brotherhood.] Now is the time to lift our national policy from the [quicksand of racial injustice] to the [solid rock of human dignity.]

> *example of a white moderate*
>
> *Silence is as bad as hateful words and actions.*
>
> *metaphor*
>
> *not moving*
>
> *¶14. Time must be used to do right.*
>
> *metaphors*

You speak of our activity in Birmingham as extreme. At first I was rather disappointed that fellow clergymen would see my nonviolent efforts as those of an extremist. I began thinking about the fact that I stand in the middle of two opposing forces in the Negro community. One is a [force of complacency,] made up in part of Negroes who, as a result of long years of oppression, are so drained of self-respect and a sense of "somebodiness" that they have adjusted to segregation; and in part of a few middle-class Negroes, who because of a degree of academic and economic security and because in some ways they profit by segregation, have become insensitive to the problems of the masses. The other [force is one of bitterness and hatred,] and it comes perilously close to advocating violence. It is expressed in the various black nationalist [groups that are springing up] across the nation, the largest and best-known being Elijah Muhammad's Muslim movement. Nourished by the Negro's frustration over the continued existence of racial discrimination, this movement is made up of people who have lost faith in America, who have absolutely repudiated Christianity, and who have concluded that the white man is an incorrigible "devil."

> 5 *King accused of being an extremist*
>
> *¶15. King in middle of two extremes: complacent & angry*
>
> *Malcolm X?*
>
> *¶16. King offers better choice.*

I have tried to stand between these two forces, saying that we need emulate neither the "do-nothingism" of the complacent nor the hatred and despair of the black nationalist. For there is the more excellent way of love and nonviolent protest. I am grateful to

> 6
>
> *How did nonviolence become part of King's movement?*

God that, through the influence of the Negro church, the way of nonviolence became an integral part of our struggle.

If this philosophy had not emerged, by now many streets of the South would, I am convinced, be flowing with blood. And I am further convinced that if our white brothers dismiss as "rabble-rousers" and "outside agitators" those of us who employ nonviolent direct action, and if they refuse to support our nonviolent efforts, millions of Negroes will, out of frustration and despair, seek(solace) and security in black-nationalist ideologies—a development that would inevitably lead to a frightening racial nightmare. 7

¶7. King's movement prevented racial violence. Threat?

Gandhi?

The church?

If . . . then . . . comfort

(Oppressed people cannot remain oppressed forever) The yearning for freedom eventually manifests itself, and that is what has happened to the American Negro. Something within has reminded him of his birthright of freedom, and something without has reminded him that it can be gained. Consciously or unconsciously, he has been caught up by the(Zeitgeist) and with his black brothers of Africa and his brown and yellow brothers of Asia, South America and the Caribbean, the United States Negro is moving with a sense of great urgency toward the[promised land of racial justice] If one recognizes this[vital urge that has engulfed the Negro community] one should readily understand why public demonstrations are taking place. The Negro has many [pent-up resentments] and latent frustrations, and he must release them. So let him march; let him make prayer pilgrimages to the city hall; let him go on freedom rides—and try to understand why he must do so. If his repressed emotions are not released in nonviolent ways, they will seek expression through violence; this is not a threat but a fact of history. So I have not said to my people: "Get rid of your discontent." Rather, I have tried to say that this normal and healthy discontent can be[channeled into the creative outlet of nonviolent direct action] And now this approach is being termed extremist. 8

spirit of the times worldwide uprising against injustice

not a threat?

¶8. Discontent is normal & healthy but must be channeled.

But though I was initially disappointed at being categorized as an extremist, as I continued to think about the matter I gradually gained a measure of satisfaction from the label. Was not Jesus an extremist for love: "Love your enemies, bless them that curse you, do good to them that hate you, and pray for them which despitefully use you, and persecute you." Was not(Amos) an extremist for justice: "Let justice roll down like waters and righteousness like an ever-flowing stream." Was not(Paul) an extremist for the Christian gospel: "I bear in my body the marks of the Lord Jesus." Was not(Martin Luther) an extremist: "Here I stand; I cannot do otherwise, so help me God." And(John Bunyan:) "I will stay in jail to the end of my days before I make a butchery of my conscience." 9

Hebrew prophet

Christian apostle

Founded Protestantism

English preacher

And Abraham Lincoln: "This nation cannot survive half slave and half free." And Thomas Jefferson: "We hold these truths to be self-evident, that all men are created equal. . . ." So the question is not whether we will be extremists, but what kind of extremists we will be. *No choice but to be extremists. But what kind?* Will we be extremists for hate or for love? Will we be extremists for the preservation of injustice or for the extension of justice? In that dramatic scene on Calvary's hill three men were crucified. We must never forget that all three were crucified for the same crime — the crime of extremism. Two were extremists for immorality, and thus fell below their environment. The other, Jesus Christ, was an extremist for love, truth and goodness, and thereby rose above his environment. Perhaps the South, the nation and the world are in dire need of creative extremists. *¶9. Creative extremists are needed.*

I had hoped that the white moderate would see this need. 10 *Disappointed in the white moderate* Perhaps I was too optimistic; perhaps I expected too much. I suppose I should have realized that few members of the oppressor race can understand the deep groans and passionate yearnings of the oppressed race, and still fewer have the vision to see that [injustice must be rooted out] by strong, persistent and determined action. I am thankful, however, that some of our white brothers in the South have grasped the meaning of this social revolution and *¶10. Some whites have supported King.* committed themselves to it. They are still all too few in quantity, but they are big in quality. Some — such as Ralph McGill, Lillian Smith, *Who are they?* Harry Golden, James McBride Dabbs, Ann Braden and Sarah Patton Boyle — have written about our struggle in eloquent and *what they did* prophetic terms. Others have marched with us down nameless streets of the South. They have languished in filthy, roach-infested *been left unaided* jails, suffering the abuse and brutality of policemen who view them as "dirty nigger-lovers." Unlike so many of their moderate brothers and sisters, they have recognized the urgency of the moment and sensed the need for [powerful "action" antidotes] to combat the [disease of segregation.]

■ **Checklist: Annotating**

1. Mark the text using notations like these:
   - Circle words to be defined in the margin.
   - Underline key words and phrases.
   - Bracket important sentences and passages.
   - Use lines or arrows to connect ideas or words.

2. Write marginal comments like these:
   - Number and summarize each paragraph.
   - Define unfamiliar words.
   - Note responses and questions.

- Identify interesting writing strategies.
- Point out patterns.

3. Layer additional markings on the text and comments in the margins as you reread for different purposes.

TAKING INVENTORY

An inventory is simply a list or grouping of items. *Taking inventory* helps you analyze your annotations for different purposes. When you take inventory, you make various kinds of lists to explore patterns of meaning you find in the text. For instance, in reading the annotated passage by Martin Luther King Jr., you might have noticed that many famous people are named or that certain similes and metaphors are used. By listing the names (Socrates, Jesus, Luther, Lincoln, and so on) and then grouping them into categories (people who died for their beliefs, leaders, teachers, and religious figures) you could better understand why the writer refers to these particular people. Taking inventory of your annotations can be helpful in writing about a text you are reading.

■ Checklist: Taking Inventory

1. Examine your annotations for patterns or repetitions such as recurring images, stylistic features, repeated words and phrases, repeated examples or illustrations, and reliance on particular writing strategies.

2. List and group the items in the pattern.

3. Decide what the pattern indicates about the reading.

OUTLINING

Outlining is an especially helpful critical reading strategy for understanding the content and structure of a reading. *Outlining,* which identifies the text's main ideas, may be part of the annotating process, or it may be done separately. Writing an outline in the margins of the text as you read and annotate makes it easier to find information later. Writing an outline on a separate piece of paper gives you more space to work with, and therefore such an outline usually includes more detail.

The key to outlining is distinguishing between the main ideas and the supporting material such as examples, quotations, comparisons, and reasons. The main ideas form the backbone, which holds the various parts and pieces of the text together. Outlining the main ideas helps you uncover this structure.

Making an outline, however, is not simple. The reader must exercise judgment in deciding which are the most important ideas. Because importance is relative, different readers can make different—and equally reasonable—decisions based on what interests them in the reading. Readers also must decide whether to use the writer's words, their own words, or a combination of the two. The words used in an outline reflect the reader's interpretation and emphasis. Reading is never a passive or neutral act; the process of outlining shows how constructive reading can be.

You may make either a formal, multileveled outline with roman (I, II) and arabic (1, 2) numerals together with capital and lowercase letters or an informal scratch outline that lists the main idea of each paragraph. A *formal outline* is harder to make and much more time consuming than a scratch outline. You might choose to make a formal outline of a reading about which you are writing an in-depth analysis or evaluation. For example, here is a formal outline a student wrote for a paper evaluating the logic of the King excerpt. Notice that the student uses roman numerals for the main ideas or claims, capital letters for the reasons, and arabic numerals for supporting evidence and explanation. (For more on the conventions of formal outlines, see pp. 328–29.)

Formal Outline

I. [T]he Negro's great stumbling block in his stride toward freedom is . . . the white moderate. . . . "
   A. Because the white moderate is more devoted to "order" than to justice (paragraph 2)
      1. Law and order should exist to establish justice.
      2. Law and order compare to "dangerously structured dams that block the flow of social progress."
   B. Because the white moderate prefers a "negative peace" (absence of tension) to a "positive peace" (justice) (paragraph 2)
      1. The tension already exists.
      2. It is not created by nonviolent direct action.
      3. Society that does not eliminate injustice compares to a boil that hides its infections. Both can be cured only by exposure (boil simile).
   C. Because even though the white moderate agrees with the goals, he does not support the means to achieve them (paragraph 3)
      1. The argument that the means--nonviolent direct action--are wrong because they precipitate violence is flawed.
      2. An analogy compares black people to the robbed man who is condemned because he had money.
      3. Analogies compare black people with Socrates and Jesus.

    D. Because the white moderate paternalistically believes
       he can set a timetable for another man's freedom
       (paragraph 4)
       1. He rebuts the white moderate's argument that
          Christianity will cure man's ills and man must
          wait patiently for that to happen.
       2. He argues that "time itself is neutral" and that
          people "must use time creatively" for constructive
          rather than destructive ends.
II. Creative extremism is preferable to moderation.
    A. Classifies himself as a moderate (paragraphs 5-8).
       1. "I...stand between...two forces": the white
          moderate's complacency and the Black Muslim's rage.
       2. If nonviolent direct action were stopped, more
          violence, not less, would result.
       3. "[M]illions of Negroes will, out of frustration
          and despair, seek solace and security in black-
          nationalist ideologies..." (paragraph 7).
       4. Repressed emotions will be expressed--if not in non-
          violent ways, then through violence (paragraph 8).
    B. Redefines himself as a "creative extremist" (para-
      graph 9)
       1. Extremism for love, truth, and goodness is creative
          extremism.
       2. He identifies himself with the creative extremists--
          Jesus, Amos, Paul, Martin Luther, John Bunyan,
          Abraham Lincoln, and Thomas Jefferson.
    C. Not all white people are moderates; some are committed
      to "this social revolution" (paragraph 10).
       1. Lists names of white writers.
       2. Refers to white activists.

Making a scratch outline takes less time than making a formal outline but still requires careful reading. A *scratch outline* will not record as much information as a formal outline, but it is sufficient for most critical reading purposes. To make a scratch outline, you first need to locate the topic of each paragraph in the reading. The topic is usually stated in a word or phrase, and it may be repeated or referred to throughout the paragraph. For example, the opening paragraph of the King excerpt (p. 339) makes clear that its topic is the white moderate.

After you have found the topic of the paragraph, figure out what is being said about it. To return to our example: King immediately establishes the white moderate as the topic of the opening paragraph and at the beginning of the second sentence announces the conclusion he has come to—namely, that the white moderate is "the Negro's great stumbling block in his stride toward freedom." The rest of the paragraph specifies the ways the white moderate blocks progress.

For each paragraph in the King excerpt, the annotations include a summary of the paragraph's topic. Here is an outline that lists those paragraph topics:

Paragraph Scratch Outline

¶1. white moderates block progress in the struggle for racial justice

¶2. tension necessary for progress

¶3. clergymen's criticism not logical

¶4. time must be used to do right

¶5. King is in the middle of two extremes: complacent and angry.

¶6. King offers a better choice

¶7. King's movement has prevented racial violence

¶8. discontent normal and healthy but must be channeled

¶9. creative extremists needed

¶10. some whites have supported King

■ Checklist: Outlining

1. Reread each paragraph, identifying the topic and the comments made about the topic. Do not include examples, specific details, quotations, or other explanatory and supporting material.

2. List the author's main ideas in the margin of the text or on a separate piece of paper.

■ PARAPHRASING

Paraphrasing is restating something you have read by using mostly your own words. As a critical reading strategy, paraphrasing can help you to clarify the meaning of an obscure or ambiguous passage. It is one of the three ways of integrating other people's ideas and information into your own writing, along with *quoting* (reproducing exactly the language of the source text) and *summarizing* (distilling the main ideas or gist of the source text). You might choose to paraphrase rather than quote when the source's language is not especially arresting or memorable. You might paraphrase short passages but summarize longer ones.

Following are two passages. The first is from paragraph 2 of the excerpt from King's "Letter." The second passage is a paraphrase of the first:

Original

    I had hoped that the white moderate would understand that law and order exist for the purpose of establishing justice and that when they fail in this purpose they become the dangerously structured dams that block the flow of social progress. I had hoped that the white moderate would understand that the present tension in the South is a necessary phase of the transition from an obnoxious negative peace, in which the Negro passively accepted his unjust plight, to a substantive and positive peace, in which all men will respect the dignity and worth of human personality.

Paraphrase

```
     King writes that he had hoped for more understanding
from white moderates--specifically that they would recognize
that law and order are not ends in themselves but means to
the greater end of establishing justice. When law and order
do not serve this greater end, they stand in the way of
progress. King expected the white moderate to recognize
that the current tense situation in the South is part of
a transition process that is necessary for progress. The
current situation is bad because although there is peace,
it is an "obnoxious" and "negative" kind of peace based on
blacks passively accepting the injustice of the status quo.
A better kind of peace--one that is "substantive," real and
not imaginary, as well as "positive"--requires that all
people, regardless of race, be valued.
```

When you compare the paraphrase to the original, you can see that the paraphrase contains all the important information and ideas of the original. Notice also that the paraphrase is somewhat longer than the original, refers to the writer by name, and encloses King's original words in quotation marks. Although the paraphrase tries to be *neutral,* to avoid inserting the reader's opinions or distorting the original writer's ideas, it does inevitably express the reader's interpretation of the original text's meaning. Another reader might paraphrase the same passage differently.

■ Checklist: Paraphrasing

1. Reread the passage to be paraphrased, looking up unfamiliar words in a college dictionary.
2. Translate the passage into your own words, putting quotation marks around any words or phrases you quote from the original.
3. Revise to ensure coherence.

■ SUMMARIZING

Summarizing is one of the most widely used strategies for critical reading because it helps the reader understand and remember what is most important in the reading. Another advantage of summarizing is that it creates a condensed version of the reading's ideas and information, which can be referred to later or inserted into the reader's own writing. Along with quoting and paraphrasing, summarizing enables you to refer to and integrate other writers' ideas into your own writing.

A summary is a relatively brief restatement, primarily in the reader's own words, of the reading's main ideas. Summaries vary in length, depending on the reader's purpose. Some summaries are very brief—a sentence or even a subordinate clause. For example, if you were referring to the excerpt from "Letter from Birmingham Jail" and simply needed to indicate how it relates to your other sources, your summary might focus on only one aspect of the reading. It might look something like this: "There have always been advocates of extremism in politics. Martin Luther King Jr., in 'Letter from Birmingham Jail,' for instance, defends nonviolent civil disobedience as an extreme but necessary means of bringing about racial justice." If, on the other hand, you were surveying the important texts of the civil rights movement, you might write a longer, more detailed summary that not only identifies the reading's main ideas but also shows how the ideas relate to one another.

Many writers find it useful to outline the reading as a preliminary to writing a summary. A paragraph-by-paragraph scratch outline (like the one on p. 347) lists the reading's main ideas in the sequence in which they appear in the original. But summarizing requires more than merely stringing together the entries in an outline. It fills in the logical connections between the author's ideas. Notice also in the following example that the reader repeats selected words and phrases and refers to the author by name, indicating, with verbs like *expresses, acknowledges,* and *explains,* the writer's purpose and strategy at each point in the argument.

Summary

```
      King expresses his disappointment with white moderates
who, by opposing his program of nonviolent direct action,
have become a barrier to progress toward racial justice. He
acknowledges that his program has raised tension in the
South, but he explains that tension is necessary to bring
about change. Furthermore, he argues that tension already
exists. But because it has been unexpressed, it is unhealthy
and potentially dangerous.
      He defends his actions against the clergy's criticisms,
particularly their argument that he is in too much of a
hurry. Responding to charges of extremism, King claims that
he has actually prevented racial violence by channeling the
```

natural frustrations of oppressed blacks into nonviolent
protest. He asserts that extremism is precisely what is needed
now--but it must be creative, rather than destructive,
extremism. He concludes by again expressing disappointment
with white moderates for not joining his effort as some other
whites have.

A summary presents only ideas. While it may use certain key terms from the source, it does not otherwise attempt to reflect the source's language, imagery, or tone; and it avoids even a hint of agreement or disagreement with the ideas it summarizes. Of course, however, a writer might summarize ideas in a source like "Letter from Birmingham Jail" to show readers that he or she has read it carefully and then proceed to use the summary to praise, question, or challenge King's argument. In doing so, the writer might quote specific language that reveals word choice, imagery, or tone.

■ Checklist: Summarizing

1. Make a scratch outline of the reading.
2. Write a paragraph or more that presents the author's main ideas largely in your own words. Use the outline as a guide, but reread parts of the original text as necessary.
3. To make the summary coherent, fill in connections between ideas.

■ SYNTHESIZING

Synthesizing involves presenting ideas and information gleaned from different sources. As a critical reading strategy, synthesizing can help you see how different sources relate to one another—for example, offering supporting details or opposing arguments.

When you synthesize material from different sources, you construct a conversation among your sources, a conversation in which you also participate. Synthesizing contributes most to critical thinking when writers use sources not only to support their ideas, but to challenge and extend them as well.

In the following example, the reader uses a variety of sources related to the King passage (pp. 339–43). The synthesis brings the sources together around a central idea. Notice how quotation, paraphrase, and summary are all used to present King's and the other sources' ideas.

Synthesis

When King defends his campaign of nonviolent direct
action against the clergymen's criticism that "our actions,

even though peaceful, must be condemned because they precipitate violence" (King excerpt, paragraph 3), he is using what
Vinit Haksar calls Mohandas Gandhi's "safety-valve argument"
("Civil Disobedience and Non-Cooperation" 117). According to
Haksar, Gandhi gave a "non-threatening warning of worse
things to come" if his demands were not met. King similarly
makes clear that advocates of actions more extreme than those
he advocates are waiting in the wings: "The other force is
one of bitterness and hatred, and it comes perilously close
to advocating violence" (King excerpt, paragraph 5). King
identifies this force with Elijah Muhammad, and although he
does not name him, King's contemporary readers would have
known that he was referring also to Malcolm X who, according
to Herbert J. Storing, "urged that Negroes take seriously the
idea of revolution" ("The Case against Civil Disobedience"
90). In fact, Malcolm X accused King of being a modern-day
Uncle Tom, trying "to keep us under control, to keep us
passive and peaceful and nonviolent" (Malcolm X Speaks 12).

■ **Checklist: Synthesizing**

1. Find and read a variety of sources on your topic, annotating the passages that give you ideas about the topic.

2. Look for patterns among your sources, possibly supporting or refuting your ideas or those of other sources.

3. Write a paragraph or more synthesizing your sources, using quotation, para-phrase, and summary to present what they say on the topic.

■ CONTEXTUALIZING

All texts were written sometime in the past and therefore may embody historical and cultural assumptions, values, and attitudes different from your own. To read critically, you need to become aware of these differences. *Contextualizing* is a critical reading strategy that enables you to make inferences about a reading's historical and cultural context and to examine the differences between its context and your own.

The excerpt from King's "Letter from Birmingham Jail" is a good example of a text that benefits from being read contextually. If you knew little about the history of slavery and segregation in the United States, Martin Luther King Jr., or the civil rights movement, it would be difficult to understand the passion for justice and impatience with delay expressed in this passage from King's writings. To understand the histori-cal and cultural context in which King organized his demonstrations and wrote his

"Letter from Birmingham Jail," you could do some library or Internet research. A little research would enable you to appreciate the intense emotions that swept the nation at the time. You would see that the threat of violence was all too real. Comparing the situation at the time King wrote the "Letter" in 1963 to situations with which you are familiar would help you understand some of your own attitudes toward King and the civil rights movement.

Here is what one reader wrote to contextualize King's writing:

Notes from a Contextualized Reading

1. I am not old enough to remember what it was like in the early 1960s when Dr. King was leading marches and sit-ins, but I have seen television documentaries showing demonstrators being attacked by dogs, doused by fire hoses, beaten and dragged by helmeted police. Such images give me a sense of the violence, fear, and hatred that King was responding to.

   The tension King writes about comes across in his writing. He uses his anger and frustration creatively to inspire his critics. He also threatens them, although he denies it. I saw a film on Malcolm X, so I could see that King was giving white people a choice between his own non-violent way and Malcolm's more confrontational way.

2. Things have certainly changed since the sixties. Legal segregation has ended, but there are still racists like the detective in the O. J. Simpson trial. African Americans like General Colin Powell are highly respected and powerful. The civil rights movement is over. So when I'm reading King today, I feel like I'm reading history. But then again, every once in a while there are reports of police brutality because of race (think of Rodney King) and of what we now call hate crimes.

■ Checklist: Contextualizing

1. Describe the historical and cultural situation as it is represented in the reading and in other sources with which you are familiar. Your knowledge may come from other reading, television or film, school, or elsewhere. (If you know nothing about the historical and cultural context, you could do some library or Internet research.)

2. Compare the historical and cultural situation in which the text was written to your own historical and cultural situation. Consider how your understanding and judgment of the reading is affected by your own context.

■ EXPLORING THE SIGNIFICANCE OF FIGURATIVE LANGUAGE

Figurative language—metaphor, simile, and symbolism—enhances literal meaning by embodying abstract ideas in vivid images and by evoking feelings and associations.

Metaphor implicitly compares two different things by identifying them with each other. For instance, when King calls the white moderate "the Negro's great stumbling block in his stride toward freedom" (paragraph 1), he does not mean that the white moderate literally trips the Negro who is attempting to walk toward freedom. The sentence makes sense only if understood figuratively: The white moderate trips up the Negro by frustrating every effort to achieve justice.

Simile, a more explicit form of comparison, uses the word *like* or *as* to signal the relationship of two seemingly unrelated things. King uses simile when he says that injustice is "like a boil that can never be cured so long as it is covered up" (paragraph 2). This simile makes several points of comparison between injustice and a boil. It suggests that injustice is a disease of society as a boil is a disease of the body and that injustice, like a boil, must be exposed or it will fester and infect the entire body.

Symbolism compares two things by making one stand for the other. King uses the white moderate as a symbol for supposed liberals and would-be supporters of civil rights who are actually frustrating the cause.

How these figures of speech are used in a text reveals something of the writer's feelings about the subject. Exploring possible meanings in a text's figurative language involves (1) annotating and then listing the metaphors, similes, and symbols you find in a reading; (2) grouping the figures of speech that appear to express related feelings or attitudes, and labeling each group; and (3) writing to explore the meaning of the patterns you have found.

The following example shows the process of exploring figures of speech in the King excerpt.

Listing Figures of Speech

"stumbling block in his stride toward freedom" (paragraph 1)

"law and order . . . become the dangerously structured dams" (2)

"the flow of social progress" (2)

"Like a boil that can never be cured" (2)

"the light of human conscience and the air of national
    opinion" (2)

"the quicksand of racial injustice" (4)

Grouping Figures of Speech

Sickness: "like a boil" (2); "the disease of segregation" (10)

Underground: "hidden tension" (2); "injustice must be exposed"
    (2); "injustice must be rooted out" (10)

Blockage: "dams," "block the flow" (2); "Human progress never
    rolls in on wheels of inevitability" (4); "pent-up
    resentments" (8); "repressed emotions" (8)

Writing to Explore Meaning

The patterns labeled underground and blockage suggest a
feeling of frustration. Inertia is a problem; movement forward
toward progress or upward toward the promised land is stalled.
The strong need to break through the resistance may represent
King's feelings both about his attempt to lead purposeful,
effective demonstrations and his effort to write a convincing
argument.

The simile of injustice being "like a boil" links the two
patterns of underground and sickness, suggesting something bad,
a disease, is inside the people or the society. The cure is
to expose or to root out the blocked hatred and injustice as
well as to release the tension or emotion that has long been
repressed. This implies that repression itself is the evil, not
simply what is repressed. Therefore, writing and speaking out
through political action may have curative power for individuals and society alike.

■ **Checklist: Exploring the Significance of Figurative Language**

1. Annotate all the figures of speech you find in the reading—metaphors, similes, and symbols—and then list them.

2. Group the figures of speech that appear to express related feelings and attitudes, and label each group.

3. Write one or two paragraphs exploring the meaning of these patterns. What do they tell you about the text?

■ LOOKING FOR PATTERNS OF OPPOSITION

All texts carry within themselves voices of opposition. These *patterns of opposition* may echo the views and values of critical readers the writer anticipates or predecessors to whom the writer is responding in some way; they may even reflect the writer's own conflicting values. Careful readers look closely for such a dialogue of opposing voices within the text.

When we think of oppositions, we ordinarily think of polarities: *yes* and *no, up* and *down, black* and *white, new* and *old.* Some oppositions, however, may be more subtle. The excerpt from King's "Letter from Birmingham Jail" is rich in such oppositions:

moderate versus *extremist, order* versus *justice, direct action* versus *passive acceptance, expression* versus *repression.* These oppositions are not accidental; they form a significant pattern that gives a critical reader important information about the essay.

A careful reading will show that King always values one of the two terms in an opposition over the other. In the passage, for example, *extremist* is valued over *moderate* (paragraph 9). This preference for extremism is surprising. The critical reader should ask why, when white extremists like members of the Ku Klux Klan have committed so many outrages against African Americans, King would prefer extremism. If King is trying to convince his readers to accept his point of view, why would he represent himself as an extremist? Moreover, why would a clergyman advocate extremism instead of moderation?

Studying the patterns of opposition enables you to answer these questions. You will see that King sets up this opposition to force his readers to examine their own values and realize that they are in fact misplaced. Instead of working toward justice, he says, those who support law and order maintain the unjust status quo. By getting his readers to think of white moderates as blocking rather than facilitating peaceful change, King brings them to align themselves with him and perhaps even embrace his strategy of nonviolent resistance.

Looking for patterns of opposition involves annotating words or phrases in the reading that indicate oppositions, listing the opposing terms in pairs, deciding which term in each pair is preferred by the writer, and reflecting on the meaning of the patterns. Here is a partial list of oppositions from the King excerpt, with the preferred terms marked by an asterisk:

Listing Patterns of Opposition

moderate	*extremist
order	*justice
negative peace	*positive peace
absence of justice	*presence of justice
goals	*methods
*direct action	passive acceptance
*exposed tension	hidden tension

■ Checklist: Looking for Patterns of Opposition

1. Annotate the selection for words or phrases indicating oppositions.
2. List the pairs of oppositions. (You may have to paraphrase or even supply the opposite word or phrase if it is not stated directly in the text.)
3. For each pair of oppositions, put an asterisk next to the term that the writer seems to value or prefer over the other.
4. Study the patterns of opposition. How do they contribute to your understanding of the essay? What do they tell you about what the author wants you to believe?

◼ REFLECTING ON CHALLENGES TO YOUR BELIEFS AND VALUES

To read critically, you need to scrutinize your own assumptions and attitudes as well as those expressed in the text you are reading. If you are like most readers, however, you will find that your assumptions and attitudes are so ingrained that you are not fully aware of them. A good strategy for getting at these underlying beliefs and values is to identify and reflect on the ways the text challenges you, how it makes you feel—disturbed, threatened, ashamed, combative, or some other way.

For example, here is what one student wrote about the King passage:

Reflections

In paragraph 1, Dr. King criticizes people who are "more devoted to 'order' than to justice." This criticism upsets me because today I think I would choose order over justice. When I analyze my feelings and try to figure out where they come from, I realize that what I feel most is fear. I am terrified by the violence in society today. I'm afraid of sociopaths who don't respect the rule of law, much less the value of human life.

I know Dr. King was writing in a time when the law itself was unjust, when order was apparently used to keep people from protesting and changing the law. But things are different now. Today, justice seems to serve criminals more than it serves law-abiding citizens. That's why I'm for order over justice.

◼ Checklist: Reflecting on Challenges to Your Beliefs and Values

1. Identify challenges by marking the text where you feel your beliefs and values are being opposed, criticized, or unfairly characterized.
2. Write a few paragraphs reflecting on why you feel challenged. Do not defend your feelings; instead, analyze them to see where they come from.

◼ EVALUATING THE LOGIC OF AN ARGUMENT

An argument includes a thesis backed by reasons and support. The *thesis* asserts an idea, a position on a controversial issue, or a solution to a problem that the writer wants readers to accept. The *reasons* tell readers why they should accept the thesis, and the *support* (such as examples, statistics, authorities, and textual evidence) gives readers grounds for accepting it. For an argument to be considered logically acceptable, it must meet the three conditions of what we call the ABC test:

The ABC Test

A. The reasons and support must be *appropriate* to the thesis.

B. The reasons and support must be *believable*.

C. The reasons and support must be *consistent* with one another as well as *complete*.

(For more on argument, see Chapter 11. For an example of the ABC test, see Christine Romano's essay in Chapter 7, pp. 273–76.)

Testing for Appropriateness

As a critical reader, you must decide whether the argument's reasons and support are appropriate and clearly related to the thesis. To test for appropriateness, ask these questions: How does each reason or piece of support relate to the thesis? Is the connection between reasons and support and the thesis clear and compelling? Or is the argument irrelevant or only vaguely related to the thesis?

Readers most often question the appropriateness of reasons and support when the writer argues by analogy or by invoking authority. For example, in paragraph 2, King argues that when law and order fail to establish justice, "they become the dangerously structured dams that block the flow of social progress." The analogy asserts the following logical relationship: Law and order are to progress toward justice what a dam is to water. If you do not accept this analogy, the argument fails the test of appropriateness.

King uses both analogy and authority in the following passage: "Isn't this like condemning Socrates because his unswerving commitment to truth and his philosophical inquiries precipitated the act by the misguided populace in which they made him drink hemlock?" (paragraph 3). Not only must you judge the appropriateness of the analogy comparing the Greek populace's condemnation of Socrates to the white moderates' condemnation of King, but you must also judge whether it is appropriate to accept Socrates as an authority on this subject. Since Socrates is generally respected for his teaching on justice, his words and actions are likely to be considered appropriate to King's situation in Birmingham. (For more on invoking authorities, see Chapter 11, pp. 368–69.)

Testing for Believability

Believability is a measure of your willingness to accept as true the reasons and support the writer gives in defense of a thesis.

To test for believability, ask: On what basis am I being asked to believe this reason or support is true? If it cannot be proved true or false, how much weight does it carry?

In judging facts, examples, statistics, and authorities, consider the following points.

Facts are statements that can be proved objectively to be true. The believability of facts depends on their *accuracy* (they should not distort or misrepresent reality), their *completeness* (they should not omit important details), and the *trustworthiness* of their sources (sources should be qualified and unbiased). King, for instance, asserts as fact that the African American will not wait much longer for racial justice (paragraph 8). His critics might question the factuality of this assertion by asking, is it true of all African Americans? How much longer will they wait? How does King know what African Americans will and will not do?

Examples and *anecdotes* are particular instances that may or may not make you believe a general statement. The believability of examples depends on their *representativeness* (whether they are truly typical and thus generalizable) and their *specificity* (whether particular details make them seem true to life). Even if a vivid example or gripping anecdote does not convince readers, it usually strengthens argumentative writing by clarifying the meaning and dramatizing the point. In paragraph 5 of the King excerpt, for example, King supports his generalization that some African American nationalist extremists are motivated by bitterness and hatred by citing the specific example of Elijah Muhammad's Black Muslim movement. Conversely, in paragraph 9, he refers to Jesus, Paul, Luther, and others as examples of extremists motivated by love and Christianity. These examples support his assertion that extremism is not in itself wrong and that any judgment of extremism must be based on its motivation and cause.

Statistics are numerical data, including correlations. The believability of statistics depends on the *comparability* of the data (the price of apples in 1985 cannot be compared to the price of apples in 2006 unless the figures are adjusted to account for inflation), the *precision* of the methods employed to gather and analyze data (representative samples should be used and variables accounted for), and the *trustworthiness* of the sources (sources should be qualified, unbiased, and — except in historical contexts — as recent as possible).

Authorities are people to whom the writer attributes expertise on a given subject. Not only must such authorities be appropriate, as mentioned earlier, but they must be believable as well. The believability of authorities depends on their *credibility,* on whether the reader accepts them as experts on the topic at hand. King cites authorities repeatedly throughout his essay. He refers to religious leaders (Jesus and Luther) as well as to American political leaders (Lincoln and Jefferson). These figures are certain to have a high degree of credibility among King's readers.

Testing for Consistency and Completeness

In looking for consistency, you should be concerned that all the parts of the argument work together and that none of the reasons or support contradict any of the other reasons or support. In addition, the reasons and support, taken together, should be sufficient to convince readers to accept the thesis or at least take it seriously. To test for consistency and completeness, ask: Are any of the reasons and support contradictory? Do they provide sufficient grounds for accepting the thesis? Does the writer fail to counterargue (to acknowledge, accommodate, or refute any opposing arguments or important objections)? (For more on counterarguing, see Chapter 11, pp. 372–75.)

A critical reader might regard as contradictory King's characterizing himself first as a moderate between the forces of complacency and violence and later as an extremist opposed to the forces of violence. King attempts to reconcile this apparent contradiction by explicitly redefining extremism in paragraph 9. Similarly, the fact that King fails to examine and refute every legal recourse available to his cause might allow a critical reader to question the sufficiency of his argument.

■ **Checklist: Evaluating the Logic of an Argument**

Use the ABC test:

A. *Test for appropriateness* by checking that the reasons and support are clearly and directly related to the thesis.

B. *Test for believability* by deciding whether you can accept the reasons and support as true.

C. *Test for consistency and completeness* by ascertaining whether the argument has any contradictions and whether any important objections or opposing arguments have been ignored.

■ RECOGNIZING EMOTIONAL MANIPULATION

Many different kinds of essays appeal to readers' emotions. Tobias Wolff's remembered-event essay (in Chapter 2) may be terrifying to some readers; John Edge's attempts to eat a pickled pig lip (in Chapter 3) may disgust some readers, especially vegetarians; and Richard Estrada's position paper (in Chapter 5) may be annoying to some readers because of his accommodating tone.

Writers often try to arouse emotions in readers to excite their interest, make them care, or move them to take action. There is nothing wrong with appealing to readers' emotions. What is wrong is manipulating readers with false or exaggerated appeals. As a critical reader, you should be suspicious of writing that is overly or falsely sentimental, that cites alarming statistics and frightening anecdotes, that demonizes others and identifies itself with revered authorities, or that uses symbols (flag waving) or emotionally loaded words (such as *racist*).

King, for example, uses the emotionally loaded word *paternalistically* to refer to the white moderate's belief that "he can set the timetable for another man's freedom" (paragraph 1). In the same paragraph, King uses symbolism to get an emotional reaction from readers when he compares the white moderate to the "Ku Klux Klanner." To get readers to accept his ideas, he also relies on authorities whose names evoke the greatest respect, such as Jesus and Lincoln. But some readers might object that comparing King's crusade to that of Jesus and other leaders of religious and political groups is pretentious and manipulative. A critical reader might also consider King's discussion of African American extremists in paragraph 7 to be a veiled threat designed to frighten readers into agreement.

■ **Checklist: Recognizing Emotional Manipulation**

1. Annotate places in the text where you sense emotional appeals are being used.

2. Assess whether any of the emotional appeals are unfairly manipulative.

■ JUDGING THE WRITER'S CREDIBILITY

Writers often try to persuade readers to respect and believe them. Because readers may not know them personally or even by reputation, writers must present an image of themselves in their writing that will gain their readers' confidence. This image cannot be made directly but must be made indirectly, through the arguments, language, and system of values and beliefs expressed or implied in the writing. Writers establish credibility in their writing in three ways:

By showing their knowledge of the subject

By building common ground with readers

By responding fairly to objections and opposing arguments

Testing for Knowledge

Writers demonstrate their knowledge through the facts and statistics they marshal, the sources they rely on for information, and the scope and depth of their understanding. As a critical reader, you may not be sufficiently expert on the subject yourself to know whether the facts are accurate, the sources are reliable, and the understanding is sufficient. You may need to do some research to see what others say about the subject. You can also check credentials—the writer's educational and professional qualifications, the respectability of the publication in which the selection first appeared, and reviews of the writer's work—to determine whether the writer is a respected authority in the field. For example, King brings with him the authority that comes from being a member of the clergy and a respected leader of the Southern Christian Leadership Conference.

Testing for Common Ground

One way writers can establish common ground with their readers is by basing their reasoning on shared values, beliefs, and attitudes. They use language that includes their readers *(we)* rather than excludes them *(they)*. They qualify their assertions to keep them from being too extreme. Above all, they acknowledge differences of opinion and try to make room in their argument to accommodate reasonable differences. As a critical reader, you want to notice such appeals.

King creates common ground with readers by using the inclusive pronoun *we*, suggesting shared concerns between himself and his audience. Notice, however, his use of masculine pronouns and other references ("the Negro...he," "our brothers").

Although King addressed his letter to male clergy, he intended it to be published in the local newspaper, where it would be read by an audience of both men and women. By using language that excludes women, a common practice at the time the selection was written, King misses the opportunity to build common ground with half of his readers.

Testing for Fairness

Writers reveal their character by how they handle opposing arguments and objections to their argument. As a critical reader, you want to pay particular attention to how writers treat possible differences of opinion. Be suspicious of those who ignore differences and pretend that everyone agrees with their viewpoints. When objections or opposing views are represented, consider whether they have been distorted in any way; if they are refuted, be sure they are challenged fairly—with sound reasoning and solid support.

One way to gauge the author's credibility is to identify the tone of the argument, for it conveys the writer's attitude toward the subject and toward the reader. Examine the text carefully for indications of tone: Is the text angry? Sarcastic? Evenhanded? Shrill? Condescending? Bullying? Do you feel as if the writer is treating the subject—and you, as a reader—with fairness? King's tone might be characterized in different passages as patient (he doesn't lose his temper), respectful (he refers to white moderates as "people of good will"), or pompous (comparing himself to Jesus and Socrates).

■ **Checklist: Judging the Writer's Credibility**

1. Annotate for the writer's knowledge of the subject, how well common ground is established, and whether the writer deals fairly with objections and opposing arguments.

2. Decide what in the essay you find credible and what you question.

11

Strategies for Arguing

Arguing involves reasoning as well as making assertions. When you write an essay in which you assert a point of view, you are obliged to come up with reasons for your point of view and to find ways to support your reasons. In addition to arguing for your point of view, you must think carefully about what your readers know and believe to argue against — to *counterargue* — opposing points of view. If you ignore what your readers may be thinking, you will be unlikely to convince them to take your argument seriously.

This chapter presents the basic strategies for making assertions and reasoning about a writing situation. We focus on asserting a thesis, backing it up with reasons and support, and anticipating readers' questions and objections (counterarguing).

■ ASSERTING A THESIS

Central to any argument is the *thesis*—the point of view the writer wants readers to consider. The thesis statement may appear at the beginning of the essay or at the end, but wherever it is placed, its job is simple: to announce as clearly and straightforwardly as possible the main point the writer is trying to make in the essay.

There are three different kinds of argumentative essays in Part One of this book. Each of these essays requires a special kind of assertion and reasoning. Here we first define each type of assertion and suggest a question it is designed to answer. Then we illustrate each assertion and question with a thesis from a reading in Chapters 5–7:

- *Assertion of opinion:* What is your position on a controversial issue? (Chapter 5, "Arguing a Position")

  When overzealous parents and coaches impose adult standards on children's sports, the result can be activities that are neither satisfying nor beneficial to children.
  — JESSICA STATSKY, "Children Need to Play, Not Compete"

- *Assertion of policy:* What is your understanding of a problem, and what do you think should be done to solve it? (Chapter 6, "Proposing a Solution")

Although this last-minute anxiety about midterm and final exams is only too familiar to most college students, many professors may not realize how such major, infrequent, high-stakes exams work against the best interests of students both psychologically and intellectually.... If professors gave additional brief exams at frequent intervals, students would be spurred to study more regularly, learn more, worry less, and perform better.

— PATRICK O'MALLEY, "More Testing, More Learning"

- *Assertion of evaluation:* What is your judgment of a subject? (Chapter 7, "Justifying an Evaluation")

Morrowind is a flawed jewel, but flawed only because its scope is so grand. Beautiful graphics, compelling stories, a huge map to explore, engaging quests, and a simple interface all add up to a premier game.

— JONAH JACKSON, "The Elder Scrolls III: Morrowind"

As these different thesis statements indicate, the kind of thesis you assert depends on the occasion for which you are writing and the question you are trying to answer for your readers. Whatever the writing situation, to be effective, every thesis must satisfy the same three standards: It must be *arguable, clear,* and *appropriately qualified.*

Arguable Assertions

Reasoned argument seems called for when informed people disagree over an issue or remain divided over how best to solve a problem, as is so often the case in social and political life. Hence the thesis statements in reasoned arguments make *arguable assertions*—possibilities or probabilities, not certainties. Argument becomes useful in situations in which there are uncertainties, situations in which established knowledge and facts cannot provide the answers.

Therefore, a statement of fact could not be an arguable thesis statement because facts are easy to verify—whether by checking an authoritative reference book, asking an authority, or observing the fact with your own eyes. For example, these statements assert facts:

Jem has a Ph.D. in history.

I am less than five feet tall.

Eucalyptus trees were originally imported into California from Australia.

Each of these assertions can be easily verified. To find out Jem's academic degree, you can ask him, among other things. To determine a person's height, you can use a tape measure. To discover where California got its eucalyptus trees, you can refer to a source in the library. There is no point in arguing over such statements (though you might question the authority of a particular source or the accuracy of someone's measurement). If a writer asserts something as fact and attempts to support the assertion with authorities or statistics, the essay is considered not an argument but a report of information.

Like facts, expressions of personal feelings are not arguable assertions. Whereas facts are unarguable because they can be definitively proved true or false, feelings are unarguable because they are purely subjective. Personal feelings can be explained, but it would be unreasonable to attempt to convince others to change their views or take action solely on the basis of your personal feelings.

You can declare, for example, that you love Ben & Jerry's Chunky Monkey ice cream or that you detest eight o'clock classes, but you cannot offer an argument to support such assertions. All you can do is explain why you feel as you do. Even though many people agree with you about eight o'clock classes, it would be pointless to try to convince others to share your feelings. If, however, you were to restate the assertion as "Eight o'clock classes are counterproductive," you could then construct an argument that does not depend solely on your subjective feelings, memories, or preferences. Your argument could be based on reasons and support that apply to others as well as to yourself. For example, you might argue that students' ability to learn is at an especially low ebb immediately after breakfast and provide scientific support, in addition, perhaps, to personal experience and interviews with your friends.

Clear and Precise Wording

The way a thesis is worded is as important as its arguability. The wording of a thesis, especially its key terms, must be clear and precise.

Consider the following assertion: "Democracy is a way of life." The meaning of this claim is uncertain, partly because the word *democracy* is abstract and partly because the phrase *way of life* is inexact. Abstract ideas like democracy, freedom, and patriotism are by their very nature hard to grasp, and they become even less clear with overuse. Too often, such words take on connotations that may obscure the meaning you want to emphasize. *Way of life* is fuzzy: What does it mean? Moreover, can a form of government be a way of life? It depends on what is meant by *way of life*. Does it refer to daily life, to a general philosophy or attitude toward life, or to something else?

Thus a thesis is vague if its meaning is unclear; it is ambiguous if it has more than one possible meaning. For example, the statement "My English instructor is mad" can be understood in two ways: The teacher is either angry or insane. Obviously, these are two very different assertions. You would not want readers to think you mean one when you actually mean the other.

Whenever you write argument, you should pay special attention to the way you phrase your thesis and take care to avoid vague and ambiguous language.

Appropriate Qualification

In addition to being arguable and clear, an argument thesis must make *appropriate qualifications* that suit your writing situation. If you are confident that your case is so strong that readers will accept your argument without question, state your thesis emphatically and unconditionally. If, however, you expect readers to challenge your assumptions or conclusions, you must qualify your statement. Qualifying a thesis makes it more likely that readers will take it seriously. Expressions like *probably, very likely, apparently,* and *it seems* all serve to qualify a thesis.

■ **Exercise 11.1**

Write an assertion of opinion that states your position on one of the following controversial issues:

Should English be the official language of the United States and the only language used in local, state, and federal government agencies in oral and written communications?

Should teenagers be required to get their parents' permission to obtain birth-control information and contraceptives?

Should high schools or colleges require students to perform community service as a condition for graduation?

Should girls and boys be treated differently by their families or schools?

Should businesses remain loyal to their communities, or should they move wherever labor costs, taxes, or other conditions are more favorable?

These issues are complicated and have been debated for a long time. Constructing a persuasive argument would obviously require careful deliberation and research. For this exercise, however, all you need to do is construct a thesis on the issue you have chosen, a thesis that is arguable, clear, and appropriately qualified.

■ **Exercise 11.2**

Find the thesis in one of the argument essays in Chapters 5–7. Then decide whether the thesis meets the three requirements: that it be arguable, clear, and appropriately qualified.

■ **Exercise 11.3**

If you have written or are currently working on one of the argument assignments in Chapters 5–7, consider whether your essay thesis meets the three requirements: that it be arguable, clear, and appropriately qualified. If you believe it does not meet the requirements, revise it appropriately.

■ GIVING REASONS AND SUPPORT

Whether you are arguing a position, proposing a solution, or justifying an evaluation, you need to give *reasons and support* for your thesis.

Reasons can be thought of as the main points arguing for a thesis. Often they answer the question "Why do you think so?" For example, if you assert among friends that you value a certain movie highly, one of your friends might ask, "Why do you like it so much?" And you might answer, "*Because* it has challenging ideas, unusual camera work, and memorable acting." Similarly, you might oppose restrictions on students' use of offensive language at your college *because* they would make students reluctant to enter into frank debates on important issues, offensive speech is hard to define, and restrictions violate the free-speech clause of the First Amendment. These *because* phrases are your reasons. You may have one or many reasons, depending on your subject and your writing situation.

For your argument to succeed with your readers, you must not only give reasons but also provide support. The main kinds of support writers use are examples, statistics, authorities, anecdotes, and textual evidence. Following is a discussion and illustration of each kind, along with standards for judging the reliability of that particular type of support.

Examples

Examples may be used as support in all types of arguments. They are an effective way to demonstrate that your reasons should be taken seriously. For examples to be believable and convincing, they must be representative (typical of all the relevant examples you might have chosen), consistent with the experience of your readers (familiar and not extreme), and adequate in number (numerous enough to be convincing and yet selective and not likely to overwhelm readers).

The following illustration comes from a book on illiteracy in America by Jonathan Kozol, a prominent educator and writer. In these paragraphs, Kozol presents several examples to support a part of his argument that the human costs of illiteracy are high.

> Illiterates cannot read the menu in a restaurant.
>
> They cannot read the cost of items on the menu in the *window* of the restaurant before they enter.
>
> Illiterates cannot read the letters that their children bring home from their teachers. They cannot study school department circulars that tell them of the courses that their children must be taking if they hope to pass the SAT exams. They cannot help with homework. They cannot write a letter to the teacher. They are afraid to visit in the classroom. They do not want to humiliate their child or themselves.
>
> Illiterates cannot read instructions on a bottle of prescription medicine. They cannot find out when a medicine is past the year of safe consumption; nor can they read of allergenic risks, warnings to diabetics, or the potential sedative effect of certain kinds of nonprescription pills. They cannot observe preventive health care admonitions. They cannot read about "the seven warnings signs of cancer" or the indications of blood-sugar fluctuations or the risks of eating certain foods that aggravate the likelihood of cardiac arrest.
>
> —Jonathan Kozol, *Illiterate America*

These examples probably seem to most readers to be representative of all the examples Kozol collected in his many interviews with people who could neither read nor write. Though all of his readers are literate and have never experienced the frustrations of adult illiterates, Kozol assumes they can recognize that the experiences are a familiar part of illiterates' lives. Most readers will believe the experiences to be neither atypical nor extreme.

■ **Exercise 11.4**

Identify the examples in paragraphs 9 and 11 in Jessica Statsky's essay "Children Need to Play, Not Compete" in Chapter 5. If you have not read the essay, pause to skim it so that you can evaluate the examples within the context of the entire essay. How well do the examples individually and as a set meet the standards of representativeness, consistency with experience of readers, and adequacy in number? You will not have all the information you need to evaluate the examples — you rarely do unless you are an expert on the subject — but make a judgment based on the information available to you in the headnote and the essay.

Statistics

In many kinds of arguments about economic, educational, or social issues, *statistics* may be essential. When you use statistics in your own arguments, you will want to ensure that they are up to date (they should be current, the best presently available facts on the subject), relevant (they should be appropriate for your argument), and accurate (they should not distort or misrepresent the subject). In addition, take care to select statistics from reliable sources and to use statistics from the sources in which they originally appeared if at all possible. For example, you would want to get medical statistics from a reputable and authoritative professional periodical like the *New England Journal of Medicine* rather than from a supermarket tabloid or an unaffiliated Web site. If you are uncertain about the most authoritative sources, ask a reference librarian or a professor who knows about your topic.

The following selection comes from an argument speculating about the decline of civic life in the United States. Civic life includes all of the clubs, organizations, and activities people choose to participate in. The author, a Harvard University professor, believes that since the early 1960s, Americans have participated less and less in civic life because they have been spending more and more time watching television. In these paragraphs, he uses statistics to support this possible causal relationship.

> The culprit is television.
>
> First, the timing fits. The long civic generation was the last cohort of Americans to grow up without television, for television flashed into American society like lightning in the 1950s. In 1950 barely 10 percent of American homes had television sets, but by 1959, 90 percent did, probably the fastest diffusion of a major technological innovation ever recorded. The reverberations from this lightning bolt continued for decades, as viewing hours grew by 17–20 percent during the 1960s and by an additional 7–8 percent during the 1970s. In the early years, TV watching was concentrated among the less educated sectors of the population, but during the 1970s the viewing time of the more educated sectors of the population began to converge upward. Television viewing increases with age, particularly upon retirement, but each generation since the introduction of television has begun its life cycle at a higher starting point. By 1995 viewing per TV household was more than 50 percent higher than it had been in the 1950s.
>
> Most studies estimate that the average American now watches roughly four hours per day (excluding periods in which television is merely playing in the background).

Even a more conservative estimate of three hours means that television absorbs 40 percent of the average American's free time, an increase of about one-third since 1965. Moreover, multiple sets have proliferated: By the late 1980s three-quarters of all U.S. homes had more than one set, and these numbers too are rising steadily, allowing ever more private viewing. . . . This massive change in the way Americans spend their days and nights occurred precisely during the years of generational civic disengagement.

– ROBERT D. PUTNAM, "The Strange Disappearance of Civic America"

These statistics come primarily from the U.S. Bureau of the Census, a nationwide count of the number of Americans and a survey, in part, of their buying habits, levels of education, and leisure activities. The Census reports are widely considered to be accurate and trustworthy. They qualify as original sources of statistics.

■ **Exercise 11.5**

In Chapter 5, identify the statistics in paragraphs 7 and 8 of Barbara Ehrenreich's essay and paragraphs 5 and 6 of Jessica Statsky's. Underline the statistics you find. If you have not read the essays, pause to skim them so that you can evaluate each writer's use of statistics within the context of the whole essay. How well do the statistics meet the standard of up-to-dateness, relevance, accuracy, and reliance on the original source? (If you find that you do not have all the information you need, base your judgments on whatever information is available to you.) Does the writer indicate where the statistics come from? What do the statistics contribute to the argument?

Authorities

To support an argument, writers often cite experts on the subject who agree with their point of view. Quoting, paraphrasing, or even just referring to a respected *authority* can add to a writer's credibility. Authorities must be selected as carefully as facts and statistics. One qualification for authorities to support arguments is suggested by the way we refer to them: They must be authoritative — that is, trustworthy and reputable. They must also be specially qualified to contribute to the subject you are writing about. For example, a well-known expert on the American presidency might be a poor choice to support an argument on whether adolescents who commit serious crimes should be tried in the courts as adults. Finally, qualified authorities must have training at respected institutions or have unique real-world experiences, and they must have a record of research and publications recognized by other authorities.

The following example comes from a *New York Times* article about some parents' and experts' heightened concern over boys' behavior. The author believes that the concern is exaggerated and potentially dangerous to boys, and she wants to understand why it is increasing. In the full argument, she is particularly concerned about the number of boys who are being given Ritalin, a popular drug for treating attention-deficit hyperactivity disorder.

Today, the world is no longer safe for boys. A boy being a shade too boyish risks find-ing himself under the scrutiny of parents, teachers, guidance counselors, child thera-pists — all of them on watch for the early glimmerings of a medical syndrome, a bona fide behavioral disorder. Does the boy disregard authority, make snide comments in class, push other kids around and play hooky? Maybe he has a conduct disorder. Is he fidgety, impulsive, disruptive, easily bored? Perhaps he is suffering from attention-deficit hyperactivity disorder, or ADHD, the disease of the hour and the most fre-quently diagnosed behavioral disorder of childhood. Does he prefer computer games and goofing off to homework? He might have dyslexia or another learning disorder.

"There is now an attempt to pathologize what was once considered the normal range of behavior of boys," said Melvin Konner of the departments of anthropology and psychiatry at Emory University in Atlanta. "Today, Tom Sawyer and Huckleberry Finn surely would have been diagnosed with both conduct disorder and ADHD." And both, perhaps, would have been put on Ritalin, the drug of choice for treating attention-deficit disorder.

— NATALIE ANGIER, "Intolerance of Boyish Behavior"

Notice the way the writer establishes the professional qualifications of the author-ity she quotes. She places him at a major research university (Emory University) and indicates by his department affiliations (anthropology and psychiatry) that he has spe-cial training to comment on how a culture treats its young men. Readers can infer from these two facts that he has almost certainly earned a doctorate in anthropology or psychiatry and that he has probably published research studies. This carefully selected quotation supports the writer's argument that there is a problem and that readers should care about it.

In this example, the writer relies on *informal* citation within her essay to intro-duce the authority she quotes. In newspapers, magazines, and some books, writers rely on informal citation, mentioning the title or author in the essay itself. In other books and in research reports, writers rely on a *formal* style of citation that allows them to refer briefly in an essay to a detailed list of works cited appearing at the end of the essay. This list provides the author, title, date, and publisher of every source of information referred to in the essay. To evaluate the qualifications of an authority in an argument relying on a list of works cited, you may have to rely solely on the informa-tion provided in the list. (For examples of two formal citation styles often used in col-lege essays, see Chapter 14.)

■ **Exercise 11.6**

Analyze how authorities are used in paragraphs 4 and 5 of Patrick O'Malley's essay "More Testing, More Learning" in Chapter 6. Begin by underlining the authorities' contributions to these paragraphs, whether through quotation, summary, or para-phrase. On the basis of the evidence you have available, decide to what extent each source is authoritative on the subject: qualified to contribute to the subject, trained appropriately, and recognized widely. How does O'Malley establish each authority's credentials? Then decide what each authority contributes to the argument as a whole. (If you have not read the essay, take time to read or skim it now.)

Anecdotes

Anecdotes are brief stories about events or experiences, recounted in an engaging way. If they are relevant to the argument, well told, and true to life, they can provide convincing support. To be relevant, an anecdote must strike readers as more than an entertaining diversion; it must seem to make an irreplaceable contribution to an argument. If it is well told, the narrative or story is easy to follow, and the people and scenes are described memorably, even vividly. There are many concrete details that help readers imagine what happened. A true-to-life anecdote is one that seems to represent a possible life experience of a real person. It has to be believable, even if the experience is foreign to readers' experiences.

The following anecdote appeared in an argument taking a position on a familiar issue: gun ownership and control. The writer, an essayist, poet, and environmental writer who is also a rancher in South Dakota, always carries a pistol and believes that other people may have an urgent personal need to carry one and should have the right to do so. To support her argument, she tells several anecdotes, including this one:

> I was driving the half-mile to the highway mailbox one day when I saw a vehicle parked about midway down the road. Several men were standing in the ditch, relieving themselves. I have no objection to emergency urination, but I noticed they'd dumped several dozen beer cans in the road. Besides being ugly, cans can slash a cow's feet or stomach.
>
> The men noticed me before they finished and made quite a performance out of zipping their trousers while walking toward me. All four of them gathered around my small foreign car, and one of them demanded what the hell I wanted.
>
> "This is private land. I'd appreciate it if you'd pick up the beer cans."
>
> "What beer cans?" said the belligerent one, putting both hands on the car door and leaning in my window. His face was inches from mine, and the beer fumes were strong. The others laughed. One tried the passenger door, locked; another put his foot on the hood and rocked the car. They circled, lightly thumping the roof, discussing my good fortune in meeting them and the benefits they were likely to bestow upon me. I felt very small and very trapped and they knew it.
>
> "The ones you just threw out," I said politely.
>
> "I don't see no beer cans. Why don't you get out here and show them to me, honey?" said the belligerent one, reaching for the handle inside my door.
>
> "Right over there," I said, still being polite, "—there, and over there." I pointed with the pistol, which I'd slipped under my thigh. Within one minute the cans and the men were back in the car and headed down the road.
>
> I believe this incident illustrates several important principles. The men were trespassing and knew it; their judgment may have been impaired by alcohol. Their response to the polite request of a woman alone was to use their size, numbers, and sex to inspire fear. The pistol was a response in the same language. Politeness didn't work; I couldn't match them in size or number. Out of the car, I'd have been more vulnerable. The pistol just changed the balance of power.
>
> —LINDA M. HASSELSTROM, "Why One Peaceful Woman Carries a Pistol"

Most readers would readily agree that this anecdote is well told. It has many concrete, memorable details. As in any good story, something happens: There is action, suspense, climax, resolution. There is even dialogue. It is about a believable, possible experience. Most important, as support for an argument, it is relevant to the writer's point, as she makes clear in the final paragraph.

■ **Exercise 11.7**

Analyze the way an anecdote is used in paragraph 2 of Natalie Angier's essay "Indirect Aggression" in Chapter 4. Consider whether the story is well told and true to life. Decide whether it seems to be relevant to the whole argument. Does the writer make the relevance clear? Do you find the anecdote convincing?

Textual Evidence

When you argue claims of value (Chapter 7), *textual evidence* will be very important. In your other college courses, if you are asked to evaluate a controversial book, you must quote, paraphrase, or summarize passages so that readers can understand why you think the author's argument is or is not credible. If you are interpreting a novel for one of your classes, you must include numerous excerpts to show just how you arrived at your conclusion. In both situations, you are integrating bits of the text you are evaluating or interpreting into your own text and building your argument on these bits.

For these bits of textual evidence to be considered effective support for an argument of evaluation or interpretation, they must be carefully selected to be relevant to the argument's thesis and reasons. You must help readers see the connection between each piece of evidence and the reason it supports. Textual evidence must also be highly selective — that is, chosen from among all the available evidence to provide the support needed without overwhelming the reader with too much evidence or weakening the argument with marginally relevant evidence. Textual evidence usually has more impact if it is balanced between quotation and paraphrase from the text. For these selective, balanced choices of evidence to be comprehensible and convincing to readers, the evidence must be smoothly integrated into the sentences of the argument. Finally, the relevance of textual evidence is rarely obvious: The writer must ordinarily explain the link between the evidence and the writer's intended point.

The following example comes from a student essay in which the writer argues that the main character (referred to as "the boy") in the short story "Araby" by James Joyce is so self-absorbed that he learns nothing about himself or other people. These paragraphs offer the reasons that the writer believes readers should take her argument seriously. She attempts to support her reasons with textual evidence from the story.

The story opens and closes with images of blindness. The street is "blind" with an "uninhabited house . . . at the blind end." As he spies on Mangan's sister, from his own house, the boy intentionally limits what he is able to see by lowering the "blind" until it is only an inch from the window sash. At the bazaar in the closing scene, the "light was out," and the upper part of the hall was "completely dark." The boy is left "gazing up into the darkness," seeing nothing but an inner torment that burns his eyes.

This pattern of imagery includes images of reading, and reading stands for the boy's inability to understand what is before his eyes. When he tries to read at night, for example, the girl's "image [comes] between [him] and the page," in effect blinding him. In fact, he seems blind to everything except this "image" of the "brown-clad figure cast by [his] imagination." The girl's "brown-clad figure" is also associated with the houses on "blind" North Richmond Street, with their "brown imperturbable faces." The houses stare back at the boy, unaffected by his presence and gaze.

–SALLY CRANE, "Gazing into the Darkness"

Notice first how the writer quotes selected words and phrases about blindness to support her reasoning that the boy learns nothing because he is blinded. There are twelve quotations in these two paragraphs, all of them relevant and perhaps not so many as to overwhelm the reader. The writer relies not only on quotes but also on paraphrases of information in the story. The second and third sentences in paragraph 1 are largely paraphrases. The quotations in particular are integrated smoothly into the sentences so that readers' momentum is not blocked. Most important, the writer does not assume that the evidence speaks for itself; she comments and interprets throughout. For example, in the first paragraph, all the sentences except the fourth one offer some comment or explanation.

■ **Exercise 11.8**

Analyze the use of evidence in paragraphs 3–5 of Christine Romano's essay in Chapter 7. (If you have not read this essay, pause to skim it so that you can evaluate the evidence in the context of Romano's full argument.) The quotes are easy to identify. The paraphrases you could identify with confidence only by reading Statsky's essay in Chapter 5, but you can probably identify some of them without doing so. Then try to identify the phrases or sentences that comment on or explain the evidence. Finally, consider whether Romano's evidence in these three paragraphs seems relevant to her thesis and reasons, appropriately selective, well balanced between quotes and paraphrases, integrated smoothly into her sentences, and explained helpfully.

■ COUNTERARGUING

Asserting a thesis and backing it with reasons and support are essential to a successful argument. Thoughtful writers go further, however, by *counterarguing*—anticipating and responding to their readers' objections, challenges, and questions. To anticipate readers' concerns, try to imagine other people's points of view, what they might know about the subject, and how they might feel about it. Try also to imagine how readers would respond to your argument as it unfolds step by step. What will they be thinking and feeling? What objections would they raise? What questions would they ask?

To counterargue, writers rely on three basic strategies: acknowledging, accommodating or conceding, and refuting. Writers show they are aware of readers' objections and questions (acknowledge), modify their position to accept readers' concerns they think are legitimate (accommodate), or explicitly show why readers' objections are invalid or why their concerns are irrelevant (refute). Writers may use one or more of these three strategies in the same essay. According to research by rhetoricians and communications specialists, readers find arguments more convincing when writers have anticipated their concerns in these ways. Acknowledging readers' concerns and either accommodating or refuting them wins readers' respect, attention, and some-times even agreement.

Acknowledging Readers' Concerns

When you *acknowledge* readers' questions or objections, you show that you are aware of their point of view and you take it seriously even if you do not agree with it. In the following example, Peter Marin directly acknowledges his readers' possible concerns. These are the opening paragraphs in an article arguing that some of America's home-less have chosen that way of life. Marin knows that readers may immediately doubt this surprising assertion. It seems inconceivable that people would choose to sleep on sidewalks and eat out of garbage cans. He acknowledges three different doubts his readers may have.

> The homeless, it seems, can be roughly divided into two groups: those who have had marginality and homelessness forced upon them and want nothing more than to escape them, and a smaller number who have at least in part chosen marginality, and now accept, or, in a few cases, embrace it.
>
> I understand how dangerous it can be to introduce the idea of choice into a dis-cussion of homelessness. It can all too easily be used for all the wrong reasons by all the wrong people to justify indifference or brutality toward the homeless, or to argue that they are getting only what they deserve.
>
> And I understand, too, how complicated the notion can become: Many of the veterans on the street, or battered women, or abused and runaway children, have cho-sen this life only as the lesser of evils, and because, in this society, there is often no place else to go.
>
> And finally, I understand how much that happens on the street can combine to create an apparent acceptance of homelessness that is nothing more than the absolute absence of hope.
>
> Nonetheless we must learn to accept that there may indeed be people on the street who have seen so much of our world, or have seen it so clearly, that to live in it becomes impossible.
>
> — PETER MARIN, "Go Ask Alice"

You might think that acknowledging readers' objections in this way — addressing readers directly, listing their possible objections, and discussing each one — would weaken an argument. It might even seem reckless to suggest objections that not all readers would think of. On the contrary, however, readers who expect writers to explore an issue thoroughly respond positively to this strategy because it makes the writer seem thoughtful and reasonable, more concerned with seeking the truth than winning an argument. By researching your subject and your readers, you will be able to use this strategy confidently in your own argumentative essays. And you will learn to look for it in arguments you read and use it to make judgments about the writer's credibility.

■ **Exercise 11.9**

Richard Estrada acknowledges readers' concerns in paragraphs 6 and 7 of his essay in Chapter 5. How, specifically, does Estrada attempt to acknowledge his readers' concerns? What do you find most and least successful about his acknowledgment? How does his acknowledgment affect your judgment of his credibility?

Accommodating Readers' Concerns

To argue effectively, you must often take special care to *accommodate readers' concerns* by acknowledging their objections, questions, and alternative positions, causes, or solutions. Occasionally, however, you may have to go even further. Instead of merely acknowledging your readers' concerns, you may decide to accept some of them and incorporate them into your own argument. This strategy can be very disarming to readers. It is sometimes referred to as *concession,* for it seems to concede that opposing views have merit.

The following example comes from an essay enthusiastically endorsing email. After supporting his own reasons for this positive endorsement, the writer accommodates his readers' likely reservations by conceding that email poses certain problems.

> To be sure, egalitarianism has its limits. The ease and economy of sending email, especially to multiple recipients, makes us all vulnerable to any bore, loony, or commercial or political salesman who can get our email address. It's still a lot less intrusive than the telephone, since you can read and answer or ignore email at your own convenience. But as normal people's email starts mounting into the hundreds daily, which is bound to happen, filtering mechanisms and conventions of etiquette that are still in their primitive stage will be desperately needed.
>
> Another supposed disadvantage of email is that it discourages face-to-face communication. At Microsoft, where people routinely send email back and forth all day to the person in the next office, this is certainly true. Some people believe this tendency has more to do with the underdeveloped social skills of computer geeks than with Microsoft's role in developing the technology email relies on. I wouldn't presume to comment on that. Whether you think email replacing live conversation is a good or bad thing depends, I guess, on how much of a misanthrope you are. I like it.
>
> – MICHAEL KINSLEY, "Email Culture"

Notice that Kinsley's accommodation or concession is not grudging. He readily concedes that email brings users a lot of unwanted messages and may discourage conversation in the workplace.

■ **Exercise 11.10**

How does Patrick O'Malley attempt to accommodate readers in paragraphs 7 and 8 of his Chapter 6 essay arguing for more frequent exams? What seems successful or unsuccessful in his argument? What do his efforts at accommodation contribute to the essay?

Refuting Readers' Objections

Your readers' possible objections and views cannot always be accommodated. Sometimes they must be refuted. When you *refute readers' objections,* you assert that they are wrong and argue against them. Refutation does not have to be delivered arrogantly or dismissively, however. Writers can refute their readers' objections in a spirit of shared inquiry in solving problems, establishing probable causes, deciding the value of something, or understanding different points of view in a controversy. Differences are inevitable. Reasoned argument provides a peaceful and constructive way for informed, well-intentioned people who disagree strongly to air their differences.

In the following example, a social sciences professor refutes one argument for giving college students the opportunity to purchase lecture notes prepared by someone else. First, he concedes the possibility of accepting another viewpoint ("Now, it may well be argued..."), and then he suggests that he even agrees with this view in part ("The amphitheater lecture is indeed...scarcely to be idealized"). Ultimately, though, he refutes this objection ("Still...").

> Now, it may well be argued that universities are already shortchanging their students by stuffing them into huge lecture halls where, unlike at rock concerts or basketball games, the lecturer can't even be seen on a giant screen in real time. If they're already shortchanged with impersonal instruction, what's the harm in offering canned lecture notes?
>
> The amphitheater lecture is indeed, for all but the most engaging professors, a lesser form of instruction, and scarcely to be idealized. Still, Education by Download misses one of the keys to learning. Education is a meeting of minds, a process through which the student educes, draws from within, a response to what the teacher teaches.
>
> The very act of taking notes — not reading someone else's notes, no matter how stellar — is a way of engaging the material, wrestling with it, struggling to comprehend or take issue, but in any case entering into the work. The point is to decide, while you are listening, what matters in the presentation. And while I don't believe that most of life consists of showing up, education does begin with that — with immersing yourself in the activity at hand, listening, thinking, judging, offering active responses. A download is a poor substitute.
>
> — TODD GITLIN, "Disappearing Ink"

As this example illustrates, writers cannot simply dismiss readers' possible concerns with a wave of their hand. Gitlin states a potential objection fully and fairly but then goes on to refute it by claiming that students need to take their own lecture notes to engage and comprehend the material that is being presented to them.

Effective refutation requires a restrained tone and careful argument. Although you may not accept this particular refutation, you can agree that it is well reasoned and supported. You do not feel attacked personally because the writer disagrees with you.

■ Exercise 11.11

Analyze the use of refutation in paragraphs 7–10 of Richard Estrada's essay in Chapter 5. (If you have not read this essay, pause to skim it so that you can evaluate the refutation in the context of the whole essay.) How does Estrada signal or announce the refutation? How does he support the refutation? What is the tone of the refutation, and how effective do you think the tone would be in convincing readers to take the argument seriously?

LOGICAL FALLACIES

Fallacies are errors or flaws in reasoning. Although essentially unsound, fallacious arguments seem superficially plausible and often have great persuasive power. Fallacies are not necessarily deliberate efforts to deceive readers. Writers may introduce a fallacy accidentally by not examining their own reasons or underlying assumptions critically, by failing to establish solid support, or by using unclear or ambiguous words. Here is a summary of the most common logical fallacies (listed alphabetically):

- *Begging the question:* Arguing that a claim is true by repeating the claim in different words (sometimes called *circular reasoning*)
- *Confusing chronology with causality:* Assuming that because one thing preceded another, the former caused the latter (also called *post hoc, ergo propter hoc*—Latin for "after this, therefore because of this")
- *Either-or reasoning:* Assuming that there are only two sides to a question and representing yours as the only correct one
- *Equivocating:* Misleading or hedging with ambiguous word choices
- *Failing to accept the burden of proof:* Asserting a claim without presenting a reasoned argument to support it
- *False analogy:* Assuming that because one thing resembles another, conclusions drawn from one also apply to the other
- *Hasty generalization:* Offering only weak or limited evidence to support a conclusion
- *Overreliance on authority:* Assuming that something is true simply because an expert says so and ignoring evidence to the contrary
- *Oversimplifying:* Giving easy answers to complicated questions, often by appealing to emotions rather than logic
- *Personal attack:* Demeaning the proponents of a claim instead of refuting their argument (also called *ad hominem*—Latin for "against the man"—*attack*)
- *Red herring:* Attempting to misdirect the discussion by raising an essentially unrelated point
- *Slanting:* Selecting or emphasizing the evidence that supports your claim and suppressing or playing down other evidence
- *Slippery slope:* Pretending that one thing inevitably leads to another
- *Sob story:* Manipulating readers' emotions to lead them to draw unjustified conclusions
- *Straw man:* Directing the argument against a claim that nobody actually makes or that everyone agrees is very weak

Strategies for Field Research

12

In universities, government agencies, and the business world, field research can be as important as library research or experimental research. If you major in education, communication, or one of the social sciences, you will probably be asked to do writing based on your own observations, interviews, and questionnaire results. You will also read large amounts of information based on these methods of learning about individuals, groups, and institutions. You also might use observations or interviews to help you select or gain background for a service-learning project.

Observations and interviews are essential for writing profiles (Chapter 3). In proposing a solution to a problem (Chapter 6), you might want to interview people involved; or if many people are affected, you might find it useful to prepare a questionnaire. In writing to explain an academic concept (Chapter 4), you might want to interview a faculty member who is a specialist on the subject. As you consider how you might use such research most appropriately, ask your instructor whether your institution requires you to obtain approval for your field research.

■ OBSERVATIONS

This section offers guidelines for planning an observational visit, taking notes on your observations, writing them up, and preparing for follow-up visits. Some kinds of writing are based on observations from single visits — travel writing, social workers' case reports, insurance investigators' accident reports — but most observational writing is based on several visits. An anthropologist or a sociologist studying an unfamiliar group or activity might observe it for months, filling several notebooks with notes. If you are profiling a place (Chapter 3), you almost certainly will want to make more than one observational visit, some of them perhaps combined with interviews.

Second and third visits to observe further are important because as you learn more about a place from initial observations, interviews, or reading, you will discover new ways to look at it. Gradually, you will have more and more questions that can be answered only by follow-up visits.

Planning the Visit

To ensure that your observational visits are productive, you must plan them carefully.

Getting Access.   If the place you propose to visit is public, you will probably have easy access to it. If everything you need to see is within view of anyone passing by or using the place, you can make your observations without any special arrangements. Indeed, you may not even be noticed. However, most observational visits require special access. Hence, you will need to arrange your visit, calling ahead or stopping by to introduce yourself, state your purpose, and get acquainted. Find out the times you may visit, and be certain you can gain access easily.

Announcing Your Intentions.   State your intentions directly and fully. Say who you are, where you are from, and what you hope to do. You may be surprised at how receptive people can be to a college student on assignment for a class or a service-learning project. Not every place you wish to visit will welcome you, however. In addition, private businesses as well as public institutions place a variety of constraints on outside visitors. But generally, if people know your intentions, they may be able to tell you about aspects of a place or an activity you would not have thought to observe.

Taking Your Tools.   Take a notebook with a firm back so that you will have a steady writing surface. Remember also to take a pen. Some observers dictate their observations into a tape recorder and transcribe their notes later. You might want to experiment with this method. We recommend, though, that you record your first observations in writing. Your instructor or other students in your class may want to see your notes, and transcribing a recording can take a lot of time.

Observing and Taking Notes

Here are some basic guidelines for observing and taking notes.

Observing.   Some activities invite the observer to watch from multiple vantage points, whereas others may limit the observer to a single perspective. Take advantage of every perspective available to you. Come in close, take a middle position, and stand back. Study the scene from a stationary position, and then try to move around it. The more varied your perspectives, the more details you are likely to observe.

Your purposes in observing are twofold: to describe the activity or place and to analyze it. Therefore, you will want to look closely at the activity or place itself, and you will also want to discover the perspective you want to take on it and develop insights into it.

Try initially to be an innocent observer: Pretend that you have never seen anything like this activity or place before. Then consider your own and your readers' likely preconceptions. Ask yourself what details are surprising and what reinforces expectations.

Taking Notes. You will undoubtedly find your own style of notetaking, but here are a few pointers.

- Write on only one side of the page. Later, when you organize your notes, you may want to cut up the pages and file notes under different headings.
- Take notes in words, phrases, or sentences. Draw diagrams or sketches if they will help you see and understand the place or activity or recall details of it later on.
- Use abbreviations as much as you like, but use them consistently and clearly.
- Note any ideas or questions that occur to you.
- If you are expecting to see a certain behavior, try not to let this expectation influence what you actually do see.
- Use quotation marks around any overheard remarks or conversations you record.

Perhaps the most important advice about notetaking during an observational visit is to record as many details as possible about the place or activity and to write down your insights (ideas, interpretations, judgments) as they come to mind. Do not focus on taking notes in a systematic way. Be flexible. Later you will have the chance to reorganize your notes and fill in gaps. At the same time, however, you want to be sure to include details about the setting, the people, and your reactions.

The Setting. Describe the setting: Name or list objects you see there, and then record details of some of them — their color, shape, size, texture, function, relation to similar or dissimilar objects. Although your notes will probably contain mainly visual details, you might also want to record details about sounds and smells. Be sure to include some notes about the shape, dimensions, and layout of the place as a whole. How big is it? How is it organized?

The People. Note the number of people you observe, their activities, their movements and behavior. Describe their appearance or dress. Record parts of overheard conversations. Indicate whether you see more men than women, more members of one nationality or ethnic group than of another, more older than younger people. Most important, note anything surprising, interesting, or unusual about the people and how they interact with each other.

Your Personal Reactions. Write down your impressions, questions, ideas, or insights as they occur to you.

Reflecting on Your Observations

Immediately after your observational visit (within a few minutes, if possible), find a quiet place to reflect on what you saw, review your notes, and fill in any gaps with additional details or ideas. Give yourself at least a half-hour to add to your notes and to write a few sentences about your perspective on the place or activity. Ask yourself the following questions:

- What did I learn from my observational visit?
- How did what I observed fit my own or my readers' likely preconceptions of the place or activity?
- What perspective on the place do my notes seem to convey?
- What, if anything, seemed contradictory or out of place?

Writing Up Your Notes

Your instructor may ask you to write up your notes on the observational visit, as Brian Cable did after visiting the Goodbody mortuary for his profile essay "The Last Stop" in Chapter 3. If so, review your notes, looking for a meaningful pattern in the details you have noted down. You might find clustering (p. 324) or taking inventory (p. 344) useful for discovering patterns in your notes.

Assume that your readers have never been to the place, and decide on the perspective of the place you want to convey to them. Choose details that will convey this. Then draft a brief description of the place. Your purpose is to select details from your notes that will help readers imagine the place and understand it.

■ Exercise 12.1

Arrange to meet with a small group (three or four students) for an observational visit somewhere on campus, such as the student center, campus gym, cafeteria or restaurant, or any other place where some activity is going on. Take notes by assigning each person in your group a specific task; one person can take notes on the appearance of the people, for example; another can take notes on their activities; another on their conversations; and another on what the place looks and smells like. Take about twenty to thirty minutes, and then report to each other on your observations. This will give you some good practice on what you will need to do when you observe on your own, and you will get to see some of the difficulties associated with observing people and places.

Preparing for Follow-Up Visits

Rather than repeat yourself in follow-up visits, try to build on what you have already discovered. You should probably do some interviewing and reading before another observational visit so that you will have a greater understanding of the subject when you observe it again. You might want to present your notes from your first visit to your instructor or to a small group from your class so that you could use their responses as well, especially if you are working on a specific assignment such as a profile. It is also important to develop a plan for your follow-up visits: questions to be answered, insights to be tested, types of information you would like to discover.

■ INTERVIEWS

Like making observations, interviewing tends to involve four basic steps: (1) planning and setting up the interview, (2) taking notes during the interview, (3) reflecting on the interview, and (4) writing up your notes.

Planning and Setting Up the Interview

The initial steps in interviewing involve choosing an interview subject and then arranging and planning for the interview.

Choosing an Interview Subject.   First, choose someone to interview. If you are writing about some activity in which several people are involved, choose subjects representing a variety of perspectives—a range of roles, for example. For a profile of a single person, most or all of your interviews would be with that person. But for a service-learning project, for instance, you might interview several members of an organization to gain a more complete picture of its mission or activities. You should be flexible because you may be unable to speak with the person you initially targeted and may wind up interviewing someone else—the person's assistant, perhaps. Do not assume that this interview subject will be of little use to you. With the right questions, you might even learn more from the assistant than you would from the person you had originally expected to see.

Arranging an Interview.   You may be nervous about calling up a busy person and asking for some of his or her time. Indeed, you may get turned down. But if so, it is possible that you will be referred to someone who will see you, someone whose job it is to talk to the public.

Do not feel that just because you are a student, you do not have the right to ask for people's time. You will be surprised at how delighted people are to be asked about themselves, particularly if you reach them when they are not feeling harried. Most people love to talk—about anything! And since you are a student on assignment, some people may feel that they are performing a public service by talking with you.

When introducing yourself to arrange the interview, give a short and simple description of your project. If you talk too much, you could prejudice or limit the interviewee's response. At the same time, it is a good idea to exhibit some sincere enthusiasm for your project. If you lack enthusiasm, the person may see little reason to talk with you.

Keep in mind that the person you want to interview will be donating valuable time to you. Be certain that you call ahead to arrange a specific time for the interview. Arrive on time. Dress appropriately. Bring all the materials you need. Express your thanks when the interview is over. Finally, try to represent your institution well, whether your interview is for a single course assignment or part of a larger service-learning project.

Planning for the Interview.   The best interview is generally the well-planned interview. Making an observational visit and doing some background reading beforehand
can be helpful. In preparation for the interview, you should consider your objectives
and prepare some questions.

Think about your main objectives:

- Do you want an orientation to the place or your topic (the "big picture") from
this interview?

- Do you want this interview to lead you to interviews with other key people?

- Do you want mainly facts or opinions?

- Do you need to clarify something you have heard in another interview, observed,
or read?

- Do you want to learn more about the person, the place, or the activity through
the interview—or all of these?

The key to good interviewing is flexibility. You may be looking for facts, but your
interview subject may not have any to offer. In that case, you should be able to shift
gears and go after whatever your subject is in a position to discuss. Be aware that the
person you are interviewing represents only one point of view. You may need to speak
with several people to get a more complete picture. Talking with more than one person may also help you discover contradictions or problems that could contribute to
the significance you decide to emphasize.

Composing Questions.   Take care in composing the questions you prepare in advance; they can be the key to a successful interview. Any question that places unfair
limits on respondents is a bad question. Avoid forced-choice questions and leading
questions.

Forced-choice questions impose your terms on respondents. If you are interviewing
a counselor at a campus rape crisis center and want to know what he or she thinks is
the motivation for rape, you could ask this question: "Do you think rape is an expression of passion or of power and anger?" But the counselor might not think that either
passion or power and anger satisfactorily explain the motivation for rape. A better way
to phrase the question would be as follows: "People often fall into two camps on the
issue of rape. Some think it is an expression of passion, while others argue it is an
expression of anger and insecurity. Do you think it is either of these? If not, what is
your opinion?" Phrasing the question in this way allows the interviewee to react to
what others have said but also gives the interviewee freedom to set the terms for his or
her response.

Leading questions assume too much. An example of this kind of question is this:
"Do you think the number of rapes has increased because women are perceived as
competitors in a highly competitive economy?" This question assumes that there is an
increase in the occurrence of rape, that women are perceived (apparently by rapists) as
economic competitors, and that the state of the economy is somehow related to acts
of rape. A better way of asking the question might be to make the assumptions more

explicit by dividing the question into its parts: "Do you think the number of rapes has increased? What could have caused this increase? I've heard some people argue that the economy has something to do with it. Do you think so? Do you think rapists perceive women as competitors for jobs? Could the current economic situation have made this competition more severe?"

Good questions come in many different forms. One way of considering them is to divide them into two basic types: open and closed. *Open questions* give the respondent range and flexibility. They also generate anecdotes, personal revelations, and expressions of attitudes. *Closed questions* usually request specific information.

Suppose you are interviewing a small-business owner, for example. You might begin with a specific (closed) question about when the business was established and then follow up with an open-ended question such as, "Could you take a few minutes to tell me something about your early days in the business? I'd be interested to hear how it got started, what your hopes were, and what problems you had to face." Consider asking directly for an anecdote ("What happened when your employees threatened to strike?"), encouraging reflection ("What do you think has helped you most? What has hampered you?"), or soliciting advice ("What advice would you give to someone trying to start a new business today?"). Here are some examples of open and closed questions:

Open Questions

- What do you think about *(name a person or an event)*?
- Describe your reaction when *(name an event)* happened.
- Tell me about a time you were *(name an emotion)*.

Closed Questions

- How do you *(name a process)*?
- What does *(name a word or phrase)* mean?
- What does *(name a person, object, or place)* look like?
- How was it made?

The best questions encourage the subject to talk freely but to the point. If an answer strays too far from the point, you may need to ask a follow-up question to refocus the talk. Another tack you might want to try is to rephrase the subject's answer, to say something like "Let me see if I have this right" or "Am I correct in saying that you feel...?" Often, a person will take the opportunity to amplify the original response by adding just the anecdote or quotable comment you have been looking for.

Bringing Your Tools. As for an observational visit, when you interview someone, you will need a notebook with a firm back so you can write in it easily without the benefit of a table or desk. You might find it useful to divide several pages into two columns by drawing a line about one-third of the width of the page from the left margin. Use the left-hand column to note details about the scene, the person, the mood of the interview, and other impressions. Head this column *Details and Impressions*. At the top of the right-hand column, write several questions. You may not use them, but they will jog your memory. This column should be titled *Information*. In it, you will record what you learn from answers to your questions.

Taking Notes during the Interview

Because you are not taking a verbatim transcript of the interview (if you want a literal account, use a tape recorder or shorthand), your goals are to gather information and to record a few quotable bits of information, comments, and anecdotes. In addition, because the people you interview may be unused to giving interviews and so will need to know you are paying attention, it is probably a good idea to do more listening than notetaking. You may not have much confidence in your memory, but if you pay close attention, you are likely to recall a good deal of the conversation afterward. Take some notes during the interview: a few quotations; key words and phrases; details of the scene, the person, and the mood of the interview. Remember that how something is said is as important as what is said. Look for material that will give texture to your writing—gesture, verbal inflection, facial expression, body language, physical appearance, dress, hair, or anything that makes the person an individual.

Reflecting on the Interview

As soon as you finish the interview, find a quiet place to reflect on it and review your notes. This reflection is essential because so much happens in an interview that you cannot record at the time. Spend at least a half-hour adding to your notes and thinking about what you learned.

At the end of this time, write a few sentences about your main impressions from the interview. Ask yourself these questions:

- What did I learn?
- What seemed contradictory or surprising about the interview?
- How did what was said fit my own or my readers' likely expectations about the person, activity, or place?
- How can I summarize my impressions?

Writing Up Your Notes

Your instructor may ask you to write up your interview notes. If so, review them for useful details and ideas. Decide what perspective you want to make on this person. Choose details that will contribute to this perspective. Select quotations and paraphrases of information you learned from the person.

You might also review notes from any related observations or other interviews, especially if you plan to combine these materials in a profile, ethnographic study, or other project.

■ QUESTIONNAIRES

Questionnaires let you survey the opinions and knowledge of large numbers of people. You could carry out many face-to-face or phone interviews to get the same information, but questionnaires have the advantages of economy, efficiency, and anonymity. Some questionnaires, such as the ones you filled out when entering college, just collect demographic information: your name, age, sex, hometown, religious preference, intended major. Others, such as the Gallup and Harris polls, collect opinions on a wide range of issues. Before elections, we are bombarded with the results of such polls. Still other kinds of questionnaires, such as those used in academic research, are designed to help answer important questions about personal and societal problems.

This section briefly outlines procedures you can follow to carry out an informal questionnaire survey of people's opinions or knowledge and then write up the results. There are many good texts on designing questionnaires. A sample questionnaire appears below (Figure 12.1).

Figure 12.1 Sample Questionnaire: Scheduling at the Student Health Clinic

This is a survey about the scheduling of appointments at the campus Student Health Clinic. Your participation will help determine how long students have to wait to use clinic services and how these services might be more conveniently scheduled. The survey should take only 3 to 4 minutes to complete. All responses are confidential. Thank you for your participation.

1. Have you ever made an appointment at the clinic?   (Circle one.)

   Yes   No

2. How frequently have you had to wait more than 10 minutes at the clinic for a scheduled appointment?   (Circle one.)

   Always   Usually   Occasionally   Never

3. Have you ever had to wait more than 30 minutes at the clinic for a scheduled appointment?   (Circle one.)

   Yes   No   Uncertain

4. From your experience so far with the clinic, how would you rank its system for scheduling appointments?   (Circle one.)

0	1	2	3	4	5
no experience	inadequate	poor	adequate	good	outstanding

5. Given your present work and class schedule, when are you able to visit the clinic? (Check all applicable responses.)

_____ 8–10 A.M.   _____ 1–3 P.M.
_____ 10 A.M.–Noon   _____ 3–5 P.M.
_____ 12–1 P.M.

6. Given your present work and class schedule, which times during the day (Monday through Friday) would be the most and least convenient for you to schedule appointments at the clinic? (Rank the four choices from *1* for most convenient time to *4* for least convenient time.)

_____ Morning (7 A.M.–Noon)   _____ Dinnertime (5–7 P.M.)
_____ Afternoon (12–5 P.M.)   _____ Evening (7–10 P.M.)

7. How would you evaluate your most recent appointment at the clinic?

8. Based on your experiences with scheduling at the clinic, what advice would you give to other students about making appointments?

9. What do you believe would most improve the scheduling of appointments at the clinic?

10. If you have additional comments about scheduling at the clinic, please write them on the back of this page.

Focusing Your Study

A questionnaire survey usually has a limited focus. You might need to interview a few people to find this focus. Or you may already have a limited focus in mind. If you are developing a questionnaire as part of a service-learning project, discuss your focus with your supervisor or other staff members.

As an example, let us assume that you go to your campus student health clinic and have to wait over an hour to see a doctor. Sitting in the waiting room with many other students, you decide that this long wait is a problem that would be an ideal topic for a writing assignment you have been asked to do for your writing class, an essay proposing a solution to a problem (Chapter 6).

You do not have to explore the entire operation of the clinic to study this problem. You are not interested in how nurses and doctors are hired or in how efficient the clinic's system of ordering supplies is, for example. Your primary interests are how long students usually wait for appointments, what times are most convenient for students to schedule appointments, how the clinic accommodates students when demand is high, and whether the long wait discourages many students from getting the treatment they need. With this limited focus, you can collect valuable information using a fairly brief questionnaire. To be certain about your focus, however, you should talk informally with several students to find out whether they also think there is a problem with appointment scheduling at the clinic. You might want to talk with staff members, too, explaining your plans and asking for their views on the problem.

Whatever your interest, be sure to limit the scope of your survey. Try to focus on one or two important questions. With a limited focus, your questionnaire can be brief, and people will be more willing to fill it out. In addition, a survey based on a limited amount of information will be easier to organize and report on.

Writing Questions

The same two basic types of questions used for interviews, closed and open, are also useful in questionnaires. Figure 12.1 illustrates how these types of questions may be employed in the context of a questionnaire about the student health clinic problem. Notice that the questionnaire uses several forms of *closed questions* (in items 1–6): two-way questions, multiple-choice questions, ranking scales, and checklists. You will probably use more than one form of closed question in a questionnaire to collect different kinds of information. The sample questionnaire also uses several *open questions* (items 7–10) that ask for brief written answers. You may want to combine closed and open questions in your questionnaire because both offer advantages: Closed questions will give you definite answers, while open questions can elicit information you may not have anticipated as well as provide lively quotations for your essay explaining what you have learned.

Whatever types of questions you develop, try to phrase them in a fair and unbiased manner so that your results will be reliable and credible. As soon as you have a collection of possible questions, try them out on a few typical respondents. You need to know which questions are unclear, which seem to duplicate others, and which provide the most interesting responses. These tryouts will enable you to assess which questions will give you the information you need. Readers can also help you come up with additional questions.

Designing the Questionnaire

Begin your questionnaire with a brief, clear introduction stating the purpose of your survey and explaining how you intend to use the results. Give advice on answering the questions, and estimate the amount of time needed to complete the questionnaire (see Figure 12.1 for an example). You may opt to give this information orally if you plan to hand the questionnaire to groups of people and have them fill it out immediately.

However, even in this case, your respondents will appreciate a written introduction that clarifies what you expect and helps keep them on track.

Select your most promising questions, and decide how to order them. Any logical order is appropriate. You might want to arrange the questions from least to most complicated or from general to specific. You may find it appropriate to group the questions by subject matter or format. Certain questions may lead to others. You might want to place open questions at the end (see Figure 12.1 for an example).

Design your questionnaire so that it looks attractive and readable. Make it look easy to complete. Do not crowd questions together to save paper. Provide plenty of space for readers to answer questions, especially open questions, and encourage them to use the back of the page if they need more space.

Testing the Questionnaire

Make a few copies of your first-draft questionnaire, and ask at least three readers to complete it. Time them as they respond, or ask them to keep track of how long they take to complete it. Discuss with them any confusion or problems they experience. Review their responses with them to be certain that each question is eliciting the information you want it to elicit. From what you learn, reconsider your questionnaire, and make any necessary revisions to your questions and design or format.

Administering the Questionnaire

Decide who you want to fill out your questionnaire and how you can arrange for them to do so. The more respondents you have, the better, but constraints of time and expense will almost certainly limit the number. You can mail or email questionnaires, distribute them to dormitories, or send them to campus or workplace mailboxes, but the return will be low. Half the people receiving questionnaires in the mail usually fail to return them. If you do mail the questionnaire, be sure to mention the deadline for returning it. Give directions for its return, and include a stamped, self-addressed envelope, if necessary. Instead of mailing the questionnaire, you might want to arrange to distribute it yourself to groups of people in class or around campus, at dormitory meetings, or at work.

Note that if you want to do a formal questionnaire study, you will need a scientifically representative group of readers (a random or stratified random sample). Even for an informal study, you should try to get a reasonably representative group. For example, to study satisfaction with appointment scheduling at the clinic, you would want to include students who have been to the clinic as well as those who have avoided it. You might even want to include a concentration of seniors rather than first-year students because, after four years, seniors would have made more visits to the clinic. If many students commute, you would want to be sure to have commuters among your respondents. Your essay will be more convincing if you demonstrate that your respondents represent the group whose opinions or knowledge you claim to be studying. As few as twenty-five respondents could be adequate for an informal study.

Writing Up the Results

Once you have the completed questionnaires, what do you do with them?

Summarizing the Results. Begin by tallying the results from the closed questions. Take an unused questionnaire, and tally the responses next to each choice. Suppose that you had administered the student health clinic questionnaire to twenty-five students. Here is how the tally might look for the checklist in question 5 of Figure 12.1.

5. Given your present work and class schedule, when are you able to visit the clinic? (Check all applicable responses.)

_____ 8–10 A.M. ~~THL THL THL~~ III *(18)*   _____ 1–3 P.M. III *(3)*

_____ 10 A.M.–Noon ~~THL~~ II *(7)*   _____ 3–5 P.M. ~~THL~~ IIII *(9)*

_____ 12–1 P.M. ~~THL THL~~ III *(13)*

Each tally mark represents one response to that item. The totals add up to more than twenty-five because respondents were asked to check all the times when they could make appointments.

Next, consider the open questions. Read all respondents' answers to each question separately to see the kinds and variety of responses they gave. Then decide whether you want to code any of the open questions so that you can summarize results from them quantitatively, as you would with closed questions. For example, you might want to classify the types of advice given as responses to question 8 in the clinic questionnaire: "Based on your experiences with scheduling at the clinic, what advice would you give to other students about making appointments?" You could then report the numbers of respondents (of your twenty-five) who gave each type of advice. For an opinion question (for example, "How would you evaluate your most recent appointment at the clinic?"), you might simply code the answers as positive, neutral, or negative and then tally the results accordingly for each kind of response. However, the responses to most open questions are used as a source of quotations for your report or essay.

You can give the results from the closed questions as percentages, either within the text itself or in one or more tables. You can find table formats in texts you may be using or even in magazines or newspapers. Conventional table formats for the social sciences are illustrated in the *Publication Manual of the American Psychological Association,* Fifth Edition (Washington, DC: American Psychological Association, 2001).

Because readers' interests can be engaged more easily with quotations than with percentages, plan to use open responses in your essay. You can quote responses to the open questions within your text, perhaps weaving them into your discussion like quoted material from published sources. Or you can organize several responses into lists and then comment on them.

You can use computer spreadsheet programs to tabulate the results from closed questions and even print out tables or graphs that you can insert into your essay. For a small, informal survey, however, such programs will probably not save you much time.

Organizing the Write-up.   In organizing your results, you might want to consider a plan that is commonly followed in the social sciences.

Reporting Your Survey

Statement of the problem

     Context for your study

     The question or questions you wanted to answer

     Need for your survey

     Brief preview of your survey and plan for your report

Review of other related surveys (if you know of any)

Procedures

     Questionnaire design

     Selection of participants

     Administration of the questionnaire

     Summary of the results

Results: Presentation of what you learned, with limited commentary or interpretation

Summary and discussion

     Brief summary of your results

     Brief discussion of their significance (commenting, interpreting, exploring implications, and possibly comparing to other related surveys)

Strategies for Library and Internet Research

Research requires patience, careful planning, good advice, and even luck. The rewards are many, however. Each new research project leads you to unexplored regions of the library or of cyberspace. You may find yourself in a rare-book room reading a manuscript written hundreds of years ago or involved in a lively discussion on the Internet with people hundreds of miles away. One moment you may be keyboarding commands, and the next you may be threading a microfilm reader, viewing a videodisk, or squinting at the fine print in an index. You may breeze through an encyclopedia entry introducing you to a new subject or struggle with a just-published report of a highly technical research study on the same subject.

This chapter is designed to help you learn how to use the resources available in your college library and on the Internet. It gives advice on how to learn about the library and the Internet, develop efficient search strategies, keep track of your research, locate appropriate sources, and read them with a critical eye. Chapter 14 provides guidelines for using and acknowledging these sources in an essay.

■ INTEGRATING LIBRARY AND INTERNET RESEARCH

Although this chapter includes separate sections on the library and the Internet, these two ways to find research information are closely intertwined. You can often use the Internet to access many of the library's resources—the catalog of books and other items, indexes to periodical articles, and other kinds of electronic databases—from your own computer in your home or dorm room. On the other hand, you will need or want to go through the library's computers rather than your own to access many Web-based resources, including those that charge fees for subscriptions or for downloading and printing out documents.

For most research topics, you will need to find source materials both in the library and on the Internet because each offers material not available from the other. The vast majority of books and articles published in print are not available online, and so you will almost certainly need to consult some of these print sources to avoid getting a skewed perspective on your topic, especially if it deals with events that occurred more than a few years ago. As discussed later in this chapter, print sources also tend to offer more reliable information than online ones. Likewise, though, very little online material ever appears in print, and especially for current topics, you will almost certainly want to check the Web for the latest developments or research findings. Compared with print sources, online sources usually take less time and effort both to find and to integrate into your own writing. So in some ways, they can help you do a more thorough job of research within the time available to you. Still, be careful not to rely too heavily on the Web just because it is easy to use.

■ ORIENTING YOURSELF TO THE LIBRARY

To conduct research in most college libraries, you will need to become familiar with a wide variety of resources. Public-access catalogs, almost all of them now electronic, provide information on books. Periodical indexes and abstracts, used to locate magazine and journal articles, are available both in print volumes and in various electronic forms: on CD-ROMs, through the library catalog, or through the World Wide Web. The materials you find may be in print, in reduced-size photographic formats like microfilm and microfiche that require special machines to read, or in electronic text files accessible through an electronic periodical index or library Web site.

Taking a Tour

Make a point of getting acquainted with your campus library. Your instructor may arrange a library orientation tour for your composition class. If not, you can join one of the regular orientation tours scheduled by the librarians or design your own tour (for suggestions, see Table 13.1). Because nearly all college libraries are more complex and offer more services than typical high school or public libraries, you will need to learn how your campus library's catalog and reference room are organized, how you can access computer catalogs and databases, whom to ask for help if you are confused, and where you can find books, periodicals, and other materials.

Nearly every college library offers a Web site and handouts describing its resources and services. Pick up copies of any available pamphlets and guidelines. Also look for a floor map of materials and facilities. See whether your library offers any research guidelines, special workshops, or presentations on strategies for locating resources. Many library Web sites offer tutorials for using the library's electronic resources.

Consulting a Librarian

Think of college librarians as instructors whose job is to help you understand the library and get your hands on sources you need to complete your research projects. Librarians at the information or reference desk are there to provide reference services, and most have years of experience answering the very questions you are likely to ask. You should not hesitate to approach them with any questions you have about locating

Table 13.1 Designing Your Self-Guided Library Tour

Here is a list of important locations or departments to look for in your college library.

Library Location	*What You Can Do at These Locations*
Loan desk	Obtain library cards, check out materials, place holds and recalls, pay fees or fines.
Reference desk	Obtain help from reference librarians to locate and use library resources.
Information desk	Ask general and directional questions.
Reserves desk	Gain access to books and journal articles that are on reserve for specific classes.
Interlibrary loan department	Request materials not available on site.
Public-access computers	Gain access to the library catalog, electronic periodical indexes and abstracts, the campus network, and the Internet.
Current periodicals	Locate unbound current issues of newspapers, journals, and magazines.
Directories of books and journals	Use directories to find the location of books and journals shelved by call numbers.
Reference collection	Find reference materials such as encyclopedias, dictionaries, handbooks, atlases, bibliographies, statistics, and periodical indexes and abstracts.
Government publications department	Locate publications from federal, state, and local government agencies.
Multimedia resources	Locate nonprint materials such as videos, CD-ROMs, and audiotapes.
Microforms	Locate materials on microfilm (reels) and microfiche (cards).
Special collections	Find rare and valuable materials not readily available in most library collections; in larger libraries only.
Archives	Find archival materials, collections of papers from important individuals and organizations that provide source material for original research (in larger libraries only).
Maps and atlases	Locate maps and atlases in a special location because of their size and format.
Copy service	Use self-service and special-function copiers.
Reading rooms	Read in quiet, comfortable areas.
Study rooms	Study in rooms reserved for individuals or small groups.

sources. Remember, however, that they can be most helpful when you can explain your research assignment clearly and ask questions that are as specific as possible. You need not do so face-to-face: Many library Web sites now offer "virtual reference" chat rooms that connect library users to a reference librarian who can offer advice, send electronic documents, and demonstrate electronic searches.

Knowing Your Research Task

Before you go to the library to start an assigned research project, learn as much as you can about the assignment. Ask your instructor to clarify any confusing terms and to define the purpose and scope of the project. Find out how you can narrow or focus the project once you begin the research. Asking a question or two in advance can prevent hours—or even days—of misdirected work. Should you need to ask a librarian for advice, have the assignment in writing. You should try to get to the library as soon as you understand the assignment. If many of your classmates will be working on similar projects, you may be competing with them for a limited number of books and other resources.

■ A LIBRARY SEARCH STRATEGY

For your library research to be manageable and productive, you will want to work carefully and systematically. Although specific search strategies may vary to fit the needs of individual research tasks, the general process presented in Figure 13.1 should help you get started, keep track of all your research, use library materials to get an overview of your subject, locate the sources you need, and read those sources with a critical eye. Remember that research is a recursive, repetitive process, not a linear one. You will be constantly refining and revising your research strategy as you find out more about your topic.

■ KEEPING TRACK OF YOUR RESEARCH

As you research your topic, you will want to keep a careful record of all the sources you locate by setting up a working bibliography. You will also want to take notes on your sources in some systematic way.

Keeping a Working Bibliography

A *working bibliography* is a preliminary, ongoing record of books, articles, Web sites— all the sources of information you discover as you research your subject. In addition, you can use your working bibliography to keep track of any encyclopedias, bibliographies, and indexes you consult, even though these general sources are not identified in an essay.

Each entry in a working bibliography is called a *bibliographic citation*. The information you record in each bibliographic citation will help you to locate the source in the library and then, if you end up using it in your paper, to *cite* or *document* it in the final *bibliography*—the list of references or works cited you provide at the end of an essay. Recording this information for each possible source as you identify it, rather than reconstructing it later, will save you hours of work. In addition to the bibliographic information, note the library location where the source is kept and any index

Know your research task
- Keep a research journal
- Keep a working bibliography
- Take notes

Get an overview of your topic
- Look in encyclopedias and subject dictionaries
- Review textbooks
- Explore Internet sites
- Check factual information, correct spelling of terms, dates, etc.
- Construct a list of keywords and phrases
- Develop a preliminary topic statement

Use subject guides to identify possible sources of information on specific topics

Conduct a preliminary search for sources, using keywords and subject headings
- Check the online catalog for books
- Check periodical indexes for references to articles
- Check Internet sites

Evaluate and refine your search by asking yourself
- Is this what I expected to find?
- Am I finding too much?
- Am I finding enough?
- Do I need to modify my keywords?
- Do I need to recheck background sources?
- Do I need to modify my topic statement?

Refine your search based on the answers

Locate sources
- Books
- Magazine and journal articles
- Newspapers
- Internet sites
- Government and statistical sources
- Other sources appropriate to your topic

Read your sources with a critical eye
- For information
- For relevance
- For accuracy
- For comprehensiveness
- For bias
- For currency

Continue to evaluate and refine your search strategy based on the research results

Figure 13.1 Overview of an Information Search Strategy

or other reference work where you learned about it, just in case you have to track it down again. (See Figures 13.2 and 13.3 below for guidelines on how to record bibliographic and other information for a book or a print article. For guidelines for Internet sources, see p. 421.)

As you locate books in the library, record this information in your working bibliography for each book you look up.

Author: _____

Title: _____

Place of publication: _____

Publisher: _____

Date of publication: _____

Library where book is located: _____

Call number: _____

Special location (such as in reference or government publications dept.): _____

Is the book available or checked out?: _____

Figure 13.2 Information for Working Bibliography—Books

As you locate articles in the library, record this information in your working bibliography for each article you look up.

Author of article: _____

Title of article: _____

Title of journal: _____

Volume number: _____ Issue number: _____

Date of issue: _____ Inclusive page numbers: _____

Library and special location: _____

Index where you found the article: _____

Figure 13.3 Information for Working Bibliography—Periodical Articles

Confirm with your instructor which documentation style is required for your assignment so that you can follow that style for all the sources you put into your working bibliography. Chapter 14 presents two common documentation styles — one adopted by the Modern Language Association (MLA) and widely used in the humanities and the other advocated by the American Psychological Association (APA) and used in the social sciences. Individual disciplines often have their own preferred styles of documentation.

Practiced researchers keep their working bibliography on index cards, in a notebook, or in a computer file. Many researchers find index cards convenient because the cards are easy to arrange in the alphabetical order required for the list of works cited or references. Others find cards too easy to lose and prefer instead to keep everything — working bibliography, notes, and drafts — in one notebook. Researchers who use computers for their working bibliography can either record the information in a file in their word processing program or use one of the software programs that format the information according to a preset documentation style (such as MLA or APA) or a customized style created by the user. These programs can also create and insert the citations that are required — within the essay text or in footnotes or endnotes — and can format the final list of works cited. Some programs can even download source information from electronic indexes and other databases into a bibliographic file and then automatically format the information.

Whether you use index cards, a notebook, or a computer file for your working bibliography, your entries need to be accurate and complete. If the call number for a book is incomplete or inaccurate, for example, you will not be able to find the book in the stacks. If the author's name is misspelled, you may have trouble finding the book in the catalog. If the volume number for a periodical is incorrect, you may not be able to locate the article. If you get the bibliographic information from a catalog or index, check it when you examine the source directly.

Taking Notes

After you have identified some possible sources and found them in print or online, you will want to begin taking notes. If you can make a photocopy of the relevant parts or download them onto your computer, you may want to annotate on the page or on the screen. Otherwise, you should paraphrase, summarize, and outline useful information as separate notes. In addition, you will want to record quotations you might want to use in your essay. (Outlining, paraphrasing, and summarizing are discussed in Chapter 10, and quoting is discussed in Chapter 14.)

You may already have a method of notetaking you prefer. Some researchers like to use index cards for notes as well as for their working bibliography. They use 3- by 5-inch cards for their bibliography and larger ones (4- by 6-inch or 5- by 7-inch) for notes, and some also use cards of different colors to organize their notes. Other people prefer to keep their notes in a notebook, and still others enter their notes into a computer file. Whatever method you use, be sure to keep accurate notes.

Careful notetaking is the most important way to minimize the risks of misquoting and of copying facts incorrectly. Another common error in notetaking is copying an author's words without enclosing them in quotation marks. This error leads easily to *plagiarism,* the unacknowledged and therefore improper use of another's words or ideas. Double-check all your notes, and be as accurate as you can. (For other tips on avoiding plagiarism, see Chapter 14, pp. 439–40.)

You might consider photocopying materials from print sources that look especially promising. All libraries house photocopy machines or offer a copying service. Photocopying can facilitate your work, allowing you to reread and analyze important sources as well as to highlight material you may wish to quote, summarize, or paraphrase. However, because photocopying can be costly, you will want to be selective. Be sure to photocopy title pages or other publication information for each source you copy, or write this information on the photocopied text, especially if you are copying excerpts from several sources. Bring paper clips or a stapler with you to the library to help keep your photocopies organized.

For electronic sources you find in the library, download the material to a disk, and print it out if at all possible, especially if the source is on the Web. Downloading gives you the same options for rereading, highlighting, and annotating as photocopying does, and the printout serves as a "hard copy" in case the source changes or disappears. Be sure the printout or the working-bibliography entry includes all the information required by the documentation system you are using.

■ GETTING STARTED

"But where do I start?" That common question is easily answered. You first need an overview of your topic. If you are researching a concept or an issue in a course you are taking, a bibliography in your textbook or your course materials provides the obvious starting point. Your instructor can advise you about other sources that provide overviews of your topic. If your topic is currently in the news, you will want to consult newspapers, magazines, or Internet sites. For all other topics—and for background information—encyclopedias and disciplinary (subject) guides are often the place to start. They introduce you to diverse aspects of a subject that might lead you to find a focus for your research.

Consulting Encyclopedias

General encyclopedias, such as the *Encyclopaedia Britannica* and the *Encyclopedia Americana,* give basic information about many topics; however, general encyclopedias alone are not adequate resources for college research. Specialized encyclopedias cover topics in the depth appropriate for college writing. In addition to providing an overview of a topic, a specialized encyclopedia often includes an explanation of issues related to the topic, definitions of specialized terminology, and selective bibliographies of additional sources.

As starting points, specialized encyclopedias have two distinct advantages: (1) They provide a comprehensive introduction to key terms related to your topic, terms that are especially useful in identifying the subject headings used to locate material in catalogs and indexes, and (2) they provide a comprehensive presentation of a subject, enabling you to see many possibilities for focusing your research on one aspect of it.

The following list identifies some specialized encyclopedias in the major academic disciplines:

ART	*Dictionary of Art*. 34 vols. 1996.
BIOLOGY	*Concise Encyclopedia Biology*. 1995.
CHEMISTRY	*Concise Encyclopedia Chemistry*. 1993.
COMPUTERS	*Encyclopedia of Computer Science and Technology*. 45 vols. 1975.
ECONOMICS	*Fortune Encyclopedia of Economics*. 1993.
EDUCATION	*Encyclopedia of Educational Research*. 1992.
ENVIRONMENT	*Encyclopedia of the Environment*. 1994.
FOREIGN RELATIONS	*Encyclopedia of U.S. Foreign Relations*. 1997. *Encyclopedia of the Third World*. 1992.
HISTORY	*Encyclopedia USA*. 20 vols. 1983 – . *New Cambridge Modern History*. 14 vols. 1957 – 1980, 1990 – .
LAW	*Black's Law Dictionary*. 1990.
LITERATURE	*Encyclopedia of World Literature in the Twentieth Century*. 5 vols. 1981 – 1993. *Encyclopedia of Literature and Criticism*. 1990.
MUSIC	*New Grove Dictionary of Music and Musicians,* 2nd ed. 29 vols. 2001.
PHILOSOPHY	*Routledge Encyclopedia of Philosophy*. 10 vols. 1998.
PSYCHOLOGY	*Encyclopedia of Psychology*. 8 vols. 2000.
RELIGION	*Encyclopedia of Religion*. 16 vols. 1987.
SCIENCE	*McGraw-Hill Encyclopedia of Science and Technology*. 20 vols. 1997.
SOCIAL SCIENCES	*International Encyclopedia of the Social Sciences*. 19 vols. 1968 – .
WOMEN'S STUDIES	*Women's Studies Encyclopedia,* rev. ed. 3 vols. 1999.

You can locate any of these in the library by doing a title search in the online catalog and looking for the encyclopedia's call number. Find other specialized encyclopedias by looking in the catalog under the subject heading for the discipline, such as "psychology," and adding the subheading "encyclopedia" or "dictionary."

Three particular reference sources can help you identify other specialized encyclopedias covering your topic:

ARBA Guide to Subject Encyclopedias and Dictionaries, 2nd ed. (1997): Lists specialized encyclopedias by broad subject categories, with descriptions of coverage, focus, and any special features. Also available online.

Subject Encyclopedias: User Guide, Review Citations, and Keyword Index (1999): Lists specialized encyclopedias by broad subject categories and provides information about articles within them. By looking under the key terms that describe a topic, you can search for related articles in any of over four hundred specialized encyclopedias.

Kister's Best Encyclopedias: A Comparative Guide to General and Specialized Encyclopedias, 2nd ed. (1994): Surveys and evaluates more than a thousand encyclopedias, both print and electronic. Includes a title index and a topic index that you can use to find references to encyclopedias on special topics.

Consulting Disciplinary Guides

Once you have a general overview of your topic, you can consult one of the research guides within the discipline. The following guides can help you identify the major handbooks, encyclopedias, bibliographies, journals, periodical indexes, and computer databases in the various disciplines. You need not read any of these extensive works straight through, but you will find them to be valuable references. The *Guide to Reference Books,* Eleventh Edition (1996), edited by Robert Balay, will help you find disciplinary guides for subjects not listed here.

ANTHROPOLOGY	*Introduction to Library Research in Anthropology,* 2nd ed. 1998. By John M. Weeks.
ART	*Visual Arts Research: A Handbook.* 1986. By Elizabeth B. Pollard.
EDUCATION	*Education: A Guide to Reference and Information Sources,* 2nd ed. 2000. By Lois Buttlar and Nancy O'Brien.
FILM	*On the Screen: A Film, Television, and Video Research Guide.* 1986. By Kim N. Fisher.
GENERAL	*Guide to Reference Books,* 11th ed. 1996. Edited by Robert Balay.
HISTORY	*A Student's Guide to History,* 8th ed. 2001. By Jules R. Benjamin.
HUMANITIES	*The Humanities: A Selective Guide to Information Sources,* 5th ed. 2000. By Ron Blazek and Elizabeth S. Aversa. Also available online.
LITERATURE	*Reference Works in British and American Literature,* 2nd ed. 1998. By James K. Bracken. Also available online.
	Literary Research Guide: An Annotated Listing of Reference Sources in English Literary Studies, 3rd ed. 1998. By James L. Harner.

MUSIC	*Music: A Guide to the Reference Literature.* 1987. By William S. Brockman.
PHILOSOPHY	*Philosophy: A Guide to the Reference Literature,* 2nd ed. 1997. By Hans E. Bynagle. Also available online.
POLITICAL SCIENCE	*Political Science: A Guide to Reference and Information Sources.* 1990. By Henry York.
PSYCHOLOGY	*Library Use: A Handbook for Psychology,* 3rd ed. 2003.
SCIENCE AND TECHNOLOGY	*Information Sources in Science and Technology.* 1998. By Charlie Hurt.
SOCIAL SCIENCES	*The Social Sciences: A Cross-Disciplinary Guide to Selected Sources,* 3rd ed. 2002. By Nancy L. Herron. Also available online.
SOCIOLOGY	*Sociology: A Guide to Reference and Information Sources,* 2nd ed. 1997. By Stephen H. Aby.
WOMEN'S STUDIES	*Introduction to Library Research in Women's Studies.* 1985. By Susan E. Searing.

Consulting Bibliographies

Like encyclopedias and disciplinary guides, bibliographies give an overview of what has been published on the subject. A *bibliography* is simply a list of publications on a given subject. Its scope may be broad or narrow. Some bibliographers try to be exhaustive, including every title they can find, but most are selective. To discover how selections were made, check the bibliography's preface or introduction. Occasionally, bibliographies are annotated with brief summaries and evaluations of the entries. Bibliographies may be found in a variety of places: in encyclopedias, in the library catalog, and in research guides. All specialized encyclopedias and disciplinary guides have bibliographies. Research articles include bibliographies to document their sources of information.

Even if you attend a large research university, your library is unlikely to hold every book or journal article that a bibliography might direct you to. The library catalog and serial record (a list of periodicals the library holds) will tell you whether the book or journal is available on site or through interlibrary loan.

■ IDENTIFYING SUBJECT HEADINGS AND KEYWORDS

To extend your research beyond encyclopedias, you need to find appropriate subject headings and keywords. *Subject headings* are specific words and phrases used in library catalogs, periodical indexes, and other databases to categorize the contents of books and articles so that people can look for materials about a particular topic. One way to begin your search for subject headings is to consult the *Library of Congress Subject Headings* (LCSH), which your library probably makes available both in print and online. This work lists the standard subject headings used in library catalogs. Here is an example from the LCSH:

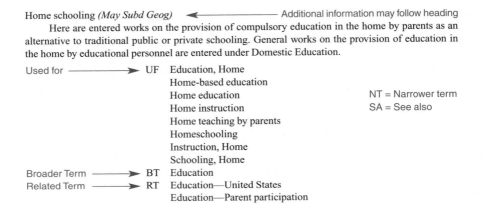

Home schooling *(May Subd Geog)* ◀──────────── Additional information may follow heading
    Here are entered works on the provision of compulsory education in the home by parents as an alternative to traditional public or private schooling. General works on the provision of education in the home by educational personnel are entered under Domestic Education.

Used for ──────▶ UF   Education, Home
                     Home-based education
                     Home education   NT = Narrower term
                     Home instruction   SA = See also
                     Home teaching by parents
                     Homeschooling
                     Instruction, Home
                     Schooling, Home
Broader Term ──────▶ BT   Education
Related Term ──────▶ RT   Education—United States
                     Education—Parent participation

This sample entry proved particularly useful because when the student researching this topic found nothing listed in the library catalog under "Home schooling," she tried the other headings until "Education—Parent participation" and "Education—United States" yielded information on three books. Note, too, that this entry explains the types of books that would be found under these headings and those that would be found elsewhere.

Instead of looking for likely headings in the LCSH, however, you can usually locate useful subject headings faster by searching the catalog or other database using *keywords,* words or phrases that you think describe your topic. As you read about your subject in an encyclopedia or other reference book, you should keep a list of keywords that may be useful. (Make sure you spell your keywords correctly. Computers are unforgiving of spelling errors.) As you review the results of a keyword search, look for the titles that seem to match most closely the topics that you are looking for. When you call up the detailed information for these titles, look for the section labeled "Subject" or "Subject Heading," which will show the headings under which the book or article is classified. (In the example that follows, this section is abbreviated as "Subj-lcsh.") In many computerized catalogs and databases, these subject headings are links that you can click on to get a list of other materials on the same subject. Keep a list in your working bibliography of all the subject headings you find that relate to your topic, so that you can refer to them each time you start looking for information. Here is an example of an online catalog listing for a book on home schooling:

| Title: | Pathways to privatization in education / by Joseph Murphy . . . [et al.] |
| Imprint: | Greenwich, Conn.: Ablex Pub. Corp., c1998 |

LOCATION	CALL NO	STATUS
MAIN	LB2806.36 .P38 1998	NOT CHCKD OUT

Description:	xiii, 244 p.; 24 cm
Series:	Contemporary studies in social and policy issues in education
Subj-lcsh	**Privatization in education — United States**
	Educational vouchers — United States
	Home schooling — United States
Add author:	Murphy, Joseph, 1949–
Note(s):	Includes bibliographical references (p. 209–236) and index
ISBN:	1567503632 (cloth)
	1567503640 (pbk.)

Determining the Most Promising Sources

As you follow a subject heading into the library catalog and periodical indexes, you will discover many seemingly relevant books and articles. How do you decide which ones to track down and examine? You may have little to go on but author, title, date, and publisher or periodical name, but these details actually provide useful clues. Look again, for example, at the online catalog reference to a book on home schooling (see above). The title, *Pathways to Privatization in Education,* is the first clue to the subject coverage of the book. Note that the publication date, 1998, is fairly recent. From the subject headings, you can see that this book focuses on various aspects of the privatization of education, which includes home schooling, and that the geographic focus of the book is the United States. Finally, from the notes, you can see that the book includes an extensive bibliography that could lead you to other sources.

Now look at the following entry from *Education Index,* a periodical index:

> **Home schooling**
> Do children have to go to school? [Great Britain]
> C. Henson. *Child Educ (Engl)* v73 p68 Mr '96
> Homegrown learning [Twin Ridges Elementary School
> District combines homeschooling with regular
> classroom instruction] D. Hill. il *Teach Mag* v7 p40-5
> Ap '96
> Should we open extracurriculars to home-schoolers?
> J. Watford; B. Dickinson. il *Am Teach* v80 p4 Mr '96

This entry lists articles that address different aspects of home schooling, briefly describing some of the articles. You can see that the first article deals with the issue from a British point of view, which might provide an interesting cross-cultural perspective for your essay. The title of the third article seems to indicate an argument on the issue; because it appears in a magazine for teachers, it might give you a sense of that profession's attitudes toward home schooling. Be careful, though, to stay focused on your specific research topic or thesis, especially if you are pressed for time and cannot afford to become distracted exploring sources that sound interesting but are unlikely to be useful.

In addition, each entry contains the information that you will need to locate it in a library. Going back to the first article, here is what each piece of information means.

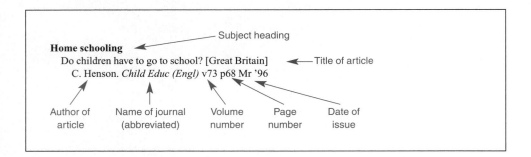

When you look in catalogs and indexes, consider the following points when deciding whether you should track down a particular source:

- **Relevance to your topic:** Do the title, subtitle, description, subject headings, and abstract help you determine how directly the particular source addresses your topic?

- **Publication date:** How recent is the source? For current controversies, emerging trends, and scientific or technological developments, you must consult recent material. For historical or biographical topics, you will want to start with present-day perspectives but eventually explore older sources that offer authoritative perspectives. You may also want or need to consult sources written at the time of the events or during the life of the person you are researching.

- **Description:** Does the length indicate a brief treatment of the topic or an extended treatment? Does the work include illustrations that may elaborate on concepts discussed in the text? Does it include a bibliography that could lead you to other works or an index that could give you an overview of what is discussed in the text? Does the abstract indicate the focus of the work?

From among the sources that look promising, select publications that seem by their titles to address different aspects of your topic or to approach it from different perspectives. Try to avoid selecting sources that are mostly by the same author, from the same publisher, or in the same journal. Common sense will lead you to an appropriate decision about diversity in source materials.

■ SEARCHING ONLINE LIBRARY CATALOGS AND DATABASES

Computerized library catalogs and other databases consist of thousands or millions of records, each representing an individual item such as a book, an article, or a government publication. The record is made up of different fields describing the item and allowing users to search for it and retrieve it from the database. Here is a record for a book from a library's online catalog, with the searchable fields in bold:

Author:	Gordon, William MacGuire, 1935–
Title:	The law of home schooling / William M. Gordon, Charles J. Russo, Albert S. Miles. Topeka, Kan.: National Organization on Legal Problems of Education, c1994.
Location:	Main
Call No:	JLL 74-383 no. 52
Description:	74 p.; 23 cm.
Series:	NOLPE monograph series no. 52.
Notes:	Includes bibliographical references and index.
Subjects:	Home schooling—Law and legislation—United States. Educational law and legislation—United States. Education—Parent participation—United States.
Other entries:	Russo, Charles J.

Using Different Search Techniques

Basic search strategies include author, title, and subject searches. When you request an *author search,* the computer looks for a match between the name you type and the names listed in the author field of all the records in the online catalog or other database. When you request a *title search* or a *subject search,* the computer looks for a match in the title field or the subject field, respectively. Computers are very literal. They try to match only the exact terms you enter, and most do not recognize variant or incorrect spellings. That is an incentive to become a good speller and a good typist. However, because most library catalogs and databases also offer the option of searching for titles and subjects by keywords, you need not enter the full exact title or subject heading. In addition, you can be flexible where the computer cannot. For instance, if you were researching the topic of home schooling, you could do a subject search not only for "home schooling" but also for "homeschooling" and "home-schooling." Table 13.2 on p. 406 describes some search capabilities commonly offered by library catalogs and databases.

Table 13.2 Common Search Capabilities Offered by Library Catalogs and Databases

Type of Search	How the Computer Conducts the Search	Things to Know
Author search (exact) • Individual (*Guterson, David*) • Organization (*U.S. Department of Education*)	Looks in the author field for the words entered	• Author searches generally are exact-match searches, so authors' names are entered *last name, first name* (for example, "Shakespeare, William"). If you enter "William Shakespeare," the computer will generate a list of authors whose last names are William. • Organizations can be considered authors. Enter the name of the organization in natural word order. • An exact-match author search is useful for finding books and articles by a particular author.
Title search (exact) • Book title • Magazine or journal title • Article title	Looks in the title field for words in the exact order you enter them	An exact-match title search is useful for identifying the location of known items, such as when you are looking for a particular journal or book.
Subject search (exact)	Looks in the subject heading or descriptor field for words in the exact order you enter them	An exact-match subject search is useful when you are sure about the subject heading.
Keyword search	Looks in the title, note, subject, abstract, and text fields for the words entered	A keyword search is the broadest kind you can use. It is useful during early exploration of a subject.
Title word search • Book title • Magazine or journal title • Article title	Looks in the title field of the record for the words entered and ignores word order	Since this is not an exact-match search, entering "home and schooling" will retrieve the same records as entering "schooling and home."
Subject word search	Looks in the subject heading or descriptor field of the record for the words entered and ignores word order	Since this is not an exact-match search, entering "education privatization" will retrieve the same records as "privatization education."

Doing Advanced Searches and Using Boolean Operators

The real power of using an online catalog or other database is demonstrated when you need to look up books or articles using more than one keyword. For example, suppose you want information about home schooling in California. Rather than looking through an index listing all the articles on home schooling and picking out those that mention California, you can ask the computer to do the work for you by linking your two keywords. Many online catalogs and databases now offer the option of an *advanced search,* sometimes on a separate page from the main search page, that allows you to search for more than one keyword at a time, search for certain keywords while excluding others, or search for an exact phrase. Or you may be able to create this kind of advanced search yourself by using the *Boolean operators* AND, OR, and NOT along with quotation marks and parentheses.

To understand the operation of *Boolean logic* (developed by and named after George Boole, a nineteenth-century mathematician), picture one set of articles about home schooling and another set of articles about California. A third set is formed by articles that are about both home schooling and California. Figure 13.4 below provides an illustration of how each Boolean operator works.

AND

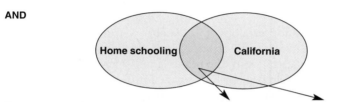

Returns references that contain both the terms **home schooling** AND **California**

- Narrows the search
- Combines unrelated terms
- Is the default used by most online catalogs and databases

OR

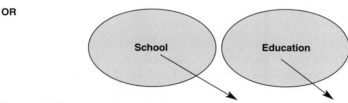

Returns all references that contain either the term **school** OR the term **education,** but not both

- Broadens the search **("OR is more")**
- Is useful with synonyms and variant spellings: ("home schooling" and "homeschooling")

NOT

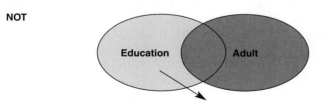

Returns references that include the term **education** but NOT the term **adult**

- Narrows the search
- May eliminate relevant material

Figure 13.4 The Boolean Operators: AND, OR, and NOT

Table 13.3 Electronic Search Tips

If You Find Too Many Sources on Your Topic:	*If You Find Insufficient Information on Your Topic:*
• Use a subject heading search instead of a keyword search.	• Use a keyword or title search instead of a subject heading search.
• Add a concept word to your search.	• Eliminate unimportant words or secondary concepts from your search terms.
• Use a more precise vocabulary to describe your topic.	• Try truncated forms of your keyword.
	• Use different words to describe your topic.
	• Check the spelling of each term you type.

The search mechanisms for catalogs and databases usually require that the Boolean operators be typed in all capital letters. Some mechanisms use the plus sign (+) or the ampersand (&) instead of AND, the minus sign (–) instead of NOT, and the | sign instead of OR; check the Help page or home page for instructions if necessary.

You can also use quotation marks around a group of words to search for a phrase (with the words in the same order). And you can use parentheses to combine the Boolean operators: for example, *home schooling* NOT (*California* OR *Texas*) will retrieve all articles about home schooling except ones that mention California and ones that mention Texas.

Using Truncation

Another useful search strategy employs *truncation*. With this technique, you drop the ending of a word or term and replace it with a symbol, which indicates you want to retrieve records containing any term that begins the same way as your term. For example, by entering the term "home school#" you would retrieve all the records that have terms such as "home school," "home schooling," "home schools," "home schooled," or "home schoolers." Truncation is useful when you want to retrieve both the plural and singular forms of a word or any word for which you are not sure of the ending. Truncation symbols vary with the catalog or database. The question mark (?), asterisk (*), and pound sign (#) are frequently used.

Table 13.3 above offers some suggestions for expanding or narrowing your electronic search.

■ LOCATING SOURCES

The following are guidelines for finding books, periodical articles, government documents and statistical information, and other types of sources.

Finding Books

The primary source for books is the library's computerized catalog. Besides flexibly searching keywords and subject headings, the catalog may tell you whether a book is currently available or checked out. It also allows you to print out source information rather than having to copy the material by hand. However, the catalog will require correct spelling for searches and may contain only materials received and cataloged after a certain date.

Whether you search a library catalog by author, title, subject, or keyword, each record you find will provide the following standard information. You will need this information to enter the book in your working bibliography and to locate it in the library.

1. *Call number:* This number, which usually appears on a separate line in the computerized catalog record, is your key to finding the book in the library. Most college libraries use the Library of Congress call-number system, and most public libraries and some small college libraries use the Dewey system. The Library of Congress system uses both letters and numbers in the call number, and both are needed to locate a book. Call numbers serve two purposes: They provide an exact location for every book in the library, and because they are assigned according to subject classifications, they group together books on the same topic. When you go to the stacks to locate the book, therefore, always browse for other useful material on the shelves around it. Call numbers also give information about special collections of books kept in other library locations such as the reference room or government publications department. If the online catalog covers more than one library, the name of the library that has the book will also be included.

2. *Author:* The author's name usually appears last name first, followed by birth and death dates. For books with multiple authors, the record includes an author entry under each author's name.

3. *Title:* The title appears exactly as it does on the title page of the book, except that only the first word and proper nouns and adjectives are capitalized.

4. *Publication information:* The place of publication (usually just the city), the publisher, and the year of publication are listed. If the book was published simultaneously in the United States and abroad, both places of publication and both publishers are indicated.

5. *Physical description:* This section provides information about the book's page length and size. A roman numeral indicates the number of pages devoted to front matter (such as a preface, table of contents, and acknowledgments).

6. *Notes:* Any special features such as a bibliography or an index are listed here.

7. *Subject headings:* Assigned by the Library of Congress, these headings indicate how the book is listed in the subject catalog. They also provide useful links for finding other books on the same subject.

Finding Periodical Articles

The most up-to-date information on a subject is usually found not in books but in articles published in periodicals. A *periodical* is a publication such as a magazine, newspaper, or scholarly journal that is published on an ongoing basis, at regular intervals (for instance, daily, weekly, monthly, or annually), and with different content in each issue. Many print periodicals now publish online versions as well, although the contents may be somewhat different. In addition, some magazines and journals are published exclusively on the Web. Examples of periodicals include *Sports Illustrated* (magazine), the *New York Times* (newspaper), *Tulsa Studies in Women's Literature* (scholarly journal), *Kairos* (online journal), and *Slate* (online magazine).

Articles in periodicals are usually not listed in the library catalog; to find them, you must use library reference works called *periodical indexes.* Some periodical indexes include *abstracts* or short summaries of articles. In the library, indexes may be available in print, in microform, on CD-ROM, through the computerized catalog, or as online databases. Many are available in both print and electronic formats, and some electronic indexes give you access to the full text of articles. Regardless of format, periodical indexes all serve the same basic function of leading the user to articles on a specific topic. If you understand how to use one, you will be able to use others.

Distinguishing Scholarly Journals and Popular Magazines

Although they are both called periodicals, journals and magazines have important differences. *Journals* publish articles written by experts in a particular field of study, frequently professors or researchers in academic institutions. Journals are usually specialized in their subject focus, research oriented, and extensively reviewed by specialists prior to publication. They are intended to be read by experts and students conducting research. *Magazines,* in contrast, usually publish general-interest articles written by journalists. The articles are written to entertain and educate the general public, and they tend to appeal to a much broader audience than journal articles.

Journals contain a great deal of what is called *primary literature,* reporting the results of original research. For example, a scientist might publish an article in a medical journal about the results of a new treatment protocol for breast cancer. *Secondary literature,* published in magazines, is intended to inform the general public about new and interesting developments in scientific and other areas of research. If a reporter from *Newsweek* writes an article about this scientist's cancer research, this article is classified as secondary literature. Table 13.4 summarizes some of the important differences between scholarly journals and popular magazines.

Selecting an Appropriate Periodical Index or Abstract

Periodical indexes and abstracts are of two types: general and specialized. Both provide you with information that will help you locate articles on a topic. In addition to the ones listed on pp. 411–15, check with a reference librarian to identify other indexes and abstracts that may be useful for your topic.

Table 13.4 How to Distinguish a Scholarly Journal from a Popular Magazine

Scholarly Journal	Popular Magazine
• The front or back cover lists the contents of the issue.	• The cover features a color picture.
• The title of the publication contains the word *Journal.*	• The title may be catchy as well as descriptive.
• You see the journal only at the library.	• You see the magazine for sale at the grocery store, in an airport, or at a bookstore.
• It does not include advertisements or advertises products such as textbooks, professional books, or scholarly conferences.	• It has lots of colorful advertisements in it.
• The authors of articles have *Ph.D.* or academic affiliations after their names.	• The authors of articles are journalists or reporters.
• Many articles have more than one author.	• Most articles have a single author but may quote experts.
• A short summary (abstract) of an article may appear on the first page.	• A headline or engaging description may precede the article.
• Most articles are fairly long, 5 to 20 pages.	• Most of the articles are fairly short, 1 to 5 pages.
• The articles may include charts, tables, figures, and quotations from other scholarly sources.	• The articles have color pictures and sidebar boxes.
• The articles have a bibliography (list of references to other books and articles) at the end.	• The articles do not include a bibliography.
• You probably would not read it at the beach.	• You might bring it to the beach to read.

General Indexes.   These indexes are a good place to start your research because they cover a broad range of subjects. Most have separate author and subject listings as well as a list of book reviews. General indexes usually list only articles from popular magazines and newspapers, although some of them include listings from basic scholarly journals. Here is a list of the most common general indexes:

The Readers' Guide to Periodical Literature (1900–; online, 1983–; updated quarterly): Covers about two hundred popular periodicals and may help you launch your search for sources on general and current topics. Even for general topics, however, you should not rely on it exclusively. Nearly all college libraries house far more than two hundred periodicals, and university research libraries house twenty thousand or more. The *Readers' Guide* does not even attempt to cover the research journals that play such an important role in college writing. Here is an example of an entry for home education:

> **HOME EDUCATION**
> Home-school kids in public-school activities. D. Brockett. *The Education Digest* v61 p67–9 N '95
> Pros and cons of home schooling. il *Parents* v70 p18 N '95
> Why homeschooling is important for America [address, August 11, 1995] S. L. Blumenfeld. *Vital Speeches of the Day* v61 p763–6 O 1 '95

Magazine Index (on microfilm, 1988–; online as part of InfoTrac, 1973–; see below): Indexes over four hundred magazines.

InfoTrac (online): Time coverage varies by subscription. Includes three indexes: (1) the *General Periodicals Index,* which covers over twelve hundred general-interest publications, incorporating the *Magazine Index* and including the *New York Times* and the *Wall Street Journal;* (2) the *Academic Index,* which covers four hundred scholarly and general-interest publications, including the *New York Times;* and (3) the *National Newspaper Index,* which covers the *Christian Science Monitor, Los Angeles Times, New York Times, Wall Street Journal,* and *Washington Post.* Some entries also include abstracts of articles. This sample InfoTrac entry is from the *General Periodicals Index:*

AUTHOR(s):	Hawkins, Dana
TITLE(s):	Homeschool battles: clashes grow as some in the movement seek access to public schools.
	illustration photograph
Summary:	An estimated 500,000 students in the US study at home, and there is an increasing tension in some communities as some of the 'homeschoolers' attempt to use the public schools on a limited basis. The parents of one homeschooler in Oklahoma have sued the school district to gain access.
	U.S. News & World Report
	p57(2)
	Feb 12 1996 v120 n6
DESCRIPTORS:	Home schooling_Cases
	Public schools_Cases
	Education_Parent participation

more follows -- press <RETURN>   (Q to quit)

Alternative Press Index (1970–; online through Biblioline): Indexes alternative and radical publications.

Humanities Index (1974–; online, 1984–): Covers more than five hundred periodicals in archaeology, history, classics, literature, performing arts, philosophy, and religion.

Social Sciences Index (1974–; online, 1983–): Covers more than five hundred periodicals in economics, geography, law, political science, psychology, public administration, and sociology. The complete text of certain articles is available on the CD-ROM.

Public Affairs Information Service Bulletin (1915–; online, 1972–): Covers articles and other publications by public and private agencies on economic and social conditions, international relations, and public administration. Subject listings only.

Specialized Indexes and Abstracts.   These publications list or summarize articles devoted to technical or scholarly research. As you learn more about your topic, you will turn to specialized indexes and abstracts to find references to scholarly articles. The following example from *Sociological Abstracts,* which indexes and summarizes articles from a wide range of periodicals that publish sociological research, is typical of entries found in specialized indexes:

> **91X2727**
> **Mayberry, Maralee & Knowles, J. Gary** (Dept Sociology U Nevada, Las Vegas 89154), **Family Unity Objectives of Parents Who Teach Their Children: Ideological and Pedagogical Orientations to Home Schooling,** UM *The Urban Review,* 1989, 21, 4, Dec, 209–225.
> ¶ The objectives of parents who teach their children at home are examined, using results from 2 qualitative studies: (1) a study conducted in Ore in 1987/88, consisting of interview & questionnaire data (N = 15 & 800 families, respectively); & (2) an ongoing ethnographic study being conducted in Utah (N = 8 families). Analysis suggests that while families have complex motives for teaching their children at home, most respondents felt that establishing a home school would allow them to maintain or further develop unity within the family. It is concluded that a family's decision to home school is often made in an attempt to resist the effects on the family unit of urbanization & modernization. Policy implications are discussed. 36 References. Adapted from the source document. (Copyright 1991, Sociological Abstracts, Inc., all rights reserved.)

When you compare this entry with the previous citations from the *Readers' Guide* and InfoTrac's *General Periodicals Index* (pp. 411–12), you will see differences in the following features:

- The format of the citations
- The authors' qualifications
- The titles of the articles
- The titles of the publications where the articles appear
- The length of the articles
- The amount of information given about the content of the articles

Here is a list of specialized periodical indexes that cover various disciplines:

ABI/INFORM (1971–; online)

Accounting and Tax Index (1964–; online)

America: History and Life (1954–; CD-ROM, 1964–)

American Statistics Index (1973–)

Applied Science and Technology Index (1958–; online)

Art Index (1929–; online, 1983–)

Biological and Agricultural Index (1964–; online, 1983–)

Education Index (1929–; online, 1983–)

Engineering Index (1920–)

Historical Abstracts (1955–; online, 1982–)

Index Medicus (1961–; online as MEDLINE)

MLA International Bibliography of Books and Articles in the Modern Languages and Literature (1921–; online)

Music Index (1949–; online, 1981–)

Philosopher's Index (1957–; online)

Physics Abstracts (1898; online as INSPEC)

Psychological Abstracts (1927; online as PsycINFO; CD-ROM as PsycLIT)

Science Abstracts (1898)

Sociological Abstracts (1952; online as Sociofile)

Most periodical indexes and abstracts use their own system of subject headings. The print version of *Sociological Abstracts,* for example, has a separate volume for subject headings. Check the opening pages or, for an electronic index or abstract, the opening screen or home page to see how subjects are classified. Then look for periodicals or articles under your most useful subject heading from the LCSH or the heading that seems most similar to it. If you are using an electronic index, the items in the subject heading field for particular articles may function as links to lists of related materials.

Indexes to Periodicals Representing Particular Viewpoints.   Some specialized periodical indexes tend to represent particular viewpoints and may help you identify different positions on an issue.

Chicano Index (1967–): An index to general and scholarly articles about Mexican Americans. Articles are arranged by subject with author and title indexes. (Before 1989, the title was *Chicano Periodical Index.*)

G. K. Hall Index to Black Periodicals (1999–); previously published as *Index to Black Periodicals* (1984–1998): An author and subject index to general and scholarly articles about African Americans.

Left Index (1982–; online only, 2000–): An author and subject index to over eighty periodicals with a Marxist, radical, or left perspective. Listings cover primarily topics in the social sciences and humanities.

Another useful source for identifying positions is *Editorials on File,* described on p. 417.

Full-Text Electronic Services.   In addition to the electronic indexes and abstracts listed earlier, many libraries subscribe to other electronic database services that provide the full text of articles, often in particular subject areas. The text is available either in the database itself (so you can see it onscreen and download it or print it out) or by mail or fax for a fee. Subscriptions to these services tend to be expensive, so they may not be available in small college libraries, and the articles available may be limited to those in recent issues. Nevertheless, be sure to check with a librarian about what is available at your library. Some of these services include the following:

ERIC (Educational Resources Information Center) (online, 1966–): Indexes, abstracts, and provides some full texts of articles from 750 education journals.

Business Periodicals Ondisc (1988–) and *ABI/INFORM* (1988–): Provide full-text articles from business periodicals that can be printed on your library's laser printer.

PsycBooks (1987–): A CD-ROM database that indexes books and book chapters in psychology.

Ingenta (1998–; www.ingenta.com): An online document delivery service that lists articles from more than 5,400 online journals and 26,000 other publications. For a fee, you can receive the full text of the article, online or by fax.

LEXIS-NEXIS Academic Universe (time coverage varies by source; www.lexis-nexis.com/lncc/academic): Provides the full text of articles from academic journals and other sources containing legal, news, and government information and statistics.

JSTOR (www.jstor.org): Provides the full text of articles from older issues of more than three hundred journals in the humanities and social sciences.

Project Muse (1996–; muse.jhu.edu): Provides the full text of articles from more than two hundred journals in the humanities, social sciences, and mathematics from Johns Hopkins University Press and selected not-for-profit publishers.

Science Direct (1997–; www.sciencedirect.com): Provides the full text of articles from more than a thousand journals in science, technology, medicine, and the social sciences from Elsevier Press.

Interlibrary networks: Known by different names in different regions, these networks allow you to search in the catalogs of colleges and universities in your area and across the country. In many cases, you can request a book by interlibrary loan, although it may take several weeks to be delivered to your library. You can also request a copy of an article from a journal to which your own library does not subscribe. Most libraries do not lend their journals but will copy and forward articles for a fee.

Searching Electronic Periodical Databases

Although you can search an electronic periodical database by author or title, you will probably more often want to do subject searches using keywords. As with subject searches for books in the library catalog, make your keywords as precise as possible so that your search results in a manageable list of sources relevant to your topic. Most databases include a thesaurus of keywords and an advanced-search mechanism or set of guidelines for using Boolean operators or other keyword-combining procedures. In addition, many databases include a browse function. When you enter a keyword, this function automatically lists the terms that are close to the keyword alphabetically. If you enter a very general keyword, the function provides a list of subtopics that you can use to narrow your search before you ask the system to retrieve records.

Once you have typed your keywords, the computer searches the database and lists every reference to them that it finds. You can usually print the results or download the records to your own disk. Because online databases contain so much information, you may want to consult with a librarian to develop an efficient search strategy. Also keep in mind that most electronic indexes cover only the last ten to fifteen years; you may need to consult older printed versions of indexes as well.

Locating Periodicals in the Library

When you identify a promising magazine or journal article in a periodical index, you must go to the library's online catalog or periodicals database to learn whether the library subscribes to the periodical, whether the article is available in print or electronic form or both, and where you can find the magazine or journal issue you need. No library can subscribe to every periodical, so as you go through indexes and abstracts, be sure to identify more articles than you actually need. This will save you from having to repeat your catalog or database search later when you find out that your library does not subscribe to some of the magazines or journals that contain your possible sources.

Although every library arranges its print periodicals differently, recent issues are usually arranged alphabetically by title on open shelves. Older issues may be bound like books (shelved by call numbers or alphabetically by title) or filmed and available in microform. Ask a librarian at the reference desk how the periodicals in your library are arranged.

Suppose you want to look up an article on home schooling from the journal *Urban Review* that you found indexed in *Sociological Abstracts* (see p. 414). Here is a typical record for *Urban Review* from a library's online catalog or periodicals database. Notice that the title search refers to the title of the journal, not the title of the article.

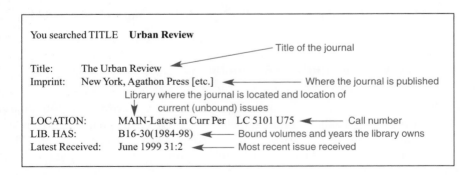

In this instance, you would learn that the library does subscribe to *Urban Review* and that you could locate the 1989 article in one of the bound volumes in the library's collection.

Finding Newspaper Articles and Other News Sources

Newspapers provide useful information for many research topics in such areas as foreign affairs, economics, public opinion, and social trends. Libraries usually photograph newspapers and store them in miniature form on microfilm (reels) or microfiche (cards) that must be placed in viewing machines to be read. Newspaper indexes such as the *Los Angeles Times Index, New York Times Index,* and *London Times Index,* which are available online as well as in print, can help you locate specific articles on your topic. College libraries usually have indexes to local newspapers as well.

Your library may also subscribe to newspaper article and digest services, such as the following:

National Newspaper Index (microfilm, 1989–; online as part of InfoTrac, 1979–) (see p. 412): Indexes the *Christian Science Monitor, Los Angeles Times, New York Times, Wall Street Journal,* and *Washington Post*

NewsBank (microfiche and CD-ROM, 1970–): Full-text articles from five hundred U.S. newspapers; a good source of information on local and regional issues and trends

Newspaper Abstracts (1988–; online, 1989–): Indexes and gives brief abstracts of articles from nineteen major regional, national, and international newspapers

Facts on File (weekly; CD-ROM, 1980): A digest of U.S. and international news events arranged by subject, such as foreign affairs, arts, education, religion, and sports

Editorials on File (twice monthly): A digest of editorials from 150 U.S. and Canadian newspapers with brief descriptions of editorial subjects followed by fifteen to twenty editorials on the subject, reprinted from different newspapers

CQ Researcher (1991–; previously published since 1924 as Editorial Research Reports): Reports on current and controversial topics, including brief histories, statistics, editorials, journal articles, endnotes, and supplementary reading lists

Foreign Broadcast Information Service (FBIS) (1980–; online, 1990–): A digest of foreign broadcast scripts, newspaper articles, and government statements from Asia, Europe, Latin America, Africa, Russia, and the Middle East

Keesing's Record of World Events (1931–; also online): A monthly digest of events in all countries, compiled from British and other reporting services; includes speeches and statistics and chronological, geographic, and topical indexes

Finding Government and Statistical Information

Although college libraries still maintain large collections of print publications by government agencies, federal, state, and local governments are making many of their publications and reference services available through the World Wide Web. Ask a reference librarian for assistance in locating governmental sources in the library or on the Web. In particular, consider consulting the following sources for information on political subjects and national trends. Although these publications are not always listed in library catalogs or databases, they can usually be found in the reference area or the government documents department of college libraries. If these works are not listed in your library's catalog, ask for assistance in locating them.

Sources for Researching Political Subjects.   Two publications that report developments in the federal government can be rich sources of information on political issues. Types of material they cover include congressional hearings and debates, presidential proclamations and speeches, U.S. Supreme Court decisions and dissenting opinions, and compilations of statistics.

> *Congressional Quarterly Almanac* (annual): A summary of legislation that provides an overview of government policies and trends, including analysis as well as election results, records of roll-call votes, and the text of significant speeches and debates

> *CQ Weekly* (online, 1998–; formerly published as *Congressional Quarterly Weekly Report*): A news service that includes up-to-date summaries of congressional committee actions, congressional votes, and executive branch activities as well as overviews of current policy discussions and other activities of the federal government

Sources for Researching Trends.   Research can help you identify trends to write about and, most important, provide the statistical evidence you need to demonstrate the existence of a trend. The following resources can be especially helpful:

> *Statistical Abstract of the United States* (annual; some content online, www .census.gov/statab/www): A publication of the Bureau of the Census that provides a variety of social, economic, and political statistics, often covering several years, including tables, graphs, charts, and references to additional sources of information

> *American Statistics Index* (1974–; annual with monthly supplements): Attempts to cover all federal government publications containing statistical information of research significance and includes brief descriptions of references

> *Statistical Reference Index* (1980–): A selective guide to American statistical publications from sources other than the U.S. government, including economic, social, and political statistical sources

> *World Almanac and Book of Facts* (annual): Presents information on a variety of subjects drawn from many sources, including a chronology of the year, climatological data, and lists of inventions and awards

> *The Gallup Poll: Public Opinion* (1935–): A chronological listing of the results of public opinion polls, including information on social, economic, and political trends

In addition to researching the trend itself, you may want to research others' speculations about its causes. If so, the reports of federal government activities described in the preceding section may be helpful.

Finding Other Library Sources

Libraries hold vast amounts of useful materials other than books, periodicals, and government documents. Some of the following library sources and services may be appropriate for your research.

- *Vertical files:* Pamphlets and brochures from government and private agencies
- *Special collections:* Manuscripts, rare books, and materials of local interest
- *Audio collections:* Records, audiotapes, music CDs, readings, and speeches
- *Video collections:* Slides, filmstrips, videotapes, and DVDs
- *Art collections:* Drawings, paintings, and engravings
- *Interlibrary loans:* As noted above, many libraries can arrange to borrow books from other libraries or have copies of journal articles sent from other libraries as part of an interlibrary network program. Ask your librarian how long it will take to get the material you need (usually several weeks) and how to use the loan service (some libraries allow you to send an electronic request to the local interlibrary loan office).
- *Computer resources:* Interactive computer programs that combine text, video, and audio resources in history, literature, business, and other disciplines

■ USING THE INTERNET FOR RESEARCH

The *Internet* is a vast global computer network that enables users to store and share information quickly and easily. The *World Wide Web* is a network of sites on the Internet, each with its own *electronic address* (called a *URL,* or *uniform resource locator*). You can gain access to the Internet through your library or campus computer system or at home through a commercial *Internet service provider (ISP)*. To search the Web, you also need a *Web browser* such as Netscape or Internet Explorer. By now, most of you are familiar with searching the Internet. This section provides some basic background information about the Net and introduces you to some tools and strategies that will help you use it more efficiently to find information on a topic.

As you use the Internet for conducting research, keep the following concerns and guidelines in mind:

- *The Internet has no central system of organization.* On the Internet, a huge amount of information is stored on many different networks and servers and in many different formats, each with its own system of organization. The Internet has no central catalog, reference librarian, or standard classification system for the vast resources available there.

- *Many electronic sources are not part of the Internet or require a paid subscription or other fees.* Computerized library catalogs, electronic periodical indexes, full-text article databases, and other electronic resources are often stored on CD-ROMs or on campus computer networks rather than on the Internet and so are available to students only through the library or other campus computers. Furthermore, some databases on the Web charge for a subscription or for downloading or printing out content. For these reasons (as well as the one discussed below), you should plan to use the library or campus computer system for much of your electronic research, since it will give you access to more material at a lower cost. You will not need to pay for subscriptions, and you may be able to download or print out material for free as well.

- *Internet sources that you find on your own are generally less reliable than print sources or than electronic sources to which your library or campus subscribes.* Because it is relatively easy for anyone to publish on the Internet, judging the reliability of online information is a special concern. Depending on your topic, purpose, and audience, the sources you find on the Internet may not be as credible or authoritative as print sources or subscription electronic sources, which have usually been screened by publishers, editors, librarians, and authorities on the topic. For some topics, most of what you find on the Internet may be written by highly biased or amateur authors, so you will need to balance or supplement these sources with information from your library or campus and print sources. When in doubt about the reliability of an online source for a particular assignment, check with your instructor. (See Reading Sources with a Critical Eye on pp. 426–29 for more specific suggestions.)

- *Internet sources are not as stable as print sources or as the electronic sources to which your library or campus subscribes.* A Web site that existed last week may no longer be available today, or its content may have changed.

- *Internet sources must be documented, and so you need to include them in your working bibliography.* A working bibliography is an ongoing record of all the possible sources you discover as you research your subject. The working bibliography becomes the draft for the list of references or works cited at the end of your essay, even if you do not include all these sources in your final list. You will need to follow appropriate conventions for quoting, paraphrasing, summarizing, and documenting the online sources you use, just as you do for print sources. Because an Internet source can change or disappear quickly, be sure to record the information for the working-bibliography entry when you first find the source. Whenever possible, download and print out the source to preserve it. Make sure your download or printout includes all the items of information required for the entry or at least all those you can find. Citation forms for Internet sources typically require more information than those for print sources, but the items are often harder (or impossible) to identify because Internet sources do not appear in the kinds of standard formats that print sources do. (See Figure 13.5 for an example of how to organize bibliographic information for an Internet source.)

As you locate potentially useful Internet sources, record this information (as much as applies) for each site:

Author(s) of work: _____

Title of work: _____

Title of site: _____

Editor(s) of site: _____

Sponsor of site: _____

Publication information for print version of work: _____

Range or total number of pages, paragraphs, screens, or other sections of the work, if numbering

appears on screen: _____

Name of database and online service: _____

Date of electronic publication or latest update: _____

Date you accessed the source: _____

Electronic address (URL): _____

Keyword(s) or sequence of links you used to access the source: _____

_____

Figure 13.5 Information for Working Bibliography—Internet Sources

■ NAVIGATING THE WEB

A *Web browser* is a software program that allows you to display and navigate Web pages on your computer. Web browsers have evolved from basic text-driven browsers such as Lynx into graphical, point-and-click interfaces such as Netscape Navigator and Microsoft Internet Explorer, which support not only text and hypertext links but also sound, images, animation, and video.

Understanding Home Pages

A particular Web site usually consists of multiple screens, or pages: a home page and other pages to which it is electronically linked. The *home page* is what you most often see first when you access a Web site; it typically provides a title heading, a brief introduction to or overview of the site, and a brief table of contents consisting of links to the information available at the site. In this way, it is like the opening pages of a book. Figure 13.6 on p. 423 shows the home page for *Home Education Magazine*. Web sites may be sponsored by companies, educational institutions, government agencies, private organizations, or individuals. The bottom of a home page usually includes the name of the group or person responsible for the site and an email address or other information about how to contact the sponsor or editor.

Using Links

On a Web page (and in other electronic documents, such as email), *links* to other pages, to other text on the same page, or to other Web sites are often indicated by underlined or boldface text. For example, the *Home Education Magazine* home page provides links to an online newsletter, a resource guide, and other material related to home schooling. Links can also appear as boxes, buttons, icons, or other graphic images. Each Web site has its own scheme for organizing and identifying links. In addition to sending your browser to another Web address, the links on a Web site can perform many other functions. For example, they may open a form to be filled out by the reader, start a video, play music or sounds, or launch a preaddressed email composition window.

Understanding URLs

Each Web page has its own address, called a *uniform resource locator* or *URL,* which allows people anywhere in the world to locate a particular Web page. The URL for the National Home Education Network follows the typical pattern: http://www .nhen.org.

- The first part of a URL usually consists of the abbreviation *http://* (meaning *hypertext transfer protocol*); it tells the sending and receiving computers how to transfer the information being sent.
- The second part of the URL usually includes the standard *www.,* to establish that the location being accessed is on the World Wide Web, and then identifies the institution, government agency, corporation, or organization that owns or sponsors the site. For example, home-ed-magazine.com indicates that the site is sponsored by *Home Education Magazine.* The three-letter suffix at the end of this part identifies what kind of site it is.

  .com = commercial site

  .edu = educational institution site

  .gov = government site

  .org = organization site

  .mil = military site

  .net = Internet service site

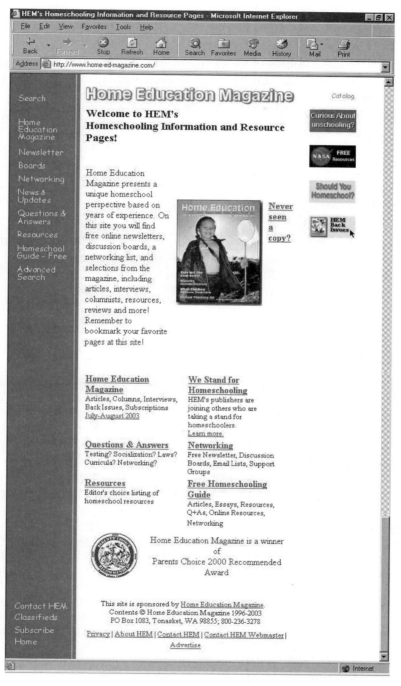

Figure 13.6 Home Page for Home Education Magazine

If the owner or sponsor of the site is outside the United States, this part of the URL will also include a two-letter code indicating the country, such as *.ca* for Canada or *.uk* for the United Kingdom.

- Many URLs have a third part, which may be lengthy, identifying the part of the site where the page is found or the kind of computer language it is written in (as in *wlcm_hemnewsltr.html* for the *Home Education Magazine* newsletter).

When you type a URL into an address box to access a site, you generally need to follow the exact spacing and punctuation of the site's address. Sometimes, though, a browser or a site will not require the *http://* or the *www.* or will require that you omit them.

Creating Bookmarks

You can store the addresses of Web pages that you may want to visit again by creating *bookmarks* for them. In Netscape, you do this by clicking on a Bookmark button; in Internet Explorer, you click on Favorites and then on Add to Favorites. This stores the name of the page in a list that you can click on whenever you want to revisit the page. If you are not using your own computer, you will need to download your bookmarks onto a disk or email them to yourself to save them.

■ USING SEARCH TOOLS

Because the World Wide Web does not have a central directory that will point you to specific resources, *search tools* are important resources for searching the Web for information on your topic. Table 13.5 lists some of the most popular search tools. To use these tools effectively, you should understand their features, strengths, and limitations.

Most search tools now allow you to look for sources using both search engines and subject directories. *Search engines* are based on keywords. They are simply computer programs that scan the Web—or that part of the Web that is in the particular search engine's database—looking for the keyword(s) you have entered. *Subject directories* are based on categories, like the subject headings in a library catalog or periodical index. Beginning with a menu of general subjects, you click on increasingly narrow subjects (for example, going from Science to Biology to Genetics to DNA Mapping), until you reach either a list of specific Web sites or a point where you have to do a keyword search within the narrowest subject you have chosen. Search engines are useful whenever you have a good idea of the appropriate keywords for your topic or if you are not sure under what category the topic falls. But subject directories can help quickly narrow your search to those parts of the Web that are likely to be most productive and thus avoid keyword searches that produce hundreds or thousands of results.

Always click on the link called Help, Hints, or Tips on a search tool's home page to find out more about the recognized commands and advanced-search techniques for that specific search tool. Most search engines either allow searches using the

Table 13.5 Commonly Used Search Tools

Name	URL
Search Tools	
All the Web	www.alltheweb.com
AltaVista	www.altavista.com
Excite	www.excite.com
Google	www.google.com
HotBot	www.hotbot.com
Lycos	www.lycos.com
Teoma	www.teoma.com
Yahoo!	www.yahoo.com
Metasearch Tools (search multiple search engines and subject directories)	
Ixquick	www.ixquick.com
WebCrawler	www.webcrawler.com
ProFusion	www.profusion.com
Zworks	www.zworks.com

Boolean operators discussed on pp. 406–8 or incorporate Boolean logic into an advanced-search page. Many also let you limit a search to specific dates, languages, or other criteria.

As with searches of library catalogs and databases, the success of a Web search depends to a great extent on the keywords you choose. Remember that many different words often describe the same topic. If your topic is ecology, for example, you may find information under the keywords *ecosystem, environment, pollution,* and *endangered species,* as well as a number of other related keywords, depending on the focus of your research. When you find a source that seems promising, be sure to create a bookmark for the Web page so that you can return to it easily later on.

■ USING EMAIL AND ONLINE COMMUNITIES FOR RESEARCH

You may find it possible to use your computer to do research in ways other than those already discussed in this chapter. In particular, if you can find out the email address of an expert on your topic, you may want to contact the person and ask whether he or she would agree to a brief online (or telephone) interview. In addition, several kinds of electronic communities available on the Internet may possibly be helpful. Many Web sites consist of or incorporate tools known as *bulletin boards* or *message boards,* in which anyone who registers may post messages to and receive them from other members. Older Internet servers known as news servers also provide access to bulletin boards or variants called *newsgroups.* Another kind of community, *mailing lists,* are groups of people who subscribe to receive email messages shared among all the members simultaneously. Finally, *chat rooms* allow users to meet together at the same time in a shared message space, using either a Web-based or generally available chat software application.

These different kinds of online communities often focus on a specific field of shared interest, and the people who frequent them are sometimes working professionals or academics with expertise in topics that are obscure or difficult to research otherwise. Such experts are often willing to answer both basic and advanced questions and will sometimes consent to an email or telephone interview. Even if they are not authorities in the field, online community members may stimulate your thinking about the topic in new directions or save you a large amount of research time by pointing you to a range of other available resources that might otherwise have taken you quite a while to uncover. Many communities provide some kind of indexing or search mechanism so that you can look for "threads" of postings related to your topic.

As with other sources, however, evaluate the credibility and reliability of online communities with a critical eye. Also be aware that while some communities and some members of them welcome guests and newcomers, others may perceive your questions as intrusive or unwanted. What may seem new and exciting to you may be old news for veterans. Finally, remember that some online communities are more active than others; survey the dates of posts and frequency of activity to determine whether a given group is still lively or has gone defunct.

You can probably access a variety of Usenet newsgroups related to your topic through your college library; go to www.groups.google.com to find a list. For mailing lists, you have to register for a subscription to the list. Remember that each subscription means you will be receiving a large amount of email, so think about the implications before you sign up.

■ READING SOURCES WITH A CRITICAL EYE

From the beginning of your search, you should evaluate potential sources to determine which ones you should take the time to examine more closely and then which of these you should use in your essay. Obviously, you must decide which sources provide information relevant to the topic. But you must also read sources with a critical eye to decide how credible or trustworthy they are. Just because a book or an essay appears in print or online does not necessarily mean that an author's information or opinions are reliable.

Selecting Relevant Sources

Begin your evaluation of sources by narrowing your working bibliography to the most relevant works. Consider them in terms of scope, date of publication, and viewpoint.

Scope and Approach. To decide how relevant a particular source is to your topic, you need to examine the source in depth. Do not depend on title alone, for it may be misleading. If the source is a book, check its table of contents and index to see how many pages are devoted to the precise subject you are exploring. In most cases, you will want an in-depth, not a superficial, treatment of the subject. Read the preface or introduction to a book or the abstract or opening paragraphs of an article and any biographical information given about the author to determine the author's basic approach to the subject or special way of looking at it. As you attend to these elements, consider the following questions:

- Does the source provide a general or specialized view? General sources are helpful early in your research, but then you need the authority or up-to-date coverage of specialized sources. Extremely specialized works, however, may be too technical.
- Is the source long enough to provide adequate detail?
- Is the source written for general readers? Specialists? Advocates? Critics?
- Is the author an expert on the topic? Does the author's way of looking at the topic support or challenge your own views? (The fact that an author's viewpoint challenges your own does not mean that you should reject the author as a source, as you will see from the discussion on multiple viewpoints.)
- Is the information in the source substantiated elsewhere? Does its approach seem to be comparable to, or a significant challenge to, the approaches of other credible sources?

Date of Publication. Although you should always consult the most up-to-date sources available on your subject, older sources often establish the principles, theories, and data on which later work is based and may provide a useful perspective for evaluating it. If older works are considered authoritative, you may want to become familiar with them. To determine which sources are authoritative, note the ones that are cited most often in encyclopedia articles, bibliographies, and recent works on the subject. If your source is on the Web, consider whether it has been regularly updated.

Viewpoint. Your sources should represent a variety of viewpoints on the subject. Just as you would not depend on a single author for all of your information, so you do not want to use only authors who belong to the same school of thought. For suggestions on determining authors' viewpoints, see the following Identifying Bias section.

Using sources that represent different viewpoints is especially important when developing an argument for one of the essay assignments in Chapters 5–7. During the invention work in those chapters, you may want to research what others have said about your subject to see what positions have been staked out and what arguments have been made. You will then be able to define the issue more carefully, collect arguments supporting your position, and anticipate arguments opposing it.

Identifying Bias

One of the most important aspects of evaluating a source is identifying any bias in its treatment of the subject. Although the word *bias* may sound accusatory, most writing is not neutral or objective and does not try or claim to be. Authors come to their subjects with particular viewpoints. In using sources, you must consider carefully how these viewpoints are reflected in the writing and how they affect the way authors present their arguments.

Although the text of the source will give you the most precise indication of the author's viewpoint, you can often get a good idea of it by looking at the preface or introduction or at the sources the author cites. When you examine a reference, you can often determine the general point of view it represents by considering the following elements.

Title. Does the title or subtitle indicate the text's bias? Watch for loaded words or confrontational phrasing.

Author. What is the author's professional title or affiliation? What is the author's perspective? Is the author in favor of something or at odds with it? What has persuaded the author to take this stance? How might the author's professional affiliation affect his or her perspective? What is the author's tone? Information on the author may be available in the book, article, or Web site itself or in biographical sources available in the library. You could also try entering the author's name into a search engine and see what you learn from the sites it finds.

Presentation of Argument. Almost every written work asserts a point of view or makes an argument for something the author considers important. To determine this position and the reason behind it, look for the main point. What evidence does the author provide as support for this point? Is the evidence from authoritative sources? Is the evidence persuasive? Does the author make concessions to or refute opposing arguments? (For more detail on these argumentative strategies, see Chapter 11.)

Publication Information. Is the book published by a commercial publisher, a corporation, a government agency, or an interest group? Is the Web site sponsored by a business, a professional group, a private organization, an educational institution, a government agency, or an individual? What is the publisher's or sponsor's position on the topic? Is the author funded by or affiliated with the publisher or sponsor?

Editorial Slant. What kind of periodical published the article — popular, academic, alternative? If you found the article on a Web site, is the site maintained by a commercial or academic sponsor? Does the article provide links to other Web resources? For periodicals, knowing some background about the publisher can help to determine bias because all periodicals have their own editorial slants. Where the periodical's name does not indicate its bias, reference sources may help you determine this information. Two of the most common are the following:

Gale Directory of Publications and Broadcast Media (1990–, updated yearly): A useful source for descriptive information on newspapers and magazines. Entries often include an indication of intended audience and political or other bias. For example, the *San Diego Union* is described as a newspaper with a Republican orientation.

Magazines for Libraries (1997): A listing of over 6,500 periodicals arranged by academic discipline. For each discipline, this book lists basic indexes, abstracts, and periodicals. Each individual listing for a periodical includes its publisher, the date it was founded, the places it is indexed, its intended audience, and an evaluation of its content and editorial focus. Here is an example of one such listing:

> 2605. *Growing Without Schooling.* [ISSN: 0745-5305]
> 1977. bi-m. $25. Susannah Sheffer. Holt Assocs., 2269
> Massachusetts Ave., Cambridge, MA 02140. Illus.,
> index, adv. Sample. Circ: 5,000.
> *Bk. rev:* 0–4, 400–600 words, signed. *Aud:* Ga, Sa.
> *GWS* is a journal by and for home schoolers. Parents and
> students share their views as to why they chose home
> schooling and what they like about it. While lesson plans
> or activities are not included, home schoolers could get
> ideas for interesting activities from articles chronicling
> their experiences ("Helping Flood Victims," "Legislative
> Intern"). "News and Reports" offers home schoolers
> information on legal issues while the "Declassified Ads"
> suggest resources geared toward home schoolers. This
> is an important title for public libraries and should be
> available to students and faculty in teacher preparation
> programs.

14

Strategies for Using and Acknowledging Sources

In addition to your own firsthand observation and analysis, your writing in college will be expected to use and acknowledge secondary sources—readings, interviews, Web sites, computer bulletin boards, lectures, and other print and nonprint materials.

When you cite material from another source, you need to acknowledge the source, usually by citing the author and page or date (depending on the documentation system) in your text and including a list of works cited or references at the end of your paper. It is necessary to acknowledge sources correctly and accurately to avoid *plagiarism,* the act of using the words and ideas of others as if they were your own. By citing sources correctly, you give credit to the originator of the words and ideas you are using, give your readers the information they need to consult those sources directly, and build your own credibility.

This chapter provides guidelines for using sources effectively and acknowledging them accurately. It includes model citations for both the Modern Language Association (MLA) and American Psychological Association (APA) documentation styles.

■ USING SOURCES

Writers commonly use sources by quoting directly, by paraphrasing, and by summarizing. This section provides guidelines for deciding when to use each of these three methods and how to do so effectively.

Deciding Whether to Quote, Paraphrase, or Summarize

As a general rule, quote only in these situations: (1) when the wording of the source is particularly memorable or vivid or expresses a point so well that you cannot improve it without destroying the meaning, (2) when the words of reliable and respected authorities would lend support to your position, (3) when you wish to highlight the author's opinions, (4) when you wish to cite an author whose opinions challenge or vary greatly from those of other experts, or (5) when you are going to discuss the source's choice of words. Paraphrase passages whose details you wish to note completely but whose language is not particularly striking. Summarize any long passages whose main

430

points you wish to record selectively as background or general support for a point you are making.

Quoting

Quotations should duplicate the source exactly. If the source has an error, copy it and add the notation *sic* (Latin for "thus") in brackets immediately after the error to indicate that it is not your error but your source's:

> According to a recent newspaper article, "Plagirism [sic] is a problem among journalists and scholars as well as students" (Berensen 62).

However, you can change quotations (1) to emphasize particular words by underlining or italicizing them, (2) to omit irrelevant information or to make the quotation conform grammatically to your sentence by using ellipsis marks, and (3) to make the quotation conform grammatically or to insert information by using brackets.

Using Underlining or Italicizing for Emphasis.   You may underline or italicize any words in the quotation that you want to emphasize, and add the words *emphasis added* (in regular type, not italicized or underlined) in brackets after the words you want to emphasize.

> In his introduction, Studs Terkel (1972) claims that his book is about a search for "daily meaning as well as daily bread, for recognition as well as cash, for astonishment rather than torpor [emphasis added]; in short, for a sort of life rather than a Monday through Friday sort of dying" (p. xi).

Using Ellipsis Marks for Omissions.   A writer may decide to leave certain words out of a quotation because they are not relevant to the point being made or because they add information readers will not need in the context in which the quotation is being used. When you omit words from within a quotation, you must use ellipsis marks — three spaced periods (. . .) — in place of the missing words. When the omission occurs within a sentence, include a space before the first ellipsis mark and after the closing mark. There should also be spaces between the three marks.

> Hermione Roddice is described in Lawrence's *Women in Love* as a "woman of the new school, full of intellectuality and . . . nerve-worn with consciousness" (17).

When the omission falls at the end of a sentence, place a sentence period *directly after* the final word of the sentence, followed by a space and three spaced ellipsis marks.

> But Grimaldi's commentary contends that for Aristotle rhetoric, like dialectic, had "no limited and unique subject matter upon which it must be exercised. . . . Instead, rhetoric as an art transcends all specific disciplines and may be brought into play in them" (6).

A period plus ellipsis marks can indicate the omission of the rest of the sentence as well as whole sentences, paragraphs, or even pages.

When a parenthetical reference follows the ellipsis marks at the end of a sentence, place the three spaced periods after the quotation, and place the sentence period after the final parenthesis:

> But Grimaldi's recent commentary on Aristotle contends that for Aristotle rhetoric, like dialec-tic, had "no limited and unique subject matter upon which it must be exercised.... Instead, rhetoric as an art transcends all specific disciplines..." (6).

When you quote only single words or phrases, you do not need to use ellipsis marks because it will be obvious that you have left out some of the original.

> More specifically, Wharton's imagery of suffusing brightness transforms Undine before her glass into "some fabled creature whose home was in a beam of light" (21).

For the same reason, you need not use ellipsis marks if you omit the beginning of a quoted sentence unless the rest of the sentence begins with a capitalized word and still appears to be a complete sentence.

Using Brackets for Insertions or Changes.   Use brackets around an insertion or a change needed to make a quotation conform grammatically to your sentence, such as a change in the form of a verb or pronoun or in the capitalization of the first word of the quotation. In this example from a student's essay on James Joyce's "Araby," the writer adapts Joyce's phrases "we played till our bodies glowed" and "shook music from the buckled harness" to fit the grammar of her sentences:

> In the dark, cold streets during the "short days of winter," the boys must generate their own heat by "play[ing] till [their] bodies glowed." Music is "[shaken] from the buckled harness" as if it were unnatural, and the singers in the market chant nasally of "the troubles in our native land" (30).

You may also use brackets to add or substitute explanatory material in a quotation:

> Guterson notes that among Native Americans in Florida, "education was in the home; learn-ing by doing was reinforced by the myths and legends which repeated the basic value sys-tem of their [the Seminoles'] way of life" (159).

Some changes that make a quotation conform grammatically to another sentence may be made without any signal to readers: (1) A period at the end of a quotation may be changed to a comma if you are using the quotation within your own sentence, and (2) double quotation marks enclosing a quotation may be changed to single quota-tion marks when the quotation is enclosed within a longer quotation.

Integrating Quotations

Depending on its length, a quotation may be incorporated into your text by being enclosed in quotation marks or set off from your text in a block without quotation marks. In either case, be sure to blend the quotation into your essay rather than drop-ping it in without appropriate integration.

In-Text Quotations.   Incorporate brief quotations (no more than four typed lines of prose or three lines of poetry) into your text. You may place the quotation virtually anywhere in your sentence:

At the Beginning

"To live a life is not to cross a field," Sutherland quotes Pasternak at the beginning of her narrative (11).

In the Middle

Woolf begins and ends by speaking of the need of the woman writer to have "money and a room of her own" (4) — an idea that certainly spoke to Plath's condition.

At the End

In *The Second Sex,* Simone de Beauvoir describes such an experience as one in which the girl "becomes as object, and she sees herself as object" (378).

Divided by Your Own Words

"Science usually prefers the literal to the nonliteral term," Kinneavy writes, "— that is, figures of speech are often out of place in science" (177).

When you quote poetry within your text, use a slash (/) with spaces before and after to signal the end of each line of verse:

Alluding to St. Augustine's distinction between the City of God and the Earthly City, Lowell writes that "much against my will / I left the City of God where it belongs" (4–5).

Block Quotations.   In the MLA style, use the block form for prose quotations of five or more typed lines and poetry quotations of four or more lines. Indent the quotation an inch (ten character spaces) from the left margin, as shown in the following example. In the APA style, use block form for quotations of forty words or more. Indent the block quotation about a half inch (five character spaces), keeping your indents consistent throughout your paper.

In a block quotation, double-space between lines just as you do in your text. *Do not* enclose the passage within quotation marks. Use a colon to introduce a block quotation, unless the context calls for another punctuation mark or none at all. When quoting a single paragraph or part of one in the MLA style, do not indent the first line of the quotation more than the rest. In quoting two or more paragraphs, indent the first line of each paragraph an extra quarter inch (three spaces). If you are using the APA style, the first line of subsequent paragraphs in the block quotation indents an additional five spaces from the block quotation indent.

```
In "A Literary Legacy from Dunbar to Baraka," Margaret
Walker says of Paul Lawrence Dunbar's dialect poems:
            He realized that the white world in the United
        States tolerated his literary genius only because
```

> of his "jingles in a broken tongue," and they
> found the old "darky" tales and speech amusing and
> within the vein of folklore into which they wished
> to classify all Negro life. This troubled Dunbar
> because he realized that white America was deni-
> grating him as a writer and as a man. (70)

Introducing Quotations

Statements that introduce quotations take a range of punctuation marks and lead-in words. Here are some examples of ways writers typically introduce quotations.

Introducing a Quotation Using a Colon

A colon usually follows an independent clause placed before the quotation.

> As George Williams notes, protection of white privilege is critical to patterns of discrimina-
> tion: "Whenever a number of persons within a society have enjoyed for a considerable period
> of time certain opportunities for getting wealth, for exercising power and authority, and for
> successfully claiming prestige and social deference, there is a strong tendency for these
> people to feel that these benefits are theirs 'by right'" (727).

Introducing a Quotation Using a Comma

A comma usually follows an introduction that incorporates the quotation in its sentence structure.

> Similarly, Duncan Turner asserts, "As matters now stand, it is unwise to talk about communi-
> cation without some understanding of Burke" (259).

Introducing a Quotation Using that

No punctuation is generally needed with *that*, and no capital letter is used to begin the quotation.

> Noting this failure, Alice Miller asserts that "the reason for her despair was not her suffering
> but the impossibility of communicating her suffering to another person" (255).

Punctuating within Quotations

Although punctuation within a quotation should reproduce the original, some adaptations may be necessary. Use single quotation marks for quotations within the quotation:

Original from Guterson (16–17)

> E. D. Hirsch also recognizes the connection between family and learning, suggesting in his
> discussion of family background and academic achievement "that the significant part of our
> children's education has been going on outside rather than inside the schools."

Quoted Version

Guterson claims that E. D. Hirsch "also recognizes the connection between family and learning, suggesting in his discussion of family background and academic achievement 'that the significant part of our children's education has been going on outside rather than inside the schools'" (16–17).

If the quotation ends with a question mark or an exclamation point, retain the original punctuation:

"Did you think I loved you?" Edith later asks Dombey (566).

If a quotation ending with a question mark or an exclamation point concludes your sentence, retain the question mark or exclamation point, and put the parenthetical reference and sentence period outside the quotation marks:

Edith later asks Dombey, "Did you think I loved you?" (566).

Avoiding Grammatical Tangles

When you incorporate quotations into your writing, and especially when you omit words from quotations, you run the risk of creating ungrammatical sentences. Three common errors you should try to avoid are verb incompatibility, ungrammatical omissions, and sentence fragments.

Verb Incompatibility.   When this error occurs, the verb form in the introductory statement is grammatically incompatible with the verb form in the quotation. When your quotation has a verb form that does not fit in with your text, it is usually possible to use just part of the quotation, thus avoiding verb incompatibility.

he describes seeing himself
► The narrator suggests his bitter disappointment when "~~I saw myself~~
"as a creature driven and derided by vanity" (35).

As this sentence illustrates, use the present tense when you refer to events in a literary work.

Ungrammatical Omission.   Sometimes omitting text from a quotation leaves you with an ungrammatical sentence. Two ways of correcting the grammar are (1) adapting the quotation (with brackets) so that its parts fit together grammatically and (2) using only one part of the quotation.

► From the moment of the boy's arrival in Araby, the bazaar is presented as a

commercial enterprise: "I could not find any sixpenny entrance and . . .

hand[ed]
~~handing~~ a shilling to a weary-looking man" (34).

▶ From the moment of the boy's arrival in Araby, the bazaar is presented as a

commercial enterprise: "~~I~~^{He}could not find any sixpenny entrance"and ~~. . .~~

^{so had to pay a shilling to get in (34)⊙}
~~handing a shilling to a weary looking man" (34).~~

Sentence Fragment. Sometimes when a quotation is a complete sentence, writers neglect the sentence that introduces the quote—for example, by forgetting to include a verb. Make sure that the quotation is introduced by a complete sentence.

▶ The girl's interest in the bazaar ~~leading~~ ^{leads} the narrator to make what amounts to a sacred oath: "If I go . . . I will bring you something" (32).

Paraphrasing and Summarizing

In addition to quoting sources, writers have the option of paraphrasing or summarizing what others have written.

Paraphrasing. In a *paraphrase,* the writer restates primarily in his or her own words all the relevant information from a passage, without any additional comments or any suggestion of agreement or disagreement with the source's ideas. A paraphrase is useful for recording details of the passage when the order of the details is important but the source's wording is not. Because all the details of the passage are included, a paraphrase is often about the same length as the original passage. Paraphrasing allows you to avoid quoting too much.

Here is a passage from a book on home schooling and an example of an acceptable paraphrase of it:

Original Source

Bruner and the discovery theorists have also illuminated conditions that apparently pave the way for learning. It is significant that these conditions are unique to each learner, so unique, in fact, that in many cases classrooms can't provide them. Bruner also contends that the more one discovers information in a great variety of circumstances, the more likely one is to develop the inner categories required to organize that information. Yet life at school, which is for the most part generic and predictable, daily keeps many children from the great variety of circumstances they need to learn well.

–David Guterson, *Family Matters: Why Homeschooling Makes Sense,* p. 172

Acceptable Paraphrase

According to Guterson, the "discovery theorists," particularly Bruner, have found that there seem to be certain conditions that help learning to take place. Because each individual requires different conditions, many children are not able to learn in the classroom. According to Bruner, when people can explore information in many different situations, they learn to classify and order what they discover. The general routine of the school day, however, does not provide children with the diverse activities and situations that would allow them to learn these skills (172).

Readers assume that some words in a paraphrase are taken from the source. Indeed, it would be nearly impossible for paraphrasers to avoid using any key terms from the source, and it would be counterproductive to try to do so because the original and paraphrase necessarily share the same information and concepts. Notice, though, that of the total of 86 words in the paraphrase, the paraphraser uses only a name *(Bruner)* and a few other key nouns and verbs *(discovery theorists, conditions, children, learn[ing], information, situations)* for which it would be awkward to substitute other words or phrases. If the paraphraser had wanted to use other kinds of language from the source—for example, the description of life at school as "generic and predictable"—these adjectives should have been enclosed in quotation marks.

In fact, the paraphraser puts quotation marks around only one of the terms from the source: "discovery theorists," a technical term likely to be unfamiliar to readers. The source of all the material in the paraphrase is identified by the author's name *(Guterson)* in the first sentence and by the page number *(172)* in the last sentence, which indicates where the paraphrased material appears in David Guterson's book. This source citation follows the style of the Modern Language Association (MLA). Notice that placing the citation information in this way indicates clearly to readers where the paraphrase begins and ends, so that they understand clearly where the text is expressing ideas taken from a source and where it is expressing the writer's own ideas (or ideas from a different source). Should readers want to check the accuracy or completeness of the paraphrase, they could turn to the alphabetically arranged list of works cited at the end of the essay in which the paraphrase appeared, look for Guterson's name, and find there all the information they would need to locate the book and check the source.

Although it is acceptable and often necessary to reuse a few key words or quote striking or technical language, paraphrasers must avoid borrowing too many words from a source and repeating the sentence structures of a source. Here is a paraphrase of the first sentence in the Guterson passage that repeats too many of the words and phrases in the source, making the paraphrase unacceptable.

Unacceptable Paraphrase: Too Many Borrowed Words and Phrases

Apparently, some conditions, which have been illuminated by Bruner and other discovery theorists, pave the way for people to learn.

If you compare the source's first sentence and the paraphrase of it, you will see that the paraphrase borrows almost all of its key language from the source sentence, including the entire phrase *pave the way for*. Even if you cite the source, this heavy borrowing would be considered plagiarism, using the ideas and words of others as though they were your own.

Here is another paraphrase of the same sentence that too closely resembles the structure of the source sentence, again making the paraphrase unacceptable.

Unacceptable Paraphrase: Sentence Structure Repeated Too Closely

Bruner and other researchers have also identified circumstances that seem to ease the path to learning.

If you compare the source's first sentence and this paraphrase of it, you will see that the paraphraser has borrowed the phrases and clauses of the source and arranged them in an identical sequence, simply substituting synonyms for most of the key terms: *researchers* for *theorists, identified* for *illuminated, circumstances* for *conditions, seem to* for *apparently,* and *ease the path to* for *pave the way for.* This paraphrase would also be considered plagiarism, even though most of the key terms have been changed and even if you cite the source.

Summarizing.   Like a paraphrase, a *summary* may rely on key words from the source but is made up mainly of words supplied by the writer. It presents only the main ideas of a source, leaving out examples and details. Consequently, summaries allow you to bring concisely into your writing large amounts of information from source material.

Here is an example of a summary of five pages from the David Guterson book. You can see at a glance how drastically some summaries condense information, in this case from five pages to five sentences. Depending on the summarizer's purpose, the five pages could be summarized in one sentence, the five sentences here, or two or three dozen sentences.

In looking at different theories of learning that discuss individual-based programs (such as home schooling) versus the public school system, Guterson describes the disagreements among "cognitivist" theorists. One group, the "discovery theorists," believes that individual children learn by creating their own ways of sorting the information they take in from their experiences. Schools should help students develop better ways of organizing new material, not just present them with material that is already categorized, as traditional schools do. "Assimilationist theorists," by contrast, believe that children learn by linking what they don't know to information they already know. These theorists claim that traditional schools help students learn when they present information in ways that allow children to fit the new material into categories they have already developed (171–75).

In this summary, the source of the summarized material is identified by the author's name in the first sentence and the page numbers of the material in the last sentence, following the citation style of the Modern Language Association. As with paraphrases, putting the citation information at the beginning and the end of the summary in this way makes clear to the reader the boundaries between the ideas in the source and the writer's own ideas (or the ideas in a different source).

Though this summarizer puts quotation marks around three technical terms from the original source, summaries usually do not include quotations: Their purpose is not to display the source's language but to present its main ideas. Longer summaries like this one are more than a dry list of main ideas from a source. They are instead a coherent, readable new text composed of the source's main ideas. Summaries provide balanced coverage of a source, following the same sequence of ideas and avoiding any hint of agreement or disagreement with them.

ACKNOWLEDGING SOURCES

Notice in the preceding examples of paraphrasing and summarizing that the source is acknowledged by name. Even when you use your own words to present someone else's information, you must acknowledge that you borrowed the information. The only types of information that do not require acknowledgment are common knowledge (John F. Kennedy was assassinated in Dallas), facts widely available in many sources (U.S. presidents used to be inaugurated on March 4 rather than January 20), well-known quotations ("To be or not to be. That is the question"), or material you created or gathered yourself, such as photographs that you took or data from surveys that you conducted. Remember that you need to acknowledge the source of any visual (photograph, table, chart, graph, diagram, drawing, map, screen shot) that you did not create yourself or of any information that you used to create your own visual. (You should also request permission from the source of a visual you want to borrow if your essay is going to be posted on the Web.) When in doubt about whether you need to cite a source for something, it is safer to do so.

The documentation guidelines later in this section present various styles for citing sources. Whichever style you use, the most important thing is that your readers be able to tell where words or ideas that are not your own begin and end. You can accomplish this most readily by taking and transcribing notes carefully, by placing parenthetical source citations correctly, and by separating your words from those of the source with *signal phrases* such as "According to Smith," "Peters claims," and "As Olmos asserts." (When you cite a source for the first time in a signal phrase, you may use the author's full name; after that, use just the last name.)

Avoiding Plagiarism

Writers—students and professionals alike—occasionally fail to acknowledge sources properly. The word *plagiarism,* which derives from the Latin word for "kidnapping," refers to the unacknowledged use of another's words, ideas, or information. Students sometimes get into trouble because they mistakenly assume that plagiarizing occurs only when another writer's exact words are used without acknowledgment. In fact, plagiarism applies to such diverse forms of expression as musical compositions and visual images as well as ideas and statistics. So keep in mind that, with the exceptions listed above, you must indicate the source of any borrowed information or ideas you use in your essay, whether you have paraphrased, summarized, or quoted directly from the source or have reproduced it or referred to it in some other way.

Remember especially the need to document electronic sources fully and accurately. Perhaps because it is so easy to access and distribute text and visuals online and to copy material from one electronic document and paste it into another, many students do not realize or forget that information, ideas, and images from electronic sources require acknowledgment in even more detail than those from print sources do (and are often easier to detect if they are not acknowledged).

Some people plagiarize simply because they do not know the conventions for using and acknowledging sources. This chapter makes clear how to incorporate sources into your writing and how to acknowledge your use of those sources. Others plagiarize because they keep sloppy notes and thus fail to distinguish between their own and their sources' ideas. Either they neglect to enclose their sources' words in quotation marks, or they fail to indicate when they are paraphrasing or summarizing a source's ideas and information. If you keep a working bibliography and careful notes, you will not make this serious mistake. (For more on keeping a working bibliography, see Chapter 13, pp. 394–97.)

Another reason some people plagiarize is that they doubt their ability to write the essay by themselves. They feel intimidated by the writing task or the deadline or their own and others' expectations. If you experience this same anxiety about your work, speak to your instructor. Do not run the risk of failing a course or being expelled because of plagiarism. If you are confused about what is and what is not plagiarism, be sure to ask your instructor.

Understanding Documentation Styles

Although there is no universally accepted system for acknowledging sources, most documentation styles use parenthetical in-text citations keyed to a separate list of works cited or references. The information required in the in-text citations and the order and content of the works-cited entries vary across academic disciplines. This section presents the basic features of two styles: the author-page system that is advocated by the Modern Language Association (MLA) and widely used in the humanities and the author-year system that is advocated by the American Psychological Association (APA) and widely used in the natural and social sciences.

In Part One of this book, you can find examples of student essays that follow the MLA style (Linh Kieu Ngo, Chapter 4, and Jessica Statsky, Chapter 5) and the APA style (Patrick O'Malley, Chapter 6). For more information about these documentation styles, consult the *MLA Handbook for Writers of Research Papers,* Sixth Edition (2003) or the *Publication Manual of the American Psychological Association,* Fifth Edition (2001).

Check with your instructor about which of these styles you should use or whether you should use some other style. A list of common documentation style manuals is provided in Table 14.1 on p. 441.

The MLA System of Documentation

Citations in Text

The MLA author-page system generally requires that in-text citations include the author's last name and the page number of the passage being cited. There is no punctuation between author and page. The parenthetical citation should follow the quoted, paraphrased, or summarized material as closely as possible without disrupting the flow of the sentence.

Dr. James is described as a "not-too-skeletal Ichabod Crane" (Simon 68).

Table 14.1 Some Commonly Used Documentation Style Manuals

Subject	Style Manual	Online Source
General	*The Chicago Manual of Style.* 15th ed. 2003.	www.chicagomanualofstyle.org
	A Manual for Writers of Term Papers, Theses, and Dissertations. 6th ed. 1996.	—
Online Sources	*Columbia Guide to Online Style.* 1998.	www.columbia.edu/cu/cup/cgos/ idx_basic.html
Biological Sciences	*Scientific Style and Format: The CBE Manual for Authors, Editors, and Publishers.* 6th ed. 1994.	www.councilscienceeditors.org/ publications/style.cfm
Chemistry	*The ACS Style Guide.* 2nd ed. 1997.	www.pubs.acs.org/books/ references.shtml
Government Documents	*The Complete Guide to Citing Government Documents.* Rev. ed. 1993.	www.lib.memphis.edu/gpo/ citeweb.htm
Humanities	*MLA Handbook for Writers of Research Papers.* 6th ed. 2003.	www.mla.org
	MLA Style Manual and Guide to Scholarly Publishing. 2nd ed. 1998.	
Psychology/ Social Sciences	*Publication Manual of the American Psychological Association.* 5th ed. 2001.	www.apastyle.org

Note that the parenthetical citation comes before the final period. With block quotations, however, the citation comes after the final period, preceded by a space (see pp. 433–34 for an example).

If you mention the author's name in your text, supply just the page reference in parentheses.

Simon describes Dr. James as a "not-too-skeletal Ichabod Crane" (68).

A WORK WITH MORE THAN ONE AUTHOR

To cite a source by two or three authors, include all the authors' last names; for works with more than three authors, use all the authors' names or just the first author's name followed by *et al.,* meaning "and others," in regular type (not italicized or underlined).

Dyal, Corning, and Willows identify several types of students, including the "Authority-Rebel" (4).

The Authority-Rebel "tends to see himself as superior to other students in the class" (Dyal, Corning, and Willows 4).

The drug AZT has been shown to reduce the risk of transmission from HIV-positive mothers to their infants by as much as two-thirds (Van de Perre et al. 4–5).

TWO OR MORE WORKS BY THE SAME AUTHOR

Include the author's last name, a comma, a shortened version of the title, and the page number(s).

> When old paint becomes transparent, it sometimes shows the artist's original plans: "a tree will show through a woman's dress" (Hellman, Pentimento 1).

A WORK WITH AN UNKNOWN AUTHOR

Use a shortened version of the title, beginning with the word by which the title is alphabetized in the works-cited list. ("Awash in Garbage" was the title in the following example.)

> An international pollution treaty still to be ratified would prohibit all plastic garbage from being dumped at sea ("Awash" 26).

TWO OR MORE AUTHORS WITH THE SAME LAST NAME CITED IN YOUR ESSAY

In addition to the last name, include each author's first initial in the citation. If the first initials are also the same, spell out the authors' first names.

> Chaplin's Modern Times provides a good example of montage used to make an editorial statement (E. Roberts 246).

A CORPORATE OR GOVERNMENT AUTHOR

In a parenthetical citation, give the full name of the author if it is brief or a shortened version if it is long. If you name the author in your text, give the full name even if it is long.

> A tuition increase has been proposed for community and technical colleges to offset budget deficits from Initiative 601 (Washington State Board 4).

> According to the Washington State Board for Community and Technical Colleges, a tuition increase . . . from Initiative 601 (4).

A MULTIVOLUME WORK

When you use two or more volumes of a multivolume work in your paper, include the volume number and the page number(s), separated by a colon and one space, in each citation.

> According to Forster, modernist writers valued experimentation and gradually sought to blur the line between poetry and prose (3: 150).

If you cite only one volume, give the volume number in the works-cited entry (see p. 447) and include only the page number(s) in the parenthetical citation.

A LITERARY WORK

For a novel or other prose work available in various editions, provide the page numbers from the edition used as well as other information that will help readers locate the quotation in a different edition, such as the part or chapter number.

> In Hard Times, Tom reveals his utter narcissism by blaming Louisa for his own failure: "'You have regularly given me up. You never cared for me'" (Dickens 262; bk. 3, ch. 9).

For a play in verse, such as a Shakespearean play, indicate the act, scene, and line numbers instead of the page numbers.

> At the beginning, Regan's fawning rhetoric hides her true attitude toward Lear: "I profess / myself an enemy to all other joys.../ And find that I am alone felicitate / In your dear highness' love" (King Lear I.i.74–75, 77–78).

In the MLA style, act and scene numbers may instead be given in arabic numerals: (King Lear 1.1.74–75, 77–78).

For a poem, indicate the line numbers and stanzas or sections (if they are numbered), instead of the page numbers. If the source gives only line numbers, use the term *lines* in the first citation and give only the numbers in subsequent citations.

> In "Song of Myself," Whitman finds poetic details in busy urban settings, as when he describes "the blab of the pave, tires of carts...the driver with his interrogating thumb" (8.153–54).

A RELIGIOUS WORK

For the Bible, indicate the book, chapter, and verse instead of the page numbers. Abbreviate books with names of five or more letters in your parenthetical citation, but spell out full names of books in your text.

> She ignored the admonition "Pride goes before destruction, and a haughty spirit before a fall" (New Oxford Annotated Bible, Prov. 16.18).

A WORK IN AN ANTHOLOGY

Use the name of the author of the work, not the editor of the anthology, but use the page number(s) from the anthology.

> In "Six Days: Some Rememberings," Grace Paley recalls that when she was in jail for protesting the Vietnam War, her pen and paper were taken away and she felt "a terrible pain in the area of my heart—a nausea" (191).

A QUOTATION FROM A SECONDARY SOURCE

Include the secondary source in your list of works cited. In your parenthetical citation, use the abbreviation *qtd. in* (in regular type, not italicized or underlined) to acknowledge that the original was quoted in a secondary source.

E. M. Forster says "the collapse of all civilization, so realistic for us, sounded in Matthew Arnold's ears like a distant and harmonious cataract" (qtd. in Trilling 11).

AN ENTIRE WORK

Include the reference in the text without any page numbers or parentheses.

> In The Structure of Scientific Revolutions, Thomas Kuhn discusses how scientists change their thinking.

A WORK WITHOUT PAGE NUMBERS

If a work has no page numbers or is only one page long, you may omit the page number. If a work uses paragraph numbers instead, use the abbreviation *par(s)*, and use a comma after the author's name.

> The average speed on Montana's interstate highways, for example, has risen by only 2 miles per hour since the repeal of the federal speed limit, with most drivers topping out at 75 (Schmid).

> Whitman considered African American speech "a source of a native grand opera" (Ellison, par. 13).

TWO OR MORE WORKS CITED IN THE SAME PARENTHESES

When two or more different sources are used in the same passage of your essay, it may be necessary to cite them in the same parentheses. Separate the citations with a semicolon. Include any specific pages, or omit pages to refer to the whole work.

> A few studies have considered differences between oral and written discourse production (Scardamalia, Bereiter, and Goelman; Gould).

MATERIAL FROM THE INTERNET

Give enough information in the citation to enable readers to locate the Internet source in the list of works cited. If the author is not named, give the document title. Include page, section, paragraph, or screen numbers, if available.

> In handling livestock, "many people attempt to restrain animals with sheer force instead of using behavioral principles" (Grandin).

List of Works Cited

Providing full information for the citations in the text, the list of works cited identifies all the sources the writer uses. Entries are alphabetized according to the first author's last name or by the title if the author is unknown. Every source cited in the text must refer to an entry in the list of works cited. Conversely, every entry in the list of works cited must correspond to at least one in-text citation.

In the MLA style, multiple works by the same author (or same group of authors) are alphabetized by title. The author's name is given for the first entry only; in subsequent entries, three hyphens and a period are used.

```
Vidal, Gore. Empire. New York: Random, 1987.
---. Lincoln. New York: Random, 1984.
```

The information presented in a list of works cited follows this order: author, title, publication source, year, and (for an article) page range. The MLA style requires a "hanging indent," which means that the first line of a works-cited entry is not indented but subsequent lines of the entry are. The MLA specifies an indent of half an inch or five character spaces.

Books

Here is an example of a basic MLA-style entry for a book:

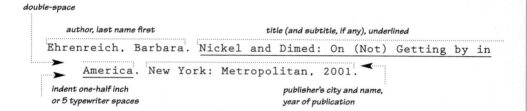

double-space

author, last name first   title (and subtitle, if any), underlined

```
Ehrenreich, Barbara. Nickel and Dimed: On (Not) Getting by in
    America. New York: Metropolitan, 2001.
```

indent one-half inch   publisher's city and name,
or 5 typewriter spaces   year of publication

A BOOK BY A SINGLE AUTHOR

```
Lamb, Sharon. The Secret Lives of Girls. New York: Free, 2002.
```

A BOOK BY AN AGENCY OR A CORPORATION

```
Association for Research in Nervous and Mental Disease. The
    Circulation of the Brain and Spinal Cord: A Symposium on
    Blood Supply. New York: Hafner, 1966.
```

A BOOK BY MORE THAN ONE AUTHOR

```
Saba, Laura, and Julie Gattis. The McGraw-Hill Homeschooling
    Companion. New York: McGraw, 2002.

Wilmut, Ian, Keith Campbell, and Colin Tudge. The Second
    Creation: Dolly and the Age of Biological Control. New
    York: Farrar, 2000.
```

A WORK BY MORE THAN THREE AUTHORS

The MLA lists all the authors' names *or* the name of the first author followed by *et al.* (in regular type, not italicized or underlined).

> Hunt, Lynn, et al. The Making of the West: Peoples and
> Cultures. Boston: Bedford, 2001.

A BOOK BY AN UNKNOWN AUTHOR

Use the title in place of the author.

> Rand McNally Commercial Atlas and Marketing Guide. Skokie:
> Rand, 2003.

A BOOK WITH AN AUTHOR AND AN EDITOR

If you refer to the author's text, begin the entry with the author's name.

> Arnold, Matthew. Culture and Anarchy. Ed. J. Dover Wilson.
> Cambridge: Cambridge UP, 1966.

If you cite the editor in your paper, begin the entry with the editor's name.

> Wilson, J. Dover, ed. Culture and Anarchy. By Matthew Arnold.
> 1869. Cambridge: Cambridge UP, 1966.

AN EDITED COLLECTION

> Waldman, Diane, and Janet Walker, eds. Feminism and
> Documentary. Minneapolis: U of Minnesota P, 1999.

A WORK IN AN ANTHOLOGY OR A COLLECTION

> Fairbairn-Dunlop, Peggy. "Women and Agriculture in Western
> Samoa." Different Places, Different Voices. Ed. Janet H.
> Momsen and Vivian Kinnaird. London: Routledge, 1993.
> 211-26.

TWO OR MORE WORKS FROM THE SAME ANTHOLOGY

To avoid repetition, you may create an entry for the collection and cite the collection's editor to cross-reference individual works to the entry.

> Boyd, Herb, ed. The Harlem Reader. New York: Three Rivers, 2003.
>
> Wallace, Michelle. "Memories of a Sixties Girlhood: The Harlem
> I Love." Boyd 243-50.

ONE VOLUME OF A MULTIVOLUME WORK

If only one volume from a multivolume set is used, indicate the volume number after the title.

Freud, Sigmund. The Complete Psychological Works of Sigmund
    Freud. Vol. 8. Trans. James Strachey. London: Hogarth,
    1962.

TWO OR MORE VOLUMES OF A MULTIVOLUME WORK

Sandburg, Carl. Abraham Lincoln. 6 vols. New York: Scribner's,
    1939.

A BOOK THAT IS PART OF A SERIES

Include the series title in regular type (not underlined or in quotation marks), followed by the series number and a period. If the word *Series* is part of the name, include *Ser.* before the number. Common abbreviations may be used for selected words in the series title.

Zigova, Tanya, et al. Neural Stem Cells: Methods and Protocols.
    Methods in Molecular Biology 198. Totowa: Humana, 2002.

A REPUBLISHED BOOK

Provide the original year of publication after the title of the book, followed by normal publication information for the edition you are using.

Alcott, Louisa May. An Old-Fashioned Girl. 1870. New York:
    Puffin, 1995.

A LATER EDITION OF A BOOK

Rottenberg, Annette T. The Structure of Argument. 2nd ed.
    Boston: Bedford, 1997.

A BOOK WITH A TITLE IN ITS TITLE

Do not underline a title normally underlined when it appears within the title of a book.

Hertenstein, Mike. The Double Vision of Star Trek: Half-Humans,
    Evil Twins, and Science Fiction. Chicago: Cornerstone,
    1998.

O'Neill, Terry, ed. Readings on To Kill a Mockingbird. San
    Diego: Greenhaven, 2000.

Use quotation marks around a work normally enclosed in quotation marks when it appears within the title of a book.

> Miller, Edwin Haviland. <u>Walt Whitman's "Song of Myself":</u> <u>A Mosaic of Interpretation</u>. Iowa City: U of Iowa P, 1989.

A TRANSLATION

If you refer to the work itself, begin the entry with the author's name.

> Tolstoy, Leo. <u>War and Peace</u>. Trans. Constance Garnett. London: Pan, 1972.

If you cite the translator in your text, begin the entry with the translator's name.

> Garnett, Constance, trans. <u>War and Peace</u>. By Leo Tolstoy. 1869. London: Pan, 1972.

A DICTIONARY ENTRY OR AN ARTICLE IN A REFERENCE BOOK

> "Homeopathy." <u>Webster's New World College Dictionary</u>. 4th ed. 1999.

> Rowland, Lewis P. "Myasthenia Gravis." <u>The Encyclopedia Americana</u>. 2001 ed.

AN INTRODUCTION, PREFACE, FOREWORD, OR AFTERWORD

> Holt, John. Introduction. <u>Better than School</u>. By Nancy Wallace. Burnett: Larson, 1983. 9-14.

Articles

Here is an example of a basic MLA-style entry for an article in a periodical:

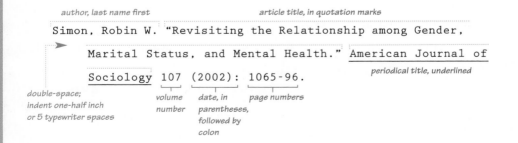

author, last name first *article title, in quotation marks*

Simon, Robin W. "Revisiting the Relationship among Gender, Marital Status, and Mental Health." <u>American Journal of</u> <u>Sociology</u> 107 (2002): 1065-96.

periodical title, underlined

double-space; indent one-half inch or 5 typewriter spaces *volume number* *date, in parentheses, followed by colon* *page numbers*

If the article is not on a continuous sequence of pages, give the first page number followed by a plus sign, as in the following example.

AN ARTICLE FROM A DAILY NEWSPAPER

Peterson, Andrea. "Finding a Cure for Old Age." Wall Street
    Journal 20 May 2003: D1+.

AN ARTICLE FROM A WEEKLY OR BIWEEKLY MAGAZINE

Gross, Michael Joseph. "Family Life during Wartime." The
    Advocate 29 Apr. 2003: 42-48.

AN ARTICLE FROM A MONTHLY OR BIMONTHLY MAGAZINE

Stacey, Patricia. "Floor Time." Atlantic Monthly Jan./Feb.
    2003: 127-34.

AN ARTICLE IN A SCHOLARLY JOURNAL WITH CONTINUOUS ANNUAL PAGINATION

The volume number follows the title of the journal.

Shan, Jordan Z., Alan G. Morris, and Fiona Sun. "Financial
    Development and Economic Growth: An Egg and Chicken
    Problem?" Review of International Economics 9 (2001):
    443-54.

AN ARTICLE IN A SCHOLARLY JOURNAL THAT PAGINATES EACH ISSUE SEPARATELY

A period and the issue number follow the volume number.

Tran, Duke. "Personal Income by State, Second Quarter 2002."
    Current Business 82.11 (2002): 55-73.

AN EDITORIAL

"The Future Is Now." Editorial. National Review 22 Apr. 2002:
    15-16.

A LETTER TO THE EDITOR

Orent, Wendy, and Alan Zelicoff. Letter. New Republic 18 Nov.
    2002: 4-5.

A REVIEW

Cassidy, John. "Master of Disaster." Rev. of <u>Globalization and Its Discontents</u>, by Joseph Stiglitz. <u>New Yorker</u> 12 July 2002: 82-86.

If the review does not include an author's name, start the entry with the title of the review and alphabetize by that title. If the review is untitled, begin with the words *Rev. of* and alphabetize under the title of the work being reviewed.

AN UNSIGNED ARTICLE

Begin with the article title, alphabetizing the entry according to the first word after any initial *A, An,* or *The.*

"A Shot of Reality." <u>U.S. News & World Report</u> 1 July 2003: 13.

Electronic Sources

Electronic sources present special problems in documentation for several reasons. Their content frequently changes or disappears without notice; and because it is not organized in the kinds of standard ways that print books and periodicals are, finding the information needed for documentation is often difficult. If you cannot find some of this information, just include what you do find. You may also be able to get answers to some of your questions by going to www.mla.org.

Much of the information required in citations of electronic sources takes the same form as in corresponding kinds of print sources. For example, if you are citing an article from an online periodical, put the article title in quotation marks and underline or italicize the name of the periodical. If the source has been previously or simultaneously published in print, include the print publication information if it is available. You also should include information specific to electronic sources, where it is appropriate and available, including the following:

- The version number of the site, preceded by *Vers.*
- The date the source was published electronically or most recently updated
- The name of any institution or organization that sponsors the site (usually found at the bottom of the home page)
- The date you most recently accessed the source
- The URL, in angle brackets. Try to give the URL for the specific part of the source you are citing, but if this URL is very long or not provided, give the URL for the search page of the site, so that readers can find the source using the author or title. (In still other situations, the best URL you can give will be a site's home page.) In MLA style, a URL that will not fit on one line should be broken only after a slash. Do not use a hyphen at the break, and delete any hyphen added by your word processor.

Here is an example of a basic MLA-style entry for the most commonly cited kind of electronic source, a specific document from a Web site:

```
Cuddy-Keane, Melba. "History of IVWS." The International
    Virginia Woolf Society Web Page. 23 June 2003.
    International Virginia Woolf Society. 2 Aug. 2003
    <http://www.utoronto.ca/IVWS>.
```

author, last name first — *title of document, in quotation marks* — *title of site, underlined* — *date of most recent update* — *date of access* — *sponsor of site* — *URL*

AN ENTIRE WEB SITE

```
Gardner, James Alan. A Seminar on Writing Prose. 2001. 15 Sept.
    2002 <http://www.thinkage.ca/~jim/prose/prose.htm>.
```

If the author's name is not known, begin the citation with the title.

```
The International Virginia Woolf Society Web Page. 31 Aug.
    2002. International Virginia Woolf Society. 20 Jan. 2003
    <http://www.utoronto.ca/IVWS>.
```

For an untitled personal site, put a description such as *Home page* (in regular type, not underlined), followed by a period, in the position a title would normally be cited.

```
Chesson, Frederick W. Home page. 1 Apr. 2003. 7 July 2003
    <http://pages.cthome.net/fwc>.
```

AN ONLINE SCHOLARLY PROJECT

For a complete project, provide the title, underlined, and the name of the editor, if given. Then give the electronic publication information—the version number (if any), the date of electronic publication or latest update, and the name of the sponsoring organization—followed by the date of access and the URL.

```
The Darwin Correspondence Project. Ed. Duncan Porter. 2 June
    2003. Cambridge U Library. 13 July 2003 <http://
    www.lib.cam.ac.uk/Departments/Darwin/>.
```

A BOOK OR SHORT WORK WITHIN A SCHOLARLY PROJECT

Begin with the author's name and the title (underlined for a book or in quotation marks for an article, essay, poem, or other short work). Follow with the print publication information, if any, and the information about the project. Give the URL of the book or short work, not of the project, if they differ.

Corelli, Marie. The Treasure of Heaven. London: Constable,
    1906. Victorian Women Writer's Project. Ed. Percy Willett.
    10 July 1999. Indiana U. 3 Dec. 2002 <http://
    www.indiana.edu/~letrs/vwwp/corelli/treasure.html>.

Heims, Marjorie. "The Strange Case of Sarah Jones." The Free
    Expression Policy Project. 24 Jan. 2003. FEPP. 18 Apr.
    2003 <http://www.fepproject.org/Commentaries/
    sarahjones.html>.

MATERIAL FROM A PERIODICALLY PUBLISHED DATABASE ON CD-ROM

Braus, Patricia. "Sex and the Single Spender." American
    Demographics 15.11 (1993): 28-34. ABI/INFORM. CD-ROM.
    UMI-ProQuest. 1993.

A NONPERIODICAL PUBLICATION ON A CD-ROM, MAGNETIC TAPE, OR DISKETTE

Picasso: The Man, His Works, the Legend. CD-ROM. Danbury:
    Grolier Interactive, 1996.

AN ARTICLE FROM AN ONLINE SUBSCRIPTION SERVICE

If you accessed the article through a personal subscription, after the date of publication give the name of the service, the date of access, and, if possible, the URL of the article or the service's search page. If the service supplies no URL that someone else could use to retrieve the article, end with either the word *Keyword,* a colon, and the keyword you used or the word *Path,* a colon, and the sequence of links you followed, with semicolons between the links.

Weeks, W. William. "Beyond the Ark." Nature Conservancy.
    Mar.-Apr. 1999. America Online. 2 Apr. 1999. Keyword:
    Ecology.

If you accessed the article through a library subscription, after the print publication information give the name of the database, underlined, if available; the name of the subscription service; the name of the library; the date of access; and the URL of the service's home page, if available. If the service provides only the first page number of the print version of the article, use a hyphen, a space, and a period after the number.

Hillenbrand, Laura. "A Sudden Illness: Personal History."
    New Yorker 7 July 2003: 56-65. ProQuest. U of South
    Florida Main Lib. 10 July 2003 <http://
    www.proquest.umi.com>.

AN ARTICLE FROM AN ONLINE JOURNAL

Include the volume number and issue number, if given, after the title of the journal and the number of pages, paragraphs, or other sections, if given, after the date of publication.

> Lankshear, Colin, and Michelle Knobel. "Mapping Postmodern Literacies: A Preliminary Chart." The Journal of Literacy and Technology 1.1 (2000). 10 Jan. 2002 <http://www.literacyandtechnology.org.v1n1/lk.html>.

A POSTING TO A DISCUSSION GROUP

For a posting to a newsgroup, include the author's name (if you know it), the title or subject line of the posting (in quotation marks), the identifying phrase *Online posting,* the posting date, and the access date. End with the newsgroup's name, preceded by the word *news:* and no space, in angle brackets.

> Rostrum, Rich. "Did Jefferson Really Wish for the Abolishment of Slavery?" Online posting. 6 July 2003. 14 July 2003 <news:soc.hist.war.us-revolution>.

For a posting to a listserv, include the list's name after the posting date. For a listserv that archives postings at a Web site or listserv address, provide the URL, enclosed in angle brackets.

> Martin, Francesca Alys. "Wait—Did Somebody Say 'Buffy'?" Online posting. 8 Mar. 2000. Cultstud-1. 8 Mar. 2000. <http://lists.accomp.usf.edu/cgi-bin/lyris.pl?visit=cultstud-1&id=111011221>.

For a listserv with no Web site, provide the moderator's email address in place of a URL.

AN EMAIL MESSAGE

The subject line of the message is enclosed in quotation marks. Identify the persons who sent and received it and the date it was sent.

> Duffy, Lynn. "Re: Pet Therapy." Email to the author. 5 Nov. 2002.

SYNCHRONOUS COMMUNICATION

For a posting in a forum such as a MOO, MUD, or IRC, provide the name(s) of any specific speaker(s) you are citing and a description of the event, along with its date, the name of the forum, the date of access, and the URL, beginning with *telnet*. (If an archived version of the posting is available, cite the *http* address instead.)

> Patuto, Jeremy, Simon Fennel, and James Goss. Online discussion
> of "The Mytilene Debate." 9 May 1996. MiamiMOO. 28 Mar.
> 1998 <telnet://moo.cas.edu/cgi-bin/moo?look+4085>.

COMPUTER SOFTWARE

> How Computers Work. CD-ROM. Indianapolis: Que, 1998.

Other Sources

A LECTURE OR PUBLIC ADDRESS

> Birnbaum, Jack. "The Domestication of Computers." Keynote
> address. Conf. of the Usability Professionals Association.
> Hyatt Grand Cypress Resort, Orlando. 10 July 2002.

A GOVERNMENT DOCUMENT

If the author is known, the author's name may either come first or be placed after the title, introduced with the word *By*.

> United States. Dept. of Health and Human Services. Building
> Communities Together: Federal Programs Guide 1999-2000.
> Washington: U.S. Dept. of Health and Human Services, 1999.

A PAMPHLET

> Boat U.S. Foundation for Boating Safety and Clean Water.
> Hypothermia and Cold Water Survival. Alexandria, VA: Boat
> U.S. Foundation, 2001.

PUBLISHED PROCEEDINGS OF A CONFERENCE

If the name of the conference is part of the title of the publication, it need not be repeated. Use the format for a work in an anthology (see p. 446) to cite an individual presentation.

> Duffett, John, ed. Against the Crime of Silence. Proc. of the
> Intl. War Crimes Tribunal, Nov. 1967, Stockholm. New York:
> Clarion-Simon, 1970.

A PUBLISHED DOCTORAL DISSERTATION

If the dissertation was published by University Microfilms International, add *Ann Arbor: UMI,* and the year. List the UMI number at the end of the entry.

Botts, Roderic C. Influences in the Teaching of English, 1917-
          1935: An Illusion of Progress. Diss. Northeastern U, 1970.
          Ann Arbor: UMI, 1971. 71-1799.

AN UNPUBLISHED DOCTORAL DISSERTATION

Bullock, Barbara. "Basic Needs Fulfillment among Less Developed
          Countries: Social Progress over Two Decades of Growth."
          Diss. Vanderbilt U, 1986.

A LETTER

Rogers, Katherine. Letter to the author. 22 Mar. 2003.

A MAP OR CHART

Mineral King, California. Map. Berkeley: Wilderness P, 1979.

A CARTOON OR COMIC STRIP

Provide the title (if given) in quotation marks directly following the artist's name.

Kaplan, Bruce Eric. Cartoon. New Yorker. 8 July 2002. 36.

AN ADVERTISEMENT

City Harvest "Feed the Kids" 2003. Advertisement. New York 26
          May 2003: 15.

A WORK OF ART OR MUSICAL COMPOSITION

De Goya, Francisco. The Sleep of Reason Produces Monsters.
          Norton Simon Museum, Pasadena.

Beethoven, Ludwig van. Violin Concerto in D Major, op. 61.
Gershwin, George. Porgy and Bess.

If a photograph is not part of a collection, identify the subject, the name of the person who photographed it, and when it was photographed.

Washington Square Park, New York. Personal photograph by
    author. 24 June 1995.

A PERFORMANCE

Proof. By David Auburn. Dir. Daniel Sullivan. Perf. Mary-Louise
    Parker. Walter Kerr Theatre, New York. 9 Sept. 2001.

A TELEVISION PROGRAM

"Murder of the Century." American Experience. Narr. David Ogden
    Stiers. Writ. and prod. Carl Charlson. PBS. WEDU, Tampa.
    14 July 2003.

A FILM OR VIDEO RECORDING

Space Station. Prod. and dir. Toni Myers. Narr. Tom Cruise.
    IMAX, 2002.

Casablanca. Dir. Michael Curtiz. Perf. Humphrey Bogart, Ingrid
    Bergman, and Paul Henreid. 1942. DVD. Warner Home Video,
    2003.

A MUSIC RECORDING

Indicate the medium ahead of the name of the manufacturer for an audiocassette,
audiotape, or LP; it is not necessary to indicate the medium for a compact disc.

Beethoven, Ludwig van. Violin Concerto in D Major, op. 61.
    U.S.S.R. State Orchestra. Cond. Alexander Gauk. David
    Oistrikh, violinist. Audiocassette. Allegro, 1980.

Springsteen, Bruce. "Dancing in the Dark." Born in the U.S.A.
    Columbia, 1984.

AN INTERVIEW

Lowell, Robert. "Robert Lowell." Interview with Frederick
    Seidel. Paris Review 25 (1975): 56-95.

Franklin, Ann. Personal interview. 3 Sept. 2002.

The APA System of Documentation

Citations in Text

AUTHOR INDICATED IN PARENTHESES

The APA author-year system calls for the last name of the author and the year of publication of the original work in the citation. If the cited material is a quotation, you also need to include the page number(s) of the original. If the cited material is not a quotation, the page reference is optional. Use commas to separate author, year, and page in a parenthetical citation. The page number is preceded by *p.* for a single page or *pp.* for a range. Use an ampersand (&) to join the names of multiple authors.

> Dr. James is described as a "not-too-skeletal Ichabod Crane" (Simon, 1982, p. 68).

> Racial bias does not necessarily diminish (Johnson & Tyree, 2001).

If you are citing an electronic source without page numbers, give the paragraph number if it is provided, preceded by the paragraph symbol (¶) or the abbreviation *para*. If no paragraph number is given, give the heading of the section and the number of the paragraph within it where the material appears, if possible.

> The subjects were tested for their responses to various stimuli, both positive and negative (Simpson, 2002, para. 4).

AUTHOR INDICATED IN SIGNAL PHRASE

If the author's name is mentioned in your text, cite the year in parentheses directly following the author's name, and place the page reference in parentheses before the final sentence period. Use *and* to join the names of multiple authors.

> Simon (1982) describes Dr. James as a "not-too-skeletal Ichabod Crane" (p. 68).

> As Jamison and Tyree (2001) have found, racial bias does not diminish merely through exposure to individuals of other races (Conclusion section, para. 2).

SOURCE WITH MORE THAN TWO AUTHORS

To cite works with three to five authors, use all the authors' last names the first time the reference occurs and the last name of the first author followed by *et al.* subsequently. If a source has six or more authors, use only the last name of the first author and *et al.* (in regular type, not italicized or underlined) at first and subsequent references.

First Citation in Text

> Dyal, Corning, and Willows (1975) identify several types of students, including the "Authority-Rebel" (p. 4).

Subsequent Citations

> The Authority-Rebel "tends to see himself as superior to other students in the class" (Dyal et al., 1975, p. 4).

TWO OR MORE WORKS BY THE SAME AUTHOR

To cite one of two or more works by the same author or group of authors, use the author's last name plus the year (and the page, if you are citing a quotation). When more than one work being cited was published by an author in the same year, the works are alphabetized by title and then assigned lowercase letters after the date (1973a, 1973b).

> When old paint becomes transparent, it sometimes shows the artist's original plans: "a tree will show through a woman's dress" (Hellman, 1973b, p. 1).

UNKNOWN AUTHOR

To cite a work listed only by its title, the APA uses a shortened version of the title.

> An international pollution treaty still to be ratified would prohibit all plastic garbage from being dumped at sea ("Awash," 1987).

SECONDARY SOURCE

To quote material taken not from the original source but from a secondary source that quotes the original, give the secondary source in the reference list, and in your essay acknowledge that the original was quoted in a secondary source.

> E. M. Forster says "the collapse of all civilization, so realistic for us, sounded in Matthew Arnold's ears like a distant and harmonious cataract" (as cited in Trilling, 1955, p. 11).

List of References

The APA follows this order in the presentation of information for each source listed: author, publication year, title, and publication source; for an article, the page range is given as well. Titles of books, periodicals, and the like should be italicized, if possible.

When the list of references includes several works by the same author, the APA provides the following rules for arranging these entries in the list:

- Same-name single-author entries precede multiple-author entries:

  Aaron, P. (1990).

  Aaron, P., & Zorn, C. R. (1985).

- Entries with the same first author and a different second author are alphabetized under the first author according to the second author's last name:

  Aaron, P., & Charleston, W. (1987).

  Aaron, P., & Zorn, C. R. (1991).

- Entries by the same authors are arranged by year of publication, in chronological order:

```
Aaron, P., & Charleston, W. (1987).

Aaron, P., & Charleston, W. (1993).
```

- Entries by the same authors with the same publication year should be arranged alphabetically by title (according to the first word after *A*, *An*, or *The*), and lower-case letters (*a*, *b*, *c*, and so on) are appended to the year in parentheses:

```
Aaron, P. (1990a). Basic...

Aaron, P. (1990b). Elements...
```

Use a hanging indent of five spaces, as in the following examples:

Books

A BOOK BY A SINGLE AUTHOR

```
Ehrenreich, B. (2001). Nickel and dimed: On (not) getting by
     in America. New York: Metropolitan.
```

A BOOK BY AN AGENCY OR A CORPORATION

```
Association for Research in Nervous and Mental Disease.
     (1966). The circulation of the brain and spinal cord:
     A symposium on blood supply. New York: Hafner.
```

A BOOK BY MORE THAN ONE AUTHOR

```
Saba, L., & Gattis, J. (2002). The McGraw-Hill homeschooling
     companion. New York: McGraw-Hill.

Hunt, L., Po-Chia Hsia, R., Martin, T. R., Rosenwein, B. H.,
     Rosenwein, H., & Smith, B. G. (2001). The making of the
     West: Peoples and cultures. Boston: Bedford/St. Martin's.
```

If there are more than six authors, list only the first six followed by *et al.* (not italicized).

A BOOK BY AN UNKNOWN AUTHOR

Use the title in place of the author.

```
Rand McNally commercial atlas and marketing guide. (2003).
     Skokie, IL: Rand McNally.
```

When an author is designated as "Anonymous," identify the work as "Anonymous" in the text, and alphabetize it as "Anonymous" in the reference list.

A BOOK WITH AN AUTHOR AND AN EDITOR

Arnold, M. (1966). *Culture and anarchy* (J. D. Wilson, Ed.).
    Cambridge, MA: Cambridge University Press. (Original work
    published 1869)

AN EDITED COLLECTION

Waldman, D., & Walker, J. (Eds.). (1999). *Feminism and docu-
    mentary.* Minneapolis: University of Minnesota Press.

A WORK IN AN ANTHOLOGY OR A COLLECTION

Fairbairn-Dunlop, P. (1993). Women and agriculture in western
    Samoa. In J. H. Momsen & V. Kinnaird (Eds.), *Different
    places, different voices* (pp. 211-226). London: Routledge.

A TRANSLATION

Tolstoy, L. (1972). *War and peace* (C. Garnett, Trans.). London:
    Pan Books. (Original work published 1869)

AN ARTICLE IN A REFERENCE BOOK

Rowland, R. P. (2001). Myasthenia gravis. In *Encyclopedia
    Americana* (Vol. 19, p. 683). Danbury, CT: Grolier.

AN INTRODUCTION, PREFACE, FOREWORD, OR AFTERWORD

Holt, J. (1983). Introduction. In N. Wallace, *Better than
    school* (pp. 9-14). Burnett, NY: Larson.

Articles

AN ARTICLE FROM A DAILY NEWSPAPER

Peterson, A. (2003, May 20). Finding a cure for old age. *The
    Wall Street Journal,* pp. D1, D5.

AN ARTICLE FROM A WEEKLY OR BIWEEKLY MAGAZINE

Gross, M. J. (2003, April 29). Family life during war time.
    The Advocate, 42-48.

AN ARTICLE FROM A MONTHLY OR BIMONTHLY MAGAZINE

Stacey, P. (2003, January/February). Floor time. *Atlantic Monthly, 291*, 127-134.

AN ARTICLE IN A SCHOLARLY JOURNAL WITH CONTINUOUS ANNUAL PAGINATION

The volume number follows the title of the journal.

Shan, J. Z., Morris, A. G., & Sun, F. (2001). Financial development and economic growth: A chicken and egg problem? *Review of Economics, 9*, 443-454.

AN ARTICLE IN A SCHOLARLY JOURNAL THAT PAGINATES EACH ISSUE SEPARATELY

The issue number appears in parentheses after the volume number.

Tran, Duke. (2002). Personal income by state, second quarter 2002. *Current Business, 82*(11), 55-73.

AN ANONYMOUS ARTICLE

Communities blowing whistle on street basketball. (2003). *USA Today*, p. 20A.

A REVIEW

Cassidy, John. (2002, July 12). Master of disaster [Review of the book *Globalization and its discontents*]. *The New Yorker*, 82-86.

If the review is untitled, use the bracketed information as the title, retaining the brackets.

Electronic Sources

While the APA guidelines for citing online resources are still something of a work in progress, a rule of thumb is that citation information must allow readers to access and retrieve the information cited. The following guidelines are derived from the *Publication Manual of the American Psychological Association*, Fifth Edition (2001), and the APA Web site.

For most sources accessed on the Internet, you should provide the following information:

- Name of author (if available)
- Date of publication or most recent update (in parentheses; if unavailable, use the abbreviation *n.d.*)

- Title of document
- Publication information, including volume and issue numbers for periodicals
- Retrieval information, including date of access and URL or path followed to locate the site

A WEB SITE

When you cite an entire Web site, the APA does not require an entry in the list of references. You may instead give the name of the site in your text and its Web address in parentheses. To cite a document that you have accessed through a Web site, follow these formats:

American Cancer Society. (2003). How to fight teen smoking. Retrieved June 3, 2003, from http://www.cancer.org/docroot/ped/content/ped_10_14_how_to_fight_teen_smoking.asp

Heims, M. (2003, January 24). The strange case of Sarah Jones. *The Free Expression Policy Project*. Retrieved April 18, 2003, from http://www.fepproject.org/commentaries/sarahjones.html

ARTICLE FROM A DATABASE

Follow the guidelines for a comparable print source, but conclude the retrieval statement with the name of the database. You do not need to indicate how you accessed the database.

Houston, R. G., & Toma, F. (2003). Home schooling: An alternative school choice. *Southern Economic Journal, 69*(4), 920-936. Retrieved July 15, 2003, from InfoTrac Onefile database.

Hillenbrand, L. (2003, July 10). A sudden illness: Personal history. *The New Yorker*, 56-66. Retrieved July 10, 2003, from ProQuest database.

AN ARTICLE FROM AN ONLINE PERIODICAL

If an article that you access through a periodical's Web site also exists in an identical print version, your citation can follow the format for the print article with the addition of "[Electronic version]" following the title of the article (before the period and without quotation marks). However, if you have any reason to believe that the format or content differs from the print version or if no page numbers are provided, then you need to include retrieval information.

Jauhar, S. (2002, July 15). A malady that mimics depression. *The New York Times.* Retrieved July 30, 2003, from http://www.nytimes.com/2003/07/15/health/15CASE.html?fta=y

Retrieval information is always required for periodicals that are published only online.

Lankshear, C., & Knobel, M. (2002). Mapping postmodern literacies: A preliminary chart. *The Journal of Literacy and Technology, 1*(1). Retrieved September 29, 2002, from http://www.literacyandtechnology.org/v1n1/1k.html

ONLINE POSTINGS

Include online postings in your list of references only if you can provide data that would allow retrieval of the source. Provide the author's name, the date of the posting, the subject line, and any other identifying information. For a message on a listserv, conclude the entry with the name of the list and complete retrieval information.

Gordon, M. (2003, January 29). Dialect mixing [Msg. 10]. Message posted to the American Dialect Society's ADS-L electronic mailing list, archived at http://listserv .linguistlist.org/archives/ads-1.html

For a message posted to a newsgroup, conclude the entry with the newsgroup name. If the author is identified only by a screen name, use this name at the beginning of the citation.

Rostrum, Rich. (2003, July 14). Did Jefferson really wish for the abolishment of slavery? [Msg. 47]. Message posted to news://soc.history.war.us-revolution

AN EMAIL MESSAGE

In the APA style, it is not necessary to list personal correspondence, including email, in your reference list. Simply cite the person's name in your text, and in parentheses give the notation *personal communication* (in regular type, not underlined or italicized) and the date.

COMPUTER SOFTWARE

If an individual has proprietary rights to the software, cite that person's name as you would for a print text. Otherwise, cite as you would an anonymous print text.

How Computers Work [Computer software]. (1998). Indianapolis: Que.

Other Sources

A GOVERNMENT DOCUMENT

U.S. Department of Health and Human Services. (1999). *Building communities together: Federal programs guide 1999-2000.* Washington, DC: Author.

AN UNPUBLISHED DOCTORAL DISSERTATION

Bullock, B. (1986). *Basic needs fulfillment among less developed countries: Social progress over two decades of growth.* Unpublished doctoral dissertation, Vanderbilt University, Nashville, TN.

A TELEVISION PROGRAM

Charlsen, C. (Writer/Producer). (2003, July 14). Murder of the century [Television series episode]. In M. Samels (Executive Producer), *American experience.* Boston: WGBH.

A FILM OR VIDEO RECORDING

Myers, T. (Writer/Producer). (2002). *Space station* [Motion picture]. New York: IMAX.

A MUSIC RECORDING

If the recording date differs from the copyright date, the APA requires that it should appear in parentheses after the name of the label. If it is necessary to include a number for the recording, use parentheses for the medium; otherwise, use brackets.

Beethoven, L. van. (1806). Violin concerto in D major, op. 61 [Recorded by USSR State Orchestra]. (Cassette Recording No. ACS 8044). New York: Allegro. (1980)

Springsteen, B. (1984). Dancing in the dark. On *Born in the U.S.A.* [CD]. New York: Columbia.

AN INTERVIEW

When using the APA style, do not list personal interviews in your references list. Simply cite the person's name (last name and initials) in your text, and in parentheses give the notation *personal communication* (in regular type, not italicized or underlined) followed by a comma and the date of the interview. For published interviews, use the appropriate format for an article.

■ SOME SAMPLE RESEARCH PAPERS

As a writer, you will want or need to use sources on many occasions. You may be assigned to write a research paper, complete with formal documentation of outside sources. Several of the writing assignments in this book present opportunities to do library or field research—in other words, to turn to outside sources. Among the readings in Part One, the essays listed here cite and document sources. (The documentation style each follows is given in parentheses.)

"Cannibalism: It Still Exists," by Linh Kieu Ngo, Chapter 4, pp. 129–32 (MLA)

"Children Need to Play, Not Compete," by Jessica Statsky, Chapter 5, pp. 176–79 (MLA)

"More Testing, More Learning," by Patrick O'Malley, Chapter 6, pp. 226–29 (APA)

Acknowledgments

Natalie Angier. "Indirect Aggression." From *Woman: An Intimate Geography* by Natalie Angier. Copyright © 1999 by Natalie Angier. Reprinted with the permission of Houghton Mifflin Company. All rights reserved.

Rick Bragg. "100 Miles per Hour, Upside Down and Sideways." From *All Over But the Shoutin'*. Copyright © 1997 by Rick Bragg. Reprinted with the permission of Pantheon Books, a division of Random House, Inc.

Annie Dillard. "An American Childhood." From *An American Childhood* by Annie Dillard. Copyright © 1987 by Annie Dillard. Reprinted with the permission of HarperCollins Publishers, Inc.

John T. Edge. "I'm Not Leaving Until I Eat This Thing." From *The Oxford American* (September/October 1999). Copyright © 1999 by John T. Edge. Reprinted with the permission of the author. Photo by Shannon Brinkman. Reproduced with permission of the photographer, www.shannonkbrinkman.com.

Barbara Ehrenreich. Excerpt from "Evaluation." From *Nickel and Dimed: On (Not) Getting By in America*. Copyright © 2001 by Barbara Ehrenreich. Reprinted with the permission of Henry Holt and Company LLC.

Richard Estrada. "Sticks and Stones and Sports Team Names." From *The Los Angeles Times*, October 29, 1995. Copyright © 1995 by The Washington Post Syndicate. Reprinted with the permission of The Washington Post Writers Group.

Trevor Hall. "The Edison Café." From *Doubletake* (Fall 2000). Copyright © 2000. Reprinted with the permission of the author. Photos by Michael Coles. Reproduced with permission.

Mark Hertsgaard. "A Global Green Deal." From *Time*, April/May 2000. Copyright © 2000 by Time, Inc. Reprinted with permission.

Stephen Holden. "A Hell for Fathers and Sons." From *The New York Times*, July 12, 2002: E1 (including *The New York Times* logo). Copyright © 2002 by The New York Times Company. Reprinted with permission. Publicity shot from *A Road to Perdition* courtesy of DreamWorks/20th Century Fox. Reproduced by permission. Screen shot of *Home Education Magazine* home page. www.homeedmag.com. Reproduced by permission of Home Education Magazine.

Jonah Jackson. Review of *The Elder Scrolls III: Morrowinds*. From www.techtv.com/splay/print/0,23102.3387959,00 and www.techtv.com/extendedplay/reviews/story/0,24330,3387950,0. Reproduced by permission. *The Elder Scrolls III: Morrowind 7*, 2002 Bethesda Softworks LLC, a ZeniMax Media Company. The Elder Scrolls, Morrowind, Bethesda Softworks and ZeniMax are registered trademarks of ZeniMax Media Inc. All rights reserved.

Martin Luther King Jr. An annotated sample from "Letter from a Birmingham Jail." Copyright © 1963 by Martin Luther King Jr. Copyright renewed 1991 by The Heirs to the Estate of Martin Luther King Jr. Reprinted by arrangement with the Heirs to the Estate of Martin Luther King Jr., c/o Writers House, Inc. as agent for the proprietor.

Katherine S. Newman. "Dead-End Jobs: A Way Out?" From *The Brookings Review*, Fall 1995. Copyright © 1995 Katherine S. Newman. Reprinted with permission.

Anastasia Toufexis. "Love: The Right Chemistry." From *Time*, February 15, 1993. Originally titled "The Right Chemistry." Copyright © 1993 Time, Inc. All rights reserved. Reprinted with permission.

Tobias Wolff. "On Being a Real Westerner." From *This Boy's Life* by Tobias Wolff. Copyright © 1989 by Tobias Wolff. Reprinted with permission of Grove/Atlantic, Inc.

Index

RISE B. AXELROD is director of English Composition and professor of English at the University of California, Riverside. She has previously been professor of English at California State University, San Bernardino, director of the College Expository Program at the University of Colorado, Boulder, and assistant director of the Third College Composition Program at the University of California, San Bernardino.

CHARLES R. COOPER is an emeritus professor in the department of literature at the University of California, San Diego, where he served as coordinator of the Third College Composition Program, Dimensions of Culture Program, and Campus Writing Programs. He has also been codirector of the San Diego Writing Project, one of the National Writing Project Centers. He is coeditor, with Lee Odell, of *Evaluating Writing* (1999) and coeditor, with Sidney Greenbaum, of *Studying Writing: Linguistic Approaches* (1986). He is also coauthor, with Susan Peck MacDonald, of *Writing the World* (Bedford / St. Martin's, 2000).

Together, Axelrod and Cooper have coauthored *The St. Martin's Guide to Writing,* Seventh Edition (Bedford / St. Martin's, 2004) and, with Alison Warriner, *Reading Critically, Writing Well,* Seventh Edition (Bedford / St. Martin's, 2005).

SUBMITTING PAPERS FOR PUBLICATION

TO STUDENTS AND INSTRUCTORS

We hope that we'll be able to include essays from more colleges and universities in the next edition of the *Concise Guide* and our accompanying anthology, *Sticks and Stones and Other Student Essays*. Please let us see essays written using *Axelrod & Cooper's Concise Guide to Writing* you'd like us to consider. Send them with this Paper Submission Form and the Agreement Form on the back to *Concise Guide*, Bedford/St. Martin's, 33 Irving Place, New York, NY 10003.

PAPER SUBMISSION FORM

Instructor's name _____

School _____

Address _____

Department _____

Student's name _____

Course _____

Writing activity the paper represents _____

This writing activity appears in chapter(s) _____
of *Axelrod & Cooper's Concise Guide to Writing*

You may also submit papers online at bedfordstmartins.com/conciseguide

AGREEMENT FORM

I hereby transfer to Bedford/St. Martin's all rights to my essay,

(tentative title), subject to final editing by the publisher. These rights include copyright and all other rights of publication and reproduction. I guarantee that this essay is wholly my original work, and that I have not granted rights to it to anyone else.

Student's signature: X _____

Please print clearly

Name: _____

Address: _____

_____

_____

Phone: _____

Please indicate the reader or publication source you assumed for your essay:

_____

Write a few sentences about the purpose or purposes of your essay. What did you hope to achieve with your reader? _____

_____

_____

_____

_____

_____

Bedford/St. Martin's representative: _____